CW00968893

HEGEL

'A series of exegetical and critical reflections on Hegelian philosophical theses, carried out with constant attention to Hegel's aims ... Even when he finds Hegel's doctrines indefensible and incoherent or Hegel's arguments sophistical, Inwood's criticisms lack the polemical atmosphere and triumphant tone common to the writings of the professional Hegel-deprecator ... Inwood has produced a very unusual book about Hegel. It is valuable in content and well-written.'

The Philosophical Review

'[Inwood] has set new standards in the explication of Hegel's thought-processes ... to write the book he has written call[s] for a rare mixture of learning, acumen and perseverance. Hegel scholarship will only have itself to blame if it does not derive great benefit from the result.'

Mind

'admirable'

Philosophical Quarterly

The Arguments of
the Philosophers

The purpose of this series is to provide a contemporary
assessment and history of the entire course of
philosophical thought. Each book constitutes a detailed,
critical introduction to the work of a philosopher or school
of major influence and significance.

Also available in the series:

*available in paperback

HEGEL

M. J. Inwood

Fellow of Trinity College, Oxford

London and New York

First published 1983 by Routledge & Kegan Paul plc

Reprinted 1998
by Routledge
11 New Fetter Lane, London EC4P 4EE

Simultaneously published in the USA and Canada
by Routledge
29 West 35th Street, New York, NY 10001

First published in paperback 2002

Routledge is an imprint of the Taylor & Francis Group

© 1983, 2002 M J Inwood

Printed and bound in Great Britain by
TJ International Ltd, Padstow, Cornwall

British Library Cataloguing in Publication Data
A catalogue record for this book is available from the British Library

Library of Congress Cataloging in Publication Data
A catalog record for this book has been requested

ISBN 0-415-27719-1

For Christiana

When you start out on the way to Ithaca,
you should wish the journey long,
full of adventures and of knowledge.
The Laestrygonians, the Cyclopes,
angry Poseidon you shouldn't fear,
such things on your way you'll never find
if you keep high your thoughts, and if exquisite
emotions touch your spirit and your body.
The Laestrygonians, the Cyclopes,
wild Poseidon you will never meet
if you are not carrying them inside, within your soul,
and if your soul does not erect them there before you.

C.P. Cavafy, 'Ithaca'
(tr. C. Sourvinou-Inwood)

How very strange he is! I don't know whether he's brilliant or crazy. He didn't seem to me to be a very clear thinker (Ottilie von Goethe, on Hegel; from *Goethe: Conversations and Encounters*, tr. D. Luke and R. Pick, London, 1966, p. 170).

Contents

CONTENTS

CONTENTS

Abbreviations

The following abbreviations have been used in the text and notes for works by Hegel:

JS 1801-7   *Jenaer Schriften, 1801-7*, ed. E. Moldenhauer and K.M. Michel.

PG   *Phänomenologie des Geistes*, ed. J. Hoffmeister, 6th ed., 1952.

M. [re *PG*]   *Phenomenology of Spirit*, tr. A.V. Miller.

NHS 1808-17   *Nürnberger und Heidelberger Schriften, 1808-1817*, ed. E. Moldenhauer and K.M. Michel.

WL   *Wissenschaft der Logik*, 2 vols, ed. E. Moldenhauer and K.M. Michel.

M. [re *WL*]   *Science of Logic*, tr. A.V. Miller.

PR   *Grundlinien der Philosophie des Rechts.* (References are to the numbered paragraphs of this work.)

Enz.   *Enzyklopädie der philosophischen Wissenschaften*, 3 vols. (References are to the numbered paragraphs of this work.)

VPG   *Vorlesungen über die Philosophie der Geschichte*, ed. E. Moldenhauer and K.M. Michel.

N.   *Lectures on the Philosophy of World History*, tr. H.B. Nisbet.

VA	*Vorlesungen über die Ästhetik*, 3 vols, ed. E. Moldenhauer and K.M. Michel.
K.	*Hegel's Aesthetics*, 2 vols, tr. T.M. Knox.
VPR	*Vorlesungen über die Philosophie der Religion*, 2 vols, ed. E. Moldenhauer and K.M. Michel.
VBDG	*Vorlesungen über die Beweise vom Dasein Gottes*. (References are to the number of the lecture and to the page numbers of *VPR*.)
S.S.	*Lectures on the Philosophy of Religion*, 3 vols, tr. E.B. Speirs and J.B. Sanderson.
VGP	*Vorlesungen über die Geschichte der Philosophie*, 3 vols, ed. E. Moldenhauer and K.M. Michel.
H.	*Lectures on the History of Philosophy*, 3 vols, tr. E.S. Haldane and F.H. Simson.
EGP	*Einleitung in die Geschichte der Philosophie*, ed. J. Hoffmeister and F. Nicolin, 3rd ed., 1959.
L.	*Introduction to the History of Philosophy*, tr. Q. Lauer, in *Hegel's Idea of Philosophy*.

The following abbreviations have been used in the notes for works by Kant:

KdrV	*Kritik der reinen Vernunft*. (References are to the pages of the 1st, 1781, and 2nd, 1787, eds, known as 'A' and 'B' respectively.)
GzMdS	*Grundlegung zur Metaphysik der Sitten*, ed. K. Vorländer, 6th ed., 1925.
KdU	*Kritik der Urteilskraft*, ed. K. Vorländer, 6th ed., 1924. (References are usually to the numbered paragraphs of the work.)

Chronological Table

1769		Napoleon born.
1770	Hegel born at Stuttgart. Hölderlin, Beethoven born.	
1775	Schelling born.	
1776		Declaration of Independence in America.
1778	Rousseau dies.	
1781	Kant: *Critique of Pure Reason.*	
1785	Jacobi: *On the Doctrine of Spinoza.*	
1787	Herder: *God, Some Conversations.*	
1788	Kant: *Critique of Practical Reason.*	
1788–93	Hegel attends Tübingen theological seminary together with Hölderlin and, later, Schelling.	
1789		Fall of Bastille.
1790	Kant: *Critique of Judgment.*	
1793–6	Hegel is private tutor in Bern.	
1794	Fichte: *Science of Knowledge.*	Danton and Robespierre die.

1796–1800	Hegel is private tutor in Frankfurt.	
1799	Schleiermacher: *On Religion: Speeches to its Cultured Despisers.*	Napoleon becomes First Consul.
1800	Hegel goes to Jena, where Schelling is professor of philosophy. Schelling: *System of Transcendental Idealism.*	
1801	Hegel's dissertation (*De Orbitis Planetarum*) gains him a lectureship at Jena. Hegel: *Difference between the Systems of Fichte and Schelling.*	
1802–3	Hegel edits *Kritisches Journal der Philosophie* with Schelling.	
1802	Hegel: *Faith and Knowledge.*	
1804	Kant dies.	Napoleon crowned Emperor.
1806	Hegel completes *Phenomenology of Spirit.*	Napoleon defeats Prussians at Jena.
1807	*Phenomenology* published.	
1807–8	Hegel edits daily paper at Bamberg in Bavaria.	
1808–16	Hegel is headmaster of a school in Nuremberg.	
1811	Hegel marries Marie von Tucher.	
1812–13	Hegel: *Science of Logic*, Vol. I.	
1814		Napoleon defeated and exiled to Elba. Congress of Vienna.
1816–18	Hegel is professor of philosophy at Heidelberg.	
1816	Hegel: *Science of Logic*, Vol. II.	
1817	Hegel: *Encyclopaedia.*	

1818-31	Hegel is professor of philosophy at Berlin.	
1818	Karl Marx born.	
1821	Hegel: *Philosophy of Right.*	Napoleon dies on St Helena.
		Greek War of Independence begins.
1827	Hegel: much enlarged, second edition of *Encyclopaedia.*	
1831	Hegel dies of cholera.	
1832	Goethe dies.	
1832-40	Hegel's works and lectures published by his friends.	

Preface

'There are not two Hegels as there are two Wittgensteins and, perhaps, several Schellings' (p.4). When I wrote these words I had in mind the differences between successive Hegels, between primarily the Hegel of the so-called *Early Theological Writings* (composed while he was a private tutor in Bern and Frankfurt) and the Hegel who, from his years as a lecturer at the university of Jena to the culmination of his career as a Professor in Berlin, produced various drafts of what purports to be a definitive 'system' of philosophy. There is, however, another sense in which we might suppose that there are two Hegels: two more or less contemporaneous Hegels. One of them is a grim, forbidding metaphysician, the author of one of the least accessible books ever written, the *Science of Logic.* He tried to reduce the world, the mind, nature, and anything else he could think of, to pure thought. He held perverse theological doctrines which, while more digestible than his logic, are no less unappetizing. He was more than just tempted to claim that history ended with himself. The other Hegel is a more amiable fellow. He wrote the *Phenomenology of Spirit*, a long and difficult book, which is, nevertheless, light reading in comparison to the *Science of Logic.* He was more interested in politics than in God, and provided, in his *Philosophy of Right*, an account of the modern state, which displays a healthy realism about social and political affairs and compares quite favourably both with earlier and with more recent accounts. (This Hegel was once thought to be a proto-Nazi, but this is no longer held to be so. His role as a politico-philosophical miscreant has been taken over by Heidegger.) He appears at his best in his posthumously published lectures. They expand on his cryptographic publications with lively and often relevant illustrations. He surveys the whole of world-history, from its beginnings in the primeval forests of Africa to the civilized, and somewhat germanic, present. He reviews the history of every religion known to him. He produced a history art, of all the architecture, sculpture, painting, music and poetry of every period with which he was familiar - and that is a great deal of art. 'I have tried', I wrote, 'to bring out the strangeness of Hegel and of his enterprise, to retain and emphasize the oddity of what he is saying rather than to dilute it to something which, though sensible and possibly true, no longer seems worth saying' (p.1). That must be Hegel Number One. There is not much strange about Hegel Number Two. Why did I prefer the repellent Hegel to his affable namesake? It was perhaps indecent to show such an unhealthy interest in the metaphysical skeletons in Hegel's attractively ornate cupboard and inconsiderate to drag them out in public. At the very least, I was unfair to Hegel Number Two. What effrontery to suggest that he had nothing worth saying! I have learnt better since.

Why only two? The number two is, as Hegel realized, an odd number. If there are really two Hegels they should be two for Hegel himself, not just *for us*. We should find a third Hegel lurking somewhere in the background. This Hegel is aware of the existence of both the Hegels we have just delineated and he unites them in a single consciousness. What does this Hegel have to say about all this? He notes, first of all, that the two Hegels we have sketched are opposite to each other. Hegel No.1 is 'metaphysical', logical, systematic. Hegel No.2, if not quite an empiricist, at least appeals to experience; apart from some irritating intrusions of logic, he is full-blooded and down-to-earth; despite his best efforts to be systematic he is somewhat free-wheeling and haphazard. Then Hegel – Hegel No.3 – reminds us that, in his view (and, more or less, in the view of the other two Hegels) opposites require each other. Not only that. Opposites turn into each other at their extreme point. North and south are opposites. But if you walk far enough to the north without changing direction, you begin to walk to the south, and if you walk far enough to the south, you begin to walk to the north. He adds, on reflection, that this is not true of every pair of opposites. East and west are also opposites. Each requires the other. But they do not turn into each other in the same way as north and south do. However far you walk to the east, you will never start walking to the west, unless you change direction; and however far you walk to the west, you will never start walking to the east. Still, let us see whether what is true of some opposites applies to the two Hegels. Perhaps if we explore each Hegel sufficiently we shall find him changing into his counterpart.

Perhaps this will not happen. But if we find only that each Hegel *requires* the other, that would at least be something.

From Thought to World

Let us start then with Hegel No.1 and try to see whether he requires, even turns into, Hegel No.2. This may seem a fairly simple task, since it is not easy to conceive of someone who is only a metaphysician, only a logician, and has nothing at all to say about the perceptible world. How would such a person find his way home at night? But there have been philosophers who come close to this ideal of a pure metaphysician. Before Kant, Hegel tells us, philosophers often held that there were two realms, a realm of reality accessible to thought alone and a realm of appearance accessible only to sense-perception. Such a view need not be especially theological, but philosophers who believed in a god usually located him in the realm of reality. No harm is done therefore, if we take their view of God as an example of more general points. I begin with some of the traditional doctrines of the theology of Hegel's day. They are standard doctrines running from Aquinas in the 13th century down to Leibniz and his German followers such as Christian Wolff, the people Hegel calls the 'older metaphysicians'. Some of the doctrines were of course disputed before Hegel's time, especially by mystics such as Meister Eckhart, but they belong to mainstream theology and to much of main-stream philosophy.

1. God is a person, a mind, or something of that sort.

2. God is distinct from the world. The world was created at some date, say 4,000 BC, but God did not come into existence then. He is eternal and unchanging. The existence of the world does not change anything in God, it does not add anything to him.

3. The world is finite, but God is infinite.

4. God is pure being, with no negation, no limitations, no gaps to be filled in.

5. God is many things: he is supremely good, wise, eternal, creative, and so on. But he is also entirely simple. We must not think of his goodness, wisdom, etc. as so many distinct properties inhering in a thing in the way that a lump of sugar is cubical, white, sweet, etc. When goodness, wisdom, and so on are raised to perfection, as they are in the case of God, they cease to be distinct properties and come to amount to the same thing.

6. We apply these terms to God, and also infer that he exists, by starting out from various features of the world. For example, in the world objects move. How do they do that? What keeps things on the move? God as a mover that does not itself move or change, the unmoved mover. Again, the world is well-organized. So God must be a good organizer. And so on.

7. Apart from these arguments from God's effects in the world, many philosophers – Descartes, Leibniz, and so on (though not Aquinas) – accept another sort of proof, from the concept of God. They did not think that God was just a concept or an abstract entity like the number two. He was a real entity, corresponding to his concept but distinct from his concept. But in this case, unlike any other, the concept guarantees his existence. He is perfect. Perfection is involved in the concept of God. But he would not be perfect if he did not exist. So he exists.

8. Even with these proofs of God, there is some residual mystery, something we do not know about him, about the essential nature of things. According to Aquinas, and no doubt other philosophers, all will become clear to us after death. Survival of death is not just a continuation of this life, it enables us to do or know what we missed in this life.

Hegel's responses to these doctrines tell us a great deal about his attitude towards the 'old metaphysics'. (1) God is not a person. In Hegel's vocabulary, 'person' has a somewhat specialized use: it denotes someone who secures recognition from others by owning property. Nevertheless, God is mind or spirit, *Geist* – a word that has, as we shall see, a fluidity appropriate to Hegel's other beliefs about God. (2) God is not distinct from the world. Hegel believes this partly because he accepts that (3) God is infinite. If God and the world were distinct, they would be two things, each bounded by the other. Then God would not be infinite, since to be infinite is to be unbounded. The infinite must in some way embrace the finite. But infinity is only the most striking example of a more general point. The metaphysician does not think about God alone and simply perceive the world. Thoughts are applied to the world as well as to God. While God is necessary, the world is contingent. And 'contingency' is a thought, not a perception. (To the naked eye, the world no more looks contingent than God looks necessary.) If that is so, the metaphysician draws a sharp contrast between two opposite thoughts. So sharp is the contrast that each thought is assigned to a distinct realm. But this, Hegel argues, is mistaken. Thoughts do not simply contrast with each other, they also involve, and sometimes even turn into, each other. To separate them in this way is comparable to separating the north and south poles of a magnet. There cannot be two distinct realms, or at least we cannot coherently *think* that there are. God and the world are related by a sort of identity in difference, comparable to the relation of the two poles of a magnet or perhaps the relation of mind and body. The incarnation symbolizes this relation. God actualizes himself in the world. Hence to do justice to God, we must also give an account of the world. This is a first sign of Hegel No.1 turning into Hegel No.2.

(4) God is not pure being. First, pure being with no negation is sheer indeterminacy, emptiness. Second, without some lack, some negativity, there is no reason for God to 'create' the world, to actualize himself in the world. There must be negativity in an acorn if it is to grow into an oak-tree. This confirms what we have just seen. An adequate account of God must involve those features of him that relate him to the world. (5) God is not a simple unity to which we give many names. This view introduces an objectionable dualism between a simple unity *in itself* that appears *to us* in many forms. If simplicity and complexity are so sharply separated, we can give no account of how this simple unity appears to us in many forms or of the relations between the different forms, between, say, God's goodness and God's power. Hegel's logic does things differently. It displays various thoughts or concepts. There is no simple unity underlying them like a peg on which they all hang. They are not the properties of a single thing, like a sugar-lump. And they are not just set out in a list. They are related by a dialectic in which each one passes over into the other owing to its internal deficiencies. So negativity is involved. That is another reason why God has to involve negativity – to connect together the names we apply to him in a sort of identity in difference.

(6) The proofs of God's existence from his effects in the world find a place in Hegel's system but in a radically altered form and in more than one version. Take for example the proof from contingency. Finite things in the world are all contingent. Each one begins to exist and sooner or later ceases to exist. At that rate they might all cease to exist at once and then the world would never get going again. So there must be some necessary being that cannot begin or cease to exist and which keeps all the rest in existence. A version of this proof occurs in at least two places in Hegel's system. First, when we ascend from everyday thought to philosophy, we start out from contingent everyday things and ascend to the necessities of logic. Second, it appears within logic itself. There contingency and necessity are two of the thoughts Hegel examines.

And contingency passes over into necessity. (Later on these concepts and the transition between them appear again in the philosophy of nature and again in the philosophy of mind.) That happens too with most of the other proofs. They appear in the ascent to Hegel's system and then again within the system. The proofs were originally intended to prove the existence of a single distinct entity, but Hegel transforms them into entry points into philosophy and transitions within philosophy, passages from one concept to another. Hegel's version of these 'proofs' differ in yet another respect. Some of the traditional proofs of God's existence from his supposed effects in the world postulate God in order to avoid an infinite regress. For example, things on earth move. What keeps them moving? The sun, say. What keeps the sun moving? The stars. But it cannot go on like that forever. So we postulate a first unmoved mover. A finite series terminating in an unmoved mover is the only alternative to an endless series of moved movers. However, Hegel introduces a third possibility, that things go round in a circle. His system has no real beginning or end. It goes from logic to nature and from there to mind, and mind concludes with philosophy, which takes us back to logic again. If we think of logic as God, he descends into nature, then rises again to mind, and eventually returns back to himself in philosophy. So the traditional proofs cannot retain their old, unilinear form. If they are to survive they have to represent stages on a circle.

(7) Hegel says he accepts the ontological proof. But he alters it entirely. Traditionally the proof establishes on the basis of a concept the existence of a real, non-conceptual entity distinct from the world. But it cannot do that in Hegel's view, since God is not a non-conceptual entity distinct from the world. In fact from Hegel's responses to points (5) and (6) it looks as if God, or at least the first stage of God, is a concept, or rather the system of concepts, unravelled in the logic. Now what can the ontological proof prove the existence of? Not the concept, since the ontological proof assumes the existence of a concept to begin with. Not God as a distinct non-conceptual entity, for there is no such entity. What it does is represent the move from logic to the natural world, the actualization of God or the concept in nature. But before that it also represents a move within logic itself, the move from the concept or subjectivity to objectivity. For in some way what happens outside logic is prefigured and explained within logic. What Hegel means by the ontological proof is not a proof of the existence of God, but an account of God's actualization in the world – something like the creation of the world.

(8) There is no individual survival or immortality. One reason

for this is that Hegel does not think that there is any fundamental residual mystery, nothing that we could learn after death that we cannot learn before death by philosophical thought. Everything is open and above board. More generally Hegel believes that people die when they have done everything they can do, so there is no point in a continuation of life. That he did not believe in immortality does not impair his belief in God. It is quite possible to believe in God without believing in immortality. But his belief that everything about God is entirely comprehensible is fairly unorthodox. He often appeals to the altar of the unknown God that was set up in Athens, in case some god were neglected in their worship. St. Paul saw this altar, according to Acts 17: 23, and said: 'Whom therefore you ignorantly worship, him I declare unto you'. So do I, says Hegel. God is not unknown. Hegel claims to tell us *all* about him. God is not 'grudging': 'All that God is, he imparts and reveals; and he does so, at first, in and through nature'.[1] Hegel brings God right down to earth – and us earthlings right up to God.

Now that the traditional theology has undergone this transformation, it is not too difficult to see how Hegel can say that his philosophy has the same 'content' as Christianity. The concept, what logic studies, corresponds to God the Father, nature is God the son, and mind is God the holy spirit – which in German is the same word as 'mind': *Geist*. Or another way of looking at it is this: the concept is God in himself, self-enclosed; nature is God become conscious, conscious of an object other than himself, an alienated God, as it were; mind is God becoming self-conscious, becoming aware of himself, as well as of his object, in the strivings of human beings. Nature and human beings are not distinct from God but essential phases in the development of God. Again, then, we cannot do justice to God unless we explore nature, the human mind, and our practical and intellectual endeavours. Hegel No.1 cannot do his job properly without the collaboration of Hegel No.2.

Objections present themselves. One is this. God, Hegel conceded earlier, is mind or spirit. But now God has become a system of concepts actualizing itself in nature and humanity. And that, surely, is not a mind, not at least a single mind. To this Hegel has two replies. First, the concept or thoughts are embedded in the world. The world has a definite logical structure. But these thoughts, this logical structure, also form the core of the human mind. Human beings are essentially thought or thoughts – not thoughts that they can explicitly unravel all at once, but thoughts that they can painfully and circuitously become aware of over history in their manifold interactions with the world. So if the thoughts that constitute the human mind are embedded in the world, the world is itself a sort of mind. Second, human minds are an essential phase of God. Without them God would not be self-conscious, not a proper mind at all. That is human *minds*, not *mind*. But the words 'mind' and 'spirit' are not, even in English, restricted to the individual human mind. We speak of the 'spirit of the age', the 'Greek mind', the 'European mind'. The mind readily spreads beyond the individual mind to become a collective or shared mind that permeates individual minds. This is not just a manner of speaking. Human beings need a culture, a shared mind, to be recognizably human at all except in their physical structure. In Hegel the shared mind expands to take in all human beings. That is another way in which God might be said to be a mind.[2]

Hegel No.1, then, requires Hegel No.2. There is no distinct metaphysical realm that might be considered quite separately from the perceptible world. God or the concept is the essence of the world. As Hegel says, an essence is no essence if it does not manifest itself as appearance. An acorn is no acorn unless it has a tendency to become an oak.

From World to Thought

But why does Hegel No.2 require Hegel No.1? Could Hegel not have written about nature, society, history, art, and even religion without such deference to logic – a logic that retains the marks of its birth from theology and metaphysics? Hegel's reply is this: All human beings think. Dogs and cats have sensory input, but they do not think. Because they do not think they have no conception of the world comparable to our own, no structured society, no history, no art, no religion. However, not all human beings think in the same way or to the same degree. In general, the more we think, the more satisfactory is our view of the world, our society, and our religion.[3] The intellectual and practical enterprise of Europeans stems from their thought and this, in turn, is intertwined with their Christian religion:

> *Europeans* ... have for their principle and character the concrete universal, the self-determining thought. The christian God is not merely the differenceless One, but the triune God who contains difference within himself, who has become man, who reveals himself. In this religious representation the opposition of universal and particular, of thought and reality, has supreme intensity and is nevertheless brought back to unity ... The principle of the European mind is, therefore, self-conscious reason, which has the confidence in itself that for it nothing can

be an insuperable barrier, and which therefore invades everything in order to become present to itself therein. The European
mind opposes the world to itself, makes itself free of it, but again
sublates this opposition, takes its Other, the manifold, back into
itself, into its simplicity. Here, therefore, there prevails this
infinite thirst for knowledge, which is alien to the other races.
The European is interested in the world, he wants to know it,
to make this Other confronting him his own, to bring into his
view the genus, the law, the universal, the thought, the inner
rationality, in the particularizations of the world. As in the
theoretical, so too in the practical sphere, the European mind
strives after the unity to be produced between itself and the
external world. It subjects the external world to its ends with an
energy which has ensured for it the mastery of the world. In his
particular actions the individual here proceeds from firm
universal principles; and in Europe the political state, by rational
institutions, exhibits more or less the unfolding and actualization of freedom, exempted from the wilfulness of a despot.[4]

Hegel here applies one of the principles expounded in his logic,
that inner and outer, subjectivity and objectivity, stand in direct
proportion to each other. As Europeans detach themselves from
the world and delve inside their own minds, they can to the same
degree master the world instead of being simply buffetted by it.
Here, then, is one reason why Hegel No.2 must, in order to
complete his task, appeal to Hegel No.1. He cannot, he believes,
fully understand what human beings do or why, say, Europeans
behave differently from other human beings, unless he explores
their thought, their 'categories'. What is it about human beings that
makes them operate differently from cats and dogs? What is it
about Europeans that impels them to explore the world? What is so
special about the Christian religion? These are questions that Hegel
believes he needs to ask, and the answers to them are supplied by
Hegel No.1.
Let us grant, then, that Hegel No.2 needs to speak about
thoughts. But why does he need a systematic 'logic'? And why
apply it, in an apparently so procrustean fashion, to empirical
material? Hegel has at least two answers to this: First, if some
human beings have different thoughts from other human beings, if,
say, modern Europeans think differently from ancient Greeks, it
seems natural to ask: How do modern thoughts differ from ancient
thoughts? Are they simply distinct types of thought or are they
intelligibly related to each other? And how does human thought
change over history? How do Greeks become Romans, Romans

become medieval, and medieval thinkers become modern thinkers? If these changes are at bottom changes in thought, and if the changes are intelligible, then there must be intelligible routes from one thought, or one type of thought, to another. If the historian, the philosophical historian, is to show the intelligibility of such changes, then he must have a command of the relations between thoughts and of their transitions into each other. Hegel's logic is a map of the logical terrain. On this map we can locate various peoples – the Greeks, the Romans, the medievals – and show the routes, at least the possible routes, by which humanity travelled from one location to another.

But it is not just to explore his subject-matter adequately that Hegel No.2 needs a logic. He needs it, he feels, even to confront his subject-matter at all in an appropriate way. The state? Nature? The history of the world, of art, of religion, of philosophy itself? These are not easy matters to deal with. One has to consider societies and events entirely remote from oneself. One has to appreciate historic deeds, styles of art, religious practices, in general mentalities, that are quite different from anything one experiences in one's immediate surroundings and with which one has initially little sympathy. Then one has to bring order into this mass of material, present it to the reader as an intelligible narrative divided into digestible segments. The task is perhaps comparable (and Hegel himself compares it) to the process by which a child reaches a conception of an objective world. An infant lacks a firm hold on the world, even on its own body, to the extent that it lacks inner depth. The child's world is initially a world centring on the child itself. Its desires come first, and then whatever satisfies those desires, those who love it with an unrequited love – for the infant has no empathy with others. Of remote places, of people unrelated to it, the infant has no conception. Even later, each of us retains, Hegel argues, an 'individual world', a world in which our familiar places and people occupy the foreground, while the rest sinks into the background.[5] But rational adults have another world as well, a world not centred on them-selves, a world in which remote times and places are as real and important as what is close to ourselves and our daily concerns. How do we reach this objective world? By thought, Hegel says, by developing our own subjectivity so as to liberate ourselves from our immediate surroundings and their impact on us. Then we can emerge from our subjectivity to reclaim the world from which we detached ourselves. Only now it is an objective world, a world ordered by thought. Entities are implicitly classified into species and genera, not viewed solely in terms of their emotional significance to us. They are related to each other in 'rational' ways – causally, spatio-temporally, and so on. The world is not just my world; it is a world for others as well as for myself. Species, genera, causality – these are thoughts, thoughts that form the core of our subjectivity but are also responsible for the objectivity of the world.

So it is with Hegel. Hegel wants to explore this objective world thoroughly and objectively. He must distance himself from his 'individual world', escape from the parochialism of contemporary Germany, its Lutheran and Catholic faiths, its art and literature, even its Kantian philosophy, in order to explore the history, religion, art and philosophy of all times and places, without any initial bias in favour of his own and without assessing everything else by the standards of his own time and place. (It does not of course follow that Hegel cannot then return to his own time and place, and decide that it is, in some respects at least, superior to other times and places. This is what he does. But then it is an objective assessment, not a local prejudice.) He does this as the child did, by descending into his own subjectivity and away from his own time and place. But at this elevated level one can only do that by explicit, philosophical thinking, by producing logic – a map of the conceptual landscape that enables him to locate the people of other times and places. By developing his own thought to a sufficient extent, Hegel can acquire a new insight into the thought – and therefore the societies, the art, the religion, the philosophy – of people who think quite differently from himself. Not, of course, *entirely* differently. Other ways of thinking are, Hegel believes, contained, at a deep and implicit level, in this own thought. This is why, by exploring his own thought to a sufficient depth he can make contact with the thought of others. Hegel thus owes his supreme objectivity, his openness to the ways of all times and places, to his correspondingly intense subjectivity, his penetration into his own mind. The subjective Hegel, Hegel No.1 perhaps, and the objective Hegel, Hegel No.2, go together – at least in the eyes of Hegel No.3.

Subjectivity and Objectivity

Hegel expresses some of his ideas about objectivity and subjectivity in an engaging story that he tells in his first major work.[6] A human being, or what Hegel calls 'consciousness', has become aware of itself as an 'I' or ego, aware of itself just as itself. It is then distressed by the contrast between its simple self and the variegated, kaleido-scopic world confronting it. So it tries to demolish the world by desiring and consuming items in it – plants, animals, fish. But that does not solve the problem. As soon as it has consumed one thing, another pops up and has to be eaten too. Consciousness sees that this is going to get it nowhere. By a lucky chance it meets another 'consciousness', somewhat similar in appearance and demeanour to itself. Each now fights the other, for no other reason than to gain 'recognition' or 'acknowledgement' from the other. The victor enslaves the other and gets a sort of recognition from him, though the recognition is not worth much, since the recognizer is now just a slave. There are two ways we might take this story. It might be a genuine narrative with a temporal progression. First I am just aware of myself as myself. Next I desire and eat things. Finally I encounter someone else, fight him, and so on. This is rather an odd story. Can anyone be self-aware without being aware of others? Surely the word 'I' goes together with the words 'you', 'he', and 'she', as well as 'it'. Hegel obviously agrees that there is something unsatisfactory about regarding oneself as 'I', if one does not recognize others, address them as 'you' and so on. That is one reason why the story moves on from mere self-awareness to recognition of others. But if we dislike the idea that there ever was a time when people were self-aware but did not recognize others, we can take the story in a different way. On this view it is not a proper story that progresses in time. It is a dramatic way of presenting logical relations, not temporal relations, between self-awareness, desire and recognition. Then Hegel is arguing as follows. I am undoubtedly aware of myself as I, as myself. That would not be possible if I did not desire and consume things. But that is not enough. It would not be possible either if I did not recognize and were not recognized by others. These two features – desire and reciprocal recognition – are logical presuppositions of self-consciousness, not temporal consequences of it. So we have these two interpretations of Hegel's story, a temporal version and a logical version. Which one is right?

They are both right. In this story Hegel is addressing at least two different problems. The first is what we now call the 'problem of other minds'. How do I know that there are any other people apart from myself? The second is the problem of the origin of society. How did we get from a state of nature to a state of society? The problem of other minds is not very obviously a historical problem. It is a problem about how we know there are other minds, whenever we do know it, whether now or in the remote past. Presumably human beings have always believed that there were other human beings and always associated with them as human beings in some way or other. The problem of the origin of society is by contrast a historical one. It is not about how people always are, or how they are now, but about some event or train of events in the remote past. But somehow or other Hegel wants to deal with the two problems together.

To see how the two problems might be brought together, let us look at what some of Hegel's predecessors and contemporaries had to say about them. First, then, other minds. Kant was generally felt to have neglected the matter of other people. Fichte and Schelling started out with the 'absolute' I or ego, the I that does not contrast with 'you', 'he' and 'she'. But they also tried to remedy this deficiency in Kant. Because there is an I, Fichte argued, there must be a you. 'No Thou, no I; no I, no Thou'.[7] His main argument is this: To be a proper person, I must be a moral agent, there must be things that I ought to do and things that I ought not to do. This is only possible if there are other people, people to whom I owe duties, to whom I ought to do some things and ought not to do others. Schelling was early on a collaborator of Fichte's, and also a close friend of Hegel's. He has two arguments for the necessity of other people and belief in them. First, without other people, I would not be conscious of an objective world. Other people perceive the world when I am asleep, they perceive parts of it that I do not, and so on. They thus guarantee that the world exists independently of me, that the world is not simply *my* world. Secondly, without other people I would not be conscious of my freedom. Without other people I can do whatever I like. The existence of others imposes restrictions on what I do. I cannot just follow my urges, I have to restrain myself. I can eat plants and animals, but not people. I cannot do so, not only because people offer resistance to me, but because it is morally wrong. In respecting this moral constraint I demonstrate my freedom, both to myself and to others. Schelling also holds that belief in other minds requires reciprocal recognition: 'I ... must recognize [other intelligences] as existing independently of me ... this relation is fully reciprocal, and no rational being can prove itself as such [as a rational being], except by recognizing others as such'.[8] He wrote this in 1800, seven years before Hegel's *Phenomenology of Spirit*. So far, then, these 'idealists', Fichte and Schelling, have two main conclusions: First, belief in the existence of other people is not an optional extra. If I do not recognize the existence of others, then I cannot regard myself as a proper person, I cannot be self-conscious or aware of my freedom. I cannot be a moral being, or even, perhaps, inhabit an objective world. Secondly, the problem of other minds is a practical matter, not just a theoretical matter. I believe in the existence of others not only because regular observation of their appearance and behaviour suggests that they are beings rather like myself, but because my own conduct, the conduct I must engage in if I am a proper person, commits me to believing in other people and would not make sense otherwise.

This second point, that to believe in other people is to act morally towards them, already brings the problem of other minds closer to the problem of the origin of society. To act morally towards others is close to, if not exactly the same as, interacting with them socially. The connection between the two problems can be clarified by reflection on the words 'recognize' and 'recognition'. The words are ambiguous. In one sense to recognize something is just to see what it is or what sort of thing it is. To recognize a dog is to see that it is a dog, to recognize Fido is to see that it is Fido. In another sense to recognize something is to acknowledge it. What I recognize in this sense is usually a person or the quality, action or product of a person. I recognize a person by saying 'hello', clapping, pinning on a medal, and so on. Let us call recognition in the first sense 'weak recognition' and recognition in the second sense 'strong recognition'. For I can recognize someone in the first sense without acknowledging them. But I cannot properly acknowledge someone unless I recognize them in the first sense, see that they're a person, a hero, or whatever. At first sight it seems as if the two problems involve different senses of recognition. To believe that there are other people is to see that there are other people, to recognize others in the weak sense. To be in society is to acknowledge other people in some way or other, to recognize them in the strong sense. But Fichte, Schelling and Hegel deny this difference. Properly to recognize people as people involves behaving morally towards them. But to treat someone morally and not just instrumentally is in a way to acknowledge them, to recognize them in the strong sense, not just to notice that they are a person. Schelling says: recognition must be reciprocal. I do not have good reason to recognize someone else as a person unless they recognize me as a person. But their recognition of me must be strong recognition, acknowledgement, for I cannot know what others think about me unless they manifest it appropriately. Recognition that is appropriately manifested must be strong recognition, not just weak recognition. Put more formally: If something is a person, it must weakly recognize others as persons. So if I weakly recognize someone as a person, I must recognize that they recognize others as persons. But then their recognition of others must be strong recognition, acknowledgement, for otherwise I could not be aware of it.

Now the two problems, other minds and society, are closer together in the following respect. One might suppose that recognition of other people and social interaction with them are two different things. One might think, for example, that people recognized the existence of other people long before they interacted with them socially. Not of course the other way round. To interact socially with people one has to recognize them as people. But one can perhaps recognize them as people without any social interaction. Fichte, Schelling and Hegel deny this. Recognition of other people and social or moral involvement with them go together.

Now let us approach this from the other side and turn to the other problem, the origin of society. Here Hegel's mentors are not Fichte and Schelling, but Hobbes and Rousseau. Hobbes' argument is roughly this: In the state of nature people were involved in constant conflict. This was bad for everyone, since even the strongest person needs to sleep and is then vulnerable to attack. So to end this state of affairs they agreed among themselves to submit more or less unconditionally and unilaterally to one of their number. This original pact of submission determines the fundamental nature of the sovereign and his rights over individuals even today. A citizen is bound to obey the sovereign without question, though Hobbes tends to qualify this by adding such conditions as that a subject is not obliged to obey the sovereign to the extent of breaking the natural law. Rousseau (as Hegel interprets him) argues as follows. In the state of nature people for some time recognized each other's existence without forming societies. They did not fight each other, so their motive for leaving the state of nature was the desire for goods that required co-operation, not fear of death at the hands of each other. They all made a contract with each other to set up a state that would secure their co-operation. This too determines the nature of the state today. The state is based on a contract. If this contractual arrangement no longer suits me, then I am free to opt out of it, to withdraw from the contract.

Hegel does not give a very explicit account of the origin of the state or of society.[9] He believed that we cannot study history seriously without written records, and there cannot be written records from a period when there was no state or society. So history cannot say much about the origins of state or society. Still, he does indicate some of his agreements and disagreements with Hobbes and Rousseau. For both Hobbes and Rousseau, human beings are fully formed people before they enter society. Hobbes' combatants and Rousseau's people, who have long recognized each other's existence but not yet got around to co-operating, are people much like us. They just have not yet formed the appropriate social arrangements. For Hegel this is not so. Before people recognize each other in the sense of interacting socially they are not proper human beings. On the question of how people behaved towards each other in the state of nature, Hegel sides with Hobbes against Rousseau. They fought. He does not have much evidence for this, except travellers tales that suggested to him that this is how people behaved in Africa. His main reason for assuming it is different from Hobbes'. Hobbes believed that in the state of nature people fought, because people in his own day, relieved of civilized restraints, fought each other in the English civil war. Hegel believed that they fought because they were, unlike us, wild and uncivilized, and fighting is what uncivilized people do. Hegel agrees more with Hobbes than with Rousseau on what gets society going. It is a pact of submission, not a general contract between equals. Only this pact does not, as in Hobbes, give rise directly to a state or even a complete society. In the *Phenomenology of Spirit* Hegel does not tell us how this happens. He moves on to other themes – stoicism, scepticism, and so on, which seem to have little bearing on the origin of the state. But he often expresses his diagreement with Rousseau's view that the state arose by a contract. Hegel also rejects an assumption made by both Hobbes and Rousseau. Each of them assumes that his theory about the origin of the state also tells us about the nature of the state in the present. Hegel disagrees. Even if the state did arise from a contract, it is not a contractual arrangement today. One is not free to opt out of the state if it does not satisfy one's requirements, not at least unless one emigrates. Perhaps the state did originate in some sort of pact of submission. But it is not like that nowadays. We are not kept in order merely by the sovereign's threat of force or by the fear that if we disobey the sovereign we shall relapse into the state of nature. We have been well educated in the schools and universities of Prussia and other German states. We go to church regularly. We have thoroughly imbibed habits of obedience and orderly conduct. We are in short quite different from people in the state of nature, quite different from the combatants in the *Phenomenology*.

This presents us with a difficulty. We saw that, in the philosophers of Hegel's time, the problem of other minds was closer to the problem of the origin of the state or society than it has since become. But now the two problems have come apart again. For the problem of other minds is not a historical problem. It is not solved by telling us how someone once discovered the existence of other people and then handed this knowledge down to us. If I do not already believe that there are other people why should I believe people who tell me that there are? It is a problem about how we know there are other minds at any time, in the remote past and now. Hobbes and Rousseau might claim to have solved it in their discussion of the origin of society, because for them people in the state of nature and people in society are more or less the same. But for Hegel they are not the same. So how can a story about the origin of society tell us about our knowledge of other people today? The answer is this: The fight in the state of nature was a fight for recognition, acknowledgement. Today, Hegel says, we do not often engage in individual combat.[10] But we still need recognition. We get it not by fighting each other but by doing our job properly and performing our civic duties. We also get it by owning property.[11] The main point of property is not so much to satisfy one's needs as to stake out a claim to being a person and to acquire recognition by others. But what about the other elements in the story, combat, fear of death, enslavement? Hegel says that he introduced these in the *Phenomenology* because he was thinking of the state of nature and our transition out of it. Combat, fear of death, enslavement have little place in modern society. So they are not relevant to interpersonal relations today. This is not exactly correct. Hegel is not doing justice to himself. Even in modern society there is a place for combat, fear of death, and enslavement. As Hobbes portrays the state of nature it is inhabited more or less exclusively by male adults. Hegel's combatants are also adult males. Rousseau brings in women and children, and his state of nature is consequently less violent. Rousseau's book *Emile* was devoted to the education of children. Hegel too has a lot to say about the education of children.[12] The type of education that Hegel favoured is not very child-centred. It involves repression and alienation. The child is not allowed to do as it likes. Its desires are to be restricted, frustrated, not invariably but often. It puts up resistance, but eventually has to give in. When it goes to school it is made to stop speaking its native German and to learn Latin, then Greek, and so on. It has to learn verbs by rote. The point of this is not at the time apparent to the child. It is a sort of slavery. If the child does not do its homework or if it flicks ink pellets at the teacher, it is made to stand outside the rector's study and there endures something like fear of death.[13] All this, in Hegel's view, makes the child into a proper human being. It comes to realize that it cannot do whatever it likes, because it is not the only person in the world and not the centre of the world. Its desires are thwarted by others and it turns back in upon itself. Eventually it escapes from this slavery and can begin to write in German. But now it does this with a knowledge of ancient languages, logic and so on behind it. So it has a better command of its native language, a more objective insight into it, than if it had been allowed to speak it all along unmolested. New recruits to the polity undergo, in a modified form, a process of conflict, enslavement and repression from which they will eventually emerge as reciprocally recognizing members of an objective social order.

Conclusion

Who wrote this story? Hegel No.1, Hegel No.2, or Hegel No.3? Not Hegel No.1, certainly. It is too light-hearted, too worldly for him. Hegel No.2, then? Not exclusively. For the story does not simply speak about our involvement with others and our formation of societies and states. It is a story primarily about the human mind. The mind cannot, immediately and without more ado, reach out to others and enter into social and political relations with them. It must at the same time descend into itself, deepen its subjectivity, become a pure I. 'Consciousness' has already got some way with this before it meets the other consciousness but, if it is enslaved, its repression by the master intensifies this condition. Similarly, frustration of the child's impulses turns it in on itself. Then the mind rebounds from subjectivity into objectivity. It recognizes and acknowledges the existence of others on a par with itself, others who inhabit the same world as itself. The social and political relations it forms with others hone it into a complete human being. They not only (at least in their European version) confer freedom on it. They enable it to achieve an objective view of the world, both guaranteeing its objectivity, independent of the individual's whims and preferences, and supplementing the meagre information about it that any isolated individual can acquire. Something similar happens to Hegel. As the philosopher telling the story of the fight for recognition, Hegel does not appear within his own story. But we might apply the story to his own case in the following way. His opponents are not his immediate contemporaries, but figures from the past: Egyptian architects, Greek sculptors and philosophers, Roman emperors, and so on. To deal with them on an equal footing, to give them recognition and to win from them a sort of recognition in return – their submission to incorporation into his system – he immerses himself in the depths of subjectivity – pure thought – in order to ascend to the height of objectivity. At every level, then, subjectivity and objectivity go hand in hand. So, therefore, do the two Hegels.

---

1 *Encyclopaedia of the Philosophical Sciences in Outline*, §140 Addition.
2 In view of Hegel's radical transformation of the tradition, it is hard to say whether he believes in God or not, whether he is a Christian or not.

We might compare the case of the atom. An atom used to be something indivisible, unsplittable. Democritus thought they were unsplittable lumps and that is what the Greek word *atomon* means. So unsplittability seems to be the essence of an atom. But now the atom has been split. Do we still believe in atoms? There are three alternatives. First, we could say that since what we regarded as atoms can be split, we have found that there are no atoms. That is comparable to saying that Hegel is an atheist. But we do not say that we now disbelieve in atoms, partly perhaps because that would confuse us with people who genuinely did not believe in atoms, such as Aristotle, who rejected Democritus' view that there were these little lumps making up everything. Second, we could say: we still believe in atoms, only we have found that the things we used to think were atoms, since they are splittable, are not the real atoms. The real atoms are electrons or quarks or whatever indivisible bits we may postulate. That is like saying: Hegel believes in God, but he found that God is not the biblical God or the God of traditional theology. God is just the world and its logical structure. Thirdly, we can say: we still believe in atoms, and they are more or less the same things as Democritus identified as atoms. But we have found that they can be split. If we could split them as easily as we can cut a cake then they would not be atoms. But since they can only be split with considerable difficulty, they still count as atoms. That is roughly what Hegel says about God: I believe in God, and the same God as the biblical God and the God of the theologians. But I have found, with good reasons, that he is not as the theologians say he is and he is not literally as he is said to be in the various strands of the bible. But no one in their right mind ever thought that he was.

3   But not, embarrassingly, our art. See my edition of Hegel's *Introductory Lectures on Aesthetics*.

4   *Encyclopaedia of the Philosophical Sciences*, §393 Addition.

5   *Ibid.* §402 Addition.

6   *Phenomenology of Spirit*, IV.A.

7   *Foundations of the Science of Knowledge* in Fichte (1971), vol.I, p.189.

8   *System of Transcendental Idealism*, in Schelling (1927), vol. II, p.550.

9   Unlike Hobbes and Rousseau, Hegel distinguishes carefully between the state and 'civil society'. My neglect of this distinction here is intended to facilitate my exposition and in no way to depreciate the importance of the distinction.

10   *Encyclopaedia of the Philosophical Sciences*, §432 Addition.

11   *Philosophy of Right*, §71.

12   *Encyclopaedia of the Philosophical Sciences*, §396 Addition.

13   Hegel was himself the rector (or headmaster) of a gymnasium (or grammar school) in Nuremberg from 1808 until 1816, when he took up a professorship at Heidelberg University.

Introduction

Hegel can be seen in a number of ways: as a metaphysician on the grand scale, as a source of insights into the history of art, religion and society, or as an acute commentator on the culture of his time. Without wishing to deny that he is all these things and more, I have preferred to stress the metaphysical elements of his thought, to see him as trying to disclose the fundamental nature of the universe. I am unsympathetic to attempts to underplay this aspect or to reduce it to a more familiar, commonsensical view of things. My reasons for this are twofold. Firstly, it seems obvious that Hegel regarded logic as central to his system, that he believed, or at any rate half-believed, that the world was a product of pure thought, that God or reason was in the world, and so on. His consideration of art, his concern with the details of science, history and society, are subordinate to this. Secondly, Hegel's peculiar fascination for subsequent generations is primarily due to our predilection for the grandiose, perhaps insane, ambition of the metaphysician over the commonplace, even where the commonplace happens to be true. I have therefore tried to bring out the strangeness of Hegel and of his enterprise, to retain and emphasize the oddity of what he is saying rather than to dilute it to something which, though sensible and possibly true, no longer seems worth saying.

Even when viewed in this way, Hegel's thought is obscure and equivocal and it is correspondingly difficult to summarize. In rough outline, however, he saw the world as a whole on the model of a mind, a mind which, as it were, projects an object ('nature') of which it can be *conscious*. This object develops by stages into men, and they become conscious not only, in various ways, of nature but of the cosmic mind itself and of its relationship to nature. The emergence of men and the growth of their understanding represents the increasing *self-consciousness* of the cosmic mind. This self-consciousness is completed by Hegel's own system, in which the whole process has become entirely transparent to us. This picture of the world has, obviously enough, a theological interpretation in terms of God's creation of the world and so on. Hegel took religion seriously. He regarded himself as an orthodox Lutheran, reasserting the rationality of theism in the face of Kant's radical and influential attacks on it and intrepidly following up its implications for our view of the world. But it can and should be translated into terms of philosophy or of 'thought' and this is how it is represented in Hegel's *Encyclopaedia*. The three parts of this work, the only complete presentation of his mature system, correspond to the three phases of the cosmic process. The first, the *Logic*, represents God as he is in himself, independently of nature and of men — God the Father, as it were. It presents us with a system of 'pure thoughts'. The second, the *Philosophy of Nature*, gives an account of the various phases of nature, beginning with space and passing through phases of greater complexity until we reach the stage of animal life — God the Son. The third part, the *Philosophy of Mind*, describes the features of human life, beginning with those characteristic of infants and of primitive men and culminating in the activity of philosophy itself — God the Holy Spirit. Unusually perhaps for a metaphysician of this type, Hegel takes history seriously and human history plays a crucial role in his system. Nature, on his view, does not develop historically and his beliefs about the origin of man are shrouded in obscurity. But men and their ways of seeing things do develop over time and this is what Hegel takes to be the advance to self-consciousness — both their own and that of the world-spirit. In addition therefore to those sections of the *Encyclopaedia* which refer to world history, and to the history of art, religion and philosophy, we have sets of lectures on each of these themes, put together by Hegel's pupils after his death from his and their own notes.

This brief summary already suggests several questions. How seriously is the theological interpretation of the system intended? What is the status of pure thoughts? Does Hegel believe that nature is generated by and/or derivable from them? These are some of the questions which I shall attempt to answer in this work.

Hegel's system is difficult to present in an orderly fashion. He often gives the impression of wanting to say everything at once, and he offers few guidelines for the unravelling of his system, of the steps which led him to it, and of the presuppositions which underlie it. Indeed, on Hegel's own view, his system forms a circle and thus has, strictly speaking, no presuppositions and no starting-point. (Marx claimed that Hegel's dialectic was standing on its head and needed to be turned the right way up again. He did not explain how a circle can be upside down.[1]) If Hegel were right, it would not be hard to organize an account of him. For he believed not only that thought about any subject worth thinking about should be systematic, but that, if one abandons one's own pre-judices and predilections and immerses oneself in the subject matter, then the subject-matter will, so to speak, organize and articulate itself. There will be no problems about how to begin and what to say next; there is only one right way to begin and, at each stage, only one right way to proceed. I criticize this belief later in this book but, in addition, my own experience has not borne it out. I have felt, rather, that there are an indefinite number of things that can be said about Hegel; that there are several more or less reasonable ways of organizing the same material; that there is no uniquely appropriate point of entry into his thought and no uniquely correct way of continuing from any given point. It is, in any case, a mistake to become wholly absorbed in Hegel's system. One should remain at a critical distance from it, retaining the capacity to raise questions which he did not ask and to make explicit what he took as read. There seems little point in simply reproducing his thought in his own terminology. My approach to Hegel, it might be objected, falls foul of another of his beliefs, the belief that informal introductions to his system are of little value, primarily because they involve the detachment of aspects of his thought from their place in the system. It is indeed important not to lose sight of Hegel's system, but questions must be asked and assumptions exposed outside the system itself, if it is to be made intelligible. In any case, Hegel did not practise what he preached. I have found those lengthy introductions and prefaces — in which he questions the value of introductions and prefaces — to be the best illuminated approaches to his thought, and I doubt whether we could understand it without them.

Immersion in the subject-matter might be attained to a not un-reasonable degree by giving an account of what Hegel says in his works in the order in which they were written.[2] I have not adopted this policy, primarily because certain crucial themes run through all his works. These common themes, the systematic structure of his thought, and the questions it was designed to answer are more important than the details. They are what Hegel would wish to be judged by. The problems of organization might, again, have been simplified by the adoption of a chronological approach to Hegel's views. This too, however, I have rejected. What we find puzzling and controversial is not the differences between what he said in 1807 and what he said in 1830, but the underlying similarities, the core of belief which in his maturity he did not question or abandon. It is only after we have understood this persistent core that we are in a position to raise questions about peripheral changes. Of course, Hegel was not born a Hegelian. His early but posthumously published 'theological' writings differ significantly in both style and content from his later works.[3] I have not, however, found these writings to be an enlightening point of entry into his system, and it is this system which is of primary historical and philosophical interest. In his philosophical maturity Hegel's beliefs did not change sharply or significantly. He saw himself, moreover, as filling out a plan which he had adopted fairly early in his career. There are not two Hegels as there are two Wittgensteins and, perhaps, several Schellings. I have therefore ignored such changes as there are or may have been, and have generally cited passages regardless of the date of their composition.

The plan of this book, then, is as follows. Part One provides a sort of introduction to the system as a whole. An attempt, in Chapter I, to elucidate the notion of a pure thought is followed by an account of the relationship of pure thoughts to the self (Ch. II) and of their corresponding relationship to what is other than the self, nature (Ch. III). Certain themes in this Part are revived later in the book. It also raises some of the problems which his system is intended to meet, in particular those suggested by his criticisms of empiricism and the natural sciences (Ch. III). Part Two deals more explicitly with Hegel's problems. A general account of his notion of a problem suggests that it and his conception of what counts as a solution are themselves problematic (Ch. IV). This is followed by a consideration of Hegel's response to some varieties of epistemological scepticism, and of his reasons for supposing that our knowledge can be genuine, secure and complete (Ch. V). What Hegel calls 'infinite' objects – God, the mind, and the universe as a whole – present special problems. The following two chapters examine his belief that we can know about them and the type of epistemic strategy which, on his view, such knowledge requires (Chs VI, VII). Part Three turns to the solution of these problems, the system as a whole. An account of the *Logic* and of the status of pure thought (Ch. VIII) is followed by an examination of the crucial transition from logic to nature (Ch. IX) and of Hegel's beliefs about the status of the phenomenal world (Ch. X). The final chapter considers some aspects of his ethical and political doctrines and, in particular, the support which they derive from his metaphysics (Ch. XI). There is, of course, some overlap between

4

these themes and some arbitrariness in the divisions. (Hegel believed that division into chapters was an artificial interruption of the stream of thought, desirable only for the reader's convenience.) I can only hope that, at any stage, nothing has been presupposed which has not already been considered sufficiently for the purpose in hand.

One feature of my procedure perhaps requires some explanation. It is commonly felt that exposition and criticism are distinct matters and that they should be pursued separately: first we need to know what a thinker says and then we can propose and consider objections to it. This division of tasks may have its place, but I have not found it to be appropriate to the case of Hegel. I have felt rather that criticisms and objections play as important a role in reaching a view about what he means as in assessing the truth of what he says as I see it. I have tried therefore to reconstruct Hegel's meaning (or meanings) by arguing with him. Even in Part One, for example — where I attempt to give a simplified overview of Hegel's system before the introduction of Hegel's problems complicates matters — I have not hesitated to propose and criticize alternative interpretations, to suggest difficulties and ways in which they might be countered. The justification of this procedure, apart from its apparently Hegelian character, is twofold. Hegel's thought is, in the first place, obscure and complex. One cannot simply read off his meaning from his text without working at it. I have felt it worth while to reveal the workings of this process so that the reader can see how I have proceeded and, if I have gone astray, where I have done so. In the second place, Hegel's thought — and not simply his words — is ambiguous. Right from the start we need to question the assumption that his words and sentences have a single clear sense. The proposal of criticisms and of alternative interpretations helps, I believe, to disclose the important ambiguities in his thought. The alternative is a bland 'rational reconstruction' of it, which fits more or less loosely on his text and represents in any case only one of several directions in which his thought might be taken. This is not the procedure I have chosen to adopt. On my view, then, it is a mistake to detach exposition from criticism and to attempt to do them separately. My criticisms of Hegel are not on the whole intended to diminish his stature as a thinker, but in part to expose his merits. These merits lie in the range of problems which he confronted, in the systematic, though perhaps not ultimately coherent, nature of his response to them, and in the wealth of ideas which he left to posterity. But arguments are needed to discover the nature of this heritage as well as to assess its value.

My sparse references to the voluminous secondary sources do

not reflect the extent of my indebtedness to them. Hegel's influence on Marx and on Kierkegaard accounts, directly or indirectly, for much of this literature. It is, however, a mistake to view Hegel through the prism of Marx, of Kierkegaard or, for that matter, of any other later thinker. I have preferred to consider Hegel in his own right. This, after all, is presumably what Marx did. The translations from Hegel, though not from other authors, are in every case my own, but I have — except where the work is arranged in numbered paragraphs — given a page reference to a published translation. (A standard pagination for the works of Hegel is, as yet, lacking.) My translations aim at literalness rather than elegance. Some of them are translations not of Hegel's own words, but of compilations produced posthumously by his pupils from his and their notes. This is true not only of the lectures, but of the 'additions' to the paragraphs in the *Encyclopaedia* and the *Philosophy of Right*. I have not hesitated to cite these additions in support or illustration of what I wanted to say when I felt that they were clearer or fuller than Hegel's published words, but I have indicated this procedure by appending 'Z' (*Zusatz*, 'addition') to the paragraph number. I can see no significant divergence between Hegel and his editors. I have avoided, both in my translations and in my text, the common practice of capitalizing the initial letter of significant Hegelian words — a practice which has no counterpart in German, where all nouns begin with a capital. It has the advantage of differentiating the Hegelian and the informal uses of a word, but it misleadingly implies that such a sharp line can be drawn. It should in general be clear from the context how I am using a word. I have, therefore, avoided the upper case, except where it is a requirement of literacy rather than of piety.[4]

Hegel is all things to all men — or at least to all those who have read him and to some who have not. This is due not only to the notorious difficulty of his writing — his great disservice to posterity is surely to have lowered the resistance to obscurity — but also to the variety of the problems he attempted to solve and to his imposition of system both on recalcitrant material and on his own essentially impressionistic mind. (If Hegel had not written aphorisms, it would be tempting to call him an aphorist *manqué*.) This is reflected in the fact that his text often licenses conflicting interpretations or models of his thought, with little prospect that they can be reconciled at a deeper level. I have acknowledged such ambiguities where I have found them. But I cannot expect that my Hegel will suit everyone's taste. The most I hope for is that he will be both an intelligible and a recognizable Hegel.

PART ONE

Prelude

I

Perception, Conception and Thought

'Thinking' and 'thought' are among the most important words in Hegel's vocabulary. Philosophy, for example, is the 'thinking consideration of objects' (*Enz.* I. 2) and, in so far as Hegel's system has a foundation, it lies in some relatively simple features of thinking.[1] This chapter will be concerned with Hegel's distinction between thinking, or more properly thoughts, and some other elements of our cognitive equipment.

1 *The sensuous*

A dog, like a person, may be able to see a telephone, but it cannot presumably think about a telephone in its absence or about telephones in general. To do this it would need to have the concept of a telephone and other concepts which this one presupposes.[2] What is it that is missing when I merely think about telephones and do not see or hear any or, to put it another way, what is it that is common to me and a dog when we both see (or hear) a telephone? It is our sensory intake or, as Hegel generally calls it, the 'sensuous' (*das Sinnliche, Enz.* I. 20). The sensuous is the object of perception or, at least, it is what makes the difference between perceiving something and merely thinking about it. Hegel is aware that our perceptual experience is organized and articulated in terms of our concepts and beliefs. A dog cannot, as we can, recognize or see a telephone *as* a telephone and does not, therefore, have the same perceptual experience as ourselves. He sometimes marks this distinction by a contrast between perception, which is concerned with our raw sensory intake, and experience (*Erfahrung*), which is this sensory material moulded by thought.[3] This is a difficult distinction and one on which Hegel sometimes casts doubt, but it does not concern us here.[4]

9

The sensuous is characterized by individuality and by asunderness (*das Aussereinander, Enz.* I. 20). What we perceive are individuals. When I see a bowl or a red patch, I see not bowls in general or bowlhood or redness, but some definite, individual bowl or some definite, individual red patch. Again, the things that we perceive are asunder, spread out, in space and time. I see, feel or hear one thing after another and I see or feel one thing next to another. The parts of the bowl are next to each other in space and the parts of it that I see at any one time occupy different positions in my visual field. Moreover, no bowl stands in isolation. There are other individual things next to it, above and below it. Unless I am so close to it that it takes up the whole of my visual field, I shall see other things spatially related to it and these things, or the parts of them that I see, occupy different places in my field of vision. (This account of asunderness has been conducted in terms both of our sensations and of the material things which produce them, since this is not a distinction which Hegel clearly draws when he speaks of the 'sensuous'.)[5]

We can, of course, think about a definite individual bowl, but we can also think about bowls in general or about a bowl, but no particular bowl. What enables us to do this is the concept of a bowl. In contrast to the individuality and asunderness of the sensuous, concepts are characterized by universality and by simple 'self-relatedness' (*Beziehung-auf-sich, Enz.* I. 20). The concept of a bowl applies not just to some particular bowl, but to any bowl whatsoever of the indefinite number that there are. Any particular bowl will have definite features and will stand in definite spatial and temporal relationships to other things, features and relationships which differentiate it from other bowls. If the concept is to apply to any bowl, it must omit or abstract from these particular features and relationships; it must be, in one sense of that elusive word, 'abstract'.[6] Concepts, moreover, are not spread out or asunder; they and their components do not stand in spatio-temporal relationships to each other in the way that items in our visual field do, nor do the universal features, redness, for example, or bowlhood, for which they can perhaps be said to stand, except in so far as they are embodied in particular individuals.

2 *Concepts and conceptions*

This distinction between the sensuous and concepts is no doubt difficult in detail, but its general drift is clear enough. Matters become more complicated when Hegel comes to distinguish between two types of concept. Indeed the concept of a bowl or of redness is not, in his terminology, a concept (*Begriff*) at all, but rather a conception (*Vorstellung*). The distinction is one between empirical or, at least, non-formal concepts such as those of a bowl, a horse or of God (*Vorstellungen*) and abstract or formal concepts such as those of being, of causality or of a thing ('thoughts', *Gedanken*). It is an important distinction. The *Logic*, the first part of Hegel's triadic system, is, among other things, an examination of (pure) thoughts, and when he says such things as that philosophy is the 'thinking consideration of objects', it is thinking in terms of pure thoughts that he primarily has in mind.

Conceptions are themselves of two types. There are empirical ones such as that of a horse and non-empirical ones such as those of God or of duty (*Enz.* I. 20). Difficulties arise even in the attempt to distinguish empirical conceptions from pure thoughts. Pure thoughts are non-empirical, but Hegel interprets this in more than one way. In the first place, pure thoughts are not given in 'immediate sensation' (*Enz.* I. 42Z. 3. Cf. 39). A lump of sugar, a particular thing, is hard, white, sweet and cubical, and we can detect these qualities by our various sense-organs. But the unity of the lump of sugar, the fact that these qualities all belong to a single thing, is not given in our sensory intake and is not, therefore, strictly perceived (*Enz.* I. 42Z. 3. Cf. *PG* pp. 89 ff., M. pp. 67 ff.). Similarly, when I watch a piece of wax melting under the application of a flame, all that is strictly given in perception is 'the individual events following one another in time', not the fact that there is a causal connection between the events, that the application of the flame causes the wax to melt (*Enz.* I. 42Z. 3). Some pure thoughts, that of a force for example, refer to entities which we do not ordinarily regard as perceptible. We can see the flash of lightning, but not the force of which it is the expression (*Enz.* I. 21Z. Cf. *PG* pp. 102 ff., M. pp. 79 ff.). These are some of the ways in which thoughts, or the features to which they refer, are imperceptible.[7]

These examples do not, however, immediately enable us to discriminate between thoughts and conceptions. For if I cannot strictly perceive things, then I cannot strictly perceive lumps of sugar or bowls. If I cannot perceive causal relations, then I cannot perceive melting, pushing, or pulling. But presumably the concepts of a lump of sugar, of melting, and so on are conceptions rather than thoughts. Hegel sometimes obscures the distinction still further by interpreting the imperceptibility of thoughts in a quite different way. For he gives as an example of a thought rather than a conception the concept of an animal, for the reason, amongst others, that we cannot perceive or point to an animal as such, an

11

animal which is no particular sort of animal (*Enz.* I. 24Z. 1). This point applies, however, to any determinable general term. I cannot see a poodle which is just a poodle and has no further features of its own; I cannot see a red patch which is just red and no specific shade of red. I may indeed see that something is a poodle or red and yet fail to notice what sort of poodle or red it is, whereas I could hardly see that something was an animal while failing to notice anything about what sort of animal it was. But Hegel has not said enough to license the attribution of this idea to him. The point would fail to apply, then, only to maximally determinate terms, a term, for example, for a specific shade of red which did not contain, or within which we could not sensorily discriminate, a range of different shades. But Hegel does not want to restrict the class of conceptions to such concepts as these.

His main point, however, is a better one than this. He can concede that bowls and sugar-lumps as well as things, melting as well as causing, and electricity as well as force, are not given in sensation. But we can distinguish within any conception a sensory element and an element of thought. A lump of sugar, for example, is a unified thing with properties. That is the element of thought which the conception of it contains and this is not given in our perception of it. But it is not simply a thing; it is also a particular sort of thing different in kind from a lump of salt. This element, which distinguishes a thing of one sort from those of another, is what is given in sensation. Similarly, while causal relations are not given in sensation, what is so given enables us to distinguish between a flame melting a piece of wax and a block of ice solidifying it. Forces, again, are not perceptible, but the empirical element enables us to distinguish between electricity and gravity.

This is perhaps what Hegel means, but it involves at least three difficulties. Firstly it still gives us no ground for drawing a sharp line between thoughts and conceptions. For granted that empirical data are required for us to tell whether something is melting something else rather than solidifying it, perceptual experience is also needed if we are to know whether one of two events causes the other and, if so, which causes which. This will be so, even if the concept of causality is regarded as universally applicable to our experience, as long as it is not randomly applicable to it. And most of the concepts which Hegel classifies as pure thoughts are of neither random nor universal application. Some of them, that of being for example, are applicable to everything and are involved in any significant utterance.[8] But many of them, though they are widely applicable, are not universally so. The concept of causality is one example of this. Hegel does not believe that this concept is properly applicable to organic nature or to human life. We should not say, for example, that damp causes fever or that Caesar's ambition caused the downfall of the Roman Republic, not because such statements are empirically false, but because causality is not the right category to employ in such cases.[9] Another example is the concept of a whole consisting of parts. This too can be applied to a wide range of entities, but not to living organisms, minds or societies.[10] There are presumably empirical procedures for deciding whether or not any given entity can be appropriately conceived in terms of causality or as a whole consisting of parts — one might, for example, attempt to dismantle and reassemble it — and, if that is so, it is hard to deny that the concept has some empirical content. As far as this goes, then, all that Hegel can claim to have shown is that there are degrees of generality in our concepts, that of causality being, for example, of greater generality than that of a horse, and that the more general a concept is, the less its applicability depends on the precise character of our sensory data.

A second difficulty is that Hegel seems to be conflating two quite different distinctions, the distinction between more general and less general concepts and that between concepts the instances of which are perceptible and concepts the instances of which are not. His treatment of the concept of an animal provides a bridge between these two distinctions but it is, as we have seen, an insecure one. For it is not true of all the concepts which he regards as pure thoughts that they are not given in sensation. The concepts with which the *Logic* begins, those of being, of becoming and of determinate being (*Dasein*) are not of this kind, though they are also of unrestrictedly universal application. The concept of being is taken by Hegel both in a predicative sense (as in 'This leaf is green', *Enz.* I. 3) and in an existential one (as in 'God is', *Enz.* I. 51), but its primary use seems to be when one simply gestures towards or focuses upon some item in one's experience by saying or thinking 'That is!' or 'There it is!' (*PG* pp. 79 ff., M. pp. 58 ff.).[11] It may be true that the fact that a creature has sensations does not guarantee that it has this concept, and that the concept cannot be acquired by abstraction from one's sensory experience. But neither of these points is sufficient to establish that being is not given in our sensations in the way that causality or forces supposedly are not. The question is not whether, if one has the requisite sensations, one will automatically have or acquire the concept, but whether, given that one has the concept and that one has the requisite sensations, the sensations alone can guarantee the applicability of the concept to them. In the case of the concept of being, there is no room for a sceptic to drive a wedge between our bare sensory intake and the claim that it *is*. That is, no doubt, little consolation, for the claim is a singularly empty one. However, the same is true of the richer claims that come under the heading of determinate being. Here we do not confine ourselves to saying that things *are*, but ascribe definite qualities to our experience, particular colours for example. There is, however, no assumption at this stage that one and the same individual has more than one quality or that it can have different qualities at different times, nor is it assumed that the qualified items are objective rather than subjective or, for that matter, subjective rather than objective (*Enz.* I. 89 ff.; *WL* I. pp. 115 ff., M. pp. 109 ff.). The claims are of the type 'This is green', 'That is red', and so on. In this case, too, it is not obvious that there is an epistemic gulf between our sensory intake and the application of these concepts, once it is granted that we have them. The pure thought is not, however, the concept of redness; that is, if anything, a conception. Rather it is the concept of determinate being itself. But again, granted that we have this concept, there can be no question that our sensory intake is determinate. Indeed the statement that something is red presumably entails that it is of some determinate quality. Hegel's claim that thoughts are not given in sensation cannot, then, provide him with the distinction he requires between thoughts and conceptions.

A third difficulty is suggested by one of Hegel's own arguments in the *Phenomenology of Mind*. There he argues that there is no way in which I can capture or express my experience without employing thoughts. Even if, as I do in the 'form of consciousness' which he entitles 'sense-certainty' (*sinnliche Gewissheit*), I confine myself to focusing upon or picking out particular items in my experience, I am committed to the use of token-reflexive terms such as 'this', 'here', and 'now' and these terms express or involve thoughts (*PG* pp. 79 ff., M. pp. 58 ff.).[12] If I go further and ascribe qualities to my experience, then the terms I employ involve the concept of determinate being. As we have seen, Hegel does not speak, in this context, of one's subjective sensory intake as opposed to objective items in the world, and this is perhaps because he feels that the distinction between what is objective and what is merely subjective is a sophisticated one, the drawing of which presupposes a richer conceptual arsenal than is available to the simple forms of consciousness which he is considering here. The point would apply, however, to our sensory intake considered as such, namely that no thought-free description, or even indication, of it can be given. But to give substance to the thesis that thoughts generally are not, or that some particular thought is not, given in our sensory intake, we should be able to suggest some way of describing our sensations such that the description does not imply or entail statements which involve thoughts or, at least, the particular thought with which we are concerned. If Hegel's argument is sound, however, then we cannot claim that no thought is given in sensory experience, since we cannot provide an entirely thought-free description of it. The thoughts of being, of negation, and of determinate being are implicit in any description of our sensory experience. The most we can hope to do along these lines is to show that certain thoughts are not involved in it when it is described in minimally thought-ridden terms. The claim, for example, that the unity and persistence of objects is not given in sensation will mean that no statement or set of statements of the type 'This is green', 'That is red', and 'This is sweet' — where 'this' and 'that' simply locate the quality rather than denote a subject, like perhaps the 'it' in 'It is raining' — entails any such statement as 'This single thing is both sweet and white' or 'This thing was red, but is now green.' The claim that causal connections are not given will mean that statements of the first type ('This is green'), together perhaps with statements of the second ('This thing was red, but is now green'), do not entail such statements as 'This made that change its colour' or 'This melted that.' This procedure cannot, however, be applied to such primitive thoughts as those of being and of determinate being, since these are involved in any statement whatsoever. Hegel cannot, then, by this route distinguish thoughts as a whole from empirical conceptions.

If something is to be said about thoughts as a whole, then the claim that they are not given in sense-experience might be taken to mean that sense-experience is different from thoughts, and this could be given more content by adding that one might, or at least an animal might, have sense-experience without having any thoughts — even that of being. A creature of this type could not, of course, describe its own sense-experience. It does not follow that *we* could not describe it, but if we do so, then we shall inevitably employ thoughts which the creature itself does not possess. This, however, is not the sense which Hegel generally gives to the claim that thoughts are not contained in sensation. Moreover, since, on his view, any creature which lacked thoughts would also lack conceptions, this suggestion too fails to supply a way of distinguishing between them. In this sense, neither thoughts nor conceptions are given in sensation.

3 *The acquisition of thoughts*

A different, though related, interpretation of the thesis that pure thoughts are not empirical is that while sensory experience is required for the formation of conceptions, it is not necessary and/or not sufficient for the acquisition of thoughts. A distinction is needed here between at least two different levels at which thoughts can occur. Firstly, thoughts are implicit in all our ordinary discourse, intertwined with empirical material. The sentence 'This leaf is green' involves at least the thoughts of being ('This leaf *is* green') and of individuality ('*This* leaf is green') (*Enz.* I. 3). Secondly, one can consider or employ thoughts in their pure form. Ordinary people do not normally do this; they do not extricate thoughts from their empirical context. It is done in different ways by philosophers, by theologians (when they claim, for example, that God is pure being) and perhaps by grammarians.

The questions about the role of sensory experience in our acquisition of pure thoughts can be asked of each of these levels at which they occur. Firstly, how do ordinary men come to acquire such concepts as those of being, negation and causality? This is a difficult question and only a few considerations can be sketched here. Some of Hegel's pure thoughts, those, for example, of being and of non-being or negation, cannot be straightforwardly derived from experience by any such process as abstraction. They are, in the first place, universally applicable, so that a language teacher could not point to one thing and say 'That is!' and to another saying 'That isn't!' in the way in which he can point to things which are, and to things which are not, red. The mere fact that a concept is universally applicable does not, indeed, inevitably mean that it cannot be taught in this way. For the teaching method exploits not so much what is the case and what is not as what is apparent to the learner and what is not. It is, however, unclear how some things, but not others, could obviously and noticeably 'be' in the way that some things are more obviously causally determined than others are. Secondly, concepts such as those of being, of negation, of qualitative similarity and dissimilarity, of numerical identity and difference seem to be involved in the learning of any word by this procedure and cannot, therefore, themselves be conveyed by it. If I teach someone the meaning of the word 'red' by pointing to a number of red things and saying 'Red', by pointing to other things and saying 'Not red', 'Green', 'Blue', and so on, the procedure presupposes that the learner has the concepts of being and of negation, though not, of course, the corresponding words. (To say this perhaps amounts to little more than saying that the language-learner, unlike a cat or a tree, is capable of learning a language.) Hegel would not claim, of course, that one could have or acquire these concepts if one had no sensory experience at all or if one did not learn a language which included empirical terms. Nor is he much attracted by the view that such concepts are innate in us; he sometimes suggests that this is a vacuous thesis, on a par with explaining why opium sends us to sleep by reference to its *virtus dormitiva* (*VGP* II. p. 107, H. II. p. 92).[13]

These arguments, such as they are, do not, however, extend to concepts like that of causality which are, on Hegel's view, of restricted applicability. The point, as we have seen, is presumably that while sensory experience is required for us to form such conceptions as that of pulling, it is not sufficient since these conceptions involve the thought of causal connection, and causal connection is not given in our sensory intake. The thought of causal connection is therefore seen as the mind's own contribution to the learning process. However, as long as causal connections are regarded not as all-pervasive, but as restricted in their occurrence to certain areas of our experience, it is quite unclear why the concept of causality differs in more than degree from those of melting and of pulling. As far as these arguments go, it may simply be that if a man is to acquire the concept of causality, that is, in this context, *some* causal conceptions *or other*, there are looser constraints on what his sensory intake has to be than if he is to acquire some particular causal conception like that of pulling.

4 *Pure thoughts*

Hegel is, on the whole, less interested in how ordinary men acquire such grasp as they have on pure thoughts than he is in the fact that philosophers can consider these thoughts in their purity. His official doctrine is that pure thoughts can be derived from each other without recourse to sensory experience and he purports to have done this in his *Logic*. It might be felt that, in the light of this, the foregoing attempts to distinguish thoughts from conceptions are superfluous. Hegel would, indeed, still have to justify the claim, in so far as he wishes to make it, that the concepts derived in the *Logic* resemble in any degree the concepts which we ordinarily designate by the same terms. But, if we grant that the concept with which the *Logic* begins, that of being, is a pure thought — and we have already seen some reason to do so — then there can be no question but that Hegel's concept of, say, causality is a pure thought.

17

There are, however, several difficulties with this line of argument. Firstly, and most obviously, no one in his right mind would claim that Hegel has in fact succeeded in doing what he set out to do. This is a difficult proposition to substantiate, if it is insisted that what Hegel calls 'causality' or 'life' might be quite different from causality and life as these are ordinarily understood. Hegel himself sometimes resorts to this manoeuvre,[14] but in the main it is clear that he means his words to have some connection with our words, and we would not understand him if they did not. Secondly, he does little more than pause for breath, when he has ended the *Logic*, and proceeds straight away into the discussion of nature. The transition from pure thoughts to nature is, of course, difficult both to interpret and to justify, but, for the moment, it is enough that there is no obvious change in Hegel's procedure in the transition and that presumably the *Philosophy of Nature* involves conceptions as well as thoughts. If, therefore, derivability from the concept of being were taken as the criterion of a pure thought, many conceptions, such as those of time and of space, might have to be counted as thoughts.

A final difficulty for this suggestion is that Hegel does not claim unequivocally that thoughts can be derived independently of sense-experience. At the beginning of the *Encyclopaedia* we are told that 'consciousness forms *conceptions* of objects earlier than it forms *concepts* of them, the *thinking* mind advances to thinking knowledge and conceptualization (*Begreifen*) only *through* conceiving (*Vorstellen*) and by recourse *to* it' (*Enz.* I. 1).[15] This might, of course, mean several things. It might mean, for example, only that the formation of conceptions is a historical precondition of our being able to think about or in terms of pure concepts. In a similar way, geometry might not have arisen if men had not needed to measure their land and to form the conceptions required for this purpose, but it does not follow that, once geometry has started, it needs to make constant reference to the measurement of land. It might mean, again, that pure thoughts are formed not by direct reflection on our sensory experience, but by reflection on the conceptions which are formed by such direct reflection. We are not taught, for example, the concepts of a thing or of causality in their abstract form by being directed to examples of things or of causal connections in our experience. Rather, we learn such terms as 'bowl', 'sugar' and 'melt' in this way. Subsequently we are taught the meanings of such highly general terms as 'thing', 'stuff', and 'cause' by being directed to the more concrete terms or to sentences which contain them. This is probably true, and it is no doubt a part of what Hegel had in mind. But it need not follow that thoughts are not also in some way derivable from each other. The following analogy will make this clear, and it will also serve to bring into relief some other features of Hegel's procedure.

5 *A mathematical analogy*

A very simple system of arithmetic consists of the positive whole numbers together with the operation of addition. A natural next step is to introduce the operation of subtraction, so that we can reverse the operations of addition that we perform. We shall, if we are confined to this system, call the numbers simply 'numbers' rather than 'positive' or 'whole' numbers, for we have as yet no notion of negative numbers or fractions with which to contrast them. This system already illustrates some of the features which Hegel ascribes to the philosophical consideration of pure thoughts. Our possession of it presupposes that we perform practical operations such as counting sheep, giving and receiving change and so on, and our initiation into the system takes place by our performing such simple operations and reflecting upon our performances. Philosophy, that is, presupposes conceptions (*Enz.* I. 1). But to add and subtract numbers as such is not the same thing as the performance of these everyday, practical operations, and we can form and manipulate far greater numbers than we would ordinarily employ in them. When we do pure calculations we have risen above the practical, empirical procedures in which the system has its roots. Philosophy, too, rises above sensory experience (*Enz.* I. 12).

Suppose, now, that we wish to extend this arithmetical system by introducing negative numbers. There are three ways in which this might be done. Firstly, we might simply decide, from, for example, reading books about arithmetic, that there should be negative numbers and add them to our system. Hegel sometimes implies that philosophers have no better reason than this for selecting certain concepts rather than others for employment or discussion.[16] Secondly, and more satisfactorily, we might reflect that there are in nature and in human affairs features which invite the application of negative as well as positive numbers. There are, for example, losses as well as gains, debts as well as credit, and movement backwards as well as forwards. On Hegel's view, natural scientists, when they claim, for example, that lightning is the expression of a certain kind of force, arrive at pure thoughts in a way analogous to this.[17] Finally, one can derive negative numbers from the simple system without reference to empirical phenomena. If one confines oneself to positive numbers, then every operation of adding one number to another has a result, and some operations of subtracting one number from another have a result (e.g. 5—3), but some (e.g. 3—5) do not. (This might be called a sort of 'contradiction' within the system. It is at least as good as some of the things that Hegel calls 'contradictions'!) Negative numbers can be introduced as the results of those operations of subtraction which previously had no result. Fractions can, of course, be introduced in a similar way if we start with a system containing whole numbers and the operations of multiplication and division. One can in this way extend arithmetic indefinitely without being dependent on empirical phenomena and ordinary ways of dealing with them.[18] This is analogous to the way in which Hegel purports to derive pure thoughts from each other in his *Logic*.

This analogy or model of Hegel's procedure is a useful one, though it does not, of course, represent everything that he is attempting to do. It should be added that the analogy is not Hegel's nor is it one of which he would probably approve. His opinion of arithmetic was, for various reasons, a fairly low one and his own attempt to systematize it is quite different from this.[19]

The main question here, however, is whether the model provides a satisfactory way of distinguishing between empirical conceptions and non-empirical thoughts. Arithmetic does not necessarily have an application at all. It would not be applicable to, for example, a universe which was entirely homogeneous, or which, although diverse and variegated, did not contain items which were relatively discrete and stable. But in such a universe we, if we existed at all, could not learn arithmetic or engage in pure calculation. If we can do arithmetic, by for example writing marks on paper, then it must have application at least to the marks we make.[20] (Numbers themselves, moreover, are among the things that can be counted, and, as we shall see, Hegel often implies that pure thoughts apply to themselves in a similar way.)[21] There are again certain features of the world to which arithmetic is not applicable; we cannot, for example, count the ripples on a lake, since ripples are not distinctly individuated one from another. But if we can get a numerical grip on some area of the world, there are no further particular empirical constraints on how we apply arithmetic to it. It seems, for example, intuitively natural to apply positive numbers to a man's income and negative numbers to his expenditure. But we could just as well represent his expenditure by positive numbers and his income by negative ones.

There seems, then, to be no counterpart in arithmetic to such empirical restrictions as Hegel places on the application of his pure thoughts. Pure thoughts are widely applicable but not universally so. The concept of causality is confined, as we have seen, more or less to inorganic nature and to pathological examples or features of organic and human life. This is not because the concept cannot get a grip on organic and social life. To say that Caesar's ambition caused the downfall of the Roman republic is not, on Hegel's view, absurd in the way that it would be to say that there were exactly 3,007 ripples on Lake Windermere between 10.00 and 11.00 a.m. on a certain day. The analogue in the case of arithmetic would be the claim that it is wrong to count the members of a team or the number of legs on a centipede because these items are organically interrelated in a way in which the lumps in a bowl of sugar are not. Hegel does indeed incline to the view that arithmetic or 'quantity' is more appropriately applicable to inorganic nature than to organic or human life for such reasons as this.[22] To this extent, however, the purity of quantity is thrown into question as much as that of the other thoughts of the *Logic*.

A further difficulty, as was suggested above, is that the assumption that the concept which is introduced by each of our three procedures will be one and the same concept is open to doubt. The assumption might be questioned even in the case of arithmetic. Even if we grant that the concept of a negative number is 'non-empirical' when it is derived in the third way, within arithmetic itself, there is no guarantee that this concept will coincide with the concept of a negative number which we derive in the second way, by reflection upon gains and losses, and so on. Why the two concepts do coincide, why the 'pure' concept has useful applications, is a remarkable fact and one that is difficult to explain. But the main point here is that we should perhaps, analogously, distinguish between the concept of causality as it is employed in our everyday transactions with the empirical world and the concept of causality which is derived within Hegel's *Logic*. The latter, it might be argued, is non-empirical, or at any rate is only very loosely connected with our sensory experience. We should look for its sense to the manner of its derivation and not to experience or to ordinary discourse. Hegel, indeed, often indicates that this is the right approach. He recognizes, for example, that the use of the term 'concept', when he discusses the concept, is not much like our ordinary use of the term (*Enz.* I. 60Z) and often urges us not to assume that his words mean what they do in everyday discourse.[23] If this is a confusion, however, Hegel does a good deal to encourage it. He often says that pure thoughts are familiar (*bekannt*), though they are not known (*erkannt*), that is, that these concepts are involved in our ordinary thought and speech, but are not explored in their abstraction (*Enz.* I. 19). Again, he constantly descends within the *Logic* from the consideration of pure thoughts to the question of their empirical application, and indeed these descents are generally the more intelligible parts of the work. Nevertheless, it may be that it would be more in the spirit of Hegel to regard these episodes as peripheral to the *Logic* and to conceive this work as an attempt to construct a formal system with only the remote and loose connections with experience and ordinary language that any formal system has. Questions would still remain to be answered, such questions as: Are the procedures whereby thoughts are derived clear and legitimate? Can we understand the system? and How does it come to have application? These questions will be discussed later.[24]

6 *Non-empirical conceptions*

So far we have considered Hegel's attempts to distinguish between pure thoughts and *empirical* conceptions, and the distinction has been found problematic. The problems are augmented by the fact that there is a second type of conception which is, on Hegel's view, non-empirical. Such conceptions as those of right, duty, and God are not empirical, apparently because instances of them cannot be perceived, and yet are distinct from pure thoughts (*Enz.* I. 20). Hegel sometimes negotiates the difficulty in terms of a distinction between form and content. The objects of perception, the sensuous, are individual, rather than universal, both in their form and in their content. Pure thoughts, by contrast, are universal both in form and in content. Conceptions are of two kinds. In the case of empirical conceptions, such as those of anger, of a rose or of hope, their content is sensuous and individual, but their form is universal or thought (*gedachter*). In the case of non-empirical conceptions, thinking is the source of their content, but their form is individual, it makes the content into a 'given' 'which comes to the mind from outside' (*Enz.* I. 24Z. 1). The point here is not, of course, that God is an individual and there can be only one individual who is God. There can be more than one duty, after all, and more than one god. But, if this is so, then it is a mistake to suggest that the conception of a god or of a duty lacks universality in any sense in which the conception of a rose possesses it; both types of conception are equally universal in form. What Hegel means becomes clearer elsewhere, though it is equally clearly mistaken. Non-empirical conceptions differ from thoughts not because their content is empirical but because their content is 'individualized' or isolated. Both types of conception again retain some

22

contact with sensory experience, empirical ones, because their content is derived from it, and non-empirical ones, because their content is individualized and discrete in a parallel way to that in which our sensory experience is individualized and discrete. Hegel mentions two ways in which this happens. Firstly, conceptions are sharply distinct from one another, with none of the fluid interconnections which, on Hegel's view, obtain between pure thoughts. Similarly the objects which correspond to them are regarded as sharply distinct from each other. Secondly, when the object of a conception is conceived as internally complex, no connection is established between the elements of this complex. God, for example, is conceived as being the creator, omniscient, almighty, and so on, but, apart from the fact that these attributes are all predicated of a single subject, they are not regarded as interconnected with each other.[25] Conceptions are arrayed in our mental space much as objects are arrayed alongside each other in physical space (*Enz.* I. 20).

In this passage, Hegel is conflating what are, on the face of it, two quite different distinctions. There is, firstly, the distinction between formal concepts and informal ones, between pure thoughts and empirical, or at any rate contentful, conceptions. Secondly, there is the distinction between reason and the understanding, between, very roughly, the treatment of concepts as fluid, as passing out of and into one another, and the treatment of them as sharply distinct from, and more or less unconnected with, each other. This second distinction is in itself problematic and more will be said about it later. For the moment it is enough that the two distinctions do not coincide. In the first place, pure thoughts may be treated as if they were sharply distinct from each other. This, on Hegel's view, was how Wolffian[26] metaphysics conceived them (*Enz.* I. 27 ff.). In terms of our analogy, negative numbers might be simply introduced into one's arithmetical system by reference to other text-books, and not derived from the system of positive numbers and the operations performed on them. Conversely, conceptions and their objects may be regarded as flowing into one another, rather than as individualized and isolated. Some pre-philosophical religious views employed conceptions in this way, on Hegel's account. By and large, the static conception of God as an entity with a number of distinct properties is an imposition of rationalist philosophy (*Enz.* I. 28 ff., 36). Again, Hegel himself purports to derive conceptions from one another and thus to exploit their interconnections in, for example, the *Philosophy of Nature* and the *Philosophy of Right*. It is, on Hegel's view, because of the thoughts which these conceptions involve that they can be treated in this way; thought is, so to speak, a 'subtle spiritual bond' (*Enz.* I. 20Z). But it is nevertheless the case that conceptions need not be kept distinct and isolated. In general Hegel regards the distinction between thoughts and conceptions and that between reason and the understanding as quite different distinctions and there seems no good reason for his running them together here apart from the need to differentiate non-empirical conceptions from thoughts.

How, then, can these be distinguished? It is not that thoughts are necessarily applicable or indispensable, whereas conceptions are not. For, on Hegel's view at least, the conception of God has as great a claim to indispensability as do our pure thoughts. He might perhaps have done well to consider the variety of the connections a concept can have with sensory experience. God is not normally held to be perceptible, but the conception is presumably modelled upon empirical objects and situations: the relationship of fathers to their children, of rulers to their subjects, of craftsmen to their products, and so on. It is, then, if not an empirical conception, at least a pictorial one. Again, the conception of a duty is related variously to acts of compulsion or of restraint, to socially established norms and institutions and to our desires. The trouble with this line of thought, however, is that pure thoughts themselves cannot be insulated against similar contacts with the empirical.

7 *Grammar and metaphor*

A final difficulty in the distinction which Hegel wants to draw is the ambiguity in his account of the relationship between thoughts and conceptions. Sometimes it is suggested that the relationship is like that between a sentence and its formal or grammatical structure (*WL* I. pp. 53 f., M. pp. 57 f.), and this seems especially plausible in the case of empirical conceptions. The sentence 'This rose is red' involves at least the thoughts of being and of individuality. The sentence 'This daisy is yellow' presumably involves the same thoughts, no more and no less. On the face of it, pure thoughts do not exhaust empirical conceptions; they cannot capture the difference between these two sentences. Hegel also says, however, that the relationship is that of the literal to the metaphorical (*Enz.* I. 3). This relationship, rather than that of grammar to language, is appropriate to the case of the conception of God and of such other theological conceptions as those of the creation and of the trinity. It is clear, for example, that, on Hegel's view, the conception of God and statements about him are entirely exhausted by pure thoughts and can be replaced by them without loss of meaning.[27] This ambiguity is both important and difficult, and it will be considered at length later on.[28] It is enough for the moment if we think non-committally of the distinction between thoughts and conceptions as that between the formal and the informal or between the pure and the applied — a better distinction perhaps than Hegel's ways of drawing it. It is tempting to regard the boundary between what is formal and what is not as a shifting one whose position depends on our interests and on the uses to which the distinction is to be put. Whether Hegel would have been content to regard the matter in this light depends in part on the ontological status which he assigns to pure thoughts.[29] But the point at least suggests that we should turn from the consideration of the distinction itself to that of the purposes which it was intended to serve, and this we shall do in the following chapter.

II

Thinking and the Self

The notion of the self has an important place in Hegel's philosophy. Two of the reasons for this apply with equal force to a good many other philosophers. If, firstly, we are concerned to give an account of the world, the self is a puzzling entity which it is difficult to accomodate in a coherent way. Secondly, Hegel is troubled by problems of an egocentric kind, such as 'Can I know what the world is really like?'[1] and 'Why should I not just do whatever I want to do?'[2] – problems whose solution requires an account of the self to which they essentially refer. The third reason is one that Hegel shares with few other thinkers. It is that the human mind, rather than the machine or the living organism, provides him with a model for understanding the universe as a whole. How literally this is to be taken is a controversial matter, which will be considered later.[3] This chapter will be concerned only with the first of these issues, namely the nature of the self, and that particularly in relation to thoughts and thinking.

1 *Form, content and object*

We have a picture of the self as the owner or locus of a number of faculties or capacities, and of states or activities which correspond to them. We can, for example, perceive, desire, remember, feel, and think. All these things are done or undergone by the self, and thinking is one, but only one, of the things it does, and the capacity for thought is only one of the faculties it possesses.

This picture is rejected by Hegel, on the ground that thought occupies a special position in the constitution of the self and is not simply one capacity or activity among others. Thinking is what distinguishes man from animals, Hegel constantly reiterates, and thinking is involved in all human states and activities.[4] This, however, is given more than one interpretation. Firstly, there is the claim that thoughts or thinking are involved in our other mental states or activities. It would be quite wrong to suppose that our capacities for perception, for desiring, feeling, imagining and remembering are something that we share with other creatures, while our capacity for thought is a superimposed extra which leaves these other capacities unaffected. Our perceiving, desiring and so on are, on the contrary, deeply thought-ridden. We can, for example, see a telephone as a telephone and want to ring up a friend, things that no animal can do.

Hegel connects this with our ability to form universal concepts. Animals focus only on individual things, and this is because sensation as such has to do only with individuals, this particular pain, for example, or this taste. By contrast:

> Man is always thinking, even when he only intuits or perceives
> (*anschaut*); if he considers anything he considers it always as a
> universal, he fixes on an individual, sets it in relief, withdraws
> his attention from other things, takes it as something abstract
> and universal, if only formally universal (*Enz.* I. 24Z. 1).

Universal concepts are involved in all our thinking, perceiving, desiring and remembering. The formation of concepts is associated with the ability to focus one's attention on one item in one's experience at the expense of others. One attends to one individual, e.g. a rose, or to one feature of an individual, e.g. its redness, and takes it in a universal way, as a member of a class which can have other members or as a feature which can be shared by a number of individuals. This, however, is problematic. The ability to focus one's attention is presumably a necessary condition of concept formation, but it is doubtful whether it is sufficient. If I attend to something at the expense of its environment, then it may be abstract in the sense that it is abstracted from its context by my concentration on it, but it is not necessarily abstract in the sense of 'universal' or 'taken in a general way'. Moreover, animals surely attend to certain items in their experience at the expense of others. What they perhaps cannot do is direct, withdraw, and redirect their attention at will, as I can, for example, deliberately withdraw my attention from some salient feature of my experience such as a tooth-ache, and redirect it to some peripheral item chosen at random (Cf. *Enz.* III. 448Z). But Hegel does not introduce this idea in this context.

A further difficulty is that it is not as obvious as Hegel believes that animals do not have any general concepts. Dogs, after all, do

27

not simply react to individual bones and cats, but respond to them in ways which are determined by certain general features of bones and of cats; they discriminate in their behaviour between bones and other types of things and between cats and other types of thing. It is hard to be sure what Hegel would say to this, since he does not discuss the criteria for ascribing awareness of universals, or the possession of concepts, except for cursory references to language.[5] It can perhaps be said that in his hands such terms as 'universal' and 'thinking' are too rough-hewn for discriminating carefully between animals and men.

Elsewhere, Hegel makes the point that our mental states and activities are thought-ridden in terms of a distinction between the form of a mental state or activity and its content. Perceiving, desiring and remembering, for example, are different forms. Seeing an apple and wanting an apple differ in form, while wanting an apple and wanting a banana differ in their content. Thinking is itself a form, one form among others. Thinking about an apple (or apples) is different in form from seeing or desiring an apple. But, secondly, thinking or thoughts are always involved in the content of any mental state or activity, even if its form is that of a desire or of perception, and not of thinking. Thinking, he suggests, is the appropriate form for any mental state or activity, for it corresponds to its content in a way in which other forms do not (*Enz.* I. 3). This distinction might be developed by expressing the content of a mental state or activity in the form of a proposition. In this way one could, for example, capture the egocentricity characteristic of many of our desires, the fact that to desire an apple is to desire an apple for me or to desire that I (should) have an apple, whereas to see an apple is not to see that I have an apple. But whatever form we gave to the propositions in which the content is expressed, they would at all events involve thoughts.[6]

Hegel does not, however, develop the point in this way, but rather proceeds to draw a distinction not simply between the form and the content of a mental state but also between both of these and its object. What the object of a mental state or activity is is determined primarily by its content. But the form also plays a part here. Two mental states which differ in form, but not in content, will, or might, have, or at least seem to have, different objects in virtue of their different forms:

> In any one of these forms or in the combination of several, the content is the *object* of consciousness. But in this objectivity *the determinacies (Bestimmtheiten) of these forms also ally*

28

themselves with the content; so that with each of these forms
a particular object seems to arise and what is in itself the same
can look like a different content (*Enz.* I. 3).

This is at first sight puzzling. In what sense do seeing an apple and
the desire for an apple have, or seem to have, different objects or
different contents? But what Hegel is concerned with here is the
distinction between the 'form' of thought and the other 'forms'.
To think about something, rather than simply to look at it or to
desire it, radically changes our conception of it. In the following
chapter, we shall consider the application of this doctrine to the
thinking involved in the natural sciences.[7] But what he also has in
mind here is this. Some of his near-contemporaries, notably F.H.
Jacobi, had maintained that those peculiarly human institutions,
morality and religion, were a matter of feeling or of immediate
awareness rather than of thought. We cannot, it was claimed, argue
in favour of God's existence or think discursively about him; we
can only succumb to our immediate awareness of him.[8] It is because of this contemporary debate that Hegel, with his persistent
preoccupation with theology, draws on religion for his illustrations
in this context (*Enz.* I. 2,8). One of the main applications of the
thesis that mental states and activities are thought-ridden is to the
belief in God. This belief, however naïve and primitive it may be,
always involves thoughts. It does not follow, however, that it must
be in the form of thought. One way of transposing this content
into the form of thought is by 'meta-thinking' (*Nachdenken*), that
is, by attempting to argue for or prove God's existence. One can,
on Hegel's view, believe in God without doing, or being able to do,
this, just as one can eat and digest without studying physiology
(*Enz.* I. 2). This type of thinking still involves, however, the pictorial conception of God and, although God may be conceived in
different ways by naïve believers and philosophers, there is initially
little temptation to suppose that they are speaking about different
'objects' There is, however, a second type of thinking – which
one equally need not engage in in order to believe in God – a type
which operates solely in terms of pure thoughts. The conception
of God is, on Hegel's view, fully exhausted by pure thoughts.
When we think about and in terms of them our thinking has the
same content as the feelings and conceptions of the unphilo-
sophical religious believer.[9] The object is, or seems to be, different
only because the *form* of our mental state or activity is different.
As we have seen, however, it does not follow that thoughts and
conceptions are *generally* equivalent, that thoughts exhaust, and
can entirely replace, the conceptions involved in, for example, our

29

beliefs about nature and our moral attitudes. It may be that thoughts are involved in all this, but it is a different matter to claim that thoughts are *all* that are involved in it. There is a crucial ambiguity in Hegel's doctrine that 'philosophy puts *thoughts*, *categories*, more precisely *concepts*, in place of conceptions' (*Enz.* I. 3). It might mean that philosophy strictly substitutes thoughts for conceptions, replacing the metaphorical by the literal, or only that it abstracts and considers the thoughts involved in them in the way that grammar abstracts the formal features of a language. Hegel never clearly disambiguates this claim.[10]

Hegel's concentration on religious belief misleads him in another respect. For the attractiveness of the thesis that our mental states and activities are thought-ridden, that our capacity for thought does not leave our perception, desires and so on unscathed, owes much to this choice of examples. The 'feelings of right, of morals and religion' (*Enz.* I. 8) with which he illustrates the doctrine do not exhaust the range of our mental states and activities. We also have or undergo more primitive states, such as pains and itches, states which are not obviously thought-ridden and which we presumably share with animals. It is true that our references to and descriptions of these states are thought-ridden, but some argument is required to show that such description, or even mere describability, necessarily contaminates the states themselves. One might counter this objection by qualifying the doctrine so that it applies only to what is peculiarly human, just as one might insist that it concerns only the mental in the strict sense and thus does not extend to pains and itches. Hegel advances, however, a second interpretation of the thesis, an interpretation in which it clearly does apply to such items as these.

2 *The subject as thinker*

This interpretation centres on the fact that it is a single ego or 'I' which has and is aware of having a diversity of states. Even if having a pain does not itself involve thought, it is at least I who have and am aware of having the pain. Hegel's account of the 'I' is intended to establish that it is a 'universal' and intimately associated with thought or, in his own words, that 'Thinking conceived as *subject* is a *thinker*, and the simple expression of the existing subject as a thinker is I' (*Enz.* I. 20). A diversity of considerations are adduced in support of this conclusion:

(i) The word 'I' applies to all persons and its use does not differentiate one from another; everyone is an I. Hegel infers that the word 'I' expresses a thought rather than a conception (*Enz.* I.

20).[11] But this does not follow from the fact that it applies universally. The expression 'donkey' or 'that donkey' applies to any donkey, but it does not follow that these terms express pure thoughts. Hegel's idea is that 'I' is an empirically empty term, not on a par with descriptive terms like 'red', 'donkey', or even 'man', but with such terms as 'this' or 'that'. This point alone, of course, does not establish that egos have any more to do with thought than do things or animals. For they too can be referred to by such terms as 'this' and 'that' which do not in themselves imply any qualitative difference between them.

(ii) Any ego has a diversity of states — perceptions, desires, etc. — at any one time, and these states change over time. The ego remains the same throughout this diversity and change. Hegel picturesquely expresses this (among other things) by saying 'The I is this void, the receptacle for anything and everything' (*Enz.* I. 24Z. 1). He infers that the ego is universal, in the sense that it contains, and persists throughout, a diversity of particular and transient states. This again, however, does not by itself differentiate egos from things and animals, for they too have a variety of states or properties and persist through changes in them. Hegel sometimes speaks of the thing which has properties as universal for this reason (*PG* pp. 95 f., M. pp. 72 f.). There is the difference that one might argue, in the manner of Kant, that the unity of a thing is something we introduce by imposing concepts on the diverse sensible material presented to us, whereas the ego is an 'original' unity which cannot derive its unity from anything else.[12] Hegel does not, however, seem to accept this account even in the case of inanimate things — his view that the unity of a thing is not given in sensation does not commit him to it — and he certainly rejects it in the case of non-human living creatures, regarding them as self-constituting unities.[13]

(iii) Mental states and activities differ, however, from the states and properties of a thing in several respects. They are, firstly, not simply states, but states of awareness of objects other than oneself. (The word 'object' is used in a very general way to include anything that I perceive, desire, imagine, or think about.)[14] Hegel's remark that the I is a 'receptacle for anything and everything' also means that anything can be the object of one of our mental states and activities.

(iv) I am aware, moreover, of the states themselves as well as of the objects of those states. This is not intended to exclude the possibility of subconscious mental states. Hegel's interest in mesmerism ('animal magnetism') and other such phenomena suggests that he would have been sympathetic to this idea (*Enz.*

III. 406). He is more concerned with the remarkable fact that I can be aware of such a variety of object-directed mental states and that I must be aware of a good many of them if I am to be an ego at all than to claim that I must be aware of all those that I have. In any case we could not claim that there were any subconscious mental states unless they could be or become objects of our *thought*, even if we are not aware of them in the ordinary way.

(v) Hegel often says that I can abstract from all my states and activities, both physical and mental, and that the I or ego is 'pure relation to itself', abstracted from everything which it does or undergoes (*Enz.* I. 20). We can, of course, abstract from all the properties and states of a thing by referring to it simply as 'this (thing)' or by thinking of it as a mere bearer of properties, but Hegel has in mind more than this. Firstly, I can speak of myself as 'I', whereas no thing or animal could refer to, or think of, itself in this abstract way. The point is not simply that an animal cannot speak of itself as 'I', as if an animal might be an ego, but be unaware of the fact. Self-awareness is essential to egohood. Necessarily if something is an I, it can speak or think of itself as an I, and if it can speak or think of itself as an I, then it is an I.[15] The I constitutes itself by being aware of itself; it is not a thing or a substratum which underlies its various states, either in the sense of a mere bearer of properties or in the way in which a bar of iron underlies or possesses its magnetic state (*Enz.* II. 312). It is pure 'actuosity' (*Enz.* I. 34Z), 'pure self-relation' (20), 'pure being-for-itself . . . this ultimate, simple and pure point of consciousness' (24Z. 1). In his account of sleep and dreams, Hegel provides the materials for an answer to the question 'What happens to me when I fall asleep?', a question which becomes pressing on this view of the self (*Enz.* III. 398), but which will not be discussed here.

(vi) There are various ways in which I can dissociate myself from my mental states, capacities and activities. I can think of my sensory experience or of my desires as leading me astray, or, again, as something I would rather be without. I can think of my senses not as me, but as instruments which I employ, though on Hegel's view it is wrong to think of one's capacity for thought or one's pure concepts in this way (*WL* I. pp. 24 f., M. pp. 35 f.).[16] My desires or passions can be seen as alien powers, by which I may be overwhelmed against my will or which I may resist (*Ibid*). In all these ways I can distinguish or dissociate myself from my capacities, states and activities. I can also distinguish other people from their capacities, etc., for I can suppose that another person's senses or desires delude or deceive him and that he may either succumb to or resist their allurements.

Hegel does not, in general, distinguish two distinct theses. The first is that I can dissociate myself, in one of these ways or other, from my desires and sensory experience as a whole. The second is that I can dissociate myself from any particular desire or from any particular item or form of sensory experience that I have, but that in doing so I have to take for granted, ally myself with, the rest of my desires or experience. It is, after all, far more common to dissociate oneself from some particular feeling, desire or visual experience that one has (one's persistent feeling, for example, that it is Thursday, when one knows that it is really Tuesday, or one's desire to smoke) than it is to dissociate oneself from, for example, one's desires as a whole. For some of Hegel's purposes the weaker thesis is perhaps sufficient. Some independent status is conferred upon the ego by the fact that it can, as it were, form shifting alliances with different desires or items of its sensory experience and that it is not irrevocably attached to any particular one. But to establish the special connection of the self with thought, he probably requires the stronger thesis.

(vii) Moreover, I can suppose that all my states and experience might have been different and yet I should still have existed.[17] It makes sense, or at least we are tempted to think that it makes sense, to suppose that two men might exchange all their states and experiences, physical as well as mental, and including their memories, while each one remains 'himself'. The change would not, of course, be detectable, but it would be a change, one that, for example, it is possible to wish for. It is again important to distinguish two theses, a weaker one to the effect that any one of my states might have been different, and a stronger one, to the effect that all of my states might have been different. The weaker thesis perhaps applies to things and animals, but the second does not. There is no temptation at all to suppose that all the properties of a thing or animal might have been different or that two things or animals might, at a certain time, exchange all their properties.

(viii) Nevertheless there is a sense in which people do not differ qualitatively from each other in so far as they are pure egos. What differentiates them is their particular states and activities. This is not the same as point (i), that the term 'I' is universally applicable, for the ego has a more substantial status than the 'thisness' of a thing.

These, then, are some of the features which Hegel ascribes to the self. It is clear that they amount to something quite different from the doctrine explained in section 1 of this chapter; the facts that it is I who have certain states, that I am aware of having them, and so on, do not entail, at any rate immediately or obviously,

33

that these states are thought-ridden. There are, then, two different ways in which thinking is involved in all our mental states and activities. They correspond, roughly, to two distinct senses of 'self-consciousness' (*Selbstbewusstsein*) to be found in Hegel. In the first sense, I am self-conscious if I can distinguish myself, as an 'I', from my states and from the objects of which I am conscious, if I am aware of these states as my states and of the objects as objects of my consciousness. The second sense involves the quite different requirement that the object or objects of which I am conscious should be, and/or be seen as, at bottom the same as myself, that is, permeated by thought.[18]

It may be that one could at this point reasonably undercut Hegel's argument by rejecting his conception of the self. His approach to it, and that of German idealism in general, is an introspective one; a person's body is seen as extrinsic to him, as simply one of the objects of which he is aware, albeit a peculiarly persistent one. The right approach, it might be objected, is to conceive of the self, from the start, as essentially embodied, or, perhaps, as a body. Hegel does, of course, deal with the 'community of soul and body' in the third part of his *Encyclopaedia* and in the *Phenomenology*,[19] but his initial perspective on the self is a first-person, introspective one.[20] This objection will not, however, be pressed here, for two reasons. Firstly, it is not obvious that Hegel's approach is the wrong one or that attempts to flatten out the self into a body of a certain type can be successful. Secondly, this account of the self is, even if incorrect, traditional and familiar, and it is more interesting to see how Hegel proceeded from this starting-point than to cut off the argument at this point.

3 *The subject as thoughts*

Even if we grant this account of the self, however, it is not yet clear why the ego is more intimately associated with thoughts and thinking, even its pure thoughts and pure thinking, than it is with its desires, perceptions and memories. It might seem that, just as I have desires, pains, perceptions and so forth, so I have certain general concepts and engage in episodes of thinking, and that there is no more reason to suppose that I, as such, *am* my thoughts than there is to believe that I *am* my desires or my perceptions. I can, after all, suppose that my episodes of thought and my concepts might have been different or that they, or at any rate some of them, lead me astray, and people differ in their episodic thoughts, and perhaps in their concepts, as well as in their perceptions and desires. If we take this view, then there is little to be said about the ego as such. The most that we can do is describe its states and activities. The ego is little more than the bare possessor of these states and activities.

Hegel was concerned to reject this view. Thinking is not something that I do or undergo, and pure thoughts are not something that I have. They are in some sense indentical with me:

> Accordingly, we can then much less suppose that the thought-forms which run through all our conceptions . . . serve us, that we have them in our possession and not rather that they have us in their possession; what remains to us against them, how are *we*, how am *I*, supposed to place myself as what is more universal, *beyond* them, when they themselves are the universal as such? When we place ourselves in a sensation, purpose, interest and feel ourselves confined in it and unfree, then the place into which we can extricate ourselves and withdraw into freedom is this place of self-certainty, of pure abstraction, of thinking (*WL* I. p. 25, M. p. 35).

This passage states Hegel's position, but it does not contain any compelling argument for it. The force of the point that if I were to extricate myself from the 'thought-forms' to the extent that I could regard or employ them as my instruments, then I would see myself as more universal than they are, is quite obscure. Among the variety of ways in which, on Hegel's view, the 'I' is universal, there is at least one in which it might be more universal than the forms of thought; it might, namely, be the receptacle that contains them along with other things. The fact that the pure thoughts are universal in the more familiar sense, that for example the concept of being is applicable to many things besides egos, does not show that the I is not more universal than they are in this different sense. There are however several arguments, or at least considerations, in favour of Hegel's view to be found in varying degrees of explicitness in his text. His view involves at least two components, firstly, that to be an I one has to have some thoughts or other, and, secondly, that to be an I one has to have just the pure thoughts that we do have. I could, after all, claim with some justice to be more universal than the forms of thought if I could suppose that I might have had quite different ones. The arguments will be considered from both of these points of view.

(i) Hegel seems to argue that, since to be an '*I*' I must be aware of myself as an I and since the concept of (an) I is a pure thought, thought is essentially involved in one's being an I.[21] He has Kant's authority for associating the I with thought. In the *Critique of Pure Reason* Kant says that it must be possible for the 'I think'

(*Ich denke*) to accompany all my representations (*Vorstellungen*).[22]
Again, when 'I am conscious of myself, not as I appear to myself,
nor as I am in myself, but only that I am', what makes me aware
that I am is, on Kant's view, a '*thought* not an *intuition*'.[23] When
Hegel discusses Kant's view, however, he regularly points to the
difficulty of deriving from the I those categories which, according
to Kant, are involved in all human experience, and he denies that
Kant ever overcame this difficulty (*Enz.* I. 42; *VGP* III. pp. 344 ff.,
H. III. pp. 438ff.). But the difficulty is Hegel's as much as Kant's.
For even if we grant that to be an I one must be able to think to
the extent of thinking of oneself as an I, it does not immediately
follow that one must have, let alone be, the pure thoughts which
Hegel presents in the *Logic*. (Hegel's pure thoughts include Kant's
categories, but also much more besides.) The *Logic* does not open
with a discussion of (the concept of) the I and Hegel argues against
beginning, as Fichte did for example, in this way (*WL* I. pp. 76 ff.,
M. pp. 75 ff.). We might, moreover, question one of the premises
of Hegel's argument, namely that the concept of (an) I is a pure
thought. For this concept does not figure explicitly among the
thoughts of the *Logic* at all. It is most closely associated with the
'concept', the discussion of which opens the third and final book
of the *Logic* (*WL* II. pp. 245 ff., M. pp. 577 ff. Cf. *Enz.* I. 160 ff.).
But although the I is considered at some length in this context, the
'concept' is not exclusively associated with the ego. It is a pure
thought which emerges, in nature, in the form of organic nature
or life and, in the realm of spirit or of human life, as the pure ego
(*WL* II. p. 257, M. p. 586). There is therefore some difficulty in
reconciling Hegel's *Logic* with his claim that the term 'I' expresses
a pure thought. The relationship between the ego and the pure
thoughts of the *Logic* is, as this suggests, a complicated matter
and more will be said about it later.[24]

(ii) It is a natural supposition that when I am aware that *I* desire
something or that *I* have a certain sensation, thought is essential
to this awareness. Many of the passages which suggest this line of
thought are concerned with conceptions rather than thoughts, but
presumably the peculiarity which Hegel ascribes to conceptions
belongs to them in virtue of the pure thoughts which underlie
them. This peculiarity is expressed in such remarks as these:
'conception (*das Vorstellen*) has sensuous material for its content,
but it is posited as mine, as in me' (*Enz.* I. 20); or again:

> the objects' character of being mine is only implicitly present
> in intuition and first becomes explicit in conception. In
> intuition the objectivity of the content predominates. Not until

I reflect that it is I who have the intuition, not until then do I occupy the standpoint of conception (*Enz.* III. 449Z).

This close and exclusive connection between conceptions and my awareness that something is 'mine' may seem puzzling. We can, after all, distinguish between desires and their objects, between the sensations involved in perception and the objects we perceive, and the former items are surely mine in a way that the latter are not. Hegel seems however to have reasoned somewhat as follows: It is only by applying thoughts to my sensations and thus organizing them in a coherent and interconnected way that I can think of them as representing external objects; and it is only if I can do this that I can distinguish between what is objective, external things, and what is subjective, my conceptions for example and my sensations; the application of thoughts to my sensations is therefore necessary if I am to be aware of what is mine and what is not. It is not easy to extract this argument from Hegel's text — possibly because, as the common currency of the time, it is assumed rather than explicitly stated — but it is implicit in such passages as this: [25]

> To *conceptualize* (*Begreifen*), means, for the reflection of the understanding, to cognize the series of *mediations* between a phenomenon and another existent with which it is connected, to grasp the so-called course of nature, i.e. in accordance with laws and relations of the understanding (e.g. causality, reasons (*des Grundes*), etc.). The life of feeling (*Gefühlsleben*) . . . is just this form of *immediacy*, in which the distinctions of the subjective and the objective, of intelligible personality in contrast to an external world, and those relations of finitude [viz. causality, etc.] between them, are not present (*Enz.* III. 406).

The argument does not establish that I require *all* the thoughts of Hegel's *Logic* if I am to be aware of what is mine. Nor of course does it imply that I cannot have 'brute' sensations, feelings or desires. [26] The point is rather that thoughts must be applied to some (or most) of my sensations, that some (or most) of my mental states and activities must be thought-ridden, if I am to regard any of them as mine.

(iii) Hegel makes much of the fact that one can think about thought(s) and about perception or sensation in a way in which one cannot perceive or sense thought(s) or, indeed, perception and sensation itself. The asymmetry between thought and perception is implied in this passage:

If individuality and asunderness have been given as the determinations of the sensuous, it can be added that these, too, are
themselves again thoughts and universals; in the *Logic* it will
emerge that the thought and the universal is essentially both
itself and its other, it overreaches (*übergreift*) its other and
nothing escapes it (*Enz.* I. 20).

To secure a special place in the self for thought, it must be added
that perception differs in this respect from thinking, that perception does not 'overreach'[27] thought in the way that thought
overreaches perception. We cannot perceive that thought is characterized by universality nor can thought be adequately described in
low-level sensory terms. Moreover, perception cannot characterize
itself; we cannot simply perceive that 'the sensuous' is characterized
by individuality and asunderness, and 'individuality' and 'asunderness' are not themselves sensory terms. There are two reasons for
this. Firstly, what we perceive is always individual and asunder.
This does not, in itself, entail that that we cannot perceive that it
is individual and asunder, for even though everything we see is
visible, we can see that a man is invisible by seeing, for example, his
clothes, or by hearing and feeling certain things, but failing to see
anything corresponding to them. But there is nothing that I fail
to see when I see only individuals and not universals. There is no
place where a universal could be, but is not, so that I could perceive its apparent absence from that place. Secondly, even if we
are prepared to say that we can perceive this, the perception
would be deeply thought-ridden, involving concepts of great
generality and sophistication, and therefore more like seeing that
a compass needle is pointing to the North than seeing a red patch.
   That thought can overreach what is other than thought is, for
Hegel, one of its most important features and the primacy of
thought in his system is in part based on it. Its significance in this
context, however, is not entirely clear. The point presumably is
something like this. A man, unlike an animal, is not wholly absorbed in his states and activities, but can reflect upon his capacities and his exercise of them and, as it were, distance himself
from them. Reflection upon my other capacities requires, however, the use of thought, and this suggests that thought is not
simply one faculty among others. But I cannot in a similar way
dissociate myself from my thought(s), for in order to reflect upon
my thought I have to employ it and cannot extricate myself from
it. This suggests that my capacity for thought is intimately associated with myself in a way that my other capacities are not. This
consideration can be applied generally to the ways in which, as we
have seen, I can dissociate myself from my sensations, my desires,

and perhaps my conceptions. I might, for example, suppose that they could all have been different, that they lead me astray, that I use them (or they use me) as instruments, and so on. But to make such suppositions as these I have to think, and think in a certain way, so that I cannot distance myself from my thought(s) by this procedure. If I suppose that my thoughts deceive me, that I employ them as instruments, that I might have had quite different thoughts or even no thoughts at all, then I am employing certain thoughts, such as those of being, of possibility and of difference, in making these suppositions and I could not make them if I did not.

But what in fact do these considerations establish? Doubt is cast on their significance if we consider their linguistic analogues. For I can speak about my capacities and activities rather than exercise or engage in them, and I can also speak about my linguistic capacities and activities. But, if I do this, I cannot refrain from using language in the way that I can temporarily suspend the normal exercise of at least some of my other capacities. Again, if I wish to say that language is defective, that I employ it as an instrument, or that I might have learnt no language at all, then I have to say it in some language or other. It does not follow, of course, that I had to learn a language. But the point might be taken to show that I would not have been an 'I' if I had not learnt a language, that my linguistic capacity is not one faculty among others, but is intimately associated with the ego. Hegel would probably not balk at this conclusion, since he regards language as a product of thought and implies that thought presupposes a language.[28] Similarly, the fact that I need to use thoughts of a certain type in order to suppose that I might have lacked these, or indeed any, thoughts does not entail that I could not have lacked them. But it might be taken to show that I would not, in that case, have been an I, that egohood requires thoughts, and thoughts of a particular kind. It is not clear, however, that the argument establishes even this much. For the considerations about language in general apply with equal force to some particular language such as English. If I know no other language than English, then my discourse about my linguistic and other capacities can only be conducted in English; if I wish to say that I might have learnt some other language, or no language at all, then I have to say it in English. Yet it evidently does not follow from this that I would not have been an 'I' if I had not learnt English; I could easily have acquired some other language instead. But if this is so, then the parallel argument does not establish that thought or the particular thoughts that we have are essential to egohood.[29]

(iv) Pure thoughts have, on Hegel's view, no empirical content and are not, or at least need not be, derived from or produced by anything other than and external to myself. They are, rather, produced by thinking itself.[30] My sensations, by contrast, and my desires are generated by things other than and external to myself. Hegel tends to equate the distinction between what I am and do independently of other things and what I am and do owing to their impact on me with the distinction between me as I am in myself, on the one hand, and my states and activities, on the other. My thoughts are not, then, something that I merely have; they are identical with me in a way that my sensations and desires are not. This equation is an instance of a general feature of Hegel's thought, namely the tendency to suppose that the distinction between a thing and its properties coincides with the distinction between the thing as it is (or would be) in itself, apart from its relationships to other things, and what it is in virtue of those relationships.[31] What a thing is in itself is sometimes referred to as the 'concept' of the thing. In discussing, for example, the metaphysical theologian's account of God, Hegel distinguishes between the concept of God and the properties of God, his power and goodness, for example. This is explained by the fact that the concept of God is, or expresses, what God is in himself, while his properties are determined by his diverse relationships to the world (*Enz.* I. 36).[32] The states and activities of the self are, in this respect, analogous to the properties of a thing; they are, or at least their empirical content is, produced by other things. But the self differs from other things, in that while little can be said about, for example, a lump of sugar unless we mention its properties, a good deal can be said about the self in itself, for it, so to speak, unravels into a complex logical system, the system of pure thoughts. The *Logic* is, among other things, a description of the pure ego.

There are however at least two difficulties in this argument. The first is that even if we grant that pure thoughts have no empirical content, it does not follow that external things and events play no part in our possession or acquisition of them. Even pure thinking, one might suppose, though it requires no recourse to empirical data, is dependent on certain occurrences in the brain, and the brain, from this perspective, counts as an external object other than myself. Hegel is not very forthcoming about the physiological basis of pure thinking. In general he enters into detail no more than this: '*thinking*, too, in so far as it is temporal and belongs to the immediate individuality, has a corporeal manifestation, is felt and especially in the head, in the brain . . .' (*Enz.* III. 401Z). He does, however, imply that when we think, what happens in the brain is determined by what we think rather than that what we think depends on events in the brain.[33] The suggestion that when we think we in some sense cut loose from our dependence on physical things is an important element in Hegel's system and more will be said about it later.[34]

The second difficulty in this argument is that while it can be plausibly maintained that what particular desires and sensations I have is determined by external factors, this is not true of my general capacities for having desires and sensations. The sight of a steak, for example, is not sufficient to produce a desire for it. Apart from special conditions such as hunger and/or a liking for steak, the observer must be capable of having desires which can be aroused in this way, and this capacity he owes as little (or as much) to external factors as he does his capacity for thought. Similarly, though external objects determine what sort of sensory intake I have, they do not produce my capacity for having some sense-impressions or other. This consideration suggests that while any particular sensation or desire is something that I have, my capacities for having them are me, or at any rate a part of me. Other arguments point in the same direction. It is for example much less easy to suppose — and Hegel himself does not suppose — that I might have had no desires or sensations at all and yet still have been an ego than to suppose that I might have had different desires and sensations. Again, people may differ widely in respect of their desires and sensations, but they invariably have some sensations or desires. It is probable that when Hegel contrasts thought with other faculties, he sometimes compares the *capacity* for thought with *particular* desires, sensations, etc. Some of the arguments suggested above do indeed discriminate between the capacity for thought and other capacities. For example, to think of oneself as an 'I' does not obviously or immediately involve sensations or desires, and, again, thought 'overreaches' the capacities for desire and sensation as well as the desires and sensations themselves. But these arguments are not very compelling. Perhaps Hegel would have been content with the following difference between thought and desire or sensation. The capacities for having desires and sensations are in themselves quite empty; to have any particular desires or sensations, I am dependent on encounters with the external world, and it is entirely a contingent matter what particular ones it will give me, for this varies widely from one person to another. There are, by contrast, certain thoughts that I must have, and I am not dependent for them on external influences, or not at least in the same way; they are, on Hegel's view, all derivable from each other in a way that desires and sensations are not. I can, moreover, actually think solely in terms of

41

and about pure thoughts without recourse to external objects, whereas I cannot on the face of it have pure, non-empirical desires or sensations. The further assessment of these claims will be reserved for later.[35]

4 *The growth of self-consciousness*

There is, however, a general difficulty in the identification of me with my thoughts which must be considered here. The distinction between me and my states depends in part, as we have seen, on the distinction between those respects in which I differ from other people and those respects in which I do not. The identification of a pure ego with its thoughts seems to require, then, that just as all persons are pure egos, so they all have the same pure thoughts. If I have some thought which other people do not, then I can detach myself from my thoughts at least to the extent of supposing that I might not have had this thought. But did Hegel in fact believe that all people at all times have the same thoughts or concepts? The evidence on this matter is not easy to interpret, but the likelihood is that he did not. The first section of the *Phenomenology*, for example, describes a form of consciousness, that of sense-certainty, in which the subject is equipped only with the thought of being and with whatever thoughts correspond to such terms as 'this' and 'that', that of individuality, perhaps, but not that of a thing with properties.[36] Moreover, although self-consciousness is not introduced explicitly until later,[37] the subject who is sense-certain is to some degree self-conscious. He distinguishes between himself and the object of which he is aware and at one stage exploits this distinction in order to pick out an item in his experience by saying something like 'It's the one *I* am aware of (now)' (*PG* pp. 83 ff., M. pp. 61 ff.). This, however, does not settle the matter in favour of the conclusion that not all persons have all the thoughts of the *Logic*. For here, as elsewhere, it is unclear whether what Hegel is doing is history, psychology or philosophy, whether he means, for example, that sense-certainty is a possible form of recognizably human consciousness, too incoherent to be adequate or stable, but coherent enough to exist for a time, in primitive people for example or infants, or whether he means that it is a form of experience described by some philosophers but too impoverished and incoherent ever to be actualized. It is hard to be certain, but the fact that the third section[38] describes fairly recent scientific conceptions, which are not available to everyone, might be thought to favour the first interpretation. And if some people are or have been at the level of sense-certainty, then not everyone has all the concepts of the *Logic*.

Thoughts can, of course, appear with varying degrees of explicitness, ranging from their occurrence in ordinary thought and discourse in combination with empirical material to their emergence in a pure form in philosophy. Between these two extremes a thought may figure in varying degrees of impurity in art, religion and the natural sciences. It is at least clear that a thought need not appear in all these forms in every epoch. It is for example anachronistic to attribute to Thales[39] the belief in a personal deity, for he lacked the concept of the 'subjectivity of the highest idea, of the personality of God' (*VGP* III. p. 510, H. I. p. 41); nor should we credit him with the doctrine that water is the cause of the world, for there is no evidence that he had the concept of a cause in this explicit form (*VGP* III. p. 512, H. I. p. 44). Similarly the natural sciences have not always employed the same thoughts; those of force and polarity, for example, have been recently brought to light or have become, at any rate, more explicit and noticeable (*WL* I. p. 21, M. pp. 32 f.). Some languages facilitate the disentanglement of a thought from its empirical trappings more than others. German for example has 'a wealth of logical expressions, specific and separate expressions [such as 'is' and 'this'] for the thought-determinations' which are lacking in Chinese (*WL* I. p. 20, M. p. 32).

This does not entail, however, and Hegel does not infer from it, that the Chinese lack the thoughts themselves, that not all peoples have all the thoughts even at the simplest level. The Greeks of Thales' time did, after all, attribute personality to their gods, though this was a case of imaginative conception (*Phantasievorstellung*), quite a different matter from grasping the pure thought and the concept (*VGP* III. p. 511, H. I. p. 41). No doubt, too, Thales and his contemporaries operated with causal conceptions, but the thought is a different matter from 'what sort of concepts govern their life' (*Ibid.*). It is, however, unlikely that Hegel believed that every human being has, at some level, all the thoughts of the *Logic*. Children presumably acquire them by degrees, as they do the ability to deploy sentences which involve them. They do not acquire them all at once any more than philosophers become aware of them all at once. Since Hegel often compares the development of mankind as a whole with that of the individual and primitive peoples with children,[40] it is plausible to suppose that on his view people acquired the thoughts they have, even at the implicit level, only gradually.

How does this affect the identification of the ego with pure thoughts? It is still the case, of course, that in order to be an I, a creature must have some thoughts and, if he has any, he must presumably have that of being. It is after this point that what he has and what he lacks becomes indeterminate. It is also true that, in principle at least, the other thoughts are derivable from the ones he already has, but, realistically enough, Hegel does not believe that people do or can, in defiance of their historical and psychological circumstances, derive whatever is in principle derivable.[41] Different egos will, then, if the thesis is to be maintained, be identical with different fragments of the system of pure thoughts. But how is this to be reconciled with the view that persons *qua* pure egos do not differ from each other? The answer seems to be that egohood, being an I, is not an all or nothing matter. There are degrees of self-awareness and therefore of selfhood – since Hegel believes that '[m]ind is essentially only what it knows itself to be' (*Enz.* III. 385Z) – and the degree one has attained to depends on the thoughts embodied in one's discourse and thinking. (It also depends, presumably, on how purely and explicitly these thoughts occur. Philosophers, for example, are more self-aware than ordinary people.)[42] This idea perhaps provides a bridge between the two conceptions of self-consciousness referred to above.[43] It is not implausible to suppose that someone who can say only such things as 'Give me that!', 'I want that', or 'That's red' is, although self-aware to some degree, less so than someone who can say 'I would like that, but I don't think you should give it to me' or 'If I had been (in) Julius Caesar('s position), I wouldn't have had the nerve to cross the Rubicon'; that what I can say or think about myself corresponds to some extent to what I can say or think about my 'object', about what is other than myself; and that these correlated capacities are a matter of what general concepts I am able to deploy.

At all events, Hegel distinguishes different grades of self-awareness both in the *Philosophy of Mind* and in the *Phenomenology*. He differentiates the self-conscious I from various stages on the road to it, from, for example, 'self-feeling' (*Selbstgefühl*), a more or less dreamlike state in which one is dominated by a fixed idea from which one cannot distance, and therefore liberate, oneself (*Enz.* III. 408). These stages are sometimes phases through which a child passes, sometimes states into which an adult can relapse – dream states, for example, and various pathological conditions such as insanity, somnambulism and hypnotically induced states – and sometimes both. They are characterized in part by the extent to which the subject has a grip on his own self and on the objective world. These stages are not, however, explicitly correlated with the development of thought or of language.

In the *Encyclopaedia* at least, these subjects are relegated to a few, relatively uninteresting paragraphs.[44] There are, however, occasional suggestions that Hegel had such a correlation in mind:

> Language as such is this airy element, at once sensuous and non-sensuous, and it is by the child's increasing command of language that its intelligence rises more and more above the sensuous, from the individual to the universal, to thought (*Enz.* III. 396Z. Cf. 458).

The thesis that the pure ego is pure thoughts can, then, be maintained in the face of the objection that different people have different concepts.[45] The self or ego, as we have seen, figures prominently in Hegel's system and more will be said about it later.[46] Enough has been said for the moment, however, to indicate Hegel's fundamental beliefs about it and his reasons for holding them. The following chapter will consider the objective counterpart of the self, namely the external world, and the relationship to it of pure thoughts.

III

Experience, Meta-thinking and Objectivity

In addition to his usual term for thinking (*Denken*), Hegel also uses the expression 'meta-thinking' (*Nachdenken*). The implication of the prefix is not that meta-thinking is thinking about thought, but that it is thought about things to which our primary and prior access was secured by some other means than thought. Meta-thinking is, as it were, the way in which we transpose some 'content' which, though thought-ridden, is not in the 'form' of thought into the appropriate form.[1] It does not cover only or even primarily philosophical thinking, for which Hegel's usual word is simply 'thinking'. It includes, for example, attempts to prove that God exists in contrast to the simple faith which preceded them. But most importantly it includes the thinking involved in the natural sciences. Hegel did not devote a special section of the *Encyclopaedia* or a course of lectures to the history of the natural sciences as such, as he did to the other ways in which men have attempted to understand the world – art, religion and philosophy. This is no doubt because the second volume of the *Encyclopaedia* is concerned with the philosophy of nature and this inevitably contains much historical material. For it is clear from references to them throughout his works that Hegel regarded the rise of the natural sciences as a crucial phase of human development and as a necessary precondition of his own philosophy.[2] This chapter will be concerned with his view of the natural sciences as such.

1 *Science and commonsense*

It is not easy to discover in Hegel an unequivocal answer to the question: What do the natural sciences do? This is, in part, because the sciences occupy a position somewhere between the everyday commonsensical approach to nature, on the one hand, and the philosophy of nature, on the other. The sciences are, of course, a 'thinking consideration of nature' (*Enz.* II. 246. Cf. I. 7), but this does not differentiate them from commonsense, for as we have seen, thinking is involved in all specifically human activity (*Enz.* I. 2).³ Nor, on the other hand, does it distinguish them from the philosophy of nature, which is also a matter of thought (*Enz.* II. 246). But empirical science must be distinguished from both of these. In practice Hegel tends to focus on different aspects of the empirical sciences, depending on whether the comparison he has in mind is with commonsense or with philosophy. In this section we shall be concerned with the contrast between science and commonsense.

Men have many dealings with nature which do not amount to scientific activity or even presuppose the findings of science. When Hegel is contrasting science with this everyday intercourse with nature, the doctrine that everything human is thought-ridden recedes into the background. What the sciences do, it is suggested, is introduce thoughts into our view of nature. Thus, in the *Philosophy of Nature*, physics is regarded as the theoretical approach to nature, whereas commonsense is the practical approach which treats nature as 'immediate and external' (*Enz.* II. 245) and is concerned with 'individual products of nature or with individual aspects of these products' (245Z). This does not mean, however, that scientists simply think about the phenomena which previously we only looked at or acted on, that what in the 'forms' of perception, etc. is merely perceived, felt or intuited is now argued for or proved to be true without any substantial change in the content or the object of these forms. Hegel's remark that the form in which a content occurs combines with the content to make the object, at least apparently, different is designed in part to avert this misinterpretation (*Enz.* I. 3).⁴ Even in the case of religion it is likely that to attempt to prove the doctrines assumed by the naïve believer involves changes in the doctrines themselves and in our conceptions of the objects with which they are concerned.⁵ It is even more obvious that the sciences change our conceptions of the phenomena with which they deal. What they do, Hegel implies, is convert perception into 'experience' (*Erfahrung*): 'the individual perception is different from experience, and empiricism [viz. the empirical sciences] elevates the content which belongs to perception, feeling and intuition into the *form of universal conceptions, propositions* and *laws*, etc.' (*Enz.* I. 38). The term 'experience' is used by Hegel in at least three ways. Occasionally its sense is such that any object of any mental state is an object of experience. Freedom, spirit and God are, for example, experienced, though not sensibly (*sinnlich*) experienced, just because they are 'in [our] consciousness', that is, in this case, thought about (*Enz.* I. 8). This is not, however, Hegel's customary use of the word, and it is introduced in the context of a polemic against attempts to downgrade entities which are not perceptible.[6] Secondly, 'experience' refers to our sensory intake before it has been worked up by thought, or at least before the particular thought with which it is contrasted has been introduced into it. Experience is what thoughts, for example proposed universal laws, are tested against (*Enz.* I. 7). In this sense, it is sometimes called '*Empirie*', especially when Hegel has some other sense of 'experience' in mind (*Enz.* I. 39). Finally it means sense-experience which has been moulded by thoughts, by the 'determinations of universality and necessity' (*Ibid.*). Experience in this sense is what the natural sciences produce. The sciences do not accept phenomena as they at first appear to us, but classify things into genera and species and propose universal laws, those for example of the movement of heavenly bodies (*Enz.* I. 21Z). Lightning is seen no longer as an ephemeral flash in the sky, but as an expression of the 'universal and permanent', of a force (*Ibid.*). The sciences are concerned with the 'fixed measure and the universal in the sea of empirical individualities' (*Enz.* I. 7). To the extent that they discover it, they elevate perception to the status of experience.

One procedure which the sciences employ in their promotion of the 'advance from perception to experience' is that of analysis.[7] There are at least three types of analysis, which, however, Hegel does not distinguish. One can, firstly, divide a phenomenon mentally into aspects or features into which it could not be physically divided — its shape, colour, size and weight, for example. One can also mentally analyse something into its physically separable constituents, water, for example, into hydrogen and oxygen. And, finally, one can physically divide something into its separable constituents. It is commonly believed, according to Hegel, that analysis leaves the object which is analysed unchanged, but this, he argues, is a mistake. When the elements of an object are separated they thereby acquire the 'form of universality', they become 'abstract determinations' i.e. *thoughts*' (*Enz.* I. 38Z). Essentially the same belief is involved in his remark that in attending to an individual thing or aspect of a thing one thereby treats it as universal.[8] It is clear, on the one hand, that universality involves analysis. One could not frame general laws or universal concepts without distinguishing different features of individual phenomena, since no universal feature or kind is ever instantiated in its purity. But it is not clear why, conversely, analysis involves universality in any special way. Water consists of hydrogen and oxygen, and so does *this* drop of water. But *this* drop of water consists of *this* bit of oxygen and *this* bit of hydrogen. The fact that the features or constituents of an individual thing are 'abstracted' from each other does not entail that they are 'abstracted' from their own individual instances and in that sense treated as universal.

A more important criticism of Hegel's remarks, however, is that he exaggerates, or at any rate mislocates, the difference in these respects between science and commonsense. It is a mistake to suppose that we owe the transition from individual and fleeting perceptions to the 'universal and permanent' to the natural sciences alone. Abstraction and classification is a feature of all human thought, even of pre-scientific thought, and Hegel's account of attention implies as much. This may be why he suggests that the result of scientific analysis is 'abstract determinations, i.e. thoughts', but he is not entitled to this conclusion, since conceptions, as well as pure thoughts, are universal. His remarks about lightning are similarly misconceived in their implication that universality is an innovation of the sciences. The phenomenon of lightning is in one sense no less universal than the force which it is, or by which it is produced. Before the discovery that lightning was (a manifestation of) electricity, men did not confine themselves to responding on individual occasions to individual flashes of lightning. They also classified them under the general heading 'lightning' and if they had not done so they could not have asked what (the cause of) lightning was. Moreover, even if we speak about some particular lightning flash, saying, for example, that it is the brightest we have yet seen, we are implicitly employing such thoughts as those of being and of individuality. Conversely, while we can speak of a force or of electricity in general, we can also speak of particular bits of force or of electricity (though we cannot pick them out except by means of the phenomena which we attribute to them). An individual flash of lightning is (the manifestation of) a particular bit of electricity with a particular location and strength, and this in part explains the difference between different flashes of lightning. It is true that a particular bit of electricity is not conceived of as transitory in the way that a flash of lightning is. But this is not because 'electricity' is a universal term, while 'lightning' is not. Lightning is, after all, a recurrent phenomenon, and Hegel obscures our pre-scientific awareness of this fact by comparing the individual lightning-flash with electricity taken as a whole.

49

The distinction between the practical and the theoretical, again, does not provide Hegel with the distinction he requires. On the one hand, science has practical motives and consequences, which — perhaps understandably in the light of his historical situation — he tended to underplay. On the other hand, while it is true that our pre-scientific attitudes to nature are influenced by our practical concerns and that our practical engagements with the world relate to particular individuals and not to general kinds of thing, it is quite wrong to imply that they are restricted to raw sensory data unadulterated by thought. Some thought, some conception of universality and of necessity, is involved in even the most primitive human transactions with nature. One eats, for example, some individual apple, while one can think about apples in general. But one eats this apple not characteristically because it is *this* individual, but because it is an individual of some more or less general kind. The pre-scientific agent has, moreover, certain rough generalizations available and acts on the basis of them. He is aware, for example, that items of a certain appearance are edible and that, if the tree is shaken hard enough, they will fall down. This is not to deny the important differences between a rule of thumb like 'If a tree is shaken hard enough the fruit will generally fall off' and a generalization like 'Every body continues in its state of rest or of uniform motion in a right line unless it is compelled to change that state by forces impressed upon it';[9] between the discovery that mud consists of earth and water and the discovery that water consists of molecules composed of two atoms of hydrogen and one of oxygen; or between the kinds of object and stuff encountered in everyday life and the pure elements each consisting solely of atoms of the same atomic number. But the point is not that the sciences introduce thought where there was none before. Terms such as 'thought', 'abstract' and 'universal' are not fine-grained enough to capture what differences there are.

Hegel does, however, discriminate more finely between common sense and the sciences than this suggests. The sciences introduce, firstly, new thoughts or at least new applications of old ones. The categories of force and of polarity for example have been brought into greater prominence and applied in new ways (*WL* p. 21, M. pp. 32 f.).[10] But, secondly, the categories, as they figure in the sciences, are not so deeply embedded in empirical material as they are in our ordinary consciousness: 'through the opposition and diversity of the phenomena compared, the external, *contingent circumstances* of the conditions fall away, and the *universal* thereby comes into view' (*Enz.* I. 16). We might begin, for example, our consideration of freely falling bodies by observing some specific type of thing such as an apple. Observation and experiment over a wider range of objects in a variety of circumstances, however, show that it does not matter whether the object in question is an apple, a stone, or a planet. These are merely 'external, contingent circumstances' and the same law holds regardless of them (*PG* pp. 191 f., M. pp. 152 f.). Electricity provides another example:

> Negative electricity, e.g., which at first becomes known as *resin*-electricity — while positive electricity becomes known as *glass*-electricity—entirely loses through experiments this significance and becomes purely *positive and negative* electricity, each of which no longer belongs to a specific type of thing (*PG* p. 191, M. p. 153. Cf. *Enz.* II. 324).

Experiment in a wide range of circumstances enables us to abstract a law or a concept from any particular type of circumstance and to widen the scope of its application. In the statement of our results we need no longer use low-level empirical terms like 'resin', 'glass' or 'stone', but can confine ourselves to relatively abstract terms such as 'mass', 'body', 'positive' and 'electricity'. Hegel believes that such concepts as these approximate to pure thoughts (*Enz.* I. 16). The distillation of thoughts into a pure form, or at least a purer form than that in which they occur in our ordinary consciousness, is an important function of the sciences and more will be said about it later.[11] For the moment, however, we shall consider some of the respects in which the natural sciences differ from philosophy.

2 *Empirical science*

One of the ways in which the sciences might be supposed to differ from philosophy is that they are empirical in some sense in which philosophy is not. Hegel, on the whole, shares this view. The sciences are sometimes referred to as the 'empirical' sciences (*Enz.* I. 7) or the 'experiential' sciences (*Enz.* I. 12: *Erfahrungswissenschaften*). It is true that he often stresses the connections of philosophy with experience, but its empirical connections are not the same as those of the natural sciences. The differences are obscured, however, by the difficulty of extracting from Hegel's texts any single, clear account of what it is for a cognitive enterprise to be empirical. There are several reasons for this, two of which will be mentioned here, and more will emerge later. Firstly, there is, as we have seen, much unclarity in Hegel's account of the relationship of thoughts to our sensory intake. This is due in part to the fact that thoughts are of different types and are related to the empirical in different ways. This unclarity is inherited by his account of the natural sciences in so far as they employ thoughts. Secondly, Hegel tends to discuss together three distinct things: what scientists do, what scientists claim to do, and empiricist philosophies based on the sciences. He perhaps has some reason for conflating at least the first two, in the light of the connection between what the mind is and what it is aware of itself as being.[12] But there is more reason to distinguish them, since his criticisms of the sciences, as well as of other cognitive procedures, often depend on the disparity between what they in fact do and what their practitioners aim or claim to do.[13] Nevertheless it is often difficult to distinguish these different themes in Hegel's text.

In what ways then does Hegel believe the sciences to be empirical? They are, firstly, empirical in the very general sense that they set out from experience: 'We call those sciences . . . *empirical* sciences from the starting-point which they take' (*Enz.* I. 7). This alone, however, does not distinguish these sciences from philosophy, for philosophy too had its starting-point in experience. This does not mean that philosophy proposed or proposes empirically testable hypotheses about the empirical world. It means rather that thinking is aroused by experience to rise above it into 'its own unmixed element, and to take on at first an aloof, *negative attitude* towards its starting-point' (*Enz.* I. 12). Clearly in this sense almost any mental activity can have experience as its starting-point, however unempirical it may be in other respects. One might be induced to engage in theology, poetry, mathematics or mystical reverie by experience, if only in order to find a refuge from it. It does not follow that these activities result in empirically testable claims, claims about experience or even claims at all.

The sciences are, however, empirical in less degenerate ways than this. They are, firstly, concerned with the empirical world. Science did not stand aloof from it, but 'turned upon the seemingly measureless material of the phenomenal world' (*Enz.* I. 7); and 'instead of seeking the true in thought inself, it derives it from *experience*, the outer and inner present' (*Enz.* I. 37). Secondly, scientific theories are empirically testable. Hegel expresses this in such ways as this: '[Experience provides a] *firm support* against the possibility of *being able to prove anything and everything* in the sphere of and by the method of finite determinations' (*Enz.* I. 37); and: 'on the *subjective* side, empirical cognition has firm support in the fact that consciousness has its *own immediate presence* and *certainty* in perception' (*Enz.* I. 38).

When the term 'experience' occurs in such contexts as these, it does not refer to experience in the sense in which this is a result of scientific activity, for in that case appeal to experience would be no genuine test of empirical hypotheses. The appeal is rather to sense-perception, not necessarily, that is, to raw sensations, but to data which are less thought-ridden than the final product of science. The hypothesis that lightning is an electrical discharge is tested for example against such facts as that the observer felt a shock in his hand similar to those felt in the laboratory when he was in contact with what is already acknowledged to be electricity.

What is the point of testing our hypotheses in this way? One point is that it enables us to know what to believe or accept; it provides, that is, a genuine criterion. If, by contrast, we argue *a priori* about a supersensible realm or, for that matter, about the empirical world without submitting our ideas to the test of experience, we find that there are no constraints on what we can accept; we can 'prove' anything and everything (cf. *Enz.* I. 37). Hegel accepted, on the whole, Kant's belief that if we argue about matters which are beyond the range of sense-experience, then we encounter antinomies. We find, for example, that equally valid proofs can be given both of the proposition that the world had a beginning in time and of the proposition that it did not.[14] This does not happen, according to the empiricists, Kant and, in some moods, Hegel, if we confine ourselves to the realm of sense-experience.

Another point, however, of adopting this epistemic attitude is that it confers on us at least one sort of freedom: 'On the subjective side one should acknowledge, too, the important principle of *freedom* which empiricism involves, namely that man should *himself* see, know *himself* to be *present* in, what he is to accept in his knowledge (*Wissen*)' (*Enz.* I. 38. Cf. 7). This type of freedom contrasts with the acceptance of propositions, or rather of dogmas, on authority, the authority primarily of the Catholic Church.[15] To decide questions for oneself, to accept beliefs only if one has made the relevant observations for oneself, is autonomy, in contrast to the servility of relying on the authority of others.[16]

There are however at least two problems involved in the association of the natural sciences with freedom in this sense. It suggests, in the first place, that science is a more individualistic enterprise than it in fact is. For if a person is to be free in this sense, he must presumably adopt only those beliefs which have undergone and passed the test of his *own* observation. If he has not himself performed a certain experiment, but accepts the testimony of someone who has, then he is relying to some degree on authority. But clearly no single person has made, or could make, all the first-hand observations on which our beliefs ultimately depend. Hegel could perhaps survey all the scientific results of his day, but he could hardly have independently tested them. Scientists rely on the reported observations of other scientists and laymen on the whole simply take their word for it. Hegel conceals this by speaking of 'man' (*der Mensch*), which looks as if it means 'each individual man', but must mean in fact 'mankind as a whole'. Mankind as a whole may believe only what it has observed for itself, but any individual cannot. Since religious beliefs are sometimes alleged to depend on observations made by some person or other, the difference between science and traditional religion is less stark than Hegel, at times, suggests.[17] One difference, perhaps, is that the observations to which religious belief appeals, those for example of eye-witnesses to Christ's miracles, cannot be repeated by anyone, whereas the observations which support scientific beliefs can in most cases be repeated by any competent individual, if he is ready to sacrifice time and expense.[18] The fact remains however that no single individual could repeat all of them, and most of us do not repeat any. The idea that science is a structure to the erection of which many individuals contribute would not, of course, be alien to Hegel. He was familiar with the notion of a division of labour in society (e.g. *PR* 198) and philosophy is a system which has been constructed by many men over centuries (*Enz.* I. 13). But to view science in this way is incompatible with ascribing to it the liberating effect which Hegel does. This kind of freedom requires that the observation on which one relies should be one's own observation.

A second difficulty with Hegel's view is that freedom, deciding questions for oneself rather than accepting the answers given by others, does not in itself require that one should decide them by any particular procedure, by observation and experiment, for example, rather than by some other method. What matters is that the decision should be one's own and based on data available to oneself, rather than what sort of data these are. If it is insisted that the data should be empirical, this will be because it is felt that there is no other reliable way of deciding such questions rather than because the adoption of some other method would impair one's autonomy. This would not matter, if Hegel had made it clear that it is so. But he is prone, rather, to associate the natural sciences with other cognitive procedures which are no less compatible with this sort of freedom:

He must himself be in contact [with the content] , be it only with his outer senses or with his deeper spirit, his essential self-consciousness. This is the same principle as has been called, in the present day, faith (*Glaube*), immediate awareness, the revelation in the outer world and especially in one's *own* inner world (*Enz.* I. 7).

The first of these sentences might be taken as referring ('his deeper spirit, his essential self-consciousness') to the evidence of intro-spection, which perhaps has as strong a claim to be called 'empirical' as has the evidence of our senses. But the following sentence suggests a different interpretation. 'Immediate awareness' includes not simply the immediate or intuitive awareness of the presence of external objects ('the revelation in the outer world', cf. *Enz.* I. 63, 76), but also and primarily faith in God's existence or the immediate awareness of God, and it would be at least controversial to regard this as empirical. It is true that Hegel rejects the doctrine of immediate awareness even in the case of God, and that he especially rejects the view that immediate aware-ness can provide us with knowledge of nature.[19] It is also true that in general he stresses the differences between immediate awareness and the procedures of scientists. But in emphasizing the freedom which the sciences confer on their practitioners and thus asso-ciating them with other procedures with which such freedom is equally compatible, he obscures the empirical character of the sciences and stops short of saying clearly in what it consists.

3 *Science and thought*

The natural sciences cannot, however, be straightforwardly empiri-cal on Hegel's view, for scientists do not confine themselves to an animal-like acceptance of their sensory intake nor merely to giving a description of it. This would be a pointless and incomplet-able task (*PG* pp. 185 ff., M. pp. 147 ff.). Rather, as we have seen, they introduce thoughts into it and this puts in question the empirical status of their findings.

But to what extent does it undermine it? Scientists themselves, on Hegel's view, suppose that it does not do so in the least: 'Universal determinations (e.g. force) are to have in themselves no further meaning and validity than they derive from perception and no connection is to be justified unless it can be pointed to in the phenomena' (*Enz.* I. 38); and: 'The *consistent* development of empiricism . . . concedes to thinking only abstraction and formal universality and identity' (*Ibid.*). The point of these claims seems to be not only to distinguish scientific thinking from the metaphysical employment of thought to secure access to a trans-empirical realm, but to suggest that (using terms which were not available to Hegel) sentences containing expressions such as 'force' are supposed to be equivalent in meaning to sentences which contain only 'empirical' terms together with such operations as universal quantification. (Whether empirical terms would refer only to our sensory experience or might also refer to macroscopic physical objects is not a question to which an answer can be derived from Hegel.)[20]

On occasions Hegel shows some sympathy for the view that science is, or at any rate should be, like this. In general, however, he rejects it, arguing that there is a conflict between what scientists purport to be doing and what they are in fact doing. This seems to be in part because he does not explicitly distinguish between those thoughts or thought-terms, such as 'force' and 'atom', which refer to unobservable or theoretical entities and those, such as 'one', 'many' and the forms of inference, which do not. The 'metaphysical' categories which the sciences employ include all of these (*Enz.* I. 38). But it is only thought-terms of the former type which the reductionist of the sort Hegel has in mind claims to be eliminable from scientific discourse. The others, universal generalization for example, would remain, and a universal generalization, even one which refers only to observable entities, cannot be strictly justified on the basis of a finite number of sensory observations (*Enz.* I. 39). Again, what Hegel often has in mind is not so much the sciences themselves as metaphysical offshoots from them such as materialism. The concept of matter is a very general thought, and sense-experience cannot conclusively validate materialism (Cf. *Enz.* I. 38Z, 62). But there are also a number of passages in which scientists themselves are charged with making claims which go beyond sense-experience. One of them, in which Hegel criticizes the theory of latent heat, is worth quoting at length, because it affords more than a glimpse of the idea of empirical falsifiability:[21]

> Specific heat capacity, combined with the category of *matter* and *stuff*, has led to the conception of *latent, unobservable, bound (gebundenem)* heat-stuff. As something *imperceptible*, such a determination lacks the warrant of *observation* and *experience*, and as an inferred entity it rests on the *assumption* of a *material independence* of heat .... This supposition of latent heat serves in its way to make the independence of heat as a matter *empirically* irrefutable, precisely because the supposition is not an empirical one. If the disappearance of heat,

or its appearance where it was not present before, is pointed out, the former is explained as a mere concealment or as its becoming latent and therefore unobservable, the latter is explained as its emergence from mere unobservability; the metaphysics of independence is *opposed to that experience*, indeed it is presupposed *a priori* independently of experience (*Enz.* II. 305).

The theory that heat is a stuff or a substance ('caloric') was cushioned against refutation by the postulation of latent heat.[22] Hegel rejects the theory, but he does so only in part because of its empirical defects. For, on his view, thought always does go beyond experience, if we take 'experience' in the sense of '(the objects of) sense-perception'. His rejection of it seems to be primarily due to the fact that it involves the category of 'matters' or stuffs, which is, in this case at least, the wrong category.

The fact that scientific hypotheses always go beyond sense-experience does not of course entail that they cannot be accepted or rejected in the light of it. Indeed Hegel seems to regard the heat-stuff theory not so much as a representative scientific theory, but as a degenerate one, simply because it falls short of this requirement. One might be tempted to say that his considered view is that while the application of a given thought or category to a given phenomenon is not an empirically testable matter, particular hypotheses within the framework of this category are. We might say, for example, that it is an empirical question whether lightning is or is not an electrical discharge, but not whether it is a manifestation of some force or other. This suggestion falls foul, however, of the fact that whether a given category is appropriately applicable to a given phenomenon is often itself an empirical question.[23] In the light of this, Hegel's thesis that thoughts transcend sense-perception sometimes seems to amount to little more than the claim that men, unlike animals, have a tendency to impose thoughts on, or to find thoughts in, things, and that this tendency is not determined by their perceptual capacities or intake.

Matters are complicated further by a feature of Hegel's thought which will be considered at length in a later chapter, but to which some reference must be made here.[24] Often enough he distinguishes between the thinking involved in the sciences and the trans-empirical thought of the metaphysician and the theologian, but he does not invariably do so. The clearest instances of this conflation occur in Hegel's account of Kant. Kant had argued that thoughts, universality and necessity, are not given in our sensory intake, but are imposed by us upon it. Hume was right, for example, in arguing that sense-perception as such does not justify our beliefs that one event causes another event or that one type of event causes another type of event (Cf. *Enz.* I. 39).[25] It does not follow, however, that we should or can dispense with causal judgments. The ordering of our sensory intake in terms of causal generalizations is necessary if we are to have knowledge, objective experience, at all, for such thoughts in part constitute objective experience (cf. *Enz.* I. 43).[26] There is, on the other hand, a use of the categories which Kant rejects, the application of them to objects which are not perceptible and which provide us with no sensory data or intuitions corresponding to the categories, to such entities, that is, as God and the soul. Some of the arguments for God's existence, for example, are based on premises about the empirical world, but proceed to a conclusion concerning an entity which transcends our sense-experience. Kant objects to any such inference.[27] Hegel however represents his objection as one based on the logical gap between our raw sensory data and thoughts:[28]

> Since . . . *perceptions* and their aggregate, the world, do not reveal in themselves as such the universality to which thinking elevates that content by purifying it, this universality is thus not justified by that empirical conception of the world. The rise of thought from the empirical conception of the world to God is thus opposed by the *Humean* standpoint . . . the standpoint which declares it inadmissible to *think* perceptions, i.e. to extract (*herauszuheben*) the universal and necessary from them (*Enz.* I. 50).

Hegel thus ignores Kant's distinction between the use of the categories in which 'the manifold in a given intuition is necessarily subject' to them[29] and their 'employment extending beyond the limits of experience',[30] and regards Kant's criticisms as an abandonment of his own doctrine that 'cognition in general, indeed *experience*, consists in the fact that *perceptions* are thought, that is, the determinations which at first belong to perception are *transformed* into thought-determinations' (*Enz.* I. 43). Kant is inconsistent in allowing us to 'think perceptions' to the extent of finding causal regularities in them, but forbidding us to infer from them the existence of God. For Hegel, in this context at least, both beliefs are on a par. To derive God from the world is simply to think (about) the world, just as the ascription of causal efficacy to objects and events is to think (about) the world.

It may not be easy to draw a sharp line between the procedures of the natural sciences and those of metaphysics and theology, between the empirical status of Dalton's atoms and that of Luther's God. But it is even harder to accept Hegel's occasional assimilation of them. He does so in part in order to justify his own type of thinking, which gains respectability from its association with the natural sciences. He may also have in mind his own radical restructuring of metaphysics and theology, which lends more plausibility to the assimilation.[31] It is, again, characteristic of Hegel's procedure to stretch doctrines which he is considering in various directions and to find affinities with apparently quite different conceptions.[32] Nevertheless, even with all these explanations, this episode says little for his grasp of the notions of the scientific and the empirical. What Hegel prided himself on was systematic understanding rather than scattered insights (*Enz.* I. 14), but what he displays, on this as on other matters, are scattered insights rather than systematic understanding. Further evidence of this will be provided in the following section.

4 *Explanation*

One natural answer to the question what the natural sciences do is that they explain phenomena. To say, for example, that lightning is an electrical discharge is to explain in part why lightning occurs. The theme of explanation has a variety of connections with the topics considered in this chapter. It might be thought, for example, that explanation distinguishes the sciences from commonsense, for if explanation is not restricted to the sciences, they at least produce more satisfying ones than those characteristic of pre-scientific thought. Hegel's treatment of explanation, again, reveals his uneasy grip on the notion of the empirical. And, finally, his account of scientific explanation points ahead to his criticisms of the sciences in general and his view of the ways in which philosophy should improve on them.[33] For, whether or not he would be prepared to use the word 'explain' to say so, the point of philosophy is, on Hegel's view, to explain things and it is a defect of the empirical sciences that they do not meet the standard of explanation which he requires of them.

While agreeing that scientists believe that they produce explanations, Hegel does not stress explanation (*Erklärung*) in his accounts of their work nor does he locate its value in the fact that they explain things. One reason for this, it might be supposed, is his belief that:

Through metathinking something is *altered* in the way in which the content is at first [presented] in sensation, intuition,

59

conception; it is thus only *by means of* an alteration that the *true* nature of the *object* comes to consciousness (*Enz.* I. 22).

This passage implies only that our view or conception of an object is changed by meta-thinking, not that the object itself is transformed. Whether we regard electricity as a force discovered by us or rather as a construct, a convenient way of describing our observations, on neither account is it true to say that our coming to believe that lightning is an electrical discharge changed lightning. What it did change was our view, conception or account of lightning.[34] But even if it is only our conception of lightning that is altered, this, it might be argued, still prevents us from regarding the thesis that it is an electrical discharge as an explanation of its occurrence. For the lightning which we originally set out to explain, lightning conceived as a phenomenal occurrence, is not the same as lightning conceived as an electrical discharge. If we try to explain lightning as it is now conceived by reference to electricity, then the explanation is vacuous or tautological. This argument, if it were sound, would imply that nothing could ever be explained in an informative way, since it could always be said that any proposed explanation of a phenomenon simply changes our conception or our description of that phenomenon in line with itself. The argument, however, seems not to be Hegel's. He interprets the claim that lightning is electricity, for example, not as involving the disappearance of phenomenal lightning, but as duplicating it: 'One duplicates the phenomenon, breaks it in two, into inner and outer, force and expression, cause and effect' (*Enz.* I. 21Z). As far as this goes, the force (or 'inner' or cause) might still explain the expression, the visible phenomenon which we initially found puzzling. If there is anything to prevent such an explanation from being informative, it is, on Hegel's view, that the force is the same in content as its expression, that the proposed *explanans* has the same content as the *explanandum*, not as it is conceived after the acceptance of the putative explanation, but as it was originally conceived.

For there are, Hegel argues, two pitfalls to which explanations of this type are exposed, vacuity and incompleteness, either one of which can be avoided only at the cost of succumbing to the other. Vacuous explanations are considered in a Remark (*Anmerkung*) of the *Science of Logic* entitled 'Formal mode of explanation from tautological grounds' (*WL* II. pp. 98 ff., M. pp. 458 ff.). Hegel cites, as examples of this, explaining the movement of the earth round the sun by the force of attraction which they exert on each other and explaining the crystalline form by the arrangement of the molecules which compose it. To such explanations he has two connected objections. Firstly, the phenomenon itself is our only evidence for the existence of the entity which is intended to explain it. The explanatory entity is derived from the phenomenon to be explained, just as much as the latter is derived from the former. Here, as elsewhere, Hegel does not distinguish carefully between evidential or epistemic grounds, the evidence for the existence of some entity or the reasons for believing some proposition to be true, and ontological or explanatory grounds, what explains or causes the existence of some entity or the reasons why some proposition is true.[35] But this seems not to affect his argument here. Secondly, and consequently, the explanatory entity (or statement) does not differ in content, but only in form, from the phenomenon (or statement) which it is to explain.[36] When we refer, for example, to the attractive force of the earth and the sun, this expresses no more 'than the phenomenon itself, the relation of these bodies to each other in their movement, contains, only in the form of a determination reflected into itself, of force. If we ask what sort of force attractive force is, the answer is that it is the force which makes the earth move round the sun.' Such explanations are thus on a par with explaining why opium sends one to sleep by referring to its *virtus dormitiva*.

It might be objected that even if the phenomenon to be explained were in these cases our only evidence for the existence of the entity which is to explain it, it would not necessarily follow that the explanatory entity did not differ in content from the *explanandum*, that, for example, the expression 'having a molecular arrangement of a certain type' was related to 'crystalline' in the same way as 'possessing *virtus dormitiva*' is related to 'tending to send one to sleep'. We are surely able to derive conclusions which go beyond the evidence on which they are based, even if the derivation is not a deductively valid one. But in any case the phenomenon to be explained is not in these cases our only evidence for the explanatory entity in question. Gravity or 'attractive force', for example, explains a wide variety of phenomena: the movement of planets, the fall of apples, the trajectory of a missile, and so on.[37] Its content is not exhausted by any single one of these phenomena, but owes something to each of them. In this way, an explanation might avoid becoming a 'tautological movement of the understanding' (*PG* p. 119, M. pp. 94 f.).

It if succeeds in doing this, however, it cannot avoid the second pitfall, that of incompleteness. Hegel deals with this in a Remark entitled 'Formal mode of explanation from a ground which is different from that which is grounded' (*WL* II. pp. 105 ff., M.

pp. 463 ff.). His examples of this type of explanation combine theological with scientific cases in his customary manner:

(i) gravity explains why a house stands up, why a house falls down, and why a projectile follows a certain trajectory;

(ii) the world is grounded upon nature, nature conceived not as identical with the world, but as something 'indeterminate, or at least the self-identical essence of the world which is determinate in the universal differences, the laws';

(iii) God is the ground or essence of nature, conceived now presumably not as in (ii), but as the empirical world.

In each of these cases the ground or *explanans* differs in content, and not in form only, from the *explanandum*. The explanation is not, therefore, vacuous or tautological. But for this very reason, the *explanans* does not fully explain the phenomenon which it grounds.

Here, again, Hegel seems to have two different, but connected, points in mind. Firstly, just because gravity, for example, explains so many different phenomena, it does not explain any of them completely, because it does not explain why a given phenomenon is of one type rather than another. It explains, for example, why, given that a stone is at certain distances from the earth's surface and from its centre of mass at a certain time and if we ignore such factors as air-resistance, the stone falls to the ground with a certain acceleration and reaches it at a certain time with a certain velocity on impact. But it does not explain why what we have in the first place is a stone in this position rather than a house, a planet, a missile or, indeed, a stone in some other position. The predictions of science are only conditional ones, predictions to the effect that, if certain conditions obtain, then such-and-such will happen, and hence if scientific laws and theories are explanatory they explain only certain aspects of any given phenomenon and not the phenomenon as a whole. This point cannot so readily be applied to Hegel's second two examples, for the *explananda* in these cases, the world and nature, include everything that actually exists or happens. An approximation to it, however, is that reference to God, nature, or even the laws of nature does not fully explain our world, since these explanatory entities are compatible with possible worlds other than our own. The laws of nature, for example, are compatible with a number of possible worlds differing in respect of the initial conditions obtaining in them, but not in respect of the laws which govern them. The existence of God is also consonant with several, perhaps with all, possible worlds and cannot, therefore, satisfactorily explain our own. Even if it is supposed that God could not have made a world different from our own and that certain features of him explain the details of the actual world, the description of his nature is unlikely to be specific enough to make the connection clear.[38]

Secondly, the content of the *explanans* differs in these cases from that of the *explanandum*. This seems to mean that the term 'gravity' is not, as in the first type of explanation, an abbreviation for whatever makes stones fall to the ground with a certain acceleration or a succinct way of saying that they do so; nor is it an abbreviation for whatever makes houses stand up, a stone fall down, and a projectile follow a certain path or a succinct way of saying that they do so; it refers, rather, to a force which is conceived of as genuinely distinct from each and all of the phenomena which it supposedly explains. Similarly, the term 'God' is not simply shorthand for (whatever produces) certain more or less general features of the world, but refers to an entity which is genuinely distinct from the world which he produces.[39] The connection of this with the first point seems to be that it is only if the entity in question is introduced to explain, and is evidenced by, a variety of phenomena that it and the terms referring to it can be independent of the phenomena. The connection is not, however, a tight one. Whether or not such terms as 'God', 'gravity' or 'molecule' are regarded as succinct descriptions of phenomena or as referring to distinct entities does not depend on how many or how few phenomena they are related to.

If, however, the content of the *explanans* differs from that of the *explanandum*, then again the explanation cannot be complete, for there is now a logical gap between the explanatory item and the phenomenon to be explained. This is independent of the first point, that the *explanans* explains a variety of phenomena. Even if we were to suppose that electricity could produce only lightning or that God could have produced only our actual world, we can still ask: 'Why does (or must) electricity produce lightning?' or 'Why did God produce a world at all?': 'that ground is neither the ground of the manifoldness which is different from it nor of its own connection with this manifoldness' (*WL* II. p. 106, M. p. 464). These questions cannot arise if 'electricity' and 'God' are abbreviations for the relevant phenomena, but then they have only descriptive and not explanatory force. If they have explanatory force, then there is a logical gap between them and the phenomena which cannot ultimately be closed.

The dilemma which Hegel presents seems a genuine one, difficult, if not impossible, to resolve. The best response is to concede that we cannot explain everything, that Hegel's ideal of what an explanation should be is not one that can be met. This is, however, a response which he was reluctant to make, believing, or at least half-believing, that everything had to be just as it is and that it could be shown why it is so. This, however, will be reserved for later. In the following section we shall consider some of Hegel's other criticisms of the natural sciences and the implications that these have for his philosophical programme.

5 *The defects of empirical science*

Hegel makes a number of criticisms of the empirical sciences as such. The upshot of these criticisms is not that the sciences should be abandoned or that some other way should have been followed of studying the world. Empirical science is an indispensable prelude to philosophy, and while Hegel has some objections to particular theories — championing, for example, Kepler and Goethe against Newton — he by and large accepted the results of the sciences, believing rather that they did not go far enough. The criticisms are intended to show why philosophy is required in addition, not as an alternative, to the natural sciences. Some of them can be fully appreciated only in the light of a fuller picture of Hegel's own system, but since they disclose some of the problems to which his system was a response, a preliminary account of them will be given here.

We can begin by dismissing two types of science or rather of quasi-science which, on Hegel's view, are wholly 'positive' and are therefore excluded from philosophical consideration. The term 'positive' in this context contrasts not with 'negative' or with 'natural', but with 'rational'. Something is positive if it just has to be accepted (or rejected), and cannot be rationally validated, explained or derived. The first type of positive science is exemplified by philology, which, on Hegel's view, is a mere aggregate of information. Sciences of the second type differ in that there is a particular reason for their being in this condition. Such sciences as heraldry 'have mere wilfulness (*Willkür*) as their ground' (*Enz.* I. 16). Heraldic designs are chosen by individuals for purely personal, or for no particular, reasons. There are, therefore, no interesting generalizations to be discovered about them or, if there are, they simply have to be accepted and cannot be theoretically explained. Hegel does not say whether he believes that these quasi-sciences could or would one day become systematic, developing, as chemistry had done, from a collection of bits of information into a full-fledged science. Presumably he does not believe that heraldry could do so unless the basis of the assignment of devices were to change. Nor does he say whether, if such developments were to occur, changes in the *Encyclopaedia* would be required in order to accommodate them.⁴⁰ It is clear, however, that he believes that a science can be systematically integrated with other sciences only to the extent that it is itself systematic. There is no place in the *Encyclopaedia* for purely descriptive sciences.

The third and main group of sciences, with which Hegel is concerned, includes physics, chemistry, geology and, perhaps surprisingly, history. These sciences have a 'positive' aspect, but they also 'have a rational ground and beginning' (*Enz.* I. 16). Most, if not all, of the defects which Hegel finds in them derive from their positive aspect. The first such defect is that the sciences assume their starting-points (*Anfänge*) and do not derive or justify them: 'the starting-points are everywhere *immediacies, a datum, assumptions*' (*Enz.* I. 9). Hegel has in mind here more than one type of starting-point. One of the things a science has to assume is the existence of the object or range of objects with which it is concerned (*Enz.* I. 1). Some sciences, for example – presumably geometry and physics – assume the existence of space and time (*Enz.* I. 17). Again a science might presuppose certain axioms, that, for example, if two things are equal to a third, then they are equal to each other (*Enz.* I. 188). A certain method of cognition is also assumed (*Enz.* I. 1). Presumably the assumption of certain forms of inference falls under this heading, and so too does the employment of categories, those of matter and force, of one, many, and universality, without a proper examination of them (*Enz.* I. 38). Hegel does not always make it clear what is wrong with assumptions, unless of course they are the wrong assumptions. The point seems to be, however, that as long as something is merely assumed it is always conceivable that someone will assume the opposite and to that extent the conclusions based on the assumption have not been properly justified.⁴¹ Again, if a science makes assumptions, if it presupposes a starting-point, it cannot give a complete account of what there is, but only of a selected fragment of it; the area beyond its starting-point will be closed to it.⁴²

A second defect of the sciences is their empirical character. This is connected with the first defect, to the extent that some of what Hegel counts as assumptions, for example the assumption of the existence of space and time, are presumably based on sense-perception. But it is not only empirical disciplines which rely on assumptions. Pre-Kantian metaphysics made them too, though Hegel is inclined to call this feature of it 'empirical' in an extended sense (*Enz.* I. 33). The sciences, as we have seen, lose something of their empirical character as they develop, replacing relatively low-level empirical terms such as 'resin-electricity' and 'glass-electricity' by abstract ones like 'negative' and 'positive electricity' by means of comparison and experiment.[43] But they do not abandon their moorings in sense-experience, the 'finitude of [their] *ground of cognition* (*Erkenntnisgrund*) which is partly argumentation (*Räsonnement*), partly feeling, faith, the authority of others, in general the authority of inner and outer intuition' (*Enz.* I. 16).

By implication, this is regarded as a defect in the sciences and one that is, ideally at least, to be eliminated by deriving their results *a priori*, without recourse to sense-experience.[44] There are several reasons for this. Firstly, if a proposition or a theory is ultimately dependent for its acceptance on our sense-experience, then it is not necessarily true, and, if we rely on our sense-experience in accepting it, whether or not its acceptance is ultimately dependent on it, then we have not shown that it is necessary, even if we have shown it to be true. This is because what sense-experience I, or we, have is itself a contingent and not a necessary matter. It might be objected that science should ideally explain why our sense-experience is as it is and thus show it to be necessary. And perhaps Hegel's ultimate objective does bear some resemblance to this. But the immediate replies to the objection are that no scientific theory in fact accounts for all the details of our perceptual experience and that, even if one did, the necessity of the theory and of the sensory data would each be conditional upon the necessity of the other; the composite of theory and sense-experience would not have been shown to be necessary as a whole and unconditionally. But if something is not necessary then it could have been otherwise, and if it is not shown to be necessary, then it is not shown that it could not have been otherwise. It follows that we do not, and perhaps cannot, explain why it is so, why what might not have been the case is in fact the case. An example of something which is not customarily shown to be necessary is the law of the acceleration of freely falling bodies: 'time and space, or distance and velocity . . . are indifferent to each other, space is conceived as able to exist without time, time without space, and distance, at least, without velocity — just as their quantities are indifferent to each other, since they are not related *as* something positive and something *negative*, and are thus not related to each other through *their essence*' (*PG* p. 118, M. p. 93).[45] If something is known only on the basis of sense-perception, there is always room for the question why it is so, and, as we have seen, Hegel's ideal is an explanation which excludes such questions.

A second consideration in Hegel's objection to the empirical is that he believes, as we shall see, that the core or essence of the world is pure thought or thought-determinations and that the sciences progressively disclose them to us.[46] The relationship between pure thoughts and the empirical is a complex one, but Hegel probably feels that to the extent that a concept or a law is a pure thought it should be possible to dispense altogether with empirical evidence for its application or truth, that, for example, if the concept of electricity is a pure thought we should be able to show *a priori* that lightning is an electrical discharge, while, if it is not, then we should purify it further until the point where we are able to do so. This argument would not withstand close examination, but it might nevertheless have had some appeal for Hegel.

Hegel's final objection to reliance on empirical evidence for one's view of the world is that it involves an impairment of one's freedom or autonomy. We saw earlier that empirical science is regarded as providing a new sort of freedom. It enables a man to decide questions for himself without relying on the authority of others.[47] But the victory is a shortlived one. This is suggested when Hegel speaks not simply of inner and outer intuition, but of 'the authority of others, in general the authority of inner or outer intuition' (*Enz.* I. 16). The point is made explicit elsewhere:

> Since now this sensuous [material] is and remains for
> empiricism something given, this is a doctrine of unfreedom,
> for freedom consists just in my having nothing absolutely
> other than myself over against me, but depending on a content
> which I myself am (*Enz.* I. 38Z).

There is more than one point at issue in this passage, but the crucial one here is that to rely on one's own sense-experience, though it appears at first sight to be making up one's own mind, is in a way as much to rely on external authority as is acceptance of the word of priests and kings. For one's sense-experience does not constitute oneself, but is something given to one, rather as a received creed or dogma is.[48] Reliance on it is therefore an abdication of intellectual autonomy. On Hegel's view, one is only truly free to the extent that one is thinking.[49]

The reliance of the sciences on sense-experience depends in part on a feature of them which is the subject of Hegel's third criticism, the fact that their 'starting-point, which is in itself rational (*an sich rationeller Anfang*), passes over into the contingent, because they have to bring the universal down to *empirical individuality* and *actuality*' (*Enz.* I. 16). The term 'starting-point' does not here refer to the same thing as it did in Hegel's first criticism, namely that the sciences assume their starting-points. What he has in mind are the general concepts, laws and theories of the sciences, and these are regarded as starting-points owing to their generality and logical priority over particular empirical facts rather than their epistemological priority in the cognitive procedures of the scientist. The zoologist, for example, perhaps has as his 'starting-point' the generic concept of an animal, and he proceeds from there to genera, species and subspecies, and from these again to individual animals; he moves from a universal starting-point to the particular and from the particular to the individual. (By 'particular', *besonder*, Hegel usually means 'of a particular or specific type', rather than 'individual', for which he uses *'einzeln'*.) But the transitions from the universal to the particular and from the particular to the individual are empirical rather than *a priori*. We cannot proceed *a priori* from the concept of a genus to those of its species, from that of one species to those of the others, or from the species to the individuals that exemplify them. We cannot tell by inspection of the concept of an animal that there are vertebrates and invertebrates, lions, elephants and bears. We discover what species, subspecies and individuals there are by empirical observation. In a not entirely dissimilar way more general laws or theories do not entail less general ones, unless certain empirically discovered, or at least empirically suggested, conditions are added to them, and laws and theories of either type do not on their own tell us what actual events occur.[50]

This also seems to be the substance of Hegel's complaints about analysis, namely that analysis does not leave the object as it is, but that the elements into which it is analysed acquire the form of universality and thus become thoughts; that analysis kills what is alive, since only the concrete is alive (*Enz.* I. 38Z. Cf. II. 246Z). The force of these complaints is not clear. That analysis changes our view of the object should not be, for Hegel, an objection to it, for all thinking does this. It may be intended as an objection to a certain *account* of analysis, to the view that it is purely descriptive and does not go beyond the empirical data. That analysis kills what is alive, however, is surely meant as an objection to analysis as such. But what objection? If a living organism is dissected then it generally dies, but this does not disqualify analysis unless one's purpose is the survival of the organism rather than knowledge about it. The fact that dissection kills an organism does not entail that it provides no information about why it was alive before it was dissected. In any case not all analysis is dissection and not all concrete objects are alive. If the objection has any literal content, it must consist in such points as that analysis always involves abstraction and selection, failing to capture all the features of an object; that it cannot explain why the particular features which it abstracts are combined in the particular way they are; and that the connection between the results of analysis and 'concrete' phenomena can only be re-established by empirical observation. Hegel's attitude towards analysis wavers between outright rejection and acceptance of it as a necessary first step which is to be complemented by some sort of synthesis. He tended to disfavour 'analytical' scientific theories when an alternative was available. He is, for example, invariably hostile to Newton (e.g. *Enz.* II. 270) and preferred Goethe's theory of colours:

> One cannot express oneself too strongly . . . regarding the
> conceptual barbarism which applies the category of *com-*
> *position* . . . even to light, and makes *brightness* consist of
> seven *darknesses*: one might as well say that clear water
> consists of seven sorts of earth (*Enz.* II. 320).

The preference is in part an aesthetic one, but the point which primarily worries Hegel is the gulf between more and less general concepts and theories, and between concepts and theories of any kind and concrete individuals. To leave such a gulf is not a fault peculiar to empirical science. It is characteristic of most religions that they postulate a universal essence underlying phenomena or a deity who is responsible for them, without establishing a precise connection between the surface richness of things and the indeterminate essence which purports to explain them. It is indeed inevitable that there should be a gap of sorts between thought and nature (cf. *Enz.* II. 246Z), but we can at least not make it wider than need be by following Newton when Goethe is available and we can, as Hegel seems to have believed, find a route from abstract thoughts to concrete things other than that of empirical observation.[51]

Another criticism which Hegel levels at the sciences is that they cannot accommodate the traditional objects of philosophy, freedom, spirit (*Geist*) and God (*Enz.* I. 8). It might be objected that he himself is making a large assumption in supposing that there are such things. But the question of the extent to which Hegel's own philosophy involves assumptions, and involves them at this point, will be considered later.[52] He oscillates between two distinct claims here, between the claim that the empirical sciences do not provide us with knowledge about these matters (*Enz.* I. 8) and the different claim that they deny that such knowledge is possible, either because these objects do not exist or because we have no

cognitive access to them: 'the *consistent* development of empiricism
. . . denies the supersensible in general or at least the knowledge
and determinacy of it' (*Enz.* I. 38). What he believes perhaps is
that the sciences simply do not consider 'freedom, spirit, God';
they do not deny that there are such entities or that there is some
other way of finding out about them, though in so far as they provide explanations of human actions and of natural events they
suggest arguments against, or undermine arguments for, their
existence. On the other hand, philosophies based on the sciences,
such as materialism and empiricism, do deny the existence or the
knowability of the 'supersensible'. In one respect, Hegel approves
of this feature of empiricism. It denies, or is at least unconcerned
with, the 'beyond' (*das Jenseits*), a world beyond the phenomenal
world which is ethically, ontologically or epistemically superior to
it. It is concerned only with this world (*das Diesseits*), and Hegel
agrees with it in this. For he is as eager as any empiricist to deny
that there are two distinct worlds. Freedom, spirit and God are
in this world and not in any other.[53]

Why, then, do the sciences fail to consider freedom, spirit and
God? Hegel concedes that such objects are not perceptible by the
senses, but is reluctant to say that their exclusion from the
sciences is due to this. This reluctance is supported, feebly, by the
argument that they are objects of experience just as much as any
other, because 'what is in consciousness in general is experienced;
this is indeed a tautological proposition' (*Enz.* I. 8). But, as we
have seen, he also regards experience, more narrowly, as the product of our introduction of thoughts into our raw sensory data,[54]
and he believes, or at least half-believes, that the postulation of a
deity does not transcend our sensory data any more than does the
postulation of molecules or the formulation of general laws.[55]
Why, then, can scientists not discover God, as they discover laws
and molecules? The primary reason, on Hegel's view, for the
sciences' neglect of freedom, spirit and God is that these objects
are 'infinite in their content', whereas the sciences employ 'finite
determinations' (*Enz.* I. 16) or 'finite categories' (62). What is
meant by saying that a concept, category or determination is
finite will be considered in more detail later.[56] It is enough for
the moment that it could, and probably does, mean a variety of
things. Some concepts, firstly, are not universally applicable, but
contrast with a contradictory or a contrary. The concept of simplicity, for example, is finite, because some things are, or at any
rate could be, not simple, but complex. Or, again, a concept
could be finite if it is not the only concept there is. The concept
of self-identity may be universally applicable, but it is not the

70

only concept there is, since many more things are true of anything than that it is identical with itself. Again, it may be that what Hegel has in mind is that some of the categories employed by the sciences, notably that of causality, imply a piecemeal approach to reality. If x is a cause, then there is something other than x, y, which is the effect of x, and, characteristically, there is something other than x and other than y, z, which is the cause of x. In so far as they are concerned to explain things by their antecedent causes, the empirical sciences are restricted not simply to the phenomenal world as a whole, but to mere fragments of a number of unending causal sequences within it. They confine themselves, then, to the finite.[57]

The employment of finite categories is not essentially connected with the reliance on sense-experience. Perception does indeed tend to be piecemeal, but it need not remain so: 'In experience, what matters is the spirit (*Sinn*) in which one approaches actuality. A great spirit (*Geist*) has great experiences and discerns in the motley play of appearance the point of significance' (*Enz.* I. 24Z. 3).[58] Conversely, the employment of finite categories is not peculiar to the empiricist. Pre-Kantian metaphysics was also prone to this and is similarly debarred from a proper understanding of God, freedom and spirit.[59]

It is, then, a defect of the sciences that they use finite determinations. It is a further defect that they do not recognize that their determinations are finite, and therefore do not 'exhibit their transition and that of their whole sphere into a higher sphere, but assume them to be absolutely valid' (*Enz.* I. 16). The criticism is not developed further and is, as it stands, ambiguous. It could mean that the sciences do not exhibit the transition of their categories and their sphere as a whole, nature, into a higher sphere, that of mind, for example, or perhaps of religion. But it is more likely to mean that no single science exhibits the transition of its category or categories and of its sphere into the categories and sphere of another, and higher, science. For example, no connection is indicated between physics and chemistry, or between the study of planetary motion and that of light. Hegel's diagnosis of this is that the categories involved in any one science, or area of science, are finite. They are, that is, bounded by the categories of other sciences or areas of science, and they should therefore be intelligibly connected with these other categories; the categories should, as it were, flow or spill over into one another. Since this is so, the sciences in which these categories are embodied should be intelligibly connected with each other. The sciences themselves, however, are oblivious to the finitude of their categories and therefore fail to provide such transitions. Hegel attempts to supply them in his *Philosophy of Nature*. His solutions may not be, on the whole, particularly impressive, but the problem which he addresses, that of the unity of science, is not a negligible one. His diagnosis of this problem is rooted in his account of logic and the discussion of such questions as why finite categories or concepts should flow into one another will be reserved for later.[60] It is enough for the moment that the problem is not, on Hegel's view, posed primarily by the empirical character of the sciences. Just as finite categories are not peculiar to empirical science, nor is the failure to detect and exploit the transitions between them. This, again, is a defect of pre-Kantian metaphysics (*Enz.* I. 33). On the other hand, to the extent that different sciences are regarded as distinct and are not in some way derived from each other, this will enlarge the area in which we have to rely on empirical observation and/or on assumptions.

To call something a 'defect' perhaps suggests that it is remediable, or at least that it might not have been. To what extent does Hegel believe that these defects are remediable? Some of them are eliminable within the sciences themselves or at least within the restructured version of them provided by the *Philosophy of Nature*. The disregard of the finitude of the categories, for example, though not the finitude itself, is repaired and Hegel purports to 'display their transition and that of their whole sphere into a higher sphere'. He also attempts to examine the starting-points of the sciences and to justify them in so far as they are justifiable, though it is far from clear whether he believes that it is possible to dispense with assumptions altogether. On the other hand, Hegel sometimes suggests that there is an irreducible element of contingency which he attributes to the 'impotence' (*Ohnmacht*) of nature (*Enz.* II. 250)[61] — misleadingly, since contingency also figures in human affairs (*Enz.* I. 16). If this is so, then contingency cannot be excluded from the sciences, though its area may be diminished. If such contingency is a defect, then it is so in contrast to the area of necessity within the sciences and to logic itself, not to the contingency-free natural science that might have been. Our concern here, however, has been the alleged faults of the empirical sciences, not the nature or merits of the solutions which Hegel offers for them. The remainder of this chapter will consider the value which, despite its defects, he nevertheless attributed to natural science.

6 *Objectivity and science*

The empirical sciences, as we have seen, involve thinking about phenomena. What is the point of doing this? The alternatives to doing so would be either to ignore empirical phenomena altogether and to think about something else instead or simply to accept them as they are without thinking about them at all. To disregard the phenomenal world entirely is no doubt a sophisticated response to it, which is preceded by and presupposes a primitive acceptance of it, but it is nevertheless an attitude which Hegel supposes some men to have adopted, and he makes an attempt to show its inadequacy (*PG* pp. 151 ff., M. pp. 119 ff.). This discussion can, however, be ignored here in the light of the evident obtrusiveness of empirical phenomena.[62] The fullest presentation of Hegel's argument against the second alternative occurs in a passage we have already considered, his discussion of sense-certainty in the *Phenomenology*.[63] If I am sense-certain, I survey the sensible world in all its concrete richness without classifying, conceptualizing or selecting, and I attempt to express what I am conscious of by the use of such words as 'this', 'here' and 'now'. The objection to this attitude is that such words fail to capture the concrete reality of which I am aware, fail even to denote particular individuals (since 'everything is a this'), and simply express very thin and general thoughts. The mere acceptance of empirical phenomena, if it is to be more than an animal-like state and involves an attempt to refer to them, will in any case involve thoughts and this minimal amount of thought will not enable us to do what we set out to do, namely to refer to items in, or features of, our sense-experience. It is this argument which Hegel has in mind when he says that Hume was unjustified in assuming 'the truth of the empirical' and in challenging 'universal determinations and laws from that position', when he should, like the ancient sceptics, have 'turned against the sensuous first of all' (*Enz.* I. 39). It also underlies such remarks as that perception provides no foothold for cognition, because 'as such it is always something individual and transitory' (*Enz.* I. 38Z). It is perhaps an objection to the argument that it does not show why we should or must attempt to express what we are conscious of at all, why we should not simply accept it in an animal-like way. After all, animals succeed perfectly well in doing so. Animals, of course, are not worth arguing with, but this in itself is not an argument against reverting to their condition. Hegel presumably simply assumed that, if one did revert to it, one would no longer be human.

To establish the value of thought is not, as we have seen, to show the need for science.[64] But the *Phenomenology* provides an answer to this, arguing that once a modicum of thought is introduced into our view of the world, we are propelled onward by the inner incoherence of successive attitudes to a scientific account of it (*PG* pp. 102 ff., M. pp. 79 ff.). The argument is obscure and unconvincing in detail, but one prominent motif is that we are impelled to overcome the sheer disarray in which the materials of perception are presented to us: 'the experiential sciences provide the stimulus to overcome the *form* in which their wealth of content is presented: it is something merely immediate and given, a manifold of one thing *next to* another, in general therefore contingent . . .' (*Enz.* I. 12). This passage probably refers to the results of the empirical sciences rather than to our pre-scientific experience, and the form in which they leave their results is to be overcome not by more empirical science, but by philosophy. Our pre-scientific experience is, however, even more chaotic, and the organizing work of philosophy is begun by the sciences; they have 'prepared the material for philosophy in advance by thinking, by finding universal determinations, genera and laws' (*Ibid.*). The sciences meet philosophy half-way. This ordering of the phenomenal world is sometimes seen as the solution, or as a part of the solution, to the problems presented by the contrast between the self and the world of which it is aware: 'In consciousness we see the tremendous *difference* between the *I*, this entirely *simple* entity on the one hand, and the infinite *manifoldness of the world* on the other' (*Enz.* III. 425Z).[65] The overcoming of this sharp contrast is required for the attainment of self-consciousness in Hegel's second sense, the sense in which I am self-conscious only to the extent that what I am conscious of is, and is seen by me to be, not wholly distinct from me but at bottom the same as myself.[66] The need to organize a world or sensory material which is in confusion and disarray, however, would not in itself account for the procedures of the sciences. The purpose might be achieved in a number of more or less imaginative ways, without any of the empirical constraints to which the sciences are subject. If the sciences are to have an advantage over poetry and if the world is to be shown, and not merely fancied, to be like myself, then what is required is truth or objectivity.

It is the objectivity of (meta-)thinking which Hegel stresses in the introductory sections of the *Encyclopaedia*. There are, however, two broad types of objectivity. The first might rather be called 'intersubjectivity' and it has some of the flavour of 'impartiality'. Hegel is referring to objectivity in this sense when he says that thinking is only true 'in respect of its form' in so far as it is 'not a *particular* being or activity of the subject, but is just consciousness' acting as an abstract I, as free of *every particularity* of other properties, states, etc. and only doing what is universal, in which it is identical with all individuals' (*Enz.* I. 23). So was Hume when he wrote that when a man takes the moral viewpoint he must 'depart from his private and particular situation, and must choose a point of view, common to him with others: he must move some universal principle of the human frame, and touch a string, to which all mankind have an accord and symphony.'[67] This reference to moral objectivity or impartiality should remind us that objectivity in this sense does not guarantee objectivity in the second sense. For even if one succeeds in 'acting as an abstract I' or in departing from one's 'private and particular situation', it may still be that one gets the wrong answer or even that there are no objectively right and wrong answers at all: moral values might be merely (inter-)subjective and Hegel might be wrong in believing that thoughts are 'objective' (*Enz.* I. 24). Though they are connected in such ways as that a fair amount of agreement between individuals is necessary if we are to be entitled to ascribe objectivity, objective truth or correctness, to the answers they arrive at, the two senses of 'objectivity' are distinct.

Hegel, or his editor, sometimes conflates them. In a discussion of the belief that 'cognition is only subjective' he remarks that 'the truth is the objective and should be the rule for the conviction of everyone, so that the conviction of the individual is bad in so far as it does not correspond to this rule.' But some people believe, he continues, that 'conviction as such, the mere form of being convinced, is good in itself — regardless of its content — since no criterion for its truth is available' (*Enz.* I. 22Z). The question whether our beliefs correspond, or can be known to correspond, to objective reality is here conflated with the different question whether there are or can be intersubjectively agreed criteria for the acceptability of beliefs. One might, for example, hold that a true belief is one which corresponds to the objective nature of things, but that since there is no way of telling whether a belief does so or not, the 'objective', if it is a rule at all, is not a rule which we can apply. But one is not obviously thereby committed to holding that it does not matter what one believes as long as one believes something or other. A distinction between good and bad beliefs can still be drawn by means of the criterion, for example, of coherence or failure to cohere with our experience and/or with the main body of our shared beliefs, even if the application of this criterion provides no guaranteed access to the objective nature of things.

Despite such occasional confusion, however, Hegel has separate arguments for the objectivity of thought in each of these senses. Thinking is objective in the sense of 'intersubjective' or 'impartial', because, to the extent that he thinks, the subject conducts himself as an 'abstract ego' and does not differ from other thinking individuals. Thinking, as we have seen, is intimately associated with the pure self, not with the perceiving, desiring self, but with the self which has perceptions and desires. Selves differ, not in their thinking, but in respect of their perceptions, desires, opinions and prejudices (das *besondere* Meinen und Dafürhalten, *Enz.* I. 23). The pure self as such is not prejudiced in favour of this or that view, or predisposed to this or that course of action. I may, of course, have certain desires and prejudices, but in so far as I think I suspend them or set them aside and consider questions with an open mind. My desires and prejudices may figure among the evidence relevant to these questions, but they are treated only as considerations among others and are not something that I automatically or unavoidably follow.[68]

There are, however, several difficulties in this. Firstly, while it may be true that people do not differ simply as pure egos, they do differ in their thinking. They differ in their intellectual skills, equipment and interests, so that not everyone will think about, for example, lightning, and, even if they did, they would not necessarily have the same thoughts about it or have them at the same time. It might be replied that differences in the way people think are the result of other differences between them, differences in their desires, perceptions and interests, and that if they did not differ in these respects, then they would all think in the same way. But this is of little practical relevance, since none of us is a pure thinker. The likelihood is that a being which had no desires or sensory intake would not think at all. In any case, if we are concerned with the meta-thinking of the natural sciences, we cannot be confined to thinking alone and be deprived of, or stand aloof from, our fragmentary and variable sensory intake. To decide whether or not lightning is electricity one needs sensory access to lightning and to the results of certain experiments. Perceptual experience, unlike thought, depends directly on one's spatial location, so that it will differ qualitatively from person to person. The remedy for this, however, is not to ignore perceptual experience, but to consider observations made from different angles, under different conditions and by different observers, in order to nullify as far as possible the contingencies of a single perceptual occasion or of a single observer. Objectivity, it might be argued, is achieved primarily by the cooperation and mutual criticism of many individual scientists. Participation in this process requires some, but not a perfect, degree of objectivity on the part of the individual.[69]

A second difficulty is that while thinking has so far been distinguished, more or less, from perceptions and desires, it has not been shown to be distinct from 'opinions and prejudices'. There is *prima facie* no reason to suppose that a prejudice, a belief to which one is predisposed and which one is reluctant to examine or jettison, need be less thought-ridden than any other belief. The belief that lightning is an act of divine vengeance is not obviously less thought-ridden than the belief that it is an electrical discharge. Either belief could become a prejudice which we were unprepared to submit to the test of observation and experiment, but this seems unrelated to the thoughts or conceptions involved in them. What connection is there between abstract thinking and the open mind? Hegel's answer presumably is that a relatively abstract belief, such as that lightning is a product of divine wrath, can become a prejudice only if it is supported by desires, whims or perceptual experience of an idiosyncratic, or at least parochial, kind. In so far as one insulates one's thinking from such influences, it is free-wheeling and immune to blockages produced by bias and prejudice. This reply is open to the objection that some desires which might buttress prejudice, the desire, for example, that hardship and prosperity should be in proportion to the deserts of their recipients, might be fairly widespread. It would be more to the point to examine the evidential value of the desirability of certain states of affairs for our scientific enquiries than to consider the extent of the desire for them. But even if Hegel's diagnosis of prejudice is correct, it can again be objected that what is required is not that any individual scientist should be entirely free of prejudice, but only that he be sufficiently so to participate in the interchange of criticism which neutralizes the prejudices and blindspots of the individual.

Finally, even if our desires and perceptions vary from person to person, it does not follow that our conceptions, the conception, for example, of (phenomenal) lightning, are more variable than our thoughts. Indeed, if they were, we would not all understand, at least in the same way, the claim that lightning is an electrical discharge, even if we all had the same thoughts of force and of electricity. Our conceptions, as we have seen, involve thoughts and thus the variations in our sensory intake are ironed out in the conceptions derived from it. But if our pre-scientific conceptions are already objective, it is hard to see what advance is made by the sciences in this respect; even if they introduce more thought, this does not necessarily involve more objectivity. The reply to this, however, might be that while conceptions and accounts of phenomena in terms of them may be shared, or at least shareable, by all men, they still embody the contingent features of human sense-organs. Other beings who are nevertheless rational might have quite different sense-experience from our own and therefore have an entirely different conception, if any, of lightning. But they would have to be capable, in virtue of their rationality, of thought and, if they were capable of thought, they would have to have, or be capable of acquiring, such concepts as those of a force and, perhaps, of electricity. We could, therefore, share with them an account of the world in terms of thought. The routes would differ, starting from different sense-perceptions and proceeding through different conceptions, but they would converge on a single vision of the intelligible structure of the world.[70] Whether or not we could communicate with such creatures does not matter, for Hegel believes that we can argue *a priori* that thinking involves certain definite concepts or at least the capacity for developing them. He does not consider explicitly the possibility of rational creatures other than ourselves, but his *Logic* is, among other things, an exposition of the necessary, even if implicit, features of the thinking of any rational being. The merits of this argument will be considered later.[71]

7 *Varieties of objectivity*

This first conception of objectivity involves the idea that if one succumbs to one's idiosyncratic desires, perceptions and prejudices, one can view the world only as it appears from one's own perspective. Only by abstracting from what is peculiar to oneself can one occupy a perspective-free position which is accessible to all rational beings, and hope to give an account of the world as it is in itself. The retort that what is needed is not bias-free men, but the critical interchange of many, more or less biased ones amounts to saying that objectivity does not require a perspective-free position, but is some function of many different perspectives. But, whichever of these views we prefer, there seems to be no guarantee of objectivity in any further sense, no assurance that from the position we adopt we shall see what is actually there or that there is anything to be seen at all. All men, even all rational beings, might be wrong, even if they are in agreement; the fact that one's answer to a question is free of idiosyncrasy does not entail that it is correct. Hegel believes, however, that objectivity in the sense of 'intersubjectivity' does involve objectivity in this further sense. The argument is indicated when he says that 'thinking is true (*wahrhaft*) in respect of its content, only in so far as it is sunk in the *subject-matter* (in die *Sache* vertieft ist)' and speaks of 'letting go one's *particular* opinions and prejudices and letting the *subject-matter* (die *Sache*) hold sway in oneself' (*Enz.* I. 23). Once I abandon or suspend everything peculiar to myself, I confront the 'subject-matter' as a bare ego. I contribute nothing of my own to the consideration of it and thus whatever results I arrive at are simply read off the subject-matter. There is no room for distortion of the subject-matter either between it and the ego or within the ego itself.

This argument recurs frequently, primarily with reference to philosophical, and especially pure, thinking.[72] It might be thought that Hegel does not intend to apply it to the thinking of the natural sciences, both because § 23 of the *Encyclopaedia*, though it purports initially to be about 'meta-thinking', is primarily concerned with philosophical thinking and because he does not in any case regard the sciences as free of assumptions:[73]

> The fundamental delusion in scientific empiricism is always this, that it uses the metaphysical categories of matter, force, also of one, many, universality, also the infinite, etc., it further proceeds to draw *inferences* on the basis of such categories, and thereby presupposes and applies the forms of inference and all the while it is not aware that it itself thus contains and operates metaphysics and uses those categories in an entirely uncritical and unconscious manner (*Enz.* I. 38).

How, in the light of this, can he ascribe objectivity, objectivity for that matter of either kind, to the sciences? The answer seems to be that it is because what the sciences deploy are pure thoughts. Some of the categories are, it is true, misapplied,[74] and some, like that of matter, are applied too widely.[75] His criticism, however, is not that they are not thoughts, nor primarily that they are the wrong thoughts, but that they are simply assumed rather than derived and justified. But since they figure in the logical system which he wishes to identify, or at least closely associate, with the pure ego, they do not have the same status as mere opinions and prejudices.

But whatever view we take of Hegel's intentions here, it is clear that empirical science does not involve an unmediated confrontation between natural phenomena and the bare ego. The subject brings with him, apart from his perceptual equipment, assumptions about what counts as evidence, about what counts as an explanation, and about what are legitimate types of inference and what are not. The laws of celestial motion are, as Hegel remarks, not written on the sky (*Enz.* I. 21Z). We are presented with, or seek out, clues which form the basis of inferences and interpretations. But the inferences and interpretations are ours. It is true that our assumptions are not necessarily fixed and that they may change in the course of our enquiry. But it does not follow that there is any time at which we have no assumptions at all. We can, again, suspend at least some of our assumptions and submit them to examination, but in so far as we do so we are no longer studying lightning or celestial bodies. As soon as we return to them, assumptions of some sort must be reinstated. It does not follow, however, that empirical science is not less blinkered, less prejudice-encrusted, than other cognitive attitudes. Hegel's language some-times suggests that objectivity of this sort is a matter of degree: 'thinking is true in respect of its content only in so far as (*insofern . . . als*) it is sunk in the *subject-matter*' (*Enz.* I. 23). He perhaps held that, while science is less objective than philosophy, it is more so than commonsense, and, for most of his purposes, this is all that he needs to claim.

It is not enough, however, if he is to establish a clear connec-tion between the two types of objectivity. There is, as we shall see, no good reason to suppose that there is such a thing as total immersion in one's subject matter, and it is hard to say what such absorption would be like. It is correspondingly difficult to say whether, if one were so immersed, any doubt could arise con-cerning the objectivity of one's thoughts. Since, however, the scientist cannot achieve this state, doubt can be cast on the objectivity, not only of particular theories, but of the scientific world picture as a whole. Some independent argument is therefore required for the objectivity of thought in this sense, and Hegel attempts to provide it.

8 *Thought and essence*

Hegel expresses his view that 'thoughts are objective' (*Enz.* I. 24) in a variety of ways: 'understanding, reason is in the world' (*Ibid*); 'νοῦς governs the world' (*Ibid.* Z; cf. 8); and nature is a 'petrified intelligence' (*versteinerte Intelligenz, Enz.* I. 24Z).[76] These claims have, as we shall see, more than one meaning,[77] but the relevant one with regard to the natural sciences is that thought, in contrast to perception, discloses the essence or the essential nature of a thing (*Enz.* I. 21-4). When we say that lightning is the expression of a force or that it is an electrical discharge, we are not only saying something true about it, just as we are when we say that it

is bright and yellow; we are also saying something more fundamental about it than when we say that it is bright and yellow, we
are giving its 'truth' or its true nature as opposed to its superficial
features.

The concept of a force and, perhaps, of electricity is just one
example of a thought and it is not Hegel's main example in his
argument for his position:

> When we speak of a definite animal, we say that it is [an]
> animal. The *animal as such* cannot be shown, but only a
> determinate animal. *The* animal does not exist, but is the
> universal nature of individual animals, and each existing
> animal is a far more concrete, determinate, particularized
> thing. But being an animal, the genus as the universal, belongs
> to the determinate animal and constitutes its determinate
> essentiality. If we take animality away from the dog, it
> would be impossible to say what it is. Things in general have
> a permanent, inner nature and an external existence (*Dasein*).
> They live and die, arise and pass away; their essentiality, their
> universality is the genus, and this is not to be conceived
> merely as something common to them all (*Enz.* I. 24Z. 1.
> Cf. *WL* I. pp. 26 f., M. pp. 36 f.).

Elsewhere Hegel gives a diverse collection of examples to illustrate
the thesis that 'the universal, as such a product of [meta-thinking's]
activity, contains the value, the *essential*, the *inner*, the *true*
[nature] of the *thing*' (*Enz.* I. 21):

(1) The child has to combine adjectives with nouns, and to do
so it must remember a grammatical rule. The rule is a universal
and the particular case is made to conform to this universal.

(2) We have ends or purposes, and we meta-think or reflect on
how to attain them. The end is the universal, the governing principle, and we manipulate our means and our tools in accordance
with it.

(3) Meta-thinking plays a similar role in moral matters. To meta-
think here means to know what is right, one's duty. This is the
universal, the fixed rule, to which our conduct should conform
in particular cases.

(4) In the case of natural phenomena, such as lightning, we
meta-think in order to discover their causes. The phenomenon is
duplicated into an inside and an outside, a force and its expression,
a cause and its effect. The force is the universal, the enduring
element, not this or that lightning-flash, but what remains the
same in them all.

(5) The case of plants and animals is similar. Individuals are born and die, but the genus is permanent. It is accessible only to meta-thinking.

(6) Laws of nature also belong here. We see the stars in different places at different times. This apparent disorder is unsatisfying to the mind, and thus by meta-thinking, we have established simple, constant and universal laws, from which their movements can be determined.

(7) The laws and institutions which govern the infinite manifold of human activity are also a dominant universal (*ein beherrschendes Allgemeines*) of this sort.

(8) Religion leads us to a universal which embraces everything else and through which everything is brought forth. It is not accessible to the sense, but only to the mind and thought (*Enz.* I. 21Z).

Hegel had a greater capacity than most men for assimilating what is different, and the criticisms which follow will stress the differences between these examples:

(i) Meta-thinking is said to produce, or at least to discover, the 'universal'. This is so in some of these cases, but not in all. The child is not said to produce or discover the rule for combining an adjective with a noun. Reflection enables it rather to apply the rule in particular cases. Similarly, although it is ends or purposes which are 'universal', meta-thinking is concerned not with forming or discovering them, but with finding ways of fulfilling them.

(ii) The examples do not involve universals in the same sense. In some cases, for example, the universal is naturally expressed as a universal proposition (e.g. grammatical rules, laws of nature), but in other cases it is not (e.g. purposes, forces). In most cases, again, the universal is to some degree indeterminate and can be exemplified or satisfied by any of several determinate states of affairs. Rules, laws and purposes, for example, are never so specific that only one fully determinate situation will satisfy them. There are, however, differences even here. We can speak of a force such as electricity in a general way and, again, electricity explains a variety of phenomena. But whereas a particular purpose will be more or less indeterminate as compared to any state of affairs which satisfies it, a particular instance of electricity is presumably as determinate as the phenomenon, e.g. the lightning-flash, which it produces.

(iii) Hegel speaks of the universal as 'governing' the particular and its doing so is a part of what he means by the claim that it is its essence. A grammatical rule governs the formation of particular sentences, a purpose governs the steps taken to fulfil it, laws govern phenomena, the genus governs the features of the individual animal, and so on. But the governing is of different sorts in different cases. A purpose which I have or a rule which I follow guides my conduct in a different way, or sense, from that in which the laws of celestial motion guide or govern the planets. It is misleading, or at least metaphorical, to speak of 'governing' here at all, since laws are, arguably, simply regularities in, or generalizations about, the behaviour of phenomena and lack the ontological status required to produce or affect this behaviour.[78] They differ in this respect from forces, which are felt to be items in the world, capable of making things happen.

(iv) What is essential to transitory phenomena must, on Hegel's view, be persistent in a way that they are not. The universals in these examples are persistent, but again they are so in different ways. A purpose generally persists throughout the time taken to achieve it, while each of the steps taken for this end can be forgotten as soon as it is taken. But a purpose does not persist in the way that a law of nature does, the same in indefinitely many exemplifications of itself. Genera, again, although they persist through many exemplifications of themselves, are not persistent in the way that laws are. Species, and even genera, can become extinct, while if planets were to start behaving in ways which could not be explained on what we currently accept as laws, we would be more likely to concede that we had all along been mistaken about the laws than to claim that the old laws had become extinct. It is true that animality does not come into and pass out of existence along with any given animal, for animals are replaced by other animals. But this does not depend on how abstract the general term is. Doghood is not, nor is poodlehood, transitory in the way that individual dogs and poodles are. Any property, F-ness, which is exemplified by different individuals, is not transitory in the way that those F individuals are. Animality, doghood and poodlehood differ from, say, triangularity in that their instances are systematically interrelated, animals reproducing animals, and so on, and Hegel may have thought of the generic or specific nature of an organism as an underlying entity which is passed on from individual to individual. But the relative persistence of the types of thing, as compared to individual things, does not depend on this. In this sense, as we have seen, a force such as electricity is no more persistent than the type of phenomenon it produces. A particular instance of electricity survives the phenomenon which manifests it, as atoms outlast the things which consist of them. But their persistence is not of the same sort as that of a genus or that of a law of nature.[79] 'Permanence', then, means different things in these different cases.

(v) Universals are, on Hegel's view, accessible to thought or to meta-thinking, but not to sense-perception. The difficulties in this thesis have already been considered. Granted that it is indeterminate how much of my theoretical knowledge is to be incorporated into what I can be said to perceive, forces are not generally felt to be strictly observable. When I see lightning, I can see that it is lightning, but not that it is an electrical discharge. But this is not true of a genus. When I see an animal, I do not see all animals, the 'animal as such', or the genetic structure of the animal, but I can see that it is an animal. Hegel's point here is not that there is something hidden from me that I am unable to see, but that I see a genus, or a law, only as embodied in some particular exemplification of it; it is entangled with particular features which are extraneous to the genus or law as such.

(vi) In what sense are these universals thoughts? Hegel often speaks as if thoughts or concepts were actually embedded in things, making no distinction between our thoughts or concepts and the objective features which correspond to them. For example: 'the *nature*, the peculiar essence . . . is the *concept* of the thing, *what is universal in it*' (*WL* I. p. 26, M. p. 36). The conflation is embodied in such dicta as: 'Understanding, reason, is in the world' (*Enz.* I. 24). *Prima facie* there is a distinction to be drawn between things and our concept of a thing, forces and our concept of a force, and so on. Forces are no more thoughts than things are thoughts or the sensible qualities of things are our sensations.[80] The relationship between thoughts or concepts and things is a problematic one, about which more will be said later.[81] But the consideration of it is not helped by the inadvertent loss of the familiar distinction between them. Hegel is perhaps misled here by his use of such words as 'universal' and 'thought-determination' (*Denkbestimmung*), which can be applied both to concepts and to the features of things. The latter term is introduced in order to avoid the implication that things actually think in the way that people do (*Enz.* I. 24Z. 1), but its general effect is to substitute confusion for argument.

There is, however, a distinct question from this, namely whether our concepts of an animal, of a force, of electricity and so on are thoughts rather than conceptions. Hegel's belief that they are depends on the argument that, since animality, forces and electricity are accessible only to (meta-)thought and not to perception, the concepts of them must be free of any sensory element and be, therefore, pure thoughts. The argument is, however, mistaken. We have already seen reason to doubt whether all the universals in these cases are imperceptible, whether if they are they are so in the same way, and whether the ways in which they are are such as to distinguish thoughts from conceptions. Even if a universal or its instances are unobservable, for example, it would not follow that the corresponding concept was a pure thought unless thinking were a sufficient as well as a necessary condition of establishing its application and sensory evidence were entirely dispensable. In cases such as that of electricity, where this is not so, the concept will involve a sensory element, even if the concept, that of a force, of which it is a specification does not and even if instances of it are not observable. The relative generality or abstractness of a concept is, as we have seen, related to the extent to which its acquisition and its applicability depend on the precise character of our sense-experience, but it is independent of whether exemplifications of it are observable or not.[82]

(vii) In what sense do universals constitute the essence of particular phenomena? There are, again, several possible senses and Hegel seems to have had most of them in mind. What matters to me, for example, is whether or not I achieve my purpose, not the particular means by which I do so — except in relation to other purposes of mine — and what matters is whether a man keeps his promise or not, not the precise way in which he does so — except in relation to other duties which he has. My purpose, again, explains the steps I take to achieve it, electricity explains (and causes) lightning, and a law explains (but does not cause) a particular exemplification of it. In some cases, however, Hegel seems to have more than this in mind: 'it would be impossible to say, if this foundation [viz. being a man or being an animal] were removed from a being, however many other predicates it was still equipped with . . . what such an individual was still supposed to be' (*WL* I. p. 26, M. p. 36).[83] But this could, and probably does, mean several things: that an individual animal could not cease to be an animal without ceasing to exist, that it would not have existed had it not been an animal, and that if such general terms as 'animal' did not apply to things, then there would be no individual things at all or at least we would have no way of picking them out. When Hegel says that the genus is 'not to be conceived merely as something common to them all' (*Enz.* I. 24Z), he probably means that a genus constitutes the individuals which belong to it, whereas we can only speak of some feature as common to all of a set of individuals if those individuals could exist without that feature.[84]

These points, or some of them at least, do distinguish the word 'animal' from such words as 'brown'. A brown animal, for example, can cease to be brown without thereby ceasing to exist, and it might have been white, instead of brown, all along. It is not obvious, however, that they suffice to differentiate thoughts from conceptions, 'animal' from 'dog' or 'poodle', and Hegel's use of the example of 'man' suggests that they do not. If one 'removed' from a dog its caninity one could still perhaps say what it was, that it was, namely, an animal. But a dog could not cease to be a dog without ceasing to exist, and it makes little sense to suppose that it might have been not a dog, but an animal of some other type, all along. Moreover, the points do not apply with the same force to Hegel's other 'universals', to those, for example, which are not perceptible in the way that animality is. We might say that whether a flash of a certain general type is an electrical discharge is our criterion for regarding it as lightning, that a flash which was not an electrical phenomenon would not count as lightning, however much it resembled it in other respects, and that a flash which was an electrical phenomenon would count as lightning, even if it lacked some of its customary phenomenal features. We might also say, of a given lightning-flash, that it would not have existed at all if it had not been an electrical discharge. But we could not justify this by the claim that, if we took away from lightning its electrical nature, we could not say what it was. We could, if we chose, continue to say that it was lightning, just as we did before we arrived at this particular theory about it. If there is such a difference between 'animal' and 'electricity', it is related to the fact that the connection of lightning with electricity was a scientific discovery, whereas the identification of certain creatures as animals and as animals of definite types is a feature of pre-scientific life. It is doubtful whether any consideration about our pre-scientific capacities and procedures can establish that science discloses the essences of things.

Why, then, in the face of these difficulties, does Hegel suppose that it is thoughts, rather than conceptions or perceptions, which are (or pick out or correspond to) the essential nature of phenomena? This question can still be usefully asked, despite the unclarity of such expressions as 'essential nature' and 'thought', and there are at least three general considerations that bear on it. Firstly, thoughts are characterized in part by their generality. But the more general a concept, F, is, the more radically counterfactual is the supposition that a given F individual might not have been F, and the more radical is the change that would occur if it were to cease to be F. Hence perhaps, if x is F, our inclination to say that x would not have existed had it not been F, or that it would cease to exist if it ceased to be F, increases with the generality of 'F'. Secondly, a pure thought and its application are, on Hegel's view, relatively independent of our variable and contingent sensory intake, either because it is very general or because its instances are unobservable. With this, however, one source of contingency and disagreement is removed. Our inclination to regard 'x is F' as necessary rather than contingent increases, according to Hegel, in inverse proportion to the empirical content of 'F', and we are more likely to disagree, ultimately, about whether a bright flash is lightning or not than about whether it is an event or not, more likely to differ about whether lightning is yellow or not than about whether it is electricity or not. Finally, the more general a law or a concept, the more closely, that is, it approximates to a pure thought, the more it relates diverse phenomena to one another, the movement of planets, for example, to falling bodies, and lightning to the Leyden jar: 'Nature shows us an infinite mass of individual forms and phenomena. We need to bring unity into this manifoldness; we therefore compare [phenomena] and try to discover the universal of each one' (*Enz.* I. 21Z). Even if this universal did not constitute the essence of the phenomenon in any further sense, it would still supply a potent motive for scientific investigation. But it is tempting to see, like Poincaré, a connection between generality in this sense and essentiality or 'depth': scientists seek 'the link that unites several facts which have a deep but hidden analogy . . . . Facts would be barren if there were not minds . . . which, behind the bare fact, can detect the soul of the fact.'[85] Hegel too speaks of the 'concept' or thought as the 'soul' (*Seele*) of the object, and for not dissimilar reasons (*WL* I. p. 27, M. p. 37).

9 Self and world

When Hegel propounds this doctrine, that 'thinking is the truth of what is objective (*die Wahrheit des Gegenständlichen*)' (*Enz.* I. 22Z), he is attempting to refute, and supposes himself to have refuted, the Kantian thesis that our thoughts correspond to no real features of things, but are imposed by us on the raw sensory material that is given to us. If this thesis were correct, then our thoughts would not be objective in the full sense; they would, if anything, be less so than our perceptions. Even if we accept Hegel's view, however, that it is by thinking that we establish, and by relatively pure thoughts that we specify, the essential nature of things, it does not follow that our thoughts are objective in this sense. The doctrines are independent of each other. Denial of the

87

Kantian thesis, on the one hand, does not involve the acceptance of Hegel's thesis. One might concede, for example, that lightning is actually and objectively an electrical discharge, that this is a genuine discovery about it and not at any level the creation of our own mental activity, while denying that the electrical character of lightning is any more essential to it than its colour. Conversely, the acceptance of Hegel's thesis does not involve the rejection of Kant's. Hegel would no doubt wonder why one should downgrade the objective status of the essential features of an object as compared with that of its superficial ones, but it is nevertheless possible to do so. We might agree that the claim that lightning is an electrical discharge gives in some sense the essential nature of lightning, but see no more in this than the projection of our thoughts onto the chaos of our sensory intake. We might admit that, if we took away an animal's animality, we could no longer say what it was, but urge that it follows not that there are individuals constituted independently of our mental activity, but only that, if we are to pick out individuals at all, then we must constitute them ourselves by the imposition of concepts on our sense-impressions. Even if we accept, then, what Hegel has said so far, he has not succeeded in refuting this sceptical thesis and has not shown thoughts to be unqualifiedly objective. His further attempts to do so will be considered later.[86]

Enough of Hegel's account of the world has emerged for our present purposes, however. The essential feature of this account is a symmetry between the self and the objective world. Just as pure thoughts constitute the essential self, so the same thoughts, or the determinations corresponding to them, constitute the essence of the world: 'Thinking constitutes the substance of external things. It is also the universal substance of what is spiritual' (*Enz.* I. 24Z. 1). The phenomenal features of the world have the same status — as we shall see, an ambiguous status — in relation to the intelligible structure underlying them as our desires and sensations have to the pure ego, the implicit system of thoughts which sustains them. The phenomenal world is initially distinct, and is seen as distinct, from the cognizing subject. But to the degree that the subject and the world are purified into thoughts, they are the same. We cannot, however, shed all at once our sensory states and the corresponding phenomenal features of the world, entering into immediate contact with the intelligible structure of things. Empirical science is one of the ways in which we gradually work ourselves loose from our sensations, or at least from our dependence on them, unravelling increasingly pure, and increasingly complex, thoughts from ourselves. In the same measure, we extricate the underlying structure of the phenomenal world from its empirical encrustations. We shall return later to the further developments of this conception. The immediately following chapters will be concerned with the problems which it is designed to solve.

PART TWO

Problems

IV

Philosophy and the Fall of Man

It is reasonable, in attempting to understand a philosopher, to ask what for him is the point of doing philosophy or, more specifically, what problems he is trying to solve. There are, however, difficulties in the way of this approach to Hegel. Philosophy, for example, is not always distinguished clearly from other types of thinking or indeed from other human activities in general, so that when a problem is located, it is often unclear whether it is to be solved by philosophical thinking or by some other means. Hegel has philosophical objections to drawing sharp distinctions between things,[1] but his blurring of boundaries is not always to be attributed to this source. Again, his belief that one should, ideally, not make any assumptions when one is philosophizing makes it difficult for him to state in advance the problems to which he is responding. For any problem or question involves assumptions. We have seen, for example, that one of the flaws which he found in the empirical sciences was their failure to give an account of, or even a place to, God, and this is one of the problems which his system is intended to solve, to establish the existence and nature of God. But to see this as a problem involves making certain assumptions, not necessarily that God exists, but that it is likely or possible that he does, that it matters whether he does or not, that the term 'God' has a certain meaning (*Enz.* I. 1), and so on.[2] If one does not make some such assumptions as these, then the problem will not seem a compelling or even an intelligible one. Paradoxically, even the problem of how to justify one's beliefs without making any assumptions involves making assumptions, for it is only if one takes a certain view of what is required if one's beliefs are to be creditable that it will be seen as a problem at all.[3] In practice, Hegel's problems are inherited from other philosophers and from

93

the cultural and social life of his times. But his view of philosophy forbids him to regard them as coherently, or at least appropriately, stateable independently of his own system. Philosophy is not a 'finite' discipline which can take its problems ready made. They, together with the assumptions which they involve, are to emerge within his philosophy and are not questions posed at the outset to which his system provides the answers. To the extent that Hegel's problems are a legacy, this means that his system must, as it were, embrace the philosophies of the past and his social and cultural environment.[4] His efforts to adhere to the programme of assumption-free thinking is one of the reasons why he is difficult to understand.

It is, however, possible to exaggerate the difficulties and the differences between Hegel's enterprise and other, more familiar ones. Most novels, for example, are self-contained in the sense that the problems they solve are not formulated or even intelligible at the outset, but arise in the course of the work.[5] Nor do empirical and mathematical sciences leave the problems which they were initially intended to solve unaffected; problems, as well as answers, arise and evolve in the course of a science in ways which we could not have predicted or understood at the beginning. But this does not mean that novels and sciences are unintelligible. Moreover, it is possible to disentangle from more or less informal remarks which Hegel, with some misgivings,[6] prefixed to his system or interspersed in it some of the problems which he was trying to overcome. These will be considered in the following chapters. In this chapter, we shall be concerned with what in general Hegel conceived to be the point of philosophy and the nature of the problems to which it is the response.

1 Problems and the fall

One of the more picturesque ways in which Hegel presents his view of the role of philosophy is by a fairly free reading of the myth of the fall — the only part of the Old Testament to which he attaches much importance. His treatment of it will be considered here, not only for the light which it sheds on philosophy and its problems — it is easy to detach his views on this from their mythical context — but also, though secondarily, as an example of his approach to popular religion.

The myth is introduced in an addition to the *Encyclopaedia* in response to an objection to Hegel's enterprise (*Enz.* I. 24Z. 3).[7] It is, the objection runs, presumptuous of us to think that we can or should know the truth by our own efforts. To suppose that we can is to adopt the 'standpoint of general disunion' and this is the origin of all evil and wickedness. We should abandon thinking and cognition (*Erkennen*) in favour of restoration and reconciliation, a return to 'immediate natural unity', to innocence. The objection is primarily concerned with religious belief, urging that it is better to adhere, or return, to a naïve, unquestioning faith than to reflect upon, and attempt to justify, one's beliefs. It is, however, of wider application than this. Why, for example, should one reflect critically upon one's moral code, social and political institutions, or commonsense beliefs about the external world rather than accept them unquestioningly as children and unreflective adults do? This is not a pointless or obsolete question and it need not be motivated only by a theological distress over the hybris of critical reflection. It is not inappropriate to describe the reflective attitude as one of separation (*Trennung*), separation from one's inherited moral, religious and other beliefs, separation, perhaps, from the world and from God. If we could abandon this attitude, then we would return to the 'immediate unity' which we have lost. Hegel believes that the myth of the fall contains the answer to this complaint. Philosophy must not take second place to religion, but it must concede that there is likely to be a core of truth in tales which have been so widely accepted for so long a time. The myth itself falls into five stages, each of which he interprets with some licence:

1. Adam and Eve are in a garden containing two trees. They are permitted to eat the fruit of the first, the tree of life, but God has forbidden them to eat the fruit of the second tree, that of the knowledge of good and evil. This means, according to Hegel, that we should not advance to knowledge, but should remain in a state of innocence. This is true, in the sense that we cannot remain in a state of separation, but false if it means that immediate natural unity is the right state for us to be in. We cannot remain in child-like simplicity, but must attain this harmony at a higher level by 'the labour and cultivation of the spirit'.

2. The serpent tempts them to eat the forbidden fruit, claiming that divinity consists in the knowledge of good and evil. They eat the fruit and acquire this knowledge. They then become ashamed of their naked bodies and cover themselves. The myth is mistaken, Hegel argues, in supposing that humanity fell from its natural unity because some third party encouraged it to do so. Rather the awakening of consciousness is rooted in humanity itself and occurs in every individual person. He acquires knowledge of good and evil, and presumably of other things as well, by breaking with the

unity of his natural being. Shame at his nakedness is a primitive expression of this breach. Mankind, unlike the beast, is separated from the natural, physical, aspect of itself. This is why we wear clothes; physical need is only a secondary consideration (Cf. *Enz.* III. 411Z).

3. God curses mankind. Man is to work, and woman is to suffer pain in childbirth. This again distinguishes people from nature and opposes them to it. Work is, firstly, something that animals do not have to do, and, secondly, it is necessary only because people are separated from nature; they have to work in order to get what animals have ready to hand. However, work itself heals the breach between us and nature, for we mould nature in order to satisfy our needs. Since the means to satisfy our needs are produced by ourselves, we are in a way related to ourselves in our interaction with nature, despite the continuing opposition.

4. God says: 'Behold, Adam is become as one of us, to know good and evil.' This, Hegel argues, means that knowledge is divine rather than forbidden. Philosophy is knowledge (*Erkennen*) and it is only through knowledge that we fulfil our original vocation, that is, to be an image of God. Philosophy cannot, therefore, be an aspect of the 'finitude' of the human spirit.

5. God drove them from the garden, to prevent them eating the fruit of the tree of life. This means, on Hegel's view, that in his natural aspect a person is finite and mortal, even though he is infinite in his knowledge. The point is presumably that continued consumption of this fruit was required for, and would have secured, physical immortality.

It is clear that this account does little to answer the original objection. That philosophy is divine, for example, might be re-garded, from a theological point of view, as increasing the impiety and pointlessness of a finite creature's indulging in it. For our present purposes, however, the relevant point is that in this passage Hegel extricates at least seven types of separation from the myth:

(i) We are different, and therefore separate, from natural beings like animals.

(ii) We have knowledge and, since this involves critical reflection rather than naïve acceptance, it implies a transcendence of, separation from, the object known.

(iii) We are alienated from our own bodies, the natural aspect of ourselves which we share with other creatures. One's body is finite in space and time, but one's knowledge is not. Our know-ledge, for example, ranges beyond the spatial and temporal limits of our bodies to spaces **and** times quite remote from them.

Because of this, Hegel implies, we are ashamed of our bodies.

(iv) Nature does not satisfy our needs effortlessly. We, alone of all creatures, have to work.

(v) As a self-conscious being, a person distinguishes himself from the external world in a way that other creatures do not: 'The departure of man from his natural being is the distinguishing of himself as a self-conscious [world] from an external world' (*Enz.* I. 24Z. 3).[8]

(vi) Individual men act on their own desires and in their own self-interest. To this extent, each is separated from the others and from the general good.

(vii) This self-seeking behaviour is countered by divine or human laws which enjoin action in the general interest. There is, to this extent, within society and within the individual a bifurcation into the natural being who tends to seek his own interests and universal laws which prescribe conduct for the common good.

2 *Evil*

The last two of these types of separation are introduced in part to give some plausibility to the claim that the myth of the fall describes a fall. For the general tendency of Hegel's interpretation is to see the departure from Eden as an unequivocal ascent towards divinity. But the attempt to insinuate evil into the account leads to confusion. For the addition presents more than one view of what evil consists in. Firstly, what makes a person evil, it is implied, is what separates him from nature. By this account to reflect and think or, indeed, to do anything specifically human would be evil. Secondly, it is when a person acts as a natural being that he is evil, and to act as a natural being is to act on one's own desires, characteristically, but not inevitably, in one's own interest regardless of other considerations. In so far as he acts in this way, however, a person acts no differently from any natural creature, since 'nature in general lies in the bonds of individualization' (*Enz.* I. 24Z. 3). These two accounts are connected in the following way. If an animal or an infant acts on its own desires, then its action, however bad it may seem, is not evil, because, oblivious to the difference between good and evil, the agent does not *will* his action. By contrast, a human adult, who does know the difference, but nevertheless acts on some desire he has, wills to act in a natural rather than a lawful way. Our departure from nature is thus a necessary condition of evil, in that only if one knows the difference between good and evil, is it evil to act in a natural way (cf. *PR* 139).

It can be objected, however, that it is not a sufficient condition of evil. For if a person restrains or suppresses his desires and acts only in accordance with the law, then he has indeed departed from nature, but no bad or natural action has been performed. One might reply that most people are able, and in the long run likely, to act on their desires, and they are in this sense evil. But Hegel's considered view seems to be that what is evil is not so much the departure from nature nor one's pursuit of one's desires rather than the law, but the internal disunion to which the divergence from nature gives rise. A simple example will illustrate this. A person starts out with a simple, unquestioning faith. Thinking, reflection upon it, produces doubt. By further thinking he overcomes his doubts, reconfirms his beliefs — in a more or less modified form — and acquires grounded faith (cf. *PR* 147; *Enz.* III. 396Z). The first stage is that of simple or natural unity. The second is that of separation, not merely separation from the first, natural condition — the naïve faith has not been straightforwardly forgotten — but separation within this second stage between the persisting faith and the reflective doubts. The third phase is that of reconciliation; the separation is repaired and we return to harmony once more, not this time a natural one, but a contrived harmony on a higher level. This pattern of unity-separation-reconciliation is omnipresent in Hegel's philosophy and represents a part of what he means by the 'negation of the negation'. Reflection and doubt are in a sense the negation of simple faith, and grounded faith, the rational resolution of doubt, is a negation of doubt. Grounded faith is similar, but not identical, to simple faith, and one cannot attain it unless one has passed through the phase of doubt and reflection.[9]

In what sense, then, is the transition from unity to separation a fall? Clearly it is unsatisfying to be involved in some of the separations which Hegel mentions. Reflective doubt, for example, is often a source of cognitive and emotional discomfort. It is, however, the disunion itself which is 'evil', and not the natural element, or one's favouring the natural element, in it. What is wrong with the reflective phase is not the attempt to suppress one's doubts and cling to one's former beliefs, but the conflict itself. There can, however, be more or less satisfactory ways of handling it. To try to smother one's doubts, for example, is a sterile response which cannot succeed for long, whereas to meet them head on and try to overcome them is a fruitful one. But only in the special case of the conflict between one's desires and the law is it plausible to suppose that evil consists in favouring the natural element over the other, and even here Hegel is less

98

interested in the difference between good people and bad people than in the human predicament in general. He does not, however, regard the disunion as unqualifiedly evil. It is clearly an advance of sorts to emerge from simple belief or simple goodness into doubt, reflection and conflict, for one is then on the way to higher things. The myth of the fall does not, on Hegel's view, record a fall, but a tortuous ascent.

3 *The fall from innocence*

The problems which confront us, then, are seen by Hegel as separations or disunions which need to be resolved. The 'fall' into disunity has already occurred and the task is to advance to a higher unity. It is, from this point of view, less important to explain why the original harmony was disturbed than to say why and how it should be restored. Hegel believes, however, that the fall into disunion was necessary and it is of some interest to consider why. He speaks of 'this standpoint of separation which belongs to the concept of spirit' (*Enz.* I. 24Z. 3), and again:

> Spiritual life appears at first in its immediacy as innocence
> and naïve trust; but now it lies in the essence of spirit that
> this immediate condition is overcome, for spiritual life
> distinguishes itself from natural, and more specifically animal,
> life by the fact that it does not remain in its being-in-itself
> (*in seinem Ansichsein*) but is rather *for itself* (*für sich*) (*Ibid.*).

Hegel considers the notions of being-in-itself and of being-for-itself in a number of passages.[10] The distinction involves at least two different ideas. Firstly, if something is merely in itself then it is an undeveloped potentiality, while if it is (also) for itself, it is a realized potentiality, an actuality. A seed, for example, or an infant is merely in itself, but a fully-grown plant or man is for itself. Seeds and infants develop into plants and men. Hegel confines his examples to entities which, with the qualification that certain external conditions must be fulfilled if growth is to take place, are self-developing. If seeds and infants were not more or less self-developing, there would be no natural tendency for the seed to become a plant and the infant to become a person, as there is, for example, no natural tendency for a pile of bricks to become a house rather than a bus-shelter. Spirits or minds, however, are regarded as more nearly self-developing than plants,[11] and this is in part due to the second idea behind the distinction. This is that if something is merely F in itself, then, although it is F, it is not aware that it is F, while if it is F for itself, then it is aware that it is F. This distinction applies only to persons, or to minds or spirits, and not to such entities as plants. Animals are presumably aware of their current states, their pains for example, at some level, but Hegel has in mind here a more reflective awareness than they are capable of. The two ideas are to be combined in the following way. In the case of people, or at least of minds, anything which is aware that it is potentially F thereby is, or becomes, actually F and, conversely, anything which becomes actually F does so by being or having been aware that it is potentially F. For example, ancient orientals were, on Hegel's view, essentially free — since all humans are essentially free — but they were free only potentially and not in actuality, because they were not aware of their (essential) freedom, but accepted despotism as a matter of course. This does not mean that they were wholly unaware of their condition, but they were not presumably fully aware that they were slaves. For to be aware that one is a slave implies an awareness of one's potential or essential freedom.[12]

The application of this to the separations associated with the myth of the fall seems to be this. When a slave becomes aware that he is essentially free, then there is a separation or conflict between his actual condition, his enslavement, and his awareness. Similarly, when a man becomes aware that his belief in God or his acceptance of a moral code is a simple ungrounded faith and, therefore, of the possibility of grounding his beliefs, there is a conflict between the naïve belief and the relatively sophisticated awareness of it. Men develop, both as individuals and over history, by successively becoming aware of what they now are. In becoming aware of what it is at stage n, a mind advances to stage $n + 1$, and so on.[13] This is an attractively simple view, but it is open to several objections. Firstly, much of our mental development does not take place in this way. A child learns its native language without any obvious awareness that it is potentially or essentially a language user or tnat it is actually not a language user. Hegel might reply that the acquisition of a language is the acquisition of the capacity for thought and that, since self-awareness is a function of thought, these considerations do not apply to the acquisition of a first language. But although awareness of what we potentially and actually are no doubt plays a greater part in more advanced learning, it is unclear why it should be essential to it. Secondly, one's awareness that one is potentially, though not actually, F does not invariably lead to one's becoming actually F. One's awareness that one is potentially, though not actually, a speaker of Chinese will not lead, without further effort, to one's becoming an actual speaker of it. And this effort is unlikely to be forthcoming unless there is some perceived difficulty in one's present condition, a separation or conflict between one's natural condition and one's awareness of what it is. A slave who is aware of his enslavement is the victim of such a conflict — though awareness alone will not resolve it — but most self-confessed non-speakers of Chinese are not.

More importantly for our purposes, however, this still leaves unanswered the question why one must reflect on one's condition, disturb the natural harmony, in the first place. Even if we grant that minds develop, if they develop, by successive acts of self-awareness, why should they develop at all? Hegel does not in general resort to the notion of a contradiction at this point, and with good reason. The most obvious way in which a contradiction can generate change or development is by the subject's becoming aware of it and taking steps to resolve it. But if one is aware of a contradiction in one's beliefs, this presupposes, and cannot therefore explain, one's reflection upon them. There is, for example, on Hegel's view a contradiction of sorts between the unity of a thing which we perceive and the multiplicity of the properties which belong to it (*PG* pp. 89 ff., M. pp. 67 ff.)[14] What is at issue here is not the plausibility of the claim that there is such a contradiction, but the point or level at which, if there is one, the perceiver becomes conscious of it. Apart from merely perceiving, e.g. looking at or tasting, an object, there are in this context four relevant stages:

1. One makes a statement about a particular object of perception, e.g. that this lump of sugar is white and sweet;
2. One can reflect upon this claim, believing, for example, that it is contradictory (or that it is not);
3. One can make general claims about the objects of perception, e.g. that any such object is a single thing with many properties;
4. One can reflect upon this claim, believing, for example, that it is contradictory (or that it is not).

The stages are distinguished from each other by the relative generality and the order of the claims they involve; 2. is a second-order claim about the particular, first-order claim, 1., while 4. is a second-order claim about the general, first-order claim, 3. In both cases the awareness that the first-order claim is (or is not) contradictory is embodied in a second-order claim about it. Such awareness cannot therefore explain the move from claims of the first order to second-order reflection upon them.

This is so even when the standpoint of 'innocent' harmony is a fairly sophisticated one. And since Hegel continually reapplies the formula of unity–separation–reconciliation, so that positions which are, from one point of view, reconciliations or even separations are nevertheless also seen as primitive unities, some positions of innocent unity are bound to be relatively complex. The pre-Kantian metaphysics of Leibniz's followers, for example, is, from one point of view, a phase of separation.[15] It does not simply accept, but reflects upon, and attempts to demonstrate, the dogmas of religion. Moreover, sharp distinctions ('separations') are drawn between, for example, the individual and his society, the knowing subject and the object known, God and the world, what is and what ought to be (*Enz.* I. 28).[16] Such dualisms are characteristic of the phase of separation. But, from another point of view, it is a position of naïve unity, since it assumes without question that thinking alone can reveal to us the truth about things; it is the *'naïve (unbefangene)* procedure, which still lacks consciousness of the opposition of thinking within and against itself and involves the *faith* that through *metathinking* the *truth* is *known*, that what objects truly are is brought before consciousness' (*Enz.* I. 26). This faith, that thinking reveals the essence of, or the truth about, things, it shares with most people throughout the ages (*Enz.* I. 22Z), but it has it on a higher, though still in a way naïve, level. (Hegel's own philosophy purports to reinstate this faith at a higher level still.) The old metaphysics contained, however, contradictions. Hegel inherited from Kant the belief that by its procedures valid, or equally valid, proofs could be given, for example, both of the proposition that there is free will and of the proposition that there is not, both of the proposition that the world is infinite in space and of the proposition that it is not, and so on.[17] The awareness of such contradictions as these, however, cannot in itself generate second-order reflection upon metaphysics and its procedures, for it presupposes it. Full awareness that one's beliefs or procedures are contradictory already involves the detachment from them that we are attempting to explain.

Awareness, however, varies in intensity, and Hegel may mean that full-scale reflection upon one's naïve position is often provoked by a hazy awareness of its inadequacy. A person whose beliefs or procedures are contradictory might have a dim consciousness of the futility of what he is doing, and a slave may be induced to consider his lot by the frustrations and hardships which he feels. Hegel seems to have held that reflection on traditional values was in part occasioned by the distressing feuds between agents who were unquestioning adherents of different, and potentially conflicting, segments of those values (*PG* pp. 318 ff., M. pp. 267 ff.),[18] and apparently unresolvable intellectual conflicts might well have a similar effect. However, he seems to have no better *systematic* answer to the question why primitive unities need ever be disturbed than that it is of the essence of a mind to disengage itself from its present state and pass it under review.

4 *The restoration of unity*

It is on the whole easier to see why we should attempt to overcome the disunities which Hegel mentions than to explain how they ever arose. Some of them are unpleasant in themselves. It is, for example, bothersome to have to work for a living and to restrain one's desires in order to conform to the law. Some of them present intellectual difficulties, the failure to resolve which is distressing to at least some people. The contrasts, for example, between the thinking self and the body and between the self and the world of which it is conscious are the source of several philosophical problems. In some cases, in that, for example, of pre-Kantian metaphysics, on Hegel's view, the disunity can be presented as a contradiction, and contradictions must be escaped or resolved.[19]

How are these disunities to be repaired? Hegel's general answer is that it is by thinking: 'it is thinking which both produces the wound and heals it' (*Enz.* I. 24Z. 3. Cf. 11). But this answer is inadequate. Not all of the disunities in question are reconciled by thinking, even if they are resolved at all. There are, again, different types of thinking and, even if we confine our attention to philosophical thought, Hegel's account of how this solves problems is thoroughly equivocal. If we reconsider the disunities, it will be clear that they involve different types of problem and that they are to be resolved in different ways and at different levels:

(i) *We differ radically from natural beings like animals.* Hegel tends not to regard our differences from animals as such, as opposed to specific respects in which we differ from them, as a problem. A problem is presented, for example, by the fact that we are able to restrain our current desires in the interests of our future welfare or the moral law, but not especially by the fact that we differ from animals in this regard. However the apparently wide gulf between humans and their closest natural neighbours might be seen as a problem, in the light perhaps of the dictum *'Natura non facit saltum'*. Hegel rejected the theories of evolution that were available to him in the interests of a distinction between static nature and developing culture: 'externality is proper to nature, letting distinct things fall asunder and emerge as indifferent existences' (*Enz.* II. 249).[20] However, even if this avenue is closed to him, there are several ways in which, he could concede, the contrast between people and brutes is mitigated or 'mediated'. Firstly, in so far as people reconcile the other disunities which distinguish them from animals, they revert on a higher level to the condition ascribed to animals, to a state of nature, but of cultivated nature. Secondly, there are the diverse responses which we make to animals, responses which narrow the gulf between the two realms. We study animals, classify them, detect similarities to ourselves, project human features onto them (and animal features onto ourselves) both in life and in fiction, selectively eat them (and conscientiously refrain from eating them), and submit them to varying degrees of domestication and of integration into a human framework. Finally, there are in fact similarities and continuities which obtain independently of human responses to animals, but are disclosed by scientists and perhaps by philosophers. By and large Hegel regards spirit and culture as the result of overcoming or transcending nature, rather than as a smooth development out of it,[21] but they are nevertheless intelligibly connected with each other and certain features or phases of human life are shared with animals (*Enz.* III. 388 ff.).

(ii) *Our knowledge involves a separation from the object.* A miscellany of problems falling under this heading arise, and are resolved, at several different levels. A problem of this sort arises, for example, within the life-span of each individual. Hegel accepts the familiar (and probably autobiographical) picture of a person as passing through the three phases of naïve acceptance of traditional beliefs in childhood, of adolescent revolt against them, and of increasing reconciliation to them culminating in the sophisticated acceptance of old age (*Enz.* III. 396 and Z). Similar patterns of separation and reconciliation can be seen in history. The French Revolution, for example, represented the disruption of a traditional harmony, which was subsequently restored on a higher plane (*PG* pp. 347 ff., M. pp. 294 ff.). These, however, are more properly cases of separation from, and subsequent reconciliation to, our inherited beliefs about objects than of separation from the objects themselves. An example of the latter would be this. Animals, infants and primitive peoples simply accept nature and are entirely at home with it. Separation arises when we begin to be surprised or puzzled by natural phenomena and attempt to explain them. The separation is repaired, over history, by the advance of the sciences and, within the life-time of the individual, by his growing acquaintance with the science of his age. Philosophy plays a part in such reconciliations. Hegel purports, for example, to reconcile us to, or at least to describe our reconciliation to, our inherited religious and moral beliefs.[22] He also attempts to dissolve the more specifically philosophical scepticism about our ability to know reality as it is in itself and about the objectivity of our thought.[23] In a quite different way the problem is resolved by thinking about thought itself, where, on Hegel's view, the subject and the object are straightforwardly the same.[24]

(iii) *There is a separation between a person's mind and his body.* This covers a range of problems, the primitive expression of which is a person's shame at his own body. Hegel attempts to soften the contrast between mind and body, arguing, for example, that the human body, unlike that of an animal, has a 'spiritual tone diffused over the whole, which immediately announces the body as the externality of a higher nature' (*Enz.* III. 411).[25] But he does not, as this might lead us to expect, advocate a return to the innocent nakedness of infancy, a sophisticatedly unashamed nudity. Clothing seems to be the best answer to this particular problem. The training, adornment and clothing of the body renders it a cultural as much as a natural object. (Hegel was opposed to asceticism and to eccentricity of dress, for the reason that the rejection of physical pleasure and the flouting of fashion exaggerate their importance as much as does the slavish pursuit of them.)[26] The account of the myth implies that Hegel is concerned with the contrast between the mortality of the body and the immortality of the soul or mind — a traditional view, on which there is a striking disparity between them. But this is misleading, for, as we shall see, he has little interest in the question of individual survival and probably did not accept the orthodox doctrine.[27] A problem which does concern him, and which, in the light of his account of the pure ego, arises for him in an acute form, is that of the relationship between the mind and the body. Various suggestions are made with respect to it throughout his works.[28]

(iv) *In virtue of their separation from nature, people have to work to satisfy their needs.* Hegel implies that it is work itself rather than thinking which bridges the gulf in this instance, much as the alienation of a person from his body is resolved at the simplest level by putting on clothes. The means for the satisfaction of his needs are 'produced and formed by himself. Even in this externality man is thus related to himself' (*Enz.* I. 24Z. Cf. *PG* pp. 148 f., M. pp. 118 f.). To the extent that a person forms and moulds natural objects according to his own designs, he has to do, in his subsequent dealings with them, with cultural objects ('himself') rather than natural ones. The restoration of unity is achieved by the humanization of nature and work of any kind achieves this in some degree. However, the trouble with work is not primarily that the worker is dealing with something other than himself, but that it is difficult and tedious, and the production and sale of manufactured articles is not obviously less so than the extraction of raw materials. Hegel's answer to this is that both over history and within a person's lifetime work becomes less burdensome. The individual grows accustomed to his tasks and the performance of them becomes an undemanding routine (*Enz.* III. 396Z). Over history, work becomes less of a stark confrontation between the individual and nature, and more of a cooperative enterprise involving the complementary operations of many individuals. The simplicity of the particular tasks enables machines to replace people (*Enz.* III. 526).

(v) *The self-conscious individual distinguishes himself from the external world.* This is a recurrent theme in Hegel's writings and is felt to be problematic. Various philosophical stances, the stoicism and scepticism of antiquity for example, are regarded as unsuccessful attempts to overcome or circumvent it (*PG* pp. 151 ff., M. pp. 119 ff.). At a non-philosophical level, it is remedied to some degree by the efforts of scientists to conceptualize and understand the world, and by our practical activities, our construction of a non-natural, human environment (*Enz.* III. 443 and Z). On a philosophical plane, Hegel arguably attempts to resolve the disunity finally by thinking about the world and/or about scientists' thoughts about the world and by deriving its main features and/or the results of scientists from pure thought, thus showing the external world not to be distinct from the thinking subject.[29]

(vi)–(vii) *A person is separated into a natural appetitive self-seeker and a respecter of universal laws.* The resolution of this dualism again seems to emerge in ordinary life rather than from philosophy. The individual's desires are satisfied within social institutions such as marriage and are governed by general laws (*Enz.* III. 519 ff., 552); even our eating is pervaded by unburdensome custom and ritual. Again, our needs, or at least our satisfaction of them, are socialized in the general division of labour (*Enz.* III. 524 ff.). The conflicts between a person's desires and the law, and between one person's desires and another's, are resolved, or at any rate muted, since the individual's desires and satisfactions are permeated, rather than suppressed, by social norms and institutions.[30] If philosophy has any contribution to make here, it is to show that this is so and to explain why it must be so.

106

5 *Philosophy and problems*

This list does not exhaust the problems which concerned Hegel. We might add, for example, the nexus of problems – practical, psychological, sociological, and philosophical – associated with one's relationship to other people (cf. *PG* pp. 133 ff., M. pp. 104 ff.). But it is sufficient to indicate their diversity and that of their resolutions. There are, for example, practical problems: 'What should I wear?', 'How am I to satisfy my needs?' Secondly, there are sociological, psychological and historical problems about, for example, the nature of work or men's attitudes towards, and adornment of, their bodies. Thirdly, there are the problems of people who, although clothed and adorned, are nevertheless distressed by their physical aspect, or who feel alienated from their work and its products, because they do not realize that the problems have already been resolved. Pointing out that a problem has already been solved can be a way of solving, if not that problem, at least a closely related one. Some of Hegel's problem-solving seems to be of this type. Finally, there are more strictly philosophical problems about, for example, the relationship of mind and body or the status of nature and its relationship to the human mind. Scientific discoveries and, on Hegel's view, our practical activities are relevant both to the form these problems take and to their solution (cf. *Enz.* III. 389), but there may nevertheless be residual difficulties which require more of the philosopher than the description of other people's work.

One of the difficulties of reading Hegel, then, is his interest in a diverse array of problems without a corresponding clear distinction between their types and those of the appropriate solutions. His encyclopaedic ambition, his desire to embrace the whole of human experience, accounts for the range of his concerns but not for the distressing intermingling of psychology, sociology, history and philosophy. Some of the reasons for this will be considered below, but for the moment our question is: granted that philosophy does not solve all of these problems, what role does it play?

Hegel's answer to this is characteristically ambiguous. He provides at least three different accounts of the function of philosophy. Firstly, there is what we might call the conception of philosophy as 'fiddling while Rome burns'. It is, on this view, only when one is actually engaged in philosophical thinking that complete reconciliation is achieved. Separation involves the estrangement of a person from something which is, or is felt to be, distinct from himself – his society, nature, his own body or the external world. One solution to this is to ignore the alien item altogether, to concern oneself not with it, but solely with oneself. Philosophy provides such a retreat from transactions with what is other than oneself. Hegel often implies that one is truly free only when one engages in pure thinking or logic, for in thinking about thinking one is dealing only with oneself.[31] Freedom in this sense is intimately connected with reconciliation. The reconciliation which a person achieves in working on natural objects is freedom in this sense. There, however, freedom is secured by making nature like oneself, whereas pure thinking reaches the same goal more directly by severing its relationship to it. Whether Hegel is justified in claiming that pure thinking makes one free, and how this is to be reconciled with his view that the citizen of a state may be free, even if he is not a philosopher or is not currently engaged in philosophical thinking, are questions which will be considered later.[32] The point for the moment is that Hegel, like Plato, Spinoza and, perhaps, the common man, believed that some of our problems can be solved by the mere activity of philosophizing, independently of the particular conclusions, if any, which we reach.

Hegel does not, however, believe that philosophy should provide only a retreat of this kind. Philosophers have characteristically concerned themselves with the other term of the relation, natural phenomena, society, or whatever (*Enz.* I. 12), and Hegel's two remaining accounts of the role of philosophy presuppose that this is so. Secondly, then, he sometimes indicates that the function of philosophy is a purely descriptive one: 'When philosophy paints its grey in grey, then has a form of life grown old, and it cannot be rejuvenated by grey in grey but only understood; the owl of Minerva begins its flight only with the fall of dusk' (*PR* Preface). This does not simply mean that philosophers do their work after non-philosophers do theirs; it also places restrictions on what they are to do. Philosophers *qua* philosophers should not attempt to change, or to prescribe changes in, their own society, because they arrive on the scene too late. Philosophy, for example, plays no essential part in the reconciliation of the individual with his society. This has occurred independently of the emergence of philosophy, so that the most it can do is to describe, at some level or other, the achievement of such a reconciliation by the activities of non-philosophical men.[33]

It is not immediately clear, however, how this account is to be extended to theoretical or intellectual problems. One of the ways, as we have seen, in which a person suffers disunity from nature is that initially it is merely given, a bewildering diversity of phenomena with no apparent organization or rational necessity (*Enz.* I. 98Z.1), and the same is true to a greater or lesser degree of scientist — to classify, conceptualize and explain phenomena by framing laws, postulating forces and so on, though no doubt practical activities such as the construction of parks and cities play a part. What, in this case, is the philosopher supposed to do? The 'Owl of Minerva' doctrine gives him equivocal directions. It might be thought, on the one hand, that it instructs him merely to describe and analyse the procedures and results of the sciences, perhaps with some criticism and re-ordering, but preserving their empirical, *a posteriori* character. Men *qua* scientists (and artists and religious believers) have already achieved whatever reconciliation they are at present capable of and all that remains is to describe what they have done, pointing out that it is the solution to the problem. On the other hand, the description advocated by the 'Owl of Minerva' doctrine contrasts with action, prescription and prophecy,[35] and it is not obvious that it would exclude the more ambitious role which Hegel sometimes assigns to the philosophy of nature, that of deriving or confirming the results of the sciences and thus depriving them of their *a posteriori* character (*Enz.* I. 12).[36] After all, the *Philosophy of Right* itself purports not simply to describe the state, but to show that it is rational and in some sense necessary (*PR* Preface, 1, 2, 341). The theoretical counterpart of this could well involve more than the description of the empirical sciences. What the doctrine does exclude is that philosophers should continue their work by deriving results which radically go beyond current scientific theories.[37]

Thirdly, however, Hegel occasionally assigns to philosophy a role which implies that it does not fly only after the fall of dusk — that, namely, of helping to bring about historic changes. The changes which in part constituted the Reformation, for example — the new significance given to marriage and the growth of industrial and commercial activity — are attributed to the influence of philosophy (*Enz.* III. 552). Since secularization generally and the devaluation of the monkish virtues of chastity and poverty are described in terms which suggest that they are a phase of reconciliation, philosophy would, on this account, assist in producing reconciliation in the actual world. This, however, is probably to be explained by a liberal use of the word 'philosophy' — a use which Hegel describes (*Enz.* I. 7), but to which he is not immune. The use has a theoretical underpinning. Religion, for example, has the same content as philosophy in the strict sense, only it presents it in the form of conception (*Enz.* I. 1).[38] Again, Newton was, on Hegel's view, a (bad) metaphysician because he employed concepts, such as that of an atom, which properly belong to logic (*Enz.* I. 98Z.1), and the same is true to a greater or lesser degree of all scientists: 'Only animals are pure physicists, for they do not think' (*Ibid.*).[39] The philosophy of an epoch, or the concepts subsequently abstracted from its culture by philosophical reflection on it, pervade the ideas, norms and institutions of that epoch, though they are more prominent in some areas, e.g. religion and science, than in others, e.g. leisure pursuits. Seen in this light, the attribution of historic changes to 'philosophy' does not contradict the 'Owl of Minerva' doctrine. Various types of change, of disunity and reconciliation, may be produced in part by ideas which are subsequently presented in a pure form by philosophy without its being the case that philosophy itself plays a role in such changes.

Even if we grant, however, that these conceptions of philosophy are not so much at odds with each other as they first appear, much obscurity remains with regard both to Hegel's multifarious problems and to the part which philosophy plays in their resolution. The justification and implications of the 'Owl of Minerva' doctrine, for example, are unclear not only in its extension to theoretical matters, but even in its primary application to social and political affairs. Why is there such obscurity on these matters? Some of the reasons for it cannot be fully explained until later, but some relevant considerations can be offered here. Firstly, there are connections between different types of problem which Hegel can exploit. Our practical activities, for example, and our theoretical endeavours are sometimes regarded as complementary responses to a single problem (*Enz.* I. 443Z).[40] The assimilation has something to be said for it. One will not, for example, attempt to resolve a theoretical question unless it has something of the urgency of an unfulfilled practical need. Again a rhetorically plausible, if empirically problematic, case could perhaps be made for the view that spring-cleaning and botanical classification, or dangerous driving and philosophical solipsism, derive from the same instinctual sources. These points should not, however, cloud the distinction between the occurrence of the activity itself and the truth or falsity of its results, a distinction which is at least more apparent in the case of theoretical activities than of practical ones.

Secondly, Hegel is inclined to underplay the novelty of his philosophy and, like some recent philosophers, to present his own beliefs as simply a restatement of those of commonsensical men. It is true that he often stresses the strangeness of philosophy, saying in an early piece, for example, that it is 'opposed to the understanding and still more to commonsense . . . in relation to it the world of philosophy is essentially (*an und für sich*) an inverted world' (*JS*, 1801–7, p. 182).[41] This, however, is not necessarily to be taken as contradicting his later belief, if we remember that what philosophy deals with may be familiar (*bekannt*) without being known (*erkannt*) (*Enz.* I. 19). At all events his mature doctrine is that the 'business of philosophy is just to bring expressly to consciousness what men have believed about thinking for ages. Philosophy thus advances nothing new; what we have brought forth through our reflection is already the immediate prejudice of everyone' (*Enz.* I. 22Z). His remark that one no more needs a formal knowledge of philosophy in order to know the truth, e.g. about God, than an acquaintance with physiology in order to digest one's food has similar implications (*Enz.* I. 2). Difficulties and doubts, about, for example, the objectivity of thinking, are raised by philosophers and by the terms in which they consider these matters rather than by ordinary men or their patterns of thought. To the extent that Hegel believes himself to be in agreement with the common man, he can represent his enterprise as a merely descriptive one. And, again, to the extent that he is not himself solving problems but simply describing the ways in which they are solved independently by others, all problems, of whatever type, are on a par.

Thirdly, Hegel's own account of mental or intellectual development hinders the drawing of a sharp distinction between description and innovative problem-solving. For he is inclined to say, as we have seen, that mental advance occurs by our becoming aware of the stage at which we currently are. This is surely mistaken. Mere reflection upon the procedures and results of the natural sciences leaves our knowledge of nature, if not of ourselves, as it is.[42] Nevertheless, since Hegel identifies, or at least closely associates, the awareness of a stage with the advance to a higher stage, it is often hard to say whether he is merely describing, or alternatively continuing, the work of others.

Finally, Hegel generally professes to be merely watching or merely describing what is happening, without making any contribution of his own. His most, but not unduly, explicit account of this occurs in the *Phenomenology*, where what he purports to be watching is the emergence of 'forms of consciousness' from one another. The forms of consciousness, which involve among other things philosophical positions, contain the standard or criterion by which they are to be assessed and carry out their own assessment in the light of it. They therefore refute themselves without any assistance from us (*PG* p. 72, M. p. 54). The claim, then, is that the problems, including philosophical ones, are not Hegel's problems and their solutions are not his solutions. The problems are solved by others or, perhaps, solve themselves; the philosopher has only to watch and record this process. Hegel's reason for adopting this stance is primarily epistemological, namely to avoid making assumptions which are not shared by the form of consciousness under examination, and it might be objected that even if he can disclaim the credit for solving other problems, he must at least acknowledge his solution to this epistemological one. His reply to this, however, would be that epistemological problems arise within the forms of consciousness which he is considering and that his own methodological standpoint is itself a form of consciousness which 'we' see developing out of the others in response to the problems involved in them. Philosophy, on Hegel's view, forms a circle and it does not have a starting-point at which decisions have to be made about our procedures. Our procedures emerge and justify themselves within the system. The coherence of this reply and of the conception of the philosopher as a mere spectator will be considered later.[43] The point for the moment is that Hegel's desire to avoid assumptions provides a further reason for his presenting his philosophy as simply descriptive and not as solving problems and advancing theses of its own.

None of this entails, however, that Hegel's system cannot be illuminated by considering the problems which exercised him. In the first place, his profession to the status of an onlooker is more or less spurious. There is, in any case, a countervailing suggestion that philosophy can provide substantive knowledge – of 'absolute objects' for example, namely God, freedom, and spirit – which is inaccessible to other disciplines (*Enz.* I. 10). Moreover, however purely descriptive Hegel's philosophy might be, its descriptions would be selected and articulated in conformity with the problems to which he attached importance and it would be concerned with them to the extent of pointing to their solutions, even if it does not itself provide them. The following chapters will therefore examine some of these problems and the main lines of Hegel's answers to them.

V

Knowledge and Assumptions

Hegel's system then is intended to answer a variety of problems and its features can be explained in part by reference to them. One such problem, or nexus of problems, is that of knowledge, the problem of what we can know, whether we can know anything at all, and so on. It is of course only after we have become to some degree reflective and self-conscious that we ask such questions as these. The primary form of the theoretical question is not 'What can I know (about x)?' or 'Can I know whether p is true or not?' but, 'What is the case (about x)?' or 'Is p true or not?', and the answers to these questions are assertions about x or of p (or its negation). Why should we ever advance from asking and answering questions about what is the case to asking and answering questions about what we can know? There are several ways in which such questions can arise. We might notice firstly that some of our beliefs must be false, both because different people hold different beliefs and because they subsequently reject beliefs which they once firmly held. What guarantee can there be that any one of our beliefs is true? A natural suggestion is that there might be some test or criterion which we could apply to beliefs in order to distinguish true ones from false ones. But then the doubt occurs that the only way of telling whether a proposed test or criterion is a good one is by seeing whether it in fact picks out all the true, and only the true, beliefs from the false ones, and this implies that we already have some way, independently of this test, of distinguishing them (cf. *PG* pp. 70 ff., M. pp. 52 ff.).[1] A second line of thought which leads to a similarly sceptical conclusion is that characteristically when I claim to know something, I have a reason or a piece of evidence on which I base my belief in the proposition which I claim to know. If we ask about the status of such a reason or premiss, then there seem to be two possible answers: either my acceptance of this reason or premiss is based upon my acceptance of some further reason or premiss or it is not. In the latter case it is, on Hegel's view, simply an assumption (*Voraussetzung*); in the former it seems that either the reason or premiss is supported by some further reason or premiss, and so on to infinity, or, sooner or later, we arrive at reasons or premisses which are simply accepted, without further justification, and are, therefore, mere assumptions.[2] The trouble with assumptions, on Hegel's view, is that it is always possible with equal justification to assume the contrary. There is *ipso facto* no more reason to make any one assumption than any other (*Enz.* I. 10; *PG loc cit.*). He has little to say in favour of the view that there are certain propositions, notably propositions about our immediate sense-experience, which anyone must accept if he understands them and on which the rest of our knowledge is founded. He presumably takes himself to have refuted the empiricist version of this doctrine in his examination of sense-certainty.[3] Finally, on the most common view of our (or my) cognitive situation, the object or realm of objects known is quite distinct from and independent of the knower and the knowing. A natural reflection on this is that there is after all no assurance that those states of the subject which are, or are believed to be, knowledge correspond to the objects to which they refer. Further reflection suggests that our cognitive states cannot present an accurate, or at any rate a reliable, picture of their objects, since these states are in part determined by our cognitive equipment, equipment which might have been other than it is. The picture I form of objects is the joint product of the object and the apparatus I bring to bear on it, and it is only one of indefinitely many pictures that could be formed of those objects depending on possible variations in the apparatus.[4] These, then, are some of the epistemological difficulties to which Hegel attempts to provide answers.[5]

1 *The rejection of epistemology*

Faced with considerations such as these, it is tempting to suppose that one should temporarily suspend one's beliefs about the world and, instead, examine one's cognitive powers to see what objects they are capable of knowing about, what questions they are competent to answer. The analogy which offers itself is that of a scientist who needs to check his instruments before using them for the work for which they are intended (*Enz.* I. 10; *PG* pp. 63 ff., M. pp. 46 ff.). Hegel takes Kant as his representative of this procedure,[6] but he himself rejects it and in that sense he repudiates the view that epistemology is prior to ontology.

Hegel has for this conclusion two main lines of argument which he does not in general distinguish. The first is directed against the recommendation that we should investigate our cognitive powers before we employ them to acquire any knowledge at all. This counsel is manifestly incoherent, for to examine one's capacities involves acquiring knowledge about them. One cannot acquire knowledge about them in advance of acquiring any knowledge at all (*Enz.* I. 10; *PG loc. cit.*).[7] This is one of the points at which the comparison with the testing of an instrument breaks down: one does not need to use an instrument, a camera for example, in order to examine its structure.

This line of argument is ineffectual, however, against a more modest epistemological suggestion, namely that one examines one's cognitive instruments not in advance of applying them to any question or object, but before applying them to a certain restricted range of questions or objects, in order to see whether they will work there as well as they do elsewhere. One might for example assume or hypothesize that one can have knowledge of a restricted kind about one's own cognitive powers and then ask, in the light of this, whether one can know about God or the structure of matter. It is hard to see how in such an inquiry one can avoid assuming a capacity to know *something*. Even if one's answer takes such a non-committal form as: 'If I know anything about my cognitive powers, then I can know nothing about, e.g., God, while if I cannot even know about them it is hard to see how I could know about anything else', one is at least assuming knowledge of certain canons of argument. In this case, too, the instrument-analogy is misleading. If one is testing a camera one has independent access to the objects which are to be photographed, either by one's senses or by some other instrument the reliability of which is taken for granted. But unless we are testing, not our cognitive powers as a whole, but some one way, among others, of acquiring knowledge, there is no such independent access to the objects of knowledge. All kinds of assumptions need to be made when we test an instrument which are forbidden to us when we are checking our cognitive apparatus.

Even if this analogy is defective, however, it does not follow that it makes no sense to ask, before attempting to answer a given question, whether we are capable of answering it or, in advance of investigating a certain range of objects, whether we are able to acquire knowledge about them. Hegel's objection to asking such questions is that there is no possibility of answering them in

115

the negative, no possibility of justifiably claiming that there is some question which we cannot answer or some range of objects which we cannot know about. There are, again, two lines of argument for this conclusion. In the first place, no such claim about the limits of our cognitive powers, even if it were coherently stated, could be justified, and secondly, no such claim can even be coherently stated. These preliminary epistemological queries must receive positive answers and are therefore hardly proper questions at all.

Firstly, then, a negative answer to them cannot be justified. A justification, if it were possible, would have to be conducted on the basis of internal features of our cognitive faculties, for there is, as we have seen, no possibility of comparing them directly with the objects and seeing that they are unsuited to each other. But Hegel refuses to allow that any such internal feature would show that certain areas are closed to us. Kant has supposed that the antinomies show this. In arguing about certain matters, about, for example, whether the world is finite or infinite, we find that we can prove contradictory conclusions, that 'the world has a beginning in time, and is also limited as regards space' and also that it 'has no beginning, and no limits in space; it is infinite as regards both time and space.'[8] But to prove each of two contradictory propositions is, on Kant's view, to prove neither, and it follows that the question whether the world is finite or infinite is a question we cannot answer. Kant does not believe that there is a correct answer to this question, that there is a world which is either spatio-temporally finite or spatio-temporally infinite, even if we cannot know which it is. For space and time are 'merely subjective conditions of all our intuition'.[9] Strictly speaking, therefore, such antinomies do not establish that there is anything which we cannot know, but Kant nevertheless argued that there is a realm of objects, of 'things-in-themselves', which underlie our merely phenomenal knowledge, but which are not themselves knowable by us.

Hegel's attitude towards Kant's antinomies is a complex one. It is not clear, for example, whether he believes that the spatio-temporal world is contradictorily both finite and infinite or whether it is neither, these being the wrong terms in which to describe it.[10] He did, however, reject Kant's view that they show that our knowledge can only be of appearances and not of contradiction-free reality. One reason for this is his belief that it is no better, or no worse, if *we* fall into contradiction than if the world does:

If our *world*-conception dissolves when the determinations of the infinite and the finite are transferred to it, still more is the *spirit* [or *mind*] itself which contains both of them in itself something which contradicts itself and dissolves itself (*WL* I. p. 40, M. p. 47; cf. *Enz.* I. 48).

It is tempting to suppose that Hegel is here confusing objective contradictions, as if it were both raining and not raining — which is a contradictory state of affairs — and subjective ones, as when a man believes that it is both raining and not raining — which is not; and that he has not made up his mind whether contradiction is a bad thing or an impossible thing.[11] But, whatever his reasons, he holds that the world is no more and no less immune to contradiction than are our beliefs, thoughts and conceptions. If this were so, then the contradictoriness of our thoughts, even if it proved to be inescapable, would not show that we were unable to answer the questions which provoked it or that objective reality was inaccessible to us.

The same is true of another of the internal features of our cognition which led Kant to confine it to appearances and exclude it from things-in-themselves. This is that the fundamental structure of the objects of our knowledge — the Euclidean properties of space, for example, and the causal order of nature — is knowable *a priori*. Since we could not have *a priori* knowledge of anything quite distinct from and independent of ourselves, our knowledge must be knowledge of objects moulded by our own minds, knowledge in the last analysis of ourselves.[12] Hegel, however, does not accept the sharp dichotomy between the *a priori* and the empirical that Kant presented to him. (It is not clear, of course, that he properly understood it.) Our knowledge of nature, for example, is, in its broad outlines at least, both *a posteriori* and *a priori*, both discovered empirically by scientists and subsequently derived from pure thought by philosophers (*Enz.* I. 12).[13] There is no suggestion that because our scientific knowledge can be treated in this way it is knowledge of appearances rather than of things-in-themselves. Hegel's readiness to grant the status of objectivity to a discovery rather increases in proportion to its supposed apriority.[14]

We do not, however, need to consider all such suggested features of our cognition in order to establish that none of them will, as far as Hegel is concerned, count in support of an assignment of limits to our knowledge. For Hegel's aversion to assumptions supplies an argument for the general conclusion that no internal feature of our cognitive powers can justify the attribution of such limits to them. For whatever feature, F, we detect in them, in the answers we give to questions or the conceptions we form of objects, it will always be only an assumption that actual objects or the actual answers to our questions possess a corresponding feature which prevents these answers or conceptions from being correct ones, that, for example, things-in-themselves are not contradictory or that they are not such as to disclose themselves to us independently of sense-perception (Cf. *Enz.* I. 47).

2 *Knowledge and reality*

The second, and more prominent, part of Hegel's attack on the claim that there are things which we cannot know about is his insistence that it is incoherent:

> It is . . . the height of inconsistency to concede, on the one hand, that the understanding knows only appearances and, on the other hand, to assert this knowledge as *something absolute*, by saying that knowledge *can* go no further, that this is the *natural*, absolute *limit* of human awareness . . . . One is aware of, even feels, something as a defect, *a limit*, only when one is at the same time *beyond* it (*Enz.* I. 60. Cf. *WL* I. pp. 144 ff., M. pp. 133 ff.).

If one knows that there are objects which one cannot know about, then *ipso facto* one knows something about them, for the statement 'There are objects that I cannot know about' is already a claim about them. The claim is a self-refuting one: if it is known, then it is not true and if it is true, then it is not known.

There are, however, at least two objections to be made to this argument. Hegel believes, in the first place, that the attempt to assign limits to our (or my) knowledge involves the assumption that there are two realms, ourselves (or myself), on the one hand, and objective reality or the 'absolute', on the other: 'the absolute *stands on one side* and *knowing stands on the other side*, on its own and separate from the absolute and yet something real' (*PG* p. 65, M. p. 47). This assumption, like all assumptions, is open to question. He also implies that it is incoherent. If our knowing is real, it cannot be wholly distinct from the absolute, but must at least form a part of it; a complete description of the universe would have to include an account of our own knowledge or beliefs.[15] The arguments we have considered so far purport to show that the claim that knowing is in this way distinct from the absolute is both unjustifiable and self-refuting. But does the assignment of limits to our knowledge necessarily involve this assumption? It surely does not. It need not involve the assertion that there are things or states of affairs which lie beyond those limits, but only the supposition that there might be. The limits could be assigned not by saying 'There are things-in-themselves and they are unknowable by us', but rather 'If there are any things-in-themselves, then they are unknowable by us.' Even if the latter claim is difficult to justify, it does not look self-refuting in the way that the former does.[16]

The second objection is this. We might grant that if we are to assign limits to our knowledge, we must be allowed a glimpse, if only in thought, beyond those limits. Statements such as 'I (or we) can know about things only as they appear to me (or us)' and 'There are (or might be) things which are unknowable' are of a different order from statements about particular appearances. It is, again, doubtful whether we can coherently suppose that none of our concepts, even those of existence and of possibility, are applicable to things-in-themselves, for the very claim that there are or might be such things involves the employment of these concepts. From the fact, however, that I know enough about things-in-themselves to know that they exist or might exist or that I could not know about them if they did exist, it does not follow that I know any more about them. Similarly I may know that a certain question has an answer or that, if it does, I cannot know the answer, without thereby knowing the answer. To say that if I know that there are unknowable objects, I *ipso facto* know all about them is on a par with claiming that if I say 'There is a number I shall never name', then I have self-refutingly named whatever number it is by using the words 'a number I shall never name' − rather than, as it might be, '1,000, 375,206' − or that if I expect the unexpected, then I expect whatever happens − whereas I might expect the unexpected without expecting the roof to fall in. We might, for example, put it to Hegel that there is one thing which we cannot know, namely the full expansion of π. We can, moreover, know that we cannot know it because we can prove that the expansion of π in the decimal system is of infinite length; and we have good reason to believe that we are unable to perform an infinite number of calculations in the finite time allotted to us. The reply might be that once we have said 'π' or 'the complete expansion of π', or, more plausibly, have stated the rule for expanding it, we have said all that there is to be said. But it is simply perverse to equate one characterization of a thing, for example '(the complete expansion of) π', with another, '3.14159 . . .', and to suppose that once we have given one of them this is as good as giving all the others. We could, by this route, answer any question, 'Q?', simply by replying 'The answer to the question "Q?" '

There might, then, be more to things-in-themselves or objective reality than is contained in the minimal characterization of them which we give when we say that they do or might exist, more, that is, which we believe ourselves unable to know. One reply to this might be that Hegel's *Logic* can be interpreted as arguing that since the concept of being (*Sein*) is applicable to objective reality, it follows that the other concepts which are derivable from it, those for example of determinate being (*Dasein*), of quantity or of causality, also apply to it. If this were so, then the minimal characterization of it would commit us to much more than is immediately contained in it and limits to our knowledge could not be drawn, or they could not be drawn, at least, at this point. This interpretation of the *Logic* is problematic, however,[17] and, in any case, it is not this argument which Hegel deploys when he explicitly discusses things-in-themselves. He maintains, rather, that if it is claimed that reality is unknown to us, that there are unknowable things-in-themselves, then this can only be because there is no more to things-in-themselves than is contained in the statement that they exist, that there is, as it were, no more to the iceberg than its tip:

> The *thing-in-itself* . . . expresses the object in so far as we *abstract* from everything that it is for consciousness, from all determinations of feeling and from all determinate thoughts of it. It is easy to see what remains – the *complete abstraction*, the entirely *void*, determined now only as *beyond*; the *negative* of conception, of feeling, of determinate thinking, etc. But just as simple is the reflection that this *caput mortuum* is itself only *the product* of thinking, just of thinking which has advanced to pure abstraction, of the empty ego, which makes this empty *identity* of its own into the *object*. The *negative* determination which this abstract identity acquires as an *object* is also enumerated among the Kantian categories and is something as entirely familiar as that empty identity. One can hence only be amazed to have read so often that one does not know what the *thing-in-itself* is; and nothing is easier than to know this (*Enz.* I. 44).

Hegel's argument involves at least three relevant points. Firstly things-in-themselves, things as they are independently of ourselves, or at least of our cognitive processes, are characterized in thin, highly abstract terms. This must be so, for otherwise we would be claiming to know something about them and allowing our cognitive processes to intrude into their characterization. Secondly, in so far as they are characterized, they are characterized in terms of the thoughts or categories which we have and which are familiar to us. Thirdly, they are a product of thinking, a mere projection of the bare ego, and this operation of projection is also intelligible to us from Kant's categories. It is the last of these points which is most obviously exposed to criticism. If things-in-themselves were merely a product of our thought, then it would presumably follow that there is no more to them than we ourselves put into them (except, perhaps, in the way in which a formal system which we construct may have properties which we have, as yet, not discovered). If, for example, we say only that things-in-themselves exist, then there would be no more to them than bare, featureless existence together with whatever is implied by the fact that they are things-in-themselves. However, no compelling reason is given for supposing that they are merely a product of our thinking. It is true that such access as we have to them is secured by relatively abstract thought. We cannot, *ex hypothesi*, perceive them nor does perception alone suggest to us that there is a reality beyond what is perceptible. But it no more follows that they are products of our thinking than it follows from the fact that something is perceptible that it is a product of our senses. Things-in-themselves are supposed to have features which go beyond our abstract characterization, features which are inaccessible to us; they are, in this sense, like a real person, rather than a fictional person who has only those features ascribed to him by his creator.

Why then, does Hegel suppose otherwise? In a number of passages he equates the idea of a thing-in-itself, in the sense of a thing as it is independently of our cognitive contact with it, with the apparently quite different idea of a thing-in-itself as a mere bearer of properties, not, that is, the sweet, white, cubical . . . lump of sugar, but the thing which is sweet, white, cubical, etc.[18] He points out that the thing-in-itself in this sense is unknowable simply because there is nothing to be known. Whatever knowledge we have about a lump of sugar counts as knowledge of its properties and not of it, the bearer of these properties. There is here no limit to our knowledge, nothing that is there but not known to us.

Hegel's equation of these apparently different notions is based on more than confusion. For it is supported by his belief that the properties of a thing derive from its relationships to other things and that the distinction between a thing and its properties therefore coincides with that between the thing as it is (or perhaps would be) in itself — apart from its relationships to other things — and those features of it which consist in or depend upon its relations to other things.[19] If this is so, a thing which was unrelated to any knowing subject would be indeterminate and propertyless. A thing as it is in itself, apart from our cognitive interactions with it, is thus equivalent to a mere bearer of properties, unknowable only

121

because there is nothing to be known. It might be objected that, even if we grant Hegel's premiss, it does not follow that a thing needs to interact with a cognizer in order to have a determinate character; if reality is diversified and interconnected, if there is more than one thing-in-itself and they are related to each other, then they could derive their determinate features from their relationships with each other and do not require the services of knowing subjects. The reply to this, however, is that, given that there are cognizers with whom things interact, it is arbitrary to suppose that a thing's relationships with other things confer its nature upon it, whereas its relationships with cognizers contaminate it. Why should *our* contacts with a thing be any worse than those of other entities?

Even if we accept Hegel's argument so far, however, the supposition that there is or might be an unknowable reality might be reinvigorated in the following way. We can readily conceive that there should be knowers with entirely different cognitive equipment from our own, who would form a quite different conception of the world.[20] Their conception need have no epistemic advantage over our own; it would simply be the product of a different set of relationships to things-in-themselves. But the mere possibility of alternative, but equally coherent, sets of beliefs, some of them perhaps inconceivable to us, is sufficient to induce scepticism about our cognitive powers.

There are, however, two distinct possibilities which need to be considered here. The first is that of a conceptual system or a 'form of consciousness' developed by historical and/or rational steps from our own by our more or less remote descendents. Such a system would be related to our own in the way that our system is related to that, for example, of Plato. It would, however, on Hegel's view, not be cognitively on a par with our outlook or incommensurable with it, any more than Plato's is. Our descendents' outlook would be superior to our own and they would be able to see that this was so. The same asymmetry of intelligibility would obtain between us and them as holds between ourselves and Plato. They would understand and embrace our thoughts and conceptions, while we cannot understand or embrace theirs.[21] This possibility will not be considered further for the moment, however. For, in the first place, it is unclear whether it licenses the assignment of limits to the cognitive powers of human beings rather than simply of any particular generation of them. Secondly, it is, as we shall see, in any case questionable whether Hegel believed that radical intellectual developments could continue into the indefinite future or even beyond his own time.[22]

The second possibility is that of a conceptual system or a form of consciousness which is different from, but historically and rationally unrelated to, our own. Such a system and our own would be inaccessible to each other; one could not proceed from one to the other by any series of rational or intelligible steps. They would also be, we shall assume, reciprocally incomprehensible and incommensurable. This possibility does not obviously entail that there is an objective reality with determinate features which none of these systems can, or can be known to, capture, but it is at least plausible to suppose that there is, if only in order to explain the finer details of the different systems.[23] Hegel has several reasons, however, for denying this possibility. He believes, as we shall see, that the points from which he begins in the *Logic*, the concept of pure being, and in the *Phenomenology*, sense-certainty or the immediate awareness of items in our sensory field, are indispensable components of any cognitive system and that there is only one way in which the series of thoughts or of forms of consciousness can be continued. It would follow that there could not be systems of thought or forms of consciousness which were rationally unrelated to our own. It is enough for the moment, however, that the supposition that there are or might be cognitive systems which are inaccessible and unintelligible to ourselves is vulnerable to the same arguments as those directed against the claim that there is or might be an objective reality unknowable by us. The existence or possibility of such a system, Hegel might initially argue, is expressed in our terms, terms which are perfectly intelligible to us: 'a different cognitive system which is unintelligible to us'. We understand this expression and if we did not we could not begin to discuss the matter. To the objection that there is, of course, supposed to be more to such a system than is contained in our abstract characterization of it and that it is this *more* that is unintelligible to us, the reply is that if such a cognitive system is to have a determinate character at all, then it must be related to other systems, for the determinate nature of cognitive systems depends on their relationships to each other, just as that of things depends on their relationships to one another. It is true that on Hegel's account conceptual and, more generally, cognitive systems are, at least to a high degree, self-developing and self-determining. The determinate nature of those systems which are known to us or of their parts is guaranteed by their internal relationships or by the relationships of the parts to each other. The concept of causality, for example, is what it is in virtue of its position in a system of concepts, its logical relationships to other concepts.[24] Again, perception in the *Phenomenology* – the view of the world as consisting of things with properties – owes its determinate character, in part at least, to its historical and/or rational relationships to other forms of consciousness. Might it not be that there are or could be conceptual or cognitive systems which have no rational or historical contact with our own but derive their determinate features from similar internal relationships? The answer to this seems to be that if two things are to be different from each other – let alone known to be different from each other – then there must be some other relationship between them apart from that of difference.[25] The internal relationships of an entity may secure for it enough determinacy for its parts to be different from each other, but not for it to be different from some other entity to which it is otherwise unrelated. This seems to be one of the points of Hegel's curious argument against the suggestion that there are two different worlds, one of which is the inverse of the other (*PG* pp. 120 ff., M. pp. 95 ff.).[26] Even if this is true, however, and two distinct cognitive systems would have to be related to each other in some more definite way, it is not clear why it should be required that they be rationally related to each other, that one of them be comprehensible from the standpoint of the other, and that their epistemic merits be commensurable.[27]

These arguments, conjecturally attributed to Hegel, for the necessary uniqueness of our own cognitive system – or perhaps rather 'system of systems' – and history are of course questionable, but they are not significantly more so than his independent arguments against the possibility that objective reality is inaccessible to us. We shall return to the question of our knowledge of objective reality on subsequent occasions, and in particular the suggestive, but elusive, principles that to assign or discover a limit is to transcend that limit, and that determinacy depends on relationships will receive further critical attention in the light of their crucial role in Hegel's thought.

Even if we are unconvinced by Hegel's arguments, however, it does not follow that there is any point in a preliminary investigation of our cognitive powers, that epistemology is prior to ontology. The fact or possibility that reality is unknowable does not entitle us to divide questions into those which we can answer and those which we cannot, or objects into those which we can know about and those which we cannot. We can of course distinguish between things as they appear to us, which we can know about, and things as they are in themselves, which are or may be inaccessible to us. But this is an empty distinction, which licenses no such definite claim as that we can answer questions about chairs, plants and planets, but not about God or freedom. It means

124

only that assertions we make about any of these items should be qualified by the tacit reminder that they are or may be true only of things as they appear to me (or to us) and not as they are in themselves. But this general qualification need not affect our cognitive procedures in the least. If there are any specific objects which we cannot know about, then specific arguments are needed to show this. Hegel, as we have seen, is inclined to believe that no such argument is ever valid.[28]

3 *Refutation and self-refutation*

It might be expected that, having decided against the view that epistemological questions are prior to ontological ones, Hegel would have proceeded directly to answer ontological questions, to present and argue for his own account of the universe. This, however, is not what he does. His approach — if it is a single approach — is an intricate one, determined in a variety of ways by his sensitivity to epistemological problems. One of the features of his procedure is that, initially at least, rather than speak directly about things, he considers men's views of things, the different forms of consciousness they have had and the thoughts or general concepts which they apply to things.

Hegel has a variety of motives for adopting this strategy. Not all of them can be regarded as epistemological but some of them can. He believes, for example, that we should inspect our pure thoughts before putting them to use in the consideration of things (*Enz.* I. 28, 46). This need not be taken as a contravention of his strictures on epistemology. To inspect a particular concept and to decide that it is not suitable for a given purpose, that it is not, for example, applicable to God or the self, is not the same thing as inspecting, and coming to a similar decision about, one's thought or one's cognitive powers as a whole. The examination of particular thoughts will, however, be considered later.[29] The feature of Hegel's procedure that will concern us in this section is that, on his view, when one examines a form of consciousness or a thought, certain sources of doubt and error that impede our study of the 'external' world are eliminated. As long as one is not concerned with the attribution of beliefs or concepts to other men, but only with the examination of them as such, one is not separated from beliefs and thoughts in the way that one is separated from external objects. There is, again, no problem about the selection and application of terms to describe beliefs and thoughts, for, unlike the external world, they are already conceptually articulated. Hegel's subsequent arguments, if they were valid, would occasion a revision of this account of the external world, but it is at least initially plausible to suppose that it is unorganized and difficult of access in a way that our own concepts and beliefs are not.

It might be objected, however, that this immunity to error, such as it is, is bought at too high a cost. If our concern is with things in the world, it is no help to redirect us to some other subject, our concepts and beliefs. It may be true in some sense that we have no direct access to Xs independently of our beliefs about Xs, but there is nevertheless a difference between studying men's beliefs about okapis and studying okapis. A part of Hegel's answer to this seems to be that at the level of generality with which he is concerned what kinds of entity there are and what is to be said about them is determined by our beliefs and concepts. Whether there are, for example, things with properties or forces which manifest themselves, though not whether there are okapis or not, depends on our conceptual framework. The relationship of our beliefs and concepts to things, forces or numbers is quite different from their relationship to okapis, magnetism and the number 7.[30] This doctrine, as we shall see, requires some qualification if it is to be attributed to Hegel,[31] but it will serve provisionally. The part of his answer which concerns us here, however, is that if one knows which set of beliefs about Xs is the correct one, one knows a good deal about Xs, and one way of finding out which set of beliefs is correct is by considering each possible set in turn, eliminating all the false ones and accepting what one is left with as the truth. Hegel's procedure is not only a process of elimination, but it is often useful to consider it in that light.

But again it may be objected that as soon as we advance from merely describing beliefs and concepts to the criticism of them, the immunity to error which the concentration on them was intended to secure is lost. Many beliefs can be criticized only empirically, and to do that we have to turn to the objects to which they refer. If the beliefs are of such a general or abstract kind that they elude empirical refutation, then doubt arises as to whether they are, in most cases, refutable at all. Hegel believes, however, for reasons which will emerge later, that we are never left with alternative beliefs or belief-systems between which we cannot rationally adjudicate. Beliefs (and, indeed, concepts) of this level of generality always involve some incoherence or inconsistency in virtue of which they can be rejected or at least put in their place. We do not need to compare them with our own beliefs or standards, assumptions which an adherent of the beliefs or concepts under examination might reject. A form of consciousness, for example, brings with it a standard or criterion of truth or coherence which it almost invariably fails to meet. We do not even need to import our own assumptions to the extent of ourselves pointing out the inconsistency in the form of consciousness in question. We can simply watch while it criticizes itself, applies its own standard to itself and, finding that it cannot satisfy it, abandons itself, so to speak, and turns into some other form of consciousness. It is not we who engage in criticism; we simply watch self-criticism (*PG* pp. 71 f., M. pp. 53 f.).[32]

This account is open to a number of objections. It is, for example, quite unclear what is supposed to be inconsistent with what. Sometimes it is said to be the object as it is in itself that is inconsistent with the object as it is for our consciousness (*PG loc. cit.*). I do indeed make a distinction within my consciousness between my view of an object and the object as it really is, and I can suppose that these might differ from each other. But if this is what Hegel means, it does not supply a proper test of my view of the object, for I have in general no substantial conception of how an object is in itself that differs from my beliefs about it. What he has in mind can be interpreted in various more plausible ways,[33] but our concern for the moment is not the particular way in which a form of consciousness is criticized, but Hegel's belief that it criticizes itself. This belief, that we can simply watch a form of consciousness refuting itself, derives its plausibility from a confusion between listening to an argument and actually arguing. Hegel purports to be doing neither. He is not merely listening to an argument, for there is no indication that it matters whether or not anyone apart from himself has actually argued in these ways. Moreover, even if he were merely listening to an argument, without assessing it by standards other than those of the person arguing, this would not in itself show that the position argued against and abandoned was untenable. The arguer might have reasoned invalidly and abandoned his position when there was no need to do so. The most that Hegel can claim is that the arguments presented in the *Phenomenology* and elsewhere are *ad hominem* arguments. In arguing in this way, one starts from a premiss that is accepted by one's opponent and derives from it a conclusion that he is not prepared to accept. If one's reasoning has been sound, then the opponent's present set of beliefs has been shown to be inconsistent and in need of some modification. But if the argument is to be sound, and not simply to succeed in persuading the opponent, the reasoning by which the conclusion is derived from the premiss must be valid, and not simply accepted by one's opponent. This means that certain standards of validity must be accepted by the reasoner; he cannot, if he himself is to be convinced

127

that the opponent's beliefs are inconsistent, disclaim all responsibility for the validity of his argument and place it on his opponents' shoulders. Hegel is surely saying how the form of consciousness in question ought to argue, rather than how it does argue, and this involves his making assumptions about standards of valid argument. The point of the fiction that it is the form of consciousness itself, and not we, that produces the argument can only be that the argument is one that the form of consciousness has the necessary cognitive equipment to produce and accept, but it does not follow that we can remain neutral about its validity. The criticism of belief-systems cannot, any more than can the study of nature, be a confrontation between the subject-matter and a bare, assumption-free ego, which holds in abeyance all laws of logic and canons of argument.[34] Further diagnosis and criticism of this aspect of Hegel's thought will be offered later.[35] In the following section we shall consider another difficulty in his process of elimination.

4 Completeness and necessity

Even if it were possible to be sure that belief-systems were false without making any assumptions of one's own, this would not in itself enable one to arrive at the truth unless one could also be sure that no system has been omitted from the elimination process. If we refute, or watch the self-refutation of, forms of consciousness just as they occur to us or present themselves historically, then there is no guarantee that all the possibilities have been considered or, therefore, that what remains, however irrefutable it may seem, is the truth. Hegel is thus concerned to secure that the forms of consciousness he examines are all that there are: 'The *completeness* of the forms of non-real consciousness will emerge through the necessity of the advance and the interconnection' (*PG* p. 68, M. p. 50). It is similarly important that the pure thoughts examined in the *Logic* should be complete. Hegel regularly criticizes his predecessors for the unsystematic way in which they introduced thoughts or categories, because among other things their procedure provided no guarantee that the list was complete.[36] There are a number of reasons for this requirement, for the *Logic* can, and no doubt should, be conceived in more than one way. But there are at least two reasons which are broadly epistemological. Firstly, if the *Logic* is regarded as an examination of concepts with a view to their applicability to ultimate reality, to God or the absolute,[37] then the list of candidates must be complete for the same reason as the forms of consciousness in the

Phenomenology must be, namely that we would otherwise have no guarantee that what was left after the unsuitable candidates had been weeded out was the right one for the job. If, secondly, the *Logic* is seen as the construction of a single conceptual system,[38] it is equally important to be certain that we have included all the concepts that there are, for otherwise the possibility remains that there are alternative conceptual systems none of which can be rationally preferred to the others.

How, then, is completeness, and the assurance of completeness, to be secured? One might suppose that, if indeed we simply watch what forms of consciousness or thoughts do, then there is no such problem. We can simply watch each element pass into its successor. But the onlooker-stance has no more plausibility here than it did in the former case. It is true that in the course of an argument a person may successively advance, or retreat, from one position to another. But this provides no warrant that he is right to do so or that the positions he occupies will be all the possible positions, unless his own procedure is governed by some rule which guarantees completeness. If it is, then it is this rule which we should consider and not the arguer's conduct. It is such a rule which Hegel attempts to provide. With some oversimplification – particularly in the light of the triadic structure of his works[39] – we may say that in the *Phenomenology* and the *Logic* each element is generated from its immediate predecessor by the application to it of a certain operation, in much the way that the natural numbers are generated by successive additions of 1. If the first element of the series and the operation itself are granted, then each element of the series, except (possibly) the first, has one and only one immediate predecessor and each, except (possibly) the last, has one and only one immediate successor. Hegel sometimes contrasts the structure of his own system with that of Euclidean geometry,[40] and geometry differs from it in these two respects. Even if we assume a certain set of axioms for geometry – and alternative sets are possible, whereas Hegel's system has a fixed starting-point – there is no single order in which the theorems must be proved. There are moreover alternative proofs of the same theorem, whereas in Hegel's system there is supposed to be only one route by which a given element can be reached.[41] It differs again from the generation of negative numbers from positive ones.[42] For there is, as that model was presented, no special reason why we should derive negative numbers from positive whole numbers together with addition and subtraction before, rather than after, we derive fractions from positive whole numbers together with multiplication and division. By contrast, Hegel's method of derivation is intended to exclude any chance of our omitting any element which belongs to the system. If we start out at the right place, sense-certainty or being, the subsequent direction and steps of our thought are determined. We cannot think about teleology before thinking about causality, or proceed directly from causality to teleology, omitting the intervening thoughts.

Even if we concede this much, of course, it would not follow that Hegel has encompassed all possible forms of consciousness or all possible thoughts. A different starting-point might have been chosen, leading to a wholly different series, or a different operation or combination of operations, generating a different series from the same starting-point. Other arguments will be required if these possibilities are to be excluded. Our concern in this section, however, is the nature of the operation which, on Hegel's view, generates each element from its predecessor. The transitions from one element to the next are often among the most difficult parts of his text, difficult both to understand and accept. Even if we understand a given element and his criticisms of it, even if the succeeding element seems a natural one to consider next, we can rarely see why it is the only possible successor or why there can be only one. Yet these transitions are crucial for Hegel's enterprise. What is the principle, if any, that underlies them?

Hegel often remarks that the passage from one element to the next is effected by negating it, that each element is the negation of its immediate predecessor. The rejection of an element is a variety of scepticism. But scepticism of the ordinary type does not, when it criticizes and rejects one position, automatically come to another position: 'It is the scepticism which only ever sees in the result *pure nothing* and abstracts from the fact that this nothing is determinately the nothing *of that* from *which it results*.' Such scepticism, therefore, does not proceed systematically from one position to its successor, but 'must wait to see whether anything new presents itself and, if so, what it is, in order to cast it into the same empty abyss'. Hegel's own conception of negation is different, however:[43]

> When, by contrast, its result is grasped as it in truth is, as *determinate* negation, a new form has at once arisen thereby, and in the negation the transition is made by which the advance through the complete series of forms automatically emerges (*PG* pp. 68 f., M. p. 51).

Hegel is here exploiting our ordinary notion of negation, the negation of a proposition or of a predicate. Negation must be, in one sense, determinate, for it must be the negation of some definite proposition or predicate. Moreover, a proposition or predicate can have only one negation. The negation of, for example, the proposition that all roses are red is the proposition that it is not the case that all roses (or that not all roses) are red.[44] But this is as much help as Hegel can derive from our ordinary conception of negation. The negation of the proposition that all roses are red does not tell us any more than that not all roses are red. Even if they were all of some other colour, it would not tell us what colour it was. Moreover, negation cannot, by repeated application, continue to generate new propositions or predicates. The negation of the proposition that not all roses are red is the proposition that it is not the case that not all roses are red and this, in standard logic, is equivalent to the original proposition, that all roses are red. (Hegel's logic is too non-standard to derive much assistance from the non-standard logics which have been developed since his time.) Some sense, as we have seen, can be made of Hegel's conception of negation in particular cases,[45] but it cannot be explained to any great extent by reference to features of ordinary negation nor is it so widely applicable as he believes.

Hegel gives other general accounts of the passage of one element into its successor. One of them is that thinking, thinking about and in terms of pure thoughts and presumably thinking about forms of consciousness, proceeds by the emergence and resolution of contradictions. Thinking gets involved in contradictions and develops by attempting to extricate itself from them.[46] The notion of a contradiction and the kind of contradiction-resolution that might be involved here will be considered later. The relevant point here is that this account does not guarantee that each element will have only one immediate successor, for it is not obvious that there is only one way in which a contradiction can be resolved. The simple case where we can derive contradictory propositions, p and not-p, from a set of beliefs can be resolved in at least three broad ways — by adjusting the set so that p no longer follows from them or so that not-p no longer follows, or, finally, so that neither proposition does. Even if we relax the notion of a contradiction (as Hegel does, in practice) so that, for example, the fact that there is no answer to the sum '5—7' counts as a contradiction, there is still no unique way of resolving it. To eliminate subtraction from the system and allow only addition would resolve the 'contradiction' as completely as the introduction of negative numbers. That it would do so less fruitfully seems beside the point unless some usable criterion of fruitfulness is provided.

Another recurrent suggestion is that the difference between any given element and its immediate successor is that the latter is one's awareness of or reflection upon the former. In the *Pheno-menology*, for example, Hegel implies that one's awareness of the (range of) object(s) of one form of consciousness is itself the object of the next form of consciousness: 'the awareness (*Wissen*) of the first object, or the for-consciousness of the first in-itself (*Ansich*), is itself to become the second object' (*PG* p. 73, M. p. 55) — though no form of consciousness, except perhaps the last, is aware that this is what its object amounts to. Again, in speaking of the history of philosophy, Hegel says: 'The architect of this work of thousands of years is the *one* living mind, whose thinking nature is to bring to its consciousness *what it is* and, when this has become its object, to be at once elevated above it and to be a higher stage within itself' (*Enz.* I. 13). The suggestion is that the awareness of stage n is or immediately becomes stage n + 1, that philosophy develops by successive acts of reflection upon its present state.⁴⁷ The plausibility of this account, as of the accom-panying, but logically distinct, claim that philosophy is, as it were, the product of a single mind, is not here at issue. The ques-tion for the moment is whether it provides a way of generating a single series of elements, with no branching in either direction. There is reason to suppose that it does not.

As we have already seen, we might doubt whether the aware-ness of, for example, a philosophical position is in itself sufficient to constitute or generate a new philosophical position. We would need to combine this account with the earlier one, namely that development is a process of contradiction-resolution, if it is to be clear why progress occurs. Then we can see why, in becoming aware of a philosophical position and of the contradictions it in-volves, we would be led to formulate a new position which resolves or eliminates them. But, as we have seen, there is generally more than one way of resolving contradictions. What Hegel has in mind, however, corresponds less closely to our ordinary conception of philosophical positions than it does to the more recent idea of a meta-language, a language in which we can say things about some other language, the object-language, that cannot be said in the object-language itself.⁴⁸ A language which contains, for example, names for objects and predicates which can be combined with them so as to produce sentences about objects need not contain any names for words and sentences themselves nor any predicates such as 'word', 'sentence', 'true' or 'false' which can be applied to them. Such a language would not enable us to speak about itself. To do so we would have to have another language, containing expressions which the first language lacks.

If this suggestion is correct, then each series of elements which

Hegel describes would correspond to the series: object-language, meta-language, meta-meta-language and so on. Some modifications of this idea are required if it is to be attributed to him or, more accurately, used as a model for understanding his thought. For example, Hegel does not believe, as we shall see, that his series of elements proceeds to infinity. It is intended to culminate in a full awareness of the whole process, the language, as it were, in which we can speak about the whole hierarchy of languages. There is also the suggestion that the series turns back upon itself, so that the last term of the series is related to the first in something like the way in which the first is related to the second, the second to the third, and so on.[49] The notion of a hierarchy of languages provides no obvious analogue of these features. This idea, again, seems quite remote from our original epistemological concerns. A form of consciousness or a philosophical system can, on the face of it, be true or false, while a language, though it may be rich or impoverished, cannot. Part of Hegel's point, however, is perhaps that forms of consciousness and philosophical systems cannot be straightforwardly true or false and that they are in this respect more like languages than has commonly been supposed.[50] It is in any case a mistake to look in Hegel's system for a single key idea. Its difficulty is due in part to the fact that he is attempting to do many things at once.

A difficulty more relevant to the concerns of this section is that it is not the case that for any given object-language there is only one meta-language in which we can speak about it, and if this is so, the idea of a hierarchy of languages cannot provide Hegel with a way of generating a unique series of elements. There may be two distinct languages, M_1 and M_2, neither of which is a meta-language with respect to the other, but both of which are meta-languages with respect to a given object-language, L. For we cannot, or at least need not, say everything that might be said about a given language, and which meta-language we adopt will depend on those aspects of it with which we are concerned. Some meta-languages, for example, enable us to speak about the syntactical properties of an object-language, others about its semantical properties.[51] If there is to be any answer to the question what meta-language we are to choose, then we must decide what features of the object-language we wish to consider. The case seems no different if, instead of speaking of languages, we revert to Hegel's notion of awareness. Unless we are to be indiscriminately aware of every aspect of a given element, this account must be supplemented by some specification of a particular aspect of it on which we are to focus if it is to provide each element with a unique successor. When Hegel broaches this suggestion, he does not supply any such specification.

That the series of elements which Hegel considers should be complete and that each element should have a unique successor is important for a variety of reasons. We have seen reason to doubt whether such completeness can be guaranteed in any of the ways he suggests.

5 Scepticism and diversity

The epistemological problem considered in the last two sections has been, roughly speaking, that presented by the fact that there are alternative ways of viewing the world, mutually inconsistent, but each of them apparently internally consistent, so that there is no obvious way for us to choose between them. So far Hegel's response to this has been treated as if it were a process of elimination. That it is more than that will emerge in the present section.

In many areas of knowledge the possibility that different men will make different and conflicting assumptions between which no rational adjudication is open to us remains a mere possibility. But in the history of philosophy itself, this possibility has apparently been realized. Different and conflicting systems, based on different and conflicting assumptions, have actually been proposed and espoused. To Hegel's contemporaries, then, scepticism in philosophical matters seemed to have a special justification.[52] Kant's formulation of the antinomies had sharpened the argument. Kant's own solution to them is drawn in terms of what Hegel saw as a two-world doctrine, the world of phenomena and the world of things-in-themselves. The solution to the antinomy is, in most cases, that both propositions concern only the realm of appearances, but that, since what is true or false of phenomena depends on what we can verify, there is in that realm no reason for either of them to be true. There is, for example, no answer to the question: 'Is the world finite or infinite in space?' It will only seem to have an answer if it is taken to be a question about things-in-themselves. But if it is taken in this way, then again it has no answer, for the world as it is in itself is not in space and time.[53] In other cases, the solution to the antinomy seems to be that one of the contradictory propositions is true of the phenomenal world, while the other is true of — or may be, or may or must be believed to be, true of — things-in-themselves. The world of appearance, for example, is entirely governed by causal laws; if there is free-will it must be assigned to the noumenal self, the self as it is in itself, and not to the phenomenal self.[54] In either case, however, the message is that our cognitive powers are not competent to venture far into the noumenal realm. Such claims about it as we are entitled to make are a matter of faith rather than knowledge.[55]

Hegel opposed this solution on two counts. He objects firstly, as we have seen, to any restriction on our cognitive capacity, and, secondly, to any two-world conception. For a variety of reasons, Hegel is hostile to every species of dualism, and is inclined to regard it as a phase of separation.[56] His own solution to the problem is of a quite different sort. Sometimes, in the interests of a striking analogy, he misrepresents his position:

> At the spectacle of so many *diverse* philosophies, the *universal* and the *particular* . . . must be distinguished. If the universal is taken formally and placed *alongside* the particular, then it becomes itself something particular. Such a position would automatically strike one as inept and absurd in the case of everyday objects, if, for example, someone wanted fruit and rejected cherries, pears, grapes, etc. because they were cherries, pears and grapes, and *not* fruit. In regard to philosophy, however, people are only too ready to justify their contempt for it on the ground that there are such different philosophies and each is only *a* philosophy, not philosophy *as such* (*Enz.* I. 13).

The force of the analogy is that it is silly to reject all particular philosophies on the grounds that none of them is philosophy as such, just as it would be silly to reject any particular fruit on the ground that it was not what one wanted, that is, fruit as such. But this is quite misleading. If a person wants fruit, he cannot choose the universal fruit, fruit as such, but must pick cherries, grapes or apples, or some combination of them. There is, moreover, no special reason for selecting one type of fruit rather than another; the choice will depend on personal tastes, dietary needs, and so on. This is because types of fruit are all on a par; they do not form an ordered series such that we have a reason for choosing one later in the series rather than an earlier one. But Hegel does not believe that the choice of a philosophy is a matter for personal taste. He pours scorn on the idea that it does not matter what religion one has, as long as one has some religion or other,[57] and philosophy does not differ in this respect from religion. This is because, on Hegel's view, the particular philosophies (and particular religions) differ from the particular types of fruit in at least three ways:

(i) Different philosophies form an ordered series. Later terms in the series are in some sense better or higher than earlier terms.

(ii) A later term in the series in some sense embraces or includes the earlier terms. It is, in this sense, 'more universal' and 'less particular' than its predecessors, and this is one of the reasons why it is more worthy of choice than they are: it involves all the advantages of its predecessors.

(iii) The final term in the series – Hegel's own philosophy – embraces all its predecessors and is therefore the universal philosophy. It stands in much the same relationship to the particular philosophies as does the universal *fruit* or fruithood, though not any particular species of fruit, to the particular types of fruit. (This is one of the things meant by the expression 'concrete universal'.)[58]

One might, of course, with equal justification regard the first term of the series as universal with respect to the later ones, for it is the highest common factor of all the terms of the series. But this does not affect Hegel's argument.

The doctrine is expressed in such passages as this:

> The *history of philosophy* shows, firstly, that the apparently diverse philosophies are only *one* philosophy at different stages of development and, secondly, that the particular *principles*, each one of which lay at the basis of a system, are only *branches* of one and the same whole. The philosophy which is last in time is the result of all preceding philosophies and must therefore contain the principles of all of them; it is therefore, if indeed it is [a] philosophy, the most developed, rich and concrete philosophy of all (*Enz.* I. 13).

On the view Hegel is opposing, different philosophies are, firstly, on a level with one another, and, secondly, they contradict each other in such a way that we can at most accept one of them and must reject all the others. One philosopher argues, for example, that men have free-will, while another denies it. Both statements are on a par with each other and no one could consistently accept both. A common feature of the history of philosophy, however, is the supersession of two opposing views by the rejection of some assumption shared by them both, and this case provides an example of it. For the opposing views that there is no free-will because determinism is true and that determinism is false because there is free-will can be transcended by the rejection of their common assumption that free-will and determinism are incompatible with each other. (The claim of the compatibilist, however, to transcend the two incompatibilist positions depends on the fact that the assumption of incompatibility remains a mere assumption. As soon as it is explicitly stated and argued for, all three positions are on a par.)[59] This is an example which Hegel in fact accepts, though not entirely for the familiar reasons.[60]

The point that is more prominent in Hegel's mind, however, is that whereas philosophers seem to make assertions which contradict each other, they are properly to be seen as expressing 'principles', principles which do not in the ordinary sense contradict one another and which are not on the same level as one another. The point can be illustrated from schematic, and relatively free, versions of the philosophies of Parmenides and Heraclitus.[61] Parmenides argued that one could truly and/or meaningfully say of the universe only that it *is* and that nothing else is truly and/or meaningfully assertible. Heraclitus, by contrast, argued that everything is becoming, everything is in a state of change. (Parmenides should avoid saying that *everything* is, owing to its implication of plurality.) As they stand, these assertions contradict each other, but we can extract from them principles which do not, or at least do not do so in such a way that we cannot rationally accept both principles. These principles may be different, but non-contradictory, propositions, the propositions, perhaps, that everything is and that everything is (in a state of) becoming, or they may be different concepts, those of being and of becoming, which we can accommodate in a single conceptual system.[62] But, more than this, the principles are not on a par with each other. The concept of becoming, on Hegel's view, presupposes that of being in a way in which the concept of being does not involve that of becoming. For something to become (F), for example, is for it not to *be* (F) at one time and to *be* (F) at a later time (*Enz.* I. 88; *WL* I. pp. 83 ff., M. pp. 83 ff.). There is the complication that the transition to becoming is made in the *Logic* by way of the concepts of being and nothing, but the triadic structure of Hegel's thought need not concern us here.[63] The point is that there is a sense in which Heraclitus is committed to Parmenides' principle, but not Parmenides to Heraclitus'; Heraclitus' philosophy is a higher stage of philosophy which includes Parmenides' principle. All other historical philosophies belong to this hierarchical series, Aristotle's embracing Plato's, and so on. Naturally enough, as philosophies become more complicated, it becomes more difficult to unearth a single leading principle and Hegel's efforts to show a detailed correspondence between the *Logic* and the history of philosophy begin to flag at quite an early stage, but this at any rate is his intention (*Enz.* I. 14).[64]

Here again, then, philosophies are regarded more as languages or conceptual systems than as statements or assertions.[65] On the ordinary view, Parmenides had the linguistic and conceptual resources to speak about change and diversity, but held for particular reasons that we ought not to speak about it. It may be argued that it was because his concept of being or his understanding of the word εἶναι was defective that he could maintain that talk about diversity and change was inevitably incoherent, so that his assertions, or restrictions on what can be asserted, derive from the poverty of his linguistic or conceptual system. But to say this means only that his understanding of the Greek language was insufficiently refined and not that he lacked words or concepts that were available to Heraclitus. On Hegel's view, by contrast, philosophies are more like linguistic or conceptual systems. They differ and are to be assessed in terms of their poverty or richness rather than of their truth or falsity, of what they can or cannot say rather than of what they do or do not say. A higher philosophy differs from a lower one in much the way that the system containing positive and negative numbers differs from the fragment of itself which contains only the positive ones.

If this were all that Hegel meant, it would perhaps be obvious why we should prefer a later and higher philosophy to an earlier and lower one. Why should one choose to speak the language of Parmenides or Spinoza when one can see and say much more when one speaks the language of Hegel? But run together with this idea is the more contentious one that in so far as one philosophy embraces another, the latter has no vantage point from which to criticize the former. As soon as a Kantian, for example, objects to a Hegelian that such-and-such is the case, the exponent of the more embracing philosophy replies that he has already said that and more. Where doctrines are concerned, at least, this seems reprehensible. This is not because a philosophy which embraces the doctrines of all its predecessors need be contradictory. We have already seen that meagre approximations of the assertions of Parmenides and Heraclitus, as well as of their concepts, can be accommodated in a single consistent system. A better example would be the way in which Einstein's system contains rough approximations not only of Newton's concepts, but of Newton's laws, whereas the Newtonian system does not provide similar accommodation for the Einsteinian. The point is rather that Einstein's theory cannot be regarded as cognitively superior to the Newtonian, and immune to criticism from it, solely because it embraces it in this way. Hegel argues in a similar way in his account of Plato's ideal state (*VGP* II. pp. 127 ff., H. II. pp. 112 ff.). We can criticize Plato's state, for although it had the necessary features of solidarity and control, it lacked any element of 'subjective freedom'. But Plato could not, conversely, criticize the modern or Hegelian state, for it includes not only subjective freedom, but also, in a modified form, the features which Plato valued. In the case of states, as well as doctrines, Hegel ascribes a special invulnerability to a combination of different ingredients. The advocate of a state or a doctrine containing only one or a few of these elements cannot find a foothold for criticizing it. This invulnerability, however, is surely illusory.[66-67]

6 Limits and intelligibility

There is, however, a better point to be extracted from Hegel's thought here. We have already referred to the principle of limits to which he subscribes, namely that to assign limits to something is at the same time to transcend those limits.[68] The principle is an elusive one and it is hard to be sure what it implies, but it perhaps would follow from it that a lower philosophy cannot understand a higher one and that a philosophy cannot understand itself. To understand a philosophy we must advance to a higher one which embraces it. For to understand something is to be aware of its limits, to see round its edges, so to speak, and to do that one must already be beyond it. Some support for this can be derived from our arithmetical analogy. If one has only a system of positive numbers, one is in no position to say that these numbers are positive or that the system contains no negative numbers. It is only when one has introduced negative numbers that one is able to say these things about the truncated system.[69]

We can revert here to the idea of a meta-language and an object-language, for this, as we have seen, gives more precision to talk about awareness and understanding. It is clear that one language may embrace and go beyond another without being a meta-language with respect to the latter. It may, for example, contain all the names and predicates of the simpler language, together with additional names and predicates of the same order, while providing no way of speaking informatively about it. Conversely, must a meta-language contain all the resources of its object-language? Clearly it need not. A syntactic meta-language, for example, in which we cannot speak about the meaning or the truth of sentences in the object-language, need only provide ways of speaking about the words and sentences of the object-language. It need not contain these words or the machinery for forming these sentences themselves. In it we can speak only about the object-language, not about the things that the object-language itself enables us to speak about.[70] A semantic meta-language, by contrast, in which one wants to speak about the meaning and truth of expressions in the object-language, must contain the object-language as a fragment of itself. For in it we wish to say not only such things as

'The word "rabbit" is a noun' or 'The sentence "Snow is white" is of the subject-predicate form', but also 'The word "rabbit" denotes rabbits' or 'The sentence "Snow is white" is true if and only if snow is white', where we speak directly about things that the object-language speaks about.[71] We have already seen that Hegel speaks undiscriminatingly of awareness in this context, and does not specify what type of awareness is at issue. Moreover, the principle of limits does not provide a decision as to which of these types of meta-language can best represent what he has in mind. There is a sense in which any meta-language transcends and presupposes its object-language, even if it is poorer in other respects. But the point that a later philosophy contains the principles of all earlier ones is best represented by the idea of a meta-language which includes its object-language. If each successive meta-language contains its immediate object-language, then clearly it will contain all the languages which precede it in the hierarchy.

The intuitive idea which this partially represents is not simply that some languages are richer than others, nor that some positions contain rough approximations of other positions, but that some positions are intelligible to other positions which are not, conversely, intelligible to them. We or Hegel, for example, can understand Parmenides and explain how his conclusions came to seem reasonable to him. But if Parmenides were resurrected, with his age-old cognitive limitations unrepaired, he would be unable to understand us or to explain why we said what we did. Similarly, Einstein can understand Newton and explain why, given his experimental and conceptual resources, he believed, and reasonably so, in the exact truth of his laws. But Newton could not do the same for Einstein. The situation is reminiscent of the story of the blind men who encounter an elephant and form different convictions as to what it is depending on what part of it they touch, one — who has got hold of the trunk — believing that it is a snake, another — who has found the tail — that it is a rope, and so on. A man who possesses both sight and touch can explain why each of the blind men believes what he does. (He may, if he is generous, agree that what he believes contains rough approximations of their beliefs. But it is not clear that understanding an opponent involves assenting to more than extremely rough versions of his beliefs, so much so that they need hardly approximate to them at all.) The blind men, by contrast, cannot, unless they feel the elephant all over or have some conception of vision, understand or explain the beliefs either of the sighted man or of each other. For the outsider, who is faced with these different accounts, the comprehensiveness of the sighted man's account is a point in its favour,

140

quite apart from the knowledge of its correctness which he otherwise has.

But can such comprehensiveness in fact be our criterion for preferring one doctrine to another? It may be that we are covertly
assuming the superiority of higher standpoints and of the explanations they provide. Parmenides could, after all, offer some
explanation of Hegel, in terms perhaps of madness or of possession
by demons. If we insist that the explanation be more discriminating, accounting for the finer details of Hegel's statements, it is
still not impossible that it should be provided. It might be entirely
false, but it need not be deficient in comprehensiveness, so that if
we rejected it, this would have to be in the light of our independent
knowledge of the situation, and not solely of internal features of
the explanation. It may be that, if I am one of the parties to the
dispute, I can appeal to my feeling of certainty that my opponent
has misunderstood me; and there no doubt are standards for
assessing understanding and explanation which transcend disagreements over particular points of doctrine. But it is nevertheless doubtful whether, in the case of belief-systems of comparable
complexity and sophistication, disputes between them can be
settled by a comparison of their respective comprehensiveness
and of the accounts they give of each other.

This question will not be pursued here, however. Our concern
in the next section will be to answer the question: What happens
at the end of Hegel's series and why do they ever come to an end?

7 *The problem of the beginning*

Hegel, as we have seen, was troubled by the apparent fact that
when we engage in any cognitive enterprise we have to start somewhere and this involves making assumptions, taking some things
for granted. The assumptions are of several kinds. We assume (i)
the meanings and coherence of certain words, we assume (ii) the
truth of certain propositions, and we assume (iii) the validity of
certain types of argument and the legitimacy of certain cognitive
procedures. The second and third of these types of assumption are
referred to in the following passage:

> Philosophy lacks the advantage enjoyed by other sciences of
> being able to *presuppose* its *objects* as granted immediately by
> conception and the *method* of cognition, for starting and for
> continuing, as already accepted.
>
> . . . [It must] show the *necessity* of its content and *prove*
> the being as well as the determinations of its objects (*Enz.* I. 1).

141

The third type, at least, is referred to here:

> Logic, however, can presuppose none of these forms of
> reflection or rules and laws of thinking, for they constitute
> a part of its very content and have to be first grounded within
> it (*WL* I. p. 35, M. p. 43).

The first type of assumption is implied in such passages as these:

> But we gradually see that such verbal to-ing and fro-ing leads
> to a murky distinction between an absolute truth and some
> other sort of truth, and the 'absolute', 'cognition', etc. are
> words which presuppose a meaning which it is our first
> business to ascertain . . . they [e.g. the idea that cognition is
> an instrument] could be rejected out of hand as contingent
> and arbitrary conceptions and the use, connected with them,
> of such words as 'the absolute', 'cognition', 'objective',
> 'subjective' and countless others, whose meaning is pre-
> supposed as universally familiar, could even be regarded as
> a deception (*PG* pp. 65 f., M. p. 48).

And again:

> On the contrary, opponents have too often and too vehemently
> attacked me, who were unable to make the simple reflection
> that their ideas and objections contain categories which are
> presuppositions and themselves in need of criticism before
> they are used . . . . Such presuppositions as that infinity is
> different from finitude, content is something other than form,
> the inner is different from the outer, mediation is similarly
> not immediacy . . . are at the same time brought forward
> didactically and narrated and asserted rather than proved'
> (*WL* I. pp. 31 ff., M. pp. 40 f.).

But how are we to eliminate such assumptions as these? An axiomatic system eliminates *implicit* assumptions of all three types by explicitly stating at the outset, or at least when use is first made of them, (i) primitive symbols in terms of which any symbol subsequently introduced is to be defined, (ii) axioms and/or postulates from which any proposition ('theorem') subsequently accepted is to be derived, and (iii) rules of inference in accordance with which any theorem is to be derived from the axioms. Moreover, the explicit assumptions of the system are to be kept as few in number and as simple as possible. Hegel's motivation for insisting that philosophy must be systematic is in part the same as that which has led to the development of axiomatic systems: 'Philosophizing *without system* cannot be scientific . . . . A content only has justification as a phase of the whole, while apart from it it is an unfounded assumption or subjective certainty' (*Enz.* I. 14). He criticizes Kant and his predecessors for their unsystematic introduction of their categories not simply because there is then no guarantee of completeness,[72] but also because 'they must then be enumerated *empirically* and *contingently*, and their more precise *content* can only be grounded on the *conception*, on the *assertion* that one means just this by a word, perhaps also on etymology' (*Enz.* I. 33. Cf. 30, 42.). In so far as the elements, whether they are propositions or concepts, are systematically derived from explicitly stated primitive elements, appeals to ordinary usage, beliefs and experience can be minimized.[73]

But this is not enough for Hegel. A system which proceeds from a minimum of primitive elements to a series of derived ones still has, from his point of view, a number of defects. One of them, as we have seen, is that there is likely to be no uniquely correct order in which the elements are to be derived. Indeed there is generally no uniquely correct set of primitive elements for a given axiomatic system. Two systems may be 'equivalent' in that the 'totality of concepts and propositions primitive or derived' of which they are composed is the same, but differ in that what is an axiom in the one is a theorem in the other and/or what is a primitive term in the one is a derived term in the other.[74] For a variety of reasons, Hegel finds the availability of such options an embarrassment. More important for our present concerns however is that while indefinables and undemonstrables are now out in the open, and as few and as simple as we can make them, they have still not been eliminated entirely. Traditionally it was regarded as enough if the denial or non-acceptance of an axiom could be shown to lead to an inconsistency. But Hegel's refusal to assume the law of contradiction prevents him from adopting this course. In any case, the application of the law of contradiction alone leaves available to us any number of axiomatic systems, so that again he would not secure the unique system which he requires.

How then does Hegel propose to dispense with assumptions? We have already seen one manoeuvre which he purports to adopt, namely that of simply looking at other people's assumptions without having any of his own. But even if this is accepted, one still has to select something to look at first of all. How is one to justify this choice? It may be because of this that Hegel proposes another solution, namely that his system forms a circle. But before we consider this solution, we shall present two further problems which point in a similar direction.

8 *Language and meta-language*

Another defect of axiomatic systems is that they are never, in one sense, complete. We have already seen that Hegel was concerned about our awareness of or reflection upon philosophical and other systems and that this feature of his thought can be represented in terms of the idea of an object-language and its meta-language. The same problem arises in the case of an axiomatic system. For the system itself is not all that we want to consider. According to Hegel's view that it is an essential feature of the mind to reflect upon its own states and activities, we shall also want to reflect upon the reasoning by which we think or talk about the system. Does our reasoning about the system — the meta-language — ever coincide with the reasoning formalized within it — the object-language? There are reasons for thinking that it cannot.[75] The meta-language can in its turn be examined and systematized, treated, that is, as an object-language, but then it will be considered in terms of a further meta-language, or meta-meta-language. This process can go on to infinity. We can never encapsulate the whole of our thought in a finite system or a finite series of finite systems. We can examine the reasoning or language we employ at any given stage, but this will always involve the use of language or thought of a higher level which does not coincide with the level which we are examining.[76]

This problem, or at least a similar one, disquieted Hegel. In the first place, he wanted our knowledge to be, as well as systematic, complete. Yet these two requirements seem to conflict. Either our desire for order or our curiosity must remain unsatisfied. In the second place, he would argue, the epistemic advantages, such as they are, of systematization are lost. However carefully we have checked our reasoning at the first level, it is always possible that the reasoning by which we check it involves a mistake or an erroneous assumption, and, if that is so, our checking is valueless. Unless we can capture all our thinking in a single system, we can never be sure that we are right. Hegel was not of course familiar with properly axiomatized systems. Euclid's geometry and Spinoza's *Ethics* are the closest approximations to which he refers with any frequency. He was not, therefore, acquainted with this problem in its modern form, and its technical details would be entirely beyond him. As we have seen, however, he has an intuitive grasp of some of the ideas involved.

The problem arises quite frequently in an informal way in the history of philosophy. Philosophers have often described the world and our thought and discourse about it without taking sufficient account of their own thought and discourse. Since the thought which they describe does not coincide with their thought about it, this has meant that their account has been at best incomplete. They have, however, sometimes supposed mistakenly that their account is a complete one, an account, that is, of all possible true, knowable, or meaningful thoughts or statements, and in doing so they have cast doubt on the truth, knowability or meaningfulness of their own thoughts or statements. The following are some examples of this:

(i) The first case is not one which attracted Hegel's attention, but it illustrates a part of what he had in mind. Plato, on a schematic and controversial interpretation of him, believed that the universe contained at least two types of entity, unchanging 'forms', concepts or universals such as beauty and changing particulars or individuals. Individuals owe what determinate character they have to their participation in, or imitation of, the forms. Forms, or propositions about forms, can be known, while propositions about individuals can only be believed and not known. [77]

The proposition:

1. Helen of Troy is beautiful

can be believed but not known, since among other things, she is not perfectly or unchangingly beautiful. By contrast, the proposition

2. Beauty, or the form of beauty, is different from ugliness, or the form of ugliness

can be known. Plato himself, however, needs to assert propositions which do not fall into either of these categories, propositions about the relationship between forms and individuals, philosophical propositions about individuals alone, and propositions about propositions about individuals:

3. If any individual is beautiful, then it is so to the extent that it participates in, or imitates, the form of beauty;
4. Helen is beautiful in so far as she participates in the form of beauty;
5. No individual is ever perfectly beautiful;
6. Helen is not identical with the form of beauty;
7. The proposition that Helen is beautiful can be believed but not known.

Can such statements as these be known or only believed? If they can only be believed, then Plato's own doctrine carries no more epistemic weight than do such propositions as that Helen is beautiful. If they can be known, then some modification or extension of the doctrine is required. His theory is similarly incomplete if some third epistemic attitude, other than knowledge and belief, is appropriate to them.

(ii) Kant, as we have seen, presents, on Hegel's account, a similar case.[78] He is interpreted as claiming that, on pain of saying what is not true, not known to be true, or meaningless, we should confine our discourse to perceptible phenomena and not discuss noumena or things-in-themselves. This is open to the criticism that this claim itself involves discourse about noumena. Kant's theory is therefore either self-refuting or incomplete, in need of modification or extension to account for the statements of which it consists.

There is, however, a further respect in which Kant, on Hegel's view, paid insufficient attention to the status of his own discourse. Kant, unlike his predecessors, did examine the categories which we apply to perceptible phenomena and to such entities as God, the world and the soul, but he examined them only with regard to their suitability for such applications: 'This critique [of the categories] does not, however, enter into the *content* and the determinate relationship of these thought-determinations to one another, but considers them only with regard to the contrast between *subjectivity* and *objectivity* in general' (*Enz.* I. 41). To restrict the examination of the categories to this feature of them is, according to Hegel, a mistake. The point seems to be that Kant himself is using categories not only to think about phenomena or about transcendent entities, but to think about categories themselves, and Hegel's argument is something like this:

1. One cannot think or know anything without using categories. (Hegel and Kant agree on this.)

2. When one thinks about categories, this is itself a type of thinking or knowing. (Hegel implies that Kant has forgotten this, when he accuses him of trying to know about knowing before knowing anything at all.)[79]

Therefore 3. When one thinks about categories, one is employing categories to think about categories.

But 4. When one thinks about categories in respect of their application to the world, one is not applying the categories one is using to the world, but to the categories themselves.

And 5. One should examine the categories in respect of every use that can be made of them. (Both Kant and Hegel agree on this.)

Therefore 6. One should consider the categories with respect to their application to categories, and not simply with respect to their application to the world.

But 7. To do this is, in effect, to consider the categories 'in and for themselves', that is, independently of any application that they may have or, at least, it involves a different sort of examination of them from the one Kant undertook (*Enz.* I. 41Z.1). The argument, as stated, concludes only that Kant paid insufficient attention to his own discourse. If we were to add (the truth of the addition is not here at issue) that he claimed that categories can be legitimately employed only in application to the phenomenal world, we could conclude that, by his own account, his own discourse is illegitimate, not, as before, because categories are used to speak about what lies beyond the phenomenal world, but because categories are employed to speak about the categories themselves.[80]

(iii) A case of a different and more complicated type, but one which nevertheless seems to belong here is that of Spinoza. One of Hegel's main criticisms of Spinoza is this:

> *Spinozism* is a defective philosophy in that *reflection* and its manifold determining is *an external thinking.* . . . In Spinoza the *definition of the attribute appears* after the definition of the absolute, and it is defined as the way in which the *intellect comprehends its* [viz. the absolute's] *essence.* Besides the fact that the *intellect* is taken to be posterior in its nature to the attribute — for Spinoza defines it as a *mode* — the attribute, the determination as determination of the absolute, is thus made *dependent on something else*, the intellect, which appears externally and immediately over against substance (*WL* II. pp. 195 f., M. pp. 536 f.).

There is, according to Spinoza, just one, all-inclusive, substance. This substance, on Hegel's interpretation of him, is in itself undifferentiated, but it appears to be differentiated because it appears to the intellect to have two distinct 'attributes', thought and extension, which in turn appear to be differentiated into distinct 'modes'. But what is the status of this intellect, to which the substance appears to have distinct attributes and modes? Spinoza himself regarded the intellect as a mode of substance under the attribute of thought.[81] But if this is so, then on the present interpretation the intellect itself is merely apparent. It cannot be what confers apparent differentiation on the undifferentiated substance, for we need first to explain how the intellect itself appears to exist. The alternative which Hegel attributes to Spinoza is to assume covertly that the intellect to which the substance appears differentiated is not itself a mode of substance, but is distinct from it and, as it were, external to it. But, if this is so, then Spinoza's system is, if not incoherent, at least seriously incomplete, for no account is given of such a transcendent intellect nor is there any room for it within his system.[82, 83]

Philosophers, then, have generally not paid enough regard to their own thought and discourse and they have occasionally made self-refuting claims which they might have avoided had they done so. But again the problem arises that our thought and discourse about thought and discourse of one level cannot coincide with it but must itself be on a higher level. The systematic reflection on one's own thought and discourse is a process which apparently cannot be completed. And, it might be argued, since the task cannot be completed, there is always the possibility of incoherence at the level at which we are presently operating, but have not yet examined.

9 *Fiction and meta-fiction*

A problem which is closely related, at least in form, to the foregoing is this. If one constructs an axiomatic system, one may be concerned to examine one's own discourse about this system, but it is no part of one's business to give an account of how the system arose historically. Axiomatic systems are not, after all, intended to explain everything. Hegel's ambitions, however, are wider in scope and it seems to have troubled him that, if one is to give a complete account of the universe, one must give an account of one's account and of how it came to be given. For one's own account of the universe is itself a feature of the universe which needs to be described and explained.[84] But can one's account of the universe ever coincide with or contain one's account of that account? If it cannot, then one is again involved in an infinite regress. First an account of the universe is given which disregards this account itself, then an account of this account, and so on. The task of describing the universe can never be complete.

An analogy will perhaps make the problem clear, as well as point to Hegel's solution to it. Most plays, novels and works of history are incomplete. They do not, that is, provide us with an account, true or fictional, of how they came to be produced. A true historical account must be completable, though some novels are incompletable. A novel, that is, may portray a world populated only by illiterates or prehistoric monsters, and, if this is so, no consistent account can be given of how it came to be written, within the world of the novel itself. A novel, or a historical account, may be written about the writing of the first novel, but it will not be a continuation of it; it will portray a different world, disconnected from the first. Many novels, however, are completable; the world they portray and the events they relate are not such as to exclude the novel's being written — as a (fictional) novel or as a (fictional) true account — within that world itself. In such cases we do not need, if we want to give an account of the writing of the novel, to produce some further novel about it, leading perhaps to an infinite series of novels, each describing or purporting to describe the composition of its immediate predecessor. The writing of the novel can be consistently described and explained within the novel itself, a novel which is now 'complete'. Typically, in novels of this sort, the (fictional) author begins to write the novel towards the end of the series of events presented in the novel, and the (actual) novelist breaks off at this point. He need not in fact do so. He could tell us what the (fictional) novelist wrote, repeating his whole novel within quotation marks. Since, however, this would be tedious to read and expensive to produce, and would in consistency have to be repeated *ad infinitum*, we are normally satisfied with the assurance that what the (fictional) novelist wrote is the same as the (actual) novel, and we are thus referred back to the beginning of the novel at its conclusion. Hegel does not himself discuss his system in terms of self-referential works of literature, but plays which refer to their own performance and novels which refer to their own composition would have been known to him. Apart from familiar examples such as *Don Quixote* and *Hamlet*, two plays by his contemporary, Ludwig Tieck, and a novel by Diderot are of this type.[85]

The actual world differs from any fictional one in that it must contain those who describe it and their descriptions of it. Can an account be given of it which is complete in the sense explained? The answer to this question will be considered in the next section.

10 *Circles and infinity*

The notion of infinity has figured in our account of all the problems of the last three sections. The idea suggests itself, for example, that although as things are we have to start with primitive indefinables and axiomatic undemonstrables, if we could perform intellectual operations of an infinite number of steps, we could define words in terms of other words and these words in terms of further words, and so on to infinity, or that we could demonstrate propositions from further propositions for ever without ever using the same proposition more than once. Again, we have seen that the problems of talking about one's own statements and of giving an explanatory account of one's own beliefs naturally give rise to the idea of an infinite series of languages and of an infinite series of explanatory accounts. Hegel was unimpressed by this conception of infinity, which he called 'bad' or 'negative' infinity

149

(*Enz.* I. 93, 104). His arguments on this matter are sometimes mis-conceived, but we can see, quite apart from this, that 'bad' infinity will not suit these cases. To say that everything can be proved, defined or explained at infinity is to say that not everything can be proved, defined or explained. With infinity of this sort Hegel contrasts 'true' or 'affirmative' infinity.[86] The model he employs for these two types of infinity is that of a straight line and a circle:

> The image of the progress to infinity is the straight *line*, at the two limits of which alone the infinite is and always is only where it [the line] — and it is determinate being — is not, and which *goes out beyond* to this its non-determinate being, i.e. into the indeterminate; the image of genuine infinity, bent back into itself, becomes the *circle*, the line which has reached itself, which is closed and entirely present, without *beginning* and *end* (*WL* I. p. 164, M. p. 149).

Despite the awkward expression, the basic idea of this passage is a simple one, that there is a sense in which a circle, or for that matter any line which encloses an area, is infinite or, as we might prefer, finite and yet unbounded.[87] The line which bounds the circle has no ends, just as a line which stretches to infinity has no ends; the difference is that, unlike the straight line, it can be drawn and surveyed by us; it does not go on for ever.

Circular infinity is not, however, simply a different type of infinity from linear infinity. A circle, as we have already seen, can be a way of avoiding an infinite regress. Instead of an infinite series of novels, each, except the first, telling how its predecessor came to be written, we can have a novel the last event in which is the writing of the novel itself and the novel then forms a sort of circle. Again, instead of supposing that definition and demonstration, if it is not to come to an end with primitives and axioms, must proceed to infinity, we might imagine a circular system in which the first terms are supported by, as well as support, the last, in which the primitive words are defined in terms of the words defined by means of them and the axioms are proved on the basis of theorems derived from them. Finally, we might imagine that the infinite series of meta-languages of ascending order could be replaced by a finite, but circular, series each member of which is the object-language of its immediate successor and the meta-language of its immediate predecessor.

Hegel claims in a number of passages that his system forms a circle or a circle of circles (*Enz.* I. 15). How many circles there in fact are, their types and their significance are matters which will be considered later.[88] Something will be said here, however, about the way in which the circularity of his system bears on these problems. One type of circle, that in which a series of events culminates in the account of that series of events, is suggested by the fact that, when we reach the end of some of Hegel's works, what we find under such grandiose titles as 'Absolute Awareness' (*Das Absolute Wissen, PG* pp. 549 ff., M. pp. 479 ff.) and 'The Absolute Idea' (*WL* II. pp. 548 ff., M. pp. 824 ff.) is not so much a new and distinct form of consciousness or concept, on a par with those that precede it, as a recapitulation of the whole series together with an account of the method by which it was generated. The same is true of the system as a whole. The final part of the *Encyclopaedia*, the *Philosophy of Mind*, concludes with a brief account of philosophy, the highest phase of mind, and it is implied that this takes us back to the beginning of the system, to logic: 'Science has in this way returned to its beginning' (*Enz.* III. 575). The *History of Philosophy* ends on a similar note. It concludes with an account of Hegel's own philosophy (*VGP* III. pp. 454 ff., H. III. pp. 545 ff.), and this is the point at which we become fully aware of the whole series of philosophies and of the relations between them. One of the things that the culmination of such a series consists in is the coincidence of the knowing subject and the object known. In the *Phenomenology*, for example, Hegel draws a distinction between 'we', the author and his readers, on the one hand, and, on the other, the form of consciousness under consideration (*PG* pp. 73 ff., M. pp. 55 ff.). While the work progresses allegedly on the strength only of arguments which are, or at least can be, proposed and accepted by the forms of consciousness themselves,[89] we are constantly reminded that we can see certain things to be true of a form of consciousness, especially concerning its relationships to other forms, that it cannot see. What seems to have happened at the end of the *Phenomenology* is that the position we occupy throughout the work has developed out of the forms of consciousness themselves, so that this final form of consciousness is capable of examining all its predecessors just as we did. The last term of the series is the awareness of the series as a whole.[90]

The second type of circle, that in which assumptions which one made at the beginning are justified at the end, cannot take, in Hegel's system, the form that we might expect. For, as we shall see, the primary elements at any rate of his *Logic* are not propositions, but concepts or conceptual systems.[91] There is also the difference that, whereas in a normal axiomatized system the axioms and theorems are to be accepted without qualification, a part of the point of Hegel's system is the criticism and rejection, at least for certain purposes, of the concepts which come up for consideration. They are not, of course, straightforwardly jettisoned, but they are not unreservedly accepted. Nevertheless, the end of the system is meant in some way or other to explain and legitimate its beginning and the procedures by which it is constructed. When, for example, Hegel is trying to explain why the *Logic* begins with (the concept of) pure being, he says: 'Through the advance, then, the beginning loses the one-sided character which it has when it is determined as something immediate and abstract in general; it becomes a mediated entity and the line of scientific advance becomes a *circle*' (*WL* I. p. 71, M. pp. 71 f.).

It is not clear, however, that, on Hegel's view, the way in which we begin requires subsequent justification at all. Pure being is not a hypothesis which we adopt tentatively at first and later see to be the right one because of the results derived from it:[92]

> It is not the case, as with those constructions which one is directed to make in order to prove a geometrical theorem, that it emerges only afterwards in the proof that one was right to draw just these lines and then to begin the proof itself with the comparison of just these lines or angles' (*WL* I. pp. 71 f., M. p. 71).

Pure being is seen to be the right place to begin independently of the results we derive from it. On the other hand, Hegel implies that we need to know things about our beginning and our procedures which will emerge in a proper form only later in the system:

> the very *concept* of *science* [viz. logic] in general belongs to its content, and indeed constitutes its final result; it cannot say in advance what it is . . . . What is given in advance in this introduction, therefore, does not aim to ground the concept of logic or to justify scientifically its content and method in advance, but to make more accessible to conception (*Vorstellung*) the viewpoint from which this science is to be considered by some elucidations and reflections in an argumentative and informal style (*WL* I. pp. 35 f., M. p. 43. Cf. *PG* p. 9, M. p. 1; *Enz.* I. 10).

Hegel presents a number of preliminary considerations in favour of starting with pure being, particularly in the section of the *Science of Logic* entitled 'With what must science begin?' (*WL* I. pp. 65 ff., M. pp. 67 ff.). Presumably his point is that such considerations, involving as they do a comparison with the pure ego and with nothing or non-being – concepts which do not emerge within the system until later – cannot be fully appreciated until we can survey the system as a whole. These two lines of thought seem to lead in different directions, but there need be no actual inconsistency on Hegel's part. The way in which a novel or a play begins and the principles of its construction cannot be fully appreciated until one has seen or read it through. But the opening and the way in which the plot proceeds may nevertheless seem entirely natural and unforced, quite unlike the lines we have to draw to prove a geometrical theorem.[93] But how does the end of the system, or of the *Logic*, legitimate the beginning? Sometimes it seems as if it explains or justifies the beginning only in the sense in which an element, a proposition, for example, or the opening of a play, becomes clearer when we see what is or can be derived from it:

> it emerges that what constitutes the beginning, since it is thereby still undeveloped, contentless, is not truly known at the beginning and that only science, science in its whole development, is the complete, contentful, and first truly grounded knowledge of it (*WL* I. p. 71, M. p. 72).

If this is so, then Hegel's epistemic circle may be a circle in no more stringent a sense than that in which the first type of circle is, namely that the last term of the series is a survey of the series as a whole. In such a survey, we see the place of the beginning in the whole system, but it does not follow that the beginning we chose is fully vindicated. There may, after all, be as many equally coherent systems as there are plays and novels.

The third type of circle, that in which a potentially infinite series of meta-languages of ascending order is replaced by a finite, but complete, series of them, similarly threatens to become a circle only in a degenerate sense. It is doubtful whether Hegel believes that pure being, for example, represents a meta-language with respect to the absolute idea. The historical embodiment of logic in the history of philosophy makes this clear. No one would suggest that Parmenides' or Thales' philosophy was the upshot of reflection upon Hegel's or even that they would have understood it if it had been presented to them. The idea seems rather to be that, whereas each element of the *Logic* or of the *Phenomenology* is, as it were, a meta-language with respect only to one or more of the preceding elements, the final stage is a language in which we can speak both about that language itself and about the whole series which it terminates. The absolute idea or absolute awareness is fully luminous to itself. Reflection upon it does not lead to a higher stage, any more than the addition of one to infinity produces a number greater than infinity.[94] It follows from this that the Hegelian circle is not homogeneous in the sense that it does not matter at which point one enters it. One cannot, after all, begin a novel whose climax is its own composition at any point one likes. One has to start at the beginning of the *Logic*, or perhaps of the *Phenomenology*, and not, for example, in the middle of the *Philosophy of Nature*.[95]

Hegel held that any (bad) infinite regress is vicious. Some infinite regresses are vicious, but so too are some circles. Some circles, however, are benign, and so too, on the ordinary view, are some infinite regresses.[96] How vicious are Hegel's circles? They sometimes seem comparable to Escher's 'Drawing Hands', where each of two hands is being drawn by the other, or to the idea of pulling oneself up by one's own bootstraps.[97] But some of them seem virtuous enough. The idea, for example, of an account of a series of events which culminates in and explains the giving of that account is coherent, unless we insist that the account is not complete until it has been written over and over an infinity of times. The problem here is rather how a series of elements, each generated by some operation on its immediate predecessor, can terminate in an awareness of the whole series, how, that is, the historical (or fictional) process can be represented by logic. The series of natural numbers does not culminate in an awareness of the series as a whole, and it is not clear how an ascending series of languages could do so. If, on the other hand, the circle is interpreted as an epistemic one, then it is on the face of it vicious, or at least ineffectual. The fact that a series of elements, of beliefs for example, is self-sustaining in this sense does not in itself guarantee that it is the only possible self-sustaining system and does not, therefore, establish that it is to be accepted in preference to some alternative. Hegel could perhaps be interpreted as meaning not that our beliefs form a strict circle of justification, but that it is a mistake to regard some of our beliefs as epistemically primary and others as resting on them, that all our beliefs both support, and are supported by, each other.[98] To this one might add that even if we could enter into an infinite series of beliefs, none of which occurs more than once in the series and each of which supports its immediate successor, we would still have no guarantee that it was the only possible self-sustaining infinite series. It is likely, however, that Hegel took his circle, or circles, more seriously than this suggests. He would still need, in any case, to establish the uniqueness of his system, and for this other arguments are required.[99]

The circles in Hegel's system and the problems they involve will be considered again in a later chapter. The following two chapters, however, will raise a further set of problems which his system is intended to solve.

VI

Infinite Objects and Finite Cognition

The problems of the preceding chapter were problems of knowledge in general, without special regard to what the knowledge is of. The problems of this and the following chapter, by contrast, are those of our knowledge of objects of a certain type, those namely which are 'infinite in their content', such as God, freedom and the soul (*Enz.* I. 8). These problems have been foreshadowed earlier. We have seen, for example, that Hegel criticized the empirical sciences for their inability to accommodate such entities as these.[1] The sciences receive support in this from some religious believers, and Hegel's myth of the fall was introduced in part in order to meet on their own ground those who claimed that it was impossible for finite man to know what is infinite and impious for him to try.[2]

In the light of Hegel's aversion to assumptions, it might seem surprising that he makes what is for us the bold assumption that God exists. There are, however, four possible replies to this objection, short of ascribing overt inconsistency to him:

(i) Hegel need not assume that God (or the soul or freedom) exists, but only that if he did exist, he would be infinite and might, therefore, be inaccessible to 'finite' cognition, to empirical science for example. If, then, we confine ourselves to finite cognitive procedures, we may be cutting ourselves off from answering the question: Does God exist and, if so, what is he like? Assumptions are no doubt still made here, but not necessarily any very controversial ones. Hegel would not care to support the claim that God is infinite by appeal to traditional usage (cf. *Enz.* I. 33), but it can in fact be simply hypothesized and not asserted at all: 'If there is an *infinite* God, then he cannot be known by finite cognition.' That infinite objects cannot be known by finite cognition is something that Hegel argues for rather than assumes.

(ii) If we disregard the criticism of the empirical sciences, Hegel's criticisms are directed primarily against the pre-Kantian meta-physicians and can be seen as *ad hominem* ones. For they themselves assumed or attempted to prove that God exists, that he is infinite and that something can be known about him, while at the same time they employed finite methods of cognition. Hegel can argue that they are inconsistent, that their procedures cannot reveal to them what they claim to know, without committing himself to any of their more substantial beliefs.

(iii) This *ad hominem* stance is connected, as we have seen, with another reply that Hegel might give, namely that such problems together with their presuppositions are not strictly preliminary to his system, but are developed within it.[3] The system properly begins with the account of pure being (*Enz.* I. 84). Conceptions such as those of God, freedom and the soul are not presupposed by it except in the sense that they are historical preconditions of its construction and of our entry into it. These concepts, and the corresponding existential claims, are to be derived within the system and it is only within it that we are in a position to take account of the problems which gave rise to it. The problems are introduced at the beginning, but only for the reader's convenience.[4] If we took Hegel seriously we would ignore these introductory remarks and read through his works as if we were infants acquiring dimly grasped knowledge, but incapable of formulating the questions which it answers. A child, after all, realizes only later, if at all, what the point is of learning a language or arithmetic, and one's entry into any complete, self-contained body of knowledge must be of that kind. Whether such an ideal is coherent or not, it is certain that Hegel's system fails to live up to it. Apart from the fact that it presupposes the meanings of certain words and certain modes of argument,[5] there are constant references throughout the *Logic* to familiar beliefs and conceptions of a non-logical kind and it would be hardly intelligible without them. The ideal, however, seems to have been Hegel's and he would appeal to it in response to the objection we are considering.

(iv) The objection to assuming the existence of God arises in part because God is conceived of in a particular, usually an anthropomorphic, way. Hegel, however, often uses the expression 'the absolute' as an alternative to 'God' (*Enz.* I. 12, 85), and this expression is meant to convey no more than 'reality as a whole' or something of that sort.[6] This concept too must be derived within Hegel's system (cf. *WL* II. pp. 187 ff., M. pp. 530 ff.), but the assumption, if we have to make it, that the absolute exists and that it is infinite in Hegel's sense is likely to occasion less initial discomfort than the corresponding assumption about God. A materialist, for example, might agree that there must be some way the world is, and that reality as a whole cannot be dependent on, or conditioned by, anything distinct from itself. The controversy is likely to centre not on the existence of the absolute, but on its nature and knowability.[7]

Hegel can, then, by one or more of these replies be relieved of at least some of the burden of presupposition which he ought not to carry. There is, however, another objection that might be raised to his enterprise. He is examining finite methods of cognition with the aim of seeing whether they are adequate to handle infinite entities. But, it might be argued, this conflicts with his prohibition on asking preliminary epistemological questions.[8] The answer to this, however, is that he does not suppose that the question 'Can we know God at all?' can receive a negative answer. His belief that, if God exists, then he is knowable, is based in part on theological considerations such as that God would not be so envious as to withold the possibility of such knowledge from us, but primarily on logical ones, especially the vacuity of the claim that God exists if we have no idea what he is, or is like.[9] But it does not follow that God, the soul or freedom can be known by any method whatsoever, and there is no objection to examining finite cognitive procedures to see whether they are adequate to the task.

This examination is based on the traditional division of the elements of cognition into concepts, judgments (propositions) and syllogisms (arguments, proofs), a division which Hegel provisionally accepts.[10] The underlying idea is that if we are to know that, for example, God is good, we need concepts, those of God and of goodness. These concepts must be combined into a judgment or proposition. And, finally, it is reasonable to suppose that some argument for, or proof of, the proposition is, or could be, given, if we are to accept it. Hegel, as we shall see, revises this picture quite radically, but his scepticism about finite cognition is expressed in terms of doubts about the appropriateness of each of these three elements to infinite entities. The question of this and the following chapter, then, is: Why can finite cognitive procedures not handle infinite objects and what, if any, is the alternative? In this chapter we shall consider Hegel's doubts about concepts and the propositional form.

1 Metaphysics and opposition

Pre-Kantian metaphysicians had, on Hegel's account, made assertions of the type 'God exists (*hat Dasein*)', 'The world is infinite' and 'The soul is simple' (*Enz.* I. 28). The subject-term in each of these cases denotes an object which is 'infinite'. The predicate-term ascribes a property or an attribute to this subject. What is needed, Hegel suggests, and what they failed to provide, is an examination of these predicates to see whether they are appropriate, before we apply them to such subjects (*Enz.* I. 28. Cf. 41). Not all of his arguments for this prescription are respectable. He argues, for example, that if the absence of contradiction is a necessary condition of the truth of a proposition, then we should make sure that our predicate-term does not contain a contradiction, independently of its application to a subject, since, if it does, then any affirmative proposition with this predicate will be false (*Enz.* I. 35). But this is a bad argument. If any contradiction in the predicate alone will emerge in the proposition, there is no special reason why we should not form and examine propositions straight away. Hegel's real reason, or at least one of his real reasons, for advocating a preliminary investigation of predicates is that he does not believe that such predicates as these are suitable for infinite subjects. The outcome of such an investigation would be negative. Why is this? He often implies that there is some single defect common to all these predicates in virtue of which they are inapplicable to infinite entities. What is wrong with them is that they are 'finite' determinations (*Enz.* I. 27, 28Z).[11] To say that a concept or a predicate is finite means, as we shall see, more than one thing. But, in this section, we shall be concerned with the fact that the predicates or thought-determinations in which Hegel is interested are inapplicable to infinite entities for a variety of different reasons, not all of which have any obvious connection with their finitude. This is clear from his detailed criticisms of the following metaphysical propositions:

(i) 'God has existence' (*Enz.* I. 28 and Z).

(ii) 'The soul is simple' or 'The soul is complex' (*Enz.* I. 28, 34Z, 47).

(iii) 'The world is infinite' or 'The world is finite' (*Enz.* I. 28, 48Z).

(iv) 'A person is free' or 'A person, like everything else, is governed by necessity' (*Enz.* I. 35, 48).

(v) 'There is evil in the world' or 'Mankind is evil' (*Enz.* I. 35Z. Hegel does not supply a definite proposition here).

Hegel's treatment of these cases will be considered in turn:

(i) '*God has existence.*' This proposition is distinguished from the others by the fact that whereas their predicates are members of contrasting pairs of concepts – finite/infinite, simple/complex, free/necessary, good/evil — the term 'exist' or 'have existence', in German as in English, is not. Its contradictory is formed only by means of the general sign for negation: 'does *not* exist' or 'does *not* have existence'. Hegel's treatment of it reflects this. In the other cases, he offers for consideration a contrasting pair of propositions, 'The soul is simple', for example, and 'The soul is complex.' But in this case he does not. Again, in the other cases, he is inclined to say that the truth, or the best approximation to it, is given by the seemingly contradictory conjunction of both propositions: 'The world is both infinite and finite', and so on (*Enz.* I. 32Z, 47Z). But he shows no similar tendency to say that God both exists and does not exist.

The reason for this is that Hegel's objection to the term 'exist' is not, as in the other cases, that it is 'one-sided', but that it is applied characteristically to such entities as giraffes and Mt Everest, finite things which have particular, limited characters excluding their possession of other characters, and which are related to and conditioned by other things in manifold ways.[12] On any reasonable view, let alone Hegel's, God is not an entity of that type. To say that God exists might be taken to imply, therefore, that he is of a piece with Mt Everest, while to say that he does not exist suggests that he is like Pegasus and mermaids, failing to exist in the way that they do. It might be less misleading, then, to say that God neither exists nor fails to exist than to say that he does, that he does not, or that he both does and does not. Hegel's own theology seems to license a conclusion of this type,[13] but this does not prevent him from speaking quite frequently of the 'existence of God'.

(ii) '*The soul is simple/complex*.' This case is more complicated, for Hegel has more than one reason for objecting to these propositions. One of these reasons assimilates this case to the first. It is that the soul is not a 'thing' on a par with ordinary things (*Enz.* I. 34Z, 47, where Kant is given credit for having realized this).[14] It is rather 'absolute actuosity' (*Enz.* I. 34Z).[15] One cannot, therefore, ask questions about its spatial location nor can one say that it is simple or that it is complex (*Ibid.*). This is not a good argument. Other entities than 'things' can be said to be simple or complex, problems, for example, concepts, propositions and theories. When we say that a theory is complex, we do not imply that it is a material thing like a maze or a jigsaw puzzle. It is not clear, moreover, that any entity, even a 'thing', can be *only* simple or *only* complex. A definite answer can be given to the question 'Does Mt Everest exist or not?' but no answer can be given to 'Is Mt Everest simple or complex?' unless we are told

159

more about the point of the question and the sort of answer required. There is a general distinction, on Hegel's view — though it is one he sometimes forgets — between those concepts or pairs of concepts which are problematic in their application to infinite entities alone and those which are problematic in their application to finite things as well. For example, the pair of terms 'mediated' (*vermittelt*) and 'immediate' (*unmittelbar*), are, on Hegel's own view, both applicable to everything. Nothing is *only* mediated or *only* immediate (*Enz.* I. 12, 66).[16] These terms do not discriminate in any straightforward way between infinite entities and finite things. On each of these counts, then, this argument fails to establish that the soul is in a special position with respect to simplicity and complexity. If it were valid, however, it would presumably license a conclusion similar to that which Hegel seems to accept in the case of God's existence, not that the soul is both simple and complex, but that it is neither.

A second consideration, however, points to a different conclusion. Hegel sometimes suggests that the reason for our inability to give a straight answer to the question whether the soul is simple or complex is that it is both simple (in one way or respect) and complex (in another way or respect):

> Thus the soul is, for example, admittedly simple identity with itself, but at the same time it, as active, differentiates itself within itself, whereas by contrast what is *only*, that is abstractly, simple is, precisely as such, also dead (*Enz.* I. 47Z).

Hegel (or his editor) may have had in mind the fact that the pure ego unravels, so to speak, into a system of pure thoughts or the fact that it has perceptions, desires and so on and does not remain only a pure ego.[17] We saw earlier that, on Hegel's account, the states of the self are produced by external objects. In some passages, by contrast, he appears to assign a more active role to the self, implying that it in some way generates its own empirical states (*Enz.* I. 34Z).[18] The case for saying that the soul is complex, as well as simple, is perhaps stronger, if the ego is regarded as in some sense generating its own states, but in either case these states provide some reason for saying that, if the self is in a way simple, it is also in a way complex.

A third reason for supposing that the soul cannot be unproblematically either simple or complex is the self-transcending character of the self. Unlike a stone or an animal, I can describe myself. I can, for example, say or think that I am a simple entity. But, again, if I reflect upon what I have just said or thought, I must concede that I am not (merely) a simple entity, but (also) an entity which says or thinks that it is a simple entity. In this particular case, there is reason to suppose that an entity which characterizes itself as simple is to that extent complex, and that an entity which characterizes itself as complex is to that extent simple. But it is also quite generally the case, for any predicate F, that if I characterize myself as F, I must be prepared to add that I am not merely F, but something which characterizes itself as F. Hegel does not explicitly formulate this argument, but it coheres in a loose way with his principle that to be aware of a limit is to transcend it, and with his view that the system of thoughts with which the self is identical is the product of reflection by each phase of thought on its immediate predecessor. It would, of course, follow from the argument that there are difficulties in the claim that I am a soul, a self or a mind: I am not, after all, only a self, but something that characterizes itself as a self. In the first place, however, the term 'self' or 'mind' is not an ordinary descriptive term on a par with 'stone', 'dog' or, on Hegel's view, 'complex', any more than the self is one thing among others.[19] Secondly, Hegel would not object to the conclusion that the self is also in some sense what is not the self. The very fact that the self is aware of what is not itself differentiates its relationship to other things from that of a stone to other things, and Hegel, as we shall see, would relish rather than reject the inference that it is related to them in an even stronger sense than this.[20] The argument then, as far as he is concerned, is not open to the *reductio ad absurdum* which first suggests itself.

A final consideration which probably influenced Hegel here is that the self has to employ concepts which contrast with each other, that of complexity as well as simplicity, of finitude as well as infinity, and so on. It might therefore be felt to be problematic if one such contrasting concept applies to the self to the exclusion of the other.[21] The problem might seem to vanish as soon as we distinguish between possessing or employing a concept and instantiating or exemplifying it. If I can apply the concepts of a stone and of a person while being a person and not a stone, why should my ability to apply the concept of simplicity have any bearing on the question whether I am simple, complex, neither or both? There may, of course, be arguments to such an effect in the case of particular concepts. Hegel might have argued, for example, that if I am to employ the concepts of infinity and of finitude, then I cannot be merely finite, that if I can apply the concept of complexity then I cannot be only simple or only complex, and so on. But any general argument to the effect that, if I can employ both a concept F and its contrary or contradictory, then neither one of them can be exclusively applicable to me is surely undercut by the distinction between employment and exemplification. It may be, however, that Hegel would have rejected this in the light of his belief that the self is the system of pure concepts, and not merely the possessor of them.[22] It is true that the distinction between employment and exemplification would reappear in the form of a distinction between those concepts which are contained in the system and those concepts which are applicable to the system as a whole. Such a distinction would seem to be required in the light of the fact, for example, that the system contains the concept of contingency as well as that of necessity,[23] since Hegel would surely wish to say that the system as a whole is necessary rather than contingent. Nevertheless it is not clear that he would have accepted such a contrast. He may have felt that the circularity of logic implies that there is a perfect match between the absolute idea and itself, that it applies to itself as a whole. In view of the importance of the ego in Hegel's system, we shall return to this point, as well as to others raised under this heading, later on.[24]

(iii) *'The world is infinite/finite.'* Hegel has two arguments against these propositions. The first of them is an objection to the thesis that the world is infinite, and not finite, in space and/or in time:[25]

> Here infinity is fixedly opposed to finitude, but it is easy to see that, if both are opposed to each other, infinity, which is yet supposed to be the whole, appears only as *one* side and is limited by the finite. A limited infinity, however, is itself only a finite entity (*Enz.* I. 28Z).

This apparently fallacious argument is of a type which occurs quite frequently in Hegel. We are told, for example, that if we form abstractly universal concepts, such as that of an animal, and distinguished them sharply from 'particular' concepts like that of a giraffe, then the universal will turn out to be just one particular alongside others (*Enz.* I. 80Z; *WL* II. p. 281, M. p. 606).[26] Such arguments involve a confusion of orders or levels. Universal, or generic, concepts may form a particular, or specific, type of concept co-ordinate with the particular type of particular concepts. But it does not follow from this that universal concepts are themselves merely particular concepts, that the concept of an animal, for example, is co-ordinate with that of a giraffe. Similarly it may be that the concept of infinity is co-ordinate with that of finitude and is therefore, in one of Hegel's senses, a finite concept. But it would not follow from this that an infinite thing is co-ordinate with finite ones, that it is really only finite. We would be making the same mistake, only in a more obvious way, if we were to infer from the fact that 'big' is a small word that big things are really only small.[27] Whether there is more to Hegel's argument than this suggests will be considered later, but *prima facie* it seems to rest on this simple error.[28]

This argument does not have the same force against the thesis that the world is only finite and not infinite, except in the sense that, if it implies that the concepts of finitude and infinity can be sharply detached from each other, it will raise problems for the concept of infinity. Hegel's reason for holding that the world is not merely finite is that there would, in that case, have to be something beyond it which bounded or limited it. Since the world as a whole cannot be bounded in this way, it must be infinite and, therefore, both infinite and finite. This conclusion is supported by the consideration that while

> we can go beyond any *determinate* space and also beyond any *determinate* time . . . it is no less correct that space and time are only actual through their determinacy (i.e. as *here* and *now*) and that this determinacy lies in their concept (*Enz.* I. 48Z).

This argument seems no better than the argument that the series 1,2,3,4, etc. is finite, as well as infinite, because each term in it is finite and any (finite) segment of it is finite. In effect Hegel believes that space and time are infinite. His assertion that they are equally finite depends on the uncontroversial point that they contain, or consist of, finite segments.[29]

The first of these arguments at least seems quite different in form from those employed with respect to God's existence and the simplicity or complexity of the soul. It was not suggested, for example, that if simplicity and complexity are sharply contrasted with each other, then simplicity becomes a sort of complexity or complexity becomes a sort of simplicity. Moreover, while Hegel does not doubt that some things exist and that some things are complex — in each case, finite things — the first argument would rule out any claim of the type 'x is infinite and not finite.' He does not believe that we can say of God, for example, that he is infinite and not finite.[30] The second argument does not, however, apply to *any* infinite entity in the same way. There is no obvious indication that God, like space or time, can be represented as an infinite series containing finite segments. The point of saying that God is both infinite and finite is presumably that he essentially generates, or particularizes himself into, finite things. But the discussion of this topic will be postponed until later.[31]

(iv) '*A person is free/governed by necessity.*' Hegel's predecessors, or at least those who primarily concerned him, had agreed that natural objects and processes are governed by necessity only, but they had differed as to whether or not people are exempt from necessity and are therefore free.[32] Hegel's answer, though not his argument for it, is not entirely dissimilar to his account of finitude and infinity. Just as some objects are merely finite, so some objects – roughly speaking, the same objects – are wholly governed by necessity. Minds, by contrast, are neither exclusively free nor exclusively necessitated in their workings; they are both free and necessitated:

> A freedom which had no necessity within itself, and a mere necessity without freedom, are abstract and thus untrue determinations. Freedom is essentially concrete, eternally determined within itself and thus at the same time necessary. When one speaks of necessity, one generally means by it primarily mere determination from without, as e.g. in finite mechanics a body moves only if it is struck by another body, and indeed in the direction imparted to it by this impact. This, however, is a merely external necessity, not truly inner necessity, for this is freedom (*Enz.* I. 35Z. Cf. 48Z, 158 and Z).

The argument is more plausible, if we think of necessity as determination and of freedom as *self*-determination.[33]

(v) '*There is evil in the world/Mankind is evil.*' Hegel's account of good and evil is different from his treatment of freedom and necessity, despite his inclination to assimilate them. He might have no objection to saying that, just as the self is both free and necessitated, so it, or the world, is both good and evil. But in this case, the opposed terms, 'good' and 'evil', are not on a par. 'Good' is the positive term, while 'evil' is negative and evil is in some sense fleeting and unreal:

> If we regard evil as something fixed and independent which is not the good, this is correct and the opposition is to be acknowledged in the sense that the apparent and relative character of the opposition is not to be taken as implying that good and evil are one in the absolute . . . that something becomes evil only through our view of it. But there is this much that is false, namely that one sees evil as a fixed positive element, while in fact it is the negative, which has no independent subsistence but only attempts to be independent and is in fact only the absolute shining (*Schein*) of negativity into itself (*Enz.* I. 35Z).

It is not true, that is, that good and evil and the difference between them lie only in the eye of the beholder, but this should not be taken to imply that evil exists on a par with good. As we shall see, this account of good and evil is formally similar to his account of infinity and finitude; finite things, like the evils with which they are sometimes equated, are less than wholly real.[34]

These, then, are some examples of Hegel's treatment of the 'one-sided' propositions attributed by him to his predecessors. This account of them has not, of course, been complete. The intention of this section has been only to convey the general nature of his strategy and some of the variations of his tactics in response to particular cases.

2 *Infinity and description*

Hegel's objections to the propositions considered in the preceding section depended for the most part on the fact that their predicates are members of contrasting pairs of concepts, each of which apparently excludes the application of the other. His solution in most cases was that both or neither of these concepts is applicable to the infinite entity in question. He has, however, a further objection to 'finite' concepts which does not depend on this feature of them and which cannot, therefore, be answered in the same way. It is that the nature of an infinite entity cannot be exhausted by the application to it of a finite number of finite concepts:

> Such predicates are *per se* a *restricted* content and already reveal themselves as inadequate to the *fulness of the conception* (of God, nature, mind, etc.) and in no way exhaustive .... The orientals sought to remedy [this] defect, e.g. in the determination of God, by the many *names* which they assigned to him; but still the names were supposed to be *infinite* in number (*Enz.* I. 29. Cf. *VPR* II. pp. 224 f., S.S. III. pp. 13 f.).

The force of this criticism does not depend on a predicate's having a contradictory or a contrary. We could, if that were the case, remedy the situation by describing God not simply as, for example, necessary, but as both free and necessary. Our description of him would then be seemingly contradictory, but it would at least be finite in length. It is clear, however, that to characterize an infinite entity as both free and necessary would, according to Hegel's argument, still leave an infinite number of things to be said about it. We have not yet said, for example, that it is both simple and complex. The argument points to the fact that such concepts are

165

finite not only in the sense that they have an opposite or a negation, but that they, together with their opposites, embrace less than the whole of the field of thought.

One immediate objection to Hegel's argument is that it applies with equal force to finite entities. It may be that a finite object cannot be fully described by a finite number of predicates; the case for saying that it cannot is strengthened if a complete account of it is to include a statement of all its relational properties. Yet in this respect Hegel contrasts finite things with infinite ones:

> Now with finite things it is indeed the case that they must be determined by finite predicates, and here the understanding (*Verstand*) is in its rightful sphere with its activity . . . . If I call e.g. an action a *theft*, then it is thereby determined in accordance with its essential content and to know this is enough for the judge. Similarly finite things are related as *cause* and *effect*, as *force* and *expression*, and when they are grasped in these determinations, they are then known in their finitude (*Enz.* I. 28Z).

He recognizes elsewhere, however, that the characterization of an action is not a simple matter. No act of theft is only an act of theft. It can always be described in an indefinite number of other ways, as, for example, satisfying the needs of oneself and one's dependents or as preventing the victim of the theft from misusing his property (*Enz.* I. 121Z; *WL* II. pp. 105 ff., M. pp. 463 ff.).

One reply to this might be that the number of predicates required for the complete description of a finite object or event is, though very large, not infinite. The variety of possible descriptions of it will present difficulties when we are trying to decide whether to punish or condemn the action or not. For then we will need to know which description is the essential or relevant one, whether it is to be regarded, for example, as a violation of property or as an act of charity or of self-preservation.[35] But if our purpose is simply to describe the action, we are not faced with such a choice and, if the possible descriptions are finite in number and in length, we can just produce them all. Since, however, Hegel generally discusses this matter from the point of view of punishment or condemnation rather than of disinterested description, he does not indicate whether he would accept this reply or not.

A second reply is that in the case of a finite event or object we can select from the possible true descriptions of it, whether they are infinite in number or not, one or more which are especially important. Thus in the case of an act of theft, Hegel remarks that, among all its diverse features, 'the violation of property which has here taken place is the decisive point of view (*der entscheidende Gesichtspunkt*), before which the others must give way' (*Enz.* I. 121Z). But how are we to determine which of the many possible points of view is the decisive one? On any particular occasion, of course, what we choose to say about something will depend on our interests and purposes. But that 'the violation of property . . . is the decisive point of view' seems not to depend, by Hegel's account, on the interests and purposes of the thief and of his victim or even on those of the probable beneficiaries and probable victims of acts of theft in general. It is determined rather by the larger social and political framework in the context of which the action occurs. It might be objected that this answer simply removes the problem to an earlier stage. For even if we grant that a certain true description of the backcloth against which an action occurs, of human society, determines the point of view from which that action is to be regarded, there are as many possible ways of describing a society as there are of describing an action, and different views of society may suggest that different features of an action be regarded as essential or decisive. Proudhon, for example, did not see what are commonly regarded as acts of theft in the same light as Hegel did,[36] and this is because he did not view society in the same way as he did, emphasizing features of it which Hegel underplayed and underplaying aspects which Hegel stressed. Such differences are not always open to empirical settlement, nor would Hegel accept the answer that the account we give of society is to be decided by men's interests and purposes. He would reject the implication that what interests and purposes men have is independent of their social life, and that it is ascertainable independently of our account of their social life.[37] His own answer seems to be that the description we give of society, or for that matter of nature, is determined ultimately by logic. The conceptual system of the *Logic*, of which we can give a single, non-arbitrary account, articulates our descriptions of the natural and social world. Thus it determines, through the intermediary of an account of human society, the decisive point of view from which a particular act of theft is to be regarded. In a not dissimilar way, it determines which of the many things that can be said about a flash of lightning are the important ones to say about it. It is, however, beyond the scope of this chapter to say how this is achieved.[38]

If we can find some non-arbitrary way of selecting the appropriate things to say about finite objects and events, why can we not do the same for infinite entities without resorting to complete and therefore infinite accounts of them? Why can we not, for example, select for description those aspects of God which suit our purposes and interests or discover the decisive point of view from which he is to be regarded? The general answer to this seems to be that infinite entities are what underlie and legitimate our descriptions of finite ones, that infinite objects transcend our interests and points of view. They cannot therefore themselves be described only in accordance with our interests or seen from one point of view among others. One might feel, for example, that since the self is that which has interests and takes a point of view, is, as it were, the repository of interests and of possible points of view, it is inappropriate to give such a selective account of it. The case of God, however, is perhaps a better one. Firstly, God is, on Hegel's account, not simply an entity which we need to describe, but is, in some sense, the whole system of possible conceptual frameworks for describing things. When we attempt to describe some finite entity or range of finite entities, it is from this system that we need to make a selection on some criterion or other. If our selection is to be a fully rational one, we must have some characterization of this system of possibilities and this characterization cannot, on pain of an infinite regress, be itself a selective one, dependent on our interests or on some other criterion by which we single out the decisive point of view from which to regard it. The range of possible points of view, that is, cannot itself be seen only from one point of view. Secondly, God himself supplies the criterion for our selection of one of these descriptive frameworks for our account of particular finite entities. God, for example, explains why men have the interests and purposes they do and it is by reference to him that we can justify some of them as representing the decisive point of view in particular cases. Again, on pain of an infinite regress, we cannot see our criterion for choosing a point of view only from a point of view. Less formally, God is conceived by Hegel as the essence of the world, as the world as it is in itself. Men see the world from various perspectives or points of view. But the point of postulating God is lost if he is seen only from a point of view or if he himself represents only one way of viewing things among others. The philosopher or the theologian purports to dig beneath our purposes and interests, our selective descriptions and points of view, to the reality that underlies them.[39]

God, then, performs a variety of functions in Hegel's system and all of them imply that a complete, perspectiveless account of him is required. More will be said later about how he, God, manages to fulfil them all.[40] The problem for the moment, however, is that even if we grant that a complete description of an infinite entity is desirable, no way of providing it has yet been shown. How could we give a description of infinite length? The answer is, of course, that Hegel has revised the notion of infinity, so that it no longer implies an infinite regress, but is a surveyable, circular infinity.[41] Whether we regard God as an entity which we describe or simply as the system of concepts or conceptual frameworks presented in the *Logic*, he is not something that goes on and on forever, but a circle, the description of which can be, as far as this goes, complete. But, even so, can it be complete? We have already argued that it may not be possible to give a complete account of a finite entity and, from this point of view, a circular entity is on a par with any finite one. We may grant that God, on Hegel's view, is identical with the conceptual system(s) of the *Logic* or at least that he cannot have properties which go beyond logic.[42] But what guarantee is there that we have said, or even can say, everything that there is to be said about this logical system? Hegel supposes that the system as a whole cannot but be adequate to characterize itself, that at the end of the *Logic* at least we arrive at a self-characterizing system, but it does not follow from this that all the implications of the system are revealed to us, any more than one's belief that the English language can be fully described in the English language entitles one to assume that one knows everything about the English language. Hegel himself may have been misled by the circularity of his system, as well as by his conviction that he is a mere spectator of its unravelling, into believing that his account of it must be complete. He occasionally concedes that it may not be so in minor respects,[43] but presumably he would argue that, since it is constructed and articulated in the course of thinking itself, its essential features must be accessible to the thinker, in much the way in which the essential character of an intentional action, its plan or intention, is accessible to the agent. Like any formal system, that of the *Logic* may have properties which surprise its originator, but these properties are logical consequences of its essential features, of the plan of its construction, and cannot be inaccessible to thought itself.

The essence of this reply is that the characterization of a formal system cannot, and need not, be partial and selective in the way that our account of the entities to which we apply it is. The problems of describing it and of discovering its implications are different from those of deciding the scope of its application, whether it is appropriately applied to some range of entities, and so on. Hegel's more surprising claims that his system is unique, that it is, as it were, the system of all possible conceptual systems, that it is guaranteed to capture the essential features of any area to which it is applied, and that it is, in effect, God, are considered elsewhere.

3 *Concepts and truth*

So far we have stressed the variety of Hegel's criticisms of the application of 'finite' concepts to infinite entities. Underlying all his particular objections, however, there is a general belief that finite concepts or categories are suitable only for finite entities, whereas infinite objects require infinite thoughts. We can see readily enough why certain finite concepts are inapplicable to an entity such as God. To say that God is a cause, for example, or *the* cause of everything, would imply in normal usage that there was an effect which was distinct from God and on which his status as a cause in some sense depended (cf. *WL* II. pp. 222 ff., M. pp. 558 ff.). Again Hegel rejects Herder's view that God is a force, for the reason that a force 'requires solicitation from without, acts blindly and because of this deficiency of form the content too is limited and contingent' (*Enz.* I. 136).[44] Hegel believes, however, not simply that some concepts suggest that what they are applied to is finite, but that these concepts together with the others that we have considered share a single defect, that of finitude, in virtue of which they are unsuitable for infinite entities.

No single, clear account of why this should be so is given, but some of the best discussions of it occur in the course of Hegel's explanations of truth.[45] Truth, in his sense, is more or less co-extensive with infinity, and in the following passage the terms are interchanged:

In the philosophical sense, truth means . . . agreement of a content with itself . . . . The deeper (philosophical) meaning of truth is in part already found in ordinary usage. Thus one speaks e.g. of a *true* friend and understands by this one whose mode of conduct conforms to the concept of friendship; likewise one speaks of a *true* work of art. Untrue then amounts to bad, inadequate within itself. In this sense a bad state (*Staat*) is an untrue state, and badness and untruth consist in general in the contradiction which obtains between the determination [or 'definition', *Bestimmung*] or the concept and the existence of the object . . . . God alone is the genuine agreement of concept and reality; but all finite things have an untruth in them, they have a concept and an existence which is inadequate to their concept. They must therefore pass away, and this manifests the inadequacy of their concept and their existence. The animal as an individual has its concept in its genus, and the genus frees itself from individuality by death.

The consideration of truth in the sense here explained, agreement with itself, constitutes the proper concern of logic . . . .

The business of logic can also be said to be to examine thought-determinations, to see how far they are capable of grasping the true. The question is therefore what are the forms of the infinite and what are the forms of the finite. In ordinary consciousness one finds no problem in finite thought-determinations and lets them pass without further ado. But all deception stems from thinking and acting in accordance with finite determinations (*Enz.* I. 24Z. 2; cf. 172 and Z; 213 and Z).

This passage does not directly explain what it is for a concept, category or thought-determination to be true or untrue. It is primarily concerned with the truth-value of things or objects. Ordinarily we suppose that some finite things, e.g. some friends, are true (friends), while others are not. Hegel gives even here two distinct accounts of what the untruth of a friend or of a work of art consists in, that, firstly, it disagrees with its concept and, secondly, it disagrees with itself or is in some way internally discordant. These accounts clearly need not coincide. Something that purports to be a friend or a work or art but fails to live up to the ideal embodied in the concept of a friend or a work of art need not be internally discordant nor, incidentally, need its life be briefer than that of a true friend or work of art. But in any case, Hegel's main point is that in the strict sense no finite entity, even a true friend or a true work of art, is true. What he has in mind is presumably this. Any finite object is environed and influenced by other finite objects. They are causally responsible for its coming into and passing out of existence and for many of the properties which it has. In the case of a finite object, therefore, such as a particular elephant, we cannot explain its existence or its particular features, e.g. the precise length of its trunk or the loss of a tusk, by reference to its concept, to the mere fact that it is an elephant. Its existence depends in part on the activities of other elephants and the particular features which it has are determined by the influence of other finite things. In the case of infinite entities, by contrast − God, for example, or the world as a whole − the object and its concept must coincide, or at least there is no reason for them not to. For there can be nothing outside an infinite entity to produce, influence or destroy it in ways that are not determined by the concept of it. God will not have particular features which are not contained in his concept. All truths about God, we might say, are analytic. He will be everlasting, for there can be nothing to explain his coming into or passing out of existence.[46] Moreover the ontological argument is applicable to God, though not to finite entities. Given the concept of an elephant

171

alone, we cannot infer the existence of some particular elephant, Jumbo, or even of any elephants at all. For causal conditions are required for the existence of elephants and of Jumbo, conditions which may or may not obtain. But no such conditions are either necessary or possible in the case of God's existence, so that there is nothing to prevent us from inferring his existence from his concept alone.[47]

It may seem odd that, having assessed the truth-value of things in terms of their conformity to concepts, Hegel goes on to give a parallel account of the truth-value of concepts. One would expect that, if the truth-value of a thing depends on its agreement or disagreement with its concept, the truth of the concept itself would not be in question. How can a test show that a candidate is defective, unless the test itself is not relevantly defective? The answer seems to be that some tests are such that no candidate could possibly pass them, that some concepts, finite ones, are such that no entity could perfectly conform to them. There not only is not, but could not be, an elephant which depended on nothing else for its existence and its properties. But what does it mean to say that a concept is true or untrue, infinite or finite? The passage is unhelpful here, for it gives or implies at least four different accounts of this. If the truth-value of a concept or thought-determination is parallel to that of a thing, then we must say either that:

1. A concept is true if and only if it agrees with itself, and is otherwise untrue,

or

2. A concept is true if and only if it agrees with *its* concept, and is otherwise untrue.

In the second half of the passage, however, an account is given which implies that the truth-value of a concept is not parallel to that of an object, but depends rather on the objects to which it is applicable:

3. A concept is true if and only if it is 'capable of grasping the true' or is a 'form of the infinite', otherwise it is untrue. Intertwined with this is the suggestion that concepts are true or untrue in the same way as objects are:

4. A concept is true if and only if it is infinite, otherwise it is untrue.

These four, apparently distinct, accounts of the truth of a concept are not the result only of careless writing. The features which they express are deeply embedded in Hegel's concepts of infinity and finitude. An example of his treatment of a finite concept in the *Logic* will illustrate this.

4 *Wholes, parts and falsity*

The concepts which Hegel examines in his criticism of pre-Kantian metaphysics are, as we have seen, for the most part pairs of concepts each of which is the apparent contrary or contradictory of the other. But while all of the concepts considered in the *Logic*, except the final one, the absolute idea, are finite, they are not in general concepts of this type, or at any rate this is not the aspect of them that Hegel emphasizes. Many of them indeed form pairs, especially those in the second Book of the *Logic*, the 'Doctrine of Essence', but the members of them are not usually such as to exclude, even apparently, the application of each other. The concept of a cause, for example, is tied to that of an effect,[48] but there is no such paradox in supposing that one and the same event can be both a cause and an effect, as there is in holding that something is both simple and complex. Of those concepts which do not fall into pairs, there is little inclination to suppose that they are incompatible with each other. The concept of being, for example, applies to everything. Concepts which occur later in the series, those of qualitative determinacy, for example, of quantity, or of causality do not exclude the application of each other and they apply to at least some of the things that 'are'.

Why, then, are such concepts finite rather than infinite? One answer is that it is because each concept is different from the others in the system and is determined by its relationships to them, by its place within the system.[49] Each concept, except perhaps the last, embraces less than the whole of the realm of pure thought. Sometimes Hegel suggests that for a concept to be finite is for it to be regarded as separated from other concepts 'by an infinite chasm' (*Enz.* I. 32Z); that if we treat apparently opposing concepts like those of freedom and necessity not as exclusive, but as jointly applicable, and if we treat different concepts like those of quality and quantity not as simply different, but as derivable from each other, then they cease to be finite and become infinite. But his considered view seems to be that such concepts are still finite even when they are treated in the proper manner. As we have seen, to say that something is both F and non-F is not necessarily to say everything that is to be said about it. And to derive one concept from another, to treat its boundaries as fluid, is not to show that it is all-inclusive, that it is the only concept there is. In the case of a particular concept, Hegel's treatment purports to demonstrate its finitude rather than remedy it. It is only the system as a whole, the 'logical idea', which is infinite and not any particular segment of it.[50]

Hegel does not, however, content himself with showing that every concept is finite in this sense, that it is, as it were, bounded by, and spills over into, other concepts in the system. Any finite concept is, in addition, internally defective or discordant, and it is these internal defects that enable us to proceed from one concept to another, rather as we are able to construct negative numbers owing to the deficiencies of positive ones. An example of this is the concept of a whole consisting of parts. The concept is a finite one, not primarily because there is some concept which contrasts with it and excludes its application, but because it is simply one concept among others. It is also, however, in 'disagreement with itself' or internally discordant. The defect or 'contradiction' is not, on the face of it, a very disturbing one, but this does not impair its merits as an illustration. The problem is that

(i) A whole must both be a whole and contain parts. But this, on Hegel's view, involves two conflicting requirements:

(ii) If the parts are to be genuine parts, then they must be parted or divided from each other

(iii) If the whole is to be a genuine whole, the parts must not be divided from one another, but together and contiguous (*Enz.* I. 135; *WL* II. pp. 166 ff., M. pp. 513 ff.).

The concept of a whole consisting of parts is then, on this view, internally inconsistent. Hegel seems, however, in line with his account of the untruth of objects, to have attempted to represent this inconsistency as a conflict between the concept and its exemplification:

> The relation of whole and parts is *untrue* to the extent that its concept and reality do not correspond to each other. The concept of the whole is to contain parts; but if the whole is posited as what it is by its concept, if it is divided, it ceases to be a whole (*Enz.* I. 135Z).

But what does this distinction between concept and reality amount to? One possibility is that the concept is that of a whole consisting of parts, while the reality is actual wholes. But, if that is so, the passage is misleading. For we do not need to examine or manipulate actual wholes in order to discover this flaw in the concept. Another possibility is that the concept is the concept of the concept of a whole consisting of parts while the reality is

174

simply the concept of a whole consisting of parts. But if this is so, it is unclear what the concept of the concept is supposed to be other than the concept itself. The text associates the first requirement, (ii), with the reality, and the second, (iii), with the concept. But this is clearly arbitrary. The division of the parts, with the consequent disappearance of the whole, is regarded as the reality; but it could just as well be the cohesion of the whole with the consequent disappearance of the parts. If there is any distinction to be drawn between the concept of a whole and the concept of this concept, it can only be the distinction between, on the one hand, the general account of what it is to be a whole, (i), and, on the other, the conflicting requirements, (ii) and (iii), implicit in (i). As it is the concept-reality distinction hovers uneasily between the two possible distinctions referred to: that between the concept of a whole and actual wholes and that between the concept of the concept of a whole and the concept of a whole. This probably reflects the fact that Hegel has not made up his mind about the answers to two questions: 'Does the truth of anything consist in its agreement with itself or in its agreement with its concept?' and 'Is a concept untrue in a way parallel to that in which things are untrue or is it untrue because no thing can agree with it?' Without an answer to these questions, no clear account can be given of the internal defects of this or any other concept. At all events, however, the *Logic* proceeds from here to the concept of a force (*Enz.* I. 136). The distinction between a whole and its parts re-emerges as the distinction between a simple force and its complex expression or manifestation. This concept in turn is of course found wanting (*Enz.* I. 137), but it does not suffer from the same defect as its predecessor. The 'contradictions' within concepts are, so to speak, the nuts and bolts which hold them together and are thus intimately connected with their finitude.[51]

Hegel has attempted to show, then, that the concept of a whole containing parts is finite in more than one sense. But even if he has succeeded in this, has he thereby shown that the concept is not applicable to infinite entities, that it is not 'capable of grasping the true'? The answer to this is unclear. One might suppose that, if he has detected a genuine inconsistency in the concept, then he has established that it is not applicable to anything, finite or infinite. But Hegel does not draw this conclusion: 'There are indeed things which correspond to this relation, but they are also for that very reason merely lowly and untrue existences' (*Enz.* I. 135Z). All that follows from its deficiency is that it is not applicable, or at least not applicable alone, to higher types of entity such as plants, animals, minds and presumably deities: 'The limbs and organs e.g. of a living body are not to be seen merely as parts' (*Ibid.*). Why a defective concept can still be applied selectively and how we are to decide where to apply it are questions to be considered later.[52] It is enough for the moment that an argument which establishes that a finite concept is unsuitable for some finite things, as well as for infinite ones, cannot establish the connection we require between the infinity of concepts and the infinity of things. Some further attempts to do so will be considered in the following section.

5 *From the concept of infinity to the infinite concept*

It would be tempting to conclude that Hegel's belief that infinite objects require infinite concepts rests on no more than a confusion between the concept of infinity and the infinite concept.[53] But it would be uncharitable to do so before considering some further arguments that he has, or might have, adduced in support of this belief. At least four such arguments suggest themselves:

(i) If a finite entity is an entity which is bounded and conditioned by entities other than itself, then a concept or a thought-determination might be finite in either or both of two ways. It might, firstly, be bounded by other concepts, either because it is opposed to them or because it is simply different from them. Secondly, it might be bounded by the things to which it applies or by the empirical data which are required for our application of it. Any concept which does not alone guarantee its own exemplification or determine the particular features of its instances will be finite in this sense.[54] We have already seen that if an object is infinite or true, then its concept must be infinite in this second sense. For an infinite entity is one which perfectly matches its concept. This, however, simply shifts the problem elsewhere. For why should a concept which is infinite in this second sense be infinite also in the first sense? What reason is there to suppose that, if a concept alone did guarantee the existence and nature of an object, then it would be exempt from bounding and conditioning by other concepts? If this question is to be answered, some further argument is required.[55]

(ii) If an object is infinite, if, that is, the concept of that object fully determines its nature and existence, then there is some pressure to identify the concept with the object. But if we are to identify them, it might be argued, then the concept too must be infinite, for otherwise it would differ in its properties from the object. This argument is valid. If an infinite entity is a concept, then the concept cannot be only a finite one. It is not, however, clear that if an entity is true or infinite in Hegel's sense, then we must identify it with its concept in such a way that whatever is true of the one is true of the other. This may of course have been one of the considerations which led Hegel to identify God with the system of concepts of the *Logic*, but even if we accept this, there may still be a distinction of sorts between this infinite system and the perhaps finite concepts which are applicable to it.[56] It is no doubt true that if an entity is infinite, then it must include or embrace the concept of finitude, for example, as well as that of infinity, but it needs to be argued that there is more reason to suppose that it could not include concepts which are not applicable to it than there is to hold that I cannot possess concepts which I do not exemplify. The English language contains the word 'French' as well as the word 'English', but it is nevertheless English and not French.

(iii) Some concepts are finite in the sense that they have a contradictory or a contrary. But, it might be argued, if anything is F — or if it makes sense to say that something is F — then there must be something — or it must make sense to say that there is something — which is non-F. If, therefore, the infinite is F, there will be — or it will make sense to say that there is — something which is non-F and which is distinct from the infinite. But if that is so, the infinite will be, or might have been, bounded by something other than itself. It will also be dependent upon it, at least in the sense that it could not be, or at least be said to be, F unless what is non-F existed or might have existed. But then the infinite is no longer infinite. The answer to this, however, is that, even if the general principle is accepted, there seems to be no reason why what is non-F, e.g. non-infinite, should not be included in what is F, e.g. infinite, distinct from it only in the way in which a part is distinct from the whole which contains it. It does not follow that the concept of non-F-ness is similarly included in that of F-ness, that the concept of infinity contains that of finitude. Or, at any rate, such inclusion as there is need only license the inference from:

x is F

to:

There is something, y, which is non-F,

and not that from:

x is F

to:

x is non-F.

(iv) Hegel has a deeply entrenched belief that the relationships between concepts mirror the relationships between things. He

177

perhaps owes something here to Spinoza: 'The order and connection of ideas is the same as the order and connection of things.'[57] A striking application of this doctrine occurs in Hegel's discussion of how we should divide a genus into species, of the principle of classification we should adopt. One answer to this is that it does not matter what we take as the distinguishing marks (*Merkmale*) of a species as long as they enable us to recognize members of that species when we encounter them. If that were so, then it presumably would not matter either what species we chose to recognize. The only requirements would be that our classification should be consistent and useful. Hegel rejects this view. He often remarks that humans are the only creatures with lobes to their ears,[58] and that, if the selection of distinguishing marks were an arbitrary matter, we could pick this entirely inessential feature as the defining feature of humanity (*Enz.* II 246Z). He does not add that we might, on this account, not count humans as a single species at all, but regard those of them who lack ear-lobes as constituting a different species – presumably because he takes it for granted that creatures which reproduce, and are reproduced by, each other form a single species. This is not, however, always taken for granted and indeed cannot be in non-biological cases. The question answered in the following passage seems to be as much: 'What species should we recognize?' as 'How should we define those species which we do recognize?'[59]

> In the case e.g. of animals the instruments for eating, teeth and claws, are used as a far-reaching ground of division in systems of classification; at first they are taken only as aspects in which the marks (*Merkmale*) can be more easily distinguished for the purpose of subjective cognition. But in fact those organs involve not only a distinguishing which belongs to an external reflection, but they are the point of vitality of the animal individuality, where it posits itself in contrast to the other of external nature as an individuality which relates itself to itself and separates itself from continuity with the other. In the case of the plant, the fertilizing organs constitute that highest point of vegetable life, whereby it points to the transition to sexual difference and thus to individual individuality (*in die individuelle Einzelheit*) (*WL* II. p. 526, M. pp. 805 f.).

The idea is that there are parts or features of organisms by means of which they enter into a conflict with their environment, a conflict which both sustains them and marks them off as distinct individuals. These features are assumed to differ from species to species and can thus be taken as the distinguishing marks of species. There is, then, a sort of parallel between actual animals and our concepts of them. Giraffes, both as a species and as individuals, are finite entities, bounded, and in part determined, by other species and individuals. They protect themselves by means of their hooves and attack other organisms with their teeth, thus marking themselves off as a distinct species and/or distinct individuals. Similarly the concept of a giraffe is a finite concept, bounded, and in part determined, by other concepts. It distinguishes itself from other concepts, that of a lion for example, by reference to the teeth and hooves of the giraffe. Hegel clearly wishes to give a similar account of other concept-ranges, arguing for example that the conceptual relationships between our concepts of red, blue, yellow, etc. mirror the physical relationships between actual red, blue and yellow things (*Enz.* I. 42Z. 1).[60] If the parallel were an exact one, it would be natural to infer that in order to grasp the infinite entity, the entity which embraces all finite ones, we need the infinite concept, the concept which similarly embraces all finite concepts.

The parallel, however, is quite imperfect. Hegel's selection of teeth and claws is not wholly arbitrary. It is true that other features of animals, their skin and fur for example, protect them from external invasion, but they do not require any aggressive activity on the part of the animal. But there are, apart from this, two main difficulties. Firstly, there is in the case of things a distinction between the species and the individual for which the case of concepts provides no obvious analogue. There is, on the face of it, only one concept of a giraffe and not a different one for each giraffe – or, at any rate, Hegel shows little sign of favouring the Leibnizian doctrine that there is.[61] As we shall see, he is sometimes inclined to deny or downgrade the individual,[62] but in this context he perhaps overstresses it. For the species is defined in terms of those features by which individual members of it distinguish and assert themselves as individuals rather than of those by means of which the species as such distinguishes and maintains itself. In the light of this, it is unclear whether the parallel is meant to be between individuals and concepts or between sets of individuals and concepts or, confusedly, both.

Secondly, although concepts are related to each other and things are related to each other, their relationships are not parallel. Individual animals are brought to an end and, despite Hegel's tendency to equate species with concepts (*Enz.* I. 24Z. 1 and 2), so are species. Concepts are not destroyed or, at least, not by each other and not in the way that animals and species are.[63] Individual

179

animals, again, do not interact only with the things suggested by our conceptual system. The conceptual neighbours of giraffes are lions, tigers, zebras and so on. But giraffes may be dispatched by other giraffes or by entities that are conceptually quite remote from them like fire and flood. In the simpler case of the colour spectrum, a colour or an object of a certain colour is characteristically environed by objects of different colours. Moreover, if an object changes its colour, then the colour it had must be supplanted by some other colour. But the change in colour is not produced by the colour which replaces it nor, necessarily, by any other object in virtue of its colour. Colours may be changed by things conceptually distant from them, such as scraping. For the interactions between things do not mirror the relationships between our concepts. Since, however, the parallel breaks down even at the level of finite things and concepts, there is little temptation to suppose that it entitles us to infer that infinite entities require an infinite concept.

6 *Truth and predication*

Hegel often speaks as if the appropriate thing to do with infinite concepts, when we find them, is to predicate them of infinite entities. But this is misleading. For, as we have seen, he believes that an infinite entity ultimately is concepts, and not a subject to which we apply them. One of the routes by which he reaches this position is his criticism of predication or the propositional form as such. Some of his objections are intimately connected with his aversion to finite concepts, for they are directed primarily against the predication of finite concepts. It is these objections which will be considered in this section.

One of them occurs in the course of his discussion of truth. It might seem odd, Hegel concludes, to inquire about the truth of thought-determinations. On the ordinary view, the question of truth does not arise until concepts are applied to 'given objects', for truth is regarded as the 'agreement of an object with our conception' (*Enz.* I. 24Z. 2). We have already seen that Hegel uses the word 'true' in a different sense from this. But, he argues, to regard judgments of this sort as true is not simply to use the word 'true' in a distinct, i.e. the usual, sense. It also embodies a philosophical mistake:

> It is one of the most essential logical prejudices that such
> judgments as 'The rose is red' or ' — is not red' can contain
> truth. They can be *correct* (*richtig*), i.e. in the restricted circle

of perception, of finite conception and thinking; this depends on the content, which is likewise a finite content which is in itself (*für sich*) untrue. But truth depends only on the form, i.e. the posited concept and the reality corresponding to it; but such truth is not to be found in the qualitative judgment (*Enz.* I. 172).

Two distinct reasons are given for this. The first is that the subject of such a judgment does not agree with or measure up to its concept and is therefore untrue in Hegel's sense.[64] This is obvious in the case of judgments about sick men, acts of theft and false friends. But, on Hegel's view, any finite entity falls short of its concept. Any rose, and not simply diseased or defective ones, falls short of the concept of a rose. Any judgment about a finite entity is therefore untrue (*Enz.* I. 172Z).

The reply to this might be that Hegel is simply using the word 'true' in a different sense, and the fact that an entity is not true in his sense does nothing to establish that a judgment about it is untrue in his or any other sense. But his second criticism goes some way towards meeting this objection. It is that the rose has many other features besides redness and many other things besides this rose are red, so that in the judgment 'This rose is red' the subject and the predicate do not coincide: 'such an individual quality does not correspond to the concrete nature of the subject' (*Enz.* I. 172). It is not quite clear whether this argument depends on regarding 'This rose is red' as an identity statement, purporting to say that this rose is (identical with) redness, just as 'Thera is Santorini' says that Thera is identical with Santorini. If it does, then Hegel reaches this conclusion by a roundabout route. He first extracts from the judgment 'This rose is red' the judgment 'The individual is a particular [quality].' He then interprets this as asserting that the individual is a (or the) particular and implies, rightly, that this judgment is false (*Ibid.*; *WL* II. pp. 311 ff., M. pp. 631 ff.). But of course the judgment 'This rose is red' does not entail the false judgment 'The individual is a particular.' If the latter expression represents its logical form, then *either* 'the individual' and 'a particular' are to be understood as variables, indicating what sort of words are to replace them — but, in that case, the words 'The [individual] is [a particular]' do not express a judgment at all, but only the form of a judgment like 'x is F'; *or* the expression is to be read as saying 'The individual exemplifies or is qualified by a particular' — but in this case there is no special reason for regarding the judgment as false. Since this is so, the truth of a qualitative judgment is not impaired by the fact that it entails a judgment of this type. Its subject and its predicate do indeed fail to coincide, and this may make such judgments unsuitable for infinite entities.[65] But unless a judgment purports to assert the identity or coincidence of its subject and predicate, their failure to coincide cannot be a reason for denying its truth.

These two criticisms of the qualitative judgment are quite distinct. Hegel tends to conflate them, in part because he concentrates on judgments like 'This body is sick' (*Enz.* I. 172Z), where the predicate both ascribes to the body a feature in respect of which it falls short of its concept — that of a body or that of life — and fails to present a complete description of it which applies uniquely to it. The first of these defects concerns the relationship between the body and its concept; neither this concept nor the respect in which the body falls short of it need be presented in the judgment itself. The second concerns the relationship between the subject and the predicate of the judgment. Even if an entity is infinite and in perfect accord with its concept, a judgment about it, such as 'God is good', would still fail to secure the coincidence of the subject and the predicate. Characteristically, Hegel is attempting to establish a connection between the defectiveness of a thought-determination, in this case the form of the qualitative judgment, and the defectiveness of the entities to which it applies.[66] He has, so far, failed to show the connection.

There are, however, further arguments purporting to show that the predicative judgment is peculiarly inappropriate for infinite objects. One argument or set of arguments is contained in such remarks as these:

> the procedure [of the pre-Kantian metaphysicans] consisted in the *attribution* of predicates to the object to be known, thus e.g. to God. But this is then an external reflection (*äusserliche Reflexion*) about the object, for the determinations (the predicates) are ready-made in my conception and are attributed to the object only externally. On the contrary, genuine knowledge of an object must be such that the object determines itself out of itself and does not acquire its predicates from without (*Enz.* I. 28).

A similar criticism is made in the following paragraph:

> [the predicates are] combined with one another in virtue of being predicates of *one* subject, but they are diverse in their content, so that they are received from *without in relation to each other* (so dass sie *gegeneinander* von *aussen* heraufgenommen werden) (*Enz.* I. 29).

It is easy to misunderstand this argument. It might be supposed, for example, that Hegel is assuming that when I predicate F-ness of some object, x, then I conceive myself as making x to be F, as conferring F-ness on x 'from without'. This assumption would clearly be false. To say that x is F is generally to say what x is like, and may have been like for some time already, independently of one's making this statement about it; it is not to confer F-ness upon it. The words 'external reflection' might also suggest the argument that, to predicate F-ness of x, I, the predicator, must be distinct from and outside x, the subject of predication. But I cannot be distinct from and outside God, for in that case God would be finite, simply one thing among others, and I cannot be distinct from my own self. The first of these propositions, however, is false. I can apply predicates to a group of which I am a member, saying that it has, for example, 32 members, including myself. It is perhaps true that my doing so implies that I distance myself psychologically to some degree from the group, but it is not obvious that Hegel would object to the implication that I can distance myself psychologically from God and even from myself. Again, it may be that I cannot describe exhaustively by means of predicative judgments a group of which I am a member, since my successive judgments, or judgings, about the group are themselves features of the group. This, however, seems more in keeping with other passages than with these.[67] It does not entail, in any case, that I cannot appropriately apply *any* predicates to a group to which I belong.

What Hegel means is, rather, this. When I make predicative judgments about a lump of sugar, saying for example that it is cubical, rough, sweet, white and soluble, I do not establish any connection between these predicates or the corresponding properties, apart from the fact that they belong to one and the same thing. Indeed I cannot do so, for colour, shape and texture are independent variables. We might suppose that in the case of some of its properties there is a deep connection between them, their conjunction being explicable by the underlying nature of sugar. But not all its properties depend on this. Its cubical shape, for example, depends on the whims of the manufacturer and has nothing to do with the intrinsic properties of sugar. One strand in Hegel's thought is that the properties of a mere thing depend on its relationships to other things,[68] and, if this is so, any connection between them can only be remote. To the extent, moreover, that the properties of a thing are disparate, we are encouraged to draw a distinction between the properties and the thing underlying them.[69] The judgment-form, 'x is F', reflects this distinction.

When Hegel discusses pre-Kantian theology, he ascribes to it the view that God has properties and that these depend on his various relationships to the world (*Enz.* I. 36).[70] If this were so, then we could predicate of God goodness, wisdom, power and so on, without establishing any connection between these predicates. We might, moreover, distinguish between God as he is in himself and the properties conferred on him by his relationships to the world. But this, Hegel implies, cannot be the way in which God's character is determined, for there can be nothing distinct from God to which he is related and with which he interacts. If he is determinate at all, he must be self-determining and, if this is so, each aspect of him must be explicable in terms of himself, of his nature or, perhaps, his concept. God, like the ego, is 'absolute actuosity'.[71] Consequently, no aspect or feature of him can be flatly different from any other aspect or feature of him, but must be intrinsically connected with it. What are we to do about this? Hegel tends to speak as if we should simply leave God in peace to develop his own nature, while we, so to speak, watch. But this, as we have seen, is misleading. It is hard to see how we can entirely escape the position of 'external reflection'. What we can do is examine what are generally taken to be predicates of God — in effect, the thought-determinations — to see what their intrinsic connections with each other are. Hegel's conception of pure thoughts as fluid and derivable from each other is in part intended to answer a theological problem about the nature of an infinite God. But once we have done this, there is still no question of predicating these concepts, even the whole system, of God, for that would imply a distinction between God and his properties, a distinction which in his case has no basis. The conclusion, then, is that God is not something to which thought-determinations apply, but is the whole system of interrelated thought-determinations. This conclusion is supported by an argument to be considered in the following section.

7 Propositions and assumptions

This final argument against predication in the case of infinite entities is a complex one and Hegel's statement of it will be quoted at length:

> Its [viz. metaphysics] objects were indeed totalities, which
> in their own right (*an und für sich*) belong to reason, to the
> thinking of the intrinsically *concrete* universal — *soul, world,
> God*; but metaphysics received them from *conception*, made

them, as *ready-made, given subjects*, the basis of the application
of determinations of the understanding and it had in that conception alone the *criterion (Massstab)* for whether or not the
predicates were suitable and sufficient (*Enz.* I. 30). The conceptions of soul, world and God seem at first to afford thinking
a *firm support*. But besides the fact that the character of particular subjectivity is mixed with them and they can have
accordingly very different meanings, they need rather to be
first given a firm determination by thinking. This is expressed
by every proposition, in which what the subject, i.e. the initial
conception, is is supposed to be first stated by the predicate (i.e.
in philosophy by the thought-determination).

In the proposition 'God is eternal, etc.' we begin with the
concept 'God'; but what he *is* is not yet known (*gewusst*);
it is only the predicate which expresses what he *is*. Consequently in logic, where the content is determined entirely in
the form of thought alone, it is not only superfluous to make
these determinations into the predicates of propositions, with,
as their *subject*, God or the more vague absolute, but it would
also have the disadvantage of suggesting another criterion than
the form of thought itself (*Enz.* I. 31. Cf. *PG* pp. 50 ff., M.
pp. 38 ff.).

This passage contains at least two objections to such propositoons
as 'God is eternal.' The first is that the concept of God is received
on authority and that this conception, together with the beliefs
traditionally associated with it, is covertly used as a criterion for
whether or not such propositions are to be accepted. The second
is that we do not know what the subject of the proposition is, do
not know what the term 'God' means or to what it refers, until we
accept the truth of the proposition. It is, on the face of it, hard to
reconcile these two criticisms. Presumably Hegel means that as
long as our concept of God is merely a received conception, we
cannot strictly know what God is. But the fact remains that unless
we have some idea of what the word 'God' means, independently
of our acceptance of such propositions as 'God is eternal', we
cannot use our received conception as a criterion for assessing
these propositions. And if we have some independent idea, however rough, of what the subject of the proposition is, there is no
case for saying that the propositional form is superfluous. Hegel
should have put his criticism in the form of a dilemma: *either* the
subject-term is a received conception and will, or may, be used as
a criterion *or* it has no meaning for us until we give it one by
accepting the truth of propositions about it, that is, *either* the

subject-term is pernicious *or* it is superfluous. The limbs of this dilemma will be considered in turn.

The first limb is in itself misleading in that it contains two distinct criticisms of a term like 'God': that it stands for a conception rather than a pure thought and that it is taken over from other people and not worked out for ourselves. We have already seen that in attempting to draw the difficult distinction between non-empirical conceptions and pure thoughts, Hegel tends to conflate it with the different distinction between concepts which are taken over from others and concepts which are constructed independently by being derived from one another.[72] We have, however, seen reason to doubt that these distinctions coincide, that there could not be a pure thought which was received on authority or, conversely, a conception which was independently derived. It may be that if a concept is accepted on authority, then we have no guarantee that it contains no empirical or pictorial element, but it may nevertheless be free of them.

Even if we grant, however, that the concept of God is both a conception and received from others, it is still not clear that it need be used as a criterion for the acceptability of propositions involving it, that Hegel is entitled to conclude that 'this metaphysics was not free and objective thinking, since it did not allow the object to determine itself freely out of itself, but presupposed it as ready-made' (*Enz.* I. 31Z).[73] After all, the rationalist metaphysicians attempted to prove propositions about God and did not just record traditional beliefs. There are, however, two replies to this. Firstly, even if we were to accept the validity of their proofs, what propositions they proved depended on their respect for tradition; their selection from the possibly provable propositions was not independently determined. Secondly, such proofs depend on axiomatic premises and what these are is determined by tradition. If one did not assume certain beliefs together with the conception, one could no more prove the applicability of these predicates to God than one could to the Loch Ness monster. The use of a contentful subject-term, then, involves unexamined assumptions both of meaning and of fact.[74]

8 *The superfluity of the propositional form*

The second limb of the dilemma, however, is that if we dispense with such assumptions, then the subject-term is superfluous, for we do not know what it stands for until we accept the truth of the propositions in which it occurs. The subject-term is dispensable and so, therefore, is the propositional form. This is one of Hegel's arguments for his decision to consider concepts or conceptual systems as such and not to apply them, at any rate immediately and in the traditional way. In a number of passages in the *Logic*, he suggests that the pure thoughts could each be taken as a definition of God or of the absolute. But apart from the fact that all of them, except the last, are inadequate for this purpose owing to their intrinsic defects, he sees no point in taking them in this way:[75]

> Being itself as well as the following determinations, not only of being, but the logical determinations in general, can be regarded as definitions of the absolute, as the *metaphysical definitions of God* . . . . But if the form of definitions were used, it would involve a substratum hovering before our imagination (*Vorstellung*); for even the *absolute*, which is supposed to express God in the manner and form of thought, remains only a *pretended* (*gemeinter*) thought, a substratum which is in itself indeterminate — in relation to its predicate, which is the determinate and actual expression in thought. Because the thought, the subject-matter which is here our sole concern, is contained only in the predicate, the form of the proposition, like that subject, is entirely superfluous (*Enz.* I. 85).

The argument under consideration in this section is here entangled with the point that a subject–predicate proposition implies an inappropriate distinction between a substratum and the properties inhering in it.[76] But since the indeterminacy of the substratum corresponds to the vacuity of the subject-term, Hegel takes the two arguments to amount to much the same thing.

Whatever view we take about the relationship of these two arguments, however, Hegel is in error. Firstly, not all propositions have an obvious subject-term. Simple examples are 'It is raining' and 'Something is red.' Indeed, it might be argued that we can eliminate contentful subject-terms altogether, for the predicate calculus dispenses with them, transferring their content into the predicate. For example, 'A cat is on the mat' can be re-expressed as 'There is something which is a cat and that thing is on the mat' or, more technically, as '$(\exists x)$ (x is a cat and x is on the mat)'. One does not, in this case, know what 'x' stands for until one understands the rest of the proposition, but it does not follow that one can dispense with the proposition. One could just as well argue that since one does not know what 'It' stands for in 'It is raining', it would be better to give up making statements about the weather and examine the concept of rain instead. The statement 'God is eternal' could be re-expressed, along these lines, as

'There is one and only one thing which is divine and that thing is eternal.' Hegel's objection might then be recast in the form: since the term 'God' has no determinate content, the same is now true of the predicate-term 'is divine'. But, of course, if we eliminate that expression, we are not left only with the concept of eternity, but with the proposition that there is something eternal.

Secondly, even if a proposition does have a contentful subject-term, its content need not be known initially by the person to whom the proposition is addressed. In saying, for example, 'God is the ground of all being', we may mean not to say something about a subject which is independently and clearly identifiable, but to say what the subject is. But it does not follow that the subject-term is dispensable. We might compare the more down-to-earth sentence 'John is (the one) drinking cider', when it is said not in order to provide information about John to someone who already knows who John is, but in order to enable someone to identify John. It would be absurd to suggest that in this case we might just as well give up asserting propositions and concentrate on the predicates alone.

9 Concepts and logic

If it were not for this recurrent argument, it would be tempting to regard Hegel's *Logic* as primarily an attempt to prove such propositions as 'Everything/something *is*', 'Everything/something is determinate', 'Everything/something is a whole consisting of parts', and so on. Indeed when he discusses the inference (*der Schluss*), he equates the definition of the absolute as (an or the) inference with the proposition that everything is an inference: 'The inference is therefore the *essential ground of everything true*; and *the definition of the absolute* is now that it is the inference, or if this determination is expressed as a proposition: "Everything (*Alles*) is an inference"' (*Enz.* I. 181). The sense of 'inference' involved in this is not at issue here.[77] The crucial point is the switch from 'The absolute is F' to 'Everything is an F.' Hegel is of course more ready to say of some pure thoughts, e.g. the inference, than of others, e.g. that of a whole with parts, that everything exemplifies them. But the question still remains why, in the *Logic*, he is not concerned, except by way of asides, with the application or embodiment of pure thoughts at all.

There are several possible answers to this, apart from the theological function which the *Logic* is intended to perform. Firstly, Hegel seems to have taken his objections to propositions of the type 'God is F' or 'The absolute is F' as extending to any proposition

188

in which thoughts are applied to things. (The distinction between definitions and propositions in *Enz.* I. 181 does not affect this issue.) Another reason, it might be suggested, is that propositions of the forms 'Everything is F' and 'Something is F' presuppose a range of distinct objects. We cannot, therefore, replace 'F' by a pure thought, because objects cannot be individuated apart from the pure thoughts which they embody. The answer to this, however, is that such propositions may be re-expressed in a way which does not imply that there are distinct objects independently of their truth, in the form, for example, 'The concept of F-ness has application.' Whatever the difficulties about the precise formulation of such propositions, there is still a difference between the mere consideration of a concept and the claim that it has some application. Finally, however, there is Hegel's official doctrine that categorial concepts should be examined before we raise questions about their application.[78] This in itself would forbid us to consider the application of a concept immediately, before examining it, but it does not prevent us from doing so in the case of each concept after we have examined it. However, an apparent corollary of this doctrine would suggest that such questions cannot strictly be raised until we have reached the end of the *Logic*. For the concept of the exemplification of a concept, as opposed to the concept itself, is itself one of the concepts considered within the *Logic*, and the examination of this does not end before the conclusion of the work.[79] Hegel may have believed that the concept of the objectivity of a concept should be examined before we consider the actual objectivity of concepts. If this is so, then the objectivity of concepts cannot be considered before the end of the *Logic* itself. For that we have to wait for the second part of the system, the *Philosophy of Nature*.

The *Logic* does of course, even on this view, express what we would call propositions. It does, after all, consist of sentences and is not simply a list of words. But these propositions are propositions about concepts, applying concepts to concepts and not concepts to things. Sometimes concepts are applied to other concepts and sometimes a concept is applied to itself.[80] It might still be objected, nevertheless, that one cannot discuss a concept without keeping an eye on its possible applications to actual things. The sense of such a concept as that of a whole consisting of parts, or that of the corresponding words, essentially depends on its possible occurrence in propositions, or sentences, about actual wholes consisting of parts. Hegel's procedure is either quite illegitimate or, in practice, he must have in view the primary application of concepts throughout the *Logic*. The answer to this, however, is that it is entirely possible to construct a formal system, arithmetic, for example, or a non-Euclidean geometry, without troubling oneself about its actual applications. One must perhaps bear in mind its possible applications, but one can hold in abeyance questions about what particular things or realms it applies to. Some of Hegel's arguments suggest that he requires a more generous concession than this, that he wants us to ignore entirely anything other than the application of concepts to concepts, but other considerations imply that he does not.[81] It is not obvious, then, that his enterprise is an illicit one. The problem, as we have seen, is that some of his arguments for embarking on it are worse than the enterprise itself.

10 *Dogmatism and antinomy*

As we have seen, Hegel conceives his task as a philosopher to be to bring about, or at least to comprehend, a reconciliation of the separation that has disturbed an original harmony. The pre-Kantian rationalists, with their naïve belief that thought can capture the truth about infinite, transcendent entities, can be seen from one point of view as innocents in the garden. Kant's challenge to their enterprise is what extrudes them from it.[82] Is Hegel's response to this challenge an adequate one?

An initial difficulty is that Kant's primary objection to traditional metaphysics is that transcendent entities, like God and the soul, do not supply us with a sensory foothold for the application of our categories. In some cases, but not in all, this is highlighted by the emergence of antinomies, by the fact that there are equally good reasons for applying opposing concepts to one and the same thing. If Hegel is undeterred by this, however, Kant could still object that there can be no sound argument for applying any concept at all to an entity which, like the soul, is beyond the reach of empirical data.[83] One problem about Hegel's response to this is that he seems to provide two answers and not simply one. He speaks, in the first place, as if he, like Kant's predecessors, believed that thought could supply surprising information about a range of entities inaccessible to sense-perception. Sometimes he supports this, as we have seen, by interpreting Kant's objection as an inconsistent reluctance to apply to our sensory intake concepts which are not 'given' in it.[84] In the same breath, however, he implies that there is no obvious reason why thought should not go its own way, even in the absence of sensory data in the relevant sense: 'If thought and appearance do not fully correspond to each other, one has in the first place a choice whether to locate the

190

fault in the one or the other' (*Enz.* I. 47). Why cannot thought supply conclusions which conflict with or transcend sense-perception? The thoughts must, however, be of the right kind. If Kant's objections to metaphysics seem compelling, it may be because the fault lies, not in thoughts or concepts in general, but in the particular thoughts which the metaphysicians employed (*Ibid.*). Kant assumed that, if one-sided dogmatism is abandoned, then we are left with no knowledge at all. But he was wrong. We can make judgments of the type: 'God/the soul is both finite and infinite.' Hegel supposes, unlike Kant, that *all* applications of concepts to transcendent entities generate antinomies of this type. There are at least two reasons for this. Firstly, he is, as we have seen, inclined to conflate the law of contradiction and the law of the excluded middle, seeing little difference between, for example, 'The soul is both simple and complex' and 'The soul is neither simple nor complex.'[85] Kant's view that we are not entitled to apply concepts to transcendent entities is more readily assimilable to the claim that they are neither F nor non-F than to the claim that they are both F and non-F. Secondly, Hegel believed, unlike Kant, that the contradictoriness of categories, indeed of every category, can be shown independently of its application to any particular entity. It follows that antinomies cannot be confined to any single type of entity. There are contradictions in '*all* objects of all kinds, in *all* conceptions, concepts and ideas' (*Enz.* I. 48). One cannot therefore find a refuge from contradiction short of ceasing to think altogether. All applications of the categories, to finite as well as infinite entities, will generate problems similar to Kant's antinomies.[86]

This, then, is Hegel's first answer. We can think about transcendent entities as long as we abandon the assumption that of two opposing predications one must be true and the other false. There is no suggestion that such problematic propositions stand proxy for unproblematic ones with flat, contradiction-free predicates — as 'It is raining and it isn't' deputizes for 'It's drizzling.' Hegel's view seems to be that the infinite is, as it were, the sum of the contradictory finite and can only be reached by means of it. Puzzling entities like God, the self, and the universe as a whole cannot be captured in paradox-free terms. His second answer is quite different. It is that we should not strictly think *about* transcendent entities at all. For we should, in their case, abandon the propositional form altogether. A proposition of the type 'God is both F and non-F' should be jettisoned along with one-sided ones of the form 'God is exclusively F.'[87]

How are these two answers to be reconciled? There is more than one possibility. One is that problematic propositions are, on Hegel's view, enunciated *faute de mieux*. Any proposition with 'God' or 'the soul' as its subject-term is objectionable, but, if we are to assert propositions about them at all, the best we can provide are seemingly contradictory ones. On this view, their contradictoriness would be one reason for the abandonment of the propositional form. A second alternative is that even if Hegel abandons propositions to the extent of identifying God and the soul with a conceptual system, it may be that they are still required in order to speak about this system. If the concepts contained in the system and the concepts applicable to it coincide,[88] propositions may even so be a way of plucking concepts out of it in order to apply them to it. Finally, God and the soul are not only a conceptual system. The soul, or, as Hegel prefers, the mind or spirit, has desires and perceptions, and of course a body. God, again, creates or, as it were, spills over into the finitude of nature.[89] Propositions about God and the soul may be required in order to express their relationships to what is other than, yet at the same time an aspect of, themselves. We have already seen that this is a part of the diagnosis of Hegel's beliefs that God is both finite and infinite and that the soul is both simple and complex.[90] Such propositions would not, in Hegel's hands, be exposed to one of his objections to propositions, that their subject-terms express received conceptions. For conceptions like those of God and the soul are, on his view, derived and refurbished within the system itself. The traditional assumptions they involve are either purged altogether or reinstated by rational argument.

Hegel's answers to Kant and his predecessors can, then, perhaps be reconciled in one or more of these ways. Even if they were unacceptable, however, it would still be unsurprising that he produces different and apparently incompatible answers to the same question. For Hegel is attempting both to revive or continue the thought of his predecessors and to transform it into something quite different. An intelligible route from their position to his is unlikely to be a smooth one. More of this will be seen in the following chapter, in which we consider his attitude to argument and proof.

VII

Faith, Proofs and Infinity

It might be thought that, since Hegel has already rejected the propositional form as a vehicle for the truth about infinite entities, there can be little to say about proof or argument. For, on the customary view, the premises and conclusion of a proof or argument are propositions. This is so, and the orthodox notion of a proof has to undergo a radical transformation before Hegel can accept its application to infinite objects. He devoted a course of lectures,[1] as well as scattered passages in his other works, to effecting this transformation. Proofs are relevant, of course, to all the infinite, as well as to finite objects. His predecessors had attempted to prove, for example, that the soul is immortal, that the world is infinite and that God exists. Most of Hegel's remarks about proof, however, concern directly only the proofs of God's existence, and this chapter will concentrate on his discussion of these. These remarks are nevertheless of relevance to our knowledge of any infinite entity, and they lead us into the heart of Hegel's system.

1 *The defects of cognition*

Before considering Hegel's account of proof, we need to examine the view that in religious, and perhaps other, matters we can and should dispense with proof and argument altogether. Hegel, as we have already seen, believed that neither traditional metaphysics nor the natural sciences could do justice to infinite objects and it was a common belief of the time that thinking, or at any rate thinking of a certain kind, was bound to omit or distort religious truths. He selects as the representative of this view his now all but forgotten near-contemporary, F. H. Jacobi. Jacobi's attitude

193

toward conceptual thought is described in such terms as these:

> [Thinking has] only the categories for its product and content. These . . . are limited determinations, forms of the *conditioned, dependent, mediated*. For thinking which is restricted to them, the infinite, the true, is not (against the proofs of God's existence) . . . . [T]o conceptualize (*begreifen*) an object thus means no more than to grasp it in the form of a *conditioned* and *mediated* entity, thus, in so far as the object is the true, infinite, unconditioned, it means changing it into a conditioned and mediated one.

Cognition (*Erkennen*) is the

> thinking progression through *series* from one *conditioned* item to *another*, in which each condition is in turn conditioned by something else . . . . [T]hus all content is merely *particular, dependent* and *finite*; the infinite, true God lies outside the mechanism of such an interconnection.

Jacobi had in mind primarily the

> cognition of natural forces and laws. The infinite cannot of course be found immanent in this territory; just as *Lalande*[2] had said that he had searched the whole heavens, but had not found God. What emerged as the final result in this area was the *universal* as the *indeterminate* aggregate of the external finite — *matter (Enz.* I. 61).

There are of course several distinct points in this mixture of Hegel and Jacobi,[3] but only enough explanation of it will be given to provide an introduction to Jacobi's solution. The citation of Lalande's remark suggests that the main problem is that God is not observable. As we have seen, Hegel himself was reluctant to admit that this is a difficulty.[4] The fact that God is not observable in the way that the planet Venus is would not in itself forbid us to infer his existence from what is observable. After all, matter, in the sense in which Hegel and Jacobi attribute a belief in it to scientists, is not observable, but its existence is inferred from empirical data. The main difficulty is that the cognitive procedures of the sciences, their finite categories and arguments which employ them, do not give us access to the infinite. The categories, particularly that of causality, enable us to explain one thing by another indefinitely, but when we follow this route we never arrive at the infinite, but only at what is dependent on something else. There is, moreover, no explanatory role for God to play in the sciences.[5] Everything is explained by something else. If any large abstraction is required, it is that of bare matter, and this, on Hegel's view as on Jacobi's, does not amount to God. The categories are finite categories, apt only for dealing with finite things, and the traditional proofs which employ them do not establish the existence of an infinite deity. There is some uncertainty about whether, as the second passage cited implies, the proofs therefore fail to establish God's existence at all or whether, as the first suggests, they reduce him to a finite entity.[6] But all that matters here is that there is no legitimate inferential route from finite things to an infinite God.

Jacobi's solution to this is that, in these matters, discursive, inferential thinking is to be replaced by immediate awareness (*unmittelbares Wissen*). There are some things, notably God, of which we are immediately aware and to which arguments and even concepts are irrelevant. If this doctrine were acceptable, therefore, it would solve not only the problem of God's existence, but also the problems associated with finite concepts and the epistemological difficulties considered earlier. Hegel, however, rejects it, and he does so for at least five reasons:

(i) Jacobi held that we are immediately aware not only of (the existence of) God, but also of (the existence of) finite things, of our own bodies, for example, and of other sensuous entities (*Enz.* I. 63). Hegel objects to this apparent assimilation of God to finite things. God, he argues, differs crucially from finite things. He is intrinsically universal, in content at least,[7] and is therefore accessible only to thought. The fact that he is a person supports the same conclusion:

> when the *individuality* as ego, the *personality*, in so far as an *empirical* ego, a *particular* personality, is not meant by this, especially when the personality of God is before one's consciousness, then the question is of *pure*, i.e. *intrinsically universal* personality; such a personality is a thought and belongs only to thinking (*Enz.* I. 63).

(ii) Immediate awareness is given several different titles by its advocates. It is variously called 'awareness', 'faith' or 'belief' (*Glaube*), 'reason' (*Vernunft*) and 'feeling' (*Gefühl*) (*Enz.* I. 63).[8] This suggests that whereas awareness, belief, intuition, thought and so on are intelligibly different from each other when they are taken in their ordinary sense, it is hard to see any difference between them at Jacobi's level of abstraction:

> Intuiting, believing, express at first the determinate conceptions which in ordinary consciousness we combine with these words;

then they are indeed different from thinking and this distinction is intelligible to almost everyone. But now believing and intuiting are supposed to be taken in a higher sense, as belief in God, as the intellectual intuition of God, i.e. abstraction is to be made precisely from everything which differentiates intuiting, believing from thinking. One cannot say how believing and intuiting still differ from thinking, once they are transferred into this higher region (*Enz*. I. 63).

(iii) Jacobi's faith is not the Christian faith. In the first place, it is a merely subjective revelation and makes no appeal to the authority of the Church. Elsewhere Hegel sees this as a merit rather than a defect,[9] but his point here may be that Jacobi himself claimed to be giving an account of Christianity. More importantly, however, while Christianity has a rich, determinate content, Jacobi's faith is thin and indeterminate. God is characterized only as the supreme being (*das höchste Wesen, Enz*. I. 63. Cf. 71) or else we are aware only *that* God exists and not of anything else about him (*Enz*. I. 73).

(iv) Immediate awareness cannot justify any one set of religious beliefs, since, if it justified any one, it would justify all:

> The Indian does not regard the cow, the ape, or the Brahmin the Lama, as God because of mediated awareness, argumentation or inferences; rather he has *faith* in them (*glaubt* daran) (*Enz*. I. 72. Cf. 63).

(v) The doctrine of immediate awareness purports to forgo not only arguments, but also one-sided, exclusive concepts. In claiming, however, that awareness can be wholly immediate, to the complete exclusion of mediation, the doctrine reverts to the rigid 'Either-Or' of the understanding. On Hegel's view, nothing is exclusively immediate and nothing is exclusively mediated, so that there cannot be any such thing as merely immediate awareness (*Enz*. I. 65, 75, 78).

In Hegel's discussion of the doctrine of immediate awareness, these criticisms are intertwined with each other. Moreover, no one of them can be adequately considered without reference to the others, for they are deeply interconnected. We shall, however, attempt to examine them separately in the above order, in so far as this is possible.

2 *Faith and its objects*

It seems at first sight a sheer mistake to suppose that the view that we are or can be immediately aware of such different things as (the existence of) God and (the existence of) sensible objects entails that they are similar to each other in any further respect. I can be aware that I have a body, that $2 + 2 = 4$, and that God exists. Why should this imply any other resemblance between God, numbers and my body than that they are all possible objects of my awareness?

A part of the answer to this is that Hegel, in the light perhaps of his criticism (ii), assimilates immediate awareness to other cognitive procedures, notably to the use of the ontological argument.[10] Jacobi, on Hegel's account, claims that we have, or can have, immediate awareness of at least three types of object:

(1) We are immediately aware of God's existence. Hegel takes this to depend on the fact that 'God's *being* is immediately and inseparably bound up with the *thought* of him, objectivity with the subjectivity which at first characterizes the thought' (*Enz.* I. 64. Cf. 76, where Hegel speaks of the 'inseparability of the conception of *God* and his *existence*').

(2) I am immediately aware of my own existence. Hegel ascribes to Jacobi the view which Descartes expressed by '*Cogito, ergo sum*' ('I think, therefore I exist'). Descartes's formula, he argues, is not intended to express an inference, but immediate, noninferential awareness (*Enz.* I. 64). Hence '*cogito, ergo sum* is entirely the same [as Jacobi's doctrine] that the being, reality, existence of the I is immediately revealed to me in consciousness' (*Enz.* I. 76).

(3) We are immediately aware of the existence of sensible objects and in particular of our own bodies. Jacobi had said such things as: 'Through faith (*Durch den Glauben*) we are aware that we have a body and that outside us other bodies and other thinking entities are present.'[11] Hegel interprets such remarks as employing an ontological argument with respect to finite, sensible objects:

> the philosophy of immediate awareness goes so far in its abstraction that not only is the determination of God's existence inseparably bound up with the thought of him, but also in intuition the determination of the *existence* of my *body* and of *external* things is likewise inseparably bound up with the *conception* of them (*Enz.* I. 64).

In each of these cases, Hegel assimilates the claim that we are immediately aware of (the existence of) an object, x, to an acceptance of the ontological argument, to the move from 'thinking' of x to the 'being' of x, from a concept or a conception to the existence of instances of it, on the ground that the existence of x is immediately involved in the concept or conception of x. The assimilation is achieved in three steps. Firstly, Hegel distinguishes reflectively between the object of awareness and the subjective mental state or activity involved in the awareness of it. Secondly, he asks why this subjective state or activity guarantees the existence of the object. And finally, the answer to this question is assumed in each case to be that the concept, conception or thought of the object is 'inseparably bound up with' its existence. An advocate of immediate awareness could well object to the first of these steps and to the question which it prompts. He might claim that we should not look for a purely subjective mental component of immediate awareness, but that the point of calling it 'immediate' is that it provides us with direct access to objects. It is, however, Hegel's third step which is most obviously objectionable.

In the case of God, for example, one might claim that we have a self-certifying awareness of him or of his existence without thereby implying that the concept of God involves his existence in such a way that it is contradictory to deny that he exists. The subjective component of this awareness, if one is admitted at all, may be some feeling or a mystical experience. The question how this subjective state can guarantee the existence of its supposed object may be difficult to answer, but it is not obvious that the answer to it will, or need, involve the ontological argument. The mental state, if it involves more than the consideration of a concept, may be said, for example, to guarantee the existence of God in something like the way in which our sensory states are ordinarily taken to guarantee the existence of physical objects. This claim is problematic but it is not obviously absurd and it is, at any rate, sometimes made.

In the case of my own existence, it is plausible to say that my immediate awareness of it, if I indeed have such an awareness, involves, or can be represented by, Descartes's *Cogito*. It is, however, a mistake to identify the *Cogito* with the ontological argument.[12] My own existence is, on Descartes's view, guaranteed not by a concept, the concept of a self or the concept of 'me', but by a piece of actual thinking which I undertake. The ontological argument, if it were valid, would establish that God exists necessarily and eternally.[13] The *Cogito*, by contrast, shows not that I exist necessarily and eternally, but only that I exist if, and as long as, I actually think, that I cannot think truly that I do not exist. Again, the *Cogito* has force only for the person who rehearses it; I am assured in this way of my own existence, but not of that of other people nor are they thereby assured of mine. The ontological argument, by contrast, purports to assure *us* of God's existence; it is not simply a way in which God can be certain of his own existence. Yet Hegel regularly associates the *Cogito* with the ontological argument.[14] As often in such cases, this is not a sheer error, but has deep roots in Hegel's system. Both God and the ego are identified with the concept, the conceptual system of the *Logic*, and, as we shall see, this prevents him from drawing a proper distinction between concepts and episodic or occurrent thinking.[15] It would, in the light of this, be surprising if Hegel were able to distinguish the two arguments. But it does not, of course, follow that he is entitled to attribute this assimilation to Descartes and Jacobi.

Hegel has no great objection to the *Cogito* and/or the ontological argument in the case of God and the self.[16] What he rejects is the implication that finite, sensible objects are in this respect on a par with God and the ego: 'But what concept is it which is inseparable from being? Not that of *finite things*, for these are just such things as have a *contingent* and created existence' (*Enz.* I. 76. Cf. 193). This is true, more or less, but it is based on a misunderstanding of the doctrine under consideration. The point of claiming immediate awareness of physical objects is not that the existence of any one of them is involved in the concept of it, but that when I perceive such objects I cannot reasonably doubt their existence. Characteristically an exponent of this view would reject Hegel's first and second steps, denying that we need to distinguish between the object itself and the purely subjective mental state or activity involved in one's awareness of it and to ask how the latter can assure us of the existence of the former. But even if he accepted these steps, he would surely reject the third. It is my sensory states, not my thoughts alone, which make it certain or probable that there are physical objects, and their doing so does not depend on a concept's involving existence. Hegel seems at times to assume that we can be certain that sensible objects exist only if we grant them the status of God. This again, as we shall see, is deeply entrenched in his thought. It arises from a tendency to conflate ontology and epistemology, in this case the questions 'What is the ontological status of physical objects?' and 'How can we be sure that they exist?'[17] But, again, he has no right to import this into his interpretation of Jacobi.

3 *The variety of faith*

This interpretation is forced and erroneous. Has Hegel any better reason for believing that we cannot be immediately aware of the existence of objects of widely different types? His view seems to be that one cannot detach the awareness of an object or of the truth of a proposition from the content of that object or proposition, and suppose that the nature of the awareness remains constant while the content varies radically. A naïve acceptance of the existence of sensible objects, such as we might attribute to a child or even an animal, is a quite different mental state from an immediate awareness of God as a person. The fact that one is capable of the first is no guarantee of one's capacity for the latter. Even if no actual inferring or describing is performed, one must have the concepts involved in the description of the object. Hegel might concede that there is such a thing as the non-inferential awareness of physical objects and of one's own body, but argue that one should not ignore the processes of education and conceptualization that underlie this awareness. To say that one is immediately aware of their existence sheds no more light on the analysis and justification of our beliefs than the fact that a trained mathematician can immediately see that $13 \times 22 = 286$ sheds on the analysis and justification of arithmetical statements:

> truths of which one very well knows that they are the result
> of complicated, highly mediated considerations, *immediately*
> present themselves to the consciousness of one who has become
> familiar with such knowledge. The mathematician, like every
> expert in a science, has solutions immediately available, which
> are the end-product of a very complicated analysis (*Enz.* I. 66).

Our use of such words as 'see' and 'feel' is misleading in this respect. One can feel a pain, a pin-prick, a hand, the presence of God, that God is merciful, that tax-evasion is wrong. One can see black patches, stones, telephones, that this black thing is a telephone, that he is absorbed in thought, that two and three make five, that this argument is invalid, that God is merciful, that tax evasion is wrong, and so on. It is, however, only at a superficial level that the feeling or the seeing is the same in all these cases. If they were the same, while only the objects differed, then a creature that can see stones should be able to see that it is wrong to throw them at passing cars, if only it could get the latter object into its field of vision. Nothing, on Hegel's view, is solved by the use of such words as 'feel', 'see' and 'awareness' in all these cases and nothing hangs on their use. To the extent that the object of awareness becomes remote from ordinary sensations and things, the awareness in question loses its contact with ordinary seeing and feeling and the term 'awareness' loses whatever explanatory value it originally had. If we forget this, we shall tend to assimilate the diverse objects of awareness to one another.

This seems to be something of the sort that Hegel had in mind. The points will not be examined here, but some of them will emerge more clearly in what follows.

4 *The Unknown God*

There is an obvious tension between Hegel's third and fourth criticisms of the doctrine of immediate awareness. If the immediate awareness of God reduces him to a bare minimum, as (iii) maintains, immediate awareness could not possibly justify a belief in the divinity of, say, the Dalai Lama, as (iv) suggests, for that is a specific, determinate belief, distinguished from other religions by its content. There are, however, several answers to this. A way of reconciling the criticisms will emerge later.[18] But a preliminary reply can be given in terms of the argument of the preceding section. The proponents of the doctrine of immediate awareness are, namely, presented with a dilemma. They can, on the one hand, claim immediate awareness of the truth of some specific religion, of a deity conceived in rich and complex terms. In that case, however, it is immediate only in the sense in which the trained mathematician's awareness that $13 \times 22 = 286$ is immediate. It is in fact mediated by education, an education involving concepts and inferences, and it is to this that we should look for the ultimate justification of the belief. They may, on the other hand, attempt to detach the awareness from these mediating processes and see it as truly immediate. But in that case, the object of the awareness is reduced to a thin abstraction, such that it hardly makes any difference whether we believe in it or not. It is this limb of the dilemma which is the subject of criticism (iii).

Hegel regularly objects to the theological efforts of his predecessors not that they fail to establish the existence of God, but that they establish the existence of the wrong sort of God, in this case a vacuous one. We shall see further evidence for this when we consider his account of the proofs of God's existence. He conceives of the reduction of God to an empty abstraction in two different ways. Firstly, God is regarded only as the supreme being (*Enz.* I. 63). But, secondly, he argues, immediate awareness guarantees only *that* God exists, and tells us nothing about *what* God is (*Enz.* I. 73). He seems not to distinguish these two claims as clearly as one might, for having said that immediate awareness tells us only that God exists and not what he is, he continues: 'Thus God as the object of religion is expressly restricted to God *in general* (*überhaupt*), to the indeterminate supersensible (*das*

201

unbestimmte Übersinnliche) and religion is reduced to its minimum in its content' (*Ibid.*). In neither case does Hegel distinguish between the claim that, though there may be more to God than that, this is all that we can know about him, and the claim that this is all there is to him.[19] Thus the reduction of God to a minimum might involve any one of four propositions which Hegel tends to conflate:

(1) God is the supreme being and nothing more is true of him that that he is the supreme being.

(2) God is the supreme being and nothing more can be known about him than that he is the supreme being.

(3) God exists and nothing else is true of him than that he exists.

(4) God exists and nothing else can be known about him than that he exists.

The conflation is perhaps intelligible in the light of the variety of arguments that lead to the reduction, but the propositions are *prima facie* distinct. (1) is not the same as (3). To say that God is the supreme being or that he is supersensible is at least to say something about him. But it is doubtful whether it makes sense to say that something could be only the supreme being and nothing else. (2) is less obviously nonsensical, but, taken literally, it evidently says very little in support of orthodox Christianity or of anything else. For all we know, for example, matter might be the supreme being and, if that were so, the truth of (2) would be compatible with materialism, though according to (2) we could not know that materialism, in this sense, was true. (3) and (4) are both absurdly vacuous. To say that x exists, but that nothing is true of x except that it exists, is to say nothing at all; it cannot be true of anything that it *only* exists. To say that x exists, but that this is all that can be known about it, is surely to say no more than that *something* exists. If these propositions are taken seriously and we do not illicitly smuggle into them the traditional connotation of the term 'God', then assent to them does not distinguish a Christian from any other religious, or non-religious, believer.

5 *Religion and consensus*

Why does Hegel believe that immediate awareness, or the doctrine thereof, entails this reduction? He has at least two arguments for this, the first of which will be presented in this section. It starts from the premiss that the doctrine takes as its 'criterion of truth' the mere 'fact of consciousness', the subjective fact that I am, or feel myself to be, aware of an object or of the truth of a proposition.

But this is clearly unsatisfactory. The consciousness of an individual contains many features which are entirely 'particular' and 'contingent'. Different men are aware, or feel themselves to be aware, of quite different things, owing in part to differences in their education. As soon as we recognize this, we can no longer confidently rely on our immediate awareness as the criterion of truth.

There are, Hegel believes, two possible responses to this. The first is to reflect upon the nature of our consciousness, separate out from it what is particular and contingent, and discover what is intrinsically 'universal' in it. This, he implies, is the correct response and the one that he adopts in his *Logic*. It does not have the objectionable consequence entailed by the second. The second is to discover empirically the highest common factor of everyone's awareness or beliefs and to infer that this is a necessary feature of consciousness:

> If the nature of this consciousness is not itself investigated,
> i.e. if the particular, contingent element in it is not separated
> out — by which laborious operation of meta-thinking alone
> can be discovered that which in this consciousness is universal
> in and for itself — then only the agreement of *all* about a
> content can ground a respectable presumption that it belongs
> to the nature of consciousness itself (*Enz.* I. 71. Cf. *VBDG*
> VI).

This second response amounts in effect to the argument *ex consensu gentium*, an argument which Hegel attributes to Cicero.[20] His own version of it seems to take the following form:

(1) All men/peoples believe in God/a god;
Therefore,
(2) Belief in God/a god is a necessary feature of human consciousness;
Therefore,
(3) God/a god exists.

Hegel does not clearly distinguish stages (2) and (3), no doubt in the light of his own belief that God is no more than a system of concepts. He shows some scepticism about the move from (1) to (2), but by and large his criticisms do not concern the validity of the argument, but the truth and interpretation of (1), the proposition that all men believe in God:

> How great one finds in experience the extent of atheism and
> belief in God to be depends on whether one is content with
> the determination of a god *in general* or whether a more

determinate knowledge of him is required. In the Christian world it is not conceded of Chinese, Indian, etc. idols at least, no more of African fetishes, or even of the Greek gods, that such idols are God; one who believes in such idols does not therefore believe in God (*Enz.* I. 71).

Hegel is interestingly confused about what attitude we should adopt towards proposition (1). His doubts centre on four distinct points:

(a) Some peoples, like the Eskimos, seem to have no religious beliefs or activity at all.[21]

(b) Not all those peoples who have some religious beliefs and activity believe in God or even a god. This seems to depend on Hegel's assumption that, if a man performs acts of devotion towards some physical or animate finite object, then what he is worshipping is not God or a god, but a cow, a piece of wood, or whatever the object in fact is. This assumption is open to question. Voltaire, for example, had argued that the 'error was not to worship a piece of wood or marble, but to worship a false divinity represented by this wood or marble. The difference between them and us is not that they had images and we have not: the difference is that their images showed fantastic beings in a religion.'[22]

(c) Even if we are prepared to grant that a people worship a god, it does not follow that they worship God. Belief in God, rather than belief in some god or other, imposes some minimum requirement of belief about him.

(d) Even if this standard is met by more than one people, so that we can agree that they both believe in God, their beliefs about him might still vary widely within certain limits.[23]

The premiss of the argument *ex consensu gentium* is therefore contentious. Not all men believe in God or even a god. One bad reason for supposing that they do is that all men, on Hegel's view, hold beliefs from which a theistic religion, and indeed the Christian religion, could legitimately be derived. But we should not attribute to a person all the beliefs which follow from beliefs he explicitly accepts. He may not have put two and two together:

> It does not depend on what is *implicitly* (*an sich*) contained in an object, but on what is *explicitly available* for consciousness (was davon für das Bewusstsein *heraus* ist). Every intuition of man, even the most ordinary, would be religion, if one accepts the interchangeability of these two determinations, because of course in every such intuition, in everything mental the principle is implicitly contained which,

when developed and purified, rises to religion (*Enz.* I. 71).

If one were to follow this procedure seriously, one would be in effect abandoning the argument *ex consensu* and opting for the first, Hegel's own, response.

It does not follow from these considerations, however, that the premiss 'All men/peoples believe in God' need be abandoned. What in fact happens, Hegel argues, is that the standards of belief in God are lowered so as to accommodate recalcitrant cases. The lower the standard, the more such cases will meet it, until even the Eskimos count as believing in God. The truth of the premiss and the validity of the argument is secured at the cost of draining the premiss, and therefore the conclusion, of its content: 'The charge of atheism has become less frequent in recent times, principally because the import and requirement of religion has been reduced to a minimum' (*Ibid.* Cf. *VBDG*, VI). The tendency of the *ex consensu* argument is to reduce the content of religion to the highest common factor of all beliefs which might be called religious and this also represents a reversion to the most primitive religion of all — rather as the number 1 is both the first of the positive integers and their highest common factor.

This, then, is Hegel's first argument for his view that the doctrine of immediate awareness reduces God to vacuity. Whatever the difficulties of detail it is clear that the argument *ex consensu gentium* is a natural response to the fact that men differ in what they are aware of or find self-evident, and that its effect, in the case of religion at least, will be to erode the content of our beliefs.

6 The vacuity of immediacy

Hegel's second reason for his belief in the vacuity of immediate awareness presupposes an acquaintance with his criticism (v), namely that everything is both immediate and mediated. We have already seen that he believes that a finite entity, or at least a thing with properties, derives its determinate, *immediate* character from its physical-*cum*-logical interactions with, or *mediation by*, other things.[24] In this context, however, he concentrates on the fact that everything is both the end-product of some process and has, at any given time, a definite nature:

A similarly trivial insight is the connection of immediate *existence* with the mediation of it; seeds, parents are an immediate, originating existence in relation to children, etc., which are products. But the seeds, parents . . . are likewise products, and the children, etc., despite the mediation of their existence, are now immediate, for they *are*. That I *am* in Berlin, this *immediate* presence of mine, is *mediated* by the journey I made here, etc. (*Enz*. I. 66).

Some nouns, like 'parent', point forward to the future developments of a thing, with no explicit reference to the process by which the thing originated. Other terms, like 'child', carry implications about the genesis of the thing. But whatever sort of term we employ, we cannot speak only of genesis and becoming. Genesis and becoming must be of something, there must be some end-product or result of a process if it is to be a process at all, and it is this that constitutes the immediacy of a thing. Conversely, we cannot concentrate exclusively on products and results, ignoring the processes that brought them about. In some cases at least the present state of a thing bears traces of the antecedent process responsible for it. Everything, then, or at least every finite thing, has an immediate, determinate character and this depends on its mediation by both past events and other things which co-exist with it.

This suggests the following argument for the view that the immediate awareness of an object must reduce it to indeterminacy. An object's mediating connections with past events and other objects are in some sense internal to it, in that they make it what it is. But they also form the basis of arguments concerning the object, arguments for its existence and for other propositions about it. In excluding arguments, therefore, immediate awareness would have to focus solely on the object itself, disregarding all the mediations which give the object its determinate character. It must, therefore, lose sight of this determinate character itself and view the object as entirely indeterminate. This argument, however, is clearly invalid. Even if we grant that a thing is determinate only if it is mediated and that if one is immediately aware of a thing, one cannot be aware of it as mediated, of its mediating connections, it does not follow that, if one is immediately aware of a thing, one cannot be aware of it as determinate. Any thing has a definite nature of which one might be aware without being aware of the processes and interactions responsible for it. We can, for example, easily know that Hegel is in Berlin without knowing how he got there. We might even believe that he has always been there or that he was created on that spot a few moments earlier.

Moreover, Hegel accepts the conclusion of this argument only in the case of the immediate awareness of God. For he believes that if immediate awareness is taken as the 'criterion of truth', then 'every superstition and idolatry is declared to be truth and the most wrong and immoral content of the will is justified' (*Enz.* I. 72); that 'since [the form of immediacy], being entirely abstract, is *indifferent to every content* and is thus receptive of every content, it can sanction idolatrous and immoral content as well as the opposite' (*Enz.* I. 74. Cf. III. 400). A person who claims to be immediately aware that stealing, or some particular act of theft, is wrong has no cognitive advantage over the person who claims immediate awareness that it is morally right or permissible. But if the above argument were sound, immediate awareness of these propositions or objects would drain them of their content and one could not be aware of anything so definite as the permissibility of theft or the divinity of the Dalai Lama. These things have a definite nature only in virtue of mediating processes and interactions and in excluding these from consideration one eclipses the nature they produce. But the answer to this, as we have seen, is that one can be aware of the determinate character of a thing while ignoring the physical and/or logical relationships which underlie it.

What does happen, however, if one's awareness is thus narrowly focused, is that the 'finite is posited as absolute' (*Enz.* I. 74). It is only if we can see stealing or any other finite thing in its dependence on other things that we can 'reduce it to its finitude and untruth' (*Ibid.*). Hegel's general account of finitude does not in itself license any distinction between, for example, property, respect for property, and stealing. All of these are equally dependent on something else and the concepts of them are finite, particular concepts. The point, however, is that when we look at respect for property and stealing in their appropriate context, that of a system of property-ownership on which they both depend, we can see theft as disruptive of the system in a way that respect for property is not.[25] If, by contrast, we detach theft and its converse from this larger background and ignore their connections with it, immediate awareness can attach itself to the one as well as to the other and we shall see no moral difference between them.[26] Similarly if, and only if, one attends exclusively to one's own religion, the divinity for example of the Dalai Lama, one will seem to have no grounds for rejecting it and no alternative with which to replace it. As soon, however, as one's awareness extends to its historical and logical relationships to other things, notably to other religions, one's attachment to it is undermined.

But why is the case different with the Christian God? Why does immediate awareness reduce him to vacuity, while it makes finite things absolute? The answer seems to be that an infinite object or a spirit cannot be related to other things wholly external to itself, and thus cannot derive its determinate nature from its mediation by them. Since, however, it does have a character or nature, this must be provided by internal or self-mediation (*Enz.* I. 74). But if the immediate nature of the object and the mediation which produces it are both internal to the object, there cannot be a distinction between them such that we could attend to the former at the expense of the latter. A spirit or ego has no definite, immediate nature apart from its mediating activity. It is 'absolute actuosity'. Terms like 'spirit', 'I' and 'ego' are not contrastive, descriptive terms like 'red', 'dog', 'box' or 'tree', because egos do not relate to other things in the way that finite things do (*Enz.* I. 42Z. 1).[27] Consequently one cannot be immediately aware of God as a spirit. If one is not aware of the mediating processes and activities involved, there is nothing to be aware of. God is reduced to the status of a mere supreme being, of an 'Unknown God' (*Enz.* I. 73) or else to that of a finite entity like the Dalai Lama. This is because

> God can only be spirit in so far as one is aware of him as
> *mediating himself* within himself *with himself* . . . . A content
> can only be known as the truth (*das Wahre*) in so far as it is
> not mediated with something else, is not finite, thus mediates
> itself with itself, and is hence mediation and immediate relation
> to itself in one (*Enz.* I. 74).

The mediation involved is of at least two broad types: 'spirit, being consciousness and self-consciousness, is in every case a distinguishing of itself from itself and from something else and is thus mediation' (*Enz.* I. 74Z). It is essential to a spirit that it should, firstly, be aware of a range of objects from which it distinguishes itself and, secondly, aware of itself as a simple ego, bifurcating itself, as it were, into two egos, one of which is aware of the other, though there is in fact only one ego 'distinguishing itself from itself'. The objects of which a spirit is aware are not flatly distinct from it, as sticks are distinct from stones, and, in the case of God at least, the objects from which he distinguishes himself seem to be projected out of himself in order to enable him to become self-conscious.[28] Nothing could be a spirit which did not undergo these mediations and we cannot distinguish an immediate state, the state of being a spirit, which could be known independently of these processes. Infinite entities cannot relax. Immediate awareness, however, would abstract God from his mediations. It detaches God from the world, thus making him finite as well as empty: 'It gives to the *universal* the onesidedness of an *abstraction* . . . . The form of immediacy gives to the *particular* the determination of *being*, of relating *itself to itself*

(*Enz.* I. 74). Immediate awareness cannot capture connections and relationships, the intermeshing of God and finite things, any more than could pre-Kantian metaphysics. Hegel thus reverts to criticism (ii): '*Abstract thinking* . . . and *abstract intuiting* . . . are one and the same' (*Ibid.*).[29]

7 *The mediated and the immediate*

Hegel's criticism (v) of the doctrine of immediate awareness falls into two parts. In the first place, he argues, Jacobi has gone back on his promise to avoid the application of one-sided concepts. He wishes to withold them from God, but is ready to apply them to our awareness of God:

> In such exclusions the standpoint in question immediately reveals itself to be a reversion to the metaphysical understanding, to its *either-or*, thus in fact to the relation of external mediation which rests on clinging to the finite, i.e. to one-sided determinations which that view falsely supposes itself to have left behind (*Enz.* I. 65).

The force of this argument is unclear. The proposition that one-sided concepts are inapplicable to God does not immediately entail that they are inapplicable to our awareness of God. It is true that, on Hegel's view, our awareness of God would in that case be finite. But why can our awareness of an infinite entity not itself be finite? To establish that Jacobi could not legitimately treat God and our awareness of him differently in this respect, that the characteristics of our awareness of an object infect our conception of the object itself, Hegel would have to fall back on his criticism (iii).[30] It is true, again, that if God is infinite, then our awareness of him cannot be wholly distinct from him. But it does not follow that it must be identical with him and therefore itself infinite. It may simply be a part of him, and there is no reason to suppose that an infinite entity cannot contain a finite one as a part of itself.[31] Hegel's general point may be that the concepts of immediacy and mediation should be examined before Jacobi subjects them to the weight he wishes to place on them, but 'such an examination leads to mediation and indeed to knowledge (*Erkenntnis*)' (*Enz.* I. 65. Cf. 78). Indeed, as we have seen, he believes quite generally that our cognitive procedures must be examined, as well as the objects which they disclose to us, both to secure completeness and to preserve us from error.[32] But why should the same cognitive procedures be employed at every stage, both in our knowledge of God and in our knowledge of our way of knowing God? There are perhaps several answers to this, one of them of course that Hegel does not believe that God is distinct from our way of knowing him.[33] For the moment, however, we can be content with the answer that, in this particular case, an examination of immediate awareness would be at odds with the purpose of appealing to it. Immediate awareness is intended to be the final arbiter of truth, and it cannot be this if its own epistemic credentials are to be examined.

8 *The conditions of certainty*

The second part of criticism (v), however, is that an examination of the notion of immediate awareness would have a result un-favourable to it. For we would find that everything is both mediated and immediate.[34] Parents, children, seeds and the mathematician's awareness of hard-won truths are all mediated as well as immediate (*Enz.* I. 65). Generally the mediation is prior to the immediacy, but Hegel considers one case where it is not, namely that of innate ideas. It is quite wrong, he argues, to suppose that the view that our ideas, or some of them, are innate, i.e. 'immediate', excludes external influences or mediation. Education and development are required, if we are to become conscious of such ideas. Opponents of the doctrine have sometimes mistakenly believed that, if ideas are innate, then 'all men would have to have these ideas, have e.g. the law of contradiction in their conscious-ness, be aware of it', while in fact 'the determinations in question, although innate, are not therefore supposed to be already in the *form* of ideas, conceptions of what we are aware of' (*Enz.* I. 67). Education is required to bring them to consciousness, an education which may, in the case of an individual or even of a whole people, be lacking. Hegel does not say how, in that case, we are to dis-tinguish between an idea which is innate and one which is not. Perhaps he would say that the difference depends on a difference in the sort of education that is required in order to bring the idea to consciousness.[35] However, as we shall see, he does not distin-guish enough, or clearly enough, between different types of mediation for this to be an easy question for him to answer.

Immediate awareness, too, is mediated as well as immediate. It is mediated in at least two ways. Firstly, what we are aware of depends on our education, as well as our innate capacities. This applies quite generally and not only to our awareness of God. Immediate awareness of '*God*, of the *right*, of the *ethical*' is in-tended to cover the 'other determinations – instinct, implanted innate ideas, common sense . . . natural reason, etc.' (*Enz.* I. 67).

All of these presuppose an education. This is true even of my immediate awareness of myself. An infant or a primitive could not formulate the thought that he exists. Self-awareness, Hegel argues, is an acquisition won by the long education of the individual and the race (*PG* pp. 133 ff., M. pp. 104 ff.). Philosophy cannot begin with it, as Descartes and Fichte believed, since the pure ego is not 'something entirely familiar, which everyone immediately finds within himself and to which he can adjoin his further reflection; that pure I in its abstract essentiality is rather something unfamiliar to ordinary consciousness, something which it does not find therein' (*WL* I. p. 77, M. p. 76). Secondly we can, if we consider directly the notion of immediate awareness of God, see that it involves mediation:

> in so far as it is awareness of God and of the divine, such
> consciousness is generally described as an *elevation* (*Erheben*)
> above the sensuous, finite, and also above the immediate
> desires and inclinations of the natural heart – an elevation
> which passes into, and culminates in, faith in God and the
> divine, so that this faith is an immediate awareness and
> acceptance (*Fürwahrhalten*), but none the less has that course
> of mediation for its presupposition and condition (*Enz.* I. 68).

Immediate awareness of God, if it occurs, is preceded by ordinary experience and is described as a transcendence of this experience.[36]

Everything, then, including all human awareness is both mediated and immediate. But does it follow that all human awareness is on a par in this respect? Hegel's language sometimes suggests that it does, that there is no difference between just seeing that there is no greatest prime number and accepting it as the conclusion of an inference, between knowing that one exists and knowing that the moon has a side which does not face us. But this would clearly be wrong. One could as well argue that all human contact is as much indirect as direct on the ground every meeting between men has a causal history. But when it is said that two people meet face to face, it is not denied that their encounter has causal antecedents, but only that their contact is mediated by telephones, cameras, letters or microphones. Similarly, not all epistemic contact need be indifferently both direct and indirect. If a person claims to have a direct vision of God, he is not denying that his awareness has a genesis or historical preconditions. Education, physical discipline, and perhaps the taking of drugs are necessary if the vision is to occur. But what he means is that his encounter with the object is not mediated by inferences nor perhaps by conceptual thought of any kind.

A more crucial distinction which Hegel fails to draw is that between epistemic and non-epistemic mediation. Jacobi has argued that if a person is, or feels himself to be, immediately aware of the existence of x or of the truth of p, he is entitled to claim that x exists or that p is true. To what extent does the fact that all immediate awareness is mediated vitiate this entitlement? The answer seems to be that some types of mediation — epistemic mediation — do, while others — non-epistemic mediation — do not. On the one hand, my immediate awareness that Athens is the capital of Greece or that $13 \times 22 = 286$ has no independent cognitive value, for it is mediated by my past education and calculations. If they had been otherwise, then what I am now immediately aware of would have been different. There is a reasonable assumption that my awareness is correct, but the justification of these propositions depends ultimately on the merits of the education and calculations from which my awareness of them derives. On the other hand, my awareness of my own existence does not draw its cognitive force only from the processes which mediate it. My immediate awareness of my own existence depends on an education, the existence of other people, an effort of abstraction on my part, and so on, but it does not follow that any more is required to justify my belief in my own existence than an appeal to my immediate awareness of it.[37] The mediations are in this case non-epistemic.

Was Jacobi's immediate awareness of God mediated epistemically or non-epistemically? Some of the mediation mentioned by Hegel is epistemically irrelevant. The fact, for example, that immediate awareness is preceded by and transcends ordinary sensory and appetitive experience does not entail that such experience plays any cognitive role in the awareness itself. On the other hand, if one's awareness is mediated by a certain type of education and discipline, its cognitive appeal is diminished by the reflection that if one had been educated and disciplined differently, then one would have been immediately aware not of these propositions, but of quite different ones. Similarly, if the use of different drugs were to produce different visions of God, then one could not appeal to one's own particular drug-induced vision in order to contradict claims based on visions produced by alternative drugs. This line of argument, as we have seen, leads to the attenuation of the notion of God. The question when, if ever, the appeal to immediate awareness is a conclusive justification of a proposition, which is not vitiated by any mediating factor, and when it is not is difficult to answer and will not be answered here. One might attempt to answer it in terms of incorrigibility, suggesting, for example, that one's (feeling of) immediate awareness of the truth of p is a sufficient justification of p if, and only if, it is logically impossible that one should feel immediately aware that p and yet p be false. Religious awareness would not satisfy this condition unless its content were exceptionally rarefied. But, again, the condition is too strong for those, like Jacobi, who wish to claim that we are immediately aware of the presence of physical objects.

At all events, Hegel himself does not begin to answer this question and cannot do so in the light of his failure to distinguish epistemic from non-epistemic mediation even in a general way. Given this conflation, he seems to hold that there is nothing of which we are immediately aware in the relevant sense — except possibly near-vacuous things like the concept of pure being — that the acceptance of any proposition requires reference to some other proposition, and that it is a mistake to distinguish between ultimate premises and the conclusions based on them. This is, as we have seen, one reason for the circularity of his system.[38] This view does not, however, follow from the fact that all our awareness or knowledge is mediated in some way or other. What needs to be shown is that it is epistemically mediated, and for this we require some distinction between reasons and causes, justification and explanation. Further evidence of Hegel's omission to supply such a distinction and some reasons for the omission will emerge later.[39]

9 Hegel's debt to Jacobi

Hegel's criticism (v) of the doctrine of immediate awareness seems at odds with some of his other objections to it. Criticisms (iii) and (iv), for example, assume on the face of it that the awareness is, or if it occurred would be, properly immediate. But now, we have learned, no awareness can be only immediate. One consequence threatened by this is that we shall be unable to distinguish between what Jacobi misdescribed as 'immediate awareness' and Hegel's own preferred mode of cognition. This latter, he argues, is both mediated and immediate: 'The *Logic* itself and the *whole of philosophy* is the *example* of the *fact* of a cognition which advances neither in one-sided immediacy nor in one-sided mediation' (*Enz.* I. 75). But so, on Hegel's account, is whatever Jacobi was doing. So is the demonstrative method of pre-Kantian metaphysics, despite its attempt to cognize in a wholly mediated way (*Ibid.*). For everything is both immediate and mediated, whether or not it admits proof and inference. Can Hegel distinguish Jacobi's awareness from his own way of knowing? It is true that he does not wish to draw a sharp line between his own philosophy and others. To do so would be to apply one-sided concepts to his own system, making it just one system among others. One of his responses to scepticism, as we have seen, is to suggest that other views are in some sense contained in his own and that, if they are pressed hard enough, they will grow over into it.[40] Nevertheless some lines, however hazy, have to be drawn. The beliefs of other men are not identical with Hegel's; non-Hegelians are implicit, not explicit, Hegelians. The question, then, is: Is Hegel's way of knowing any more than Jacobi's correctly described?

The answer to this lies in the distinction between external and internal mediation. The phenomenon of immediate awareness is mediated in all kinds of ways. But these mediations are excluded from, and therefore external to, the content of the awareness itself. Hegel's cognition purports, by contrast, to gather up into itself the mediating factors which determine it. The history of philosophy, for example, which underlies and mediates any philosophy, however radical it may appear, is explicitly taken up into Hegel's system both as a distinct phase of it[41] and as a supposed correlate of the *Logic*.[42] This absorption of mediating factors may explain in part his reluctance to distinguish the epistemic from the non-epistemic ones. For he may believe that their integration into the system makes them all, as it were, steps in the argument, whatever their status originally was. Apart from this, however, the procedure has two distinct merits. Firstly, while the naïve believer or the person who is immediately aware of something is, as it were, the plaything of such external factors as the education he happens to have had, the Hegelian philosopher achieves liberation from such contingencies by becoming aware of them. When a factor is explicitly introduced into the system, it is, so to speak, put in its rightful place and it does not have the same determining influence as it would have had if it had not been incorporated, or at least its influence on the system now corresponds to its epistemic entitlement, namely its position in the system. This idea is an extension of the familiar one that one achieves a certain disengagement from factors which mar one's objectivity, from one's prejudices for example, by becoming aware of them.[43]

Secondly, as we have seen, God, if he is to be determinate and genuinely infinite, must be internally mediated, self-mediating.[44] It is only if our cognition is similarly internally mediated that it can reflect the structure of God. Immediate awareness cannot do so, both because what mediates it is external to it and because there is no guarantee that these external mediations correspond to those within the deity. It is only if we become aware of these factors and assign them their place within the system that we can be sure that the mediations of our cognition correspond to those within the object of it.

This, then, is the general contribution which Hegel's examination of the doctrine of immediate awareness makes to his own system. How this programme is to be worked out will become clearer when we have considered his account of mediated cognition, of cognition by means of proofs or arguments.

10 *Proofs, grammar and physiology*

It might be thought that, in the light of his substantial agreement with Jacobi's criticisms of the proofs of God's existence, Hegel should discard them altogether. This expectation could be reinforced by his remark that to suppose that meta-thinking is essential for 'the conception and acceptance of the eternal and the true', that only the proofs can produce 'faith in and conviction of God's existence' is like saying that 'we could not eat until we had acquired knowledge of the chemical, botanical and zoological features of foodstuffs and that digestion would have to be postponed until we had completed the study of anatomy and physiology' (*Enz.* I. 2).[45] The proofs are regarded as the product of sophisticated reflection on naïve beliefs, presupposing them, rather than producing them, in much the way that a grammarian's reflections on language presuppose ordinary linguistic behaviour. It does not follow, however, from this analogy or from Hegel's that the proofs should be abandoned, any more than we should give up the study of physiology or of grammar. The analogies are of course inexact even on Hegel's view. The study of anatomy does not substantially alter our digestive processes or our eating habits, and the study of grammar need not change our primary linguistic behaviour. But naïve faith is disrupted by our reflection upon it. We cannot persist in it or return to it once we have subjected it to meta-thought, nor should we resort to any such spurious reconstruction of naïve faith as immediate awareness.[46] The road to reconciliation is longer than that.

What we must do, rather, is examine the proofs and attempt to overcome the difficulties they involve. The proofs, as Hegel repeatedly points out, had come under attack in his own day from Kant and his followers, and were widely supposed to have been discredited. Hegel does not share this belief and he attempts to reinstate them. His treatment of the proofs, however — like his treatment, perhaps, of almost everything else — operates on more than one level. In the first place he presents objections to Kant's criticisms of the proofs, objections of a sort which might be made by someone who accepted the proofs in their traditional form. Most of these objections seem hopelessly inadequate unless we remember the other level or levels at which he is working. Secondly, however, he presents criticisms of his own, the result of which is a radical, if not explicit, reinterpretation of the proofs, such that both Kant's criticisms and his own replies to them are quite beside the point. Before we consider this in detail, however, we must present his account of the traditional proofs.

11 The traditional conception of the proofs

This account is an odd one, infected by Hegel's own beliefs and preconceptions, and it will be quoted at length. It falls into three subdivisions, concerned with the 'concept of God or his possibility', the proofs of his existence, and his properties. These correspond to the logical items, concept, proof and proposition:

(a) The main question in the understanding's consideration (*verständigen Betrachtung*) of God is which predicates suit or do not suit what *we conceive* (*vorstellen*) God to be. The contrast between reality and negation is here taken as absolute; therefore all that remains for the *concept*, as the understanding takes it, is in the end the empty abstraction of the indeterminate essence (*Wesens*), of pure reality or positivity, the dead product of the modern enlightenment. (b) The *proving* of finite cognition in general displays the inverted position (*verkehrte Stellung*) that an objective ground of God's being is to be stated, and God's being thus presents itself as something which is *mediated* by something else. This proving, which has the identity of the understanding for its rule, is embarrassed by the difficulty of making the transition from the *finite* to the *infinite*. Thus it was either unable to free God from the persistently positive finitude of the existing world (*von der positiv bleibenden Endlichkeit der daseienden Welt*), so that God had to be determined as the immediate substance of the world (pantheism) — or he remained an object over against the subject, thus in this way a *finite* entity (dualism). (c) The *properties*, whereas they are supposed to be determinate and diverse, have strictly disappeared in the abstract concept of pure reality, of the indeterminate essence. But in so far as in conception the finite world still remains as a *true* being with God over against it, the conception of God's diverse relations

216

to the world also arises, relations which, determined as properties, must on the one hand be themselves of a finite kind (e.g.
righteous, benevolent, powerful, wise, etc.), since they are
relations to finite states, but on the other hand are supposed
also to be infinite. This contradiction admits, at this standpoint, only of the nebulous resolution through quantitative
increase — pushing them into indeterminacy, into the *sensus
eminentior*. But this in fact reduces the property to nothing
and merely leaves it a name (*Enz.* I. 36).

Hegel is trying to say too many things in this passage, but his
general conception of the traditional proofs is this. God as he is
in himself is a pure, featureless essence — the concept of God. He
is not, however, the only entity in the universe, but co-exists with
a world which he in some sense supports or underlies and to
which he is related in various ways. The relationships between
God and the world confer on each of them certain properties.
The world has certain general features, its contingency, for example,
and its apparent purposiveness, and God has the corresponding
properties of being a necessary being and a purposive demiurge.
Each of these general features of the world forms the basis of a
proof of the existence of a transcendent being identified as the
bearer of the corresponding property. If, for example, we start
from the fact that all the things and events in the world are contingent, then we arrive at the conclusion that there exists a necessary being; if we begin from the apparently purposive ordering
and interlocking of things in the world, we infer the existence of
a purposive designer; and so on (cf. *VBDG* VIII). The proofs,
then, might be conceived not so much as establishing the existence
of an entity of which we have a clear and complete conception,
but as filling out our conception of God.[47] This is not, of course,
how the rationalist theologians in fact conducted their enterprise.
On Hegel's view, they tacitly presupposed the full-fledged traditional conception of God and, far from giving a free rein to
thought, used this conception as the criterion of the direction and
correctness of their reasoning.[48] But this factor need not be taken
into account here.

The picture becomes more complicated when we learn that the
inferential traffic between God and the world runs in both directions and not only one. We start, as before, with a more or less
empty concept of God:

For the understanding, all determination, as opposed to simple
identity, is only a limit (*Schranke*), a negation as such; thus all
reality is to be taken only limitlessly, i.e. indeterminately, and

217

God, being the sum of all realities (*Inbegriff aller Realitäten*) or the most real being (*das allerrealste Wesen*), becomes a *simple abstraction* and all that is left for determination is the similarly entirely abstract determinacy of *being*. Abstract *identity*, which is also called here the concept, and *being* are the two elements the unification of which is sought by reason . . . . This unification admits of two *ways* or forms; one can begin from *being* and pass from there to the *abstraction* of *thinking* or, conversely, the transition can be effected from the *abstraction* to *being* (*Enz.* I. 49, 50).

The proofs which pass from being to abstract identity or the concept are the proofs we have already considered, those namely which take as their premises statements about the world and the finite things in it, and infer from them the existence of God. The proof which passes from the concept to being is the ontological proof, one which purports to establish the existence of God from premisses about the concept of God. There is then, on Hegel's view, a pleasing symmetry between these two types of proof. They both establish a connection between the concept and being, but they do so by proceeding in contrary directions. The symmetry is shattered as soon as we ask: 'Is the being in question the being of God or the being of the world?' But this question will be postponed until we consider the ontological proof.[49] For the moment our concern is with those proofs which pass from being – the being of the world – to God.

12 *Concept and properties*

A curious feature of Hegel's account of the proofs is his distinction between the concept of God and his properties. We would normally think of the (or a) concept of God as involving some account of his properties. One may, after all, have the concept of an elephant without knowing everything about elephants, but one must be able to say something about their generic properties. The contrast reflects a variety of factors. It depends in part, firstly, on Hegel's own belief that in the case of an ordinary finite thing, the distinction between the thing and its properties coincides with the distinction between the thing as it is, or would be, in itself and the effects on it of its relationships to other things.[50] The next step is to identify the thing or the inner core of the thing, apart from its development and its entanglements with other things, with its concept. What makes this natural, if not legitimate, is firstly the fact that in a statement in which a predicate is ascribed to a thing, such as 'The cat is happy', it is easy to suppose that while the predicate-term denotes a property of the thing, the subject-term denotes the thing itself, using of course the concept of the thing as an intermediary. Since any feature of the thing can be predicated of it, the thing itself and the concept of it are emptied of their content. Secondly, Hegel's account of the untruth of finite things[51] suggests the coincidence, if not identity, of the thing as it is, or would be, in itself and its concept. A finite entity falls short of its concept owing to those very relationships to other entities in virtue of which it has a determinate character. If *per impossibile* it were unrelated to other things, then it would fully correspond to its concept.

God, the rational theology implies, is a finite entity distinct from, and dependent upon, the phenomenal world. It follows that we can draw the same distinction between him, or his concept, and his properties as we make in the case of any other finite thing. If his relationships with the finite world are for any reason severed, then he becomes an indeterminate, featureless essence. Pre-Hegelian theology provides at least two examples of this. First there is the tendency, brought to a head by Newton and his followers, to explain natural phenomena in natural terms and thus to dispense with the need for divine intervention in the world. Hegel concedes that Newton himself continued to regard God as the creator and director of the world, but adds that

> it is a consequence of this explaining in terms of forces that the inferential understanding proceeds to fix each one of these individual forces in its own right and to maintain them in this finitude as an ultimate; over against this finitized world of independent forces and stuffs only the abstract infinity of an unknowable, supreme, other-worldly essence remains for the determination of God. This then is the standpoint of materialism and of the modern enlightenment, whose awareness (*Wissen*) of God renounces the what (*das Was*, viz. the question what God is) and reduces itself to the mere that (*das blosse Dass*) of his being (*Enz.* I. 136Z. 2).

It is only in virtue of his relations to the world that God has a determinate nature, or at any rate one that we can know about. If these relations are severed by explaining events in the world solely in terms of each other, then God is reduced to a bare, featureless entity.[52]

The same thing can happen, however, if, instead of being cut off from the world, God is regarded as the only entity there is, with nothing distinct from himself with which he can interact.

There is an escape-route here, as we have already seen, namely that provided by internal self-mediation. But if no self-mediation occurs, an isolated entity can only be a blank, featureless entity. This is at least a part of the diagnosis of Hegel's treatment of Spinoza. As we have seen, one of his complaints against Spinoza is that if he is to explain how his single substance can have attributes and modes, he must assume that there is something outside this substance, an intellect to which the modes and attributes appear.[53] Support for this is found in Spinoza's definition of an attribute: 'By *attribute*, I mean that which the intellect perceives as constituting the essence of substance.'[54] Hegel interprets this as implying that it is only because there is an intellect which perceives substance that substance has attributes at all, that the attributes are appearances to an intellect. This intellect cannot itself be only a mode of substance, as Spinoza claims,[55] but must be external to it. That this is a misinterpretation of Spinoza is suggested by a fact which Hegel glosses over, that substance has an infinite number of attributes, all but two of which, namely thought and extension, are inaccessible to our intellect and cannot therefore be constituted by it.[56] But the doctrine that the properties of a thing are constituted by its relationships to other things suggests another reason, apart from sheer misunderstanding, for Hegel's puzzlement over Spinoza's attributes. Since substance is unique and is not related to anything else and since Spinoza supplies no account of a way in which it 'mediates itself with itself', it should be simply indeterminate and have no modes or attributes at all. Only the tacit assumption of something outside it can remedy this deficiency.

13 *Perfection and abstraction*

The distinction between the concept of God and his properties does not, however, depend only on Hegel's own beliefs, but also reflects genuine tensions within theology itself. There is pressure, from more than one direction, on the theologian to give a thin account of God, claiming no more for him than that he is the supreme being or that he exists.[57] The source of pressure to which Hegel adverts in this context is the need to exclude from God and from our account of him any limit or negation. Leibniz exemplifies this position:

God is absolutely perfect, *perfection* being only the magnitude of positive reality taken in its strictest meaning, setting aside the limits or bounds in things which have them.[58] . . . Hence

God alone (or the necessary being) has this prerogative, that
he must exist if he is possible. And since nothing can hinder
the possibility of that which possesses no limitations, no
negation, and, consequently, no contradiction, this alone is
sufficient to establish the existence of God *a priori*. [59]

Hegel would not disagree that we can establish the existence of
such a deity *a priori*, but he would argue that it is not worth
establishing. For he accepts Spinoza's dictum that 'All determination is negation'[60] and, by this principle, a negation-free
entity can only be an indeterminate being or essence, something
which belongs, as it were, only to the highest genus of all and has
no further *differentia*. The exclusion of negation from God's
nature reduces him to a mere will-o'-the-wisp, unknowable only
because there is nothing to be known: *Das reine Licht ist die reine
Finsternis* (*Enz.* I. 36Z).[61]

In so far as God is related to the world, he must of course have
properties corresponding to definite states of the world. But this,
Hegel argues, does not help matters. For since these properties are
those of a supposedly infinite entity, they must again be understood as infinite in degree, without any limitation or negation.
Leibniz again illustrates the point:[62]

> The perfections of God are those of our souls, but he possesses
> them without limits: he is an ocean of which we have only
> received drops; there is in us some power, some knowledge,
> some goodness; but these perfections are all complete in God.

But this again, Hegel argues, leads by the same principle to the
utter indeterminacy of our conception of God. He does not enter
with any great precision into the question why this is so, but presumably his idea is that if a property is taken in an infinite degree
without any negation or limitation, then it is no longer limited or
negated by other such properties, so that infinite power, for
example, is just the same as infinite wisdom or as infinite goodness (cf. *VBDG* VII). The result is not the rich, dialectical ferment
which Hegel's *Logic* purports to provide, but simply an indeterminate mess. We are back then with the empty conception
of God with which we began, and it is only by giving way to the
power of *Vorstellung* and suppressing the intimations of thought
that we can think of God as possessing a diversity of attributes.
The position is an unstable one, hovering between thought and
conception, between the vacuous and the picturesque.

In general terms, the dilemma here seems genuine. If God is
described in rich, concrete terms, then some predicates apply to

him to the exclusion of others. But if that is so, then God is only one thing among others or, at any rate, one thing among other possible things. If, on the other hand, negation and contrast are excluded from his nature and, as far as possible, from our description of it, then the description is vanishingly thin and intangible. It hardly makes sense to ask whether such an entity exists or not, for there is no intelligible difference between its existing and its not existing.[63]

14 *Theology and geometry*

A possible third reason for the contrast between the concept of God and his properties brings us to the nature of proof itself. We have already suggested that the proofs can be regarded not so much as establishing the existence of an entity of which we have an antecedent clear conception, but as filling out our hazy, preliminary conception of that entity. If that is so, then the concept of God may correspond to the vague notion of him with which we begin, and his properties to the richer conception which we acquire in the course of arguing for his existence. That Hegel sees the proofs of God's existence in this way is implied by the fact that he criticizes the customary proofs not because they are invalid, but because they prove the existence of the wrong sort of God, generally a finite God.[64] It is also suggested by his criticisms of proofs in geometry:

> When we prove a geometrical proposition, each individual part of the proof must carry its own justification with it, ... but it is no less true that the whole course of the procedure determines itself and justifies itself by the end (*Zweck*) which we have therein and by the fact that this end is attained by such a procedure (*VBDG* II, in *VPR* II. p. 358, S.S. III. p. 166).

Or again:

> The *essentiality* of the proof, however, even in mathematical cognition has not yet the meaning and nature of being an element in the result itself, but in this result it is rather past and vanished.... But philosophical cognition ... contains both [the existence and the essence of the object], whereas mathematical cognition exhibits only the becoming of *existence*, i.e. of the being of the nature of the subject-matter in *cognition* as such (*PG* pp. 35 f., M. pp. 24 f.; cf. *WL* II. pp. 533 ff., M. pp. 811 ff.).

222

These passages have of course more than one point. One of them, however, seems to be that the meaning of a theorem to be proved is fixed and understood independently of the proof given of it. It is in the light of our desire to establish this theorem that we decide what the steps of our proof are to be.[65] Each step must of course be a legitimate one, but the theorem to be proved determines which of the indefinitely many legitimate steps is taken at each stage. Philosophical proofs, by contrast, and these should include the proofs of God's existence, differ in this respect. The theorem to be proved is not antecedently given and some other way, intrinsic to the proof itself, must be found of deciding what the steps of the proof are to be.[66]

Something of what Hegel has in mind can perhaps be seen from a consideration of our attempts to establish empirically the existence of ordinary physical entities. Suppose, firstly, that one sets out to show that there is a dolphin in Lake Windermere. In this case one has a more or less clear conception of what one wants to detect before one has detected it. Even here of course one's initial conception of what needs to be shown will be less definite and determinate than what one eventually shows once the evidence is forthcoming. If there is in fact a dolphin in Lake Windermere, then it will have all kinds of particular features and relationships that were not conveyed by the proposition which one undertook to establish. Merely possible objects can be indeterminate in ways that actual ones cannot. This in itself provides some basis for a distinction between the concept, that of a dolphin in Lake Windermere, and the properties, those features of the actual dolphin which are not determined by the mere fact that it is a dolphin in Lake Windermere. This distinction should not arise in the case of God, for as an infinite entity he is fully determined by his concept. But if, like the rationalist theologians, we assume that God is distinct from the world, then he can have surprising properties, in virtue of his relationships to it, that could not have been derived from his concept alone.

Hegel's conception of proof, however, is better illustrated not by this case, but by the attempt to seek evidence for the existence of some unfamiliar entity such as the Loch Ness monster. We start out, not with a full-grown concept like that of a dolphin, but with a vague, embryonic conception of something large and animate. If evidence emerges for the existence of the monster, then this evidence will not only increase the probability of the creature's existing, but will also fill out our conception of it. Our initial conception − the 'concept' − is not of course wholly indeterminate and cannot be if we are to know what is to count as evidence for or against its exemplification. There are indeed few restrictions on the nature of the Loch Ness monster apart from location, size and animality, but it could not be a log, a sunken ship or an eel. If one of these things turned out to be the closest approximation to a monster contained in the Loch, then we would say that there is no Loch Ness monster. Hegel's ideal of proof sometimes seems to be a limiting case of this, a process of reasoning whose beginning imposes itself on the thinker and each subsequent step of which is determined by its predecessor, so that no appeal is required to a thesis to be proved however vaguely conceived that thesis may be.

15 *Hegel's reply to Kant*

The proofs of God's existence, then, or at least those which proceed from premises about the world, may be seen, provisionally, in this light. The differences between the proofs depend on the different ways in which their premises characterize the world. The cosmological proof, for example, characterizes it as a collection of contingent objects and events, and infers from it the existence of a necessary being (*Enz.* I. 50).[67] The teleological proof, by contrast, conceives the world as a 'collection of infinitely many *purposes* and *purposive* relationships' and consequently arrives at the conception of God as a purposive designer (*Enz.* I. 50).[68] These are, on Hegel's view, only two of very many proofs, each of which proceeds from some feature of the world to a god with the corresponding property, establishing his existence and building up our picture of him at the same time.[69]

Does this way of regarding the proofs entail that they are all valid? Hegel sometimes seems to assume that it does, since he hardly ever criticizes a proof in respect of its validity, but rather the conclusion it establishes. If our understanding of a conclusion were always tailored to fit the arguments or evidence for it, then no argument could be invalid. If, for example, 'There is a Loch Ness monster' were understood to mean only something like 'There is something or some collection of things responsible for the peculiar ripples, bulges, etc. on the surface of the Loch', then, if we granted the existence of the ripples, etc., we would have to grant the existence of the Loch Ness monster. If an argument contains several steps, of course, one step might still be invalidly derived from its predecessors, but this can be met by arguing similarly that our understanding of each step is to be trimmed to suit the manner of its derivation. One difficulty would be to secure a unique interpretation of any given step, for indefinitely many things are entailed by any single proposition. But, again, this difficulty could be met by making the interpretation suitably vague or general.

In practice, however, the determination of the sense of a conclusion by the arguments for it is not taken this far. We have some understanding of statements like 'God exists' or 'The Loch Ness monster exists' independently of the arguments for them. Even if we did not, we would still have an understanding of the propositions which fill out these conceptions, propositions of the form 'x is a purposive designer' or 'x is covered with green scales', apart from such arguments. Since this is so there can still be in such cases a gap between the premises and the conclusion. A person might well argue illegitimately that there is something green and scaly in Loch Ness or that there is a purposive designer of nature, even if these features are not involved in his initial conception of God or of the Loch Ness monster.

Kant and his followers had argued that the proofs of God's existence are invalid in this way. Hegel's answer to this is, on the face of it, inadequate. It is, as we have seen, that Kant's criticisms are based on a radical Humean scepticism about the legitimacy of thought. What the proofs effect, or perhaps describe, is the subjection of the world to thought and this means to 'strip off it the form of individualities and contingencies and to grasp it as a universal, active being which is intrinsically (*an und für sich*) necessary and determines itself in accordance with universal purposes . . . to grasp it as God' (*Enz.* I. 50). Kant's criticism of such thinking amounts to no more than the objection that it involves a transition from one thing to another, from perceptions to thoughts. He is simply inconsistent in rejecting Hume's account of causality, while accepting his view that we cannot legitimately infer the existence of a deity from features of the perceptible world (*Enz.* I. 50).[70] To the obvious reply that these are quite different types of thinking, between which both Hume and Kant distinguished, Hegel seems oblivious, speaking only in general of thinking (about) the world:

> The rise [to God] has for its basis nothing more than the *thinking* of the world, not merely the sensuous animal-like consideration of it. The *essence, substance,* the *universal power,* and *final purpose* (*Zweckbestimmung*) of the world is for thinking and *only* for thinking. The so-called proofs of God's existence are to be seen only as *descriptions* and analyses *of the course of the spirit* within itself, a *thinking* spirit which thinks the sensuous. The *elevation* of thinking above the sensuous, its

225

transcendence of the finite to the infinite, the *leap* which is
made with the breaking off of the series of the sensuous into
the supersensible, all this is thinking itself, this transition is
only thinking. If such a transition is not supposed to be made,
then this means that we are not supposed to think. In fact
animals make no such transition; *they* stick to sensuous feeling
(*Empfindung*) and intuition; they therefore have no religion
(*Ibid.*).

This, however, is a muddle. The person who argues for the existence of God from some feature of the world is not simply imposing thoughts on his raw sensory intake. The premiss of the
argument, that the world is, for example, apparently purposively
organized or that it is causally ordered, already involves thoughts
and presupposes that this type of thinking has been done. Animals
cannot entertain the premisses of such arguments, let alone derive
conclusions from them. What Kant finds problematic is the next
step, involving thinking of a different type, namely the derivation
from this premiss of a conclusion about a transcendent entity.
From the muddle, however, we can perhaps extract three arguments against Kant:

(i) If we can legitimately engage in thinking of the first type,
why can we not embark on thinking of the second type? As we
have already seen, Kant has an answer to this which Hegel does
not meet directly.[71]

(ii) The proofs are not strictly proofs at all, but simply descriptions of mankind's 'rise to God'. (This expression is ambiguous
and, as we shall see, intentionally so.)[72] The question of their
validity does not therefore arise. They are to be assessed only in
terms of their historical or psychological accuracy. This is the on-
looker-pose which, as we have already seen, Hegel regularly adopts.
It might still be objected of course that what is described is the
acceptance of invalid arguments rather than valid ones, that the
'spirit' took the wrong 'course' and it is the philosopher's job to
say so. But Hegel's point seems to be that the course of the spirit
within itself is not strictly a single argument at all, but more a
process of development by self-correction. Bad arguments may
occur within this process, but they are also abandoned or reno-
vated within it.[73] The proofs are descriptions of this whole process,
rather than of individual arguments that arise in the course of it.

(iii) There really are not, in any case, two distinct types of
thinking here. To rise to God is not, as Kant supposes, to infer the
existence of some entity which is numerically distinct from the
perceptible world. It is, rather, to continue the process of thinking

226

about this world, and to object to the proofs, as Kant does, is to cut off this enterprise at a quite arbitrary point. This reply is problematic for two reasons. Firstly, there are, on Hegel's view, distinct types of thinking which his talk of 'thinking the world' helps to conflate. To engage in one of these types of thinking does not necessarily involve all the others.[74] The answer to this, however, is that these types of thinking are not related to each other in the way that the premiss and conclusion of an argument are, so that to criticize the validity of the proofs is quite beside the point. Secondly, what are we to make of Hegel's jocular suggestion that only animals have no religion, in the light of his objection to the decline in the standards for the ascription of a religion?[75] The answer seems to be that it *does* matter what sort of thinking one engages in, that men are exposed to. a variety of theological defects.[76] Where we draw the line between religion and irreligion, between belief and atheism, is, however, irrelevant. In any case, Kant's criticisms are intended to apply to some believers whose thought in fact remains at a primitive level, that of a vacuous and/or a finite deity. Kant's objection to them is the wrong one. They think too little and not too much.

Hegel's reply to Kant makes some sense, then, if we remember that he is radically transforming the proofs and the conception of God which they involve. This transformation is often carried out behind a smokescreen of verbiage. But the cover is not impenetrable and the way in which the change occurs will appear more clearly when we consider Hegel's own criticisms of the traditional proofs.

16 *Criticisms of the traditional view*

What, then, are Hegel's criticisms of the proofs? There are, firstly, three closely connected objections, which are presented separately but point to the same solution:

(i) The proofs in their orthodox form are based on the 'identity of the understanding', and this means that they cannot pass from the finite to the genuinely infinite. God either remains entangled in the finite world, giving a version of pantheism, or he is an object distinct from the world, giving a dualistic position (*Enz.* I. 36).

(ii) In arguing for the existence of God from the nature and existence of finite things, the rationalist theologians conceive God as dependent on or grounded in finite things. This is unsatisfactory, since God is supposed to be not dependent on anything else, but rather the ground of everything (*Enz.* I. 36Z, 62).

(iii) This is because the way in which the proofs are expressed implies that their starting-point, the finite world or a certain view of it, remains the same at the end of the proof as it did at the beginning. The proofs must be restructured or reconceived so that this implication does not hold (*Enz.* I. 50).

These objections will be considered in turn.

17 *Finitude and deduction*

The first criticism is relatively straightforward. When Hegel says that the proofs are governed by the 'identity of the understanding', he seems to mean that they are, or purport to be, ordinary deductive arguments. Identity covers a variety of things. For example, comparing geometrical figures and showing them to be congruent, similar, or equal in area, is regarded as an application of the principle of identity, not because it is the result of a deductive argument, but because it brings out an identity between the figures (*Enz.* I. 80Z). Again, dividing things up into distinct species and genera is an application of the same principle (*Ibid.*). However, the proneness of the understanding to make sharp distinctions between things and between concepts is regularly associated with deductive argument. Why this is so is not entirely clear. It is true that one of the criteria for the distinctness of genera is that nothing can belong to more than one genus and that a sharply defined concept contrasts with a contradictory or contrary concept which excludes its application.[77] But this implies only that we should not contradict ourselves, and not contradicting oneself is a different matter from confining oneself to deductive arguments. The point, however, is that non-empirical arguments depend on relationships between concepts, and cannot range beyond the paths that these provide. If we insist on sharp, rigid distinctions between concepts, then the only relations between them are those of complete identity, partial identity and sheer difference, relations, that is, which license only deductive arguments, together perhaps with inductive ones (*WL* II. pp. 384 ff., M. pp. 689 ff.).[78] Given, then, that the proofs of God's existence are deductive arguments, they cannot establish the existence of an infinite entity from premises which refer only to finite things. There is a logical gap between the finite and the infinite which the principle of identity cannot surmount.

As we have seen, however, Hegel does not conclude from this that the proofs fail to establish their independently understood conclusion. Rather, what they establish is to be understood in the light of the proofs — the existence of a finite God. The problem is not so much whether God exists or not, but what sort of God exists. And a finite God is the wrong sort. There are, however, two alternatives here. A finite God might be simply identical with the finite world, and then what is established is a version of pantheism, a version which amounts to atheism.[79] There is no difficulty in the claim that deductive arguments with premises concerning the world can show the existence of God in this sense, for all that this amounts to is the existence of the finite world, and, obviously enough, premises which refer only to the finite world can entail its existence. What is questionable is Hegel's assumption that the phenomenal world as a whole, if there were no deity or other supersensible entity distinct from it, would be finite rather than infinite. Some reasons for this assumption will be suggested later.[80]

The alternative to this is that God is distinct from the world and therefore again finite. In contrast to pantheism, however, this conclusion cannot be established by deductive arguments whose premises concern only the world. Although God is, on this account, finite, his finitude does nothing to clear the logical gulf between him and the world. For there is no smoother logical path between two distinct finite entities than there is between a finite entity and an infinite one. This point is blurred when we speak, as Hegel often does, only of 'the finite' without stressing that God and the world are distinct finite entities. If he had noted it, he might have taken more seriously Kant's objection to the traditional proofs. It does not follow, however, that Hegel's own version of the proofs is open to the same objection, so that his failure to notice it may not matter in the long run.

For the moment, the main consequences to be drawn from this criticism are that something must be done to establish a proper relationship between God and the finite world, and that a form of argument which transcends the 'identity of the understanding' is required for this purpose.

18 Grounds and dependence

To argue for the existence of God from the nature of finite things implies, Hegel suggests, that God is dependent on finite things. We have already seen that he blurs the distinction between epistemic and non-epistemic mediation.[81] This criticism seems at first sight to rest on a similarly gross confusion between epistemic grounds or reasons — as in 'He's ill, because he has spots' — and non-epistemic or ontological grounds — as in 'He has spots, because he's ill.'[82] If one argues for the existence of God from features of finite things, this no more implies that God is dependent on finite things than, if one infers the presence of a person from the sight of a footprint, one need suppose that the person depends on the footprint rather than the footprint on the person. Nor does it follow that one conceives God to be distinct from the world, any more than, when one infers the presence of a person from the sight of a foot, one need conceive the person to be distinct from the foot rather than a whole of which the foot is a part. The doctrine that the meaning of a conclusion depends on the arguments for it does nothing to undermine this distinction. The ripples on Loch Ness may help to form our conception of the monster as well as constituting evidence for its existence. But the epistemic and semantic dependence of statements about the monster on statements about the ripples does not entail that the monster depends on the ripples rather than the ripples on the monster. Nor again does the doctrine imply that the entities which constitute our evidence for the existence of the monster must be distinct from it. The fin on which, or on our glimpse of which, our statements about the monster are semantically and epistemically dependent may be a part of the monster, just as the foot is a part of the person.

Why, then, does Hegel assume that the logical or epistemological relationships within our arguments must, in the case of God at least, correspond to the ontological relationships of the entities with which they are concerned? To see this, we must consider another criticism which Hegel makes of proofs in geometry:

> The movement of the mathematical proof does not belong to the object, but is an activity *external* to the subject-matter. Thus the nature of the right-angled triangle itself does not divide itself in the way exhibited in the construction which is necessary for the [viz. Pythagoras'] proof of the theorem which expresses its ratio; the whole production of the result is a procedure and means of cognition' (*PG* p. 35, M. p. 24).

It is only because we in our proofs make moves which the object of the proof does not that there can be so many different proofs of, for example, Pythagoras' theorem (*VBDG* VIII).[83] If the proofs of God's existence are taken to be, in this respect, philosophical proofs and unlike the proofs of geometry, then it would indeed follow from the structure of the proofs as they stand not simply that God is dependent on finite things, but that he develops out of them in some way corresponding to the development of our conclusions about him out of premises about finite things. But why should we take the proofs in this way? Hegel does not, after all, believe that geometrical proofs are remediable in this respect.

Their defects are the result of the nature of their subject-matter (*PG* pp. 37 ff., M. pp. 25 ff.). Why should it be any different with the proofs of God's existence?

Hegel seems to believe that the answer lies in his remark that for rationalist theology God 'remained an object over against the subject' (*Enz.* I. 36). This consideration is introduced in the course of his brief account of dualism. He objects to the view that God is distinct from the birds, flowers, sunsets and other finite entities to which the premises of the proofs refer, but he has special reasons for his hostility to the view that God is distinct from the subject, his proofs and his provings. If my proofs or provings differ in structure from God himself, then I and my provings cannot be identical with God. I cannot, moreover, be wholly absorbed in my subject-matter in the way that a philosopher should be,[84] but must retain an element of wilfulness in order to decide how the proofs should run independently of the movement or structure of the subject-matter. Hegel's point is, then, more properly expressed in the form of a dilemma: *either* the proofs are of the philosophical variety and in that case they imply that God depends on finite things *or* they are of the geometrical type and in that case they imply the distinctness of the knowing subject from God.

But why should the rationalist theologian hesitate to accept the second limb of this dilemma? It is only if our proofs are to be identical with God that their structure must coincide with his. The infinity of God, however, does not require this identity, but only that our proofs and provings should be in some sense a part of God.[85] And there is no special reason why a part should have the same structure as the whole to which it belongs. It may be difficult to think of the wilful, independent theologian as a part of God as he is traditionally conceived, but surely no more difficult than it is to assign this status to the wilful, independent mathematician. It may, again, be desirable that our arguments should, if possible, reflect the ontological structure of the object we are arguing about. But it does not seem necessary, nor may it be even possible, that they should.

There are, however, at least two reasons why Hegel cannot accept this reply. The first is that, as we have seen, there is in the case of God, at least when he is properly conceived, no distinction between his immediate state and his mediations.[86] Mediations, however, are what arguments capture, and if we do not embody them in our arguments about God, they will be lost to us. Right-angled triangles have an immediate nature which persists, even if we ignore the mediations responsible for it, but God does not. The second is that none of the replies that we have so far made to Hegel's argument has assigned an adequate relationship to God and finite things. To suggest that he is related to finite things in the way that monsters are to ripples or people are to footprints is to propose a dualistic view, with a God as finite as men and monsters. To suggest, on the other hand, that he is related to them as people are to feet or monsters are to fins is to propose a version of pantheism, in effect of atheism. But what alternatives are there and how are they to be encapsulated in our proofs of his existence? To see this, we must turn to Hegel's third criticism of the traditional proofs and the theological problem which underlies it.

19 *Identity, difference and Spinoza*

This theological problem emerges most explicitly when Hegel considers Spinoza. Spinoza had been generally regarded as an atheist on the ground that he identified God, i.e. substance, with the world. But this, Hegel argues, is not necessarily so. There are in fact three possible views that may be taken about God and the world:

(i) The finite world exists and God does not.

(ii) God exists and the finite world does not, but is only 'phenomenon, illusory being'.

(iii) God exists and so does the finite world (*VGP* III. pp. 162 f., H. III. pp. 280 f.).

Position (iii), that God and the world co-exist, is unsatisfactory because it makes God a finite object alongside other finite objects. Positions (i) and (ii) can be regarded as different versions of pantheism, of the view that God is identical with the world. A statement of the form 'x is identical with y' or 'x = y' does not necessarily amount to or imply a denial of the existence of x or a denial of the existence of y. The statement, for example, 'Thera is the same (island) as Santorini' does not imply that Thera does not exist or that Santorini does not, nor does 'Water is H_2O' involve denying the existence of water or of H_2O. Some identity-statements do, however, involve a denial of the existence of, or at least an ontological downgrading of, one of the identified items. For example, 'Flying saucers are (simply/nothing but) certain cloud formations' implies that flying saucers do not exist and 'The Loch Ness monster is the ship that sunk in 1789' implies that the monster does not exist. Again, to say 'The mind is (just) the brain' or 'Physical objects are (just) our sensations' suggests at least an ontological downgrading of minds or of physical objects. Whether or not a statement of the form 'x = y' downgrades x or y or neither presumably depends on whether the properties which we ascribe to the single object or type of object once we have accepted the truth of the identity-statement are more closely associated with our antecedent conception of x or of y or are equally associated with both. The standard symbol for identity is '=' and this can be retained for those cases where the identity-statement does not imply the downgrading of either of the identified terms. Thus 'Thera is Santorini' can be written as 'Thera = Santorini.' But in those cases where one or other of the identified terms is downgraded, the statement can be symbolized as 'x ⇒ y' or as 'y ⇒ x' depending on whether it is x or y that is demoted. It is perhaps more natural to write 'x ⇒ y' than 'y ⇐ x', but these can be taken as equivalent. Thus 'The Loch Ness monster is the sunken ship' can be written as 'The Loch Ness monster ⇒ the sunken ship' or 'The sunken ship ⇐ the Loch Ness monster.'

What about the pantheistic statement 'God is the world'? It cannot, Hegel implies, be read as a non-reductive identity-statement of the type 'Thera is Santorini' and symbolized as 'God = the world.' This is primarily because our antecedent conceptions of God and of the world are so different that no single entity could straightforwardly be both God and the world. It can, then, be interpreted in either of two ways, as 'God ⇒ the world', implying the ontological demotion of God, or as 'The world ⇒ God', implying that the world does not strictly exist. Spinoza was customarily taken to have meant 'God ⇒ the world', an assertion of atheism. Hegel believes that, on the contrary, he meant 'The world ⇒ God', a position which Hegel entitles 'acosmism' (*Enz.* I. 50). This cannot properly be regarded as atheism, and Spinoza has only been interpreted in that way because 'it is found more intelligible that God should be denied than that the world should be denied' (*Ibid.*).

This interpretation of Spinoza is no doubt more nearly right than that of his detractors, but it is, as we have seen, probably incorrect.[87] (Hegel has of course a vested interest in interpreting his predecessors so that their views come close, but not too close, to his own.) The trouble in this case is that the three alternatives which he offers to Spinoza:

    (i) God ⇒ the world
    (ii) The world ⇒ God
    (iii) God ≠ the world.

are not regarded by him as exhaustive. Hegel's own view is not identical with any of these, but involves some sort of dynamic interaction between God and the world, which, if it is to be symbolized in these terms at all, would be expressed as:

(iv) God ⇔ the world, i.e. God ⇒ the world and the world
⇒ God
or perhaps as:
God ⇒ the world ⇒ God.

This, however, has not been provided with an interpretation by what we have said in this section and it looks, on the face of it, incoherent. This perhaps is why Hegel does not offer it to Spinoza, a philosopher primarily of the understanding rather than of reason. More will be said to clarify it later.[88] For the moment it is enough that, although not himself an acosmist, Hegel regarded it as the most satisfactory of the three alternatives, and his discussion of the proofs which proceed from the world to God is conducted in terms of it.

20 *The rise to God*

How does this affect the interpretation of the proofs? The force of an ordinary argument, Hegel implies, depends on the truth of the premisses. An argument such as:

All philosophers are wise
Hegel is a philosopher
Therefore, Hegel is wise

may indeed be valid even if the premisses are false, but in that case the argument does nothing to establish the truth of the conclusion. We cannot, at the end of the argument, claim that the premisses are false or in some way faulty without to that extent undermining our argument for accepting the conclusion. In their traditional form, the proofs of God's existence are similar in this respect to an ordinary argument, but if they are taken in this way then they inevitably lead to dualism or to atheistic pantheism. For their premisses assert or imply the unqualified existence of the finite world. The proofs, then, are to be taken in a different way, as proceeding from premisses which, although they are at first accepted as true, are seen to be false, or half-false, in the light of the conclusion that is derived from them. This provides the answer to Jacobi's difficulty. He argued that in the proofs conditions, namely the world or some aspect of the world, are sought for the unconditioned God, thus reducing it to something grounded and dependent, and because of this he rejected thinking altogether in favour of immediate awareness. But if we interpret the proofs properly, then our knowledge is in one way mediated or conditioned, but in another way there is no mediation or transition at all. The conditions are negated, are, as it were, absorbed into that which they condition, so that it is after all something unconditioned:

The proving of reason [*Vernunft*, as opposed to *Verstand*, the understanding][89] also has something other than God as its starting point, only it does not in its advance leave this other as an immediate and existing entity, but rather shows it to be mediated and posited, and thus it emerges that God is to be seen as something that contains mediation sublimated within itself, truly immediate, original and self-dependent — If one says: 'Consider nature, it will lead you to God, you will find an absolute final purpose', what is meant is not that God is a mediated entity, but only that *we* take the course to God from something other than God, such *that* God is at once both the consequent and the absolute ground of that first item, that the position is thus reversed and what appears as the consequent reveals itself also to be the ground and what at first appeared to be the ground is reduced to the consequent (*Enz.* I. 36Z).

When we consider Hegel's detailed account of the proofs, however, it is not at all clear how this is supposed to be reflected in them. The point seems to be that the 'rise to God' alters the view or conception of the world embodied in our premises, rather than that it changes the world itself. One might suppose that Hegel believes that the conclusion which we derive from our initial characterization of the world leads us to reject this characterization. If that were so, his account of the cosmological proof, for example, would have to be something like this. The premiss is: 'The world is a collection of contingent things and events.' From this, it is inferred that there is a necessary being on which they all depend. But, if this is so, the premiss is false, or at least misleading, since what depends on, or is necessitated by, a necessary being is itself in one sense necessary rather than contingent. This, however, cannot be what Hegel has primarily in mind, for he remarks that 'it is involved in the very [proposition, viz. that the world is a collection of contingent things and events] that the world is *contingent*, that it is only something *deciduous* (*Fallendes*), phenomenal and intrinsically *nugatory* (*für sich Nichtiges*)' (*Enz.* I. 50). This characterization of the world is just the one that is required by acosmism and it is not to be abandoned in favour of the ascription to it of some sort of necessity. Secondly, this procedure cannot be applied to the other proofs, to, for example, the teleological argument. The premiss of this argument is 'The world is purposively organized', and the conclusion that is derived from this, namely that there is a purposive director of it, does not incline us to suppose that the world is not, after all, purposively organized, but has some other character instead.

There are, nevertheless, still two distinct ways in which, on Hegel's view, the rise to God changes our view of the world, and not, as he implies, only one. These correspond to the two types of thinking which are *prima facie* involved in the proofs.[90] Firstly, there is the thinking involved in, or presupposed by, our acceptance of the premises of the proofs. Our view of the world is changed when we cease merely to perceive it, and begin to conceptualize or understand it in terms of scientific laws, the concepts of a force, of causality, of purposive organization, and so on. Secondly, there is the thinking involved in inferring from the world thus characterized the existence of a deity on which it depends. This leads to the rejection not of our initial characterization of the world, but of the implication that the world, however character-ized, is self-sustaining and fully real. If God exists, then the finite world is in some sense unreal, a mere manifestation of God: 'the world has indeed being (*Sein*), but it is only illusory being (*Schein*), not genuine being, not absolute truth' (*Enz.* I. 50).[91] Both types of alteration are involved in Hegel's claim that when we 'think the empirical world', we

> alter its empirical form and convert it into a universal; thinking at the same time exerts a *negative* activity on that basis . . . .
> The inner substance (*Gehalt*) of what is perceived is brought out with the removal and *negation* of the shell (*Ibid.*).

Obviously enough, the two types of thinking are, on the tradi-tional view, different, and thinking of the first type does not commit one to that of the second type. Why does Hegel conflate them? We have already seen that the general reason for his doing so is the radical transformation of the proofs and of our con-ception of God which he is attempting to bring about. But a local reason for it, a pretext, as it were, under which the transformation is conducted, is a special feature of the cosmological proof. For the premiss of this argument, that the world is an aggregate of contingencies, characterizes the world, on Hegel's view, as it is for mere perception, for animals; it describes the world as it is or would be independently of any thinking characterization of it. It might be supposed, therefore, that in inferring the existence of a necessary being from this premiss, we are at the same time conceptualizing our raw sensory intake. But this is a mistake. Even if we grant that the word 'contingent' does imply this, to characterize the world as it is independently of thought is already to think about it in a way that no animal can do. Thought over-reaches what is other than thought.[92] Secondly, the teleological proof cannot plausibly be regarded in this way. Hegel himself would agree that the world's purposive arrangements are accessible only to thought and not to perception alone.

There are, then, two quite distinct ways in which thought alters our conception of the finite world. It, firstly, subjects our sensory material to conceptualization of various kinds, and, secondly, it declares that the world thus conceptualized is less than fully real, a mere offshoot of God. Hegel runs these together for reasons of his own.

21 *Philosophical arguments*

If we ignore, for the moment, this confusion, the idea that some arguments proceed from premises which are modified in the light of the conclusion derived from them is not an implausible one. An example of what Hegel perhaps has in mind is provided by Russell:[93]

> We all start from 'naïve realism', i.e., the doctrine that things are what they seem. We think that grass is green, that stones are hard, and that snow is cold. But physics assures us that the greenness of grass, the hardness of stones, and the coldness of snow, are not the greenness, hardness, and coldness that we know in our own experience, but something very different. The observer, when he seems to himself to be observing a stone, is really, if physics is to be believed, observing the effects of the stone upon himself. Thus science seems to be at war with itself: when it most means to be objective, it finds itself plunged into subjectivity against its will. Naïve realism leads to physics, and physics, if true, shows that naïve realism is false.

Arguments for physics start from naïvely realistic premises which are shown to be false, or only half-true, in the light of the conclusions they imply.

Philosophical arguments, and not just those for the existence of God, often proceed in this way. Philosophical arguments about perception, for example, often begin with a commonsensical distinction between veridical and illusory perception, between how things look to an observer and how they actually are, and proceed from this to draw the conclusion that our senses are invariably unreliable or that statements about physical objects are to be understood phenomenalistically, in terms of statements about one's own sense-data. The distinction drawn at the beginning is not necessarily abandoned in the light of the conclusion derived from it, but it is reinterpreted as, for example, a distinction between how things look to a normal perceiver in normal circumstances and how they look to an abnormal perceiver and/or in abnormal circumstances, where 'normal' and 'abnormal' are suitably defined in terms of the theory which is argued for. This new interpretation of the premiss of the argument is not one that would be accepted by someone who had not already accepted the conclusion of the argument. Nor perhaps could it be understood at the outset, for the point of such arguments is as much to explain or introduce a new theory or viewpoint as to establish the truth of one which is antecedently well understood. The premisses could of course be hedged with qualifications so that they stand in no need of subsequent revision, but again the ability to see what qualifications are required and the incentive to introduce them are lacking until one has understood and accepted the conclusion. Arguments in favour of a novel viewpoint must begin from premisses which can be accepted by someone who still occupies the old viewpoint.

Arguments such as these, however, provide only a partial parallel to Hegel's enterprise. They differ from it in perhaps three respects. Firstly, these arguments are arguments for some conclusion which was true all along. On Russell's view, for example, if physics is true, then naïve realism was false even before our discovery of its falsehood. Similarly, if phenomenalism is true, it is true quite independently of our formulation and acceptance of it. Does Hegel believe that the subordinate status which finite things are seen to have in the light of the theological conclusions we derive from them is a status which they had all along, independently of our thought about them? As we shall see, his answer to this question is irremediably ambiguous.[94]

Secondly, proponents of such arguments as these are not inclined to stress the ontological significance of their proposal of the argument. They are more concerned about the truth of its conclusion and the validity of the argument than the arguing itself as a historical event. Even if we suppose, however, that Hegel held that our arguments leave finite things unchanged and alter only our conception of them, the fact of our coming to see the world differently is nevertheless one of crucial theological importance. It is in itself a change in the world, in so far as we are a part of the world, but it is also a change in God, for we cannot, on Hegel's view, be distinct from God himself. Our cognitive activities are not external to God, but are an aspect of him, of the reality which is to be known.[95] In this sense, the 'rise to God' is something that God himself does.[96]

Finally, these arguments proceed, as it were, only in one

direction. They start, for example, with physical objects and end up with sensations, or they begin with observable physical objects and conclude with unobservable scientific entities. They do not characteristically travel also in the reverse direction. One can think of various ways, both vicious and innocuous, in which they might do so. A harmless 'reversal' of Russell's argument would be to explain, in terms of the laws and entities of physics, why stones feel hard, grass looks green, and snow feels cold, to make the return journey, so to speak, from physics to phenomena. A less harmless one would be to argue that the entities postulated by physics are no more than 'logical constructions out of', or simplified ways of describing, the entities of naïve realism. This, however, would clearly run counter to Russell's argument, establishing that naïve realism was true and physics, strictly speaking, false. Analogously, one might argue that sensations or sense-data are no more than physical entities or aspects of physical entities, that they are for example states of, or events in, our brains. But such an argument would normally be held to be at odds with its counterpart, the argument to the effect that physical objects and events are no more than sensations or sense-data. The two arguments are not normally proposed by the same philosopher at the same time. Hegel, by contrast, seems to be doing just that. How this is to be interpreted will be considered in detail later.[97] In the following section, however, we shall examine the theological version of this reversal, namely the ontological argument.

22 *The traditional ontological proof*

The ontological proof, the proof which proceeds from the concept or 'abstract identity' to being, runs, in its orthodox form, somewhat as follows:

1. God is an absolutely perfect/supremely great being.
2. A being which did not exist would not be absolutely perfect/ supremely great.

Therefore,

3. God exists.[98]

The concept of God is supposed to be such that it is contradictory to say that God does not exist in much the way that the concept of a triangle is such that it is contradictory to say that there is a triangle which does not have three sides. The argument has met with little support in recent times and it is at first surprising that Hegel should be so confident of its validity, especially in the light of his familiarity with Kant's objections to it. The answer again is that Hegel's version of the proof is entirely unlike the orthodox version, but the metamorphosis occurs under the cover of a series of replies to Kant's objections, replies such as might be made by a devotee of the traditional argument.

Kant had illustrated the 'distinction between thinking and being' with the example of a hundred dollars in my pocket. The concept of a hundred dollars is the same whether they exist or not, whether they are actual or merely possible. However great a difference their existence would make to my finances, it cannot be derived from the mere concept of them. Similarly the existence of God cannot be derived from the concept of him (*Enz.* I. 51).[99] Hegel's reply to this is that God is an entity of a different order from a finite object such as a hundred dollars. To say that a thing is finite means or implies that its existence is different from its concept or conception. But God is supposed to be that which can only be 'thought as existing', the concept of him involving his existence. It is this unity of the concept and being which constitutes the concept of God. He is, then, unlike finite things in that he is by definition something that cannot but exist.[100]

This is a familiar reply, a reply that might be made, for example, to the objection that, if the ontological argument were valid, then by framing our concepts of a lion or of a unicorn so that they included existence as a defining feature, we could establish that unicorns or lions exist necessarily.[101] We could not do that, since lions and unicorns are, or would be, finite entities whose existence is dependent on other entities. The reply is still open to the further objection that the concept of an infinite being, of a being which cannot but exist, might be a contradictory one or that, even if it is not, it might nevertheless fail to be exemplified. Hegel might have this objection in mind in what follows, but, as often happens on crucial occasions, he lapses into obscurity:

> This is of course still a formal determination of God, which therefore contains in fact only the nature of the *concept* itself. But it is easy to see that it already includes in itself *being* in its wholly abstract sense. For the concept, however it is determined, is at least the *relation* to itself which emerges through the elimination (*Aufhebung*) of mediation and is thus itself *immediate*; but being is nothing else than this. It would . . . be strange, if the innermost essence of spirit, the concept, or if even I or, above all, the concrete totality which is God were not even rich enough to contain in itself so poor a determination as being is — it is the poorest, most abstract of all. As far as content goes (*dem Gehalte nach*), there can be nothing less significant for thought than *being*. The only thing that may

240

be even less significant is what one first of all means by being, namely an *external sensible* existence like that of the paper which I have here before me; but a sensible existence of a limited, transitory thing is not in question here (*Enz.* I. 51).

There are several reasons for the obscurity of this passage and of Hegel's other treatments of the ontological argument. Firstly, there are a number of different words, all of which might be loosely translated by the term 'existence' and might be used to formulate the ontological argument. We do not generally distinguish carefully between such words as 'being', 'determinate being' (*Dasein*), 'existence', 'actuality', 'reality' and 'objectivity', or at least we do not do so in the way that Hegel does in his *Logic*. What looks like an attempt on his part to defend the ontological argument is often no more than a discussion of the appropriateness of one or other of these terms for application to God.[102] Thus in the passage quoted above, a good deal is made of the distinction between the sort of being which can properly be attributed to God and the 'sensible existence' of a finite thing. But when he says that the concept 'already includes in itself *being* in its wholly abstract sense', it is unclear whether he is saying that the ontological argument is valid or, on the contrary, that the term 'being' is unsuitable for the use which both the proponents and the critics of the argument wish to make of it.

A second obfuscating factor is Hegel's tendency to issue a shower of distinct points without pausing for breath. In the passage quoted, for example, at least three points are made about being and God:

(i) The concept, God or the concept of God *is* or has being in the sense that it is immediate, for we have, as it were, abolished the steps by which we arrived at it: 'the concept . . . is . . . the *relation* to itself which emerges through the elimination of mediation and is thus itself *immediate*; but being is nothing else than this.'[103] Hegel is referring primarily to what happens in the *Logic*,[104] but the point is only a re-statement in terms of pure thought of what he has said about man's 'rise to God', namely that it involves the demotion of the finite things from which the rise begins and the ascription to God of the substantial, unmediated status which they at first seemed to have. Clearly this has nothing to do with the ontological argument as traditionally conceived. If the being of anything is in question here, it is the being of the concept itself rather than the being of what the concept is the concept of. If it tells us anything about God, it tells us what he would be like if he existed and not that he exists.

(ii) The concept or system of concepts with which God is to be identified includes the concept of pure being: 'the concept . . . contain[s] in itself . . . being.' This again tells us nothing about God's existence. It tells us neither about the ontological status of the concept nor about its exemplification or embodiment in things.

(iii) So large and important an entity as God can hardly fail to be when trivial entities such as pieces of paper succeed in doing so. If this means only that, if God existed, then he would *be*, it is unexceptionable, but irrelevant. If, on the other hand, it means that God must *be*, then it is no more than a jejune re-statement of the ontological argument.

The primary reason, however, for Hegel's imperspicuity and apparent irrelevance is the unacknowledged fact that the ontological proof, as he understands it, has more to do, in theological terms, with God's creation of the world than with his existence.

23 *Hegel's ontological proof*

The evidence that Hegel interpreted the argument in this way is circumstantial, but compelling none the less.

(i) We have already seen that there is, on his view, a symmetry between the ontological and the other proofs, that the former proceeds from the concept to being, while the latter go from being to the concept.[105] Moreover, Kant's objection to the ontological proof is taken to be the converse of his criticism of the other proofs, namely that, just as universal concepts are not given in empirical phenomena, so conversely 'the determinate' cannot be derived from universal concepts (*Enz.* I. 51). On the ordinary interpretation of the proofs, however, this symmetry does not obtain. The premises of the cosmological and teleological proofs concern not the being of God, but the being of the phenomenal world, and what they derive from this is not, or not only, the concept of God, but his existence or being. Hegel concedes as much when he says of them that '*being* is common to both sides and the opposition concerns only the distinction between what is individualized (*dem Vereinzelten*) and the universal' (*Ibid.*). By contrast, the ontological proof moves from the concept of God, not to the being of the world, but to the being of God. Correspondingly, Kant's criticisms of the proofs are not mirror-images of each other. His criticism of the first type of proof is roughly that one cannot infer the being of an infinite entity from the being of finite ones. His criticism of the second is that one cannot derive the being of anything, finite or infinite, from the concept of it.

The symmetry, then, seems to hold only if 'being' is taken equivocally as the being of God and the being of the world. When the ontological proof is reinterpreted, however, as deriving the empirical world from God or from the concept, the symmetry does obtain, for the being is in both cases the being of the world.

(ii) Hegel believes, as we have seen, that the point of unifying the concept with being is not just to establish the existence of an entity of which we have a clear and determinate conception, but to fill out or determine a near-vacuous concept of God. This makes a good deal of sense in the case of those proofs which infer God's existence from features of the observable world, but it is in-applicable to the traditional ontological proof. If a concept is vacuous, it is not made any less so by the claim that it is actualized. The emptiness of the concept is inherited by the corresponding existential claim. Hegel may be acknowledging this when he speaks of being as the 'similarly entirely abstract determinacy' (*Enz.* I. 49). It is true that a finite entity is always more determinate than the concept of it, having properties the possession of which is not entailed by the fact that it exemplifies that concept. But this should not be what Hegel has in mind here, since an infinite entity like God fully conforms to its concept, so that his being could not determine his concept in this way.

The point makes more sense, however, if the ontological proof is restructured after Hegel's own fashion. So does his report of Kant's objection to it: 'the determinate (*das Bestimmte*) is not contained in the universal, and the determinate is here being. Or being cannot be derived from and analysed out of the concept' (*Enz.* I. 51). The first sentence here cannot mean that the in-spection of a concept alone cannot tell us that the concept is exemplified. It seems rather to mean *either* that specific concepts cannot be derived from generic ones, that, for example, the con-cept of an animal cannot be derived from that of an entity nor that of an okapi from that of an animal;[106] *or* that generic concepts alone do not tell us what individuals or specific types of individual exist, that, for example, the inspection of the concept of an entity or of an animal cannot guarantee the existence of okapis. It can hardly mean what the second sentence seems to mean, that, for example, the concept of an okapi does not involve the existence of okapis. This is what Kant meant, but it has nothing to do, as the other points have, with the determination of concepts. It is this second sentence, however, which reflects the traditional concerns of the ontological proof. The first is more relevant to whatever it is that Hegel is doing in the *Philosophy of Nature*, attempting to derive specific concepts from more general ones, deriving claims about nature from the consideration of pure thoughts, or whatever.[107] The development of nature out of pure thoughts or, in theological terms, the consideration of God's creation of the world, can plausibly be seen as a determination, a filling out, of God or of pure thought. The ascription of existence to something of which we already have a concept cannot.

(iii) If the arguments are taken in their usual sense, it is unclear why both types of proof are required. We would, if Hegel is right, need all the proofs which proceed from the world to God, since each of them provides us with different information about him. But the ontological proof, as we have seen, makes no additional contribution to the concept of God, unless it is reinterpreted. It may be true, as Kant argued, that the cosmological argument presupposes the validity of the ontological proof.[108] But Hegel rejects this view and, in any case, his account does not suggest that he would want the ontological proof to play only a subsidiary role (*VPR* II. pp. 421 ff., S.S. III. pp. 237 ff.). On his new interpretation, however, it plays an essential part. For the creation of the world is quite a different matter from the concerns of the other proofs.

(iv) Hegel's preferred term for the statement of the ontological argument seems to be 'objectivity' rather than 'being', 'existence' or any of the other alternatives, and the argument is especially associated with the transition in the *Logic* from the 'concept' to the 'object' (*Enz.* I. 193; *WL* II. pp. 402 ff., M. pp. 705 ff.). What the concept and the object are will be considered in more detail later.[109] It is enough for the moment that the concept is not much like the concept of God as it is traditionally understood and that the object, though it is connected with God, is not much like the familiar biblical figure whom we associate with the term:

> the object in general is the *one* whole which is not yet further
> determined within itself, the objective world in general, God,
> the absolute object. But the object also has distinction in
> itself, falls apart within itself into indeterminate manifoldness
> (as objective *world*), and each of these *individualized* entities
> is also an object, an existence (*Dasein*) which is internally
> concrete, complete, and independent (*Enz.* I. 193).

Since logic deals with pure thoughts, the object is presumably meant to be understood just as the object if we confine ourselves to logic, and we are not supposed to replace it with a conception such as that of God or that of the natural world.[110] The *Logic*, however, is intended, as we shall see, to represent Hegel's system as a whole, his account of the entire universe, at the level of pure thought, and we are therefore entitled to step outside logic and to look for an interpretation of the transition from the concept to the object in the system as a whole. The most obvious counterpart to it here is the passage from the *Logic* as such to the *Philosophy of Nature*, from pure thought to nature. In traditional theological terms, this transition has more to do with God's creation of the world than with his existence. Scattered evidence for this association occurs throughout the compilations from Hegel's lecture notes.[111] The significance of these passages and of the transition from logic to nature will be considered later. The point for the moment is that, at least as his immediate pupils understood him, Hegel does not distinguish clearly between the existence of God and the existence or 'creation' of the world. In so far as he does distinguish them he associates the ontological argument with the latter rather than the former.

Why is this so? There are at least two reasons. Firstly, the question whether God exists and the question whether the world exists cannot be, for Hegel, two distinct questions. For God and the world would in that case be two distinct entities and God would be finite. But, again, Hegel is not, as we shall see, an acosmist.[112] He believes that the natural and human world exist in a sense in which, on his interpretation, Spinoza did not. There is, therefore, a proper question to be asked about the existence of the world, and it supplants the corresponding question about God. Secondly, God, as we have seen, is, at one level at least, simply the system of concepts portrayed in the *Logic*. What existential questions can we ask about this? We can ask: 'Are these concepts instantiated?' and 'Are they embedded in things or somehow separate from them?' But these are questions about the existence and status of the world, about, so to speak, the creation. We might ask, again, about the ontological status of the concept or concepts as such, and this is perhaps the closest approximation that Hegel's system allows to the question 'Does God exist?' The answer to this question is a complicated one.[113] Indeed, since Hegel regularly contrasts being or existence with concepts or the concept, it is not one that he can easily ask. But it is at any rate clear that the ontological argument in its standard form can shed no light on it. This argument presupposes a concept and says nothing further about *its* ontological standing. Indeed, it applies quite trivially to concepts themselves: if there is the concept of a concept then of course there is a concept. But this tells us nothing about the sense in which concepts exist. Hegel's reason, then, for not taking the ontological proof as a proof of God's existence is that, if it is seen in that way, there is nothing for it to be a proof of.

24 *God as spirit*

We have, then, two types of theological proof, one of them proceeding from the empirical world to the concept or God, and the other proceeding in the reverse direction. How are these to be integrated into a single account of God? The answer lies in Hegel's conception of God as a spirit.

The proofs, he argues, are traditionally presented as proofs of one and the same conclusion, but this, as we have seen, is inaccurate. Each proof provides us with a different conception of God, and these conceptions are of varying degrees of adequacy. If, for example, we regard the world as a mass of contingencies, then God is seen as a necessary being. He is, of course, that, but he is also more than that. If we also go on to take account of organic structures and their purposive character, of life, then we shall view him, more satisfactorily, as a purposive directing cause. This, however, is both dangerous and inadequate. The danger is that we shall seek for trivial, 'external' purposes in nature, explaining, for example, the cork-tree by our need to stop up wine-bottles: 'The purpose-concept is not merely external to nature . . . for trivial things often result from this, when e.g. God's wisdom is admired because, as is said in the *Xenia*,[114] he made cork-trees grow for bottle-stoppers, etc.' (*Enz.* II. 245Z. Cf. I. 205Z). As we shall see, Hegel is concerned not with external teleology of this sort, which seems to imply that God is distinct from the world he has designed, but only with so-called internal teleology.[115] His main objection to the purposive account, however, is that God is more than alive, more than a purposive agent; he is a spirit, and to acquire this conception of him the appropriate starting-point in the world is spiritual nature, man and his works (*Enz.* I. 50). Someone, like Spinoza, who does not regard God as a spirit is not on that account an atheist, but his conception of God is inadequate.

What Hegel means by the claim that God is a spirit is not, of course, that he is a person distinct from and above the physical world. He means rather that the universe as a whole is, or is to be regarded as, a mind. A mind involves, on Hegel's view, three phases:

(i) A thinking self or a pure ego. This is God the Father, in theological terminology.

(ii) An object, seen as distinct from itself, of which it is conscious – nature or, with qualifications, God the Son.[116]

(iii) The acquisition of self-consciousness by means of a progressive awareness that this object is no more than a projection of itself – God the Holy Spirit.

Since no mind can become self-conscious without an apparently distinct object of which it is conscious, God is crucially dependent on the world, on, as it were, the creation, and could not be a mind without it. At the same time, however, the world is not conceived as fully and blankly distinct from God, so that his dependence on it does not impair his infinity.

This account of Hegel's beliefs, however, is presented in terms of conceptions and not of pure, or at least literal, thoughts. His account of his system as such does not contain any extended, explicit account of God. Religion does indeed figure in the *Philosophy of Mind*[117] and in his lectures on the subject, but there the account is primarily of men's beliefs about God, not of God himself. This is because the system as a whole is supposed to run parallel to the religious account of the universe, as an interpretation of it in terms of thought: 'thinking has to move freely within itself, but we should note at once that the result of free thinking agrees with the content of the Christian religion, for this is a revelation of reason' (*Enz.* I. 36Z).[118] The three parts of Hegel's system, then, correspond to the three phases of the cosmic mind:

(i) The system of pure thoughts presented in the *Logic* corresponds to the pure ego or God the Father:

Logic is thus to be understood as the system of pure reason, as the realm of pure thought. *This realm is the truth, as it is in and for itself without any veil.* One can therefore express it by saying that this content is *the exposition of God, as he is in his eternal essence before the creation of nature and of a finite spirit* (*WL* I. p. 44, M. p. 50).

The plausibility of this identification is supported by our earlier account of the ego.[119]

(ii) These pure thoughts are embodied in nature, which forms a hierarchical system corresponding in structure to logic. This is presented in the *Philosophy of Nature* and it corresponds to God the Son.

(iii) The development of the human mind has a similar structure. The *Philosophy of Mind* deals in part with phases of human life which do not develop over time, except during the life-span of the individual. But the most important parts of it, from the point of view of Hegel's cosmic mind, are those which present the growth of human awareness over history, a growth which corresponds to God's acquisition of self-consciousness, God the Holy Spirit.

The proofs of 'God's existence' are seen by Hegel more or less as accounts or descriptions of various phases of this system. The ontological proof represents the transition from (i) to (ii), from God or thought to nature. It is presented primarily in the transition from the *Logic* to the *Philosophy of Nature* and in the account of nature which follows. What it describes is not so much the rise to God as the descent of God. The descent is not of course thought of as occurring at some particular time, and nature does not, on Hegel's view, develop over time. The transition to nature is one of the most difficult points in Hegel's system and it will not be considered further here.

The rise to God is, on the face of it, harder to locate than the descent of God. We have already seen that Hegel tends to conflate at least two types of thinking, the conceptualization of raw sensory material and the inference from the conceptualized world to a transcendent entity on which it depends. But the question is even more complicated than this suggests, for there are more than two types of thinking in which people engage. There is, firstly, the thinking of ordinary consciousness, expressed in such statements as 'This rose is red', 'The fire will melt the butter' and so on. This sort of thinking already involves the conceptualization of raw sensory material. As we have seen, the question whether it develops over history is not one that Hegel explicitly answers.[120] Secondly, there is the historically developing thought of scientists, who subject the commonsensical world to higher and more general concepts. As we have seen, Hegel sometimes runs this together with the first type of thinking, implying that before scientists come upon the scene we are confronted by a chaos of unconceptualized sensations.[121] Thirdly, there are our progressively higher religious beliefs, consisting of increasingly satisfactory, but nevertheless still pictorial or metaphorical, conceptions of some sort of divinity, explaining the sensible world and our place in it. Finally, there is the thinking of pure thoughts themselves in abstraction from sensory material, the sort of thinking done by philosophers. These are not, of course, the only historical developments which we undergo. There is also the development of art-forms and of social institutions, both of which involve thought.[122] But enough of them have been mentioned to illustrate the difficulty.

Similarly there are a variety of ways in which a person might be theologically defective. He might, firstly, fail to think at all, even at the simplest level, and then he would be an atheist in an animal-like way.[123] One might, again, think in some way or other, but think at the wrong level, at the level of commonsense, for example, or of empirical science, but not at that of theology or of philosophy. Thirdly, one might think at the right level, but remain at a

fairly early stage of the thought-series. This is what happened to
Spinoza. He was thinking on the highest level, but stopped short
of the end of the thought-series, thinking in terms only of substance. It is even more obviously the case with those who regard
God only as the supreme being. Fourthly, the relationship between
God and the world or between thought and the world might be
misunderstood. This happens if one believes that God and the
world co-exist or adheres to atheistic pantheism, or, for that
matter, to acosmic pantheism.[124] A related mistake is made by
those who postulate a gulf between thought and the world, who
ignore the empirical world, or fail to do justice to its complexity:

> [Thinking] thus at first finds in itself, in the idea of the
> *universal* essence of these appearances, its satisfaction; this
> idea (the absolute, God) can be more or less abstract . . . . If
> thinking remains at the *universality* of ideas — as is neces-
> sarily the case with the first philosophies (e.g. the being of
> the Eleatic school, the *becoming* of Heraclitus, etc.) — it is
> rightly charged with *formalism*; it can also happen with a
> developed philosophy that only abstract propositions or
> determinations are grasped, e.g. that everything is one in the
> absolute, the identity of the subjective and the objective, and
> are simply repeated in the face of the particular (*Enz.* I. 12).

Finally, there might be recalcitrant people who do not accept
Hegel's account of the relationship between different thought-
series, who deny, for example, that philosophy represents religion in the form of thought. The nearest that Hegel comes to
considering this possibility is his acknowledgment that at certain
periods philosophy and religion appear at odds with one another
(*Enz.* I. 19Z. 3; *VBDG* I).

This diverse array of theological shortcomings presents us with
a number of possible locations for the rise to God, even in the case
of any particular proof. The cosmological proof, for example,
might represent a transition from not thinking at all to thinking
at some level or other, a shift from thinking at one level, that of
the natural sciences, for example, to thinking at a higher, the
theological or the philosophical level, or a transition from contingency to necessity within a single thought-series. For the
concepts of contingency and of necessity are both contained, as
are other pairs of contrasting concepts, within the system of pure
thoughts itself. Hegel, as we have seen, gives us no help in deciding
between these alternatives.

If we ignore the particular proofs and consider only the rise to
God in general, Hegel sometimes suggests that the types of thinking

themselves form a single series through which men progress, making no sharp distinction between advance in one type of thinking and shifting from one type to another. The *Phenomenology* and the *Philosophy of Mind*[125] present in. a single series various forms of consciousness or of increasingly adequate ways of making sense of the world.[126] Different types of thinking — commonsensical, scientific, philosophical, religious, political and artistic thinking — form a hierarchical series which is intended to correspond in structure to the *Logic*, just as any one type of thinking corresponds to logic.[127] In so far as this is so, however, the account can correspond only very roughly to any historical sequence of events, since political life, art, religion and philosophy have obviously occurred concurrently rather than successively in time. The account may show us why we ought to proceed from one type of thinking to another, but it cannot be a description of our rise to God.

Another possible answer is that the thought-series run parallel to each other in human history. Each of them has the same structure as the system of pure thoughts and represents the unravelling of this system in a particular medium. At any given historical epoch, thinking of any kind should have reached more or less the same stage of this system. It does not, of course, follow that any given individual must have reached the same point on each thought-series. A given individual may be scientifically progressive, but theologically atavistic, or indeed he may not engage in religious thinking at all. But the dominant, or at least the most advanced, trends of an epoch should be in line with each other. The rise to God can, if this is so, be seen as a sort of unilinear advance by humanity as a whole.

It is also true that the various theological defects are interrelated with each other in a number of ways. This again does not mean that any given individual must be equally defective in all respects, but rather that if he is defective in one way he is likely to be deficient in others. A natural or social scientist, for example, who does not engage in religious or philosophical thinking will be unable to produce ultimately satisfying explanations of the sort that Hegel requires.[128] Or, again, if one conceives God in a certain way, as, for example, a substance, as pure being or as the essence of the world, then one is bound to misconceive his relationship to the world, lapsing into dualism, atheism or acosmism. Conversely if one misconceives the relationship of God or of thought to the world, it must be due in part to deficiencies in one's thought or one's conception of God. Pure thoughts themselves provide models of the relationship between God or thought and what

250

is other than God or thought, namely the world.[129]

Similarly if one misapprehends the relationships between the different types of thinking, believing for example that religion and philosophy are distinct from, or at odds with, one another, this can be only because one has not got far enough with thinking of either kind. For the thought-series not only run parallel but, in a certain sense, intersect. When, and only when, people have completed their scientific and religious thinking, they can complete their philosophical thinking, and, when they have done this, they can see the true relationship between all the series, that, for example, the system or series of pure thoughts is embodied in them all, that it underlies the progress of natural science and expresses the true meaning of our religious beliefs. The culmination of all these intellectual developments is Hegel's own philosophy, in which the whole system of pure thoughts, their relationship to nature and the meaning they give to human history becomes transparent to us.[130] At this stage, all the deficiencies vanish. If one attempts, for example, to drive a wedge between Hegel's system and Lutheran orthodoxy, the 'absolute religion', arguing that Hegel's thought is too remote from it to count as an adequate interpretation, then this shows only that one cannot have properly completed the course of pure thought.

Mankind as a whole, then, rises to God, works its way up by degrees to a survey of the conceptual structure of the world. The process by which it does so is, on Hegel's view, the converse of the descent of God, the 'process' by which the world is, as it were, generated by that conceptual structure.[131] Has the problem presented by the different kinds of thinking been solved? As we shall see, it has not. Hegel's conflation of different types of thinking represents, in part, an attempt to make it seem obvious that one should rise to God, when it is not. For it is obvious that one should think in some way or other, but it is not obvious that one should think in all the ways recommended by Hegel. It also reflects, however, a deep confusion over the answer to the question: 'What is nature like independently of our thinking?' This confusion will re-emerge later.[132] In the following section, however, we shall consider some of the merits of Hegel's conception of the universe.

25 Minds, machines and organisms

Philosophers who have accepted the Christian revelation have not in general been content to appeal to faith or authority in defence of their beliefs. They have attempted to argue for them, bringing reason to the aid of faith (cf. *VBDG* I). Characteristically, however, they have not attempted to prove the whole of Christian doctrine in this way. Much of what is peculiar to Christianity cannot be argued for from first principles, but has to be accepted on faith and/or authority. In modern times, at least, philosophers have resigned themselves to proving the existence of a supreme being, characterized perhaps as the purposive creator and sustainer of the world, as supremely good and so on. But reason, it has been felt, cannot take one much further than this — the highest common factor, if not of all religions, at least of several of them (*Enz.* I. 36Z). Hegel, by contrast, believed that the whole content of Christianity, in particular the doctrine of the Trinity, could be expressed and justified in philosophical terms, and this is what the conception of God as a spirit, or its literal counterpart in terms of thought, provides.

The theological advantages of Hegel's system, however, are unlikely to have a wide appeal. Even if we care whether or not Christian dogma is justified by philosophy, his account of Christianity is wildly unorthodox, and its translation into terms of thought might be felt to transform it into a wholly secular doctrine. It is nevertheless worth asking what general reasons there may be for accepting his conclusions. The universe has been regarded as analogous to a machine or an organism. God has been conceived as a supreme being, as a purposive demiurge or as a substance. To view the universe as a person or a mind may be no less absurd than any of these, but is there anything special to be said in its favour?

In the first place, Hegel's model, he believes, gives a better account of the fact that there is a phenomenal world at all. On some other views, at least, the connection between the *explanans* and the *explanandum* is unclear.[133] If God is merely a necessary being, it is unclear why he should create a world, generate a collection of contingent things and events. If he is a being capable of purposive production, it is unclear why he should ever exercise this capacity. If he is a substance, it is, on Hegel's view, unclear why he should have modes and attributes.[134] The generation of a phenomenal world is, by contrast, built into Hegel's model. God must 'create' some world or other, something 'external, spiritless, outside of God', if he is to be a person at all (*VPR* II. p. 534. S.S. III, p. 366).

Secondly, the other models, even if they explain why there is some world or other, leave it a mystery why it has the features it does have rather than others. Some of them indeed would seem to exclude a number of the objects which the world contains and of the changes which it undergoes. If God is, for example, merely a necessary being or a purposive designer, it is clear how he could produce contingent things or organic nature, but not how he could produce anything so much more advanced than himself as the human mind. Hegel's idea seems to be that, if God is to explain the highest phenomena, the human mind and its works, he must share their essential feature, be, as it were, a projection of the *explanandum* onto a higher plane: '*Spiritual* nature alone is the worthiest and truest *starting-point* for the thinking of the absolute' (*Enz.* I. 50). Similarly the conception of the universe as a machine or as an organism is inadequate unless we are prepared to regard people as merely mechanical or merely organic entities, ready to assume their place as parts of a machine or of an organic whole. These models seem also to exclude a proper account of human history, for they will lead us to regard it as monotonously repetitive like the working of a machine or as a recurring cyclical process like those found in nature.

Even if these models do not exclude the features of the world which they purport to explain, they generally do nothing to explain them. Hegel more or less shares Spinoza's view that 'Nothing in the universe is contingent, but all things are conditioned to exist and operate in a particular manner by the necessity of the divine nature'.[135] Spinoza, however, does not begin to explain the general features of the world of which we are aware, and it is hard to see how he could do so, with his view of God as a mere substance. The same is true of the conceptions of him as a necessary being or as a purposive demiurge. Even if God must create something and even if he *could* create what we have, why *did* he create what we have?

It might, however, be objected to Hegel's spirit-model that although it may provide an explanation of people or their minds, it cannot do justice to the non-spirits contained in the world such as machines and organisms. How can it be right to assign to the universe as a whole features which belong only to some parts of it, to people, that is, but not to others such as stones? The answer to this seems to be that a mind or spirit can accommodate different features or, perhaps, different characterizations of itself in a way that other types of entity cannot. If God is regarded as a necessary being, it is unclear how we could characterize him in any other way. How could God be *both* a necessary being *and* a purposive creator? One way of accommodating both these features would be to regard them as different properties belonging to a single thing, but, as we have seen, this conception of God leaves a problematic disunity in him. Why should one thing have just these properties? The answer that they depend on its relationships to other things is not available in the case of an infinite entity. If God is a spirit, by contrast, there is room for different characterizations of him integrated in a single system. This can be seen, in terms of our anthropomorphic conception, in more than one way, both of which were probably in Hegel's mind. We can imagine God as simply having thoughts which are ordered and interconnected in the way that the concepts of Hegel's *Logic* are. Alternatively, and more picturesquely, God can be seen as characterizing himself successively in different ways, transcending, as it were, each self-characterization and proceeding to another, higher one. He begins by regarding himself as pure being and traverses in this way the whole system of concepts of the *Logic*.[136] His final self-characterization, as the absolute idea, will amount to his awareness of himself as involving all the earlier ones, as well as of the logical connections between them. Since these thoughts include those appropriate for non-spirits, for stones, machines, and organisms, as well as for spirits, the answer to the objection raised above is that, if God is conceived as a thinker, a spirit, then we can assign to him the features required for the explanation of non-thinkers.

Seen in this way, then, God can both allow for, and explain, at least the general features of our world. The levels in the hierarchy of nature, the steps on the *scala naturae*, correspond to the series of thoughts which he has or of which he consists. The requirement that he is to become self-conscious places certain restrictions on what the world can be like. A spirit must have an object which is or appears other than itself, which is, like nature, 'external, spiritless, outside of God'. But, again, if he is to become self-conscious, there must be rational beings who are capable of thinking about nature and of becoming aware of God. This, in turn, implies that nature has such features as are required for the existence of people and of their cognitive powers. This explanatory model provides a better account of the hierarchy and development of the world than the others do.

In particular, the picture of a mind, transcending itself in a way that other entities do not, makes more sense, on Hegel's view, of human history than its competitors. He is notoriously prone to attribute single strands of human history and even history as a whole to one mind. The history of philosophy is, as we have seen, assigned to a single 'architect', to 'the *one* living mind' (*Enz.* I. 13).[137] The attribution to a single mind implies that the development of philosophy over the ages has the sort of coherence and cumulative nature that we might find in an individual mind and, indeed, that it might in principle be the thinking of a single person endowed with great longevity or speed of thought. Similarly we can imagine a single chemist who successively postulates Democritus' atomic theory, Boyle's, Dalton's, Rutherford's and so on, becoming dissatisfied with each in turn and replacing it with a more adequate view. This does not entail what Hegel also believes, namely that different philosophies or atomic theories do not contradict, or are at least compatible with, one another. For what a person believes at one time may well contradict what he believes at another. All that is implied by the spirit-model is that the history of philosophy or of any other intellectual sphere should be consequential enough to constitute the train of thought of a single, coherent, thinker. This does, however, impose some conditions on what history can be like. It could not, for example, be regressive, beginning with Einstein, Rutherford or Hegel and ending up with Thales. If it were like that, we could not understand the history of thought, since we would be equipped by now only with Thales' mental furniture.[138] It follows that God, the single spirit whose intellectual development this was, would not be advancing towards self-consciousness, but lapsing into senility. Again, it could not be an inconsequential history, with each successive thinker producing a theory which bore no relationship to those of his predecessors or to the problems raised by them. On Hegel's view, these conditions are satisfied. In many areas at least a thinker attempts to solve problems raised by his predecessors and improves on their efforts. His own view has intelligible connections with previous ones such that if a single thinker were to adopt all these views in succession he could not be accused of incoherence, irrelevance or regression into senility.

It might be objected to this account that it implies that the development of any intellectual sphere is autonomous, proceeding only in response to internal stresses and problems, and remaining unaffected by other cultural processes or indeed by natural factors such as the climate. And, firstly, this is an empirical question which cannot be settled as hastily as Hegel wishes, and, secondly, his account might imply that there are several world-spirits, each of them at work in a different area. Hegel's reply to this, however, is that, firstly, to the extent that men are civilized and undergo historical development at all, they are fairly well insulated against constant or recurrent natural factors such as the climate (*Enz.* III. 392 and Z.). Their intellectual history develops more or less autonomously. Secondly, a single spirit, in a different sense of 'spirit', pervades the whole cultural life of a people at any given period. All the branches of its culture have reached approximately the same stage, and there are intelligible connections between the different types of thinking in

255

which it engages.[139] Such effects as other intellectual processes have on, for example, philosophy only confirm and perhaps hasten what its autonomous development would have been. But apart from this, the different aspects of intellectual life are sufficiently connected to be contained in a single, coherent mind. The world-spirit is not a narrow specialist. Hegel is thus inclined to see not only particular branches of our development, but also human history as a whole as the manifestation of the progress of a single mind.

If, then, we are to give some single picture of God or of the universe as a whole, then, on Hegel's view, the cumulative, coherent character of cultural history, as well as the complexities of nature, are captured more adequately by the model of a mind or spirit than by any of the available alternatives.

26 Substance and subject

The third merit, in Hegel's eyes, of the spirit-model is that it provides an account of the relationship between God and finite things that avoids the unsatisfactory alternatives which he presented to Spinoza. These alternatives were dualism, atheism — God ⇒ the world — and acosmism — the world ⇒ God. We have already suggested that, although of these alternatives Hegel prefers acosmism, what he is in fact seeking is some fourth alternative which secures the existence both of God and of finite things without thereby lapsing into dualism. This, then, is what the spirit-model has to supply.

This is what Hegel seems to have in mind when he criticizes Spinoza for making God only a substance and not a subject as well: 'Everything depends . . . on grasping and expressing the true (*das Wahre*) not as *substance*, but just as much as *subject*' (PG p. 19, M. p. 10; cf. *VGP* III. pp. 164 ff., H. III. pp. 287 ff.). The primary sense of 'subject' here is that of a cognitive subject as opposed to an object, that is a mind or an ego. This sense, however, is conflated with that other sense of 'subject' in which it is the subject of a proposition or judgment and is contrasted with the predicates ascribed to it. Hegel's predecessors set him a bad example in this respect. Kant is using 'subject' in both senses in this passage: 'I, as a thinking being, am the *absolute subject* of all my possible judgments, and this representation of myself cannot be employed as the predicate of any other thing.'[140] The two notions are entangled in Fichte's *Wissenschaftslehre* in sentences like this: 'The judging ego predicates something not strictly of A, but of itself, that it finds A in itself: and therefore the second

A [viz. in the judgment "A = A"] amounts to the predicate.'[141] Hegel himself attempts to bridge the gap between the two senses by exploiting the etymological connection between the German words for 'judge' or 'make a judgment' (urteilen) and 'divide' (teilen), seeing an analogy between the way in which a judgment, or the subject of a judgment, divides itself into a subject and a predicate and the way in which a subject divides itself into a subject and an object.[142] He seems to think of the object of a mind as in some sense a predicate of it, nature, for example, as a predicate of God.[143]

One might regard this as leaving finite entities where Spinoza put them. What is the difference between being a predicate of God and being a mode or accident of God? The force of the claim that the absolute is a subject, however, seems to be not only to explain how the absolute generates finite entities, but also to confer on them a more substantial status than Spinoza was prepared to grant them. Spinoza's view that finite things are modes of substance implies that they are related to God in much the way that my blushes and smiles are related to me. Despite frequent suggestions to the contrary, Hegel does not support this view. He objected at least to the reduction of the finite ego to an accident of substance, a blush on the cheek of the absolute:[144]

> The conception of the freedom of the subject rebels against (empört sich) the Spinozist universal substance; for that I am subject, spirit, etc. – the determinate is, according to Spinoza, all only a modification (VGP III. p. 193, H. III. p. 287).

If, on the other hand, God is a subject or a mind, the ontological position of finite things and persons is, on Hegel's view, more secure. Things and men are not flatly accidents of God nor are they flatly distinct from him. They are, as it were, projections of him, God himself regarded as his own object, and the cognitive (and practical) activities of men are the means whereby these projections are brought back to their source. The idea of consciousness already involves a part of Hegel's point. If I am conscious of x, then x is not distinct from me in the way that a stick is distinct from a stone, nor is it just a feature of me like my smile. But another part of his point is that if we provide for the 'return' of finite things to the absolute, then we can initially give them more independence of it. A ball can be thrown further and thus achieve greater independence of the thrower, if it is attached to him by elastic which will guarantee its return, whereas if its recovery is not secured in this way it cannot be thrown at all except at the cost of its breaking loose from the thrower altogether. (The absolute does not need elastic. It throws boys after the balls who bring back the balls to it.) Spinozism is, on Hegel's view, static, while his own account is dynamic, ascribing to the universe a tripartite, 'syllogistic' structure which turns back on itself in a circular manner. The relationship of God to the world is sometimes compared with that of an author-director to the performance of his play. On Hegel's account the simile continues thus: the characters in the play become aware that they are no more than characters in a play and the author-director's production of the play is the final scene of the play itself.[145] In orthodox Christianity it would be Christ who performs this role, but in Hegel's version, if any single individual can claim it, it is Hegel himself.[146]

This, then, is Hegel's system, presented in terms of metaphorical conceptions. There are, obviously enough, weak spots in it, which would not resist much critical probing. But to see more clearly where they lie, we need to translate it back into literal thoughts, and to do this we must return to the beginning again, to the *Logic*.

PART THREE

The System

VIII

Logic: Thinking about Thinking

As we would expect from the variety of problems which it is intended to solve, Hegel's *Logic* is a puzzlingly complex and grandiose construction. Its details are intricate, often obscure and sometimes interesting, but we shall not be concerned with them here. More important than these is the question: 'What in general is Hegel attempting to do in the *Logic*?' and it is this question which we shall try to answer in this chapter. We begin with a general survey of the structure and contents of the work.

1 *The structure of logic*

There are two versions of the *Logic*. The first and fuller version, the *Science of Logic,* was published in two parts, the first, the 'Objective Logic', in 1812, the second, the 'Subjective Logic', in 1816. Both parts were republished together, with some revisions, in 1831. The second, briefer and generally more manageable version constitutes the first part of the *Encyclopaedia* which was first published in 1817 and reappeared in 1827 and 1830 with many additions. There are differences in the arrangement of the two versions, but they are not major ones and are not in themselves of much significance.[1] Logic is intended to form the first part of Hegel's system, but since this system is meant to form a circle, it is also in a sense the culmination of it. This is related to the fact that the *Science of Logic* was preceded, in 1807, by the *Phenomenology of Mind,* a work which purports to show how, by passing through various more or less inadequate forms of consciousness, we should end up doing logic. The contents of the *Phenomenology* recur in an abbreviated form in the third part of the *Encyclopaedia (Enz.* III. 413 ff.), and this culminates in philosophy itself (572 ff., esp. 577). Philosophy itself, of course, starts with logic, so we are back at the beginning again. The significance of this will be considered later.[2]

With regard to the contents of the work a few obvious remarks must here suffice. The contents of the Objective Logic are in their broad outlines familiar enough. They are the concepts of traditional metaphysics, those of being, for example, of quality, quantity, essence and causality, concepts which are applicable to things, whether ordinary sensible things or extraordinary supersensible ones. It is with reference to these concepts that Hegel can most plausibly say that logic coincides with metaphysics (*Enz.* I. 24).[3] The Subjective Logic, by contrast, opens with a discussion of the traditional concerns of formal logic, of concepts, judgments and forms of inference. Kant had distinguished sharply between general logic, corresponding roughly to the contents of the first section of Hegel's Subjective Logic, and transcendental logic, which broadly corresponds to the concerns of Hegel's Objective Logic.[4] But for Hegel they form a single process of thought. There is no obvious break in continuity between the two parts of the *Logic*. The last sentence of the 1831 version of the Objective Logic marks the transition to Subjective Logic: 'This is the *concept*, the realm of *subjectivity* or of *freedom*' (*WL* II. p. 240, M. p. 571). The Subjective Logic does not, however, confine itself to the concerns of traditional logic. Its second section is entitled 'Objectivity' (*WL* II. pp. 402 ff., M. pp. 705 ff.). or 'The Object' (*Enz.* I. 194) and seems to revert to the theme of Objective Logic, with a discussion of mechanism, chemism and teleology. The final section, 'The Idea' (*WL* II. pp. 462 ff., M. pp. 755 ff.; *Enz.* I. 213 ff.), contains an account of life, of cognition and volition, and concludes with the absolute idea. The transition to the Subjective Logic, to the 'concept', and the switch of perspective which it seems to involve, is one of the most puzzling features of the *Logic*. So too is the apparent return to objective logic. An attempt to explain these features will be made later.[5]

More remarkable still is the structure of the *Logic*. The work is divided into three books: 'The doctrine of being', 'The doctrine of essence (*Wesen*)' and 'The doctrine of the concept (*Begriff*)'. The first two of these books constitute the Objective Logic, the third coincides with the Subjective Logic. Each of these books is, in turn, divided into three sections; each section into three chapters, each chapter into three segments, each of which is again divided into three. In most cases, though not in all, the subdivision goes no further than this. The *Logic* consists, then, of a system of nested triads and its structure can be represented by the diagram

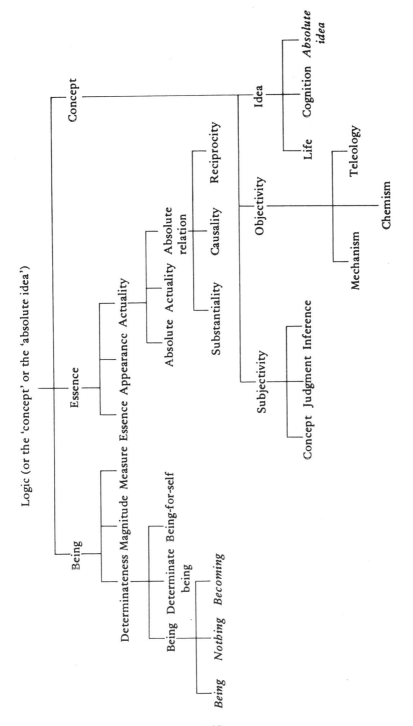

Logic (or the 'concept' or the 'absolute idea')

Being
Essence
Concept

Determinateness Magnitude Measure Essence Appearance Actuality

Being Determinate Being-for-self
being

Being Nothing Becoming

Absolute Actuality Absolute
relation

Substantiality Causality Reciprocity

Subjectivity
Objectivity
Idea

Concept Judgment Inference

Mechanism Chemism Teleology

Life Cognition *Absolute idea*

on page 263. The organization of the *Logic* is not there given in full. Only in the case of the first branch, the one that terminates in being, nothing and becoming, is it pursued to its ultimate subdivisions. (The absolute idea, too, is not further subdivided.) But this is enough to convey its overall structure.

A noticeable feature of this structure is the tendency for the same heading to recur at different levels of the hierarchy. 'Being', for example, is the title of the first book, of the first chapter of the first section of that book, and of the first division of that chapter. 'Determinate being' too occurs at three levels: as the title of the second chapter of the first section of the first book, as the title of the first subdivision of that chapter ('Determinate being as such'), and as the title of the first subdivision of that subdivision ('Determinate being in general'). Again, the second section of the first book is entitled 'Magnitude (Quantity)', its first chapter is 'Quantity', and the first subdivision of this chapter is 'Pure Quantity'. The recurrence of the same heading at different levels is found throughout the work. It is not, however, always the first member of a triad which has the same title as the triad as a whole. Sometimes it is the second member which has this privilege. The second section of the second book, for example, is entitled 'Appearance' (*Erscheinung*). But its first chapter is 'Existence'; it is the second chapter which is again 'Appearance'. Again, the third section of this book is called 'Actuality', and the second chapter of it, not the first, has this title. With the third book, at least in its overall plan, we again find the first member of the triad assuming the title of the triad as a whole. This book is 'Subjective Logic or the Doctrine of the Concept'. 'Subjectivity' reappears as the title of its first section and the 'Concept' as that of the first chapter of this section. Perhaps the most significant of these recurrences are those of 'Concept' and 'Absolute Idea', the title of the last chapter of the work. For the *Logic* itself, or rather the system of concepts which it presents, is often spoken of as the 'concept' or as the '(absolute) idea'.[6]

Hegel's logical system is different, then, from an ordinary classificatory system which divides genera into species and species into subspecies. In such a system genera do not re-emerge as species nor species as subspecies. The genus 'Animal', for example, is not a type, species or subspecies of itself. It is divided perhaps into vertebrates and invertebrates and, again, neither of these is a species of animal. In Hegel's system, by contrast, although it is difficult to find a single coherent pattern, it looks as if one idea is that we pass from the last subsegment of a segment not simply into the first subsegment of the next segment, but into the next segment itself. For the first subsegment of a segment is itself the segment as a whole. Since genera figure among their own species, we can capture the articulation of a hierarchical, triadic system in a single unilinear process of thought. In an ordinary system of classification we cannot derive the species from the genus or species from species. Division and subdivision depend on empirical inquiry, on the actual differences which we encounter in nature (*WL* II. pp. 519 ff., M. pp. 800 ff.). This, on Hegel's view, is not so in logic. We can derive species from genera and species from species in a single sweep of thought.[7]

The organization of the *Logic* has connections with several other features of Hegel's thought. That it forms a single classificatory system is related to the fact, for example, that it is sometimes thought of as presenting a unique, self-differentiating concept, the concept, perhaps, of God or of the universe.[8] That higher divisions form subdivisions of themselves is obviously connected with the intention that the *Logic* as a whole should be the culminating scene of the *Logic*.[9] It is also related to Hegel's fondness for applying concepts to themselves, regarding, for example, the universal and the particular as two particulars or specifications of the universal.[10] But enough has been said for the moment about the overall structure of the work. The next question to ask is whether logic in Hegel's sense is possible at all.

2 *Form and content*

Hegel gives a number of apparently different accounts of what logic is. It is, he says, 'the science of *the pure idea,* that is, of the idea in the abstract element of *thinking*' (*Enz.* I. 19). But this definition, he continues, presupposes an acquaintance with his system if it is to be understood. A better account for our purposes is that logic is thinking about thinking, thinking about pure thoughts; the mind 'gives satisfaction to its highest inwardness, *thinking,* and acquires thinking as its object' (*Enz.* I. 11. Cf. 17). There is, however, an initial doubt as to whether this is possible at all. Kant had argued that the categories have no meaning or at any rate cannot provide us with knowledge unless they are supplemented by empirical data: they are, 'as unities merely of subjective consciousness, conditioned by given material, empty in themselves and have their application and use only in experience' (*Enz.* I. 43).[11]

Hegel maintains, on the contrary, that the 'thought-determinations' are not 'external forms', external, that is, to the content which gives them a concrete meaning (*WL* I. pp. 26 f., M. pp. 36 f.).

Some of his arguments for this are bad ones. The categories, one argument runs, cannot be in themselves empty (*für sich leer*). It is true that their content is not perceptible or spatio-temporal, but since they are determinate, they must have a content apart from their application. He illustrates this with the example of a book. A work of fiction may contain a mass of individual characters and events, and yet lack content. More is needed for content than sensuous material, namely thoughts or categories. A book is contentful to the extent that it contains 'thoughts, universal results, etc.' (*Enz.* I. 43Z). The analogy is an imperfect one, however. The distinction between pure thoughts and our bare sensory intake does not coincide with the contrast between 'general results' and individual events, for, on Kant's view – and Hegel's – thoughts are involved even in a humdrum narrative of individual events. But, more important than this, what Hegel would need to show if he is to establish that pure thoughts are contentful on their own is not simply that a contentful narrative must contain thoughts, but that it could be contentful even if it contained only thoughts and no 'individual events and situations' at all. The analogy shows at most that, if an experience involves some sensory data, then its contentfulness varies in proportion to the thoughts which it contains. But this does not entail that thoughts or categories are contentful when taken on their own.

But why, in any case, is Hegel so anxious to show that pure thoughts have an independent content? Sometimes, as we have seen, he speaks as if it is to secure our cognitive access to supersensible objects.[12] Thus Kant is seen as arguing as follows:

1   All knowledge involves categories.
2   The categories have no content unless they are supplemented by intuitions.

But

3   The absolute, God or things-in-themselves provide no intuitions.

Therefore

4   The absolute, God or things-in-themselves cannot be known (*Enz.* I. 44).

Hegel accepts premiss 1 of this argument and more or less agrees to premiss 3. As we have seen, he directly attacks the conclusion 4, involving as it does the notion of an unknowable thing-in-itself.[13] But if the conclusion is faulty there must be something wrong either with the argument itself or with one of its premisses, and Hegel is here locating the fault in premiss 2.

However, as we have also seen, Hegel does not ultimately believe

that the absolute is something distinct from thoughts themselves
to which thoughts are to be applied. Why then can they not be
purely formal? It is not as if we cannot think about what is purely
formal, about mere external forms. A propositional form, represented for example by the expression 'Fx', is formal in the sense
that it is not itself a proposition, but needs to be supplemented by
some content or other if it is to become one. But it does not follow
that we cannot think about the form expressed by 'Fx'. Many
logic books manifest such thinking. The answer, or at least a part
of it, is that if we think about pure thoughts, then we must use
pure thoughts to do so, our thoughts about pure thoughts must
themselves be pure thoughts:

> The activity of the thought-forms and the criticism of them
> must therefore be united in cognition. The thought-forms must
> be considered in and for themselves; they are the object and the
> activity of the object itself; they examine themselves, they must
> determine their limits and exhibit their defects within themselves
> (*Enz.* I. 41Z. 1).

But if this can be done, the categories cannot be purely formal,
they cannot always stand in need of external intuition (*WL* I. p.
36, M. p. 44). A purely formal thought cannot be employed to
think about itself. One cannot, for example, use the form 'Fx' to
think about the form 'Fx', not just because it is an insufficiently
rich thought, but because it is not a complete thought at all. Hegel
often criticizes traditional formal logic on the grounds that it is
'finite' (*Enz.* I. 20Z), and a part of what he means is that it is not
reflexive, that the thinking which the logician himself engages in
is quite different from the thoughts or thought-forms which he
thinks about. But this can only be because the object of his
thinking is a mere fragment of the thought of which he is capable.
His enterprise is incomplete. Thinking of the proper sort is infinite
and self-contained (*Enz.* I. 28Z). The claim that thought is infinite
means more, for Hegel, than that it is self-reflexive, but this much
is enough for the moment.[14]

By Hegel's account, logic is close to being an example of what
Kant called an 'intuitive understanding' or 'intellectual intuition'.
Kant supposed that in contrast to our own discursive understanding,
which can 'only *think*, and for intuition must look to the senses',
we can form the idea of, though we do not in fact possess, an
'understanding in which through self-consciousness all the manifold
would *eo ipso* be given, [which] would be *intuitive*'.[15] He believes,
however, that[16]

were I to think an understanding which is itself intuitive (as, for

267

example, a divine understanding which should not represent to itself given objects, but through whose representation the objects should themselves be given or produced), the categories would have no meaning whatsoever in respect of such a mode of knowledge. They are merely rules for an understanding whose whole power consists in thought, consists, that is, in an act whereby it brings the synthesis of a manifold, given to it from elsewhere in intuition, to the unity of apperception — a faculty, therefore, which by itself knows nothing whatsoever, but merely combines and arranges the material of knowledge, that is, the intuition, which must be given to it by the object.

If an understanding were intuitive, then its possession of a concept or acquaintance with a universal would automatically imply acquaintance with its instance or instances. There would be no contrast between possibility and actuality. Thinking about something would *ipso facto* guarantee the existence and accessibility of what was thought about.

Hegel does not discuss the idea of an intuitive understanding at great length or with much appreciation of the problems involved. But when he does so, he pays tribute to it as one of Kant's better insights.[17] Moreover, Hegel's remarks about it invariably imply that we actually have it. If this is so, then pure thinking, as he describes it, has many of the features which Kant ascribes to intuitive understanding. Since thinking is its own object, the thinking itself would automatically secure the existence of what is thought about. Pure thinking does not require supplementation by a sensory or any other sort of 'given'. There is no contrast between the actuality and the mere possibility of what is thought about, nor is there any distinction between those features which the object must have if it is to satisfy the concept which is applied to it and variable features which are not determined by its concept.[18] The application of thought to the object will fully determine it, for there can be no looseness of fit between pure thinking and itself.[19] Logic, moreover, is a form of cognition and not merely a preliminary to it. Pure thinking provides us with knowledge about the forms of thought (*Enz.* I. 41Z).[20] It does not, of course, as on Kant's view an intuitive understanding would, dispense with concepts altogether nor does it, as Kant implies, reveal its object all at once, like Jacobi's immediate awareness. It involves a slow unravelling of the system of pure thought, which is only revealed to us as a whole at the end.[21,22]

3 The point of logic

Granted that pure thinking is possible, why should we indulge in it? Hegel gives various answers to this question, some of which we have already considered. A common reply is that we should examine our concepts before we apply them to infinite objects (*Enz.* I. 28).[23] The interests of a systematic derivation of such concepts are often invoked (*Enz.* I. 33, 42). This type of answer is given when Hegel purports to be arguing within the philosophical tradition and thinks of his logic as a continuation of that tradition which resolves certain problems or contradictions within it. Other answers which he gives tend to assume that philosophy as a whole is a sort of pure thinking and attempt to meet the question: Why should we engage in pure thinking rather than, for example, empirical scientific thinking? One of them depends on Hegel's view that the ego is identical, or intimately associated, with thought. The mind 'gives satisfaction also to its highest inwardness, *thinking* . . . . Thus it comes to its *very self* . . . for its principle, its unadulterated selfhood is thinking' (*Enz.* I. 11). To think purely, to think about and in terms of pure thoughts, is to attain the highest level of self-consciousness.

A second answer of this type is that other types of cognitive and practical attitude involve contradictions, the attempt to resolve which impels us on to pure thinking. We have already said something about this type of answer in relation to the disturbance of primitive harmony which Hegel postulates in his account of the human predicament in general.[24] We have since seen, however, that Hegel often blurs the distinction between different types of thinking.[25] In particular, his answer to the question why we should think purely rather than at some other level is bedevilled by his failure to distinguish it from the distinct question: Why should our thinking at any one level advance once we are engaged in it? The two questions are confused, for example, in the context of a discussion of three types of cognition: experiential cognition, 'reflection', and cognition 'in the form of thinking':

> That the form of thinking is the absolute form and that the truth appears in it as it is in and for itself is the assertion of philosophy in general. The proof of it has the primary point of showing that those other forms of cognition are finite forms . . . . All the forms of finite thinking will occur in the course of the logical development [and will be shown to be in some sense inadequate] (*Enz.* I. 24Z.3).

On the face of it, the word 'form' is here used in two ways. It denotes, firstly, a level of thinking, experiential cognition being, for example, a different form of cognition from pure thinking. Secondly, it denotes concepts which occur as phases within each level of thinking. It is not obvious that when we pass within the *Logic* from one form or concept to another, showing each in turn to be inadequate, we thereby establish that other levels of thinking, the experiential type for example, are inadequate. The form of 'reflection', which involves the thinking characteristic of pre-Kantian metaphysics, thinking in terms of hard and fast concepts, is indeed found to be deficient if concepts can be shown to flow into one another by the *Logic*. But there is, as we have seen, no necessary connection between the rigidity of thinking and whether or not it is experiential or pictorial.[26] Goethe is cited as an example of someone who 'looks into nature or into history, has lofty experiences, discerns the rational and expresses it' (*Enz.* I. 24Z.3).[27] There is no suggestion here that Goethe dealt in rigid, exclusive concepts in the way that the practitioners of reflection do. If this is so, however, it is hard to see how we could be dislodged from experiential thinking of this sort, or indeed from pictorial religious thinking of the appropriate type, by encountering contradictions in it which we feel impelled to overcome. For Hegel regularly maintains that contradictions have their source in rigid, fragmented concepts.[28] They can explain, therefore, the move from Newton's physics to Goethe's physics (*Enz.* II. 330), or from Catholic christianity to Lutheran christianity, but not from physics to philosophy or from religious thinking to pure thinking. It may be that once we raise the question 'What type of thinking or cognitive approach is the right one?' we are *ipso facto* already thinking at a philosophical level. But it still needs to be asked what compels us to raise this question or, indeed, what prevents us from lapsing back into a lower level of thinking once we have asked it.

Hegel seems to have believed that all such questions as this are answered within his system. Once one has entered his circle, all one's doubts about the wisdom of doing so will be allayed. One will see for example, in the *Philosophy of Nature*, why one cannot remain at the level of Goethe. But why should one enter the circle in the first place? Hegel probably has no better answer to this than he has to the question why primitive harmonies need ever be disrupted. Again, we should perhaps be less scrupulous than he is about explaining everything and simply accept that there is at least some reason within the existing philosophical tradition for thinking about thinking.

4 *Thought and reflexivity*

Hegel makes large claims on behalf of thought about thought, primarily on the basis of its reflexivity. Unlike other sciences it does not have to begin with a 'subjective presupposition':

> For the beginning (*Anfang*) which philosophy has to make, it might seem that it begins in general with a subjective pre-supposition just as the other sciences do, namely that it must make a particular object, as in other cases space, number, etc., so in this case *thinking*, into the object of thinking. But it is the free act of thinking to place itself at the standpoint where it is quite independent (*für sich selber*) and thus *produces and gives itself its own object.* Further, the standpoint which thus appears as *immediate* [viz. as the result of a free decision to think] must make itself into the *result* within science and indeed into its final result, in which it [sc. science, viz. philosophy] reaches its beginning again and returns into itself. In this way philosophy reveals itself to be a circle which returns into itself, a circle which has no beginning in the way that other sciences do, so that the beginning is a beginning only in relation to the subject, that which decides to philosophize, and not in relation to the science as such. Or, in other words, the concept of the science and thus the first phase — and because it is the first phase it contains the separation between the (as it were, external) philosophizing subject and the thinking which is its object — must be grasped by the science itself. This indeed is its unique purpose, activity and goal, to attain to the concept of its concept and thus to its return and satisfaction (*Enz.* I. 17).

The rest of this chapter will amount in effect to a commentary on this passage and others like it.[29] Even at this stage, however, Hegel's claims for logic may seem inflated if we consider other branches of learning which are reflexive in much the way that logic is. Linguistics, for example, consists of language about language and psychology involves the exercise of at least some of the psychological functions which it studies. Any given piece of linguistic or psychological research is likely to be 'finite', in the sense that it will not consider the sentences produced by the linguist himself or the psychological powers displayed by the psychologist. But it will not be viciously finite, unless it excludes or denies the linguistic or psychological capacities involved in its own production.[30] These sciences are at least potentially 'infinite', for they can legitimately be included among their own objects.[31]

Can these sciences, then, dispense with 'subjective presuppositions'? And if they cannot, why should we assume that logic is capable of doing so? To institute a comparison in this respect, we shall distinguish four of the types of assumption or presupposition which Hegel has in mind. Not all of them are at issue in the passage quoted, but all of them, and more, are referred to at some point in Hegel's works:

(i) *The object with which the science is concerned.* This is what he has in mind when he mentions number and space, the objects of arithmetic and geometry respectively (*PG* pp. 35 ff., M. pp. 24 ff.). Most sciences have to assume the existence of their objects. The mere practice of logic, by contrast, guarantees the existence of its objects.[32]

(ii) *Rules of procedure or method.* Other sciences presuppose certain rules or laws in accordance with which they proceed. They do not examine these rules themselves, for that is no part of their proper business. Logic, by contrast, has to examine its own rules and cannot, therefore, presuppose them (*WL* I. p. 35, M. p. 43).[33]

(iii) *The starting-point of the course of our thinking.* Should we begin by thinking about pure being or about something else? That this is what Hegel has in mind is suggested by his use of the word 'beginning', and it is certainly what is involved in the section of the *Logic* entitled 'With what must science begin?' (*WL* I. pp. 65 ff., M. pp. 67 ff.).

(iv) *Engaging in pure thinking at all.* This is the question which we considered, inconclusively, in the last section. Hegel ascribes it at first to a free act on the part of the thinker, but he also suggests that if we think for long enough the initial decision to do so will eventually be legitimated within philosophy itself. This seems to be one of the points involved in the claim that the science arrives at its own concept, a claim which recurs in the *Science of Logic* (*WL* I. p. 35, M. p. 43).[34]

What is the position of linguistics and psychology in each of these respects? It is roughly as follows:

(i) The very fact that a linguist speaks or writes about language entails that there is something for him to write or speak about and the fact that a psychologist is studying psychology involves the existence of something for him to study. But this dispensation from the first type of assumption is of dubious value. Even if a linguist supposes that he is writing about English in English, he cannot embark on an assumption-free investigation of his own utterances. He might after all be mistaken in his belief that his own discourse is English rather than some other language or a dialect peculiar to himself. Again, a psychologist can be sure that his mental states are psychological, but not that they are not wholly idiosyncratic but are representative of those of a wider group. Unless the research of the linguist or psychologist is strictly autobiographical, they must make empirical assumptions of this sort, which are open to empirical refutation.

(ii) These sciences as such do not study the rules of their own procedure except in so far as these rules are expressed in the language under consideration or are features of the psychological phenomena under observation. In practice, of course, the practitioners of such disciplines reflect upon their own procedures and perhaps select from among available alternatives. But they would not, at any rate, claim that, in virtue of doing so, they are dispensed from assuming certain rules of procedure, of evidence and validity.

(iii) The reflexivity of linguistics and psychology does not automatically tell the linguist or the psychologist where to begin. If either is to begin at all, then some sentence must be uttered or some psychological activity performed. But there is no guarantee that the first sentence written or the first mental act performed will be the appropriate point to start. It may, for example, be too complicated to receive their first consideration.

(iv) The linguist and the psychologist do not hope, however far they advance in their researches, to discover why they do, or should, engage in linguistics or psychology, except in the trivial sense that they may find out more about what makes the disciplines worthwhile. Nor do they expect to arrive at the 'concept' of their sciences, except again in the sense that one finds out what a subject is by doing it rather than from the relatively uninformative definitions with which textbooks begin.

Can logic do any better than this? Hegel believes that it can and his answer, in terms of our four headings, would run something like this:

(i) It is true that the linguist and the psychologist have to appeal to empirical evidence to support their statements about languages and minds. But this is because what language an individual speaks and what psychological states he has are contingent matters, dependent on all kinds of factors extraneous to the individual himself. The linguist has to consider sentences like 'This leaf is green.' But this sentence, firstly, contains words like 'leaf' and 'green' which express conceptions rather than pure thoughts, conceptions which depend in part on our sensory intake and which we might not have had. Secondly, even in the case of those parts of the sentence which express pure thoughts, 'This', 'is' and the overall structure of the sentence, it is a contingent matter how any particular language expresses them and even whether they use separate words to express them at all (*Enz.* III. 459).[35] It follows from this that the ego is distinct from the particular language it employs. Any given language is something that I have rather than what I am. Linguistics is language about language, but there are still two distinct terms involved, the linguist and the language he happens to speak. Similarly psychology involves two terms, the psychologist and the psychological states he happens to have. By contrast, what pure thoughts I have is not a contingent matter, and, as we have seen, there is on Hegel's view, no distinction to be drawn between the ego or thinker and his thoughts. Thinking about thinking is, therefore, reflexive in a way that linguistics and empirical psychology are not. This in itself does not guarantee, of course, that I am not eccentric, having, or rather consisting of, thoughts which others do not, but this, as we have seen, Hegel attempts to rule out by arguing that there is only one possible system of pure thoughts.[36] *Qua* pure thinker no individual differs from any other except in respect of the extent to which he has explicitly unravelled the system. Idiosyncracies and eccentricities depend on our empirical states, on the effects on us of external things.[37]

(ii) That the rules and procedures of logic are not presupposed but are examined and established by logic itself is not a consequence only of the reflexivity of logic, but of the fact that such rules and procedures are themselves thoughts and therefore fall within the domain of logic. Logic, in this respect, too, differs from linguistics and psychology. One might, however, be more ready to accept that it is the business of logic to *state* and *consider* the rules of its own procedure than that it can succeed in *justifying* them. Must it not either follow certain rules in attempting to justify rules or else do so in a quite haphazard, ruleless manner? In the first case, the rules followed in the justification will either be the same as the rules to be justified or will differ from them. But the justification is, then, either circular (if the rules are the same) or involves an infinite regress of justifications (if they are different). If, on the other hand, the justification itself is not governed and constrained by any rules, then there seems no reason to accept it. Random thoughts cannot justify anything. The circularity of the system does not help here, since how the circle develops will depend on the rules by which it is constructed.[38] What would Hegel say in reply to this? The question will be considered again later,[39] but for the moment we can notice that the answer will depend on the identification of the thinking ego with the thoughts themselves. For to suppose that the ego, in considering a certain subject-matter, must follow certain rules presupposes a distinction between subject-matter, on the one hand, and the ego, on the other, which is faced with a number of possible ways of dealing with this subject-matter, only some of these ways being in accordance with the rules. If, as Hegel believes, thinking of this sort involves the total immersion of the ego in its subject-matter, namely itself (*Enz.* I. 23), then questions about what rules or procedures we should follow can hardly arise. Doubts have already been cast on this supposed absorption of the ego into its subject-matter. These will be elaborated later.[40]

(iii) The 'free act' of engaging in pure thinking need not automatically set one off at the right point any more than the 'free act' of studying a language does. One might suppose that the identification of the ego with pure thoughts implies that questions about where the ego should begin cannot be asked. But Hegel seems, nevertheless, to ask them. For when deciding to think purely one has to begin somewhere, and the circularity of the system does not entail that it does not matter at what point the cognizing subject enters it. One cannot break into the *Logic* at any arbitrarily chosen point any more than one can start reading an autobiography, whose final episode is the writing of the autobiography, at a random page.[41] Why does Hegel's *Logic* begin with being? Three types of answer are given to this. Firstly, he argues that if one starts with something else, with nothing, for example, or becoming, then one will, if one continues thinking, find oneself back at being, and will then go through logic in the right order (*WL* I. pp. 73 ff., M. pp. 73 ff.). This, however, is problematic. Why should one go backwards to being rather than forwards to something else? Does not the suggestion that there are different routes through the *Logic* imply a distinction between the ego and its thoughts? There does not seem to be any satisfactory answer to these questions. Secondly, pure being is implied to be a self-validating starting-point. It is a peculiarly empty thought, simple and immediate rather than complex and concrete. It is, as it were, the blank space of thought rather than an actual, definite thought: 'What makes the beginning, the beginning itself, is therefore to be taken as something unanalysable, in its simple unfilled immediacy, thus *as being*, as what is entirely empty' (*WL* I. p. 75, M. p. 75). Thirdly, it is suggested that the beginning of the *Logic* is somehow legitimated by its conclusion. As we have seen, it is quite obscure how this works, but it is implicit in such remarks as these:[42]

Thus then logic too has returned in the absolute idea to this simple unity which is its beginning; the pure immediacy of being, in which at first all determination appears to be extinguished or omitted by abstraction, is the idea which has come by mediation, that is by the sublimation (*Aufhebung*)[43] of mediation, to its corresponding likeness to itself (*WL* II. p. 572, M. p. 842).

(iv) It might seem unsurprising that logic does not begin by giving an account of what it is or a definition of logic. Definitions of a science are generally unilluminating unless one is already familiar with the science in question, and most of them do not waste much time in providing such a definition. It would not be very significant, then, if logic did not supply the concept of itself in advance, but relied on informal understanding or on our actually doing the subject to tell us what logic is. What is significant is Hegel's belief that we can arrive at the concept of logic as the final result of logic. Linguists and psychologists tend not to make analogous claims on behalf of their own disciplines, but, if they did, they would have to say that the final feat which a linguist performs is the analysis of the sentences which he, as a linguist, produces and that the psychologist completes his work by analysing and explaining the mental processes which he undergoes when he is doing psychology. The pure thinker can, and eventually does, think not simply about particular thoughts, but about the whole system of thoughts as such and his thinking of them.

5 *The advance of thinking*

What has been said so far implies that if one is thinking about thoughts, then one's thinking progresses. One does not remain transfixed to a single thought, but successively thinks about different thoughts. Similarly the linguist successively considers different sentences or different features of sentences, and the psychologist considers different aspects of our mental make-up. How do they proceed from one topic to the next? There is some sort of order of increasing complexity. One would not, for example, consider conceptual thought before perception or the subjunctive before the indicative mood. But apart from this, there are presumably few constraints on the order in which topics arise. Different authors take them in different orders. Moreover, different topics do not arise out of each other without further assistance. An appeal to experience is generally required for the introduction of a new topic as well as for something to say about it. One might agree, for example, that linguistics is reflexive, the production of sentences about sentences, but insist that the different types of sentence or features of sentences are more or less distinct from each other, with no obvious non-empirical transitions between them.

Might one similarly agree that pure thinking is reflexive while maintaining that thoughts are sharply distinct from one another, that an appeal to experience is required if we are to proceed from one thought to the next? Hegel sometimes suggests, not quite this, but something that might be taken to imply it, namely that the development of philosophy is not autonomous, but advances in response to developments in other areas of thought, notably in the natural sciences. This is perhaps the point of the Owl of Minerva conception of philosophy considered earlier.[44] It is also implied in the following passage:[45]

> [Thinking] *rises* into its own unmixed element and thus at first takes on a distancing, *negative relation* to that beginning [viz. experience] . . . . Conversely the empirical sciences carry with them the incentive to overcome the *form,* in which the wealth of their content is presented as merely immediate and found . . . therefore as in general *contingent,* and to raise this content to necessity — this incentive drags thinking out of that universality and the satisfaction secured in itself and drives it on *to the development out of itself* (*Enz.* I. 12).

Philosophy, then, in its historical development is dependent on advances in the empirical sciences. Since Hegel believes that his logic mirrors the history of philosophy, the thoughts of the logic are related to each other in the same way as historical philosophies are. But then this suggests that logic too is dependent on experience, that it does not develop autonomously, but is devised in order to provide a framework for empirical discoveries in the natural and social sciences.

This argument is, however, mistaken. The fact that empirical discoveries were required in order to provoke philosophers into moving from one theory to another does not entail that the move could not in principle have been made autonomously, without appeal to experience. Conversely, then, the fact, if it is a fact, that Hegel's *Logic* needs no assistance from experience does not entail that the history of philosophy is similarly self-contained, even if we grant Hegel's view of the relationship between logic and history. For even if certain things can in principle be derived, deduced or constructed *a priori* from what we currently accept, it is historically unrealistic to assume that we shall be both able and willing to do so without outside help. Arithmetic, for example, is *a priori*, but its development required stimuli of various types and degrees of intensity from practical affairs and scientific problems. Afterwards and in retrospect we can see that it is *a priori*, but we should not therefore expect its original discoverers to have developed it without recourse to experience.[46] This does not mean, of course, that Hegel's *Logic* proceeds *in fact* without any prodding from experience. It seems to require it at several points. But this can hardly have been his intention, and the fact that the initial historical development of these concepts depends on such prodding does not entail that it should be so.

Even if we grant this much, however, why should we suppose that it is possible to proceed from one thought to the next without resorting to experience, when psychology and linguistics cannot do so? It is true that if thoughts are to be thought about, then they must be surveyable together, they must, as it were, be in the same field. But this consideration provides only the weakest of connections between different thoughts, a connection which must obtain between the objects of any science, however disparate and disconnected they are in other respects. A stronger connection than this is required if Hegel's objections to finite concepts, for example, are to be met and if his desire to find systematic inter-connections between the different aspects of God is to be satisfied.[47] Can such a stronger connection be found? Hegel seems to have at least two reasons for supposing that it can. Firstly, if pure thoughts are themselves non-empirical in one or more of the senses discussed earlier,[48] one would expect that, when we are thinking about them, we need not rely on external empirical indications about how we are to proceed. But this implies that there are fluid transitions from one concept to another rather than hard and fast barriers between them, footpaths, as it were, and not fences which we cannot cross without assistance. In terms of the analogy suggested earlier, if we are not to introduce negative numbers empirically, by an appeal to losses and debts or to what we already find in textbooks, then there must be some *a priori* route to them from positive numbers. One of the points of the claim that logic is infinite is that it requires no reference to external, empirical factors.

This alone, however, would not guarantee that pure thoughts can be surveyed only in one order. A system of footpaths can be traversed in several different ways. This possibility is excluded, however, by the second consideration, namely that the self just is pure thoughts. If this is so, then there can be no appeal to experience for a ruling on how to proceed, for there is no residual ego to make such an appeal. There cannot, moreover, be alternative routes that we might take through the network of pure thoughts, for there is no ego which could make a choice, even an arbitrary choice, about the route to follow.

Something has already been said about the way in which logic proceeds, and we shall return to the topic later.[49] In the following section, however, we must consider a question suggested by its non-empirical character, namely: Can we understand what the *Logic* means?

6 *Meaning and metaphor*

Hegel's *Logic* is probably the most difficult of all his writings. Other works owe much of their obscurity to the influence on them of the *Logic*. This difficulty derives in large measure from Hegel's resolution to philosophize without making any assumptions, a resolution which no doubt remained unfulfilled, but which he pursued with just enough success to make life difficult for his readers.[50] One of the types of assumption which he was anxious to avoid was, as we have already seen, assumptions about what we mean. He was concerned to answer not only the traditional philosophical questions: 'What is the case?' and 'What can we know?' but also the question: 'What do we mean?' This is a familiar question in recent philosophy, but Hegel's answer to it is less familiar. For, he seems to believe, the avoidance of assumptions in this case excludes appeals not only to the language of philosophical tradition, but to ordinary locutions and ordinary experience of any kind (*Enz.* I. 33).[51] Can we, in this case, understand what Hegel says in the *Logic*?

Sometimes he suggests that it is simply a mistake to ask what the *Logic* means at all:

> The complaint is made that one does not kr.ow what one is to *think* in a concept which has been grasped; there is nothing more to be thought in a concept than the concept itself. But the point of that complaint is a yearning for a *commonplace conception which is already familiar* (*Enz.* I. 3).

The request for a familiar conception is, he implies, misguided. The reason why this is so is given in a passage which is concerned primarily with the meaning of philosophy, but which applies with equal force to the meaning of pure thoughts:[52]

> In what sense, i.e. in what meaning, is the history of thinking reason to be regarded? And to this we can reply that it can be

279

presented in no other meaning than in the sense of thought itself; or we can say that the question itself is out of place. In the case of anything we can ask for its sense or meaning; thus in the case of a work of art [we can ask for] the meaning of the form (*Gestalt*), in language for the meaning of the word, in religion for the meaning of the conception or the ritual, in other actions for their moral value, etc. This meaning or sense is nothing but what is essential, or universal, substantial in an object, and this substantial aspect of an object is the concrete thought of the object. We always have here two types of thing, an external and an internal element, an outer appearance, which is sensibly perceptible, intuitable, and a meaning which is just the thought. But now since our object is itself the thought, these two elements are not present, but rather the thought is what is meaningful in its own self. The object is here the universal; and thus we cannot ask here for a meaning separate or separable from the object. The history of philosophy thus has no other meaning, no other determination, than thought itself. The thought is here itself what is innermost, highest and one cannot therefore establish a thought above it. In the case of a work of art we can reflect, advance considerations, about whether the form corresponds to the meaning; we can therefore place ourselves above it. The history of free thought can have no other sense, no other meaning, than to speak about thought itself. The determination which appears here in place of sense and meaning is thought itself (*EGP* pp. 95 f., L. pp. 71 f.).

The nub of this argument is that concepts or thoughts are meanings and it does not make sense to ask what *they* mean. One can ask for the meaning of a word, but not for the meaning of its meaning. Hegel does not, however, have in mind primarily the relationship between a word and its meaning, but rather that between a metaphor and its literal meaning. Concepts are, so to speak, the literal meaning of conceptions, religious beliefs, rituals, works of art and so on. It is, on this view, inappropriate to seek for a conception in order to understand a thought or a concept, because the relation of meaning, when *x* means M, is asymmetrical. It is not always so. If the meaning of a word is given by another word, then the relation is a symmetrical one. If '*Begriff*' means (the same as) 'concept', then 'concept' means (the same as) '*Begriff*'. But if the meaning of a word is thought of as a concept or a thought rather than another word, or if what we are giving is the literal meaning of a myth, ritual or metaphor, *x*, then *x* means M in a sense in which M does not mean *x*. Someone might of course fail to understand M because the terms which it involves are unfamiliar to him, and then we might refer him back to x, if he is familiar with that. But this is to make a special concession to his defective understanding.[53] It does not imply that M means x.

This account of the intelligibility of the *Logic* is, however, inadequate. We might, in the first place, cast a general doubt on Hegel's confident belief that pure thoughts or the words that express them are the literal meanings of rituals, myths, works of art and so on. The distinction between the literal and the metaphorical is difficult to draw in general, quite apart from the question whether in any particular case we have assigned the correct meaning to a metaphorical term. But in any case, even if we grant that thoughts or thought-words are the literal meaning of religious beliefs and styles of art, it is, as we have seen, a mistake to suppose that the relationship of thoughts or thought-words to ordinary conceptions and to sentences like 'This leaf is green' is that of the literal to the metaphorical.[54] Literal words and sentences can in principle be understood quite apart from metaphors, even perhaps if we had no metaphors at all. But there could be no thoughts or thought-words if there were no conceptions or sentences involving them, and we cannot understand thoughts or thought-words without reference to them.[55] The relationship of thoughts or thought-words such as 'being' or 'individuality' to a sentence like 'The leaf is green' is less like that of the literal to the metaphorical than that of grammar to a language. No one would suppose that the abstract grammatical form of a sentence is its true, literal meaning or that we could understand expressions of such forms unless we understood some of the sentences in which they are embodied. Finally, however, Hegel misconstrues the question of someone who asks what the *Logic* means. He is not asking, as we have seen, for the literal interpretation of metaphors, nor is he asking for the meaning of a thought or for the meaning of the meaning of Hegel's words. He is asking for the meaning of his words. For what we are presented with in the *Logic* is not immediately pure thoughts, but with words, such as 'being', and with sentences, such as 'The pure concept is the absolutely infinite, unconditioned and free' (*WL* II. p. 274, M. p. 601). Even if we grant that these expressions are literal rather than metaphorical, we might well fail to understand what they mean. And how can Hegel explain to us what they mean, if he is not prepared to point to ordinary locutions or experience?

One reply that might be made is that in order to understand Hegel one has to forget about his words and attempt to reproduce his own thought for oneself. One will then have the thoughts

which correspond to his words. To do this one need understand
only his prefatory remarks, for if one thinks purely, then there
is only one way of doing it. This might be supported by the
suggestion that language is a defective medium for the expression
of thought. This, however, appears not to be Hegel's solution. His
remarks about language do not suggest that he regarded it as an
inadequate medium which we would do well to abandon.[56] His
comments on the German language are invariably favourable in
this respect, and his argument is often supported by untranslatable
puns.[57] Moreover, thought and its product, language, share an
inability to denote or pick out particular individuals.[58] Most
of his remarks about the inadequacy of language for the
expression of thought are directed against undeveloped languages,
such as Chinese,[59] or the symbolic languages of mathematics and
logic.[60] Indeed we do not find him attacking language as such
where we would perhaps most expect it, namely where he presents
his view that infinite entities can be described only in paradoxical
propositions. The fault lies in finite concepts and in the form of
the proposition, not in language as such. None of this, of course,
entails that our thought is dependent on our language rather than
simply that language is a good way of expressing what we happen
to think. But Hegel does not appear to believe that thinking is
independent of all linguistic expression. This would go against the
general views of the time, as we find them presented, for example,
in the writings of Herder.[61] We are, then, entitled to look at Hegel's
written words for a solution to the problem of meaning.

7 The construction of meaning

A partial analogue of what Hegel is attempting to do is, as we have
seen, a formal system such as arithmetic or Russellian logic in
which symbols are defined in terms of other symbols chosen as
primitives. Such a system is, however, loosely connected with our
ordinary language and experience and we could not understand it
if it were not. The primitive terms of a system, for example, are
explained by reference to ordinary locutions and one could not
gain access to arithmetic unless one were familiar with its simple
applications in such everyday activities as counting. It does not,
however, follow that the system is empirical. Once we have won
access to it, ordinary language and experience can be left behind —
aufgehoben, as Hegel would say. Extensions to the system can be
made independently of them, perhaps even before we have thought
of an appropriate application. This sort of account fits much of
what Hegel says about logic, that it presupposes, for example, that

we have experience and form conceptions from it which involve or correspond to pure thoughts, but that we leave these behind when we engage in logic itself.[62]

Pure thoughts, Hegel tells us, are involved in all our everyday speech and experience (*Enz.* I. 3). Logic is, from one point of view, easy because it deals with what is familiar: 'they are also what is most familiar (*Bekannteste*), being, nothing, etc., determinacy, quantity, etc., being-in-itself (*Ansichsein*), being-for-itself (*Für-sichsein*), one, many, etc.' (*Enz.* I. 19). The thought-determinations are the

> innermost essence, but they are also what is ever on our lips and therefore seems to be thoroughly familiar . . . . It is naturally supposed that the absolute must lie in the far beyond (*jenseits*); but it is just what is entirely present, what we, even if we are not expressly conscious of it, always carry with us and use (*Enz.* I. 24Z. 2).

Hegel concedes that it is difficult to think about what is most familiar to us and to range freely among abstractions like pure being (*Enz.* I. 3, 19, 24Z. 2), but he does not doubt that the categories of the *Logic* are more or less the same as those involved in our everyday speech.

We might ask what guarantee there can be that they are the same, if pure thoughts are derived *a priori*. How can we be sure, for example, that the concept of pure being which figures in the *Logic* is the same as that which is involved in such sentences as 'This leaf is green'? The answer seems to be that we cannot. Moreover the connections between the *Logic* and the familiar are in fact far looser than Hegel suggests. Pure being no doubt has something to do with humble uses of the word 'is', and thoughts such as those of determinate being and of quantity correspond to our uses of such expressions as 'red', 'sweet', 'big', 'two feet long' and 'how many?' But many of his categories do not occur very obviously in our everyday discourse. An example of this is the syllogism. Considerable ingenuity would be required to show that the syllogism is in ordinary employment even in its usual sense, but any confidence that we might have in Hegel's claim is quenched when we read such passages as this:[63]

> [the syllogism (*Schluss*)] is the determination that the particular is the middle-term which unites the extremes of the universal and the individual. This form of inferring (*Schliessens*) is a universal form of all things. All things are particular and combine themselves as a universal with the individual. The feebleness

(*Ohnmacht*) of nature, however, involves that the logical forms are not exhibited purely. Such a feeble exhibition of the syllogism is e.g. the magnet, which in the middle, its point of indifference, combines its poles, which are thus immediately one in their distinctness (*Enz.* I. 24Z.2).

Despite the fact that what Hegel first introduces looks like a type of argument,[64] he concedes that the syllogism in his sense bears little resemblance to that of the 'old formal logic' (*Enz.* I. 24Z. 2). But more important than this is the unlikelihood that the syllogism in either sense is 'ever on our lips'.

It may be, however, that such connections as there are between ordinary discourse and Hegel's *Logic* are sufficient to secure our access to it. It is not, after all, essential that every category in it should be 'ever on our lips', but only that what is already familiar to us should enable us to understand what Hegel is saying. The categories are to be derived or reconstructed within the *Logic* and not drawn from everyday speech and experience at every stage. Concepts and words are, then, to be given a meaning independently of them. How exactly does Hegel purport to pursue this programme? There are, unfortunately, a variety of possibilities and it is entirely unclear which, if any, was dominant in his mind:

(i) One obvious idea is that, since each thought is derived from its predecessor or predecessors, the meaning of the word which expresses the thought is determined solely by the way in which it is derived and any other connotations of the word are to be excluded. This corresponds to Hegel's belief that the sense of the conclusion of a proof is determined by the proof itself.[65] We might suppose, on this view, either that the meaning of pure 'being' is taken as given or that it is in turn derived at the end of the *Logic*.[66]

(ii) Another idea is that, conversely, one understands a concept by understanding what can be derived from it. This is perhaps what Hegel has in mind when he says: 'This further determination [of being into other categories] is at once both a *putting-forth* and thus an unfolding of the concept which is *in* itself and at the same time the *withdrawal* of being *into itself*' (*Enz.* I. 84).[67] An analogue of this would be the suggestion that one cannot fully understand a proposition unless one sees what other propositions, or at least types of proposition, it entails. But Hegel is fonder of organic similes: just as one cannot understand what a seed is, if one knows only that it is produced by a plant and not also that it grows into one, so one's grasp of a concept depends on one's knowing what is derived from it (e.g. *Enz.* I. 161Z).

(iii) A thought together with those which are derived from it and those from which it is derived forms a system of thoughts, and one of Hegel's ideas is that one cannot fully understand any thought unless one can see its place in the system as a whole. There is an organic analogue of this as well. On Hegel's view, the parts of a plant or an animal form a cohesive system such that no one of them can be detached from it without ceasing to be what it is, and no one of them can be understood without reference to the others.[68] But he also refers to relationships between colours (*Farbenverhältnisse*) as a 'symbol' of logic (*WL* II. p. 295, M. p. 618). A part of what he means is presumably that one could not understand the word 'red' unless one understood the meaning of some other colour-words which contrast with it. There are, however, several differences between a system of colours or colour-words and Hegel's *Logic*. One is that colour-words exclude the application of each other whereas Hegel's thoughts in many cases do not. To allow for this feature, one would have to extend the analogy, by saying, for example, that one could not fully understand colour-words unless one also understood words which described some other aspects of things, their shapes, for instance, or their sizes. Another difference, however, is that, while the word 'red' must figure in some system of colour-words, it is indeterminate which one. How many other colour-words there are to be and what colours they are to stand for is left open, and how it is settled will depend on what colours are found in the speakers' environment and what discriminations they need to make. In Hegel's *Logic*, by contrast, any concept can figure in only one system and its meaning is fully determined by its position in that system. There can be no appeal to the objects in our environment or to our needs and purposes in the *a priori* construction of logic.[69]

A final difference is that there is in the colour spectrum no obvious direction from lesser to greater complexity, as there is in Hegel's *Logic*. To capture this feature of it we must revert to the analogy of the system of numbers or, perhaps, of grammatical constructions. For these do display an order of increasing complexity, such that the system can be built up by proceeding from simpler elements to more complex ones. There is of course a corresponding loosening of the ties between a simple element and the system as a whole, since simple ones can be understood without one's understanding complex ones. But we can nevertheless suppose that simple elements cannot be *fully* understood in isolation from more complex ones, and Hegel may require no more than that. We can, perhaps, combine our two organic metaphors, if we imagine that a plant develops from simple states to more complex ones and that its past states are encapsulated in its present one, so that the organs of a fully-developed plant are ordered in terms of increasing complexity, each one involving in some way its simpler predecessors.[70] We need not suppose, however, that nature provides an exact analogue of Hegel's logical idea.

(iv) A general difficulty with all the foregoing accounts is that Hegel uses in the *Logic* many words apart from those that stand for pure thoughts and he also uses at certain stages of the work thought-words which are not derived or examined until a later stage. The discussion of pure being, for example, opens with the sentence: '*Being, pure being* — without any further determination (*Sein, reines Sein* — ohne alle weitere Bestimmung)' (*WL* I. p. 82, M. p. 82). The concept of being is here introduced and the word for it is presupposed. But, apart from this, some of the words which are used to introduce it express thoughts which have not yet been considered and are not considered here, but only later in the *Logic*. The concept of determination, for example, is examined further on in the work (*WL* I. pp. 131 ff., M. pp. 122 ff.). The word 'without', moreover, is not obviously examined in the *Logic* at all, unless we take 'without . . . determination' as a single expression and locate the investigation of it in the section on determination. This suggests a different conception of the way in which meaning is conferred on the terms used in the *Logic,* a conception corresponding to the idea of a series of languages of increasingly higher order.[71] On this view, the words which are used to speak about the concept under examination at any given stage would not themselves be examined at that stage, but only at a later one. We would have, of course, a partial understanding of such words even at the stage at which they are simply employed and not actually examined, an understanding based on the use of these words in ordinary language. But the understanding would be only partial, and the terms are to be reconstructed at a subsequent stage. At the end of the *Logic* we would reach a stage at which every term has been purified and is defined in terms of the others. At that point we can talk about the whole system in terms of itself. There is no misfit between the thoughts thought about and the thoughts about them to generate a move to a distinct, higher stage.

On all of these accounts of how the *Logic* works, except the first, it would of course be the case that we cannot fully understand any part of it until we have read it right through. This would, however, only be objectionable, if it meant that one could not understand any of it *at all* until one had understood all of it. But understanding is a matter of degree. One cannot fully understand a detective novel until one has reached its dénouement, and one's introduction into a formal system or an unfamiliar science is mediated by imperfect or incomplete insights which are revised and improved as one progresses further into the system.[72]

But which of these conceptions of the *Logic*, or which combination of them, is the correct one? This is hard to say. The difficulty stems in part from the fact that Hegel has left no presentation of even a part of logic which is purged of all attempts to explain it to outsiders by reference to ordinary conceptions. It is generally unclear what is a part of the system proper and what is simply informal talk about the system which could in principle be jettisoned. But it also derives from the unclarity of his own intentions. His general purpose is clear enough. It is to use ordinary language and experience in order to rise above (*aufheben*) them and discover the underlying structure of all experience and language. But how, in detail, he supposed that this could be done is obscure. A partial analogue of what he hoped to achieve by the end of the *Logic* is a natural language such as English or German. A natural language can be seen as containing various 'finite' sub-languages which are not capable of speaking about themselves, but it is itself infinite, capable of speaking about itself in a way that most formal systems are not. It has the additional feature, moreover — if Hegel in fact requires it — that the process of definition is circular. A dictionary of the language will use a term x in its account of y and y in its account of x. It is unnatural to divide the expressions of such a language into primitive terms and defined ones when it is in fact an interlocking system of expressions which may be explicated in terms of each other according to taste. The analogy is of course imperfect. The connections between Hegel's concepts are intended to be tighter and their links with experience looser than is the case with the expressions of a natural language. But it conveys his intentions at least as well as his occasional suggestion that what he requires is a strict circle of explication.

This, then, is Hegel's general solution, or solutions, to the problem of the intelligibility of logic. More needs to be said, however, about the way in which the *Logic* proceeds, and this will occupy the following sections.

8 *Complexity and transcendence*

How does pure thinking advance? How do we get from one thought to the next? Hegel often speaks as if thought about thought were quite unproblematically reflexive, as if the thoughts about thoughts were always the same as the thoughts they are about. But this of course is not so, any more than the linguist's sentences are the same as the sentences they are about or the psychologist's own mental processes are precisely the same as those he is describing. The linguist's sentences about a sentence like 'The cat is happy' will display greater complexity and a richer vocabulary than that sentence itself. Similarly it is, on Hegel's view, thinking as a whole which is 'infinite', and not the particular thoughts that one thinks about. We have already seen, for example, that when the logician thinks about *'being, pure being'*, his own thought about it is of a higher order of complexity. If it were not so, if there were a complete fit between the object-thought and the meta-thought, it is hard to see how pure thinking could advance at all except by arbitrary leaps and bounds. It is suggested, moreover, by Hegel's principle of limits, namely that to see that something has limits or to see what its limits are is to go beyond those limits. If I think about a thought of a certain definite content, my thought about it cannot have the same content, the same limits, but must transcend them.[73]

This, then, is, as we have already seen, one way of looking at Hegel's *Logic.* The idea would be that the thought which one considers at any one stage, thought$_n$, is the thought one had about the thought of the previous stage, thought$_{n-1}$. This procedure would generate a continuous supply of new object-thoughts. It is as if the linguist were to move from considering a sentence, S_n, immediately to the examination of the sentence he produced about S_n, sentence S_{n+1}. The concepts or conceptual systems which are considered in the *Logic* are finite, both in the sense that they are of definite, restricted content and are thus extendible, and in the connected sense that they are not adequate for thought about themselves. This is evidently true, for example, of the concept of pure being which enables us only to gesture towards items in our experience, saying that they *are.*[74] It is also true of determinate being, *Dasein,* whether this is regarded as a possible predicate in sentences like 'This has existence' or as shorthand for a system of quality words, such as 'red', 'green', 'square' and 'circular', which enables us to describe features of our experience. A *Dasein*-system is finite in that it does not enable us to say what we want to say about its own general structure and the possibility and scope of its own application. If, therefore, it is possible to think about *Dasein* at all, then the *Dasein*-system must be finite in the further sense that it can be extended and enriched. The obvious way of doing so is to supplement it with the concept or concepts which we require in order to think about it. The goal of the whole process would be, as we have seen, the infinite system which is capable of describing itself and which cannot be extended. Since it has, in a sense, no limits, there is no reason why our awareness of it should involve our transcending it.[75]

Does the fact that thought is one step ahead of the thought which it is about reintroduce a distinction between thoughts and the self? Not necessarily. The distinction need only be between two thoughts, an earlier, lower one and a later, higher one, not between the thoughts and an ego which has them. In fact this corresponds quite well to the self-transcending character of the self, a feature of it which the *Logic* must capture if it is to be regarded as an account of the self.[76] The idea also coheres well with some of the other purposes which the *Logic* is intended to serve. The history of philosophy, as we have seen, and also the histories of art, religion and political institutions, are supposed to constitute the development of human self-consciousness, advancing by reflection upon their present state and culminating in an understanding of the whole process.[77] It also captures the asymmetry of intelligibility which obtains between different levels of thinking:

> Philosophy as the conceptual (*begreifendes*) thinking of this
> content has the advantage over the pictorial conceiving
> (*Vorstellen*) of religion that it understands both; it can
> understand religion, it understands also rationalism and super-
> naturalism, and also itself; but the converse is not the case.
> Religion, standing at the standpoint of conception, understands
> only what is at the same standpoint as itself, not philosophy,
> the concept, the universal thought-determinations (*VGP* I. p.
> 101, H. I. pp. 80 f.).

Philosophy or logic is a meta-language with respect to the language of religion. If we remember that the progression from one type of thinking, e.g. religion, to another, e.g. philosophy, is supposed to mirror the progression within logic itself, then this confirms the suggestion that this is the principle on which the *Logic* operates.[78] Finally, the suggestion gives some account of the increasing richness or 'concreteness' of the pure thoughts themselves. As we might expect from the fact that they are intended to reflect the history of philosophy, the pure thoughts are not seen by Hegel as being on a par with one another. Each one, roughly speaking, embraces more of the realm of pure thought than its predecessors. For example, mechanism, chemism and teleology are not simply alternative ways of explaining things but have an ascending order in a hierarchy. Teleological explanations presuppose or include mechanistic and chemical explanations. We could not, for example, explain how a purposive agent fulfils his plan unless we referred to mechanical and chemical processes: 'This relation [viz. that of the means to the material] is a sphere of mechanism and chemism which now *serve* the purpose which is their truth and free concept' (*Enz.* I. 209).[79] We might say, roughly, that if one concept or conceptual system, x, is the immediate predecessor of another, y, then the following relationships hold between them:

(i) If y applies to a thing or to an area, then x applies to it too, but the converse does not necessarily obtain;
(ii) One cannot have or employ y without having and employing x, but the converse does not necessarily obtain;
(iii) There is a sense in which one cannot explain y without referring to x, but one can explain x without referring to y.
These relationships are not, of course, explicable only on the view that each thought is, as it were, a meta-language with respect to its immediate predecessor, but they are, as we have seen, compatible with it.[80]

There are, however, apparently insuperable objections to this account of how the *Logic* works. Some of them concern its attribution to Hegel. The most promising case for the account is perhaps that of the transition from being and nothing to becoming, which is made primarily for the reason that being *becomes* nothing and nothing *becomes* being. The concept of becoming is introduced because it is required in order to think about the concepts of being and nothing.[81] But, as we have seen already, some of the concepts required to think about pure being are considered only much later in the *Logic*, if at all. Moreover, the pattern is not to be seen, at any rate clearly, in the rest of the *Logic*. Concepts are, as we would expect, applied to each other, but the way in which this happens, looks haphazard rather than systematic. Sometimes concepts are applied to themselves. In the following passage, for example, Hegel appears to be deriving the (concept of the) particular from (that of) the universal or generic by arguing that the universal is itself a particular:[82]

The particular is the universal itself, but it is its difference or relation to an other, its shining outwards (*sein Scheinen nach aussen*); but there is no other present, from which the particular would be distinguished, except the universal itself. The universal determines itself, thus it is itself the particular; the determinacy is its difference; it is distinguished only from itself. Its species are therefore only (a) the universal itself and (b) the particular (*WL* II. p. 281, M. p. 606).

In another passage, the concept of difference is applied to itself in a parallel way:

> Difference in itself is the difference which relates to itself; thus it is the negativity of itself, difference not from an other, but from its own self; it is not itself, but its other. But what is different from difference is identity. It is therefore itself and identity. Both together constitute difference; it is the whole and its aspect (*WL* II. pp. 46 f., M. p. 417).

Such applications of concepts to themselves are a recurrent feature of the *Logic*. They explain in part why a member of a triad often has the same title as the triad as a whole.[83] But it is not a procedure which is applied very systematically. It may be, for example, that a part of the point of the distinction between the concept and the reality in the case of a whole consisting of parts[84] is that we are meant to be considering the applicability of this concept to itself. But it is not very clear how this is to be done. The concept of a whole containing parts is not very obviously applied by Hegel either to itself or to its immediate predecessor, appearance (*Erscheinung*). We can see how, in a general way, Hegel is thinking about thoughts. But it is hard to find any regular, systematic relationship between the object-thoughts and the meta-thoughts.

It is not clear, in any case, that the model of languages of ascending order provides everything that Hegel requires. We have already seen that there is no unique meta-language for any given object-language, while each thought is intended to have a unique successor.[85] Another requirement, however, is that the boundaries or limits between one concept and another should be, as it were, shifting and fluid rather than sharp and fixed.[86] But this is not guaranteed by the language-model. For a thought$_{n+1}$ which reflects upon thought$_n$ need not be supposed to shift or remove the limits of n, but only itself to have wider limits than n. This fact is obscured by our analogy of arithmetic. For in the case of the positive whole number system it is true both that certain things cannot be said about it unless we have a language which countenances negative numbers and that the boundaries of the system are fluid, that negative numbers can be derived from it. But the first point does not entail the second. The fact that we can say that the numbers are positive implies only that we have some access to negative numbers; it says nothing about what sort of access this is. Similarly a syntactic or a semantic meta-language need not be in any way derivable from the object-language; it may simply have to be invented. Hegel's idea, however, seems to be rather that, as in the case of arithmetic, the thought required to think about a thought must be derived from the object-thought itself. To see how this works we must revert to the notion of a contradiction.

9 Progress and contradictions

Thinking, and indeed everything else, develops, on Hegel's view, by the emergence of contradictions and the attempt to overcome them:[87]

> it happens that thinking gets involved in contradictions, i.e. gets lost in the fixed non-identity of thoughts, thus it does not attain to itself (*sich selbst nicht erreicht*), rather remains caught in its opposite. The higher need [to think and thus to satisfy one's 'highest inwardness'] counters this result of the thinking of the mere understanding (*des nur verständigen Denkens*) and is grounded in the fact that thinking does not give up, it remains true to itself even in this conscious loss of its being-at-home with itself (*Beisichseins*), '*that it may overcome*', that it may produce the dissolution of its own contradictions within thinking itself. — The insight that the nature of thinking itself is dialectic, that, as understanding, it must fall into the negative of itself, into contradiction, is a main feature of logic (*Enz*. I. 11).

We have already seen an example, thought not perhaps a very impressive one, of a thought-determination which Hegel finds to be contradictory, namely that of a whole consisting of parts.[88] We have also considered an analogy, that of the system of positive whole numbers, in which something like a contradiction arises if it is taken on its own and is not supplemented by negative numbers. Something even more like a contradiction is provided by the example — again not an example used by Hegel himself — of a tribe which counts according to the system '1', '2', '3', '4', 'Many', which has, that is, no numerals for any number greater than 4, but indiscriminately counts any group with more than 4 members as many. If such a tribe can add and subtract then contradictions will arise in their system. For example:

$$(i) \quad 3 + 4 = \text{Many}$$
$$(ii) \quad 2 + 4 = \text{Many}$$
$$(iii) \quad \text{Many} = \text{Many}$$
$$\text{Therefore, (iv)} \quad 3 + 4 = 2 + 4$$
$$\text{Therefore, (v)} \quad 3 = 2$$

This false conclusion can be evaded if they deny the apparently tautological proposition (iii) and accept the apparently contradictory proposition: 'Many $\neq$ Many'. This true proposition can be stated in an obviously non-contradictory way if the system is extended to include numerals for all the positive whole numbers. Then we can explain that 'Many $\neq$ Many' simply means that no number greater than 4 is equal to every other number greater than 4, and then propositions like '3 = 2' cannot be derived.[89]

These arithmetical cases display some of the features which Hegel requires. The 'contradictions' in a system are, for example, associated with its finitude, with the fact that it is a mere fragment of the field of thought, and the contradictions are resolved by extending the system in the appropriate way. There is, again, a connection of sorts between this account of the way in which Hegel's *Logic* works and our previous account in terms of successive meta-languages. For the extended system which resolves the contradictions of the primitive system can, together with certain other terms, be seen as a meta-language with respect to the simpler system, for many things can be said in terms of it about the primitive system which cannot be said in terms of the primitive system about itself.[90] This account makes sense of a number of things which Hegel says.

It faces, however, at least three difficulties. The first is that, as we have already seen, there is not in general only one way of disposing of a contradiction. Hegel might exclude simplifying or retrogressive solutions — such as giving up counting altogether — by appealing to his belief that the most primitive concept of all, that of pure being, is inherently unstable, so that one cannot avoid contradictions by trimming down one's thinking unless one is prepared to give up thinking entirely. But even if the solution must be a progressive one, it does not follow that there is only one such solution available. Why, for example, should the concept of a whole containing parts be remedied or supplanted by the concept of a force and its expression rather than by that of an organic whole? A second is that Hegel cannot supply any obvious answer to the question: Why should we overcome contradictions in our thinking and not simply accept them as they are? Logic is not, on his view, to assume rules or laws such as the law of contradiction, but is to examine them with an open mind. But if that is so, then it cannot advance in accordance with such rules until it has examined and justified them. Moreover Hegel is not as convinced as most of us are that the world is self-consistent, so that he cannot appeal to the falsity of contradictory propositions or to the inapplicability of contradictory concepts in order to justify extricating oneself from contradictions.[91] The passage quoted above appears to explain why contradictions are intolerable only by using such ambiguous expressions as '[thinking] remains caught in its opposite (*in seinem Gegenteil befangen bleibt*)' and 'fall into the negative of itself (*das Negative seiner selbst*)'. These could mean *either* that thinking falls into the opposite or the negation of the thought which it has just had — that is, that it contradicts itself — *or* that it falls into the opposite or the negation of thinking as such — that is, that it ceases to be thinking altogether. One might therefore assume that these two conditions coincide, that a thinker who contradicts himself thereby ceases to think, and, if this were so, then any reason one had for thinking at all would be a reason for not contradicting oneself or at least for resolving contradictions as quickly as possible when they arose. But the two conditions are not the same. We have no more right to assume that a thinker who contradicts himself *ipso facto* ceases to think than we have to say that a speaker who utters contradictory sentences thereby ceases to speak. Does Hegel have any better reason for believing that contradictions must be overcome? We shall return to this crucial question later.[92] For the moment our concern is a third difficulty, or group of difficulties, which arises out of the triadic structure of Hegel's *Logic,* and this will be considered in the following section.

10 *Hegel's triads*

The Hegelian triad is reminiscent of the pattern of unity–disunity–reconciliation which we considered earlier,[93] and Hegel does indeed describe the triad as if it represented the disruption of a primitive harmony and the restoration of it at a higher level. He associates it with three elements which the *Logic* involves. They are, firstly, the 'abstract' element or that of the understanding, secondly, the dialectical or the 'negatively-rational' element, and, thirdly, the 'speculative'[94] or 'positively-rational' element. The first element is rooted in the understanding, *Verstand,* while the second two are functions of reason, *Vernunft.*[95] These elements or aspects do not form distinct parts of logic nor are they sharply contrasted with each other. To see them in this way would be to see them only from the point of view of the understanding; the first element alone would govern the relationship between itself and the other two. Rather each element is involved at every stage of logic and because of this each of them is involved in their relationships to one another (*Enz.* I. 79). The elements are described by Hegel as follows. The first, 'thinking as *understanding*', 'sticks to the fixed determinacy and the distinctness of it from others; a restricted abstraction such as this is regarded by it as having a subsistence and being of its own' (*Enz.* I. 80). Initially concepts are treated in the *Logic* as having sharp, well-defined boundaries with respect to each other. This is quite legitimate. Logic is not supposed to be an undifferentiated mystical haze. The second element, however, involves the demolition of these barriers: 'The *dialectical* element is the very self-elimination (*Sichaufheben*) of such finite determinations and their transition into their opposites' (*Enz.* I. 81). Finally the third element supplies the new term which emerges from this process: 'The *speculative* or *positively-rational* aspect grasps the unity of the determinations in their opposition, the *affirmative* element which is contained in their dissolution and their transition' (*Enz.* I. 82).

How, on this account, are the members of a triad related to each other? Hegel gives two answers in this passage. The first is that the second term of a triad is the negation of the first, and the third the negation of the second, the negation of the negation. The dialectic, when it is employed properly,[96]

> has a *positive* result, because it has a *determinate content* or because its result is really not *empty, abstract nothing*, but is the negation of *certain determinations*, which are contained in the result precisely because this is not an *immediate nothing*, but a result (*Enz.* I. 82).

We have already seen, however, that Hegel can derive little help from our ordinary concept of negation here.[97] The second answer is that the second term is the opposite of the first, and that the third term is in some sense the unity of these two opposites: 'This rational aspect is therefore . . . also a *concrete* element, because it is not *simple, formal unity*, but rather the *unity* of *distinct determinations*' (*Enz.* I. 82). Presumably the *Logic* is supposed to continue in virtue of the fact that the last term of one triad itself has an opposite and can therefore be the first term of the next triad.

Our arithmetical analogy can easily be adapted so that it models the triadic form of Hegel's argument. We start, as before, with positive numbers and find that our inability to solve equations such as $2 - 5 = x$ leads us to introduce negative numbers. But now instead of immediately adopting both positive and negative numbers as we did before, we abandon positive numbers and retain only negative ones together with addition and subtraction. We then find, however, that our new system involves the same difficulties as the old one. We can now solve such equations as $(-2)+(-5) = -7$ and $(-5)-(-2) = -3$, but not ones like $(-2)-(-5) = x$. There is also the difficulty that the new and the old system are isomorphic. Just as $2+5 = 7$ and $5-2 = 3$, so $(-2)+(-5) = -7$ and $(-5)-(-2) = -3$. Nothing has changed except that '—' is prefixed to every numeral. How are we to express the difference between these two systems? The answer is that each can be defined only in terms of the other. There is no sense to the symbols '+' and '—' as prefixes of numerals except in the light of the contrast between them. This argument in fact occurs in the *Logic*:[98]

> In the positive and the negative one supposes that one has an absolute distinction. In themselves, however, both are the same and one could therefore call the positive also the negative and conversely the negative the positive. Thus assets and debts too are not two particular, independent types of property. What for the one, the debtor, is negative is positive for the other, the creditor. The same is true of a road to the east, which is equally a road to the west. Positive and negative are thus essentially conditioned by each other and only exist in their relation to each other. The north pole of the magnet cannot be without the south pole nor the south pole without the north pole' (*Enz.* I. 119Z. 1).

The solution to both these difficulties, the isomorphism of the two systems and the fact that either taken on its own cannot solve certain equations, is to combine positive and negative numbers in a single system. This new, 'concrete' system raises new problems of its own, for otherwise thinking would come to a halt. But it is not burdened with the difficulties of either of the simpler systems taken on its own.

This analogy resembles some of Hegel's triads. We might, for example, compare the way in which the concepts of pure being and of pure nothing or non-being are supposed each to 'become' the other.[99] Naturally enough, however, many of the triads do not fit this pattern. Only rarely does the second term of a triad seem to be the opposite of the first. In what sense, for example, is causality the opposite of substantiality or quantity that of quality? Again, the third term is not generally the only possible combination of the first two, even if it is a combination of them at all. In the discussion which follows, however, we shall be concerned with two special features of the analogy and with the extent to which they are appropriate to Hegel's *Logic*. The first is that the third term of the arithmetical triad is not a new term, but is simply the combination of the first two terms, the system of positive and negative whole numbers. The second is that the mere combination of the first and second terms resolves the defects of each of them taken alone. The system of positive numbers, for example, is unable to solve certain equations only as long as it is detached from the negative number or system. In the 'synthesis'[100] this defect disappears. Do the triads of the *Logic* share these two features? An attempt to answer these questions will be made in the following two sections.

11 *The ambiguity of the triad*

A Hegelian triad can be represented provisionally as x, y, x/y. The third term, as the symbolism indicates, in some sense involves the first two terms. The first question then is whether this third term is simply the combination of the first two or is a significantly novel concept. The answer seems to be that in most cases at least it is a new concept, the nature of which we would not have guessed simply from the information that it is the synthesis of the first two terms. We have already seen one example of this, namely the concept of teleology or purposiveness. Obviously this is not just the result of combining mechanical and chemical modes of explanation, even if it also involves one or both of them.[101] Another example, which initially looks more favourable to the view that the third term is just the first two in a single system, is the triad quality, quantity, measure. One might naturally suppose that Hegel's criticism of quantitative ways of conceiving things[102] amounts to the point that we could not apply quantitative or numerical terms to the world unless it also displayed qualitative variations. Our ability to count things and to measure them depends on perceptible qualitative differences between them and their environment, between, for example, a measuring rod and what is not the measuring rod. There is no natural break between the first six feet of something and the next six feet of it as there is between the green part of it and the red part. If we are to employ quantitative terms, then, we must combine them in a single system with qualitative ones. This, however, is not all that Hegel has in mind. The third term of the triad, measure (*Mass*), does not simply combine quality and quantity but changes our view of the relationship between them. So far the quality of something and its quantity have been regarded as indifferent to each other (*gleichgültig*), as independent variables. Within limits, how big something is does not affect its nature or quality, what kind of a thing it is. There are big horses and little horses, and little horses become big horses without thereby ceasing to be horses (*Enz.* I. 99; *WL* I. pp. 210 f., M. p. 186). Measure, by contrast, is concerned with those cases where in a variety of ways the quality of a thing depends on its quantity. If a house is big enough, for example, it is a mansion rather than a house. Again, in the case of higher organisms, the nature of the thing depends on a proportion between the sizes of its parts, and this places certain limits on its overall size (*Enz.* I. 107Z). Significant changes in the size of a country's population will bring in their train qualitative changes in its constitution (*Enz.* I. 108Z). Or again, quantitative variations in the temperature of substances result, at certain points, in qualitative alterations, from a liquid to a solid state for example. The occurrence of such qualitative changes enables us to measure temperature (*Ibid.*) The concept of measure, then, does not simply combine qualitative and quantitative terms in a single framework, but is a new concept applicable to a different, and narrower, range of phenomena.[103] In a similar way, the final term of each triad is a more or less new term, involving its two predecessors with varying degrees of explicitness, but more than the mere combination of them. If this were not so, it is hard to see how the third term could display some new defect which neither of the first two terms alone had, a defect which is required if the *Logic* is to continue.

On this account, however, it is not clear what happens to earlier terms in the *Logic* when we have reached later terms. Quantitative concepts are involved fairly explicitly in the concept of measure, for example, but they have all but vanished by the time we arrive at the concepts of substance or of causality. Are we to suppose that when we reach the stage of causality we have abandoned quantitative concepts altogether except in so far as they are implicitly involved in causal concepts, or are they to be deployed alongside causal concepts, forming together with them a single conceptual system? In the former case, the structure of the *Logic* can be represented like this:

$$x_1, x_2, x_3, \ldots x_n.$$

Each thought-determination replaces its predecessor, though it will develop out of it and in some sense incorporate it. In the latter case, it will look more like this:

$$x_1, x_2(+x_1), x_3(+x_1+x_2), \ldots x_n(+x_1+x_2+x_3 \ldots +x_{n-1}).$$

Each concept here carries with it all of its predecessors. Hegel's answer to this is equivocal. Sometimes he speaks, as we have seen, as if his enterprise is one of testing concepts and rejecting them if they are found to be faulty, much as we test and reject scientific theories. If this is so, then a concept like that of a whole containing parts is simply abandoned. All that is left of it is the traces of it in the more adequate concepts which develop from it.[104] But in other contexts, it is implied that the concept is not to be rejected entirely, but kept in reserve for application to finite entities of an inferior sort (*Enz.* I. 135Z).[105] Another source of this ambiguity is the requirement that the *Logic* should correspond to historical development — to history generally and also the history of particular types of thinking. We can start with a simple representation of, for example, the historical series of philosophies:

$$x_1, x_2, x_3, \ldots x_n.$$

Each philosophy incorporates its immediate predecessor, in something like the way in which a thought-determination of the *Logic* does. This, however, is not an adequate representation of the history of philosophy. For any philosophy assures to its adherents a certain degree of insight into the whole past history of philosophy and of the way in which it has developed. We might attempt to represent this by writing:

$$x_1, x_2(+x_1), x_3(+x_1+x_2), \ldots x_n(+x_1+x_2+x_3 \ldots +x_{n-1}).$$

But this again is unsatisfactory, since it would imply that at every stage there is an equal degree of understanding of the whole series of preceding stages. But this is not so. Such understanding is, before the final stage, always more or less fragmentary and incomplete. Insight into history is minimal at the early stages of it. It does not necessarily increase steadily over time. Aristotle, for example, may well have had a better conception of the past and of what he owed to it than some of his successors did.[106] But, apart from peaks and troughs of this sort, there is a progression from negligible to complete understanding of the course of philosophy as a whole. Complete understanding is represented by Hegel's own standpoint, and this is one of the reasons why all the concepts of the *Logic* resurface at the end of it in the absolute idea. But it is quite unclear how much of the preceding course of the *Logic* is to be incorporated into any given stage of it — except the last — if it is to supply the underlying structure of history.

12 *Contradictions and organisms*

However we answer this question, it is clear that at the end of the *Logic* we are presented with a single, comprehensive conceptual system or system of systems. The contradictions within each element of it are not simply the way in which we advance from one element to another, but they are also what holds them together in a single system. Contradictions are, as it were, the rivets of the edifice: 'The dialectical element constitutes therefore the moving soul of scientific advance and is the principle by which alone *immanent connection and necessity* enters into the content of science' (*Enz.* I. 81). Each element is determined by its position in the system and is held in place by its internal contradictions.

But how are these contradictions to be conceived? Are they removed by the incorporation of the concept into the system or do they persist? Hegel's answer is again equivocal. We have already seen that he often thinks of the conceptual system of the *Logic* as forming an organic whole. A non-organic whole is such that a part can be detached from it and still retain its fundamental character. Certain descriptions will, of course, no longer apply to, for example, a stone which is removed from a pile of stones. It will not be contiguous with the other stones and it may no longer be a part of that whole. But its removal will not deprive it of its essential nature. An organic whole is different:[107]

> The individual members of the body are what they are only through their unity and in relation to this unity. Thus as even *Aristotle* notes, a hand e.g. which is severed from the body is now only a hand in name, but not in fact (*Enz.* I. 216Z. Cf. 135Z).

Another model which Hegel employs here is the magnet. One cannot break a magnet in half in such a way that one half is the north pole and the other is the south pole. Any magnet must have both a north and a south pole. The system of pure thoughts is, in this respect, not unlike a magnet:

> Magnetism is one of the determinations which had to come into special prominence when the *concept* was suspected in determinate nature and the idea of a *philosophy of nature* was conceived. For the magnet exhibits in a simple, naive way the nature of the concept (*Enz.* II. 312. Cf. *WL* II. p. 295, M. p. 618).

Different things happen in different cases if we attempt to break up such a whole. In the case of a living organism, the severed part, though not necessarily the rest of the organism, ceases to be what it was, for example a hand. In the case of a magnet, we simply cannot detach the north from the south pole. Either both poles disappear or both parts of the original magnet are now fully magnetized, each having both a north and a south pole. What happens if we attempt to sever a thought-determination from its context in the system? Some sort of contradiction or other awkwardness arises.[108]

One might suppose, from this account, that a concept is only contradictory so long as it is detached from the system, that Hegel is engaged in an enterprise of contradiction-elimination, of integrating concepts which are faulty, if severed from their context, into frameworks in which their faults are dissolved. But this does not seem to be the case. A concept like that of a whole containing parts retains the defects which it had before Hegel dealt with it. If this were not so, we could not explain why the entities to which this concept applies are themselves of an inferior kind, are indeed faulty or 'contradictory'. Defective concepts mirror the defects of things.[109] It might be argued that in applying a concept to a finite entity while withholding from it many of the other concepts of the *Logic*, we are in effect detaching the concept from the system and it is because of this that it displays a contradiction. There are, however, two replies to this. Firstly, if we employ positive numerals in order to count a group of objects, we are in a sense severing positive numbers from the numerical system to which they belong. But the defect which positive numbers have when they are detached from negative ones does not re-emerge here. We probably do not need to subtract a greater from a lesser number, but, if we do, negative numbers are always available to supply the answer. In this respect, then, the concept of a whole containing parts would, on Hegel's view, still diverge from our analogy. Secondly, Hegel believes, as we have seen, that concepts and their relationships mirror things and their relationships to each other.[110] As we shall see, there are at least two possible alternative views which he might want to propose concerning the contradictoriness of things. The first is that, while no given entity is actually contradictory, it would be contradictory if it were detached from its relationships to other things, if it did not interact with them at all or even if it did not interact with them in the particular way that it does. This is the counterpart of the view that a thought-determination is or seems contradictory only if it is detached from the whole conceptual system. The second is that any given finite thing actually is contradictory, even when we have taken into account its relationships to other things and, in part, because of them. The counterpart of this is that concepts are contradictory even when they have their proper place in the system. Since the second of these views about the contradictoriness of things is the one that Hegel most likely held,[111] the probability is that he also believed that thought-determinations involve contradictions even when they are appropriately embedded in the conceptual system of the *Logic*.

To get some idea of the complexity of the *Logic*, we might

compare it with the way in which, ideally, science advances. Each successive theory is shown to be inadequate — generally, of course, by empirical refutation rather than *a priori* argument — and is replaced by a better theory. Each theory incorporates the merits of its predecessor, explaining for example the empirical observations which its predecessor explained as well as it did or better. Refuted theories are abandoned, except perhaps as rough approximations to the truth in certain areas, and are of interest only to the historian. But if this is to be analogous to Hegel's *Logic,* it requires at least two substantial modifications. Firstly, refuted theories would, on his view, play a crucial role in our account of the world. For certain things, more or less defective things, correspond to defective, 'refuted' theories. Secondly, Hegel would want to incorporate an account of the growth of our historical and logical understanding of science into this account of the growth of science. Roughly speaking, better theories go hand in hand with a better understanding of the historical development of science. Perhaps they do. But the difficulty is to give a coherent logical schema of this. The complexities of Hegel's *Logic* owe something to his attempt to do so.[112]

13 *Criticism and self-criticism*

In the preceding section, as well as on a number of previous occasions, attention has been drawn to Hegel's tendency to assimilate subjective contradictions, contradictions in our beliefs or concepts, to objective contradictions, contradictions or, more loosely, flaws in things and in states of affairs.[113] The idea that there are contradictions in things will be considered later at greater length.[114] But it needs to be introduced here, because Hegel's conflation of objective and subjective contradictions helps to explain several features of his thought. This consideration, for example, supplies at least a part of the answer to the following three questions:

(i) Why does Hegel believe that any thought-determination in the *Logic* has only one possible immediate successor?[115]

(ii) Why does he suppose that it is possible to think without subjecting oneself to any presupposed rules?

(iii) Why does he believe that the rational structure of logic mirrors the historical development of human thought?

These questions will be examined in turn in this section.

(i) Hegel believes that things, as well our thoughts about things, involve contradictions, and these contradictions explain why things change, why one state of affairs gives way in time to another state of affairs (*Enz.* I. 81Z). We need not, for our present purposes, press the questions how things can be contradictory or in what sense Hegel believes them to be. We need only concede that, in any series of states succeeding each other over time, one state supplants another because there is some sort of defect or tension in the earlier state which prevents it from persisting. If a man dies, for example – of natural causes, for the sake of simplicity – then there is some defect in him before his death occurs which prevents his continuing to live. If a car breaks down from internal causes, there is similarly some flaw in it before the breakdown occurs. Hegel prefers, of course, such examples of change as the growth of a plant, for there is here a progression to higher states of affairs and not a degeneration into a corpse or a heap of rubble.[116] But it is similarly reasonable to suppose that a plant changes its state because there is something wrong with its current state which prevents it from continuing. In each of these cases of change, any given state can be followed only by some one state or other. We need not assume that it could only be succeeded by the particular state which does occur. It might have been followed by some other state. But it could not have been followed immediately by more than one state. If, then, the series of concepts in the *Logic* is seen on the model of such actual, physical courses of change as these, it is natural to assume that each element has only one immediate successor. And since what is at issue is logic, with all the associations of necessity that this term carries, an obvious next step is to suppose that there is only one possible successor available at each stage.

(ii) Is Hegel's pure thinking subject to any rules at all? That it is not governed by rules, or at least not by rules that are not of its own making, might seem to follow from the principle of limits, the principle that to be aware of a limit is to transcend it (*Enz.* I. 60).[117] If thought had a limit, a rule, for example, that it could not infringe, it could not be aware of that limit and examine it on its merits. But any proposed rule of thought is itself something that we can think about. We might then decide to subject ourselves to it or we might not. In the meantime, however, thought about the rule has entirely free play. We could not adequately think about the rule if we were already subject to it in doing so. How can we be sure that our thinking is correct? The answer seems to be that thought as a whole is immune to correction, except from itself, because there is nothing else against which it can be checked. Any standard of correct thinking must first be accepted by thinking itself. Thought is therefore self-criticizing and self-correcting, or else it is not open to criticism and correction at all.

To the objections that entirely unconstrained thinking has no cognitive value and that, in any case, self-correction presupposes some rule or standard in the light of which the correction is carried out, Hegel's reply seems to be this. The thinking ego simply immerses itself in the subject-matter, so that there is no difference between the ego and pure thoughts, between my thinking and the concepts I think about. Logic is not a matter of my criticizing concepts; the concepts criticize themselves. Hegel puts it like this:

> Dialectic is usually regarded as an external art, which wilfully introduces confusion into determinate concepts and a mere *illusion* of *contradictions* in them, so that it is not these determinations which are null and void (*ein Nichtiges*), but rather this illusion, whereas the product of the understanding (*das Verständige*) by contrast is rather what is true. Often, too, dialectic is nothing more than a subjective see-saw of toing and froing argumentation, where the content is lacking and the nakedness is clothed in the subtlety which produces such argumentation. In its proper character dialectic is rather the very own, true nature of the determinations of the understanding, of things and of the finite in general. Reflection is primarily what goes beyond the isolated determinacy and relates it, thus putting it into a relationship, while for the rest it is preserved in its isolated validity. Dialectic by contrast is this *immanent* going beyond, in which the onesidedness and limitedness reveals itself for what it is, namely, as its negation. It is the nature of everything finite to sublimate (*aufheben*) itself (*Enz.* I. 81).

The addition which follows this paragraph provides a diverse collection of cases of superficial, 'external' dialectic and of 'reflection'. The procedure of reflection, by which a determinacy is 'preserved in its isolated validity', is illustrated by its treatment of death:

> One says, e.g. that man is mortal and then regards death as something which has its ground only in external circumstances. According to this way of looking at things there are two particular properties of man, vitality and *also* mortality. But the true conception is this, that life as such bears the seed of death in itself and that in general the finite contradicts and thereby eliminates itself.

The former view is characterized as the policy of '"live and let

live", so that the one is valid and *also* the other' (*Enz.* I. 81Z. 1).
Someone who treats the concepts of life and death in this way is
too tender-hearted towards them. He fails to see how the concept
of life breaks down into that of death. Hegel's examples of superficial, bogus dialectic, or sophistry, are generally derived from the
sphere of moral reasoning. Its

> essence consists in making onesided and abstract determinations
> valid on their own in isolation . . . . Thus it is e.g. in connection
> with action an essential element, that I exist and that I have the
> means of existence. But if I then emphasize this aspect, this
> principle of my welfare, on its own and draw the conclusion
> that I may steal or betray my country, then this is sophistry.
> Similarly my subjective freedom, in the sense that I am present
> in what I do with my insight and conviction, is an essential
> principle in my actions. But, if I argue from this principle
> *alone,* then this is likewise sophistry and thus all principles of
> ethics are overthrown (*Ibid.*).[118]

What is involved here is the selection of one feature of an action
or of a type of action, that it will, for example, secure my survival
– a feature which is a reason for performing the action, but not a
sufficient or an overriding reason – and justifying the action on
the basis of it.[119] Hegel does not mention the theoretical counterpart to this, where we infer for example that someone is, or
probably is, a protestant from the fact that he is a Swede, ignoring
such further evidence as his regular visits to Lourdes. Here we
similarly make 'one-sided and abstract determinations valid on
their own in isolation' by taking what is some evidence for the
truth of a proposition to be conclusive or overriding evidence for
it.

These, then, are some examples of 'external' reasoning or dialectic, as opposed to 'immanent' dialectic. But they are also cases in
which the dialectic, criticism or reasoning is faulty or incomplete.
Why must this be so? Why could there not be external dialectic
which was, in other respects, correct? The answer is that there is,
in the case of concepts and propositions, no genuine distinction
between external and immanent dialectic. We might say that to
criticize a concept or a proposition externally is to do so by
reference to empirical phenomena while if we criticize them
internally we attempt to show that they are contradictory or in
some way incoherent. But both types of criticism are in a sense
external, for it is always we who demonstrate that concepts or
propositions are defective in these ways and we do so by appeal
to assumed standards of evidence and coherence. We can bring

out the faults implicit in them, deriving, for example, an explicit contradiction from the proposition that there is a greatest prime number or refuting the proposition that the sea always obeys our commands by acting on it. But concepts and propositions do not do this work on their own, unfolding, as it were, their own implicit defects. It is rather we who do this, following the paths that they provide, and we need to refer to canons of criticism and argument to show that even explicit defects are defects.[120]

Hegel's examples of external reasoning must, then, be cases of faulty or incomplete reasoning just because there is no proper distinction between external and immanent reasoning. Why did he believe that there was? One reason perhaps is that there is, in the case of things, a distinction to be drawn between our external criticism of them and their own 'immanent self-criticism'. If one examines, for example, a motor-car, one may find all kinds of faults in it, faults which may or may not lead to its breakdown. This is external criticism. If, on the other hand, the car breaks down as a result of its defects, this is the car's self-criticism, its 'immanent dialectic'. External criticism cannot result in the breakdown of the car, but its self-criticism does. We can check external criticism against internal criticism, by seeing whether or not the car breaks down and does so owing to the faults identified by external criticism. External criticism may be specious in ways analogous to those in which the criticism of concepts and propositions may be. It may find faults which are not there or pick on superficial faults which will not affect the performance of the car. It may argue that the car cannot move, because, as Zeno has shown, motion is impossible — the car itself will show that this criticism is defective.[121] It may pick on an isolated feature of the car, which would on its own make the car work or, alternatively, lead to a breakdown, ignoring countervailing features which will inhibit this effect. External criticism need not in this case be faulty or incomplete, though it is unlikely to give an exact estimate of all the faults and their effects. But even if the external criticism corresponds completely and exactly to the actual condition and subsequent fate of the car, it is still distinct from the car's self-criticism. The self-criticism, by contrast, is immune to error and inexactitude. Leaving aside chance collisions, if the car breaks down, its overall condition must have been sufficient for it to do so and it must have broken down for exactly the reasons it did. Hegel seems to believe that if his method is properly applied, then thinking is similarly beyond criticism:

> I could not suppose that the method which I follow in this system of logic . . . is not capable of much more completeness,

of much elaboration in detail; but I also know that it is the only true method. This is clear from the very fact that it is not at all distinct from its object and content — for it is the content itself, *the dialectic which it contains in itself*, which moves it forward (*WL* I. p. 50, M. p. 54).

Thinking no doubt would be immune to criticism if it were as Hegel describes it. But there is in the case of concepts, theories and propositions no relevant sense in which they criticize themselves or succumb to an immanent dialectic as there is in the case of physical things.

(iii) This last statement requires qualification, however. For there is a sense in which concepts, theories and propositions undergo, like motor-cars, what we have called self-criticism. They may be abandoned, modified, or reinterpreted in much the way that motor-cars may break down, change and so on. This happens when men, either individual men or large groups of men over history, abandon or change them. An individual thinker, for example, does not, on Hegel's view, simply criticize concepts, he also abandons or modifies them. If a concept is rejected or altered, then it, like anything else which changes or perishes, must contain some objective flaw or 'contradiction' which accounts for its doing so. There is here no distinction between the disappearance or change of a concept and the criticism of it, for the criticism is self-criticism. This criticism of concepts does not require an appeal to assumed rules or standards any more than the breakdown of a car does. No external check is needed. Concepts perish or change because of the faults they actually have and not because of our ascription of faults to them. A similar account can be given of changes over history. If a concept, theory or philosophical position is altered or abandoned, then it must contain some objective defect or contradiction which accounts for this. If now we confuse objective flaws or contradictions with subjective ones, we shall be tempted to suppose that the defects in concepts, philosophies, and so on which result in their demise or alteration are always logical contradictions or at least epistemic flaws of some kind or other. Moreover we shall assume that the concept or philosophy which replaces it or emerges from it provides the solution to whatever epistemic faults it contains. This is perhaps a part of the explanation of Hegel's confidence that the history of philosophy follows the course of logic.

Objective flaws or contradictions are, however, distinct from subjective ones, and there is no *a priori* reason to suppose that they coincide. The subjective or epistemic flaws of a concept or a theory, even if they are perceived by its adherents, need not lead to its abandonment or modification, they need not, that is, also be objective flaws. Conversely, concepts and theories might be rejected, jettisoned or altered for all kinds of reasons apart from their known epistemic faults. A theory might disappear, for example, because it is too difficult to remember or because the books which contain it are burnt and its exponents slaughtered. That it met such a fate would show, on Hegel's view, that it was objectively flawed or contradictory in some way or other. How else could we explain its disappearance? But it would not show that it was subjectively contradictory or otherwise epistemically defective. Similarly an individual thinker might abandon or modify his concepts and beliefs for a variety of reasons. He may, for example, wrongly believe that they are contradictory or he may simply forget them. If we are to understand the history of thought at all, then the thinking of those whom we attempt to understand and in particular our own thinking must presumably be coherent to some degree. But beyond this, what makes for changes in beliefs and concepts is an empirical question.

Hegel's reply to these criticisms is that, in the case of pure thinking at least, there can be no distinction between the objective and the subjective contradictions of concepts, between our criticism of them and their own self-criticism. For at the level of pure thought there is no distinction between logic and psychology. Any reasons there are for our changing our concepts or, more generally, for our train of thought's continuing in one way rather than another, can only be valid logical reasons. Any other sort of cause or reason would have to derive from perception, imagination or desire, and their influence has been excluded by the fact that we are engaged in pure thinking. This reply depends on the identification of the self with the system of pure thoughts, and it is this that we shall consider in the following section.

14 *Thoughts, thinking and the ego*

We have already seen some of Hegel's reasons for equating the ego with pure thoughts.[122] We have also seen that the equation explains several features of his system. The plausibility of identifying God as a spirit with the system of thoughts, for example, depends heavily upon it.[123] So does Hegel's rejection of Kant's view that the pure ego is unknowable.[124] It also helps to explain a number of features of the *Logic* itself. 'When I think, I abandon my subjective peculiarity, I bury myself in the subject-matter, I let thinking take its own course, and I think badly if I add anything of my own' (*Enz.* I. 24Z. 2. Cf. 23). It follows from this that, in the case of any given individual, there is only one way in which he can think purely. The point is not simply that if there were alternative ways of thinking, alternative routes to the same conclusion as there are in geometry, there could be nothing to explain why he thought in one way rather than another, no perceptions or desires to recommend one route over another. It is also that the very fact that there were alternative paths through the field of pure thoughts would imply that there was a residual ego in some sense standing outside the system of thoughts. Moreover, unless we are prepared to concede that different men might consist of different thoughts, it follows that all pure thinkers think in the same way. People may differ in the extent to which they are capable of pure thought, but once they have disengaged themselves from everything to do with the external world, their perceptions, desires, interests and so on, there is only one route for them to take. Just as all persons are the same *qua* pure egos, so they do not differ *qua* pure thinkers.

The identification of the self with pure thoughts faces, however, at least two serious difficulties. The first is that it excludes any distinction between episodic or occurrent thinking on the one hand and thoughts or concepts on the other, between the moves I make and the moves made by my subject-matter. This confusion infects the *Logic* from the very beginning. The work starts, for example, with pure being and a transition is made to (the concept of) nothing or non-being. The transition depends on the emptiness and indeterminacy of the concept of being: 'There is *nothing* in it to intuit . . . or it is only this pure, empty intuiting itself . . . . Being, the indeterminate immediate, is in fact *nothing*, and no more and no less than nothing.' By a similar argument, (the concept of) nothing is seen to be the same as (that of) being: 'To intuit or to think nothing therefore has a meaning; both are distinguished, thus nothing *is* (exists) in our intuiting or thinking; or rather it is empty intuiting or thinking itself and the same empty intuiting or thinking as pure being is.' We might expect Hegel, in the light of this, to conclude that (the concepts of) pure being and pure nothing are straightforwardly the same. But he does not draw this conclusion. The conclusion is rather this:

What the truth is is neither being nor nothing, but rather that being does not pass over, but rather has passed over, into nothing, and nothing into being . . . . Their truth is therefore this immediate *movement* of the immediate disappearance of the one in the other: *becoming*; a movement in which both are

309

distinct, but with a distinction which is just as much immediately dissolved (*WL* I. pp. 82 f., M. pp. 82 f. Cf. *Enz.* I. 86 ff.).

To speak of the concept of being *becoming* that of nothing is to run together our thinking and the concepts about, or in terms of which, we think. Concepts may of course be closely associated with each other without being identical. The concepts of a husband and of a wife, for example, are intimately linked. When we think of, or in terms of, the one we automatically think of, or in terms of, the other. But neither of these concepts becomes or passes into the other. Any movement involved is that of our thinking, following the conceptual pathways provided. It is illegitimate therefore to derive the concept of becoming from those of being and nothing, or indeed from any other two concepts, solely in virtue of the fact that there are conceptual routes from one to the other.[125] Concepts and their interrelationships are static in a way that our thinking is not. But if this is so, it follows that the thinking ego cannot be straightforwardly identical with concepts.

The second difficulty is how we are to conceive the relationship between different egos, including that ego which is God, if each of them is identical with the 'absolute idea'. Does it follow that all egos are numerically identical, that there is ultimately only one ego? Or does it follow only that every ego is qualitatively identical with every other? If we distinguish between occurrent thinking and thoughts as concepts it is difficult to allow that two pure thinkers need be even qualitatively identical. For while concepts may be in the relevant sense atemporal or unchanging, pure thinking, as anyone who has read Hegel's *Logic* knows, takes time. Thus even if any two pure thinkers have, or are, implicitly the same system of thoughts, they may have reached at any given time different points in the process of explicitly unravelling them. At 6.00 p.m. I may be thinking about substance while you are thinking about the syllogism. Moreover, even if our thinking happens to coincide in time, we are still numerically distinct from each other: I am here and you are there, I am me and you are you.

If this is so, however, then the ego cannot be identified with its pure thoughts, unless we are prepared to say that concepts can be qualitatively identical with each other, but numerically distinct, that my concept of being, for example, is exactly similar to yours but numerically distinct from it, my concept of being as opposed to yours. In that case each ego could be identical with its system of concepts without thereby being identical with every other ego. Ordinarily we do not have occasion to speak of numerically distinct but qualitatively identical concepts; if a distinction is drawn between A's concept of x and B's concept of x, this is normally taken to imply some qualitative difference between the two concepts. But there seems to be no reason in principle why we should not distinguish between numerically distinct, but exactly similar concepts if we can find some use for the notion. The individuation of concepts would of course be parasitic on the individuation of persons. It would make no more sense to say that one and the same person had two exactly similar concepts at one and the same time than it would to say that a person had two exactly similar virtues at one and the same time. Does Hegel want to take this course? There is no evidence that he does. He does not generally speak of a concept as a psychological entity at all. Indeed, he does not on the whole speak about the concept of being, of causality and so on, but rather of (thought-)determinations, in general, and of being, causality or the cause, in particular.[126] His terminology does not, therefore, invite questions of the kind which we have been asking. But, in any case, he seems more inclined to take the alternative course of denying that egos, in so far as they are engaged in pure thinking, are numerically distinct from each other at all.

It is a familiar idea that when men engage in a certain type of intellectual activity, characteristically abstract thinking, they become in some sense one with God and with one another. Generally the sense in which they are supposed to do so is that each becomes a part of a single divine entity. There is, for example, more than a trace of this in Spinoza:[127]

> The intellectual love of the mind towards God is that very love of God whereby God loves himself, not in so far as he is infinite, but in so far as he can be explained through the essence of the human mind regarded under the form of eternity; in other words, the intellectual love of the mind towards God is part of the infinite love wherewith God loves himself.

Hegel's position is not wholly dissimilar to this. He presents, however, a novel argument for it, and this will be examined in the following section.

15 Thought and individuals

The argument is this:[128]

> Since *language* is the product of thought, nothing can be said in it which is not universal. What I only *mean* (*meine*) is *mine* (*mein*), belongs only to me as this particular individual; but if

311

language expresses only what is universal, I cannot say what I only *mean.* And what is *unsayable,* feeling, sensation, is not the most excellent, the most true, but rather the least significant, the least true. If I say: 'the *individual*', '*this* individual', 'here', 'now', then these are all universalities; *anything* and *everything* is an individual, a this, and, if it is sensuous, it is here and now. Similarly when I say 'I', I *mean* myself *as this* self which excludes all others; but what I say, 'I', is just everyone; [everyone is an] I, which excludes all others from itself (*Enz.* I. 20. Cf. *PG* pp. 79 ff., M. pp. 58 ff.).

The argument of this passage can be set out as follows:

1. The only thoughts which purport to refer to particular things and persons are those expressed by such words as 'I', 'this (individual)', 'that (individual)' and so on.
But, 2. these words and the corresponding thoughts apply to every individual person or thing. Everyone, for example, speaks of himself as 'I'.
Therefore, 3. these words and thoughts do not enable us to distinguish different individuals, to refer to or denote one particular person in contrast to another one.[129]
Therefore, 4. when egos are engaged in pure thinking, they are not distinct individuals.

Clearly a parallel argument can be constructed in reply to the objection that two pure thinkers might think thoughts at different times or in different places:

1. The only thought-terms, or at least the closest approximations to thought-terms, which refer to particular times and places are 'now', 'then', 'here' and 'there'.[130]
But, 2. these terms apply to any place or to any time whatsoever. Any time is now and any place is here.
Therefore, 3. they cannot be used to pick out any particular time or place as opposed to any other. We cannot express in terms of pure thoughts any temporal or spatial differences between my thinking and yours.
Therefore, 4. there are no temporal or spatial differences between the thinking of different thinkers.[131]

To put the arguments in this form may be unfair to Hegel, for in the passage quoted above he does not explicitly draw the final conclusion, 4, nor does he do so in any other passage. Indeed his expressed view seems to be not that pure thinkers are not numerically distinct from each other, but that their distinctness is trivial and unimportant. But even if he himself did not wish to carry the arguments as far as the conclusions which we have attributed to him, it is worth considering whether the arguments do in fact lend any support to them. In any case, Hegel probably requires something like these conclusions. For his overall view seems to be that, in thinking purely, men become identical with each other and with God; that it is only when we descend from pure thoughts to the derivation or construction of nature and of human and social life that distinct individuals emerge, differentiated by their bodies and by their desires, perceptions and feelings; and that, finally, they rise again to the level of pure thinking and become once more identical with God.[132] The arguments will be examined, then, with this thesis in mind.

(i) When Hegel speaks of 'the *unsayable*, feeling, sensation', he seems to be suggesting that language does not enable us to convey the exact quality of our feelings and sensations, or indeed of external objects. This is no doubt true, but it has no obvious bearing on the question whether we are able to refer to a given, individual entity. For our ability to do this probably does not depend on that entity's being qualitatively different from every other entity and it certainly does not depend on our being able to describe or express such differences. What he means is presumably that we can only 'mean' a given individual in virtue of a feeling or sensation which is directed upon that object, so that our inability to refer to the object and our inability to express the corresponding feeling or sensation go hand in hand. But why should the fact that we cannot convey the precise quality of our sensations have anything to do with this? We can refer to our sensations without fully describing them, and it is not clear that we even need to do this in order to refer to the objects on which they are directed. The plausible thesis that we cannot describe our feelings and sensations in all their rich particularity lends no support to the thesis that we cannot refer to individual objects in public discourse. The latter ability does not presuppose that our descriptive resources are unlimited.

(ii) It is entirely unclear which of two distinct theses Hegel is advancing:

Thesis A: If we confine ourselves to thought-terms alone, in particular to token-reflexive expressions like 'I' and 'this (individual)', then we cannot refer to a given individual. We can do so, however, if we introduce conception-terms such as 'red', 'paper', 'man' and so on.

Thesis B: We cannot, whatever linguistic resources are presupposed or employed, refer to a particular individual. If we identify it as 'the bit of paper on the desk' or 'the man smoking the pipe', the expression is still universal and applies to an indefinite number of actual, or at least possible, individuals. Even proper names do not help. For, firstly, a name may be common to several actual, or at least possible, individuals, and, secondly, our ability to pick out individuals by the use of proper names depends on our being able to pick them out in other ways.

Thesis A is likely to be true. That it is this thesis that Hegel had in mind is suggested by the fact that in the passage quoted he is discussing thought rather than conception. Moreover, the parallel passage in the *Phenomenology* is a discussion of sense-certainty, the form of consciousness in which we attempt to capture reality in all its concrete richness and therefore forego the use of descriptive terms which classify things in only one of indefinitely many possible ways, selecting some features for our attention and leaving others in the background.[133] Hegel's arguments in that passage would need more elaboration if sense-certainty involved the use of such terms as '6 o'clock' as well as 'now'. Again, the view which we have tentatively attributed to him, namely that persons *qua* pure egos or thinkers are or become identical with each other, while persons *qua* active, embodied people with desires and perceptions are different from each other, clearly requires thesis A rather than thesis B.

Other considerations, however, imply that Hegel was proposing thesis B as well as thesis A. He regards the inability to identify particular individuals as a feature of language in general, and any natural language includes terms for conceptions as well as for thoughts. He is not, of course, arguing from the nature of language alone. The reason why we can argue from features of language is that language is a product of, and mirrors, thought. But this does not affect the point that the introduction of language into the discussion implies that what is at issue is thesis B rather than A alone. Moreover, it is not only thought-expressions like 'this (thing)' which fail to apply to only one individual. Every bit of paper can be referred to as 'this bit of paper', just as everything can be referred to as 'this thing' (*PG* pp. 88 f., M. p. 66). There is little room for doubt that Hegel also held thesis B.

Why, then, does he often speak as if he held only thesis A? A part of the answer is that the two theses serve different purposes in his system, and some of these purposes require thesis A alone. Thesis A is needed, if Hegel is to show that there are numerically distinct pens and pipe-smokers in a way that there are not numerically distinct pure-thinkers or egos. But thesis B comes into play, when he attempts to assign a status to finite entities like pens and pipe-smokers. Their status is, as we shall see, problematic.[134] But it is clear that Hegel wants to downgrade them in some way or other, and one argument for doing so is that they cannot be referred to as distinct individuals:

> They do indeed mean, therefore, *this* piece of paper . . . but they say 'actual *things, outer* or *sensuous objects, absolutely individual* entity', etc., i.e. they say of them only what is *universal*; therefore what is called the inexpressible is nothing more than the untrue, irrational, merely meant (*PG* p. 88, M. p. 66).

Clearly the introduction of thesis B defeats the purpose which thesis A is meant to serve. For if Hegel accepts thesis B, he cannot maintain that there is in this respect a difference between egos and pens, between pure thinkers and pipe-smokers. Numerical distinctions will be in both cases, if not non-existent, then at least insignificant.

(iii) Thesis B is doubtless false. The resources we have — token-reflexive expressions, descriptive terms, proper names and physical gestures — enable us to refer to particular individuals. We can, for example, refer to a cat by saying 'that cat' and pointing to what may be the only cat perceptible by our audience. Any cat can be referred to as 'that cat', but in appropriate circumstances the context makes it clear which cat is referred to.[135] Hegel would reply that such reference is not secured by thought or language alone, but relies on perception, a perceptual context, and on tacit understandings between the speaker and the hearer. The meanings of words do not on their own guarantee the reference, and the tacit conventions could be systematically disrupted by a sufficiently perverse audience. But it is hard to see what force this has, once we have seen how such words as 'I', 'this', and 'now' are used, that language is employed in concrete, perceptual situations and that tacit understandings must obtain if it is to work. Thesis B, however, need not be considered at length here. For we are concerned in this chapter with pure thinking and pure thoughts, and it is only thesis A which is directly relevant to these.

(iv) Thesis A, let alone thesis B, seems barely compatible with some of Hegel's other doctrines. The thesis is introduced in the *Encyclopaedia* in the course of a discussion of the doctrine that thought cannot assign limits to itself without thereby transcending them. The passage quoted above is preceded by the claim that the terms in which we describe the essential features of the sensuous themselves express thoughts, that thought 'overreaches its other and nothing escapes it'.[136] But if thought enables us to think or speak about definite individuals only in a general way, but not to refer to any particular individual, has not something escaped it? Hegel's answer to this seems to be that particular individuals, and therefore references to them, are unimportant, and that thought succeeds in capturing everything of consequence. But the claim that definite individuals are unimportant or 'untrue' requires further backing. One cannot, on pain of circularity, base it only on the fact that they escape the net of thought. What further support Hegel gives to it will be seen in a later chapter.[137]

This objection, if it is sound, establishes that, if thesis A is correct, then there are limits to thought. A more serious objection is that Hegel cannot state thesis A without himself transgressing the limits which the thesis assigns to thought. The claim that thought cannot focus on a particular individual is, it might be said, self-refuting, for to say 'We can never refer to x' is already to refer to x. We could not understand what it was that thought or language could not do, unless we had some idea of what it was that it could not do. For example, when Hegel writes: 'when I say "I", I *mean* myself *as this* self which excludes all others; but what I say, "I", is just every one', how are we to understand his statement of what I mean but cannot say? I *mean* 'myself as this self', etc. But I can also *say* 'myself as this self', and Hegel has himself said it in saying what I mean. If we are to grasp the difference between what is meant and what is said, we must rely on tacit understanding, for *ex hypothesi* the difference cannot be expressed in thought-language. Hegel might reply to this that in order to state thesis A he does not need to refer to any definite individual nor to presuppose that we can do so, but only to assume some idea of what it is to refer to an individual, an idea of sufficient precision to enable us to know when we have not succeeded in doing it. Analogously to claim that we cannot give a complete description of the concrete particularity of any individual is not itself to give such a description or to presuppose that one can be given. All that is presupposed is a sufficiently precise idea of what such a description would be for us to say what does not fulfil its requirements. To suppose that the claim actually provides such a description on the grounds that it speaks of 'the concrete particularity of x' would be like supposing that 'a number I shall never name' is itself the name of the number in question.[138] This reply seems apt. It is doubtful, however, whether Hegel is entitled to make it. For his use of the principle that thought 'overreaches' what is not thought, that thought transcends its own boundaries, seems to involve just this error.[139]

(v) Whatever the merits of thesis A in itself it cannot license the conclusion that when egos are engaged in pure thinking they are not distinct individuals. There are at least two reasons for this. Firstly, although according to this thesis we cannot in terms of pure thought refer to any given individual as opposed to others, we can say such things as 'Pure egos are numerically distinct from each other' or even 'This thing is different from that thing'. The category of difference or distinctness is, like all the other categories of the *Logic*, an unstable one.[140] But the concept of numerical difference is nevertheless a pure thought, however defective it may be, and, if it can be used at all, it can surely be used to say that there are numerically distinct egos or thinkers. Secondly, even if we could not, within pure thought, express the proposition that egos are numerically distinct from each other, it would not follow that they are numerically identical. The fact that two or more people are engaged in some activity which does not enable them to refer to themselves as distinct or even to say that they are distinct − pure mathematics, for example, or slumber − does not entail that they are not distinct individuals. One could as well argue that we are immortal, on the grounds that no one, if he is dead, can say or think that he is dead.

This argument does not, then, establish that pure thinkers or egos are not numerically distinct from each other. Yet this conclusion seems to be required, if the ego is to be identified with the system of pure thoughts. It is also deeply involved in Hegel's conception of the circularity of his system, a matter to which we shall turn in the following section.

16 *Hegel's circles*

The circularity of Hegel's system is one of its most remarkable features and has already been referred to several times.[141] He sometimes speaks as if only one circle is involved:

> Philosophy forms a circle; it has a first, immediate term − since it must begin somehow − something unproved, which is not a result. But what philosophy begins with is immediately relative, since it must appear as a result in another end-point. It is a sequence which does not hang in the air, is not something which begins immediately, but turns back into itself (*PR* 2Z).

It is clear, however, that there are in fact several circles. Each of the three main parts of the system, as well as the system as a whole, forms a circle:

the whole therefore presents itself as a circle of circles, each one of which is a necessary aspect, so that the whole idea is constituted by the system of its particular elements, but also appears in each individual element (*Enz.* I. 15).

The application of the *Logic* to nature will be considered at length in the following chapter, but some of that discussion must be anticipated here. Hegel's system is, as we have seen, tripartite. The *Logic* presents the 'idea' in its abstract form, independently of the empirical material in which it is embedded. The *Philosophy of Nature* considers the idea as it is expressed in the element of nature; it is the *'science of the idea in its otherness'* (*Enz.* I. 18). Finally the *Philosophy of Mind* considers the idea as it is found in human life, the idea *'which returns into itself from its otherness'* (*Ibid.*). The logical idea is embodied as a whole both in nature and in mind or spirit. Thus different stages of nature correspond to different stages of logic:

> Nature is to be regarded as a *system of stages,* each of which emerges necessarily from the others and is the proximate truth of that stage from which it results, but not in such a way that the one is *naturally* produced from the other, but rather in the inner idea which constitutes the ground of nature (*Enz.* II. 249).

Nature, for example, has three main spheres: mechanics, physics and organics (*Enz.* II. 252). These correspond roughly to the three main divisions of logic: being , essence and the concept. Each of these main spheres is again divided into three. Mechanics, for example, is trisected into the consideration of space and time, that of matter and motion — finite mechanics — and that of matter in 'free motion' — absolute mechanics (*Enz.* II. 253). Ideally, these should correspond to quality, quantity and measure in the *Logic*.

Naturally enough logic and nature fit together fairly loosely. We might expect, for example, space, with which the *Philosophy of Nature* begins, to correspond to pure being, and Hegel would presumably like it to do so. He concedes, however, that it does not:

> [Space] is in general pure *quantity,* no longer only as a logical determination, but as immediately and externally existing (*seiend*). Nature begins, therefore, not with the qualitative but with the quantitative, because its determination is not, like logical being, what is abstractly first and immediate, but is essentially already what is *mediated* within itself, outer-and other-being (*Enz.* II. 254).

The idea here is that, since pure being is unmediated while nature is mediated by logic, no stage of nature can correspond only to pure being. If this is intended as an explanation of the fact that nature fails to begin with a counterpart to the beginning of logic, it is unsuccessful. It would imply that no pure thought can be found in nature at all, for no pure thought is mediated in quite the way that a phase of nature is. It cannot license the detachment of only the first stage of the *Logic*, which is, in any case, mediated in virtue of the circularity of the system. However, these obvious and intelligible discrepancies between logic and nature will be ignored in the discussion which follows. Hegel does not mention them in his general remarks about the structure of his system and it is clear that what he wanted was a systematic correspondence between nature and logic.

The *Philosophy of Mind* similarly has three main divisions corresponding to those of the *Logic,* namely subjective mind, objective mind and absolute mind. Again, a detailed correlation with the *Logic* is intended. The first stage, for example, appears to be the 'soul' (*Seele*) in its 'immediate *natural determinacy* – the natural soul which merely *is* (*seiende*)' (*Enz.* III. 391). In this 'first spiritual life no distinction is yet posited between individuality and universality or between soul and the natural . . . it itself as such only *is,* has as yet no existence (*Dasein*), no determinate being, no particularization, no actuality' (*Enz.* III. 391Z). There is no difficulty here in finding a psychological counterpart to pure being. But again, to Hegel's credit perhaps, the intention of correlating the sphere of mind with logic is not executed with any great rigour.

These are not the only applications of the *Logic* which Hegel makes. Within the *Philosophy of Mind* itself various historical processes are indicated – 'world history' (*Enz.* III. 548 ff.), the histories of art (556 ff.), of religion (564 ff.), and of philosophy (572 ff.). These, as we have seen, are meant to correspond in their development to the structure of logic.[142] But the two main embodiments of logic in Hegel's system are in nature and in mind or spirit as a whole.

To what extent is the unravelling of logic in nature and mind itself a historical process? In nature, not at all:[143]

It is an inept conception . . . to regard the development and transition of a form and sphere of nature into a higher one as an externally actual production, which is, however, relegated to the *obscurity* of the past in order to make it *clearer*. . . . Thinking consideration must reject such nebulous, at bottom sensuous conceptions as, in particular, the so-called *emergence* of e.g. plants and animals out of water and then the *emergence* of more developed animal organisms out of lower ones, etc. (*Enz.* II. 249).

The *Philosophy of Mind* is ambiguous in this respect. Many of the features with which it deals successively, sense-perception, for example, and desire (*Enz.* III. 418 ff., 426), are presumably supposed to be contemporaneous both in the life of the individual and in the development of man as a biological species. Some features, however, are at least more pronounced in primitive men — the 'natural soul', for example (*Enz.* III. 392) — or in young children — for example, the 'feeling soul in its immediacy' (*Enz.* III. 405); the feeling soul is especially prominent in dreams, in the condition of the embryo, and in pathological adult states (405Z, 406).[144] It is therefore unclear whether the *Philosophy of Mind* is presenting contemporaneous aspects of the human mind, the history of the development of the human race, or the development of the human individual. Elements of all three types of enterprise are to be found in it. The important point, however, is that mind or spirit corresponds to the logical idea in the way that nature does, but it does so in a different element and at a higher level. In so far as mind develops over history, while nature does not, this is due to the difference in the element in which the idea is embodied.

Against this background, we can now ask: What circles did Hegel believe were to be found in his system? There seem to be several circles of different types, more perhaps than one would guess from his references to a 'circle of circles':

(1) Each of the three main spheres of the system can be seen as a circle in the sense that it spills over into another sphere which again follows the course of the *Logic* from the beginning. The *Logic* itself begins with being and ends with the absolute idea, but it then passes into the *Philosophy of Nature,* which, ideally at least, should start with the counterpart of being in nature. The *Philosophy of Nature* ends with the natural counterpart of the absolute idea, the animal organism or perhaps rather the animal genus or species (*Enz.* II. 350 ff., 367 ff.), and then progresses into the sphere of mind (367), where we begin once more with the spiritual embodiment of pure being. Finally the climax of the *Philosophy of Mind* seems to direct us back to the beginning of the *Logic* again (*Enz.* III. 577). Each sphere of the system, then, involves a movement from being to being and thus forms a sort of circle.

(2) It is clear from this that the system as a whole forms a circle in the sense that at the end of the system we are directed back to its beginning. The highest phase of our mental development, philosophy, culminates in Hegel's *Logic*. His own *Logic,* and more generally his system as a whole, is both a description of reality and the highest phase of the reality which it describes.[145]

(3) The *Logic* itself forms a circle in the distinct sense that its culminating phase, the absolute idea, is or involves a survey of the *Logic* as a whole. The end of the work thus directs us back to its own beginning and not simply on to nature. This, as we have seen, coheres with some of the applications of logic, with its embodiment in historical processes, for example, which culminate in an understanding of the process as a whole.[146] It is also required, however, by circles of type (1). Since each of the three parts of the system forms a circle and since each of these parts follows the course of the *Logic*, we would expect the *Logic* to form a circle in a way which reflects the way in which each of these parts, itself included, turns back upon itself.

(4) The circularity of the *Logic* is, however, also a consequence of circle (2). For the *Logic* is intended to represent not only each of the three parts of the system, but also the system as a whole, logic itself and its relationship to nature and mind. Logic is meant to prefigure its own applications. Thought overreaches what is other than thought.[147] Since the system as a whole forms a circle, a circle of circles, logic must form a circle — and perhaps a circle of circles — in order to represent the fact that the system ends with Hegel's own philosophy and therefore with logic itself.

Something has already been said about the purposes which are served by the circles in Hegel's system. But further consideration must be given here to circles (2) and (4), the circularity of the system as a whole and the logical reprsentation of this. The first is important in an account of the *Logic*, because it helps to explain the ontological status of pure thoughts; the second because it enables us, if not to unravel, then at least to see the point of, some of the complexities of the work. We begin, then, in the following section, with an attempt to explain the circularity of Hegel's system as a whole.

17 *From logic to logic*

Hegel's system begins with logic and, after giving an account of nature and mind, concludes with men doing logic. What is the significance of this? It might simply represent the reasonable, if egocentric, enterprise of concluding one's account of the world by giving an account of one's own account, an explanation of how it arose and so on.[148] On this view, of course, the system does not form a strict circle. For its beginning, logic, is not the same as its end, men doing logic. But it is sufficiently like a circle to account for Hegel's claim that it is a circle. The last sentence of the *Encyclopaedia* suggests, however, that he has more in mind than this, even if it does not make it very apparent what it is:

> The *self-partition* [or '*self-judging*', *Sich-Urteilen*][149] of the idea into both appearances [sc. nature and mind] determines them as its (self-knowing reason's) manifestations, and a unification is effected in it [sc. the idea]: it is the nature of the subject-matter (*Sache*), the concept, which advances and develops, and this movement is just as much the activity of cognition, the eternal idea which is in and for itself, eternally activates itself as absolute mind, produces and enjoys itself (*Enz.* III. 577).

What exactly is happening here? The answer seems to be something like this. There are two distinct standpoints from which we can view our own cognitive activities, the third-person standpoint and the first-person standpoint. If I take up a third-person standpoint, then I can ask about, for example, my thoughts such questions as: Whose thoughts are they? When and where is the thinker having them? Do they correspond to anything in the world? Are they determined by events in the thinker's brain of which he is unaware? From this standpoint thoughts can be attributed to definite people, they occur at definite times, and so on. If, on the other hand, I adopt a first-person standpoint, then such questions as these are out of place. Whose thoughts are these thoughts? One answer might be that they are my thoughts. But this, on Hegel's view, is no answer at all, because everyone is (an) I. And from this standpoint he is right, for while distinct individuals occur within thought, can be thought about, it does not make sense to ascribe the thought which is about them to some one of these distinct individuals as opposed to the others. Another answer might be that they are Hegel's thoughts. Hegel, however, is not simply a distinct individual, but an embodied individual who, for example, lives in Berlin in 1830. Pure thoughts cannot be assigned to Hegel, because, firstly, pure thinking is not concerned with anything so definite as the human body, space or time, let alone with Hegel's body, Berlin and the year 1830, and, secondly, even when we do come, in the second and third parts of the *Encyclopaedia,* to think about such matters, they are things that we think about and this cannot entitle us to, as it were, step outside the thinking that is about them, assigning to it a definite owner, place and date. For the same reason we cannot ask about the dependence of thinking on the brain. The brain is something which is to be thought about, and, even so, not until we leave the realm of logic. We cannot, at this level, ask questions about its relationship to the thought which is about it. From the first-person perspective, (my) thinking is ownerless and unlocated in much the way that (my) visual field is ownerless and unlocated. I am not an item within my visual field, nor is the eye which is in fact the bearer of it. My own body may indeed figure within my visual field, but it does so only as one item, albeit a peculiarly persistent item, among others. Whatever special relationship there is between my visual field and my body does not manifest itself within my visual field.[150] To ask and answer questions of this sort I must, so to speak, step outside my own visual field and take up a third-person viewpoint upon it.[151]

In terms of this distinction we can now see what Hegel is attempting to do. At the outset of his system he adopts, and invites us to adopt, a first-person stance, thinking alone without considering the relationship of this thinking to definite embodied people, brains, times and places. The thinker develops an abstract logical system, and then goes on to consider the natural world. This leads into the realm of mind, society and history, where we become aware of distinct, embodied individuals who eventually engage in pure thinking of the sort with which the system opened. At some point in this process — from about *Enz.* III. 445 onwards — we have shifted into a third-person perspective on thoughts and thinking, that is we are thinking (first-person) about men thinking (third-person). But what is the connection between my thinking and the thinking of the individual men that it is now about, between the first- and the third-person perspectives on thinking? If Hegel's system is to form a genuine circle, then he must not only legitimize the first-person stance from within the third-person point of view. He must identify the two standpoints. The thoughts must, as it were, be detached from individual, distinct thinkers, so that the system closes, as it began, not with men doing logic, but with logic.

The conclusion which Hegel requires is expressed in such ways as this:

In fact in the idea of life the self-externality of nature is *implicitly* (*an sich*) sublimated (*aufgehoben*) and the concept, the sub-stance of life, is subjectivity, but only in such a way that existence or objectivity has still at the same time succumbed to that self-externality. But in mind, which is the concept whose existence is not immediate individuality but absolute negativity, there is freedom, so that the object or reality of the concept is the concept itself; self-externality, which constitutes the basic feature of matter, is entirely dissolved into the subjective ideality of the concept, into universality. The mind is the existing truth of matter — that matter itself has no truth (*Enz.* III. 389).

This difficult passage is ambiguous in several ways, but the important ambiguity for our purposes is that between the following two theses:

(i) When a person thinks, his thought is wholly autonomous, undetermined by his physical environment and his physical body.

(ii) When thinking mind(s) come(s) on the scene, there really is no such thing as matter at all, except as a projection or a construct of thought. Thus not only is thinking independent of physical bodies and matter, it is not done by distinct, embodied individuals at all.

Thesis (i) derives no support from the first-person standpoint. It is true that at that standpoint we cannot answer the question: 'Does our thought depend on the brain?' But this does not mean that we are entitled to give a negative answer to it. Hegel does, however, argue for the thesis in other ways. Our thought does indeed have something to do with the brain (*Enz.* III. 401Z).[152] But the brain, rather than determining the course of our thinking, is, as it were, putty in our hands, conforming to the autonomous movement of thought and offering no resistance to it:[153]

but brain and spinal cord may be regarded as the immediate presence of self-consciousness, a presence which remains within itself — which is not objective, which also does not pass outwards . . . . But this *being-within-itself* [sc. the brain] is according to its concept a fluidity in which the circles which are cast into it immediately dissolve and no distinction expresses itself as *existent* (*seiender*) (*PG* pp. 239 f., M. pp. 196 f.).

This seems to be an instance of the general rule that matter becomes more fluid and insubstantial the higher we progress up the *scala naturae*:

In recent times matter has become thinner even in the hands of the physicists; they have come upon *imponderable* stuffs like warmth, light, etc. . . . These imponderables have lost the essential attribute of matter — weight — and also in a certain sense the capacity to offer resistance, but they still have a sensuous existence, a self-externality; but life-matter

324

(*Lebensmaterie*) . . . lacks not only weight, but also every other determinate existence (*Dasein*) which would enable it to count as *material* (*Enz.* III. 389).

The matter of which the brain consists is presumably the limiting case of this progressive rarefaction of matter. The autonomy of thought with respect to the thinker's physical environment is also supported, as we have seen, by the claim that pure thoughts are non-empirical.[154]

Hegel's defence of thesis (i) is unimpressive. For example, the fact that pure thoughts are in a sense non-empirical does not entail that one's having such a thought is independent of physical conditions, whether necessary or sufficient conditions. But, more important than this, the arguments advanced so far do nothing to establish thesis (ii). It seems to be an ineluctable fact that pure thinking is done by individuals with more or less material bodies, whatever we take to be the precise relationship between the thinking and the body. But as long as this is so, we still have to distinguish between logic and logicians, thoughts and thinkers. Hegel, however, seems to have at least two types of argument in favour of thesis (ii). The first depends on an appeal to such phenomena as waterdivining, clairvoyance and premonitions. These, he believes, are explicable only on the hypothesis that there is only one soul and that matter is in some sense unreal or at least wholly subordinate to it:

The understanding (*Begreifen*) of this relationless and yet completely filled-out connection becomes impossible on the assumption of personalities who are independent both of each other and of the content as an objective world and on the assumption of the absoluteness of spatial and material asunderness in general (*Enz.* III. 406).

Or more explicitly:

The soul is the *all-pervasive*, not merely existing in a particular individual; for . . . it must be regarded as the truth, as the ideality, of *everything material*, as the *completely universal*, in which all distinctions are only *ideal* and which *does not stand onesidedly opposed to the other*, but *overreaches the other* (406Z).

But this is not Hegel's main argument for thesis (ii). The soul is concerned, on his view, with our feeling and sensibility, not with higher functions like thinking (*Enz.* III. 390 ff.).[155] The primary support for the thesis seems to depend on a confusion of the first-

and the third-person standpoints on thinking, on inferences from what cannot be thought or said from the first-person perspective to what is actually true from the third-person perspective.[156] At the first-person standpoint we cannot say that our thought depends on matter and bodies; matter and bodies are just things that we think about. Our thinking, therefore, is independent of them. From a first-person viewpoint thinking cannot be assigned to a definite individual, to me rather than you or to Hegel rather than Kant, for definite individuals are again simply things that are thought about, and in any case no definite individual can be picked out by thought.[157] Thinking, therefore, is in fact ownerless, or, if we are pressed to find an owner for it, it is God's thinking, the thinking of a single, all-embracing individual. In this way the circle is closed. The system ends, as it began, not with thinkers thinking pure thoughts, but simply with pure thought as such. These inferences are, as we have seen, defective. The first-person perspective cannot license conclusions about the ontological status of thinking, thoughts or matter any more than it allows the corresponding inferences concerning visual fields and eyes.

18 'A tale that tells itself'

The oddity of Hegel's procedure can be brought into sharper focus, if we compare his theory with a more recent one with which it has some features in common. This theory is phenomenalism, the view that the world consists of, or, more properly, is a logical construction out of, sense-data. Phenomenalism can be represented initially as a programme for translating sentences about physical objects, such as 'There is a table in the next room', into sentences which refer only to sense-data, along the lines of: 'If I were to have such-and-such sense-data' — whatever sense-data I would have if I were in the next room — 'then I would have such-and-such other sense-data' — whatever sense-data are associated with the perception of a table. This form of translation is, however, unsatisfactory as it stands, primarily because the status of I myself, the force of the word 'I', is left unclear. The translation implies that I am something that has sense-data, and this leaves open the possibility that I am an embodied person and not a logical construction out of sense-data. A proper translation should eliminate references to myself in favour of terms which refer only to sense-data. Moreover, if we are not to end up with a plurality of independent egos whose sense-data and logical constructions out of them somehow coincide, people other than myself must be logical constructions out of sense-data. My belief in the existence of other people is based, after all, on my sense-experience. But if the reference to myself is retained in the translations of statements about other poeple, this confers a strange privilege on myself over them. I am the bearer or owner of sense-data, whereas others are merely logical constructions out of them. Which self has this privilege will, of course, vary according to who the phenomenalist is. One solution to these difficulties is to eliminate the reference to myself altogether and simply to speak of the possible occurrence of sense-data:[158]

> [O]nce the sense-datum language has been accepted as basic, then observers, like everything else at the physical level, must be reduced to sense-data. For to allow them to stand outside 'having' or 'sensing' the sense-data would be to bring sense-data themselves up to the physical level and so vitiate the whole phenomenalistic programme . . . . I do not see, for example, why the phenomenalist's version of such a proposition as 'there is a book-case in the dining-room' should contain the description of any sensory manifestation of a human body. It has to identify the dining-room in question and also to specify some period of time, but that should be enough. It may, indeed, be argued that unless some human body were present no sense-experiences would occur at all. But the analysis does not state that any sense-experiences do occur; only that given certain sense-experiences, then . . . certain others. That no experiences at all would be 'given' unless there were an observer is indeed a physical fact: but there is no reason why that physical fact should be prefixed to every sensory analysis. On the contrary, the phenomenalist must hold that it is itself to be analysed in purely sensory terms. The only cases, therefore, in which the analysis will contain a sensory description of an observer are those in which there is some reference to an observer in the proposition which is to be analysed. In such cases the observer will figure *in* the sensory story, but in no case will there be an observer *of* the story. The phenomenalist's tale does not include the author; it is, in that respect, a tale that tells itself.

The possible or hypothetical sense-data in terms of which the analyses of this theory are to be conducted are, then, an analogue of Hegel's pure thoughts. Questions about their ownership, when and where they occur, or would occur, are not to be asked. There are, however, several points at which the two theories diverge:

(i) Hegel deals in thoughts rather than sense-experiences and this has some bearing on other respects in which his theory differs from phenomenalism. Thoughts, on his view, do not differ from person to person in the way that actual sense-experiences do. It is therefore plausible to present the thoughts of the *Logic* as the thoughts of any and every person, though not every person will think them explicitly in the way that Hegel does.[159] Actual sense-data, by contrast, differ from person to person. The phenomenalist avoids this difficulty by dealing in terms of hypothetical sense-data rather than actual ones, and what sense-data one would have if one had certain others does not vary from person to person nearly as much as what sense-data they actually have. It will, of course, vary to some degree, but then the phenomenalist can fall back on the idea of an ideal or a normal observer. Alternatively, he may argue that, since in any case he can only hope to produce sense-datum statements the truth of which is a sufficient condition of the truth of physical object statements and not an exact translation of them,[160] such differences as there are between the perceptual powers of more or less normal observers do not matter. The phenomenalist has, in any case, at least as much right to say that his sensory language represents the perceptual capacities of all human observers as Hegel has to the analogous claim concerning pure thoughts.

(ii) Sense-data enter into phenomenalism in two different ways. Firstly, there are the hypothetical sense-data in terms of which the analyses are conducted. Secondly, there are statements about the actual and hypothetical sense-data of physical observers, statements like 'Tom had such-and-such sense-experiences', 'Dick would have had such-and-such a visual experience if he had entered the room' and even 'I would have such-and-such a sense-experience, if I had such-and-such other sense-experiences.' The phenomenalist can hardly avoid making statements of this latter type, since his use of sense-datum statements of the first type has to be explained initially in terms of them. What is the relationship between these two types of sense-datum statement? The second are to be analysed in terms of the first, but that seems to be all. There is no direct route from such statements as 'Tom has such-and-such sense-data' to the, as it were, disembodied sense-data in terms of which these statements are to be analysed. The phenomenalist is not, therefore, committed to any special theory about the relationship of a man's sense-experiences to his body and to his environment. He may, for example, accept that what sense-experiences we have depends on states of our brains, on the presence of physical objects in our environment, and so on. He can, at this level, be as materialistic as he chooses. There is no point in attempting to prize sense-data loose from the physical people who have them. But such claims about the relationship of sense-experiences to people and their brains must in their turn be analysed in terms of sense-data, so that at a higher level the phenomenalist is an idealist.

Hegel, by contrast, attempts to find a route back from third-person statements about thoughts like 'Hegel is thinking about causality at the moment' to the ownerless thinking-cum-thoughts of the *Logic*. This means that Hegel cannot be a materialist at the level at which the phenomenalist can be a materialist, but must maintain that a pure thinker in some sense disengages himself from his physical condition and environment, and, so to speak, 'rises to God'. Whereas earlier we occupied a first-person viewpoint on thoughts and thinking, at which questions about their ownership, time and place were merely suspended, we have now shifted into a third-person position in which these questions are asked and answered. The answers are that pure thoughts have no owner at all or, if they do, it is a single super-ego, God; that they are outside space and time altogether. If Hegel's tale *does* include the author then he emerges from the tale in order to tell it. The phenomenalist does not provide any analogue of this. Hegel's move is perhaps facilitated by the fact that thought is reflective upon itself in a way that our sense-experience is not. Thought can proceed from thinking about x to thinking about thinking about x, from thinking in the first-person to thinking (first-person) about thinking (third-person). In so far as the phenomenalist does provide a transition from third-person statements like 'Tom is (or even 'I am') having a certain sense-experience' to first-person sense-datum statements in terms of which all third-person statements are to be analysed, he does it by thinking rather than by having sense-experiences. But even if we grant this difference between thought and sense-experience, there is no reason to suppose that Hegel's move is at bottom any less incoherent than its phenomenalist counterpart would be.

(iii) Phenomenalism is relatively indifferent to history. In particular it attaches little significance to the rise of phenomenalism as a theory or even to the emergence of perceivers in a world of unconscious matter. Such statements as 'There were physical objects before there were any observers', 'Phenomenalism arose in the 18th century', and 'The first time anything had a sense-datum was in 4,000,000 BC' must be analysable in terms of possible sense-experience, but they are of no special importance. It is no essential part of phenomenalism to give an account of the world in which the culminating event is the provision of a phenomenalist account of the world and of its history, and in which the emergence of creatures capable of sensory experience is an important milestone.

The status of physical objects was not changed by either of these events. Physical objects always have been logical constructions out of sense-data, even before there were any *actual* sense-data or any logical constructers. The question whether a phenomenalist account is or is not to be given of the world is quite distinct from the question whether we actually do give such an account. Moreover, the building-blocks of the theory, sense-data, offer less promise of a framework for organizing history, or indeed the *scala naturae*, than do thoughts. For human sensory experience does not develop over history in the way that their thoughts or conceptual systems do.

Hegel, by contrast, is vitally concerned with the emergence of thinking creatures and with the development of his own theory. His accounts of nature and of history are structured in terms of this. Indeed nature and history are seen as in some sense teleologically directed towards the occurrence of these events.[161] Apart from the desire to explain the emergence of his own theory − a desire which a phenomenalist might incidentally share − there are at least two reasons for this. Firstly, while nature, for the phenomenalist, is what it is independently of the perceiving of men and of the theorizing of the phenomenalist, Hegel implies that nature or the world in general is crucially altered by men and by their cognitive (and practical) endeavours.[162] Whether this alteration consists merely in the fact that men are entities of an ontologically distinct order from that of non-human objects − whereas, for the phenomenalist, all entities, as logical constructions out of sense-data, are ontologically on a par − or whether men are supposed to change the status of non-human objects is not a question which Hegel can easily answer.[163] But it is, at any rate, clear that the emergence of men and their intellectual growth are of high theological significance. This is how God becomes self-conscious.[164] Phenomenalism provides nothing comparable to this. Secondly, Hegel is committed to giving some such account of nature and of history by his desire to return to the beginning of his system at the end of it. For it is only with the emergence of thinkers and in particular of pure, Hegelian thinkers that the opening of the system is reached within the system itself. The point of this seems to be not only to avoid assumptions by justifying the beginning at the end, but also to give a complete and yet − in our sense − finite explanation of the existence and nature of the universe as a whole.[165] This, of course, is something that the phenomenalist does not aspire to do.

It is a familiar fantasy that a snake could begin by swallowing the tip of its own tail and then, by consuming more and more of its own body, eventually vanish into thin air. If this process were possible, then presumably it could be reversed: a snake could come into existence simply by disgorging itself. The circularity of the process would provide a complete explanation of the existence of the snake without reference to anything other than the snake. Similarly, Hegel seems to believe, the universe exists in virtue of, as it were, disgorging itself. But neither process is possible in the case of a snake. It is hard to see why this type of explanation should work any better in the case of the universe as a whole.

19 Maps, infinity and self-reference

The universe, then, on Hegel's view forms a circle of the type:

Thought → Nature → Mind → Thought.

The circularity of his system is intended to reflect this:

Logic → Philosophy of Nature → Philosophy of Mind → Logic.

As we have seen, however, the circularity of the universe is represented not only by the system as a whole, but by the *Logic* itself.[166] The *Logic* presents the underlying structure not just of each part of the system, but of the system as a whole and therefore of the whole universe. The relationship between thought and what is other than thought, nature and mind, is prefigured within thought itself. This feature of the system has a theological counterpart:[167]

> The movement of the concept is to be regarded, as it were, merely as a play (*Spiel*); the other which is posited by it is not in fact an other. In the doctrine of the christian religion this is expressed by the fact that God has not only created a world, which stands opposed to him as an other, but that he has also produced a son from eternity, in whom he is, as spirit, at home with himself (*bei sich selbst*) (*Enz.* I. 161Z).

Our earlier picture of Hegel's theology is, then, to be qualified to this extent. God the son is the analogue not of the world or nature itself, but of, roughly, the thought of the world, the world as it is prefigured in thought.[168] What is the non-theological, literal significance of this? Hegel's fundamental idea is quite a simple one. It is that thought 'overreaches' what is other than thought. We can think not only about or in terms of particular thoughts, but also about thought in general, what is other than thought and the relationship between the two. Analogously, we can frame propositions not only about the world and not only about particular propositions, but propositions about propositions as such and about the relationship between propositions and the world.

Again, some of the complexities of Hegel's account of teleology may be due to the presence of the similar idea than when a purposive agent forms a plan, he also has some notion of the realization of the plan and of its relationship to the plan itself (*Enz.* I. 204 ff.; *WL* II pp. 436 ff., M. pp. 734 ff.). The relationship between thought and what is not thought can be anticipated within thought, just as the relationship between propositions and what is not a proposition can be expressed in propositions or the relationship between a plan and its realization is foreshadowed within the plan itself.

Pure thought then, on Hegel's view, must represent within itself both itself in its purity and its two-fold embodiment in the different elements of mind and nature. The *Logic* is similar, on this inter-pretation of it, to Josiah Royce's 'map of England, contained within England, [which] is to represent, down to the minutest detail, every contour and marking, natural or artificial, that occurs upon the surface of England'.[169] Such a map would represent not only England, but the map itself, as a feature of the surface of England, and we could see from an inspection of the map the relationship between England and the map. In a similar way, Hegel's *Logic* is intended to represent not only the system as a whole, but itself as a part of the system and the relationship between itself and the rest of the system. Royce's map, however, is a perfect map, representing every detail of the surface of England, and it follows from this that it would contain an infinity of ever smaller maps, each map_n containing a representation of itself which is map_{n+1}. Hegel's *Logic*, by contrast, is not infinite in this (bad) sense. It contains only a finite number of pure thoughts. It cannot, therefore, represent the system as a whole in full detail, with each concept of the *Logic* and each phase of nature and of mind paired off with a distinct concept of the *Logic,* for in order to do this it would need to contain an infinity of concepts. We should not expect to find, then, a reiteration of the whole of the *Logic* within the *Logic.* Instead of that we are simply directed to a re-reading of the work. Logic is, nevertheless, 'infinite' in one of Hegel's senses. It overreaches both itself and what is other than itself. We can think about the world, about our thinking about the world, about our thinking about our thinking about the world, and so on indefinitely. How does the *Logic* represent all this? The following section will attempt to answer this question.

20 *The standpoint of the concept*

Since Hegel's system ends with philosophy and this amounts to logic, we would expect the final term of the *Logic*, the absolute idea, to represent in some way logic as a whole. This is conveyed in such ways as this: 'The *determinacy* of the idea and the whole course of this determinacy has constituted the object of logical science, from which course the absolute idea itself has emerged *on its own account (für sich)*' (*WL* II. p. 550, M. p. 825). It is not, of course, to be interpreted only in this way, since logic represents not only the system as a whole, but also each part of the system. The absolute idea corresponds, for example, to the highest phase of nature, generic animal life.[170] It has, then, a variety of loosely related interpretations. Some idea of the diversity of ways in which the absolute idea is to be understood is conveyed by such passages as this:

> The idea can be conceived as *reason* . . . further as *subject-object*, as the *unity of the ideal and real, of the finite and the infinite, of the soul and the body,* as the *possibility which has its actuality in it,* as that the *nature* of which *can only be conceived as existing,* etc. because all relations of the understanding are contained in it, but in their *infinite* return and identify within themselves (*Enz.* I. 214).

The important point for our present purposes, however, is that the absolute idea represents the climax of Hegel's system — men doing philosophy — and this, as we have seen, implies that it represents logic as a whole.

If the *Logic* is to foreshadow the system as a whole, however, it is not enough that it should conclude with a term standing for logic. Logic, as we have seen, occurs twice in the system as a whole: once at the beginning and once at the end. In the interim, logic is embodied in nature and in mind. How does the *Logic* represent all this? It is initially tempting to suppose that the three main divisions of the work, the doctrines of being, of essence and of the concept, respectively stand for pure thought, nature and mind. The concepts considered in the 'Doctrine of Being' are flat, unidimensional ones, while in the 'Doctrine of Essence' we find dyadic concepts, concepts which come in pairs such as those of the essential and the inessential, of identity and difference, and of substance and accident. These concepts might be taken to represent the rift which opens up at the end of the *Logic* between pure thought or the logical idea and nature.[171] The 'Doctrine of the Concept' would, on this account, indicate the closing of this rift. The concept itself could, for example, denote the pure ego which gradually makes nature intelligible: 'The concept, in so far as it has developed to such an *existence* as is itself free, is nothing but the *I* or pure self-consciousness' (*WL* II. p. 253, M. p. 583).

This way of taking the *Logic* is, however, probably incorrect. In the first place, it is not very easy to see the logical idea, pure thought as such, represented in the 'Doctrine of Being'. Secondly, although Hegel speaks about the ego a good·deal in the course of his discussion of the 'concept in general' (*WL* II. pp. 245 ff., M. pp. 577 ff.), he does not, of course, mean to identify it with the ego and other interpretations are available to us:

> the concept is not to be regarded here as the act of the self-conscious understanding, as the *subjective understanding,*
> but as the concept in and for itself, which constitutes a *stage*
> of *nature* [viz. life or organic nature] as well as one of *mind* . . . .
> Its logical form is independent of those non-spiritual forms, as
> well as of this spiritual form (*Gestalt*), of the concept (*WL* II.
> p. 257, M. p. 586).

The interpretation of the concept as the pure ego is more in place if we take the *Logic* to represent the realm of mind, rather than the system as a whole, and interpret the doctrines of being and of essence in psychological or spiritual terms:

> The pure determinations of being, essence and concept also
> constitute indeed the basis and simple inner framework of
> the forms of mind; mind as *intuiting,* similarly as *sensuous
> consciousness,* is in the determinacy of immediate being, just as
> mind as *conceiving* and also as *perceiving* consciousness has
> risen above being to the stage of essence or reflection (*WL* II.
> p. 257, M. p. 586).

While we are at liberty to interpret the *Logic* in a variety of ways, any given interpretation of one part of it carries commitments about the interpretation of other parts.

It is in fact the concept itself which represents the logical idea, the subject-matter of the *Logic* as a whole. It is clear enough that when Hegel speaks of *the* concept, he does not in general mean ordinary concepts like that of a horse. He does indeed pass from a discussion of the concept to an account of concepts, but he regularly draws a distinction between them: 'I *have*, it is true, concepts, i.e. determinate concepts; but the I is the pure concept itself, which as concept has come to existence' (*WL* II. p. 253, M. p. 583); and: 'the concept is more than all this; its determinations are determinate *concepts,* essentially itself the *totality* of all determinations' (*WL* II. p. 295, M. p. 618). That it is, or stands for, the logical idea as a whole is suggested by the fact that it is said by Hegel to remedy and complete Spinoza's account of God or the universe as a substance: 'The great intuition of Spinozist substance *is* only *in itself* the *liberation* from finite being-for-self; but the concept itself is *for itself* the power of necessity and *actual* freedom' (*Enz.* I. 159).[172] Again, it is implicitly identified with Kant's categories: 'Then again Kant's philosophy has got only as far as the psychological reflex of the concept and has returned again to the assertion of the permanent conditionedness of the concept by a manifold of intuition' (*WL* II. p. 261, M. p. 589).[173] In general the concept is described in terms similar to those which Hegel applies to the logical idea as a whole:

> The standpoint of the concept is in general that of absolute idealism, and philosophy is conceptualizing (*begreifendes*) cognition in so far as in it everything which passes for ordinary consciousness as something which is and is independent in its immediacy, is known as merely an ideal element (*Moment*) . . . it is just the concept which contains all the earlier determinations of thinking sublimated (*aufgehoben*) within itself . . . . Of course, the concept is to be regarded as a form, but as an infinite creative form, which includes the fullness of all content within itself and releases it from itself . . . the concept is what is entirely concrete, and indeed in so far as it contains being and essence and thus the whole wealth of these two spheres an ideal unity within itself (*Enz.* I. 160Z).

The concept, then, represents, among other things, the logical idea as a whole, conceived in abstraction from its embodiment in nature and mind. But it does not expand, in the *Logic* itself, into a reiteration of the whole of logic. Rather, Hegel takes the opportunity to give an account, in the first section of the 'Doctrine of the Concept' ('Subjectivity'), of concepts, judgments and forms of inference. The second section, 'Objectivity' (*WL* II. pp. 402 ff., M. pp. 705 ff.) or the 'object' (*Enz.* I. 194 ff.), represents, on this account, nature, conceived of as distinct from the logical idea but as in some sense embodying it. This section itself falls into three parts — mechanism, chemism and teleology — and these stand for progressively higher stages of nature, leading into the third and final section, the 'idea'. The idea represents the increasing unification of the logical idea itself with the objective world, by way of life, our cognitive and practical activities, and finally the absolute idea. This, as we have already seen, denotes philosophy, especially Hegel's own philosophy and hence logic itself.

This account explains several features of the third book of the *Logic* which are initially puzzling. It explains, for example, the apparently abrupt transition from the metaphysical concerns of the first two books to the more properly logical subject-matter of the third. It also makes sense of the duplication of material already presented in the first and second books. The discussion of mechanism and chemism, for example, is sufficiently similar to the account of causality and reciprocity in the 'Doctrine of Essence' to provoke the questions why they are both required and, if they are, why they occur in such different contexts. The answer is that in the earlier passage Hegel is concerned with the pure thoughts of causality and of reciprocity in abstraction from their application to objective nature, whereas in the third book he is considering the thought of the objective realm to which these and other concepts apply. The account of mechanism, chemism and teleology is a brisk rehearsal, within the sphere of pure thought, of the *Philosophy of Nature*.

We have arrived, then, as Hegel promised, at the 'concept of the science', the concept which 'produces itself in the course of [science] and thus cannot be presupposed in advance' (*WL* I. p. 35, M. p. 43).[174] In the course of thinking about and in terms of pure thoughts, we ascend to the reflective standpoint of conceiving of the whole system of pure thoughts as such. Each pure thought, on Hegel's view, embraces its predecessors.[175] But the concept itself embraces *its* predecessors in a quite different way. It is the whole system of which they each form a part, rather than — or as well as — a further element in that system. But how does Hegel make this transition? In terms of our earlier analogy, if one is working through pure arithmetic, one is likely at some point to reflect on numbers as such and their relationship to things which are not numbers, but such a leap of reflection cannot be derived within arithmetic itself from the systematic interrelationships of types of number. Or, again, no doubt when one is considering a series of languages each of which is the meta-language of its immediate predecessor, one sooner or later becomes aware of the series as a whole and, perhaps, of the idea of an infinite language in which one can speak about it. But it is hard to see how such awareness can be generated as a member of the series itself.[176] The human mind can perform these feats. The difficulty is to see how it can provide a logical representation of them. Hegel, however, appears to believe that he has done it. How? This question will be considered in the remaining sections of this chapter.

21 Concepts and the concept

Hegel's introduction of the concept becomes easier to understand when we consider that it has a variety of interpretations apart from the one on which we have concentrated so far:

(1) The introduction of the concept is followed by an account of concepts, the ordinary, determinate concepts which, on Hegel's view, figure in our judgments. *The* concept is, as we have seen, not to be confused with a concept of this sort, but ordinary concepts must be borne in mind, when we consider the interpretations which follow.

(2) In the *Philosophy of Mind* the concept corresponds, as we have seen, to the pure ego (*Enz.* III. 424 ff.). There is an obvious connection between this interpretation of the concept and Hegel's identification of the ego with the system of pure thoughts.[177]

(3) In the *Philosophy of Nature* the concept corresponds, or at least should correspond, to organic nature, especially the plant (*Enz.* II. 343 ff.).

(4) The political state is sometimes associated with the concept (e.g. *Enz.* I. 156Z), and sometimes with the absolute idea (e.g. *PR* 257, 269). This is perhaps puzzling in the light of the fact that the state does not occupy either of the relevant positions within the *Philosophy of Mind,* but there are at least two reasons for it. Firstly, Hegel tends to regard the state as an organic entity, assimilating it to a plant or an animal (e.g. *PR* 269).[178] Secondly, he is evidently attempting to structure the *Philosophy of Right*, his account of man's social and political life, in terms of the *Logic*. The *Philosophy of Right* corresponds to only a fragment of the *Philosophy of Mind* (*Enz.* III. 483–552), but this is one of those cases where the *Logic* is reiterated within the application of it to the sphere of mind as a whole (*PR* 2).[179]

These are not the only interpretations of the concept to be found in Hegel. There should be a counterpart to it in each of the applications of the *Logic* — in the history of the world and in the histories of art, religion and philosophy. But the present list is sufficient for our purposes. There is the complication that, in the case of interpretations (3) and (4), Hegel is at least as likely to associate organic life and the state with the idea as with the concept (e.g. *Enz.* II. 337). There are at least three reasons for this. Firstly, as we have seen, when the *Logic* is taken as representing the system as a whole, the absolute idea involves a reversion to the concept, the logical idea. If the circularity of the system is taken seriously, then there should be no ultimate difference between the concept and the absolute idea. Secondly, in virtue of its function of representing the system as a whole, the *Logic* considers the concept of life, and it regards it as a phase not of the first section of the 'Doctrine of the Concept', 'Subjectivity', nor of its second section, 'Objectivity', but of the idea itself. Why the concept of

337

life occurs at this point, or indeed in the *Logic* at all, is difficult to explain. But, given that it does, it is easy to see how it could lead Hegel to refer organic nature to the idea rather than the concept. Thirdly, the idea is regularly presented as the unification of subjectivity and objectivity, as the actualization of the concept. The idea in general is

> the absolute unity of the concept and of objectivity. Its ideal content is nothing but the concept in its determinations; its real content is only the exhibition of this ideal content, an exhibition which the content gives itself in the form of external existence and, by enclosing this form (*Gestalt*) in its ideality, in its power, thus preserves itself in it (*Enz.* I. 213).

This has a special meaning in the case of the absolute idea, where, because what we are concerned with is thought about thought, the concept is, as it were, its own object:[180]

> The idea as unity of the subjective and the objective idea is the concept of the idea, the concept whose objective counterpart (*Gegenstand*) is the idea as such, whose object (*Objekt*) is the idea – an object in which all determinations have converged. This unity is thus the *absolute truth, all truth,* the idea which thinks itself, and indeed here *as* thinking, as *logical* idea (*Enz.* I. 236).

But Hegel also believes that the concept somehow realizes itself without any outside help (*Enz.* I. 160Z, 161Z).[181] The point of associating an entity with the concept is to stress the fact that it is self-contained and self-actualizing. It follows that the distinction between the concept and the (absolute) idea is to this extent a hazy one. It does not make much difference whether, for example, the plant is referred to the concept or to the idea. This complication does not, then, significantly affect the discussion which follows.

22 *Reciprocity and purpose*

How, then, is the concept introduced? The answer seems to be that the transition to it is effected primarily by way of interpretations (3) and (4), by reflection upon the nature of living organisms and societies. Towards the end of the 'Doctrine of Essence', Hegel gives an account of causality (*Enz.* I. 153 f.; *WL* II. pp. 222 ff., M. pp. 558 ff.). This leads on, intelligibly enough, to the notion of reciprocity (*Wechselwirkung*), of two or more interacting substances, the states of each being both the causes and the effects of the states of the other (*Enz.* I. 154 ff.; *WL* II. pp. 237 ff., M. pp.

569 ff.). Reciprocity is a more adequate concept than causality, but even it is not wholly adequate. The concept is a higher and altogether more satisfactory category:

> Thus in historical researches the question is first considered whether the character and customs of a people are the cause of its constitution and its laws or, conversely, their effect, and then the step is taken to conceiving both of these, character and customs on the one hand and constitution and laws on the other, from the point of view of reciprocity, such that the cause is at the same time the effect in the same connection (*Beziehung*) as that in which it is the cause, and the effect is at the same time the cause in the same connection as that in which it is the effect. This happens too in the consideration of nature and especially of the living organism, the individual organs and functions of which similarly prove to stand to each other in the relationship of reciprocity. Now reciprocity is indeed the immediate truth of the relation of cause and effect, and it stands, as it were, on the brink of the concept; however for that very reason one should not be content with the application of this relation, in so far as one is concerned with conceptual (*begreifende*) cognition . . . . If one does not get beyond it . . . one then has to do only with a dry fact, and the requirement of mediation . . . remains again unsatisfied . . . . [What should happen is] that the two sides of the relation are not left as something immediately given, but . . . are known as elements of a third, higher entity, which is just the concept. If we regard e.g. the customs of the Spartan people as the effect of its laws and, conversely, the latter as the effect of its customs, this may doubtless be correct, but this conception provides no ultimate satisfaction, because in fact neither the constitution nor the customs of this people are understood (*begriffen*) in this way. This happens only if those two aspects, and all the other particular aspects which the life and history of the Spartan people display, are cognized as grounded in this concept (*Enz.* I. 156Z).

Hegel seems to be making three fairly distinct points in this passage. Firstly, if a set-up is explained in terms of reciprocity, then it is not fully and ultimately explained. This point is supported by a pun: if one ignores the concept of something, then one cannot conceptualize or understand (*begreifen*) it. But Hegel also has an argument for it. The items which stand in a relation of reciprocity to each other are conceived of as each having a nature which is independent of its relationship to the other. The nature of each item explains why it responds in the way that it does to the successive states of the other item. Each of two boxers, for example, makes movements – evasive, defensive, offensive and retaliatory – which are in part caused by the movements of the other. But equally each of the boxers is an entity with certain characteristics independent of his interaction with the other, characteristics which in part explain his responses to the other's movements. The course of the boxing-match is not therefore fully explained in terms of reciprocity. Causal interaction between the boxers does not explain those prior features which each of them brings to the conflict, nor, of course, does it explain why just these two men are fighting each other. It does not follow that there are no entities which are related in this way. A boxing-match seems to be a clear case of reciprocity. It does follow, on Hegel's view at least, that the universe as a whole cannot be adequately conceived only in terms of reciprocity. For, if the universe as a whole is to be fully explained, there is nothing outside it – as there is in the case of the boxers – to which we can resort in order to account for the recalcitrant, independent natures of the reciprocally related entities.[182]

Secondly, there are some items within the universe – plants and societies, for example – the relationship of whose parts cannot be satisfactorily seen as one of mere reciprocity. This is not simply because this category cannot provide an ultimate explanation of any entity or situation, but because the parts or aspects of these entities have no stubborn core of independence, no characteristics that are not determined by their relationship to the other parts. A society or a living organism constitutes a special sort of unity. Its parts are intimately interconnected in a way that two boxers are not.[183] Hegel introduces here the notion of purposiveness or teleology, not 'external' or 'finite' purposiveness, where the organism is seen as serving the purpose of some entity other than itself, but 'internal' or 'infinite' purposiveness. In the case of external purposiveness, the purpose is extrinsic to the material in which it is realized, the means by which it is fulfilled. If, for example, the existence of grass is explained by reference to the dietary needs of cows, we shall have to distinguish between those features of grass which are strictly necessary for the purpose in hand, in this case the survival of cows, and those features which are not. Why does grass exist rather than some functionally equivalent substance, differing from grass in some respects but sharing its nutritional value for cows? External teleology can supply no answer to this question and the explanation which it provides remains incomplete. It is also incomplete in another way. If the survival of cows is to explain the existence of grass, we shall have to go on to ask, 'What are cows for?' and we shall either proceed in this way *ad infinitum*, each entity serving the interests of some further entity, or we shall eventually arrive at an entity which is in some sense self-explanatory or self-justifying.[184] In the case of internal purposiveness, by contrast, the purpose is a 'determination and an activity which is immanent in the matter, and all the members are reciprocally both ends and means' (*Enz.* I. 57). Each part of the organism is, ideally at least, necessary for the existence and survival of each of the other parts and of the whole organism. The genesis and workings of an organism, unlike those of a machine, a pile of stones or a boxing-match, cannot be understood in a piecemeal way, but only holistically. The parts are to be understood, as it were, in terms of the whole and not the whole in terms of the parts. For it is the whole which determines the existence and nature of the parts, and all the parts are required for the proper functioning of any of them. Hegel prefers teleological explanations, where they are available, to causal or mechanistic ones. For causal explanations, being of a piecemeal kind, do not explain the unity of the elements, why they are conjoined in the way they are. Teleological explanations, by contrast, give an account of this.[185]

Another idea which Hegel introduces in this context is that of freedom. We have already seen that necessity in its full degree is not incompatible with freedom, but rather involves it.[186] One of the thoughts underlying this claim is that if two entities are related to each other only mechanistically, by reciprocal causal interaction, then each can be said to be determined by the other, though it is, of course, not fully determined by it, since it has a nature of its own independent of the relationship. When, by contrast, the entities or aspects of an entity are as intimately associated as they are when they form an organic whole, then, firstly, each of them is fully determined by the others — the necessity is complete — but, secondly, since the whole nature of each consists in its being related in this way to the others, they can no longer be regarded as 'others'. Each part of an organic whole is, as it were, self-determining:

> the process of necessity is such that through it the rigid externality which is at first present is overcome and that its inner side is revealed, which then makes it clear that the terms which are bound to each other are not in fact alien to one another, but are only aspects (*Momente*) of *one* whole, each of which, in its connection with the other, is at home with itself, and combines with itself (*Enz.* I. 158Z. Cf. *WL* II. p. 251, M. pp. 581 f.).

Hegel's concept, or concepts, of freedom will be considered in detail later.[187] It is introduced here only in order to explain the initially puzzling fact that freedom is seen as emerging from reciprocity and is regularly associated with the concept.

Hegel's account of organisms and societies is open to criticism. His conception of living organisms has been overtaken by subsequent scientific developments. The picture is in any case overdrawn. Not all the parts of an organism are necessary for its survival. If Hegel is concerned about what happens to a part when it is detached from the whole to which it belongs, it is tempting to suppose that there is no such radical difference between organic wholes and mechanical ones as he believes there is. A boxer who is extricated from a fight stops boxing. A hand which is severed from the body dies. The laws of a society can hardly be detached from its customs at all, but members of a society can emigrate. A boxer can return to the fight, a severed hand could not, in Hegel's day, be sewn on again, émigrés can return home. We need more than Hegel provides us with if we are to make much of this. Even if we accept his account of organic wholes, however, it is still not obvious that we are committed to granting the third point which he makes in the passage quoted above, namely that entities of this type must be explained by reference to their concept. What have the purposive interrelationships of social life and of non-conscious nature got to do with concepts?

23 *Teleology and concepts*

There are several converging answers to this question. Firstly, conscious human purposes are closely associated with concepts. If a person sets out to produce some state of affairs, it is not unreasonable to suppose that he has an idea or concept of the state of affairs which he wishes to bring about, that someone who makes, for example, a clock must have the concept of a clock or of the particular type of clock which he is constructing: 'The end is therefore the subjective concept, as essential striving and urge to posit itself externally' (*WL* II. p. 445, M. p. 740). The concept of the clock plays an essential part in the production of the actual clock and when the clock has been produced, the concept is 'posited externally'. Societies and plants are not, however, purposively produced by any single agent or group of agents. Why should we suppose that concepts are involved in their growth? Hegel does not hold to the traditional view, not at least in its literal form, that they are produced by a purposive deity. In any case, a purposive deity would be responsible for heaps of sand as much as for living organisms. There is no warrant for assigning some features of the cosmos to his purposive, 'conceptual' production, but not others. The answer seems to be that if we think of an organism as *intrinsically* purposive, then it is tempting to transfer the concept into the organism itself, to suppose that there is in it something corresponding to a human plan or project. This transposition of the concept is made smoother if, like Hegel, we conflate thoughts or concepts with species and genera (*Enz.* I. 24Z.1) or think of the concept as a sort of plan which is embodied in the seed, as, perhaps, the genetic code of the organism (*Enz.* I. 161Z).[188]

Secondly, there is a tendency to associate the concept of a thing with the thing as a *whole*. This is not an unfounded tendency, since our ability to identify wholes depends in part on our concepts. We can say whether x is red or not, even if we do not know what kind of thing x is. But we cannot say whether x is a whole thing or only a part of a thing until we know what kind of a thing it is, until, that is, we apply a concept to it. A whole engine is only a part of a ship and a whole ship is only a part of a fleet. But, more than this, Kant had argued that it is our concepts which make our diverse sensory data into distinct, whole things.[189] It is not essential to this view that what is thus unified and articulated should be our subjective sensory manifold. The material for unification might be regarded rather as physical stuff. But, on either of these accounts, it is at least plausible to suppose that where the lines are to be drawn between things is not something decided by the nature of things themselves, but by us, guided by our practical purposes, the desire for simplicity, the urge to discover regularities and so on. Our decisions are recorded in our concepts and the ways in which we apply them. This is a correct account of the unity of some of the things which we individuate. A constellation such as the Great Bear obviously does not constitute a single entity as such and in itself, but only because we have decided to count it as one. It would be no affront to nature if we were to cease to organize the stars into constellations altogether or were to do so in quite a different way, since we have introduced them only for our own convenience. This account of the unity of things does not, however, suit some entities — crystals, for example, magnets, and especially higher living organisms. If it were unrestrictedly true, then we could as well count a person not as a single entity, but as two distinct half-persons, or as a series of distinct temporal 'person-slices', or we could count a person and his clothes as a single, unified object. If we did so, then we would regard a half-person or a person-slice or a person-plus-clothes as a distinct object in just the way that we now regard a person as a distinct object; we would think of a person either as a collection of objects, of half-persons or of person-slices — in much the way that we now regard a pile of apples as a collection of distinct objects — or as an incomplete fragment of a person-plus-clothes — in the way that we now regard half an apple as merely a part of a complete object. To articulate things in this way, however, would not only be inconvenient; it would ride roughshod over the organic, functional relationships which hold between the two halves of a person and between the temporal segments of a person, but which fail to obtain between a person and the clothes he is currently wearing. We can discover these relationships empirically by seeing what happens when we cut things in half, by watching the effects of damage to one temporal slice of a thing on later ones, and so on.[190] Hegel's conclusion at any rate seems to be that living organisms and certain other entities are self-constituting unities.[191] On the rejected view, however, it is the concept of a thing which makes it a single, unified thing. There is, therefore, once again a temptation to transfer the concept from our minds into the thing, to suppose that what unifies the thing is no longer a subjective concept, but an objective one at work within the thing itself.

A third reason for Hegel's introduction of concepts in this context is this. We have already seen that he tends to equate the distinction between the thing as it is in itself and the effects on it of its external relationships with the distinction between the concept of the thing and its properties. The linking idea seems to be that if a thing is unrelated to other things, then it must be fully determined by, and fully correspond to, its concept. To the extent that it fails to conform to its concept, this is because of the effects upon it of other things. The concept of a thing and its environment compete for influence over it and, in the case of finite entities, they both have a share in the outcome.[192] Some finite entities are relatively exposed to, and dependent upon, the influence of other things. A lump of sugar, for example, is sweet, white, solid and cubical owing to different processes to which it has been subjected.[193] But this is because the properties of a lump of sugar, or at least its taste, shape and colour, are more or less independent of each other. Organic wholes, however, are not like this. Their diverse features, especially their organic parts, are purposively or functionally related to one another and their harmonious development is essential to the growth and survival of the organism. Unlike the parts of a purposive, but mechanical, object like a clock, they cannot be removed without impairing the other parts and they cannot survive once they have been detached from the whole. It follows that the features of an organic whole do not depend on its contingent encounters with other objects in the way that those of a lump of sugar do. Living organisms develop in relative independence of their environment, the more so, roughly speaking, the higher the organism. They require only certain favourable conditions in order to develop in a definite, genetically determined way. If it is not the influence of the environment which makes the organism develop in one way rather than another, then it can, on the picture with which Hegel has presented us, only be its concept. Self-determination amounts to determination by a concept, the 'active *concept*, the universal which is intrinsically determinate and determining' (*Enz.* I. 57). Hegel seems to regard this concept as in some way embodied in the seed, the seed which grows, with a minimum of external assistance, into a complex differentiated organism: 'In nature it is organic life which corresponds to the stage of the concept. Thus e.g. the plant develops from its seed. The seed contains already the whole plant in itself' (*Enz.* I. 161Z).[194]

24 *The concept vindicated*

The argument so far, then, is this. We start off with the notion of reciprocity, of two or more causally interacting entities. We then tighten the relationship between the interacting entities so that they are constituted, and not only affected, by their relationship to one another, so that what we have is an intrinsically purposive, organic whole. Such a whole, we infer, is determined — to a relatively high degree, at least — by its concept. And so we have arrived at the concept.

This argument can clearly be challenged at a number of points, and some of the weak links in it have been indicated in the preceding discussion. It is also, however, incomplete. For what we have now arrived at is not *the* concept, but ordinary determinate concepts. A dandelion, for example, is determined by the concept of a dandelion, Sparta by the concept of Sparta, the concept of a state or of a particular type of state. Since what we are doing is logic or pure thinking, we should not mention anything so definite as the concept of a dandelion, but rather adhere to abstract expressions like 'determinate concept'. But the concept of a determinate concept is not equivalent to Hegel's logical idea, to the system of pure thoughts taken as a whole. It is itself only one determinate concept, albeit a relatively abstract one, among others. There is nothing in it to direct our attention to concepts like that of being, causality and so on, let alone to the whole system of them taken together. How do we get from here to *the* concept?

There seem to be at least two answers to this. Firstly, since logic is thinking about thinking, we are intended to be continually aware of the possibility of applying thoughts to thoughts themselves. Some thoughts are criticized because they cannot appropriately fulfil this role. Hegel insists, for example, that the logical idea cannot be adequately conceived in quantitative terms, primarily for the reason that arithmetic presupposes that the items to which it is applied are distinct and discrete in a way in which pure thoughts or, for that matter, the parts of a plant are not.[195] If, then, we come across a thought which is applicable to thought as a whole, our attention does not need to be especially drawn to this fact. We have had it in mind all along. But the logical idea, as we have already seen, exemplifies the concept in a way in which it does not exemplify substance, for example, or reciprocity. The pure thoughts hang together rather in the fashion of the parts of an organism. Each one is fully determined by the others and none of them can be detached from the whole.[196] Like a living organism, again, the logical idea develops autonomously. Hegel probably sees an analogy between the growth of a plant from an apparently undifferentiated seed and the emergence of the logical idea from the thought of pure being. The introduction of the concept leads us to reflect, then, on the logical idea as such because it is, on Hegel's view, the prime example of an entity which is determined by its concept.

The second answer is that, despite Hegel's occasional disavowals, we should bear in mind when considering any given thought the possibility of applying it to God or to the universe as a whole. The universe, as we have seen, cannot be adequately understood only as a collection of causally interacting substances, as a force which expresses itself or as a set of quantitative relationships. If it is to be explained or understood at all, then this must be done in terms of its concept. The universe as a whole is not situated in an environment with which it interacts; it is wholly self-determining and this, Hegel believes, means conceptually determined. But where are we to look for the concept of the universe? It cannot be some particular, determinate concept, like that of a dandelion. For, firstly, the universe contains a diversity of particular things of that sort. The concept of the universe must in some sense embrace all particular, determinate concepts if it is to account for all particular, determinate things. It must be, as Hegel has argued, an 'infinite' concept.[197] Secondly, the concept of the universe cannot contain any explicit empirical content. For, on Hegel's view, the empirical content of our concepts, or rather conceptions, derives from our perceptual encounters with particular determinate entities, and it is just the existence of entities of this type which the concept is meant to explain. To put this point in picturesque, theological terms, God's plan of the universe must be such that he could develop it independently of any sensory contact with items in the universe which he has not yet created. The only candidate which fulfils these requirements is the logical idea itself, the system of pure thoughts which we are currently unravelling. Hegel believes, as we have seen, that it is the only possible system of pure thoughts that can be developed.[198] The logical idea, then, is the concept of the universe or of God. Once again the emergence of the concept within pure thought provokes reflection upon the system of pure thoughts as a whole.

This, then, is how Hegel introduces the concept. It has, as we have seen, a variety of resonances and interpretations which are connected with each other only tenuously. It stands at the junction of several different strands of thought. We have seen, in this chapter, the ontological status which the circularity of Hegel's system is intended to confer upon it. We have also seen how, in the *Logic,* it initiates his attempt to prefigure within logic the system as a whole, to represent within the logical idea the relationship of the logical idea to what is other than itself, the empirical world. The next step, then, is to ask: How does Hegel ever get beyond the logical idea to the empirical world? This question will be considered in the following chapter.

IX

Thought and Things: the Transition to Nature

1 *An ambiguous transition*

The transition from the *Logic* to the *Philosophy of Nature* has generally been regarded as a major difficulty in Hegel's system. The actual world, it is felt, and empirical scientific knowledge about it are irreducibly non-logical and cannot be derived from pure thought alone. There is, however, room for doubt about the nature of Hegel's enterprise. To what extent did he believe that features of the empirical world can be derived from logic? There are at least four possibilities here:

(i) Hegel did not wish to make any *a priori* claims about the world at all, except perhaps that there must be some world or other and that it must display the sort of general hierarchical structure that can be termed 'dialectical'. The concepts presented in the *Logic* are otherwise selected only because they are the concepts which we have found to be required by our empirical discoveries about the world. The *Philosophy of Nature* does no more than organize the results of the sciences in the framework provided by the *Logic*. It does not purport to supply any logical or *a priori* support for them. Hegel's enterprise is, on this view, that of systematic reflection on the findings of the special sciences. We might question some features of his execution of it, and it would of course have to be revised in the light of scientific developments since his time. But there is no radical problem about the transition from logic to nature.[1]

(ii) The *Philosophy of Nature* is, as in (i), simply an attempt to systematize the results of the empirical sciences, whatever they happen to be. But what the world is like is not only a matter for empirical inquiry. The *Logic* argues for a series of general claims

348

about the world independently of the findings of the special sciences. The argument of the *Logic* proceeds in some such way as this. The concept of being has application. For, if it did not, there would be nothing, and nothing is not intelligibly different from being. But if anything *is,* then it must be determinate. For, if it were not, there would be no difference between its being and its not being. And so on. The arguments are of the form: If such and such is the case, then so and so must be the case. It is possible, but less likely, that they are of the form: If such and such is known or believed by me/us to be the case, then so and so must be known or believed to be the case. This is less likely for two reasons. Firstly, arguments of this type involve a reference to the knowing subject. But, whereas in the *Phenomenology* the forms of consciousness are intended to have a view of the knowing subject as well as of the object known and to be concerned about the relationship between the two, in the *Logic* the subject is supposed to be entirely absorbed into the subject-matter and no reference to it seems possible.[2] Secondly, arguments of this form establish conclusions not about what the world is like, but about what it must be believed, or seem, to be like. This raises the possibility that the world is different from what it seems to be, but this, as we have seen, is a possibility that Hegel will not countenance.[3] However, uncertainty over the form of argument employed in the *Logic* does not affect the main point, namely that Hegel took himself to have shown in that work that the world must display certain general features. If he does not stress this explicitly, it is perhaps because of his misplaced doubts about the 'propositional form'.[4] A contributing factor is his use of the term 'determinations' to describe the concepts of the *Logic*, a term which already implies that they are features of the world and not simply concepts. (In fact the term 'thought-determination', *Denkbestimmung,* is ambiguous. It could mean either a 'determination of thought', viz. a concept, or a 'determination of the world which is accessible to thought'.[5]) Even this relatively modest conclusion, that the concepts of the *Logic* necessarily have some application to the world, may be found unacceptable. It implies, for example, that there necessarily are living creatures, for life is one of the categories of the *Logic* (*Enz.* I. 216 ff.; *WL* II. pp. 469 ff., M. pp. 761 ff.). It is perhaps a necessary truth that, if anything is believed or known by me/us to be the case, then something is alive. But it is a contingent matter whether anything is alive or not. Hegel's ambition, however, goes no further than this. When it comes to the details of things, whether, for example, there are elephants or not, whether there are such things as crystals and magnets or not, then we have to resort to empirical investigation. Logic tells us what general requirements any possible world must satisfy; the sciences fill in the details of our actual world. One might quarrel with Hegel's location of the boundary between logic and the special sciences, but, on the whole, the enterprise is a respectable one. Again, the passage from logic to nature raises no special problem.

(iii) Hegel's *a priori* claims about the world are not confined to the *Logic*. In addition, he wishes to establish the results of the special sciences *a priori*, to derive them in some way or other from logic. It would not follow from this that we could derive from logic the finest details of the empirical world, the fact, for example, that Hegel died of cholera in 1831. For the sciences with which the *Philosophy of Nature* is concerned do not provide us with particular facts about the world. They do, on Hegel's view, tell us that there is a solar system and make general claims about the earth. But the law of falling bodies, for example, does not supply details about particular falling bodies:[6]

> This realm of laws is indeed the truth of the understanding, . . .
> but it is at the same time only its *first truth* and does not fill
> out appearance. The law is present in appearance, but it is not
> its whole presence; under different circumstances the law has
> a different actuality (*PG* p. 115, M. p. 91).

The whole body of scientific laws together would not entail a complete description of the world. Even on a rigorously determinist view, laws need to be supplemented by a detailed description of some part of the world, of a temporal stage of it for example, before they provide an account of the details of the world as a whole. Even so, Hegel's programme would, on this view, be ambitious enough. It would commit him, for example, to mantaining the necessity not only of Kepler's laws of planetary motion, but of the existence of such entities as crystals and magnets. All these matters would be derivable from logic and ultimately from the simple concept of pure being.

(iv) Hegel wishes to derive from logic not only certain very general features of the world and not only those features of it with which scientists are concerned but also its finest details, the fact for example that I am holding a black pen at 6.15 p.m. on 27 April 1980.

Which of these enterprises did Hegel himself have in mind? Many commentators have attributed to him position (i) or position (ii). The textual evidence, however, is not in their favour. The main motive for doing so seems to be that one or other of these positions is more easily defensible than the more ambitious (iii) and (iv). But it is not clear that Hegel gains in stature from this interpretation of him. He becomes more sensible, but what he has to say is of less interest. Positions (i) and (ii) will be examined again later, when we consider the question: What, on Hegel's view, is supposed to happen after Hegel?[7] But some of the arguments against their attribution to him will be presented here.

Some of Hegel's own remarks suggest that it was (i) or (ii), and nothing more, that he had in mind. He says, for example that 'besides the fact that the object is to be presented in the course of philosophy according to the *determination* of *its concept,* we must further name the *empirical* phenomenon corresponding to it and show that it does in fact correspond to it' (*Enz.* II. 246). This might be taken to mean that, having worked out our logic, we should simply look to find counterparts of the various pure thoughts in nature, relying either on our own observations or on the findings of empirical scientists. We find, for example, crystals, magnets and plants, but we might have found quite different entities exemplifying the same pure thoughts. Hegel continues, however, in a way which seems to exclude this interpretation:

> This, however, is not an appeal to experience with regard to the necessity of the content. Still less is an appeal admissible to what has been called *intuition* and tends to be simply a procedure of conception and imagination (*Phantasie*) . . . in accordance with *analogies,* which may be more contingent or more significant, and which impress determinations and schemata on the objects only *externally* (231. Remark) (*Ibid.*).

The target of Hegel's criticism in the second sentence is not entirely clear, but the passage to which he refers suggests that it is Schelling's *Naturphilosophie.* But at any rate the general sense of the passage seems to be that an appeal to experience is not essential to the philosophy of nature, that such of the details of nature as are recorded in it can be derived from logic. The following account of the *Philosophy of Nature* implies that Hegel held to position (iii):

> On the one hand the empirical sciences do not stop at the perception of the *individualities* of appearance, but have rather worked up the material by thinking to meet philosophy half-way, by finding the universal determinations, genera and laws; they thus prepare the content of the particular so that it can be received into philosophy . . . . On the other hand . . . [w]hile philosophy thus owes its development to the empirical sciences,

it gives to their content the most essential form (*die wesentlichste Gestalt*) of the *freedom* (of *apriority*) of thinking and the *warrant* of *necessity* instead of the testimony of empirical encounter (*des Vorfindens*) and of the experienced fact, so that the fact (*die Tatsache*) becomes the exhibition and copy of the original and completely independent activity of thinking (*Enz.* I. 12).

Hegel could not legitimately claim to be showing that the results of science were necessary and *a priori*, if all he intended to do was to establish empirically that they exemplify logic.

The possibility of deriving scientific statements about the world from logic has an ontological counterpart. The concept is supposed in some way or other to generate or produce the empirical world. There is something of this in such passages as this:

We should remark in this context that the assertion that the categories are on their own account empty has indeed a correct sense to the extent that we must not stop at them and their totality (the logical idea), but must advance to the real realms of nature and of mind; this advance is not however to be conceived as if a content which is alien to the logical idea comes to it from outside, but rather in such a way that to determine itself further and unfold into nature and into mind is the logical idea's own activity (*Enz.* I. 43Z).

This becomes more apparent if we consider Hegel's theological views. The traditional belief, expressed for example by Leibniz and his followers, is that God was free to create any one of several significantly different, but equally possible, worlds, or indeed to create no world at all. On this account, the nature of our world could not be derived from logic alone. How, then, are we to explain why the actual world instantiates one of these possibilities rather than some other one? Characteristically at this point divine providence is invoked. Leibniz, for example, held that God freely chose to create the best of all possible worlds. Hegel himself speaks often enough of divine providence.[8] But he does not take this to mean that God freely chose to actualize one of several logical possibilities. Nor could he consistently do so, for such a view implies that God is in some sense distinct from the world he creates and is therefore, on Hegel's account, finite. Rather he seems to share Spinoza's conviction that things 'could not have been brought into being by God in any manner or in any order different from that which has in fact obtained'.[9] Hegel believes, as we have seen, that necessity and freedom are not incompatible

352

with each other, and he holds too that divine providence is entirely compatible with necessity:

> One must not regard the conception of the world as determined by necessity and the belief in a divine providence as mutually exclusive. What underlies divine providence as far as thought is concerned will emerge shortly as the *concept*. This is the truth of necessity and contains it sublimated in itself . . . . The naive religious consciousness speaks of God's eternal and inviolable decrees, and this involves the express acknowledgement that necessity belongs to the essence of God. Man, as distinct from God . . . proceeds in accordance with caprice and wilfulness and thus it happens that in his activity something quite different emerges from what he supposed and willed, whereas God knows what he wills, is not determined in his will by any inner or outer contingency, and he also irresistibly brings about what he wills (*Enz.* I. 147Z).

This passage makes two relevant points. First, there is in the case of God no contingency about what he wills, as there is in the case of a man. Whatever God wills to happen, he necessarily wills to happen. Secondly, whatever God wills to happen necessarily happens in precisely the form in which he wills it. It seems to follow that the character of the world is fully determined by the nature of God. Translated into philosophical terms, this means that the empirical world is fully determined by the concept or the logical idea.

It does not of course follow from this that we shall be able to derive or infer the details of the world from the nature of God or of the logical idea. But Hegel seems to have felt that we should not speak about divine providence if we believe this task to be an impossible one. In the context of a discussion of world history he writes:

> The question of the *perfectibility* and *education of the human race* arises here. Those who have asserted this perfectibility have seen something of the nature of the mind, of its nature of having know Thyself as the law of its *being*, and of being, when it grasps what *it is*, a higher form than that which constituted its being. But for those who reject this thought, mind has remained an empty word, just as history has remained a superficial play of *contingent*, so-called *merely human* strivings and passions. If they also in this connection express a belief in a higher power by the expressions '*providence*' and '*plan*' of providence, yet these remain unfilled conceptions, since they also expressly

declare the plan of providence to be unknowable and incomprehensible (*PR* 343).

It is, again, one of Hegel's most frequent complaints against Spinoza that while he held that everything in the universe is necessary, determined by the 'divine nature', no attempt is made in practice to show how particular features of the world are necessitated by the nature of God. They are rather left for empirical discovery:[10]

> cognition is external reflection which does not comprehend and derive what appears as finite, the determinacy of the attribute and the mode, as also in general itself, from the substance, but rather is active as an external understanding, receives the determinations as *given* and *leads* them *back* to the absolute without taking their beginnings from it (*WL* II. pp. 195 f., M. p. 537).

This, he argues, is a consequence of the fact that Spinoza

> confines himself to *negation* as *determinacy* or quality; he does not proceed to knowledge of it as absolute, i.e. as *negation which negates itself;* thus *his substance does not itself contain the absolute form,* and the knowledge of it is not immanent knowledge . . . it contains therefore thinking itself, but only in its unity with extension, i.e. not as *separating* itself from extension, thus in general not as determining and forming nor as the movement which returns and begins from itself (*WL* II. p. 195, M. pp. 536 f.).

Something has already been said to shed light on this complex and obscure passage and a further suggestion relevant to the interpretation of it will be made later.[11] The main point, however, is that Hegel strongly implies that he intends to do what Spinoza omitted to do.

Some of the passages cited are, of course, compatible with the attribution to Hegel of position (ii). To discover that the universe has a certain general logical structure which the special sciences fill out empirically is after all more than most proponents of divine providence have done. But the general tendency of the passages, together with Hegel's criticisms of the natural sciences,[12] is to suggest that the *Philosophy of Nature* is an attempt to derive features of nature from logic, a logic moreover which is itself necessary and *a priori* rather than contingent and empirical. There are, however, difficulties in the way of this view of his enterprise. In particular does Hegel adhere to position (iv) or to position (iii)?

Does he believe that the finest details of the world can be derived from logic or that only the results of the sciences can? This question will be considered in the following section.

2 *Nature and contingency*

Hegel's theological beliefs seem to imply that the empirical world is fully determined, right down to the smallest blade of grass, by the nature of God and therefore by the concept (iv). If this is so, then we should be able in principle to derive our knowledge of it from logic. This accords with Hegel's account of truth.[13] Any finite object, as we have seen, does not fully measure up to its concept. Other things with which it interacts explain both its existence and particular features of it. This is one reason, he suggests, for the apparent contingency in nature; 'In nature not only has the play of forms its unbounded, unbridled contingency, but each form (*Gestalt*) on its own lacks the concept of itself' (*Enz.* II. 248). All finite entities are more or less exposed to, and dependent on, the influence of other entities. Hegel's account of truth, however, implies that contingency of this sort is ultimately eliminable. For God or the universe as a whole is not finite in this way. There is nothing outside it to bound and interact with it. It cannot, therefore, have particular features which are due to the influence of other things nor, if it comes into and passes out of existence, can its doing so be explained by reference to them. In the case of an infinite object there is no reason for there to be any mismatch between it and its concept. If it is determined by anything at all, then it is fully determined by its concept.[14] There is a natural epistemological corollary to this. Given only the concept of an elephant, I cannot tell whether there are any elephants or how many there are, nor, in the case of any particular elephant, can I know in advance of experience what its individual features are. But when there are no extraneous factors — as there are no factors extraneous to the universe as a whole — it should be possible to discover what it is like by simply examining the concept of it. Since elephants are themselves transitory features of the universe as a whole, we should be able to ascertain the character and fate of elephants in general, or indeed of any particular elephant, by inspecting the concept of the universe. There will then be two ways of finding out about elephants or anything else, an *a posteriori* way, that is, by observation and experiment, and an *a priori* way, namely inspection of the concept of the universe. These two routes to knowledge would correspond respectively to the empirical sciences and the philosophy of nature. The *Logic*, on this account, would be an attempt to unravel or construct the concept of the universe. The *Philosophy of Nature* would be Hegel's derivation from it of the corresponding object. This again implies, then, that he is engaged in enterprise (iv), the deduction of the *minutiae* of the universe.

This, however, seems not to have been Hegel's intention. What he actually attempts in the Encyclopaedia is the more modest programme (iii), that of deriving the results of the sciences. The contingencies of nature are, he often implies, ineliminable: 'This impotence of nature sets limits to philosophy and it is quite inappropriate to require the concept to comprehend such contingencies and, as it has been called, construct or deduce them' (*Enz.* II. 250). The most obvious cases of such contingency are particular matters of fact, the fact for example that I am holding a black pen at 6.15 p.m. on 27 April 1980. But some matters which are the proper concern of the sciences are also irreducibly contingent, the number, for example, of the species of parrot (e.g. *WL* II. p. 375, M. p. 682).

Why does Hegel make this concession to contingency? There are several answers to this. One obvious answer is that it is natural enough that he should have embarked on the more ambitious enterprise (iv), but, finding himself unable to fulfil it, abandoned it for a more modest one. There are, however, at least four considerations of a systematic kind:

1. If the nature of the world or a complete description of it were derivable from pure thought, it would seem to follow that the nature of the world is necessary and not at all contingent. Hegel, however, has reasons for wishing to say that it is also contingent. His criticisms of finite concepts, for example, commit him to denying that the world is wholly necessary and not in the least contingent.[15] Moreover, the concept of contingency figures in the *Logic* as a pure thought, contrasting with such thoughts as that of necessity (*WL* II. pp. 202 ff., M. pp. 542 ff.; *Enz.* I. 145). As such, it should be exemplified in the world: 'Although contingency . . . is only a one-sided aspect of actuality and is therefore not to be confused with it, it still has its due right, as a form of the idea in general, also in the objective (*gegenständlichen*) world' (*Enz.* I. 145Z.). Presumably this requirement could have been met by the admission of the contingency of finite things on other finite things, the sort of contingency that can ultimately be reduced to necessity. But Hegel nevertheless allows an irreducible sphere of genuine contingency both in nature (*Enz.* I. 145Z, II. 248-50) and in human life (*Enz.* I. 145Z).

But if this is so, how can it be true that the world is determined by necessity, that the logical idea does not acquire any content alien to itself, but develops into nature and mind without external assistance? One of Hegel's ideas may have been that necessity 'overreaches' contingency in the sense that it is necessary that there should be some contingency or other and that, if some particular fact, thing or event is contingent, then it is necessary that it should be contingent. We might say, similarly, that it is a necessary truth that there are some contingent truths, and that, if some particular proposition is a contingent proposition, then it is necessary that it should be contingent. In this way, it might be argued, the all-embracing claims of necessity can be reconciled with the restricted claims of contingency. But surely they are not. We need, in addition, some account of how contingency arises, and of how large the realm of contingency is to be. Are contingent matters decided by factors which are in some way beyond the control of God or the logical idea? Or does he have to toss a coin, as it were, at certain points in the realization of his plan? If so, why does he have to toss a coin at those points and not at others? Why what is contingent takes one form rather than another will be inexplicable, necessarily so, and the difficulty is to see how Hegel can concede that there is anything which is ultimately inexplicable.[16]

2. Should the *Philosophy of Nature* attempt to derive the empirical world in all its detail or only the general results which scientists have arrived at? There are, if we look at Hegel's system as a whole, considerations in favour of both these answers. Schematically, he views the universe on the model of a mind, a mind which at first or 'in itself' is simply the system of pure thoughts. It then projects these thoughts, as it were, outwards so as to produce an unrefined natural world as its object, a natural world which actualizes the thoughts. Finally men emerge from nature and refine the natural realm in various ways — in empirical science, social institutions, art, religion and philosophy. Nature is reclaimed for mind, so that the world reverts to the first stage, only at a higher level.[17] It is an important feature of the *Philosophy of Nature,* as it is of Hegel's system as a whole, that it is *both* a description of this process *and* a phase of it — the culminating phase. Hegel's account of the world is to include an account of his own account.[18] The *Philosophy of Nature,* then, should be, firstly, an account of the second phase of the cosmic cycle, of the natural realm which is generated by the logical idea. But, secondly, it is a part of the third phase of the cycle, of the reclamation of nature by mind. (Incidentally, it is also a *description* of that part

of the third phase which is constituted by the activities of natural scientists.)[19]

These different roles suggest different tasks which the work is required to perform. In so far as the *Philosophy of Nature* is an account of the second phase of the cycle, we would expect an account of nature as it is independently of the activities of natural scientists, and not simply of the theories which they superimpose on it. This implies that the details of nature should be explained, that it should be shown, if it is possible, why the logical idea generates just this world and no other. In so far, however, as the work is a part of the third phase of the cycle, we need not expect so much of it. Its task is to complete the work of the empirical sciences, that is, to organize their results and show them to be necessary and *a priori*. It need not involve an account of what nature is like independently of those results. Of course, the completion of the work of the sciences might be interpreted as requiring that what the sciences left aside as contingent should be shown to be necessary.[20] If that is so, the task of such a completion would include the task of deriving from logic the details of raw nature. But it is at least not obvious that the reclamation of nature for mind requires the derivation of all its empirical *minutiae* rather than some sort of transcendence of them.

Why are these two roles of the *Philosophy of Nature* not clearly distinguished by Hegel? One reason is that both tasks involve thinking about nature and, he believes, to think about nature is to alter it or, at least, to alter one's view of it (*Enz.* I. 22).[21] But nature as it occurs in the second phase of the cycle is not yet thought about. How, then, can one give an account of it? This line of argument makes it difficult to distinguish between giving an account of nature as it is 'in itself', independently of men's cognitive activities, and giving an account of what men make of nature, namely the results of the sciences. The answer to this, however, is that there are different ways in which one can think about nature. First, we can frame general laws and ascribe natural phenomena to such entities as forces. This is the type of thinking characteristic of the natural sciences and it is what Hegel has in mind when he says that thinking alters the way in which the object is immediately presented. Secondly, we can describe nature in various general ways which contrast it with pure thought or the logical idea. Nature can be thought of, for example, as 'asunder' or as containing individuals.[22] To think of nature in this fashion is, of course, a different matter from simply perceiving it, but it does not alter our conception of it in the way that thinking of the first type does. Thirdly, we can give detailed descriptions of natural phenomena, of, for example, particular volcanic eruptions or flashes of lightning which occur at particular times and places. This, again, is more than simply perceiving phenomena, but it does not involve alteration in the way that the first type of thinking does. Roughly speaking it is statements of this third type which Hegel would need to consider and to derive from pure thought if he were giving an account of the emergence of nature from the logical idea. There are no doubt restrictions on the accuracy and completeness of our descriptions of phenomenal nature. Our perceptual and linguistic resources and the time available to us are not unlimited. But any true statement about nature should, on this view, be derivable from the logical idea. If, on the other hand, Hegel is attempting only to complete the work of the natural sciences as a part of the third phase of the cosmic cycle, then he perhaps needs to derive only statements or theories of the first type. These, however, are two distinct enterprises. To fulfil the second is not necessarily to fulfil the first. Hegel may have believed that it was, owing to his conflation of different types of thinking.[23]

3. The *Geist-* or mind-model of the universe generates some ambiguity in the nature of Hegel's enterprise. If any type of entity within the universe is taken as our model of the universe as a whole, then certain modifications will be required in our conception of that entity. Ordinary machines, for example, need to be oiled and wound up, but, if the universe as a whole is a machine, it is a machine which requires no oiling or winding — unless the model is a dualistic one in which God is the oiler, winder and repairer. Living organisms need food, water and sunlight, but the universe, if it is an organism, can dispense with this input — unless, again, God provides it. Ordinary minds, finally, do not have perceptions or sensations except in virtue of their encounters with external objects. There are in Hegel glimpses of the view that the states of the ordinary, finite mind are generated by itself. In a discussion of the pre-Kantian distinction between rational psychology — the study of the nature of the soul — and empirical psychology, we find the following:

> The mind is activity in the sense in which the scholastics said that God is absolute actuosity. But now since the mind is active, this involves its externalizing itself. One should not therefore regard the mind as a processless *ens*, as happened in the old metaphysics, which separated the processless inwardness of the mind from its externality. The mind is essentially to be seen in its concrete actuality, in its energy, and indeed in such a way

that its manifestations are cognized as determined by its inwardness (*Enz.* I. 34Z. Cf. 140 and Z).

This and similar passages perhaps need not be taken to imply that the mind itself determines the precise content of its perceptions and desires. This is in general regarded as dependent on things other than the mind itself. In this passage, Hegel may be saying only that the mind must have some perceptual states or other, some desires or other; their content depends on external things. In other passages (e.g. *WL* II, 179 ff., M. pp. 523 ff.), he is more concerned with the distinction between 'inner', mental states and their 'outer', physical expression than with the relationship between the pure self and its contingent states. Inner states, for example intentions, must have some outer manifestation in, for example, actions. But this has no bearing on the question whether or not the pure ego generates its own states.

The finite mind is analogous in some respects to the cosmic mind. The perceptions or states of a finite mind are not, as we have seen, simply other than the pure ego. It is, firstly, aware of them or 'overreaches' them. Analogously, thought overreaches what is other than thought, characterizing it, for example, as 'asunder'.[24] Secondly, pure thoughts are involved in our perceptual states, our perceptions are thought-ridden.[25] The analogue of this is the claim that thoughts are embedded in things, that an individual such as a dog is in part constituted by a pure thought, that of animality.[26] But what about the details of things? Nature seems to be the cosmic counterpart of the perceptions or perceptible objects of a finite mind. Is nature fully determined by and derivable from the cosmic ego, the logical idea? Here there will be two conflicting tendencies. If, on the one hand, we stress the similarity of the universe to a finite mind, then we shall be inclined to suppose that it is not, that all that we can explain in terms of pure thought is the general structure of nature, its form. On the other hand, there cannot be any objects external to the cosmic mind by reference to which we could account for its states. Hegel's model of the universe is intended, as we have seen, to exclude dualism.[27] If we stress this aspect of the model, then we shall suppose that it generates its own states in a way that a finite mind does not. The details of nature must then be explicable in terms of pure thought. This ambiguity has deep roots, then, in Hegel's conception of the universe.

4. W. T. Krug once challenged philosophers of nature to deduce the pen he was writing with. One might think that Hegel is committed to performing such feats as this, if he is to show that the

logical idea generates nature and mind without external assistance. But Hegel rejects the challenge (*Enz.* II. 250).[28] Why does he do so? Krug's pen was, of course, as Hegel points out, a trivial entity as compared with, for example, the solar system.But it is not clear that this entitles him to dismiss the challenge, or what his reasons are for doing so. One reason, perhaps, is that Krug's pen was an individual entity, which, unless it has some perceptible feature to distinguish it from all other pens, can be referred to only by using token-reflexive expressions or proper names. As we have already seen, Hegel believes that there are difficultues in the way of picking out or referring to some definite individual, at least if we confine ourselves to pure thoughts.[29] If this is so, however, statements about definite individuals cannot be derived from pure thought alone, unless the individual in question has some unique character- istic. Not all of the contingencies which Hegel finds in nature are of this type, of course. The statement that there are sixty different species of parrot makes no reference to individuals, but it is, on Hegel's view, contingent. Many contingent statements, however, are statements about definite individuals and these, if Hegel is right, are beyond the reach of thought. But what is the significance of this? It might be taken, on the one hand, to mean that there really are no definite individuals, even in the raw nature produced in the second phase of the cycle. If this is so, then the task of deriving the details of nature from the logical idea will be easier than it otherwise would be.[30] On the other hand, it might mean that, although there really are definite individuals, they elude the net of thought and we should therefore attempt to derive only the general results of the sciences and not the details of things. But, if this is so, a gap opens up between ontology and epistemology, between the necessary and the *a priori.* For definite individuals are produced by God or the logical idea and, unless he creates them randomly, they and their features are necessary. In practice, Hegel seems to hover between these two positions, invoking the triviality of definite individuals and the alleged impossibility of thinking about what nature is like independently of our thought about it.

These, then, are some of the reasons for the ambiguous nature of Hegel's enterprise. It is, however, clear, on any tenable view of it, that he supposed that much of what we would regard as contingent and *a posteriori* is in fact necessary and *a priori.* What general arguments does he have to support this belief? Much of the weight is borne not by argument, but by equivocation in the use of certain key words, particularly the words 'infinite' and 'concrete'.

These terms will be examined in the following two sections.

361

3 *Infinity reconsidered*

Hegel defines finitude in such ways as this: '"Finite" means, expressed formally, what has an end, what *is*, but ceases where it connects with its other and is thus limited by it. The finite therefore subsists in relation to its other, which is its negation and shows itself to be its limit' (*Enz.* I. 28Z. Cf. 94, 95). The term 'infinite' is the negation or contradictory of 'finite', and thus the definition of 'infinite' can be derived from that of 'finite' by simply negating it: 'Infinite' means what does not have an end, etc. There is, of course, the complication that, on Hegel's view, any infinite entity must also be finite, but this can be ignored in the present context.[31]

These definitions leave a number of questions unanswered. Could there be, for example, more than one infinite entity? We might suppose, on the one hand, that there could not. If there are two distinct entities, x and y, then x must cease to be where y begins and y must cease to be where x begins. Each of the two will then be finite. On the other hand, it is not obvious that two distinct entities must 'connect' with, or be 'limited' by, each other. Might they not be distinct, yet independent and unrelated and, therefore, infinite? The best examples of this come from the sphere of what Hegel would call 'bad infinity'.[32] The numerical series

$$1, 3, 5, 7, 9, \ldots$$

and

$$2, 4, 6, 8, 10, \ldots$$

are both, in one sense, infinite. Neither of them comes to an end. Yet they are distinct. However far we continue one of the series, we shall never arrive at the other. Neither of them connects with or limits the other. A more interesting example is provided by the recent suggestion that it is logically possible for there to be two distinct, but spatially unrelated, spaces.[33] No part of a single space, even if it is infinite in extent, could be infinite in the sense of Hegel's definition. It is spatially bounded or limited by other parts of the same space. If it were not, then it would not be a part of it. But neither of the two distinct spaces would be spatially bounded by each other or by anything else. Each of them would, as far as this goes, satisfy Hegel's requirements for infinity. Nor need it be bad infinity. Each of the spaces might be spherical or, as it were, finite but unbounded.[34] If this were so, then travelling for long enough in a straight line in either one of the spaces would bring one back to one's starting-point, but, since each is spatially unrelated to the other, it would never take one into the other space.

Another example of distinct, yet infinite, entities — this time one with which Hegel was familiar — is supplied by Spinoza's account of the attributes of substance. Thought and extension are two of the attributes of God, the only two to which we have access, but each of them is infinite in the sense that each is, as it were, co-extensive with substance as a whole and neither limits or depends on the other.[35] Neither of them is infinite in the way that substance is, 'absolutely' infinite, but each of them is infinite 'after its kind':[36]

> A thing is called *finite after its kind*, when it can be limited by another thing of the same nature; for instance, a body is called finite because we always conceive another greater body. So, also, a thought is limited by another thought, but a body is not limited by thought, nor a thought by body.

Thought as a whole and extension as a whole evidently cannot be finite in this sense.

What would Hegel say about such cases as these? Firstly, he would argue, as we have seen, that if something is the case, then it must be possible for us to know that it is the case.[37] This implies that if there are two distinct entities, then they must be related to the extent that *either* one is cognitively accessible to the other *or* both are accessible to some third entity. In the case of two distinct spaces, it is a third entity which would have such access, namely the observer who can move (non-spatially) from one space to the other, successively inhabiting each space in turn and drawing the distinction between them.[38] But if this is so, then the spaces are distinct in virtue of a relation between them, not indeed a spatial relation, but one that is sufficient to render each of them finite in Hegel's sense. Each one in a sense ends where the other begins, is bounded or limited by the other. In the case of Spinoza's attributes, by contrast, one of the attributes 'overreaches' the other, we can, that is, think about extension. Thought and extension are not two distinct, co-ordinate entities. Thought is, as it were, all-embracing and, therefore, infinite in a sense in which extension is not.[39] Secondly, Hegel would argue that if two entities are qualitatively different from each other, then there must be some relationship between them which makes them different. We might be inclined to suppose that this relationship need be no more than the conceptual one between the different descriptions applicable to the two entities. But, as we have seen, Hegel believes that actual relationships mirror conceptual relationships.[40] If x is different from y, then x must be related in some way or other to y. But if this is so, then x and y cannot be both distinct from each other and infinite. The probability is, then, that Hegel believes that there can only be one infinite entity. We have already seen that, although he holds that the ego is — from one point of view, at least — infinite, he also believes that to the extent that men think purely they cease to be distinct, countable entities.[41]

Thought, Hegel repeatedly tells us, is infinite. It presumably follows from this that the logical idea is infinite 'after its kind'. There could not be more than one system of thoughts, each of them conceptually unrelated to the others. The logical idea embraces the whole field of pure thought.[42] But what are its implications for the relationship between thought and what is, *prima facie* at least, other than thought? Does it mean only that thought is in some sense autonomous and self-contained? If that were so, then it leaves open the possibility that nature is entirely distinct from thought and that statements about nature cannot be derived from logic alone without recourse to experience. Does it mean that we can think about nature? Or does it mean that nature is generated or constituted by thought? The answer is that Hegel believed thought to be infinite in several apparently different ways, ways which he nowhere clearly distinguishes:

(i) Pure thinking or thought is non-empirical; it does not depend on sensory data derived from external objects for its occurrence or character.[43]

(ii) It does not have an object which is distinct from itself, but is self-reflexive; it is its own object (*Enz.* I. 28Z).[44] Thought can in this way be conceived of as a circle, for reflexivity, the relatedness of a thing to itself, is naturally represented by a circle, a figure which is, on Hegel's view, the symbol of true infinity.

(iii) Thought cannot assign limits to itself, but, as it were, transcends them in the very act of setting them (*Enz.* I. 28Z, 60). This, as we have seen, has a variety of implications. It means, for example, that it does not presuppose any fixed rules which it cannot itself justify.[45]

(iv) It does not treat thoughts or concepts as rigid and exclusive, but as in some sense flowing into one another (*Enz.* I. 25).[46]

(v) It overreaches what is other than itself. When the 'sensuous' is characterized as 'individual' and 'asunder', individuality and asunderness are pure thoughts (*Enz.* I. 20).[47]

(vi) Thought or thoughts are embedded in what is other than thought. The thought of animality, for example, is essentially involved in a particular dog and thought is involved in our other psychological states and activities (*Enz.* I. 3, 24Z, 25).[48]

(vii) Thought 'freely releases itself' into the empirical world without any external assistance (*WL* II. p. 573, M. p. 843). If, and only if, thought is infinite in this way, we might be able, in principle at least, to derive the details of the world from thinking alone.

When Hegel speaks about the infinity of thought or thoughts, more than one sense of 'infinity' is generally in play. It is often difficult to tell which sense he has in mind. The following passage, for example, seems to involve senses (iv) and (vi) or (vii):

> If the thought-determinations are encumbered with a fixed opposition, i.e. are of a merely *finite* nature, then they are unsuitable to the truth which is absolutely in and for itself, then the truth cannot enter into thinking. Thinking which brings forth only *finite* determinations and operates with them is called *understanding* [(iv)] . . . . More precisely the *finitude* of thought-determinations is to be conceived of in two ways: the one, that they are *only subjective* and have a persistent opposite in the objective [(vi) or (vii)], the other that they, being of a *restricted content* in general, remain in opposition to each other [(iv)] as well as to the absolute [(vi) or (vii)] (*Enz.* I. 25).

In this passage some attempt is made to distinguish different senses of 'finite', though they are assumed to coincide. No such attempt is made in the following passage:

> But thinking is at home with itself, is related to itself and has itself for an object [(ii)]. When I have a thought as my object, I am at home with myself. I, thinking, is (*ist*) accordingly infinite, because it relates itself to an object which is itself. An object in general is an other, a negative over against me. If thinking thinks itself, then it has an object which is yet no object, i.e. a sublimated, ideal object [(ii)]. Thinking as such, in its purity, therefore has no barrier in itself [(iii)?]. Thinking is only finite in so far as it sticks to limited determinations, which it regards as ultimate. Infinite or speculative thinking, by contrast, also determines, but in determining, limiting, it again eliminates this defect [(iv)] (*Enz.* I. 28Z).

Hegel often associates 'finite' thinking, thinking which is conducted in such a way that it fails to be infinite, with 'formal' thinking or 'formal' logic, and the word 'formal' has many of the same ambiguities as 'finite' does.[49] When he says that the 'idea is thinking not as formal, but as the self-developing totality of its peculiar determinations and laws, which it gives to itself and does not already *have* and find in itself' (*Enz.* I. 19), he means that thinking is infinite in sense (iii), that it does not presuppose any rules or laws of thought. Elsewhere, however, the denial that thinking is formal has a different point. Hegel criticizes the view that the thinking of which logic is the science

> constitutes the *mere form* of a cognition, that logic abstracts from all *content* and the so-called second *constituent* . . . the *matter,* must be given from elsewhere, that therefore logic, of which this matter is entirely independent, can give only the formal conditions of true cognition, but cannot contain real truth nor even be just the *way* to real truth, because the essential of truth, the content, lies outside it' (*WL* I. p. 36, M. pp. 43 f.).

In this passage, the denial that thinking is formal seems on the face of it to mean that it is infinite in sense (vii), that nothing other than thought or thought-determinations is required for there to be an empirical world. In the following paragraphs, however, several distinct senses in which thinking is infinite, or is not merely formal, are at issue: (ii) and, perhaps, (v) and (vi). Hegel tends to claim that thinking, if it is done properly, is infinite in a sense which is naturally understood as (vii), and then to support this claim with arguments which establish only that it is infinite in some different, weaker sense.

We have already seen that there are connections between at least some of these ways in which thinking might be said to be infinite.[50] But, on the face of it, (i)–(vii) are distinct types or senses of 'infinity'. In particular, if thinking is infinite in any of ways (i)–(vi), this does not supply any immediate or obvious reason for supposing that it is infinite in sense (vii), that it generates the empirical world of its own accord. If there is any transition from (i)–(vi) to (vii), then it should be substantiated by argument and not shrouded in ambiguity.

4 *The concrete universals*

Another term whose ambiguity clouds these issues is 'concrete', particularly when it is used in the expression 'concrete universal'. These expressions contrast respectively with 'abstract' and 'abstract universal'. Hegel has in mind several different points when he contrasts the abstract with the concrete and, correspondingly, what counts as abstract and what as concrete differs with the context.

(i) The adjective 'abstract' is connected with the verb 'to abstract' (*abstrahieren*), and one strand in Hegel's thought is his hostility to the idea of forming concepts by abstracting from those respects in which a group of individuals differ from each other and retaining those features which they have in common. This matter is complicated. There are, firstly, three distinct types of concept with which he is concerned: (a) non-empirical, pure thoughts such as those of being and of causality; (b) empirical concepts such as those of a plant, a man or a house which apply to individuals of a certain type (*Enz.* I. 163Z.1, 164); (c) empirical concepts such as that of redness which pick out a single feature of 'concrete' individuals, individuals which may be of widely different types. Secondly, there are three distinct theses which he might be advancing with respect to each of these types of concept. The theses are not in general clearly distinguished by Hegel himself:

1. Such concepts never are formed by abstraction from sensible individuals, but they are wrongly believed to be.

2. Such concepts sometimes are formed in this way, and that is a mistake. They should be formed in some other way.

3. Such concepts always are formed by abstraction, and this is inevitable, since there is no other way in which they could be formed. This means, however, that they are defective or second-rate concepts.

With respect to pure thoughts, concepts of type (a), Hegel does not, of course, hold thesis 3. For, as we have seen, he believes that pure thoughts can be constructed independently of the sensible individuals to which they apply. The probability is that he holds thesis 2, namely that pure thoughts can, but should not, be formed by abstraction. But his views about empirical concepts, especially those of type (b), are equivocal. In the following passage, for example, he leaves it quite unclear which of the three theses is being asserted:

> When we speak of the concept, it is usually only abstract universality which we have in mind .... One speaks accordingly of the concept of colour, of the plant, of the animal, etc., and these concepts are supposed (*sollen*) to arise by our leaving out the particular, by which the different colours, plants, animals, etc. are distinguished from each other, and retaining what is common to them. This is how the understanding conceives concepts, and feeling (*das Gefühl*) is right when it regards such concepts as hollow and empty, as mere phantoms and shadows. But the universal of the concept is not something that things have in common (*ein Gemeinschaftliches*), confronted by the particular which takes its stand over against it, but rather it particularizes (specifies) itself and, in its other, remains

at home with itself in undisturbed clarity (*Enz.* I. 163Z.1).

A later passage, however, suggests that what Hegel has in mind is thesis 3:

> What are also called concepts, and indeed determinate concepts, e.g. man, house, animal, etc., are simple determinations and abstract conceptions. Abstractions which take from the concept only the element of universality and leave out particularity and individuality are then not developed within themselves and thus abstract precisely from the concept (*Enz.* I. 164).

There is no suggestion here that the concepts mentioned are not really, or need not be, abstract. They are implied to be irretrievably abstract, though it is not, of course, specified that their abstractness depends on their having been formed by a process of abstraction. Elsewhere, by contrast, Hegel maintains that our concepts of biological species are not derived by abstracting from what differentiates the members of a species from each other and retaining what they have in common. His argument is that some members of a species lack one or more of the defining features of the species to which they nevertheless belong, because they are defective — damaged or freakish — specimens. We might, for example, wish to make it a defining feature of a horse that it is a quadruped, despite the fact that there are freak or damaged horses with more or fewer than four legs. We might, again, define a man as a rational animal capable of thought, despite the existence of defective men who are incapable of thought. But, if we do this, then we cannot be putting into our concept of a horse or of a man only what all horses or all men have in common:

> The impotence of nature to hold fast to the concept in its realization involves the difficulty and in many spheres the impossibility of finding fixed distinctions for classes and orders from empirical inquiry. Nature everywhere blurs the essential limits by intermediate and defective structures, which always provide instances against any fixed distinction, even within determinate genera (e.g. that of man), through freaks, which must be assigned to this genus and yet lack determinations which should be regarded as the essential characteristics of the genus. — To enable us to consider such structures defective, imperfect, deformed, a fixed type (*Typus*) is presupposed, but this could not be derived from experience, for experience presents those so-called freaks, deformities, intermediate things etc. as well: it would rather presuppose the independence and worth of the determination of the concept (*Enz.* II. 250).

Hegel often attributes to the 'impotence of nature' features such as contingency and determination from without which occur in the realm of mind as well. This is a case in point. For in the parallel passage in the *Science of Logic,* he adds that states or governments may fail to live up to their concept or definition:

> If therefore what is bad (*das Schlechte*) is also supposed to be covered by the definition, then empirical inquiry is eluded by all properties which it wanted to regard as essential through instances of freaks which lack them, e.g. the essentiality of the brain for physical men through the instance of acephalous men, the essentiality of the protection of life and property for the state through the instance of despotic states and tyrannical régimes (*WL* II. p. 518, M. pp. 799 f.).

In these passages, then, Hegel seems to be denying thesis 3 with respect to the concepts of biological species and of the state. It does not, of course, follow that experience plays no part in the formation of such concepts nor even that it plays as limited a role as it does in the formation of pure thoughts, and this may be one reason for the apparent conflict with other passages. But Hegel's assertions here, especially in the light of his characteristic over-statement − 'this could not be derived from experience' − are hard to reconcile with his other account of the formation of empirical concepts of type (b). One might be tempted to resolve the conflict by saying that, on Hegel's view, empirical concepts can be formed in two different ways, first by abstraction from empirical phenomena, and secondly by deriving them from pure thought. On this account concepts would have to be formed empirically before we could derive them *a priori* in the *Philosophy of Nature.* But this suggestion cannot be correct, for two reasons. Firstly, concepts of biological species which presuppose a 'type' are, on Hegel's view, employed by empirical naturalists before they encounter the philosophy of nature. Our ordinary concepts do not simply express the highest common factor of all the members of a species. But if this is so, then, on Hegel's view, they cannot be derived from experience even initially. Secondly, Hegel does not in practice purport to derive anything more than very general biological concepts like those of an animal, a plant, and a man. Specific concepts like those of a lion, a tiger, and a parrot find no place in the *Philosophy of Nature.* But these specific concepts presuppose a type just as much as the more general ones, a type which cannot, according to Hegel, be derived from experience. If concepts which presuppose a type were supposed to be derived *a priori* in the *Philosophy of Nature,* he should show no hesitation over assigning specific biological concepts a place in it. There is, then, little chance of associating these two accounts of concept-formation with the two epistemic routes to nature which Hegel's system seems to provide. The truth is that Hegel has not provided us with enough information to decide what he really thought. Here, as elsewhere, he supplies isolated insights rather than a systematic account.

(ii) Hegel regards a number of actual individual entities as universal and he uses the expression 'concrete universal' or 'concrete concept' in this context. There seems to be no single feature or pair of features which makes them both universal and concrete. Rather, a diverse variety of considerations are in play:

1. The intelligence (*die Intelligenz*) is regarded as universal and concrete not because it is a faculty common to indefinitely many human beings, but for such reasons as the following:

> To grasp the intelligence as this nocturnal mine in which a world of infinitely many images and conceptions is stored without being in consciousness is, firstly, the universal requirement of conceiving the concept as concrete, like e.g. the seed, which *affirmatively* contains all the *determinacies* which come to *existence* only in the development of the tree in *virtual* potentiality. The inability to grasp this universal which is internally concrete and yet remains *simple* is what has given rise to talk about the storing of particular conceptions in particular fibres and areas [of the brain]; what is diverse, it is supposed, essentially has, too, an individual existence in space. But the seed emerges from the existing determinations to *return* to its simplicity, to the existence of being-in-itself (*des Ansichseins*), only in something else, the seed of the fruit. But the intelligence is as such the free *existence* of the *being-in-itself* which recalls itself into itself in its development. Therefore the intelligence is to be conceived, secondly, as this *unconscious* mine, i.e. as the *existing* universal, in which what is diverse is not yet posited as discrete (*Enz*. III. 453).

The general idea of this passage is that images and conceptions are implicit in one's mind even when one is not actually conscious of them, in much the way that the features of a full-grown tree are implicit in its seed. The seed differs from the mind in that once the features of the tree have become explicit, have emerged from the seed, they cannot be withdrawn back into it. The return to primitive simplicity requires a distinct seed, produced by the tree which emerged from the first seed. A man, by contrast, can call up an image and then let it lapse again into his unconscious mind. The intelligence and the seed are each both universal and concrete. They are universal owing to their simple indeterminacy. They are concrete both because of what they contain implicitly and because they actually exist.

2. The will is regarded as universal and concrete for rather different reasons, but, again, not because it is common to all men:

[The will] is *universal,* because in it all limitation and particular individuality is sublimated, for these lie only in the difference between the concept and its object or content, or, in other words, in the difference between its subjective being-for-itself – and its being-in-itself, between its *exclusive* and resolving individuality – and its very universality (*PR* 24).

If the will were universal for the same reason as the intelligence is, then we would expect Hegel's point to be that it can choose between a variety of alternatives, but is not inextricably bound to any one of them. The point, however, is not this, but rather that, if the will is genuinely free, then it has, in some obscure sense, itself as its own goal. There is then no mismatch between the indeterminacy of the will as such – its 'universality' – and the particular, determinate option which it chooses.[51] Hegel goes on to distinguish this sort of universality from 'abstract and external' universality:

It is the universality which is internally *concrete* and thus for itself, the universality which is the substance, the immanent genus or the immanent idea of self-consciousness – the concept of the free will, as the universal which *overreaches* its object, *runs through its determination* and in this determination is identical with self (*Ibid.*).

3. For similar reasons, the mind is universal and yet concrete: 'The absolutely-concrete is the mind . . . – the concept, in so far as it, as concept, distinguishing itself from its objectivity, which remains despite the distinguishing *its* objectivity, *exists*' (*Enz.* I. 164. Cf. 20, 24Z). This is what we would expect, for Hegel does not regard the thinking ego and the will as two distinct entities, but rather as different aspects or attitudes of the same entity (*PR* 4Z, *Enz.* III. 443 and Z). We have already seen that he has a variety of reasons for ascribing universality and concreteness to the ego.[52]

4. A society or a state is generally regarded as universal and yet concrete (e.g. *PR* 258). There are several reasons for this:

(a) One accepts, generally, the laws and norms of one's own society unquestioningly and does not, or need not, look beyond them for their justification (*Enz.* I. 82Z).

(b) The laws and institutions of a society embody thought and are, therefore, universal (*Enz.* III. 485).

(c) A state or a society outlives the particular individuals who make it up at any one time. It is replenished by successive generations of them in something like the way in which a biological species is.

(d) A developed state is self-organizing or self-articulating, like a biological organism. It does not depend on external influences and contrasts for its inner character (*Enz.* III. 536 ff.; *PR* 263Z, 269Z). We have already seen that Hegel associates this feature with determination by a concept.[53]

(e) A developed state is insulated against external, especially natural, influences to the extent that it 'overreaches' nature. Nature is transformed and absorbed by cultivation, decoration and so on, and men's natural needs and instincts are socialized and utilized in its workings (*Enz.* III. 485).[54]

Hegel is clearly prepared to assign concrete universality to actual things for a variety of reasons. The expression has hardly any meaning at all independently of the context in which it occurs. There are, however, several more precise points which the phrase is intended to convey:

(iii) The distinction between abstract and concrete universality is sometimes equated with the distinction between a universal which merely characterizes individual entities and a universal which constitutes them. We have already seen that, on Hegel's view, animality constitutes the individuals to which it belongs. The word 'animal' differs in this respect from words such as 'red', 'bachelor' or 'king'.[55] This is one of the points made in the following passage:

> This common element is either some *particular* aspect of the object raised into the *form* of *universality*, as e.g. the *red colour* in the rose, or *the concretely universal,* e.g. the *plant* in the rose — but in each case a conception (*Vorstellung*) which comes about through the *dissolution,* proceeding from the intelligence, of the empirical connexion of the manifold determinations of the object (*Enz.* III. 456Z).

Planthood and redness are here on a par in the sense that they are both universals which may inhere in indefinitely many actual roses, but they differ in their relationship to actual roses. How they do so becomes clearer in the following passage:

If we consider e.g. Gaius, Titus, Sempronius and the other
inhabitants of a town or country, then their all being men is
not merely something common to them, but their *universal,*
their *genus,* and all these individuals would not exist at all
(*wären gar nicht*) without this genus. It is otherwise however
with that superficial, merely so-called universality which is in
fact merely what belongs to all individuals [of a certain class]
and is what they have in common. It has been noted that men
are distinguished from animals by the fact that they all have
ear-lobes. It is clear however that if some man or other were
supposed to lack ear-lobes, his being in other respects, his
character, his capacities etc., would not be affected, whereas
it would be senseless to suppose that Gaius could fail to be a
man and yet be courageous, learned, etc. The individual man is
what he is in particular only in so far as he is before everything
else a man as such and in general and this universal is not only
something outside and next to other abstract qualities or mere
determinations of reflection, but rather what permeates and
embraces in itself everything particular (*Enz.* I. 175Z).

Hegel is here arguing that the general features of a thing are of
two sorts: those features its possession of which is a necessary
condition of its possession of very many other features and those
features for which this is not the case. Features of the first type
e.g. animality, planthood and personhood, are concrete universals,
those of the second are abstract universals. On the face of it, this
difference seems to be one of degree. My being an animal, for
example, is more fundamental than my being a person in the sense
that more of my other properties depend upon it. A person is
necessarily an animal, but an animal is not necessarily a person.
Many of the things I currently do, such as walking, could be done
just as well if I were not a person, as long as I remained an animal.
Similarly my being a person is more fundamental than my being
English or lazy, and so on. Hegel seems to require, however, a
difference of kind and not simply one of degree, a difference, for
example, between those of my properties which are such that, if
I lacked one of them, then I would not exist and those properties
which, although I possess them, are not necessary for my existence.
We have already seen that the pure thought-determinations are, on
Hegel's view, essential in this sense to the entities to which they
belong. For example, it is essential to lightning that it is the
manifestation of a force in a way that it is not essential to it that
it is yellow.[56] We have also seen, however, that there is no reason
to believe that it is only thought-determinations which are essential

in this sense. Rosehood, for example, might be as essential to roses as planthood or life.[57] Whether such a distinction can be drawn or not is a difficult matter. More will be said about its implications later.[58]

(iv) The distinction between abstract and concrete universals is sometimes drawn in a different way. An abstract universal involves only a single feature of a thing, which is kept sharply distinct from, is abstracted from, other features of it. A concrete universal, by contrast, involves several distinct, but intertwined, universal features. Hegel has this sense of 'concrete' in mind when, in the context of a discussion of the question whether a concept can be true or false, he argues that a concept can be contradictory because 'the concept, being a concrete entity (*als Konkretes*), and even every determinacy in general is essentially within itself a unity of distinct determinations' (*Enz.* I. 33). He also has it in mind when he contrasts a rose with its redness: 'Red e.g. is an abstract, sensuous conception . . . . But a rose which is red is a concrete red, in which many such abstract features can be distinguished and isolated' (*VGP* I. p. 45, H. I. p. 26. Cf. *Enz.* I. 172Z). The actual rose is concrete, but Hegel does not say, in this passage, that it is also universal. The concept of a rose, however, would presumably be both concrete and universal, for unlike redness it involves several distinct features.

One might be tempted to suppose that this distinction coincides with the previous one, namely that between universals which are essential to the entities in which they inhere and universals which are not. Essential universals such as personhood, planthood and animality are, after all, on the whole concrete in the sense that they involve several features. This temptation must be resisted, however. For, firstly, whereas there is, on Hegel's view, a case for saying that the distinction between essential and inessential universals is one of kind, this new distinction is clearly one of degree and not of kind. Secondly, some universals or concepts are concrete in the sense that they are complex, but abstract in the sense of inessential. The concept of a bachelor, for example, is a relatively complex one, but a man does not cease to exist when he ceases to be a bachelor.

Are the concepts of Hegel's *Logic* concrete in this sense? There are at least two ways in which this notion of concreteness and abstractness applies to the *Logic*. Firstly, pure thoughts which figure earlier in the system are more abstract and less concrete than later ones. The concept of pure being is abstract, because it is simple and 'empty' (*Enz.* I. 36, 49, 86). The historical philosophies, which embody pure thoughts, run parallel to the logical idea in this respect:

> Just as the unfolding of the logical idea proves to be an advance
> from the abstract to the concrete, so too in the history of
> philosophy the earliest systems are the most abstract and thus
> also the poorest ... the later contain the earlier sublimated in
> themselves (*Enz.* I. 86Z.2).

The earlier, simpler thoughts are involved in the later, more
complex ones. As we have seen, one of Hegel's ideas seems to be
that the culminating thought of the *Logic*, the absolute idea, is
supremely concrete in the sense that it embraces the whole realm
of pure thought and there is no thought which it does not already
contain.[59] Secondly, since the pure thoughts hang together so as
to form a single system, the logical idea as a whole is concrete; it
is, like the absolute idea, supremely concrete (*Enz.* I. 14). The
concept of pure being, for example, though it is in itself abstract,
is a part of a single, concrete idea.

(v) A universal may also be called abstract if it is distinct from —
abstracted or cut off from — the things which possess, exemplify
or embody it. The concept of redness or the universal *redness* is
abstract in this sense because it is distinct from, or treated as
distinct from, actual red things. The concept of a rose, however,
would also be abstract in this sense, although it is concrete in
several other senses ((i), (iii) and (iv)). For the concept of a rose
or the universal *rosehood* is not the same as actual roses. Nor, on
the face of it, can we infer from a consideration of the universal
or the concept that there are any actual roses at all. Is the logical
idea abstract in this sense? Hegel sometimes says that it is:

> Nothing is said more frequently than that the concept is
> something *abstract.* This is correct, firstly, in so far as thinking
> in general and not the empirically concrete sensuous is its
> element, secondly, in so far as it is not yet the *idea* (*Enz.* I. 164).

Part of the point of this is that the logical idea or the concept is
not the empirical world and that an account of it is not the same
as an account of the empirical world. But the logical idea might
nevertheless be concrete in the sense that the actual world, or
statements about it, are in some way derivable from it without the
assistance of additional sensory material. It is with the question
whether the logical idea is concrete in this sense that this chapter
is primarily concerned.

These contrasts between the abstract and the concrete are, on
the face of it, distinct from each other. Hegel and/or his editors
tend to run them together. The following passage, for example,
involves at least three different senses of these terms:

It is perverse to assume that there are first the objects which form the content of our conceptions and then afterwards along comes our subjective activity which by the aforesaid operation of abstracting and collecting together what is common to the objects forms the concepts of them [(i)]. The concept rather is what is truly first and things are what they are through the activity of the concept which dwells in them and reveals itself in them [(iii)?]. This is expressed in our religious consciousness by our saying that God has created the world out of nothing or, in other words, that the world and finite things have emerged from the fullness of divine thoughts and divine decrees. This is a recognition that the thought and more precisely the concept is the infinite form or the free creative activity which needs the presence of no stuff outside itself in order to realize itself [(v)] (*Enz.* I. 163Z.2).

There is, however, no obvious connection between these three notions. One might suppose that if a universal constitutes the individuals in which it inheres, is concrete in sense (iii), then we cannot derive it, or the corresponding concept, from them by abstraction. The argument would run as follows. If we are to form a concept by considering a group of individuals which exemplify it, then we must recognize them as distinct individuals. But if the concept is a constitutive one, then the individuals could not be distinct individuals if they did not exemplify it. To recognize them as distinct individuals we must, therefore, already possess the concept in question, if not the word for it, and we cannot, therefore, acquire it by abstraction from them. This argument is, however, unsound. It is doubtful, firstly, whether our ability to acquire such concepts does presuppose that we are already able to individuate things in the way indicated by the concept. We might, for example, acquire the concept of a man by being shown men, even if we could not, as yet, distinguish one man from another or count the number of men before us.[60] Secondly, even if the acquisition of such a concept did presuppose an ability to individuate instances of it, it would not follow that we needed to possess the concept already in order to do this. The fact that x could not be a distinct individual if it were not an F does not entail that we could not pick it out as a distinct individual unless we could recognize it as an F.

Again, the fact that a universal or a concept constitutes the individuals in which it inheres or to which it applies, that it is concrete in sense (iii), does not entail that it is concrete in sense (v), that it 'needs the presence of no stuff outside itself in order to realize itself'. One cannot, on the face of it, infer from a consideration of the concept of an animal or of a man that there are any animals or any men, even if we grant that animality and manhood in some sense constitute individual animals and individual men.

Perhaps the most important confusion is this. Hegel tends to run together the question whether universals (or concepts) are distinct from each other, whether, that is, they are abstract in sense (iv), with the question whether they are distinct from the individuals which exemplify them, whether, that is, they are abstract in sense (iii) and/or (v). In his discussion of the three aspects of logic, for example, he remarks that the understanding 'sticks to the fixed determinacy and the distinctness of it from others' (*Enz.* I. 80).[61] What is at issue here is the distinctness of one 'determinacy' from another, but the addition which follows has in mind its distinctness from actual things. It says that the 'activity of the understanding' is to 'give to its content the form of universality' and adds that such a universal is[62]

> an abstract universal, which as such is kept firmly opposed to the particular, but is thereby itself determined as something which is again particular. Since the understanding approaches its objects by separation and abstraction, it is thus the opposite of immediate intuition and sensation, which has to do entirely with what is concrete and sticks to it (*Enz.* I. 80Z).

But what is the connection between these two types of separation, separation from other universals and separation from concrete particulars? One line of thought might be that an actual particular is not only concrete in the sense that it *has* very many universal features, but *is* simply a combination of universal features which intertwine so as to form an actual individual. If, therefore, our universal concepts were concrete in sense (iv), they would not be distinct from actual things, for they too would be or involve a combination of universal features. But this argument is mistaken. Even if actual things are combinations of universals, they are not the same sort of combination as our concepts involve. The universal *unicorn* or the concept of a unicorn is, for example, relatively concrete in sense (iv). But it is wholly distinct and separate from actual unicorns, since there are no actual unicorns.

Another line of thought to be found in Hegel is that if one separates in thought the various features of a concrete object from one another, then they are regarded as universal. This, as we have seen, is supposed to happen in analysis: 'Analysis proceeds from the concrete . . . . It establishes distinctions [which] then become once more only abstract determinations, i.e. *thoughts'* (*Enz.* I. 38Z).[63] We have also seen that, on Hegel's view, the ability to attend to one feature of a thing to the exclusion of others involves the ability to form general concepts.[64] This in itself is questionable. We can, for example, speak of the redness of a particular thing or of its surface as well as of redness or surfaces in general. There seems to be no reason why one should not be able simply to attend to such features even if one lacks general concepts or even the capacity to form them. But even if Hegel were right about this, it would establish only that anything that was abstract in the sense of separated from entities of the same general order, abstract, that is, in sense (iv), was also universal: only universals can be abstract. It does not follow from this that a universal which is concrete in sense (iv) is also concrete in sense (v) or even (iii).

This confusion seems to play a part in the transition from logic to nature. The notion of concreteness is connected with that of a totality (*Totalität*), and this term is used, with apparent ambiguity, to license the transition. The logical idea is, firstly, a concrete totality in sense (iv):[65]

> The free and genuine thought is internally *concrete,* and thus it is [an] *idea,* and in its whole universality *the* idea or *the absolute.* The science of it is essentially a *system,* because the true as *concrete* is only as unfolding itself within itself and drawing and holding itself into unity, i.e. as a *totality,* and the necessity of it and the freedom of the whole depends on the distinguishing and determining of its distinctions (*Enz.* I. 14).

It is not obvious, however, that the fact that the logical idea is a concrete totality in this sense, and that logic is correspondingly an interlocking system, entails the possibility of a transition to nature. Similarly the fact that arithmetic can be constructed *a priori,* with different types of number being derived from one another, does not entail its applicability to the world, let alone the concrete details of the world to which it is applied. In the next paragraph, however, the fact that the idea is a totality in this sense is taken to explain the transition to nature:

> Each of the parts of philosophy is a philosophical whole, a circle which closes upon itself . . . . The individual circle, because it is a totality within itself (*in sich*), also breaks through the barrier of its element and grounds (*begründet*) a further sphere (*Enz.* I. 15).

We would have understood this more readily, if, instead of saying that each of the circles is a 'totality within itself', Hegel had said that philosophy as a whole, the 'circle of circles', forms a single totality in just the way that each individual circle does. This would mean that just as we can move from any phase of the *Logic* to any other phase of it without recourse to experience, so we can move from any part of philosophy to any other part. This would, of course, still leave some problems. How, for example, can we legitimately pass from the relatively general concepts of the *Logic*, which stand at least some chance of being *a priori*, to the empirical concerns of the rest of the system? How can we establish, in this way, that the conceptions we derive are actually exemplified, that the world corresponds to our system? But, in any case, this is not Hegel's argument. He seems to believe that the transition from logic to nature is different in kind from transitions within logic itself:

> When . . . the idea posits itself as the absolute *unity* of the pure concept and its reality, thus contracting itself into the immediacy of *being*, then it *is* the totality in this form — *nature*. This deter-mination is not, however, a *having-become (Gewordensein)* and *transition,* as . . . the subjective concept in its totality *becomes objectivity,* and *subjective purpose becomes life.* The pure idea, in which the determinacy or reality of the concept itself is raised to the concept, is rather an absolute *liberation,* for which there is no longer any immediate determination which is not just as much *posited* and the concept; in this freedom, therefore, no transition takes place; the simple being to which the idea determines itself remains fully transparent to it and is the concept which, in its determination, remains at home with itself. The passage is, therefore, here to be understood rather in the sense that the idea *freely releases* itself, absolutely sure of itself and at rest within itself (*WL* II. p. 573, M. p. 843).

It is clear from this otherwise obscure passage that something special is supposed to happen at the end of the *Logic*, something of a kind which has not happened within the *Logic*. The fact that logic is a totality, and a circular totality at that, explains why it spills over into another totality, nature. But how does it do that? There is, on the face of it, no reason to suppose that a self-generating, interlocking system of one kind will necessarily 'freely release itself' into other such systems. One might be tempted to conclude that Hegel is using the word 'totality' ambiguously to mean, firstly, an interlocking, self-contained system and, secondly, an all-embracing system, and that he is wrongly assuming that if the logical idea is a totality in the first sense, then it is a totality in the second sense too.

But this is not the whole story. The transition from logic to nature does indeed take place under the cover of such terms as 'infinite', 'concrete', 'universal' and 'totality', terms which have a number of unclear senses. There are, however, arguments for the transition to be found in Hegel and some of these will be considered in the following sections.

5 'Conceiving a thing which is unconceived'

One argument depends on the fact that the relationship between thought and what is, *prima facie* at least, other than thought is prefigured within thought itself. Thought, so to speak, overreaches both itself and what is other than itself.[66] Thought is, for example, universal, while nature is individual and particular; thought is necessary, whereas nature is contingent; thought is the subject or it is subjective, while nature is the object or is objective. But the concepts which we apply to what is not thought, those of particularity, individuality, contingency, objectivity, and so on are themselves pure thoughts (*Enz.* I. 20).[67] Hegel objects, as we have seen, to any form of dualism: 'In every dualistic system, but especially that of Kant, a basic flaw can be seen in the inconsistency of *unifying* what a moment before was declared to be independent and thus *ununifiable*' (*Enz.* I. 60). One of the points which he has in mind is that if there is, or is known to be, a dualism of, for example, thought and nature, then both of the terms and the relation between them must be accessible to one or both of the terms. The duality of thought and nature, for example, is accessible to thought, is something which we can think about.[68] But, since this is so, there is no proper duality, for one of the terms embraces and unifies both of them. There is perhaps a generic resemblance between Hegel's argument and the following argument of Berkeley:[69]

> *Philonous.* But . . . I am content to put the whole upon this issue. If you can conceive it possible for any mixture or combination of qualities, or any sensible object whatever, to exist without the mind, then I will grant it actually to be so.
> *Hylas.* If it comes to that, the point will soon be decided. What more easy than to conceive a tree or house existing by itself, independent of, and unperceived by any mind whatsoever? I do at this present time conceive them existing after that manner.
> *Phil.* How say you, Hylas, can you see a thing which is at the same time unseen?
> *Hyl.* No, that were a contradiction.

Phil. Is it not as great a contradiction to talk of *conceiving* a thing which is *unconceived*?

Hyl. It is.

Phil. The tree or house therefore which you think of is conceived by you?

Hyl. How should it be otherwise?

Phil. And what is conceived is surely in the mind?

Hyl. Without question, that which is conceived is in the mind.

Phil. How then came you to say, you conceived a house or tree existing independent and out of all minds whatsoever?

Hyl. That was, I own, an oversight; but stay, let me consider what led me into it . . . . As I was thinking of a tree in a solitary place, where no one was present to see it, methought that was to conceive a tree as existing unperceived or unthought of, not considering that I myself conceived it all the while. But now I plainly see, that all I can do is to frame ideas in my own mind. I may indeed conceive in my own thoughts the idea of a tree, or a house, or a mountain, but that is all. And this is far from proving that I can conceive them *existing out of the minds of all spirits.*

Phil. You acknowledge then that you cannot possibly conceive how any one corporeal sensible thing should exist otherwise than in a mind.

There are important differences between Hegel's argument and Berkeley's. Berkeley's argument is stated in terms of perception and the visual imagination, whereas Hegel is concerned primarily with thoughts, specifically pure thoughts. Berkeley, unlike Hegel, shows no inclination to suppose that the details of the world can be derived *a priori*. Berkeley takes exception to such postulates as matter or material substances on the grounds that they are not accessible to sense-perception. Hegel, by contrast, is prepared to accept them, in so far as they are thoughts, though he regards them, on other grounds, as inadequate thoughts.[70] Again, it has often been pointed out that, whereas Berkeley wishes to argue only that nothing could exist unless it were actually perceived by *someone or other*, his argument, if it were valid, would establish that nothing could exist unless it was actually perceived *by me*.[71] Hegel does not expose himself to this objection, however. Firstly, Hegel does not argue that in order to exist an object has to be actually thought about. In so far as he makes a distinction between being thinkable and being actually thought about, a thing needs only to be thinkable, if it is to exist, and not to be thought about. Secondly, his argument does not focus, in the way that Berkeley's does, on what any given individual can or does think. Indeed, as we have seen, he is inclined to the view that the individual self disappears in so far as it thinks. He would not, if this is so, be prepared to accept the distinction between *me* and *someone or other*.[72]

Berkeley concludes that sensible things exist only 'in a mind'. What conclusion Hegel wants to draw from his parallel argument is less clear. But we can nevertheless ask: Even if we grant that what is other than thought can or must be thought about, what follows from that? It does not follow that the precise details of whatever exists are derivable from pure thought; that thought or thoughts are in some sense constitutive of particular things; nor even that anything apart from thought exists at all. The logical idea can, as we have seen, be compared with a novel or a play which contains a reference to itself and considers its own relationship to the events which it portrays.[73] In the second part of *Don Quixote*, for example, Don Quixote is portrayed as reading the first part of *Don Quixote*. The distinction between actual events and the report of them is made within the report, and the relationship between the report and the events is considered in it.[74] But it does not follow from this that *Don Quixote* presents fact rather than fiction, nor indeed that there is anything outside the novel which resembles in the least the places, characters, and events portrayed within it. What happens within thought or within a piece of fiction cannot license any moves of this kind to what is outside thought or outside the fiction.

As we have seen, the concepts which apply primarily to the physical world are not simply contained in the *Logic*, but are also applied to thoughts themselves. The logical idea is, for example, not only subjective, but also objective, an object, in the sense that it is an object for itself. We can, that is, think about thoughts.[75] Again, while particularity and individuality apply primarily to what is other than thought and thought itself is universal, universality is a *particular* or specific type of feature alongside particularity and individuality. Universals are a *particular* type of entity contrasting with particulars and individuals.[76] But these applications of pure thoughts to themselves do not establish that there are any individuals or any objective entities apart from thoughts or concepts, any more than the fact that the word 'small' is a small word and the word 'big' is not a big word entails that there are any small things or any big things apart from words. Still less do they tell us what particular types of thing there are in the world, what individuals there are, and so on. None of the tricks that one can perform within thought — thinking about thought itself, thinking about what is other than thought, and so on — warrant any moves outside of thought, except of course in thought.

It might be objected, however, that in speaking in this way, we are drawing a sharp contrast between such thoughts as those of objectivity and subjectivity. Hegel has shown, in the *Logic,* that such sharp contrasts are illegitimate. Pure thought is, on his view, concrete or infinite in the sense that thoughts are not rigidly cut off from each other but are fluid and intermeshing.[77] But this implies that thought is concrete or infinite in the sense that it is not sharply distinct from the empirical world.[78] For the terms in which the distinction between thought and what is not thought is drawn are themselves thoughts. If these thoughts are not sharply distinct from each other, then the contrast between thought and the world cannot be drawn. The point of Hegel's argument, then, is not simply that the thoughts of objectivity and subjectivity, of universality and particularity, occur within logic. It is that they are seen to be in some way interdependent or complexly intertwined. There are, however, at least two replies to this argument. Firstly, Hegel himself wants to draw some sort of distinction between pure thought and the actual, empirical world. He concedes, as we have seen, that 'the concept is something *abstract* . . . in so far as thinking in general and not the empirically concrete sensuous is its element' (*Enz.* I. 164).[79] But, if he is to do this, he must leave enough space, as it were, between concepts for the distinction between thought and the objective world to be drawn. If this is so, however, it is open to us to ask how this space is to be spanned, how we can get from the concept to the world. Secondly, Hegel's reflections within the *Logic* on such contrasts as that between subjectivity and objectivity or that between universality, particularity, and individuality do not seem to do enough to span this gap. We can easily understand that these concepts involve one another. One could not, for example, have the concept of subjectivity unless one also had the concept of objectivity. But this does not entitle us to infer that concepts or thoughts are in any of the relevant senses objective: that thoughts are exemplified in the world, that thoughts constitute individuals, or that the details of the world are derivable from thought. To suppose that it does is to confuse the thought of objectivity with objective thought or the thought of existence with actual existence. Analogously, one can think about the concept of a unicorn and about the exemplification of that concept by actual unicorns, but our ability to do this does not secure the existence of unicorns. Hegel would of course reply that the concept of a unicorn is at best a finite concept and in fact a mere conception, while *the* concept is infinite, and so on (cf. *Enz.* I. 51, 164). But the particular argument under consideration here would, if it were sound, apply to finite concepts as well as to infinite ones, and we have yet to find an argument which discriminates between them.

6 *Form, matter and ineffability*

Hegel believes that the logical idea does not need 'a content foreign to itself from outside, but . . . it is the logical idea's own activity to unfold and further determine itself to nature and to mind' (*Enz.* I. 43Z).[80] One argument which he deploys in support of this view depends on the impossibility of specifying or describing any such material or 'content' independently of thought itself. What more is there to an actual thing than thoughts? If we try to answer this question, we shall always find that we need to employ thoughts. The argument is summarized by R. P. Wolff:[81]

> The problem which Kant faces is a perennial one in philosophy. If one distinguishes a formal and a material element in cognition, and if one identifies the formal with the conceptual, then it will always appear paradoxical to say anything about the material element. Whatever one says will be expressed by means of concepts, and hence will fall on the side of the formal. Eventually, the material becomes ineffable and indeterminate. The next step, which is frequently taken by the disciples of such a philosophy, is to drop out the material element altogether since it plays no assignable role. Thus Kant's theory tends to degenerate into an idealism, *à la* Hegel or Fichte, in which the mind generates its own world without the aid of a given manifold of intuition. An historical parallel to Kant's theory can be found in Aristotle's doctrine of form and matter. The distinction is pressed until Aristotle arrives at prime matter, which has no specifiable characteristics. How such an un-thing as prime matter can serve to individuate substances is one of the mysteries of ancient philosophy.

Does Hegel follow some such line of thought as this? There are two initial obstacles in the way of attributing it to him. Firstly, even if Hegel accepts the rest of the argument, it is not obvious that he accepts the conclusion that 'the mind generates its own world', with or without the aid of intuition − or not, at least, if 'the mind' means *me*. For even if the material element is allowed to drop out, it would not follow that the world is generated by the mind unless it were also granted that the mind generates the formal features of the world. Is this latter premiss not secured by the identification of the formal with the conceptual? Not necessarily. If this means only that the formal features of the world are those features of it which correspond to or are expressible by means of concepts, then even if concepts are produced by the mind, this does not entail that the formal features are. Hegel, as we have seen, tends to blur this distinction by speaking of '(thought-) determinations'.[82] If, on the other hand, it means that the formal features of the world are strictly identical with concepts, it still might be held that concepts are not produced by the mind. It is only if we regard concepts as generated by the mind and, initially at least, as imposed by it on the material element, that, when the material element drops out, we are left with a picture of the mind generating the world by projecting its concepts not onto something given, but, as it were, into empty, undifferentiated space.

Hegel's position on this is hard to gauge. He clearly does not regard pure thoughts as produced by me or by anyone in particular. It is only when one abandons what distinguishes oneself from other individuals that the pure thoughts emerge in their proper form and order. Moreover, in his discussion of Kant, Hegel rejects the view, which he attributes to Kant, that the thoughts are merely *our* thoughts.[83] Were it not for his insistence that that absolute is a (sort of) objective mind − the correlate of objective thoughts − Hegel could plausibly be seen as propounding a healthy realism. It is clear, however, that the objective mind is not my mind or your mind. Something has already been said about its relationship to them.[84]

7 The elimination of the material

A second difficulty about the line of thought suggested by Wolff is that it is unclear whether what we are left with, once the material element has dropped out, are pure thoughts only or, alternatively, concepts of all kinds, conceptions as well as thoughts. This distinction corresponds to two different ways in which we might attempt to distinguish between the formal and the material features of, for example, an oak-tree:

1. We might, initially at least, suppose that the distinction between the formal and the material amounts to a distinction between general and specific ways of describing the tree. If we say that it is a thing, an organic whole, a living organism, a particular individual, then we are drawing attention to its formal element. If we proceed to more specific descriptions of it, characterizing it as a plant, a tree, an oak, gnarled, and so on, then this is an account

of its material element. We then notice that what we have supposed to be an account of the material element consists, just as does our account of the formal element, of a set of descriptions or concepts, which, although they are more specific than the formal concepts, do not differ from them in kind. All we have are concepts of varying degrees of generality. It might nevertheless be objected that we require a non-conceptual element in order to account for the difference between two very similar trees and between a tree's existing and its not existing. But the reply is that this, again, is simply a matter of producing further descriptions or concepts, the concepts of existence, of what makes the difference between a thing's existing and its not existing, of numerical difference and of what makes one thing numerically distinct from another. These are themselves concepts and, indeed, relatively unspecific concepts.

2. We begin, as before, by specifying the formal element of the tree in descriptions of it as a thing, a particular individual, an organic whole, a living organism and so on. But we do not go on to indicate the material element by giving more specific descriptions of the tree. Rather we turn directly to the material element, to what, when added to the formal element, makes a specific, definite tree. We do this by using such expressions as 'the material element', 'the specific properties of the thing', and 'the sensuous asunderness of the thing'. Again we notice, however, that these expressions convey thoughts, just as much as the expressions used to indicate the formal element.

The first of these arguments would, if it were sound, establish that there is no more to actual things than concepts, where concepts include both pure thoughts and what Hegel calls 'conceptions'. The second suggests that there is no more to things than pure thoughts, and that conceptions, as well as actual things, are in some way generated by pure thoughts. Which, if either, of these two positions does Hegel hold? He does not always maintain, as clearly as we would wish, the distinction which he claims to have established between pure thoughts and conceptions. When he does draw the distinction, however, it seems clear that it is thoughts, pure thoughts, which play the important, distinctive role in his system, and not thoughts together with conceptions. Indeed he could argue that once we accept position 1, we are committed to accepting position 2, so that the positions are at the bottom one and the same. The argument would run as follows. In our preliminary distinction between thoughts and conceptions, we assumed that there was a material element – the sensuous.[85] It was this element which made the difference between a pure thought and a conception.

A conception involves a material or an empirical element, whereas a pure thought does not. It is, again, this element which makes the difference between one conception and another. The conception of a rose and that of a daisy both involve the same pure thoughts. What differentiates them is the difference in the material or empirical element which is incorporated in them. But now, according to argument 1, there is no non-conceptual material element which can perform this role. What, then, explains the difference between a pure thought and a conception which specifies it, or between two different conceptions both of which specify the same pure thoughts? There seem to be only two alternatives. *Either* there is no special explanation of these differences; we simply generate certain specific conceptions without following any definite conceptual route to them from the pure thought which they specify. *Or* conceptions are in some way derivable from pure thoughts. Hegel is reluctant to admit that anything is inexplicable, and it therefore seems likely that he would opt for the latter alternative. An argument in favour of the view that conceptions are derivable from pure thoughts will be examined in the following section. For the moment, however, we shall consider some of Hegel's arguments for eliminating, or at least downgrading, the sensible or material given. For only if this can be done can we accept position 1 *or* position 2. At least five types of consideration are adduced in favour of such an elimination. They do not, unfortunately, converge towards a single, unambiguous conclusion:

(i) The terms in which we describe the sensory given, or at least those which indicate the respects in which it differs from thought, terms such as 'asunderness' and 'individuality', themselves express pure thoughts (*Enz.* I. 20).[86] It is quite unclear what conclusion Hegel intended us to draw from this, but if it is meant to support either of the lines of argument suggested by Wolff, it is likely that he had in mind position 2, namely the more ambitious claim that conceptions, as well as actual things, are generated by pure thought.

(ii) The argument against sense-certainty in the *Phenomenology* is in part an argument against the attempt to capture the sensory given without recourse to concepts:

> The awareness (*Wissen*) which is at first or immediately our object, can only be that which is itself immediate awareness, *awareness* of the *immediate* or *of what is*. Likewise we have to conduct ourselves *immediately* or *receptively* (*aufnehmend*); thus we must alter nothing in it as it presents itself and keep conceptualization (*das Begreifen*) out of apprehension (*von dem Auffassen*) (PG p. 79, M. p. 58).

As we have seen, Hegel has, roughly speaking, two arguments against this attempt. Firstly, we cannot indicate the sensory manifold without resorting at least to such thin thoughts as those expressed by 'this', 'here', 'I' and 'now'. Secondly, even with this equipment, one cannot coherently pick out features of the manifold, since token-reflexive expressions apply to everything.[87] Whatever the merits of these particular arguments, it can be agreed that there are difficulties in the way of indicating or describing the sensory or material element in the world or in our perceptions of it. To do so is indeed impossible, if what is required is a non-conceptual description of it. But it does not follow from this that there is no such sensory or material element. Even if we cannot pick it out as a separate constituent, we can still say, for example, that it is what makes the difference between a cat and a dog, between this cat and that cat, and between a cat's existing and its not existing.

(iii) This section of the *Phenomenology* is also taken to show that thoughts, and words which express thoughts, cannot refer to or pick out particular individuals (*PG* pp. 87 ff., M. pp. 65 f. Cf. *Enz.* I. 20). One might suppose that, if this is so, Hegel would be more willing to countenance an independent material element in order to account for the fact that there are distinct individuals and for our ability to pick them out. But, as we have seen, he tends to regard this feature of thought as support for his claim that 'the thought and the universal is essentially both itself and its other, it overreaches its other and nothing escapes it' (*Enz.* I. 20).[88] Again, it is not clear what the implications of this doctrine are supposed to be. Hegel certainly refers to it in order to side-step the challenge to 'deduce' some particular individual. But does this mean that there really are no distinct individuals — except in a sense for which pure thought can make provision? If this were so, then he could argue that there is no need for an extra-conceptual material element to differentiate them. We would be able to speak about distinct individuals and even to say that this thing is different from that thing. But we would not be able to pick out a particular individual to the exclusion of others, and there would be no individual entities beyond our ability to speak about them. Alternatively, he may simply mean that distinct individuals are of no importance. Thought, in that case would provide us not with everything, but only with everything of importance. If, however, there are distinct individuals which escape the net of thought, it is hard to see how Hegel can claim that the concept realizes itself without the assistance of any extra content.[89]

(iv) Hegel believes, as we have seen, that certain thought-determinations constitute, or are essential to, the individuals which exemplify them. If we were to deprive a dog of its animality or Gaius of his humanity, they would not be anything at all — or, at least, we would be unable to say what they were (*Enz.* I. 24Z.1, 175Z).[90] One of the conclusions that he might have drawn from this is that there is no way of indicating or describing the other constituent which, when it is combined with animality, results in a dog, or the constituent which, when combined with humanity, produces Gaius. Any attempt to describe these constituents will implicitly involve the concept of animality or that of humanity, or it will at least involve some thoughts or other. Though there is little warrant for it apart from the point under consideration, Hegel regards concepts like those of animality and of humanity as pure thoughts, so that he probably took this consideration to support position 2 rather than simply position 1. Again, however, the fact that there is no way of describing the sensory or material element which does not already imply that it forms a part of a certain thought-ridden object does not entail that there is no such element.

(v) Hegel makes a similar point when he discusses the distinctions between form and matter[91] and between form and content. Matter can be so regarded, he argues, that all differences in it are merely differences of form, but then this 'one, determinationless matter is also the same as the thing-in-itself, except that the latter is intrinsically entirely abstract, while the former depends on a relation to something else, primarily the form' (*Enz.* I. 128). 'Matter', the *Logic* continues,

is here regarded as in itself entirely indeterminate, but as capable of any determination and at the same time quite permanent and uniform in every change and alteration. This indifference of matter to determinate forms is found, of course, in finite things; thus it is a matter of indifference to e.g. a block of marble whether it receives the form of this or that statue or even of a pillar. We must not overlook, however, the fact that such matter as a block of marble is indifferent to the form only relatively (in relation to the sculptor), and is not at all formless in general . . . . [It is] a determinate formation of stone, in distinction from other, similarly determinate formations, like e.g. sandstone, porphyry, etc. It is thus only the abstracting understanding which fixes matter in its isolation and as in itself formless, whereas the thought of matter includes the principle of form throughout and, therefore, a formless matter nowhere occurs as existing in experience. The conception of matter as originally present and in itself formless is very ancient and we meet it in the Greeks, at first in the mythical form of Chaos, conceived as the formless basis of the existent world. It follows from this conception that God is to be regarded not as the creator of the world, but as a mere world-former or demiurge. The deeper intuition, by contrast, is that God created the world out of nothing, which in general expresses, firstly, the fact that matter as such has no independence and, secondly, that form does not come to matter from outside, but as a totality carries the principle of matter in itself; this free and infinite form will come before us later as the *concept* (128Z).

Similar remarks are made about form and content:

> the content is not formless, but the *form* is just as much *in it as* it is *something external* to it. We have a duplication of form; firstly, it is the content and then it is reflected into itself, and, secondly, it is external existence which is indifferent to the content and then it is not reflected into itself (*Enz.* I. 133).

Hegel's point here is not, as in (iv), that the material constituent must have the form which it does and cannot be described in terms which do not imply that it has it. It is rather that, although a given piece of matter or a given content need not have the particular form which it does have, it must have some form, even if, in relation to the first form, it is 'formless'. A formless lump of marble has a form in virtue of which it is marble rather than some other sort of stuff. However far we go, we shall never arrive at pure matter or pure content with no form whatsoever. But why does it follow from this that 'form . . . as a totality carries the principle of matter in itself,' that matter or content is generated by form? One might rather infer that the distinction between form and matter or between form and content is an artificial, or at least a relative, one, that we cannot separate out a purely formal element and a purely material element and ask about the relationship between the two. Sometimes it looks as if this is what Hegel is saying. Some of the passages in which he criticizes Kant's view, that we project concepts onto the sensory manifold, might be interpreted in this way (*Enz.* I. 41Z.2, 42Z.1).[92] This conclusion is not, however, the one that Hegel drew, and what seems to have prevented him from doing so is this. The relationship between form and matter or content is an asymmetrical one. We cannot distinguish a purely material element and say something significant about it. The same is not true, however, of the formal element. For we can distinguish what looks, at first sight, like a purely formal element, namely the pure thoughts of the *Logic*. Since we cannot describe independently the matter or content which needs to be added to this in order to produce the empirical world, it is natural to conclude that the material element of things, their content, is generated by their formal element and is therefore derivable from pure thought. If there is a material element, albeit an undetachable one, it will of course follow that this formal element is not purely and exclusively formal any more than the unhewn block of marble is purely material, since such matter or content as there is will be implicit in it. We shall then hesitate over whether to say that the logical idea is purely formal or that it is jointly formal and material.[93] But this is an unimportant terminological question. Whichever we decide to say, it will still be the case that the empirical world is in some way the product of pure thoughts or thought-determinations.

It might be doubted whether this (position 2) is Hegel's thesis rather than the more modest view that the world is generated by concepts, by conceptions, that is, as well as pure thoughts (position 1). After all, most of the 'forms' which Hegel refers to correspond to conceptions rather than pure thoughts. The concepts of a statue, of marble, sandstone and porphyry are empirical conceptions, and argument (v) does nothing to eliminate *them* along with the purely material element. We have already seen, however, that when Hegel turns from finite entities like statues to the universe as a whole, he speaks of the 'free and infinite form' and equates this with *the* concept (*Enz.* I. 128Z). This suggests that he is advancing to the more ambitious position 2 on the basis of what is at most an argument for position 1. In any case, there are traces of an argument for the view that conceptions are generated by pure thoughts. This argument will be considered in the following section.

8 Relations and the inverted world

We saw earlier that there is some doubt as to whether the relationship of thoughts to conceptions is that of the literal to the metaphorical or that of abstract grammar to a language.[94] Hegel believes that religious conceptions, for example, are '*metaphors* of thoughts and concepts' (*Enz.* I. 3). This, as we have seen, involves a radical, and perhaps implausible, reinterpretation of traditional religious beliefs and conceptions.[95] But the problems confronting the view that empirical conceptions are metaphors of thoughts are of a different order. How can Hegel substantiate the claim that, in the case of such conceptions as that of green or of such propositions as 'This leaf is green', philosophy 'puts *thoughts, categories*, but more precisely *concepts*, in the place of conceptions' (*Enz.* I. 3)? We might indeed write, instead of 'green', something like 'a definite property of a particular determinable range of properties', and, instead of 'This leaf is green', 'This determinate organic individual had a definite property of a particular determinable range of properties.' But these are not adequate translations of the original expressions. They do not capture their difference from 'red' and 'This petal is red'. One could, of course, speak about such differences in terms which express pure thoughts alone. One could say, for example, that this definite property is a different definite property from that, even though both belong to the same particular determinable range of properties. But this is as far as we can go in terms of pure thoughts.

The argument so far is analogous to Hegel's argument that, while one can express in terms of pure thought the numerical differences between individuals, one cannot refer to any definite individual. He might, as in that case, stop at this point and say that pure thought captures everything that there is or, at least, everything worth capturing, that thoughts overreach conceptions in much the way that they overreach actual individuals. There is, however, an important difference between the two cases. Hegel argues that references to definite individuals are impossible not only in terms of thought-words alone, but even in terms of all our linguistic resources, conception-words as well as thought-words.[96] But this could not be argued in the case of different conceptions. We have perfectly good words, words like 'red', 'green', 'lion' and 'tiger', for expressing the difference between conceptions. Why should we restrict our vocabulary to pure thought-words, when the conceptions which we have and features of the world can be better expressed in the more extensive vocabulary which we customarily employ?

There are some indications that Hegel would reply to this by claiming that our various conceptions are generated by pure thoughts. The argument can be illustrated by our range of colours and colour-words. It is commonly argued that, if someone's colour-vision were to differ radically, but systematically, from one's own, there would be no way of detecting the difference: content is incommunicable, only structure is communicable. The structure of our system of colours and colour-words is given by such propositions as these:

(1) Red is different from green
(2) Nothing can be red and green all over
(3) Green is more like blue than it is like red
(4) Blue and yellow mixed together produce green

If the difference between two perceivers is to be undetectable, then both must assent to such propositions as these. They must also apply the same words to roughly the same things, agreeing, for example, that grass is green and that this leaf is green. Yet the perceivers might nevertheless differ in what they see. What the one sees as red and calls 'red', the other might see as (what the first calls) green and yet himself call it 'red'.

Various responses are possible to this problem:

(i) It is possible that there should be such differences in the content of what we see, despite the identity of structure. If it were so, then the meanings of our colour-words would differ from one person to another. You might mean by 'red' what I mean by 'green', though we shall never be able to detect the difference.

(ii) Although it is possible that there should be such differences in the content of our colour-vision, this would not affect the meaning of our colour-words. For the meanings of our words are determined by our public and detectable use of them. If one person applies the word 'red' in the same way as another person, and both are prepared to assent to all the relevant structural propositions, then both mean the same thing by it, whatever the differences in the content of what they see.

(iii) There could not possibly be two perceivers whose colour-vision differed systematically yet undetectably. Not only would such a difference be undetectable, it would also be inconceivable. This is because such a difference would be *ex hypothesi* a matter of our private sensations. Sensations with an incommunicable quality or content cannot possibly occur. All genuine differences, therefore, must be public, detectable differences.

(iv) Such a difference in the content of our colour-vision is again inconceivable. But this is not only because of the privacy of the difference and of the sensations in which it is alleged to reside. It is rather because the content of a quality is wholly determined by the structure of the range in which it occurs and by its position in this range. Thus in the case in question we could write, in place of 'red' and 'green', 'colour$_n$' and 'colour$_m$'. For each colour, colour$_1$, . . . colour$_n$, is fully constituted by its position in the range of colours and by its relationships to other colours in the range. The meanings of our colour-words are similarly determined by their position in a range. There is no sense to the suggestion that the content of the range might alter, while its structure remains the same. For structure determines content. This position differs from position (iii). An adherent of position (iii) could, for example, admit that here might be two or more ranges of colours each of which had the same structure, but differed in content. If all the objects in our world were to change their colours overnight, switching from their present colour to the corresponding colour on some other range, then this might be a publicly detectable change; it is only if such a difference is private, and publicly undetectable, that it is no difference at all. An adherent of position (iv), by contrast, could not admit the possibility of such a change in content alone. As long as structure remains the same, there is no change and no difference.

Which of these positions would Hegel have opted for? Some of his remarks suggest that he would prefer (i) or (ii). When he says that 'what is *unsayable*, feeling, sensation, is ... the least significant, the least true', this implies not that the unsayable does not exist, but that it is unimportant. Neither of these positions nor, indeed, position (iii) amounts to a claim that conceptions are generated by pure thoughts. Position (iv), however, is more promising in this respect and there are some signs that Hegel held it. The following passage, for example, suggests, though it does not entail, that colours are constituted by their relationships to one another:

> The sensuous, however, is the asunder, what is outside itself (*das Aussereinander, das Aussersichseiende*); this is strictly its fundamental determination. Thus e.g. 'now' only has being in relation to a before and an after. Similarly red is only present (*vorhanden*) in so far as yellow and blue are opposed to it. But this other [viz. yellow and blue] is outside the sensuous [viz. red], and this subsists only in so far as it is not the other and only in so far as the other subsists (*Enz.* I. 42 Z.1 Cf. *WL* I. pp. 131 ff., M. pp. 122 ff.).

This view need not of course be restricted to ranges of simple properties like colours and sounds. It can be extended to, for example, the species of plants and animals. We have already seen that Hegel appears to hold that the specific features of things are determined by the relations which hold between them and that this is, or at least should be, mirrored by the concepts which we form of them.[97]

A difficult, but vivid, episode in the *Phenomenology* may well be relevant in this context. In that work Hegel considers the case of a world which is the inverse of our own:

> Thus according to the law of this inverted world what is *like-named* (*das Gleichnamige*) in the first world is the *unlike* (*das Ungleiche*) of itself, and the *unlike* of the first is similarly *unlike itself*, or it becomes *like* itself. In determinate aspects

this will mean that what in the law of the first world is sweet is sour in this inverted in-itself (*Ansich*), what in the former is black is white in the latter. What, in the law of the first world, is the north pole of the magnet is, in its other, supersensible in-itself . . . the south pole; but what is there the south pole is here the north pole. Similarly what in the first law of electricity is the oxygen pole becomes in its other supersensible essence the hydrogen pole; and, conversely, what is there the hydrogen pole becomes here the oxygen pole (*PG* p. 122, M. p. 97).

The significance of this passage is obscure and no attempt will be made to unravel it here.[98] It might, however, be seen as, in part, a reply to an objection to the view that structure determines content. The objection runs as follows. If we concentrate, for the sake of convenience, on the simple structure of polar opposition, we can conceive of two significantly and detectably different worlds which are nevertheless structurally identical. The relationship between the two worlds would be such that anything which, in the one world, had a certain quality would, in the other, have its polar opposite. Black things in world 1, for example, would be white in world 2. The case becomes more complicated, but not essentially different, if we introduce ranges of properties and not simply polar opposites. Anything which, in world 1, was qualified by a property which stood in a certain relationship to one of the opposites would, in world 2, be qualified by the property which bore the same relation to the other opposite. The content of these two worlds would be detectably different, despite the identity of their structure. It follows, therefore, that structure cannot determine content.

Some of the examples of opposites which Hegel gives suggest that his answer to this objection would be that there would be no conceivable difference between a world and its inverse, let alone a detectable difference. The north and south poles of magnets, for example, are not detectably different from one another.[99] The only way in which they can be distinguished from each other is by the tendency of like poles to repel each other and of unlike poles to attract each other. If all the north poles of magnets were to become south poles and all the south poles were to become north poles, they would continue to attract and repel each other in exactly the same way as they do at present. It follows that no discernible change would have occurred in the world. The content of north poles and south poles is determined solely by their relationship to one another, by the structure, and, as long as this structure remains the same, no change in the content can possibly occur. The same is true of positive electricity (the 'oxygen pole' or anode) and negative electricity (the 'hydrogen pole' or cathode). If positively charged entities were to become negatively charged and negatively charged entities positively charged, then again no detectable change would have occurred.[100]

It is, however, a mistake to assimilate all opposites to opposites of this sort. The opposition of black and white and that of sweet and sour are different from those of north and south poles and of positive and negative electrical charges. If all black things became white and all white things became black, and if things similarly exchanged sweetness for sourness and sourness for sweetness, then the change would be a discernible one. Consequently, two worlds, each in these respects the inverse of the other, would be noticeably different from each other. Perhaps if we were to change a sufficient number of the features of things, the number of them, for example, their shapes, sizes, species and spatial locations, then the resultant world would be indistinguishable from our present one. We would notice, for example, if black swans became white and white swans became black, but not if, in addition, the white — now black — swans moved to Australia, and the black — now white — swans migrated to Europe. But Hegel does not suggest that the indiscernibility of the two worlds is to depend on the number of changes or differences which occur, and in any case it is hard to see some of the changes or differences required to secure indiscernibility as a matter of inversion or polar opposition. Changes in the number of black and white swans, for example, or changes in their geographical location are not like changes from black to white. It looks, then, as if Hegel's case depends in part on the illegitimate assimilation of different types of opposition. In any case, the indiscernibility of a world and its polar inverse, even if it were a fact, would not establish that structure determines content. More drastic changes might occur even within the polarized structure which would certainly be detectable. Swans, for example, might become magnetized.

9 The primacy of relations

Hegel's general position seems to be a natural extension of Spinoza's dictum: *Omnis determinatio est negatio* (*WL* I. p. 121, M. p. 113).[101] Each colour in the range, for example, is not what the other colours are. We might go on to say that each colour is *just* that colour which the other colours are not, that its whole content is determined by its filling the place in the range left free by the other colours. But, since this is true of every colour in the range, no colour has a content which is in any degree independent of the structure of the range: Structure determines content. But structure, it might be argued, is a matter of pure thought. It is, then, pure thought which determines the content of e.g. colours and of our conceptions of them.

There are, however, several criticisms to be made of this argument.

1. While it is true that every colour is not the other colours, it does not follow that it is fully determined by the other colours and by the structure of the range in which it occurs. This is shown, for example, by the fact that the range of colours might have been narrower than it now is. Things might have been only red, yellow and blue, and our system of colour concepts might have contained only these three members. The structure of this system would presumably be different from that of our present one, at least in the sense that it contained fewer members, but the content of the colours and the colour-concepts which it did contain need not be different from that of their counterparts in our present system. The content and boundaries of the conceptions would be determined in part by empirical phenomena and not by the structural relationships of the system alone. This objection presupposes that there is a sensory or material element which can perform this role, but, as we have seen, Hegel's arguments for its elimination are not compelling.[102]

2. Even if we were to agree that a certain range of conceptions was determined solely by its structure, it might still be a contingent matter which particular things exemplify which conceptions or even whether any given conception is exemplified at all. Hegel has two arguments to fall back on at this point. Firstly, he might claim that if anything is F, then something must be non-F, or, in a different version, that if we are aware of anything as F, then we must be aware of something as non-F.[103] These principles are, however, questionable. They are more plausible in the case of opposites of a polar kind, like the north and south poles of magnets or positive and negative electricity, though even here Hegel has not established the logical impossibility of non-polar magnetism or electricity. But even if the principles were acceptable, they would show only that, if anything were of a certain colour, then there must be something not of that colour. They would not show that every colour must be exemplified nor would they disclose which things are of which colours. Secondly, Hegel believes not only that our conceptions derive their content from their relationships to each other, but that things depend on their relations with other things for their content.[104] This is more plausible in the case

397

of biological species or human groupings than in that of colours. For things of different colours do not in general interact with one another, causally or otherwise, in significant ways, whereas biological species depend on each other for their survival and human groups define themselves by reference to each other. We could, however, grant this much, without conceding that it is logically impossible for there to have been an entirely different set of biological species or even no life at all. Nor does it follow that our present biological species could not have found some acceptable substitute for their survival, if one or more of their number had not existed.

3. Why should we suppose that the relationships between conceptions or between things are any more pure thought-determinations than is the content of the things or conceptions itself? On the face of it, the structural relations between terms are just as empirical as the terms themselves. Red, for example, is not simply different from grey, it is also brighter than grey. Animal species do not simply interact with each other, they also fight and eat each other. But 'bright', 'fight' and 'eat' express conceptions rather than pure thoughts. If we describe the structure in such terms as these then we shall not reduce differences of content to pure thought, for empirical content re-emerges in the structure. The reply to this, however, might be that such residual empirical content as the relationships between things seem to contain depends on the content of the related terms. If the relations between entities are to determine their content and not depend on it, then these relations must be evacuated of their empirical content. They must, that is, be expressible in terms of pure thoughts alone.

4. But if the structure of, for example, our system of colours is described in such general terms, might it not be that other entities satisfy the same structure? Even if we ignore the possibility of different, but structurally identical, colour-systems, it seems likely that a system of sounds or of tastes might have the same structure as our system of colours. This is reflected in the point that the initial scepticism about another person's vision of colours can be extended to the query whether, when he says he sees colours, he might not in fact be hearing sounds, tasting tastes or smelling smells. The incommunicability of content cannot be confined within a single sensory modality, but ranges across our whole sensory intake.[105] Just as different colours were conceived of only as colour$_1$, colour$_2$, . . . colour$_n$, so now the different determinables or ranges of properties are to be thought of as determinable$_1$ (e.g. colour), determinable$_2$ (e.g. sound), . . . determinable$_n$. Hegel's answer to this, however, would presumably

be the same as before. The different determinables together form a system, with a structure which determines their content. The content of each determinable, what differentiates colours from sounds or smells, is fully constituted by the abstract structure of the system of determinables and its position in it. The structure of the system of determinables need not be the same as the structure of e.g. the system of colours. All that is required is that the structure should be expressible in terms of pure thought and that the structure, whatever it is, should determine the content which fills it. This process can be continued. The concept of colour is a conception rather than a pure thought, while that of a determinable type of property is presumably a pure thought. But the distinction between a qualitative determinable and a quantitative determinable would again be determined by the relationship between them. For, as we have seen, Hegel seems to believe that the content of pure thoughts themselves is determined by the structure of the whole system of thought and their position in it.[106] There is no special reason to suppose that the determination of content by structure should end when we enter the realm of pure thoughts themselves. The whole system of pure thought generates itself, as it were, by opposition and contrast from the concept of pure being and then descends, by the same procedures, to our specific conceptions of things.

This extension of the theory, however, seems open to the same objections as before. It is, for example, surely a logical possibility that the range of determinable properties which things display should have differed in content from that which they actually have without differing from it in structure. Things might not have had, that is, colours, sounds, or tastes, but some quite different types of property which we can barely imagine. Or, again, they might have had colours and shapes, but no sounds or smells. We can perhaps also imagine various complex inversions, or at least perversions, of our own world in which objects exchange their properties not for other properties within the same range, their colour, for example, for some other colour, but for properties in a different range. Each object might, for example, exchange its present position on the colour-spectrum for some corresponding position on the range of tangible qualities and its present position on this range for the corresponding position on the colour-range. The view that structure determines content presumably implies that such worlds, as long as they shared the same logical or abstract structure as our own, could not be detectably, or even conceivably, different from it. But this implication seems to be false, and, if it is, then it cannot be true that structure, in the relevant sense, determines content. There is an irreducible sensory or material element which must be added to the logical idea before it can generate our world rather than some other sort of world. Hegel might argue that content is insignificant, but this amounts to a refusal to derive the world from thought rather than a way of doing it.

10 *Reciprocal reductions*

Hegel does not, of course, explicitly present the argument considered in the preceding two sections nor does he claim to be able to derive the details of the world from pure thought. His position is, as we have seen, an ambiguous one and it derives much of its initial plausibility from this. He does, however, seem to believe that it is possible to derive some claims about the empirical world from pure thought, if it is only the results of the sciences. But we cannot do this immediately. The results must first be discovered empirically and only subsequently can they be shown to be *a priori*. Why is this? Why, if it is possible to establish claims about the world from pure thought, is it necessary for the logician to wait for and use the results of the empirical sciences? The answer to this question does not depend on how much can be shown to be *a priori*. Whether it is the details of things or only the general results of the sciences that can be so derived, the question in either case is why philosophers could not have derived from pure thought whatever it is that they can show to be *a priori* without resorting to empirical investigation or to its results.

There are several possible answers to this question. It may be, for example, that Hegel has conflated the notions of necessity and a priority, and that he intends only to show that the results of the sciences, or whatever, are *necessary*. This does not entail, though he may have thought that it did entail, that they are not *a posteriori*. Another answer is that, on his view, we cannot acquire the appropriate pure thoughts until they have emerged in the guise of conceptions and this involves the application of thoughts in empirical scientific theories. This answer, however, simply invites the further question: Why, if pure thoughts are *a priori,* must the acquisition of *them* depend on empirical inquiry? Or, again, it is just a matter of historical realism to recognize that not everything that can in principle be derived *a priori* can in practice be so derived unless people have reached a certain level of intellectual maturity. Hegel would perhaps add that what men can and cannot do at various stages of their development is itself, like any other fact, or at least general fact, ultimately a matter of logic. Finally we might suppose that Hegel is simply making a virtue of necessity, that finding that we cannot do what, according to his theory, we should be able to do, he supplies *ad hoc* a reason for resorting to empirical investigation.

There does, however, seem to be a deeper reason for Hegel's belief that empirical science and the philosophy of nature are both required, that the former must meet the latter half-way. Certain other features of his system require that both procedures should occur. To show this is not, of course, to defend the view in question, but it does establish that it is not merely *ad hoc*. We saw earlier that Hegel considers three accounts of the relationship between God and the world, and these accounts will, on his view, also be accounts of the relationship between the logical idea and the world:

(i) God and the world co-exist
(ii) God $\Rightarrow$ the world, i.e. only the world exists
(iii) God $\Leftarrow$ the world, i.e. only God exists.

Of these alternatives, Hegel prefers (iii). But he does not believe that this is the final answer. What he does believe is best formalized as:

(iv) God $\Leftrightarrow$ the world.

But what does this mean? If we interpret it as the conjunction of (ii) and (iii), namely as:

(v) God $\Rightarrow$ the world and God $\Leftarrow$ the world

then it seems to be contradictory. For it claims both that the world alone — and not God — exists and that God alone — and not the world — exists. Reductions of one type of entity to another must, we tend to feel, be asymmetrical. As we have seen, if someone were to argue that our sense-experiences are no more than brain-processes, but that, conversely, brain-processes, like all physical objects and events, are simply logical constructions out of our sense-experiences, we would not know what he meant, unless he were prepared to concede primacy to one of the reductions and to one of the terms, seeing the other reduction as a subordinate theory within the larger metaphysical framework established by the first. He might assign primacy, for example, to sense-experiences and to the reduction: 'Physical events, including brain-processes $\Rightarrow$ sense-experiences.' Within that framework, he has a choice of alternative theories about the relationship of sense-experiences to brain-processes, and one of them is perhaps something approximating to 'Sense-experiences $\Rightarrow$ brain-processes.' There is, as we have seen, something of such a double reductionism in Hegel's account of the relationship between thoughts and the world.[107]

In some passages Hegel goes further than in others in the direction of assigning equal status both to the logical idea and to the world:

> What this [viz. Jacobi's] standpoint maintains is that neither the *idea* as a merely *subjective* thought nor merely a being on its own (*für sich*) is the truth — being which is only on its own, a being which is not that of the idea, is the sensuous, finite being of the world. What is therefore immediately asserted thereby is that the idea *is the truth* only *by means of* being and conversely being *is the truth* only *by means of* the idea. The proposition of immediate awareness rightly does not want indeterminate, empty immediacy, abstract being or pure unity on its own, but the unity *of the idea* with being. But it is thoughtless not to see that the unity of *distinct* determinations is not merely purely immediate, i.e. entirely indeterminate and empty unity, but that what is involved in it is that the one determination has truth only when it is mediated by the other — or, if one prefers, each is mediated with the truth only by the other (*Enz.* I. 70).

There is no suggestion here that Hegel is an acosmist, believing that the idea exists, but that being really does not, any more than there is that he is an atheist, believing that being exists, but that the idea does not. Each of the terms of the unity exists, but they do not, for all that, merely co-exist. It is, of course, difficult to spell out in literal terms the sort of unity or identity which he has in mind, but presumably he would fall back on such partial analogues as a mind and its object, the unity of the two poles of a magnet, and the unity of the parts of a living organism.

The sort of unity or reciprocal dependence which the terms have in these examples licenses inferences from one term to the other. If, for example, one end of a bar of iron is known to be magnetic, one can infer that the other end has the opposite form of magnetism. If one can see only one half of an organism, then one can infer a good deal about the features of the other half. These possibilities of inference are, moreover, symmetrical. If x and y have the type of unity in question, then one can infer the existence and nature of y from that of x and, conversely, that of x from that of y. It is characteristic of Hegel that when he believes that something, x, is identical with something, y, he argues both that $x = y$ or, rather, that $x \Rightarrow y$, and that $y = x$ or, rather, that $y \Rightarrow x$. He attempts to show, for example, both that being is the same as nothing and that nothing is the same as being.[108] This in itself indicates that the identity in question is not the flat identity which obtains between courage and bravery or between Thera and Santorini. For we do not need to establish both that Thera = Santorini and that Santorini = Thera.

The fact that we can show that $x \Rightarrow y$ and that $y \Rightarrow x$ is essentially connected with the fact that x and y both exist and yet do not merely co-exist. A mere dualist, for example, could not establish either that God $\Rightarrow$ the world or that the world $\Rightarrow$ God. An acosmistic pantheist could establish that the world $\Rightarrow$ God, but not that God $\Rightarrow$ the world. An atheistic 'pantheist', by contrast, could establish that God $\Rightarrow$ the world, but not the converse. If the ontological status both of God and of the world is to be secure, then we must show that God $\Leftrightarrow$ the world, and to do this we need to show both that the world $\Rightarrow$ God and that God $\Rightarrow$ the world. The first of these tasks is performed by natural scientists and, to some extent, by artists and religious believers, the second by philosophers. The first is *a posteriori*, the second *a priori*. Both of these operations are, however, incorporated into Hegel's system. For the work of scientists, artists and religious believers in elevating the world to thought, in showing namely that the world $\Rightarrow$ thought, is itself a part of the cosmic process which the philosopher needs to describe. Within this process nature, as it were, rises up to meet thought, just as thought descends into nature. Hegel's views about the *a priori* and the *a posteriori* are intimately connected with this circular movement.[109]

In this chapter we have considered one phase of this process, the transition from logic to nature. This leaves unanswered, however, a number of questions about the status, in Hegel's system, of the world, of actual physical things. To answer them, in so far as they can be answered, will be the object of the following chapter.

X

Idealism, Appearance and Contradiction

Hegel's account of the universe is, as we have seen, a complex and ambiguous one. It bears the marks of his encounters with a variety of different problems. Can we, in the light of this, find a single, coherent account of the status of the world? There are, as we shall see, conflicts and tensions in Hegel's thought on this matter. Indeed, one might expect the circularity of his system alone to throw it into disarray.[1] Nevertheless certain intelligible themes emerge from the chaos, and, where there is conflict or confusion, one can by and large see the reason for it.

1 Subjective idealisms

It is tempting in the case of a philosopher whose thought is as complex as Hegel's to interpret him in the light of categories derived from more accessible thinkers, from Spinoza, for example, from Kant or from Berkeley. It has sometimes been supposed, for example, that Hegel adheres to a version of subjective idealism, holding that, apart from myself (or ourselves), there is nothing but my (or our) sense-experiences and that I (or we) impose concepts on them to give rise to a quasi-objective world, apparently, but only apparently, distinct from myself (or ourselves).[2] This interpretation might be supported by the fact that the concepts which we might employ in order to say what more there is to physical objects than my (or our) sensations, the concept of matter for example, are regarded by Hegel simply as pure thoughts. In some passages at least, he implies that we convert our sensory intake into 'experience' by imposing such thoughts upon it.[3] If this is so – it might be argued – then such concepts as these are simply our contribution and

404

cannot describe a reality which is independent of our own thought and sensations.[4]

Hegel himself, however, regularly disowns what he calls 'subjective idealism' and it seems not to have occurred to him that he might be vulnerable to such an interpretation. It is not quite clear, however, why he rejects this position, or indeed what position he takes himself to be rejecting. In fact when he says that Kant is a subjective idealist,[5] he seems to have in mind at least three different doctrines:

(i) The empirical world is merely subjective in the sense that it is constructed or projected by us.

(ii) Our sensations are given to us in a pre-conceptual form and objects are constituted by our imposition of thoughts on them. Our sensations are thus objective in a way in which our thoughts are not.

(iii) There is an objective reality underlying the empirical world which we produce, a reality which we do not produce and which is inaccessible to us.

These are not one and the same doctrine. (i), for example, does not entail (iii). One might believe that the world is subjective, without also believing that there is an objective world which underlies it. (i), again, does not obviously entail (ii). In holding that the world which I or we know is merely subjective, one is not necessarily committed to any particular view of the relationship between thoughts and sensations. In this section we shall be primarily concerned with Hegel's attitude towards (i).

Hegel's discussion of these matters is sometimes marred by a failure to distinguish properly between perceptible, but physical, things and our sense-impressions. The following passage, for example, is considering the Kantian doctrine, (ii), that it is the application of thoughts or categories to our subjective sensations which transforms them into quasi-objective things. In stating this position it is important not to conflate things and sensations, but this is nevertheless what happens:

> To ordinary consciousness, what stands over against it, the sensuously perceptible (*das sinnlich Wahrnehmbare*) (e.g. this animal, this star, etc.), appears as what is self-subsistent, independent, and thoughts are regarded, by contrast, as what is insubstantial and dependent on something else. But in fact it is the sensuously perceptible that is strictly insubstantial and secondary, and thoughts on the contrary are truly independent and primitive . . . . [T]he sensuously perceptible is, of course, the

subjective in so far as it does not have its support in itself and is fleeting and transitory, just as thought has the character of permanence and inner subsistence (*Enz*. I. 41Z.2).

The expression 'the sensuously perceptible' could in any case refer either to perceptible, physical objects or to sense-impressions. But in this passage it is used ambiguously to refer to both. In its first occurrence it refers to physical things, since it is glossed by 'e.g. this animal, this star, etc.'. In its second and third occurrences, however, it refers primarily to sense-impressions. This is clear from the fact that the 'sensuously perceptible' is contrasted with thoughts. Physical things cannot properly be contrasted with thoughts, because thoughts are in some sense embedded in them.[6] The conflation is perhaps assisted by the fact that both things and sensations may be regarded as transitory — things in comparison with the laws and genera which they exemplify, sensations in comparison with things. It owes something, too, to Hegel's characteristic attempt, while purporting to endorse Kant's position, to insinuate his own quite different views. Something similar seems to be happening in the following passage:[7]

> As for the similarly immediate consciousness of the existence of *outer* things [in the philosophies of Descartes and Jacobi], this means nothing more than *sensuous* consciousness; to have such a consciousness is the slightest of cognitions; all that we need to know is that this immediate awareness of the *being* (*Sein*) of external things is deception and error and that the sensuous as such contains no truth, the *being* of these external things is rather a contingent transitory being, a *show* (*Schein*), — they essentially have an existence which is separable from their concept, essence (*Enz*. I. 76).

Hegel is not concerned, as Descartes and Jacobi were, to establish the existence of external objects. He unhesitatingly equates the immediate awareness of them with 'sensuous consciousness', thus blurring the distinction between the contents of our consciousness and the things of which we are conscious. This conflation has something in common with Hegel's recurrent failure to distinguish between a thought or a concept, on the one hand, and the feature or characteristic to which it refers, on the other. Expressions like 'the sensuous' or 'the sensuously perceptible' play, in this context, the same role as 'thought-determination'.[8] The reasons for the conflation are, however, rather different. For, whereas Hegel never questions the importance of thoughts, it is a recurrent theme of his treatment of the sensuous that, since perceptible objects are in any case transitory and unimportant, it does not matter whether they are objective or subjective:

> One might at first suppose that objects lose their reality by the fact that their unity is transferred into the subject. However neither we nor the objects gain anything by their mere possession of *being.* What matters is the *content,* whether this is *true* or not. It does no good to the things that they merely *are.* Time overtakes what *is,* and it also soon *ceases to be.* One could also say that man can according to subjective idealism be very proud of *himself.* But if his world is the mass of sensuous intuitions, then he has no reason to congratulate himself on such a world. In general, therefore, nothing depends on the distinction between objectivity and subjectivity; what matters is the content, and this is both subjective and objective. Even a crime is objective in the sense of mere existence, but it is an intrinsically nugatory existence and it emerges as such in the punishment (*Enz.* I. 42Z. 3. Cf. *PG* pp. 178 ff., M. pp. 142 ff.).

Hegel is here arguing not that subjective idealism is true, but that, in sense (i) at least, it does not matter whether it is true or not. The core of his argument is that whether any importance should be attached to the claim that x exists depends on what x is, its 'content'. The point can be made in terms of Hegel's simile of a book (*Enz.* I. 43Z).[9] It does not matter, he is in effect saying, whether a book is a work of fiction or a factual narrative. What matters is the content of the book, what 'thoughts, general results' it contains and how well integrated they are with the 'individual events, situations, etc.'. This, however, is a mistake. It is, of course, true that unless some specification of x is given, it does not matter whether x exists or not, and if a book has no content then it does not matter whether it is fact or fiction. In those cases, 'Does x exist?' and 'Is it fact or fiction?' are not intelligible questions. But once we have decided that x is a pound note rather than a speck of dust, it does matter whether it exists or not, and similarly with a narrative of some content, it makes sense to ask, and it is perhaps important to answer, whether it is factual or fictional. It might be objected that there are special reasons for supposing the question 'Does the world as a whole really exist or is it just my (or our) ideas?' to be an unimportant one. For it makes no empirical difference what the answer is. But if this is Hegel's point, he has not given it adequate expression. For he adds that the reason why the question of being or existence is unimportant is that transient entities which pass out of existence nevertheless possess it, and that crimes have it, even though their nullity is established by the penalties which they incur. But even if a book describes only crimes and other fleeting events, it might none the less matter whether it is fact or fiction. There is after all a difference between a high and a low crime rate. It is in any case arbitrary to introduce in this context special considerations about crime and punishment or about good and evil. Good or lawful actions are quite as transient as crimes are.[10]

At all events, however, Hegel is less interested in the question whether the world as a whole is subjective or not than in the status of things within the world. This change of concern is reflected in the use to which he puts the notion of 'appearance', as we shall see in the following section.

2 Appearance and actuality

Kant held that the objects with which we are acquainted are appearances.[11] So too does Hegel, or at least he regards some of them as appearances. But he does not mean the same by 'appearance' as Kant does. Kant distinguishes carefully between the words 'appearance' (*Erscheinung*) and 'illusion' (*Schein*). All phenomenal objects are appearances, in the sense that they are merely the way in which reality as it is in itself appears to us. But we can, nevertheless, distinguish between the illusory and the real within our experience, within the realm of appearances:[12]

> When I say that the intuition of outer objects and the self-intuition of the mind alike represent the objects and the mind, in space and in time, as they affect our senses, that is, as they appear, I do not mean to say that these objects are a mere *illusion*. For in an appearance the objects, nay even the properties that we ascribe to them, are always regarded as something actually given. Since, however, in the relation of the given object to the subject, such properties depend on the mode of intuition of the subject, this object as *appearance* is to be distinguished from itself as object *in itself*.

Hegel, too, distinguishes between *Schein* and *Erscheinung*, but not in the same way as Kant does. The word *Schein*, for example, does not mean only 'illusion', but has connotations, over and above those which Kant ascribed to it, in virtue of its association with the verb *scheinen*, 'to shine'.[13] Moreover, unlike Kant, Hegel calls physical entities *Schein* at least as often as he characterizes them as *Erscheinungen*, though this is due in part to his liking for the pun on *Sein*.[14] The important point, however, is that when Hegel claims that objects are appearances he does not mean what Kant meant:[15]

[T]he objects of which we are immediately aware are mere appearances, i.e. . . . they have the ground of their being not in themselves but in something else. But then the further question is how this something else is determined. According to the Kantian philosophy the things of which we are aware are only appearances for *us,* and their *in-itself* (*Ansich*) remains for us an inaccessible beyond . . . . The true situation is in fact this, that the things of which we are immediately aware are mere appearances not only *for us* but *in themselves* (*an sich*) and that the very essence (*Bestimmung*) of things which are thereby finite is to have the ground of their being not in themselves but in the universal divine idea. This conception of things is then also to be denoted as idealism, but, in contrast to that subjective idealism of the critical philosophy, as *absolute idealism.* This absolute idealism, although it goes beyond ordinary, realistic consciousness, is yet in substance so little to be regarded as the property of philosophy that it rather forms the basis of all religious consciousness, in so far as this too regards the sum of everything that exists (*da ist*), in general the world we see, as created and governed by God (*Enz.* I. 45Z).

We might infer from this passage that everything except the logical idea is an appearance. Or we might suppose that at most those features of phenomenal things which are expressible in terms of pure thoughts are not appearances, that trees and rocks, for example, are appearances, while the existence of things with properties and of organic wholes is not. However, Hegel also displays a tendency to distinguish within the empirical world between those things or features of things which are appearances and those which are not. In a discussion, for example, of his controversial dictum that 'What is rational is actual and what is actual is rational' (*PR* Preface), he defends himself against the charge of supporting whatever happens to be the *status quo* by arguing that only some of the things, or features of things, that exist are actual, while others are mere appearances:

An intelligent consideration of the world already distinguishes between what in the wide realm of outer and inner existence (*Dasein*) is only *appearance,* transitory and meaningless, and what in itself truly deserves the name of actuality (*Enz.* I. 6).

But where is the line between actuality and appearance to be drawn? God, the logical idea itself, is the supreme case of actuality: 'he is the most actual thing . . . he alone is truly actual.' But, apart from this 'existence is in part *appearance* and only in part actuality.'

What is actual seems to include far more than those features of things which can be directly described in terms of pure thoughts:

> In ordinary life one randomly calls every brain-wave, error, evil, and everything connected with it, and similarly every existence, however degenerate and transient, an *actuality*. But even ordinarily we feel that a contingent existence does not deserve the emphatic name of something actual; the contingent is an existence which has no greater value than that of something *possible*, an existence which can as well *not be* as be (*Ibid.*).

It is of course a mistake to identify the contingent with the merely possible. After all, what is contingent exists, even if it might not have existed. But, more important than this, is the fact that Hegel is implying that some empirical things — good things, long-lasting things and things which are, in whatever sense, necessary — are actual and are not, therefore, appearances. In particular the leading features of the modern European state are, on Hegel's view, actual, for the point of linking actuality with rationality is to exclude criticism of them.[16]

There is, then, a good deal of ambiguity in Hegel's views on how far the realm of appearance extends. This is explained in part by the variety of strands in his conception of an appearance:

(i) There is, firstly, an ethical strand. The consignment of evil to the realm of the non-actual cannot be justified on 'scientific' grounds. An individual crime is indeed transitory, but crime as such is not. It is as predictable and explicable that there will be crimes and evil as it is that there will be good actions and punishments, while the status of any particular good act or intention is as contingent as that of a bad one. Hegel's motive here is an ethical one.

(ii) What is necessary is actual, and what is contingent is merely an appearance. The boundary between the necessary and the contingent is, however, an unclear one. In one sense only the logical idea and features of it are necessary, so that the line between the actual and the apparent could be drawn between God and things. In another sense, those things or features of things are necessary which can be explained by the empirical sciences, while the area of contingency is restricted to such matters as the number of species of parrot.[17]

(iii) An object is an appearance if, and only if, it is fleeting and transitory. There is some connection between transience and contingency. After all, if a thing does not exist at a certain time, then it cannot be necessary at that time, and it is a natural step

410

from there to the conclusion that it is not necessary *simpliciter.* It is clear that if something 'appears' in this sense, it does not follow that there is something of which it is the appearance, but which does not itself appear. This sense of 'appear' is similar to that of the word in the sentence:

'He unexpectedly appeared on my doorstep.'

His appearance on my doorstep is not the appearance of something which is itself hidden. By contrast, in the sentence:

'His appearance betrayed overwork'

there is an implicit distinction between the appearance and an underlying condition which is indicated by, but not manifest in, the appearance. Roughly speaking, Kant uses 'appearance' in this second sense, but Hegel uses it in the first.

(iv) An object is an appearance if it depends on something else. This idea, as well as (iii), is present in Hegel's remark that 'we all have cause to be pleased that in the things which surround us we have to do with appearances and not with fixed and independent existences, since in that case we would soon starve both physically and mentally' (*Enz.* I. 131Z. Cf. PG pp. 87 f., M. p. 65). Physical things are not self-sustaining, but dependent on other things and vulnerable to their influence:

> When we speak of appearance, we combine with it the conception of an indeterminate manifold of existent things, the being of which is entirely mediation and which thus are not self-supporting, but have their validity only as aspects (*Momente*) (*Enz.* I. 131Z).

Things depend on other things, and this dependence is essential to them:

> Ordinary consciousness regards the objects, of which it is aware, in their individuality as independent and self-supporting, and when they prove to be related to one another and conditioned by each other, then this reciprocal dependence on each other is regarded as something external to the objects and not an aspect of their essence (*Enz.* I. 45Z.).

(v) Hegel does not stop at the conclusion that things depend on other things, however. They are, as we have seen, dependent on the logical idea: they have 'the ground of their being not in them- selves but in the universal divine idea' (*Enz.* I. 45Z. Cf. 131Z). What constitutes 'idealism' is not simply the claim that things depend on each other, but the view that there is an essence on which they all depend. Philosophers, Hegel contends, have almost invariably taken this step, and have to that extent been idealists:

> A philosophy which ascribed true, ultimate, absolute being to finite existence as such would not deserve the name of philosophy; principles of ancient or modern philosophies, water or matter or atoms, are *thoughts*, universal, ideal, not things as they immediately present themselves, i.e. in sensuous individuality – even Thales' water; for although it is also empirical water, it is in addition the *in-itself* or *essence* of all other things, and these are not independent, self-grounded, but *posited* by something else, water, i.e. ideal (*WL* I. p. 172, M. p. 155).

It does not follow, however, that the essence is something hidden from us which we merely postulate in order to explain phenomena, but which is not manifest in them:

> But it is also involved in this that the essence does not remain behind or beyond appearance, but rather that it is, as it were, the infinite goodness which releases its show (*Schein*) into immediacy and accords it the joy of existence (*Enz.* I. 131Z).

It is, of course, true even of Kant's things-in-themselves that they do not remain entirely inaccessible, but reveal themselves in a certain way in phenomena. Hegel, however, means that the essence manifests itself in the stronger sense that no residual question or doubt about its real nature remains unresolvable. A partial analogue of what he has in mind would be the 'appearance' of a book. The printed copies of the book, in virtue of which it appears, are manifestations of an authoritative manuscript or, perhaps, of the book *in abstracto*. There is, however, nothing hidden which is not given in the appearance of the book. If I read an accurate copy, then I read the book. This analogy is incomplete, since, among other things, the distinct copies of the book do not in any obvious way depend on each other. From this point of view a better analogy would be that of a structured institution (the logical idea), the positions in which are occupied, successively and contemporaneously, by different people (empirical phenomena). It is not, however, natural to use the word 'appear' in this context.

It is intelligible enough that, given these different strands in his notion of appearance, Hegel should hover between saying that all empirical phenomena are appearances and saying that only some of them are. Some objects are less transient than others and can be regarded as permanent in contrast to them. Some objects are more nearly self-developing, better insulated against external influences and more resistant to invasion from without than others are.[18] All of them, however, are grounded in the logical idea and, from this point of view, all of them are appearances. Indeed, if any entities elude its embrace, it is more likely to be those deviant or contingent ones which Hegel regards as appearances *par excellence*. We should also remember, however, that, if the circularity of Hegel's system is taken seriously, then not only are empirical objects dependent on the logical idea; it is also dependent on them. For, as we have seen, the logical idea with which the system begins is supposed to emerge, at the end of the system, from the empirical world which it generates.[19] Since this is so, it is at least intelligible that Hegel should wish to say *both* that all empirical objects are appearances — for they are all dependent on the logical idea — *and* that some of them are actual — for they need a more substantial status in order to sustain the logical idea which emerges from them.

These matters will be reconsidered later.[20] In the following section, however, the question to be asked is this: Why should we accept the move from granting that things depend on each other to the conclusion that they have 'the ground of their being in the logical idea'? Why does acknowledgment of the interdependence and transience of things commit us to any form of idealism?

3 *Appearance and the concept*

Hegel has two general lines of argument for his belief that things depend on the logical idea. The first, roughly speaking, corresponds to his belief that all finite things are appearances and starts from the facts of universal interdependence and transience. The second corresponds to his conflicting belief that some things are not mere appearances, but are relatively independent and self-determining. It is the first of these lines of argument that will be considered in this section.

We have already seen that, if we start from thought, Hegel has some reason for believing that the empirical world can be derived from it. But, if we start from the empirical world itself, what reason is there to suppose that it has an essence at all, or, if it does, that that essence is thought? What support can idealism derive from the transience and interrelatedness of things? Hegel has at least three arguments which help to mediate this transition. The first two have already been considered. Firstly, we have already seen that, on Hegel's view, the universe as a whole, the totality of interacting, reciprocally dependent objects, is self-determining and self-sustaining and that anything which determines and sustains itself is determined and sustained by its concept, in this case the logical idea.[21] Interdependence and transience are taken, in this argument, as showing that the universe is in fact one single entity. The connection between self-determination and concept-determination is supplied by traditional confusions, between, for example, holistic explanation and conceptual explanation and between God's being *causa sui* and his being fully determined by his concept.[22] Hegel's belief that the concept of a thing explains in part, and might *wholly* explain, its character, that what cannot be explained in terms of other things must be referred to concepts, is, of course, objectionable. What makes it even seem plausible is his mistaken identification of a concept with a sort of seed, or a plan embodied in a seed, which competes with external influences for the determination of the thing. Before we speak of the logical idea as the seed of the universe, we should recall that seeds are material entities, that they need water and sunlight, and that the way to find out what plan is embodied in them is to watch them grow.[23]

The second argument for the view that, if things depend on each other, then they depend on the logical idea is the converse of the argument for the conclusion that structure determines content.[24] If the relations between things are of their essence and are not simply peripheral to them, then these relations must be of a general, abstract sort, corresponding to the pure thoughts of the *Logic* rather than to empirical conceptions. Empirical phenomena are, in that case, dependent on the scaffolding of the logical idea. We have, however, already seen that this argument is exposed to serious objections.

Thirdly, and finally, Hegel assumes that the empirical world is finite. An empiricist who ignores or denies the existence of a supersensible world concerns himself only with the *finite* (*Enz.* I. 38).[25] Again, a pantheist who believes that God ⇒ the world is identifying God with the finite (*Enz.* I. 36).[26] On Hegel's account of finitude, it is of course absurd to suppose that there are only finite things and no infinite one. If the empirical world is finite, then there must be something else which bounds and influences it. But why is Hegel so sure that the empirical world is finite? It must be so, if there is anything else — God or a supersensible realm — which limits and determines it. An empiricist who believes that there is a supersensible realm, but who simply disregards it, must concede that he is concerned only with the finite and that his knowledge is incomplete. But an empiricist who denies that there is such an other-worldly realm can insist that the phenomenal world is infinite, unbounded and self-sustaining. If, but only if, the world as a whole is finite can we infer that there is something else which bounds and sustains it.

414

Why, then, did Hegel assume that it was finite? There are several possible reasons:

(i) He may have supposed that it was finite on the ground that it *would* be finite if there *were* a supersensible realm. This, however, is a mistake. Whether something is finite or not depends on whether there actually is anything else.

(ii) He may have been misled by the fact that the world of appearances in Kant's sense must be finite — for it is the appearance of something else which is not an appearance — into supposing that the world of appearances in his own sense is finite. This, again, is a mistake. To say that something is an appearance in Hegel's sense need only mean that it is transitory and/or dependent on other things. But this does not entail that there is anything which is not an appearance, except, of course, the whole collection of appearances.

(iii) He may have inferred that the world as a whole is finite from the fact that any and every proper part of it is finite. Such a confusion is suggested by Hegel's account of what he believes to be a common misinterpretation of pantheism:

> [T]he expression *pantheism* or rather the German expression into which it is roughly translated, that God is the one and *all* (*das Eine und alles*) . . . leads to the false conception that in pantheistic religion or philosophy *everything*, i.e. each existence in its finitude and individuality is declared to be God or a god, the finite as *being* (*als seiend*) is deified' (*VBDG* XVI, in *VPR* II. pp. 492 f., S.S. III. pp. 318 f.).

The misinterpretation consists in taking the sentence 'All things are God' to mean, not 'All things together are God', but 'Each thing taken separately is God': 'All, i.e. all things in their existing individualization are God — thus it [viz. the understanding] conceives pantheism, when it takes the πᾶν in this determinate category of each and every individual' (*VBDG* XVI, in *VPR* II. p. 493, S.S. III. 319). This interpretation of pantheism would commit us to saying such things as 'This table is (a) God', 'This tree is (a) God', and so on. It seems to have the consequence that there is more than one god, one in fact for each finite entity. This, however, is not the misinterpretation of pantheism which Hegel usually has in mind. Atheistic pantheism (God ⇒ the world) identifies God not with each finite bit of the world, but with the world as a whole, in such a way that God is 'reduced to the mere finite, external manifold of existence' (*Enz.* I. 50).[27] But why finite? Apparently it is because Hegel identifies these two misinterpretations, believing that both can be refuted by pointing to the essential impermanence and dependence of each and every finite thing. This may not be the result of sheer confusion. He may feel that if no single finite entity is self-supporting, then no collection of them, however large, can be self-supporting, but must depend on something else — an essence — which supports them all. If this were correct, then to believe that the empirical world as a whole needs no further support and is thus infinite is in effect to assume that at least some of its finite parts are self-sustaining — which, on Hegel's view, they are not. A persistent empiricist, however, could reject the proposition that a collection of dependent entities cannot be self-supporting, and it is difficult to refute him.[28] The inference from the interrelatedness of things to their dependence on an essence, the logical idea, is of questionable validity.

4 Actuality and the concept

Hegel's second type of argument for the dependence of things on the logical idea takes its start not from the interdependence of all things, but from certain relatively independent items in the world, in particular living organisms.[29] He represents himself, in this context, as arguing against 'subjective idealism' (*Enz.* I. 42Z.3). What he means by this, however, is not the view that the whole of our experience, the combination of thought and sensation, is subjective. As we have seen, he is inclined to argue that the truth or falsity of subjective idealism in this sense is irrelevant. He means, rather, the view that thoughts or categories have a less secure, more 'subjective', status than our sensory intake. Sensations or intuitions are, on this view, given to us and we convert them into objects by projecting thoughts onto them. What makes subjective idealism of this type seem plausible is a premiss which Hegel shares with Kant, namely that 'the categories are not contained in immediate sensation' (*Enz.* I. 42Z.3).[30] It is tempting to infer from this that objects are at bottom no more than our sensations, that the thoughts are what we contribute to them. This type of idealism, however, Hegel believes to be false. He has at least three arguments against it:

(i) The fact that thought-determinations are not given in our sensations, but are accessible only to thought, does not entail that they are merely subjective and do not really belong to objects. Thought and sensation might, as far as this goes, be on a par with respect to objectivity and subjectivity. This argument does not, of course, establish that they are, but only that no conclusive reason has yet been given for supposing that they are not.

(ii) Objects, especially living organisms, are, as we have seen, constituted by the generic concepts which they exemplify: if 'we take animality away from the dog, it would be impossible to say what it is' (*Enz.* I. 24Z.1).[31] What does Hegel believe that this argument establishes? His general conclusion is this:[32]

> The indispensable foundation, the concept, the universal, which is — if one can only abstract from the conception in the word 'thought' [i.e. consider what are strictly thoughts and ignore conceptions] — thought itself, cannot be regarded *only* as an indifferent form which is *in* a content (*WL* I. pp. 26 f., M. p. 37).

The point is presumably that objects of this type are not to be viewed as arising from our imposition of concepts on a material or sensory given. The argument does not, however, establish this. It may be true that one could not say what an individual dog was unless one applied the concept of animality, but this need not be because there was an individual which we were unable to describe, but rather because there would be no individuals at all, and therefore no dogs, until we produced them by our conceptual activity. All that there is, according to this view, is a material or a sensory given. Until thoughts have been applied to it, it is ineffable. Until thoughts such as that of animality have been applied to it, it is describable only in such terms as 'red', 'hazy' and so on. The argument does not, moreover, show that we should or must apply the concepts we do in roughly the way we now do, if we are to have identifiable individuals and to give a correct account of the world. It may be that there are a variety of alternative ways in which we can conceptualize the material or sensory element, some of which would leave no room for dogs or animals. The most that this argument establishes is that, if there are to be individuals, then we must apply *some* general, sortal concepts *or other*.[33]

(iii) Hegel, however, believes that there actually are dogs, animals, men and so on quite independently of the particular conceptual system which I or my culture happen to employ. A conceptual system which lacked the concept of an animal would be defective, however rich and elaborate it was in other respects. For reality is in fact not simply differentiated, but also articulated into relatively discrete objects such that one description of it, though it may do justice to our sensations as much as another, may still be less appropriate. This conclusion is supported, however, not by argument (ii), but by drawing attention to the cohesive relationships obtaining between the parts of an organism, to the power of higher animals to move freely through, and in relative independence of, their environment, to fend off and devour items in their surroundings, and so on.[34] Might we not, nevertheless, regard an animal or a plant as consisting of a material or a sensory element — identified, perhaps, in terms of certain low-level thoughts[35] — and the complex thoughts which confer on it the status of a plant or an animal? According to Hegel, we cannot. In the case of the material element, he would argue, the appropriate description of it, as for example 'flesh' and 'blood', already implies that it is the material of an *animal*. If the material were detached from the animal, then it would cease to have the characteristics ascribed to it. The flesh, for example, would not be alive and would not therefore be, properly speaking, flesh (*Enz.* I. 126Z).[36] The material of which an organism consists differs in this respect from the marble of which a statue is made, though, as we have seen, Hegel has other objections to the form–matter distinction which apply more generally.[37] In the case of our sensory intake, Hegel need not deny that living organisms, like anything else, can provide us with sensations which are minimally thought-ridden. The point is that it is not up to us how we proceed to conceptualize these further. There are wrong ways of doing it and a right way, a way which corresponds to the independent structure of the reality which produces them.

This, then, is a part of what Hegel means by claiming that thoughts are 'objective' (*Enz.* I. 24). Argument (iii) on its own does not, of course, establish that thoughts or thought-determinations constitute the individuals in which they are embedded, that it is thoughts that are primarily responsible for the articulation of the world. As far as argument (iii) goes, thoughts may play no greater role in this than conceptions or sensations. All that has been shown is that thoughts and sensations cannot be disentangled from each other, that they are, with respect to objectivity, on a par. This, however, is where argument (ii) comes into play. For having shown, by argument (iii), that thoughts are 'objective', we can now show, by argument (ii), that they constitute the individuals which exemplify them, that their part in the articulation of the world is the dominant one. Thoughts, then, or the features corresponding to thoughts, are, on Hegel's view, *both* objective *and,* as it were, essential or constitutive.

5 *Purpose and subjectivity*

This, then, is Hegel's argument against the second component of Kant's 'subjective idealism'. It is, however, hard to feel that the dispute has yet been settled in Hegel's favour. In the first place the argument seems to rely heavily, though not exclusively, on the conception of living organisms as intrinsically purposive which he shares with Kant.[38] Kant's own account of this matter is complex, but he nevertheless seems to have believed that the purposiveness of living organisms is subjective in a way that the mechanistic, causal ordering of nature is not:[39]

> We are right, however, in applying the teleological estimate, at least problematically, to the investigation of nature; but only with a view to bringing it under principles of observation and research by *analogy* to the causality that looks to ends, while not pretending to *explain* it by this means. Thus it is an estimate of the reflective, not of the determinant, judgement.

If this were correct, then it would presumably do some damage to Hegel's arguments for the objectivity of thoughts. For even if the purposiveness of organisms implies that thoughts are objective, the objectivity of thoughts is only established if the purposive account is true or objective and not merely a convenient way of looking at things. Hegel criticizes Kant's view in the following way:

> Now although in such an idea the understanding–relation of end and means, of subjectivity and objectivity, is sublimated, still in contradiction to this the purpose is again declared to be a cause which exists and is active *only as a conception*, i.e. as something *subjective* — thus purposive determination too is declared to be only a principle of judgment which belongs to *our* understanding.
> Once critical philosophy has arrived at the result that reason can know only *appearances,* still one would at least have a choice for living nature between two *equally subjective* ways of thinking and, according to Kant's exposition, even an obligation not to cognize natural products merely according to the categories of quality, cause and effect, composition, constituents, etc. The principle of *inner purposiveness,* had it been adhered to and developed in scientific application, would have introduced an entirely different, higher way of looking at them (*Enz.* I. 58).

This passage contains at least two arguments against the subjectivity of teleology. The first is that to regard it as subjective contradicts the very notion of inner purposiveness. For it involves making a distinction – between a purpose and the means of its realization, between subjectivity and objectivity – which the concept of inner purposiveness forbids us to draw. Secondly, there is no reason to give the categories of quality, of causality, and so on – 'mechanical' categories – priority over that of inner purposiveness. We would have a choice between two ways, perhaps two equally subjective ways, of looking at things.

There are genuine difficulties in Kant's account which cannot be entered into here. But he seems to have a reply to each of these objections. The reply to the first might run as follows: An organism as a whole, and each of its organs, is both end and means. Whereas an 'extrinsic' purpose can be realized by alternative means – a letter, for example, can be written on this or that kind of paper, in ink, pencil or typed – an organism has to consist of just this (type of) material organized in just this way.[40] But why does it follow that the view of an entity as intrinsically purposive in this sense cannot be merely subjective? If an entity actually is internally purposive, then it is not we who make it into a unity or give it the diverse properties which it has. But this does not entail that we cannot adopt the teleological viewpoint simply as a useful way of looking at a certain type of entity, without committing ourselves to the belief that it really is purposive. Kant is not distinguishing, within a purposive entity, between its subjectively introduced purpose and the material (the 'means') on which this purpose is imposed. He is rather placing a question mark by the whole teleological account of the entity as one in which end and means are inextricably intertwined. Hegel's objection, however, can perhaps be reformulated. If we are to distinguish between entities which can be appropriately regarded as if they were internally purposive and those entities which cannot, then we must give a description, in terms of non-teleological categories, of those features which invite a teleological account of some entities but not of others. Our description of these features will be as objective as any description of empirical phenomena ever can be. But then, according to Kant, if we proceed to view such entities in a teleological manner, it is because they are otherwise inexplicable, at least in the present state of our knowledge. We are not entitled to claim that these entities really are intrinsically purposive. But does this not introduce a rift between the material or means and the end or purpose, a rift which the teleological viewpoint forbids? Surely not. The distinction is rather one between different levels of our understanding of living organisms. The features which suggest a teleological account are not themselves an organ of a

420

living creature or the material of which it consists, but such things as the interlocking and articulation of its parts. Hegel himself must, in any case, draw some such distinction between the empirically discoverable characteristics of things and the categories in terms of which they are to be understood, if he is to insist that some things, but not others, are to be viewed teleologically.

To the second objection, namely that teleology is on a par with the mechanistic categories and there is no reason to suppose the one is any more subjective than the other, Kant's answer might be this. Living organisms, as even Hegel agrees, presuppose causal processes in a way that causal processes do not presuppose living organisms. Organisms inhabit a causally ordered environment and exploit causal regularities for their survival. Causal regularities, Kant believes, are necessary if we are to have any experience of an objective, or quasi-objective, world at all, whereas purposiveness is required only for the explanation of certain contingent items in our experience. Living organisms are recalcitrant to explanation in causal, mechanistic terms and would be unintelligible if we did not employ the notion of purposiveness. We might, however, have had objective experience which did not contain such pockets of incomprehensibility and we would not then have needed to invoke teleology for this purpose. Kant thus has some justification for placing purposiveness at a different level of subjectivity from causality.

What Hegel's answer would have been to this is not clear. Any adequate reply should, however, begin by distinguishing between the empirically ascertainable features of certain entities, features which tempt us to give a teleological account of them, and, on the other hand, the purposive account itself. One might, for example, agree that there objectively are such entities — we might call them, non-committally, 'organic entities' — while insisting that the teleological account of them is merely subjective. We can then ask, firstly, Is the existence of organic entities necessary? Hegel might have questioned the association of objectivity with necessity or with indispensability for objective experience. Organic entities, he might have argued, may not be necessary in this sense, but it does not follow that they are not objective. And, if they are objective, there seems no reason to doubt that the categories in terms of which they are to be understood are any less objective than that of causality. It is more likely, however, that Hegel would argue that the existence of organic entities is necessary. To do so is presumably a commitment which his programme for a philosophy of nature entails (*Enz.* II. 343 ff.). He also believes that the existence of living organisms is a necessary condition for the development of the self-conscious ego (*PG* pp. 135 ff., M. pp. 106 ff.). Since the ego, at least, is indispensable for objective experience, it would follow that so too are organic entities. The ego, however, is not only dependent on organic entities. It is also, like the logical idea itself, a far better example of the type of unity characteristic of organic entities than is any merely natural organism (*Enz.* I. 164; II. 248). Living organisms occupy a position on the *scala naturae* some way below the higher unity of the human mind and mediate the gulf between sheerly mechanistic nature and the ego.

Even if we grant, however, that the existence of organic entities is necessary, it does not follow that the category of inner purposiveness is the appropriate one to apply to them. Hegel believes that the category of teleology has been derived *a priori* within the *Logic*, but we might nevertheless question whether anything exemplifies it, let alone living organisms. The answer to this, however, is that the argument of the preceding section for the view that thoughts are objective does not require the premiss that living organisms are intrinsically purposive. To establish that it is not we who unify things, that nature is organized and articulated independently of our conceptual activity, it is enough if we concede that things, especially organic things, display a special sort of unity, a unity which can be discovered by observation and experiment.[41] We do not need to go on to attribute this unity to any kind of purpose. For most of Hegel's arguments for the objectivity of thought do not depend on our taking this further step.[42]

6 Hegel, Kant and objectivity

We might perhaps have inferred from Hegel's mind-model of the universe that things as they are in themselves, independently of our cognitive activity, are entirely free of thought, are perhaps merely the brute sensations of the cosmic mind, and that it is we who first introduce thoughts into them. But this, as we have seen, would be a mistake. Hegel believes that thoughts are in some sense in the things themselves. In any case, unlike Kant, he does not regard the self-conscious ego as an 'original identity', capable of conferring unity on other things (*Enz.* I. 42).[43] The unified, self-conscious ego is the product of a complex psychological development and its emergence goes hand in hand with its discovery of unities in nature.[44] Hegel sometimes marks his difference from Kant by claiming that 'thoughts are not merely our thoughts, but are at the same time the *in-itself* (*das Ansich*) of things and of the objective in general' (*Enz.* I. 41Z.2). Just as God is no longer something which we merely think about, but rather thoughts themselves, so the essence of things, what things are in themselves, is not just something which we think about, but thoughts. There is, in this respect, a certain parallel between Hegel and Kant. Kant's thing-in-itself is, on Hegel's view, merely a projection of the simple, indeterminate ego; the thing-in-itself is thus similarly simple and empty.[45] Hegel, on the other hand, regards the logical idea as the structure both of the ego and of the 'in-itself' of things. The ego unravels itself into the logical idea and is therefore luminous and knowable. Since things-in-themselves share the same structure, they too are knowable.[46] Hegel, however, believes, as we have seen, that he can undertake an enterprise which Kant could not, namely to trace the path by which things-in-themselves, the logical idea, develop into the phenomenal world of nature and mind.[47]

A Kantian might object, however, that, even if this is how the world seems to be, it might at bottom be quite different. Hegel may have refuted subjective idealism in one sense, by showing that thoughts are as objective as sensations are and that they are the essence or in-itself of phenomenal things. But there is another sense of 'subjective idealism', the doctrine, namely, that there is a reality underlying the phenomenal world which is inaccessible to us. Hegel's considerations about the relationship between thoughts and sensations within our experience do nothing, it might be argued, to refute this doctrine, to show that our experience is the experience of what is actually and objectively real. We could agree, for example, that phenomenal things have essences, that they belong to genera, manifest forces, and so on, but argue that these are not the things as they are in themselves, but, as it were, things as they are in themselves *for us*. The distinction between things as they appear to be and things as they really or essentially are can indeed be drawn within our expereince. But, in so far as we can give an account of things as they are in themselves, as well as of how they appear to us, this account is still, at the deepest level, subjective. Things as they are in themselves lie entirely beyond our experience and any account we can give of it.

We have already seen, in an earlier chapter, some of Hegel's arguments against this version of 'subjective idealism', and there is no need to repeat them here.[48] We can, however, summarize his main lines of objection to it. The first depends on his failure to draw a distinction between thoughts and the features or entities which correspond to thoughts.[49] The opening sections of the *Phenomenology* are accounts, among other things, of the various ways in which we distinguish, within our experience, between things as they are in themselves and things as they appear to us, between, for example, forces and the perceptible manifestations of these forces (*PG* pp. 102 ff., M. pp. 79 ff.). But these accounts of the relationship between things and our awareness of things are, we might suppose, all accounts only of the relationship between 'things-in-themselves-*for-us*' and 'things-as-they-appear-to-us'. Both of these are to be placed on the side of things as they appear to us, and it does not follow that there is no genuinely inaccessible reality lying beyond them. If, however, we refuse to distinguish between thoughts and what the thoughts are thoughts of, then this point cannot be made. The essences of things as they appear to us, forces, for example, or genera, are simply thoughts. But so, too, is the thought of an unknowable reality simply a thought. There can be no more in it than there is in the thought itself and, since it is supposed to be unknowable, the thought is an extremely thin thought, readily accessible and transparent to us.[50]

A second factor in Hegel's rejection of the doctrine is his refusal to distinguish sharply between the question whether our knowledge can be of things in themselves and the question whether, at the level of appearances, it can be complete. To know things as they are in themselves would be to have complete knowledge and to have complete knowledge of appearances would be to know things as they are in themselves. Kant himself provides considerable licence for the association of these two ideas:[51]

[W]hat necessarily forces us to transcend the limits of experience and of all appearances is the *unconditioned*, which reason, by necessity and by right, demands in things in themselves, as required to complete the series of conditions.

The two notions are conflated in Hegel's concept of the infinite, and, as we have seen, he believes that we can know the infinite:

precisely the designation of something as finite or limited involves the proof of the *actual presence* of the infinite, the unlimited . . . the awareness of limit can only be in so far as the unlimited is *on this side* in consciousness (*Enz.* I. 60).

This argument is unsound, however. It does not establish that we can know the infinite, either in the sense of reality as in itself or in the sense of the complete range of appearances. For one can say that something is finite or limited simply on the ground that one has found, or can think of, something the limits of which are staked further out. Even if the infinite must be in some sense within our consciousness, this need not involve complete knowledge of it, but only a vague or indeterminate thought of it, such as Kant is prepared to ascribe to us with respect to things in themselves. It is, moreover, hard to see how our knowledge could be complete. For, we might suppose, the world stretches to infinity in several directions: in space, the infinite series of objects; in time, the endless series of causes and effects; and, in depth, the potentially endless series of explanatory laws and entities. Is our knowledge not inevitably restricted to a finite segment of these series? Hegel believes that it is not. The universe forms, on his view, a circle, and so does our knowledge of it. Together they also form a circle, or rather a circle of circles. The world is therefore infinite, but only in the sense of being finite and unbounded, and so too is our knowledge of it. Our knowledge, then, is, apart from some contingent but unimportant details, complete. There is, therefore, no space left for unknowable things-in-themselves, if these are conceived as the completion of an infinite series, for there is no such series to be completed. Nor is there any need for them as the ultimate explanation of what there is. For, as we have seen, the circularity of our account of the universe ensures, Hegel believes, that it is a complete and final explanation of it.[52]

It can be objected that this vision of a wholly transparent and intelligible cosmos is secured only at the cost of blurring or rejecting certain important questions. Are space and time, for example, finite or infinite? Hegel answers that they are *both* finite *and* infinite, but this, as we have seen, does not amount to a satisfactory reply to the question.[53] Sometimes he suggests that it is a trivial question and that to concern oneself with it, or with the series of spatial and temporal objects, is just a waste of time, like devoting one's energies to the expansion of π (*WL* I. pp. 264 ff., M. pp. 228 ff.). In that case, however, there may nevertheless be an answer to the question, just as there is an answer to the question whether the expansion of π is infinite or not. Alternatively, one might suppose that, since the world is a projection of atemporal and aspatial thoughts, there is, on Hegel's view, no answer to the question beyond the meanderings of thought itself — any more than there are answers to questions about fictional characters beyond the words and intentions of their creators. It seems essential to Hegel's system, however, that he should give no straight answer not only to the question itself, but not even to the question whether the question has an answer or not. For he cannot give an unequivocal reply to the question: 'Is the world thought?' Or not, at least, in terms of the identity ('=') and difference ('≠') of the understanding. The best we can do is to say that the world ⇔ thought.

This, then, is Hegel's answer to the subjective idealism which he finds in Kant. The next step is to consider in more detail how his account of finite things is related to the *Logic,* and we shall do this in the sections which follow.

7 Logic and things

The logical idea is related to finite things in a variety of ways:

(i) It is contrasted with them. Thought as such is conceived as infinite, self-determining and fluid, whereas the phenomenal world is finite and separate or 'asunder'. Thought, as we have seen, over-reaches this contrast, prefiguring within itself the distinction between itself and its other.[54]

(ii) There is a parallel between the logical idea and the world of finite things. A concept like that of a whole consisting of parts is finite in the sense that it is bounded by and contrasts with other concepts, just as a finite thing is bounded by and contrasts with other things. The fate of finite concepts at the hands of pure thinking is mirrored by the mobility and transience of finite things.[55]

(iii) Apart from its general finitude, any concept has intrinsic defects. It is properly applicable only to entities which are them-selves defective in ways which mirror the defects of the concept. Defectiveness is a matter of degree. Concepts are more or less defective, and so are the things which correspond to them.[56]

(iv) Some of the concepts are applicable only to finite things, because they imply by their very nature that there is something else distinct from the entity to which they apply. If, for example, something is a force, there must be something else which induces it to manifest itself. If something has a certain quality, there must be something else with a contrasting quality in the same range. The examination of such concepts as these is intended to explain why change and dissolution occur.

We have already found it useful to compare the concepts of the *Logic* to scientific theories.[57] Some of the oddity of the relationship between the logical idea and finite things emerges more clearly if we do so here. If scientific theories were related to things in all the ways that Hegel's concepts are related to things, we would have to say something like this:

(i) Scientific theories as a whole contrast with the finite things they are about.

(ii) The finitude of things is a reflection of the finitude of theories, of their distinctness from one another, and the transience and mutability of things reflects the refutation and modification of theories.

(iii) Finite things are more or less accurately described by false or inadequate theories and this explains why the things themselves are false or inadequate.

(iv) Some theories explain why things change and perish.

The first of these points of contact between the logical idea and finite entities has already been considered at length.[58] The fourth is sufficiently obvious to require no extended discussion. The following account will therefore focus on points (ii) and (iii) — the parallel between the logical idea and the finite world, and the embodiment of defective concepts in defective things.

8 *Objective understanding and objective reason*

First, then, how is the parallel between the logical idea and the finite world to be conceived? As we have seen, logic involves three elements or aspects. First, there is 'thinking as *understanding*', which 'sticks to the fixed determinancy and the distinctness of it from others' (*Enz.* I. 80). Secondly, the '*dialectical* element is the very self-elimination of such finite determinations and their transition into their opposites' (*Enz.* I. 81). Finally, the '*speculative* or *positively-rational* aspect grasps the unity of the determinations in their opposition, the *affirmative* element which is contained in their dissolution and their transition' (*Enz.* I. 82). Roughly speaking, these three aspects concern respectively the sharp boundaries which a concept is initially supposed to have, the breakdown of such a concept or pair of concepts, and the emergence of a higher concept from this breakdown.[59]

These aspects or elements have been considered so far only with a view to the part they play in logic. They are involved, however, not only in logic, but in practically all forms of human activity. In cognition, for example, it is the understanding which is responsible for our distinguishing substances, forces and genera, regarding them as quite different from one another. It is also associated with the deductive arguments which we employ in, for example, mathematics and jurisprudence.[60] In art, religion and philosophy we owe to the understanding clarity, definiteness and precision. In the realm of practice, again, the understanding is manifested in a person's having a single, clear aim or interest and neither acting with only a vague and indefinite purpose nor flitting from one thing to another. A judge who rigidly applies the law and delivers verdicts in accordance with it is guided by the understanding (*Enz.* I. 80Z).

Passages like this are of interest in so far as they show how far Hegel was removed, in intention at least, from the romantic, the mystical and the murky. For our purposes, however, a more relevant fact about the understanding is that it, like the logical idea as a whole, is objective as well as subjective. Its characteristic features are to be found in things as well as in our ways of looking at things:

> The understanding is accordingly to be regarded as corresponding to what is called the *goodness* of God, in so far as this is taken as meaning that finite things *are,* that they have a subsistence. Thus one recognizes e.g. in nature the goodness of God in the fact that the different classes and genera of both plants and animals are equipped with everything they need to preserve themselves and prosper. This is also the case with man, with individuals and with whole peoples, for whom the indispensable prerequisites of their existence and development are in part found immediately available (as e.g. climate, quality and products of the country, etc.) and are in part in their possession as dispositions, talents, etc. Conceived in this way the understanding is displayed in general in all areas of the objective world, and it is essential to the completeness of an object that the principle of understanding should get satisfaction in it. Thus e.g. the state is incomplete if it has not arrived at a differentiation of classes and callings and if functions of politics and government which are different in concept have not yet acquired particular organs, in the same way as is the case in the developed animal organism with its different functions of sensation, movement, digestion, etc. (*Enz.* I. 80Z).

An aspect of logic or of thought is correlated with an aspect of things. But which aspect of things? The passage provides no unequivocal answer. It suggests, rather, two distinct answers. The first answer is that the understanding is manifested in the fact that there are any finite things at all, that 'finite things *are,* that they have a subsistence (*dass die endlichen Dinge sind, dass sie ein Bestehen haben)*'. We would expect finite things to include humble entities like crimes, stones, and lightning-flashes, as well as more elevated ones like plants and animals. Hegel does not deny that such entities have being, and the goodness of God is generally held responsible for finite things as a whole: 'God as the essence is the goodness of creating a world in virtue of the fact that he confers existence on the elements of his shining into himself (*den Momenten seines Scheinens in sich Existenz verleiht)*' (*Enz.* I. 131Z). The second answer is that the understanding is manifested not in all

428

finite things, but only in a special sub-set of them. This includes, firstly, those things which are relatively long-lasting and self-supporting, because they have special equipment with which they ensure their own survival, and, secondly, those things which are relatively well articulated and organized such as developed states and animals. Conversely, it excludes transient entities like waves and lightning-flashes and also things like stones which, although fairly durable, have no special survival equipment; it excludes simple, undeveloped entities such as egalitarian communes and earthworms. Why Hegel is tempted to give these two distinct answers will emerge later in this section.

The second aspect of logic, the dialectical, is similarly found in cognitive and practical attitudes other than logic. It appears, for example, in various types of scepticism and sophistry.[61] It is, however, also objective. Just as the understanding corresponds to the fact that finite things *are,* so the dialectic is manifested in the fact that they change and pass away:

> We are aware that everything finite, far from being fixed and ultimate, is, rather, changeable and transient, and this is just the dialectic of the finite, by which it, being in itself what is other than itself, is also driven beyond what it immediately is and veers into its opposite . . . . [T]he principle of dialectic corresponds to the conception of the *power* of God. We say that all things (i.e. everything finite as such) go to judgment (*zu Gericht gehen*) and we have here the intuition of the dialectic as the universal irresistible power before which nothing, however sure and firm it may seem, can stand fast (*Enz.* I. 81Z.1. Cf. 131Z).

The dialectic of things does not consist, however, in the mere fact of change and transience. It is important to see, on Hegel's view, that change and destruction are not simply the result of external and accidental encroachments on a thing, but are essentially involved in its nature: '[T]he finite is not only limited from without, but eliminates itself through its very own nature and passes into its opposite of its own accord' (*Enz.* I. 81Z.1). This point is illustrated, as we have seen, with the case of human mortality. Men die, Hegel argues, not primarily as a result of external contingencies, but because 'life as such bears the seed of death in itself' (*Ibid.*).[62] A simpler case of what Hegel has in mind is that of an acid:

> The finitude of things consists, then, in the fact that their immediate existence (*Dasein*) does not correspond to what they are in themselves. Thus, e.g. in inorganic nature, the acid is in itself at the same time the base, i.e. its being is just to be

related to its other. But then the acid is accordingly not something that persists peacefully in the opposition, but strives to make itself what it is in itself (*Enz.* I. 191Z.2. Cf. *Enz.* II. 332 and Z).

An acid is regarded as an acid just because of what happens to it when it encounters an alkali. Until it meets an alkali, it is unfulfilled, its 'immediate existence does not correspond to what it is in itself', that is, perhaps, to its 'concept'. But when the encounter actually occurs, it ceases to be an acid. As this example suggests, Hegel prefers those cases where the change involves opposition, in particular where 'the extreme of a state or activity tends to veer into its opposite' (*Enz.* I. 81Z.1). The examples which he gives of this are derived on the whole from the social and psychological realm. He cites such dicta as '*Summa ius summa iniuria*' and 'Pride goes before a fall', and suggests that the extremes of despotism and of anarchy tend to lead into one another. Dialectic does not, however, always involve opposition or even dissolution. In the realm of nature, for example, it is responsible for the quite different phenomenon of motion:

A planet stands now at this place, but in itself it is also at another place, and it brings this other-being (*Anderssein*) to existence by moving. Similarly the physical elements show themselves to be dialectical, and the meteorological process is the appearance of their dialectic.[63] The same principle forms the basis of all other natural processes and at the same time drives nature beyond itself (*Enz.* I. 81Z.1).

The third aspect of logic, the speculative or positively-rational aspect, is also involved in ordinary things and in ordinary ways of looking at things. Since the understanding is, on one account at least, responsible for the being of finite things and the dialectic for their change or dissolution, we might expect the speculative aspect to manifest itself in the results of the changes and processes brought about by the dialectic: the next position occupied by a moving object, the neutral product of an acid and a base — a salt — a corpse or, perhaps, the seed or infant with which the species makes good the loss of one of its members. This, however, is not so. Only certain special entities represent the speculative element in the world. To view something in a speculative way is to be aware of what is rational:

The empirically universal way of being aware of the rational is at first that of prejudice and assumption, and the character of the rational is . . . in general that of something unconditioned which thus contains its determinacy within itself. In this sense man is aware of the rational above all in so far as he is aware of God and is aware of him as something which is determined entirely through itself. Similarly, then, a citizen's awareness of his fatherland and its laws is an awareness of the rational, to the extent that these are regarded by him as something unconditioned and at the same time universal, to which he has to subject his individual will. In the same sense even the awareness and will of the child is rational, since it is aware of the will of its parents and assents to it' (*Enz.* I. 82Z).

Hegel's examples here are examples, primarily, of speculative attitudes towards things. The state, for instance, is regarded as rational when it is seen from the point of view of the citizen, who is, as it were, embraced by it and the boundaries of whose life are set by it. But he also means, presumably, that the state is a counterpart of the speculative aspect of logic in the objective world. The state is, as we have already seen, an especially significant entity for a number of reasons.[64] It is perhaps surprising that it should figure as an example of the objectivity of the positively rational, when it has already been cited as an instance of the objective understanding. This may have something to do with Hegel's uncertainty as to whether all finite things or only some of them correspond to the understanding. If *all* finite entities manifest the understanding, then the state needs to be marked out, in virtue of its special characteristics, as 'rational' in a way that other things are not. If, on the other hand, only some of them do, then the state is likely to be one of them and it is hard to see why, in addition, it needs to be seen as rational. The answer, presumably, is that Hegel has in mind different features of the state on different occasions. The state manifests understanding in so far as it is internally differentiated and articulated, while it is rational in so far as it and its laws are, from the point of view of the citizen at least, 'something unconditioned and at the same time universal'.

9 Appearance and change

This, then, is an abbreviated account of the parallelism which Hegel finds between logic and the phenomenal world. There are, as we have seen, at least two difficulties in it. Firstly, he is uncertain whether all finite entities or only some of them correspond to the understanding. Secondly, what corresponds to the speculative aspect of logic is not, as we would expect, the entities or states

431

of affairs which result from the changes produced by dialectic, but awesome entities like God and the state. Each of these difficulties can be explained, however. The first corresponds to the similar hesitation over the dividing line between the apparent and the actual. As we have seen, Hegel is inclined to say *both* that all finite entities are mere appearances *and* that some finite entities are actual.[65] If a finite entity is regarded as actual, he tends, of course, to underplay its connections with other entities and to suggest that it is infinite. If all finite entities are appearances, then we might suspect Hegel of acosmism, of the belief that 'the world is determined only as a phenomenon (*Phänomen*), to which actual reality does not belong' (*Enz.* I. 50). But this, as we have seen, is not his dominant view. Even if all finite entities are appearances, this need only mean that they are mutable and transitory. Finite entities have as secure a position in the universe as do sharp conceptual boundaries in the *Logic*. This seems to be what Hegel has in mind when he attributes to the understanding the fact that 'finite things *are*, that they have a subsistence.' The dialectic then demolishes them and thus shows that they are only appearances. If, on the other hand, some objective entities are actual and not mere appearances, then presumably those things which are appearances are mere phenomena, 'to which actual reality does not belong'. Hegel's claim to reject acosmism then rests on his ascription of actuality to some finite entities. This seems to be what he has in mind when he attributes only certain finite entities to the understanding. In that case, the dialectic has no special role to perform with respect to those entities. For what makes them special is, in part, their relative immunity to the processes of change and dissolution which affect other, humbler entities. Hegel's account of the status of finite things is, then, deeply ambiguous.

The explanation of the second difficulty seems to be something like this. Logic consists of only one type of series, a series of concepts of increasing richness and adequacy. The objective world, by contrast, presents us with two types of series. Firstly, there are temporal series of change and dissolution: the successive movements of planets, for example, and the repeated cycle of birth–life–death. Secondly, there is the series of higher and higher types of entity or levels of existence, proceeding, roughly, from merely physical or mechanical entities to organic ones, and so on. In nature, at least, this series is not a temporal one. Organic entities have been in existence for as long as merely mechanical ones.[66] This second type of series reflects, on Hegel's view, the increasing complexity of logic. The first type of series, in nature at least, does not. The changes which occur in nature are of a cyclical, repetitive kind. In the human realm, however, Hegel is inclined to argue, as we have seen, that the two types of series coincide, that historical processes embody the structure of logic and, with less certainty, that any series which reflects the increasing complexity of logic is a historical one. But even here the series do not in fact coincide. A case can be made for the view that historical processes, the development of philosophy or of religion, for example, follow the course of the *Logic*.[67] But the converse, namely the view that if one phase of human life or thought is higher than another then the second must precede the first in time, is difficult to maintain, and Hegel does not argue for it with any great consistency or enthusiasm. Philosophy and religion, for example, or the state and the family generally co-exist in one and the same society. There are, then, in the realm of nature and in that of mind two distinct types of series.

Which type of series does Hegel have in mind in drawing a parallel between the three aspects of logic and the three aspects of the objective world? The answer is: confusedly both. His account of objective *dialectic* is concerned, for most part, with the first, temporal, series. Dialectic changes or demolishes the entities set up by the understanding. The dialectic has, on Hegel's view, a '*positive* result' and we would naturally suppose that the result is, in this case, the next term in the temporal series. The result of the destruction or alteration of a natural entity is not a higher type of entity. The speculative aspect, however, cannot be confined to this role, for it is concerned with the transition to a higher level (*Enz.* I. 82).[68] At this point, then, Hegel switches to the second, atemporal, series, and implies that the destruction of entities at one level provides a transition to entities of a higher level. As we shall see, the confusion between these two types of series infects his account of objective contradictions.[69] The matter is complicated further by the fact that Hegel has *three* different views about the role which the speculative aspect plays in logic. These are:

(i) It provides a successor for any thought-determination, ensuring that the criticism of it has a positive result. On this account the speculative aspect would be as much involved in the emergence of the second term of a triad from the first as it is in the emergence of the third from the first two.

(ii) It is involved only in the emergence of the third term of a triad, the term which, as it were, embraces the other two.

(iii) It is involved only in the final stage of logic, the absolute idea. Hegel clearly has this third account in mind when he writes:

433

[T]he speculative in its true meaning is neither provisionally nor definitively something merely subjective, but is, rather, expressly what contains sublimated in itself those oppositions to which the understanding adheres (thus also that of the subjective and the objective) and thus proves to be concrete and a totality. A speculative content cannot therefore be expressed in a one-sided proposition (*Enz.* I. 82Z).

It is this third account which explains why Hegel gives as examples of the rational, not any entity of a higher type than those below it, but only supremely elevated entities like God and the state. This, however, concerns the point at which the speculative aspect figures on the second type of series, the atemporal hierarchy. The main point of interest is Hegel's tendency to switch from the first type of series to the second.

The parallelism between logic and the objective world is, then, marred by two things. Firstly, it is unclear where the line is to be drawn between the apparent and the actual. Secondly, whereas logic presents only one type of series, the objective world provides us with two. These two factors are connected with one another, though only loosely, in the following way. When Hegel is thinking of the first, temporal, type of series, he tends to regard all finite entities as appearances. For a series of this type depends on the fact that the terms of it arise, or appear, and then pass away. Even states and civilizations succumb to this process. When, on the other hand, he has in mind the second, atemporal, type of series, he is more inclined to regard higher entities as self-contained and long-lasting, and thus as actual rather than merely apparent. In the following section, something will be said about this second type of series and about this connection between the status of an entity and the nature of the pure thought which it exemplifies.

10 *Degrees of truth*

We saw earlier that, on Hegel's view, it is things and concepts, rather than propositions or sentences, that are primarily true or untrue.[70] Varying, not obviously equivalent, accounts are given of what the untruth of a concept consists in. A concept or a category may be untrue because it is finite, because it is a 'form of the finite', or perhaps because it fails to conform to *its* concept.[71] A thing is true if and only if it 'agrees with its concept' (*Enz.* I. 24Z.2). It is also the case, however, that if, and only if, an entity exemplifies some untrue concept or category, then it is itself untrue. It is, in that case, finite and undergoes the sort of change, in most cases eventually a fatal change, to which finite things are subject. Hegel's idea seems to be that if a thing falls under a finite category, then it is not fully determined by its concept, but is determined by, dependent on, and vulnerable to other things. It does not matter which of the concepts instantiated by a thing we consider. They may be pure thoughts like that of a whole consisting of parts or conceptions like that of a rose, a jigsaw puzzle or an acid. As long as the entity in question is a finite entity, enmeshed in its relationships with other entities, it is bound to fall short of any concept we apply to it.

If something does agree with its concept, then, Hegel implies, it lasts forever. For finite things, he argues, must 'pass away, and this manifests the inadequacy of their concept and their existence' (*Enz.* I. 24Z.2).[72] He often identifies the concept with a genus or a species (*Enz.* I. 24Z.1,2).[73] But this does not help his case. For although a genus or a species last longer than any individual member of it, it is quite possible for it to become extinct. A genus or a species is, after all, dependent on other things for its existence and survival and is not, in that sense, fully determined by *its* concept. A concept, by contrast, cannot, in one sense at least, perish. Suppose, then, that an entity were fully determined by its concept, that it did not, that is, depend on anything else for its character, existence and survival. Would it necessarily last for ever? If such an entity were to come into existence at a certain time, then its doing so would be inexplicable. There is nothing outside it which could explain its genesis, and, since it does not yet exist, its coming into existence could not be explained by its internal features. It does not, of course, follow that it is logically impossible that such an entity should come into existence, but only that, if it did so, there would be no explanation for it. By contrast, an entity which was infinite in this sense might come to an end without its doing so being inexplicable. For its passage out of existence, unlike its entry into it, could be explained, not, of course, by external factors, but by the internal nature of the entity itself. Its nature, programme, or concept might prescribe a course of decline, just as the nature of a living organism prescribes decline and eventual death, quite apart from any external invasion which may occur. The infinite object might die, as it were, of old age. Its demise would be explicable in terms of its previous states and these would in turn depend, on Hegel's account, on its concept. Why its concept should be as it is is another matter, but if it is logically possible for such a self-determining decline and extinction to occur, it is hard to see why Hegel should simply assume that it is logically impossible for the concept of an entity to prescribe it.

Our primary concern here, however, is not with the infinite object, but with finite entities, those entities which, apart from awkward exceptions like the planets, are obviously of finite duration. What is the connection between their finitude and the thoughts or categories which they exemplify? As we have seen, Hegel believes that some categories, all categories in fact except the absolute idea, are untrue, but he does not infer from this that they cannot have instances. The category of a whole with parts, for example, is untrue, yet applicable (*Enz.* I. 135Z).[74] Some things, however, living organisms for example, are not, or are not only, wholes consisting of parts. Even more surely, it is wrong to speak of the 'parts' of the soul or of the mind, to enumerate 'the diverse forms of mental activity in isolation as so-called particular forces and capacities' (*Enz.* I. 135Z).[75] The entities which do correspond to the category of a whole with parts are themselves untrue, and, more generally, if a category is untrue, then so are the things which correspond to it. It does not follow, however, that if an entity is too elevated to correspond to a given untrue category, then it is wholly true. Some types of organic whole, for example, although they are more than wholes consisting of parts, are nevertheless untrue. Individual animals are untrue in comparison with the genera to which they belong (*Enz.* I. 24Z.2), and living organisms generally are inferior to minds with respect to truth (*Enz.* II. 248).[76] The untruth of finite things seems, then, to be a matter of degree and so does that of the thought-determinations which they exemplify. Animals, though not strictly true, are truer than stones, and the corresponding categories, those of inner purposiveness and of life, are truer than that of a whole consisting of parts. The following discussion of mechanism, chemism and teleology implies that truth is not a matter of all or nothing:[77]

> Earlier metaphysics treated these concepts (*Begriffen*) like the others; first, it presupposed a conception of the world (*Welt-vorstellung*) and tried to show that the one or the other concept fits it and the opposite concept is defective, because the world-conception cannot be *explained* (*erklären*) by it; secondly, it did not examine the concept of mechanical cause and of purpose to see which has truth *in and for itself*. When this has been established independently (*für sich*), the objective world may well present mechanical and final causes; their existence is not the standard of the *true*, but rather the true is the criterion for which of these existences is the true one. Just as the subjective understanding also displays errors, so the objective world too

displays those aspects and stages (*Seiten und Stufen*) of truth which on their own (*für sich*) are at first one-sided, incomplete, and only relations of appearance. If mechanism and purposiveness are opposed to each other, they cannot for that very reason be taken as *equally valid* (or 'indifferent': *gleichgültige*), each of them being on its own a correct concept and having as much validity as the other, with the only question being where each can be applied. This equal validity rests only on the fact that they *are*, namely that we *have* both. But the necessary first question, because they are opposed, is which of the two is the true one; and the proper and higher question is, *whether a third term is their truth or one is the truth of the other. But* the *purposive relation* has proved to be the truth of *mechanism* (*WL* II. pp. 437 f., M. pp. 734 f.).

Truth, then, has 'aspects and stages'. When Hegel says that teleology is the truth of mechanism, this presumably implies that teleology is more true than mechanism. It does not follow from this that teleology is wholly and strictly true. It may well be that there is something else which is in turn the truth of, and therefore truer than, teleology. The same sort of thing is said about earlier categories in the *Logic*: 'Absolute necessity is therefore the truth into which actuality and possibility in general, as well as formal and real necessity, withdraw' (*WL* II. p. 215, M. p. 552). In general, it looks as if the third member of any triad is the truth of the first two.

A good deal has already been said about the way, or rather ways, in which one category may be higher, or truer, than another. But how can it be that some objective, finite entities are more true than others? When Hegel speaks in general terms about the untruth of finite things, he offers no satisfactory account of degrees of truth. Some things may indeed fit the particular concept which we choose to apply to them better than others do. Hegel's introduction of the notion implies, for example, that true friends are more true than false ones (*Enz.* I. 24Z.2).[78] Again, the association of untruth with transience suggests that a thing is true in proportion to its duration or, at least, to what its duration would be barring accidents. But neither of these points would license the idea of a hierarchy of entities in which butterflies are higher than pebbles. Moreover, if the untruth of a thing consists in its being bounded and determined by other things, then all finite entities are just simply untrue:

The essential relation is the determinate, entirely universal mode of appearing. Everything that exists stands in relation and this relation is what is true in each existence (*das Wahrhafte jeder Existenz*). The existing thing is thereby not abstractly on its own, but only in another (*Enz.* I. 135Z).

In a passage which is designed to downgrade the status of nature in comparison with that of the mind, Hegel insists that even living creatures are caught up in this process:

> The highest level to which nature comes in its existence is *life*; but being only a natural idea, this is subject to the unreason of externality, and the individual living creature is in each aspect of its existence caught up with an individuality other than itself; by contrast in each expression (*Aüsserung*) of mind there is contained the element of free, universal relation to itself (*Enz.* II. 248).

How, in the light of this, can there be degrees of truth in nature?

The answer seems to be that some things are less, or at least less directly, dependent on and vulnerable to external influences than others are. Hegel makes this point in a number of contexts, but most clearly perhaps in his account of causality. We might suppose that whenever one thing influences another, the influence is always a causal influence. But this, on Hegel's view, is a mistake. Rather, the effect produced by a cause must always be a simple continuation of the cause in a different form. Rain, for example, is the cause of wetness, but when the streets are wet from rain, the wetness is just the rain in another form (*WL* II. p. 226, M. p. 560). Again, when a moving body strikes another body, the same quantum of motion or of energy which the first loses is transmitted to the second (*WL* II. p. 226, M. p. 561). Hegel reveals his uneasy grip on traditional philosophical concepts by inferring from this that causal statements are analytic: '"Rain makes things wet", this is an analytic proposition.' But he has not, of course, shown that it is necessarily or analytically true that rain makes things wet or even that it has any effect at all. He has shown only that rain does in fact have an effect and that this effect is just rain in a different form. There are, again, obvious differences between the case of rain and the behaviour of billiard balls. Hegel's main point, however, is not affected by these difficulties. It is that some things do not, or do not only, receive external influences in the way that cobblestones and billiard balls do. It is, on his view, inadmissible to apply the category of causality to the *'relations of physico-organic and of spiritual life'* (*WL* II. p. 227, M. p. 562). Thus food is not the cause of blood; damp is not the cause of fever; the Ionian climate did not cause the production of the Homeric epics; and Caesars's ambition did not cause the downfall of the Roman Republic. Hegel is not denying that such factors as these play a part. The point is, rather, that the 'cause' in these cases has a different content from the 'effect' and this is because 'what acts on the living thing is independently determined, changed and transformed by it'. The living creature does not *receive another original thing into itself* or let a cause continue into itself, but breaks it off and transmutes it'. 'Spiritual' entities like people and societies do this 'in a far higher sense' than living organisms do (*WL* II. p. 228, M. p. 562). Elsewhere Hegel expands on the theme that animals, primitive people and sick people are more open to the influence of their natural environment than are civilized, healthy people. They are, for example, impressed or influenced to a greater extent by the movements of the planets, the phases of the moon, and the changes of the seasons (*Enz.* III. 392Z). Some types of thing, then, are less vulnerable to neat causal impacts, more independent and self-determining, than others. No finite entity, however, is entirely immune to outside influences, however much it may transform them.

It might be objected to this that the distinction between causal and non-causal influence is an unreal one. For nothing receives external influences purely, without making any contribution of its own. The surface of a street must be of a certain texture, if it is to become wet. Rain would not have this effect on it if it were, for example, smeared with oil. Similarly a billiard ball must have certain properties if it is to be propelled by the impact of another ball. In general, the effect that an impact x has on an object y depends on the nature of y as well as on that of x. We can, nevertheless, still distinguish between those objects whose nature is such that the effect of an external influence on them has the same 'content' as the cause and those objects which transmute the influence into something quite different. If it rains, then by and large only one sort of thing can happen to the surface of a street; it gets wet. But a variety of things can happen to a person exposed to it. He may, like the street, get wet; he may become depressed; he may put up an umbrella. Getting wet is, on Hegel's view, an effect. The wetness, of the street or of the person, seems intuitively more like the rain than does the depression. Indeed it just is some part of the rain in a different position. A person, unlike a street, can respond to rain in ways which, on Hegel's view, do not count as effects. Even so, it may be objected, it is not clear that a person has any special advantage over streets and billiard balls, if, as a physical entity, he is, like them, vulnerable to causal invasions such as drenching and propulsion and if, in addition, results like depression automatically follow upon climatic events such as rain, however much the influences have been transformed in the process. He would still be exposed both to causal encroachments and to external invasions of a non-causal kind. Hegel's answer to this, however, seems to be that living organisms are to a greater or lesser extent self-regulating, and are able to avert causal intrusions or to reduce their effect by responding to them in an appropriate way. The response may be automatic, as in the case of the body's regulation of its own temperature, or the result of choice and purposive activity, as in the case of dwellings, umbrellas and central heating. A human being in particular can, even if he is not insulated against his natural environment in these ways, at least stoically resist the onset of depression which it tends to induce and remain cheerful or indifferent in the face of such external factors. This is a part of what Hegel has in mind when he speaks of our ability to 'abstract' from external circumstances and from states of ourselves such as desires.[79] Persons differ in this respect, as in others, from other living creatures and thus stand on a higher plane of truth.[80]

Even if we grant, however, that some sense can be given to the claim that the truth of things is a matter of degree, Hegel's thesis is still exposed to a number of difficulties. In the first place, it is generally unclear what the untruth of things has to do with the untruth of the thought-determinations to which they correspond. The absence of such a connection is apparent in two cases which we have already considered, namely the qualitative judgment and the concept of a whole consisting of parts. Hegel finds two faults in the qualitative judgment: firstly, the subject is an untrue or finite thing and, secondly, the predicate of the judgment does not 'coincide' with its subject. It is, as we have seen, hard to see a connection between the first defect, a defect of things, and the second, a defect of a type of judgment or, more generally, a thought-determination.[81] The same is true of the concept of a whole consisting of parts. What is wrong with the concept is that nothing can *both* be a proper whole *and* contain proper parts. The corresponding defect of things should therefore be that, if there are any wholes consisting of parts, they fail to be proper wholes with proper parts, that they fall short of the concept which they nevertheless primarily exemplify. But the defect which Hegel finds in them is quite different. It is that they are not self-determining and self-regulating, that their parts are not subtly and purposively interconnected in such a way that they cannot, for example, be dismantled and reassembled.[82] If Hegel were proposing his thesis today, he would need to pay more attention to machines. Refrigerators, for example, can be dismantled and reassembled.

They are, in one sense at least, objects whose 'different elements are indifferent to one another (*verhalten sich als gleichgültig gegeneinander*) and are combined only in an external way' (*Enz.* I. 194Z.2). They are, on the other hand, self-regulating to a relatively high degree. They 'transmute' the cause, as well, for they produce coldness by means of heat. Hegel's categories seem insufficiently refined to handle such cases as this. The main difficulty, however, is the lack of any intuitive connection between the defects of those categories and the defects of the things which exemplify them.

In the second place, since the finitude or untruth of things is invariably associated with their transience, one might expect a thing's natural duration to correspond to its degree of truth, to its position on the *scala naturae*. Indeed one might suppose *a priori* that the longevity of a thing is proportionate to the extent to which it can regulate and adapt itself in the face of external pressures. It is obvious, however, that there is no such correspondence. Pebbles last much longer than animals. Animals die, and, when they do, they revert, as it were, to the mechanistic stage:

> When the soul has left the body, the elementary powers of objectivity begin their play. These powers are so to speak continually at the ready (*auf dem Sprunge*), waiting to begin their process in the organic body, and life is a persistent struggle against them (*Enz.* I. 219Z).

We can of course see roughly why animals might eventually succumb to the pressures which surround them, but Hegel does not explain satisfactorily why they should do so sooner than many types of entity which are lower in the natural and logical hierarchy. In particular, people or their minds, occupying as they do the summit of this hierarchy, might be expected to last for a very long time, if not for ever. Does Hegel believe that people are immortal? In the light of its ethical and religious associations, this question deserves extended discussion.

11 *Death and immortality*

The mind, on Hegel's view, has a special sort of unity surpassing that of any natural object:

> The absolutely-concrete is the mind . . . . Everything else concrete, however rich it is, is not so intimately identical with itself and therefore not so concrete within itself, least of all what is

441

commonly meant by the concrete, a manifold externally held together (*Enz.* I. 164).

This suggests that a mind lasts at least far longer than any natural entity, and much else that Hegel says converges on this conclusion. Firstly, the death of animals provides the transition from nature to the human or spiritual sphere (*Enz.* II. 376; *WL* II. pp. 486 f., M. p. 774), and this carries an implication, albeit a weak one, that people, unlike animals, are immune to death. So, again, does Hegel's explanation of the death of animals:

> In general the overcoming and passing of individual inadequacy [viz. the recovery from illness] does not eliminate the universal inadequacy of the individual, which consists in the fact that its idea is the *immediate* idea, that, as an animal, it stands *within nature* and its subjectivity is only *in itself* the concept and not *for itself* (*Enz.* II. 374. Cf. *WL* II. pp. 484 ff., M. pp. 772 ff.).

The 'universal inadequacy' of individual animals is clearly what makes them liable to disease and death. People, however, surely remedy this inadequacy, as Hegel describes it, by their cognitive and practical activities, particularly when they engage in pure thought. Why, then, do pure thinkers die or even catch colds? Finally, Hegel argues that minds can sustain contradictions. Sometimes he attributes this capacity to animals as well, in virtue of their susceptibility to pain (*WL* II. p. 481, M. p. 770).[83] But elsewhere he seems to confine it to minds:

> The *essence* of mind is . . . *freedom* . . . . [I]t *can* abstract from everything external and its own externality, from its very existence (*Dasein*); it can endure the negation of its individual immediacy, infinite *pain*, i.e. preserve itself affirmatively in this negativity and be identical for itself (*Enz.* III. 382).

> . . . What belongs to outer nature perishes through contradiction; if e.g. gold were given another specific gravity, it would have to perish as gold. But the mind has the power to sustain itself in contradiction, and consequently in pain ([power] over both good and evil) (382Z).

Hegel's notion of contradiction is, of course, a flexible one. We would not call it a contradiction for gold to have, or to acquire, a different specific gravity; for a man to be in pain, or evil; or for him to have the conception of a house — 'something which fully contradicts my ego' (*Ibid.*). This, however, does not affect the main point. Hegel maintains that a mind can survive contradictions

442

which destroy other things. But if contradictions do not destroy minds, it is not clear how anything else could.

These considerations, then, suggest that Hegel believes that the human mind, at least, is immortal. It is true that, on his view, an ego must be self-conscious, and full self-consciousness presupposes the physical and sensory interplay of at least two persons, each of whom is aware of, recognizes, and interacts with the other (PG pp. 133 ff., M. pp. 104 ff.). But it is presumably possible that an ego which has once acquired self-consciousness should retain it even after the conditions for its acquisition have disappeared. At all events Hegel claims that the mind, though not the embodied person, is immortal:

> Spirit is immortal, it is eternal; it is so just in virtue of the fact that it is infinite, that it has not the finitude of space, the finitude of a body which is five feet high, two feet wide and thick, it has not the now of time, its knowledge is not a content in it of these innumerable midges, and its will, its freedom is not the infinite mass of resistances (*Widerständen*) nor of the purposes and activities which these resistances and hindrances encounter. The infinity of spirit is its being-within-itself, abstractly its pure being-within-itself, and this is its thinking, and this abstract thinking is an actual, present infinity, and its concrete being-within-itself is the fact that this thinking is spirit (*VBDG* XIV in *VPR* II. p. 479, S.S. III. p. 302).

Nevertheless Hegel is relatively indifferent to the question of individual survival and it plays no part in his system.[84] There are at least two reasons for this. Firstly, an ego *qua* thinker is, on Hegel's view, identical with any other ego *qua* thinker and is in fact no more than the system of pure thoughts.[85] There can, therefore, be no sense or interest in the idea of individual survival. Nor can there be any question of mental activity's continuing *after* the death of the body, if the mind does not have 'the now of time (*das Jetzt der Zeit*)'. The immortality of the self can amount to no more than the atemporality of concepts and the ability of a mind to 'transcend' physical time by engaging in pure thought. Such an attenuated version of the doctrine of immortality offers few of the consolations which it traditionally provides.

Secondly, however, such consolations are not, on Hegel's view, required. Traditionally, individual immortality plays an important ethical role. Kant, for example, held that the belief is a presupposition of morality. Moral satisfaction, the perfection of the individual and the assignment of advantages in accordance with moral merit, cannot be expected in this world of appearances, but only in a future, or at least another, life:[86]

> Now since we are necessarily constrained by reason to represent ourselves as belonging to such a [viz. 'an intelligible, that is, *moral*'] world, while the senses present to us nothing but a world of appearances, we must assume that moral world to be a consequence of our conduct in the world of sense (in which no such connection between worthiness and happiness is exhibited) and therefore to be for us a future world.

Hegel, as we shall see, undercuts this argument by insisting that the world is more or less all right as it is. It is a mistake to locate moral satisfaction in another world or to postpone it into the indefinite future.[87] Even if individual immortality were possible, therefore, there would be no special point in it. Hegel is a this-worldly philosopher, concerned to find God, moral worth and rationality in the world of our experience and not in the future or in the beyond. Characteristically, he is more interested in why people believe that they are immortal and in the conception of the self that this belief involves than in whether or not the belief is true.[88] If the spirit endures in any sense which interests Hegel, it is the spirit which is embodied in human society, institutions and intellectual achievements. Spirit endures, that is, in roughly the sense in which an animal endures, if the species to which it belongs is continually replenished and survives the extinction of particular members of it. There is, perhaps, more reason to regard humanity as a whole, or a particular nation, as a substantial individual. For, on Hegel's view, whereas successive generations of animals are hardly affected by the fate of their predecessors, humanity develops in a mind-like way, by reflecting upon and transcending, as well as preserving, its past states.[89] However, the connection of this view with the orthodox doctrine of individual, personal immortality seems no more than metaphorical.[90]

Nevertheless the death of human individuals is, as we have seen, a problem for Hegel, and it may be that a residual unease about it underlies those passages in which he maintains that people are responsible for what happens to them. Thus 'everyone is the architect (*Schmied*) of his own fate' (*Enz.* I. 147Z). Rather than blame other people or external circumstances, a person should realize that 'what happens to him is only an evolution of himself and that he has only himself to blame'. If he does this, then 'he conducts himself as a free man and has faith that in everything that he encounters no injustice is done to him' (*Ibid.*). On the face of it, the belief which Hegel here recommends is simply false. A person is not necessarily responsible for everything that happens to him. Why does Hegel believe that he is? There is no doubt a weak sense in which everyone is responsible for what happens to him, namely that if something happens to a person, then he must be such that it could happen to him. In that sense, however, anything whatsoever is responsible for what happens to it. If x affects y in a certain way, then y must be capable of being affected in that way by x.[91] It may be that Hegel is saying no more than that a person is the sort of thing that is vulnerable to certain contingencies and offering the sensible advice that we should resign ourselves to this fact. However, there may be more at stake. He is perhaps attempting to explain the vulnerability of such self-determining creatures as ourselves by suggesting that a person, unlike other entities, in some sense wills his own fate or at least brings it upon himself by his own autonomous thoughts and deeds. This would make some sense, for example, of his fanciful association of Spinoza's death with the nature of Spinoza's own thought: 'He died on 21 February 1677 at 44 years of age, of consumption, from which he had long suffered – agreeing with his system, in which, too, all particularity and individuality disappear in the *one* substance' (*VGP* III. p. 160, H. III. p. 254). It is indeed absurd to suppose that Spinoza's system had anything to do with his death. That Hegel suggested otherwise becomes more intelligible, if we remember that for him it is a problem why Spinoza ever died at all.

This, then, concludes our discussion of one aspect of the relationship between the world and the logical idea, namely the hierarchy of entities corresponding to the hierarchy of concepts. In the following section we turn to another aspect of this relationship, the idea that there are contradictions in things as well as in our concepts.

12 *Varieties of contradiction*

We have already seen that the notion of a contradiction plays an important part in Hegel's system. So far we have been concerned primarily with subjective contradictions, contradictions in our concepts or in our beliefs.[92] Contradictions of this type can certainly occur. Indeed, it is not implausible to suppose that our thinking proceeds, at least to some extent and in some areas, by means of our recognition and resolution of contradictions in our previous beliefs or concepts. Hegel no doubt mishandles this idea in detail and exaggerates the extent of its applicability, but the idea in itself is not an objectionable one. He does not, however, stop at *subjective* contradictions. There are also *objective* contradictions, contradictions in things. Indeed, everything is contradictory.[93] Objective contradictions are, on Hegel's view, no more and no less objectionable than subjective ones, and, as we have seen, he criticizes Kant for supposing that contradictions are more tolerable if they are located in our minds rather than in things.[94]

Before we consider this doctrine in greater detail, we need to distinguish at least four types of objective contradiction. The first two affect only infinite entities:

1. An infinite object cannot be adequately described by any single 'finite' concept. It is therefore to be characterized by both, or neither, of any pair of opposing concepts. God, for example, is *both* infinite *and* finite.[95] Since Hegel is inclined to identify an infinite entity with the logical idea, it is perhaps doubtful whether contradictions of this type should be regarded as objective rather than subjective, but this difficulty does not greatly matter here. These contradictions do not indicate a defect in the object. They are rather a mark of the grossness of our concepts.[96]

2. An infinite object in some sense contains or embraces finite ones. But finite objects are, as we shall see, contradictory. If they were not contradictory, then they could not hang together so as to constitute a single infinite entity. An infinite entity, therefore, seems to contain or embrace the contradictions which infect its finite constituents.

Neither of these types of contradiction destroys an infinite entity. An infinite entity is, as we have seen, immune to external attacks, because there is nothing external to it. It cannot be extinguished by its contradictions, since there is, as it were, nowhere for it to go.

Finite objects similarly suffer from two distinct types of contradiction:

3. Just as finite, 'one-sided' concepts cannot be applied unproblematically to the infinite, so *some* one-sided concepts cannot be applied unproblematically to finite things. This is true, for example, of the concepts of immediacy and of mediation. Nothing whatsoever is, or can be, *only* immediate or *only* mediated. The general diagnosis of this is the same as that of contradictions of type 1, namely that our concepts are too coarse-grained to capture the true state of affairs in strict, either-or terms. Contradictions of this type do not, any more than contradictions of type 1, destroy the objects which they infect. The defect lies in the concepts rather than in the thing. The contradiction does not depend on the finitude of the thing, but is something which it shares with the

infinite – though, as we have seen, an infinite object is mediated, or 'self-mediated', in a different way from that in which finite objects are.[97]

4. Finite things also suffer from contradictions which obtain in virtue of their finitude. It is contradictions of this type which are responsible for their disappearance, or at any rate their change.

Hegel himself does not classify contradictions in this way, and it is not always easy to say, of any given contradiction which he mentions, to which category it should be assigned. Pain, for example, is, on Hegel's view, a contradiction, but is it a contradiction of type 4 or of some other type? On the one hand, physical pain, although it does not necessarily destroy a creature, is at least the sort of thing, or associated with the sort of thing, that can destroy it, and this suggests that it is of type 4. On the other hand, Hegel wants to associate the ability to feel and endure pain with the capacity to transcend one's own limits:[98]

> Living things have the advantage of pain over lifeless ones; even for them an *individual* determinacy becomes the sensation of a *negative*, because, being alive, they have in them the *universality* of vitality which *transcends* the individual, they still preserve themselves in the negative of themselves and perceive this *contradiction* existing in them (*Enz.* I. 60).

This suggests that animals feel pain because they are something more than simply finite entities and that, perhaps, this 'contradiction' has something in common with those of type 1 or type 2. Again, contradiction is involved, on Hegel's view, in one's having the conception of a house.[99] This contradiction has, of course, no tendency to destroy or weaken the entity which suffers from it and Hegel is, in any case, more inclined to say that minds are infinite than that animals are (cf. *Enz.* III. 386 and Z). It has, therefore, a stronger claim to be allocated to category 1 than pains do. In general, however, the line between the infinite and the finite is, for Hegel, a hazy and shifting one, and since he associates contradiction both with infinity and with finitude, the classification of such contradictions as these is bound to be a difficult matter. But this difficulty does not much affect the discussion which follows. The contradictions with which we shall be primarily concerned are those which indicate a defect in things rather than in our concepts. Some of our terms and some phenomena are such as to tempt us to describe the phenomena in contradictory ways. A thing might be, for example, both simple and complex, or both simple and not simple. Or if one wants to avoid overt contradiction, one can introduce qualifications, saying that it is simple in one sense, way, or respect, but not simple in another sense, way or respect. Such ways of expressing oneself do not amount to assertions of contradictory propositions nor could their truth explain why things disappear, die or change. For our need to resort to such seemingly contradictory manoeuvres indicates defects in our concepts rather than in things. Hegel believes, however, that there are contradictions in things, contradictions which are responsible for transience and change. Why did he? This question will be considered in the following section.

13 *Contradictions and the finite*

There is no single explanation of Hegel's belief in the occurrence of objective contradictions. It stands at the juncture of several distinct lines of thought:

(i) There were a number of antinomies which had not been resolved in Hegel's time, arguments suggesting that the world or some feature of it is contradictory. Kant's antinomies have already been referred to, though, since Hegel interprets these as showing the inappropriateness of finite concepts for infinite objects, they are more properly relevant to contradictions of type 1.[100] The paradoxes of Zeno,[101] by contrast, are concerned with finite entites. The most famous of them purports to show that Achilles could never overtake a tortoise in a race in which the tortoise starts, for example, 100 yards ahead of him. For by the time Achilles has reached the tortoise's starting-point, the tortoise will have covered some finite distance, and, by the time Achilles has covered this distance, it will have moved a further finite distance, and so *ad infinitum*. Achilles, therefore, will never catch up with the tortoise.[102] Another argument leads to the more overtly contradictory conclusion that a moving body is, at any given instant, both in motion and at rest; in motion, because if it were at rest at every instant in a given period of time, it could not move during that period; at rest, because there is, in an instant, no time for it to move.[103] There are three possible responses to these arguments. One is to grant their validity and to accept that motion does not really occur. Another, more common, response is to insist that motion occurs, that Achilles would overtake the tortoise, and so on, and to say that, since what actually occurs cannot be contradictory, there must be some flaw in the arguments, even if we have not yet discovered it. Hegel's response, however, is to insist that motion occurs, but to concede that it is contradictory:[104]

A thing only moves, not when it is at this instant here and at another instant there, but when it is at one and the same instant here and not here, when it both is and is not at this point at the same time. One must concede to the ancient dialecticians the contradictions which they reveal in motion, but it does not follow from that that motion does not occur, but rather that motion is *existent (daseiende)* contradiction itself (*WL* II. p. 76, M. p. 440).

The claim here, then, is that motion occurs and motion is contradictory. Hegel tends to confuse this with the quite different proposition that motion occurs and it is the contradictions in things which make them move. Thus in the same passage he writes:

[Contradiction] is not to be taken merely as an abnormality which occurs only here and there, but is the negative in its essential determination, the principle of all self-movement, which consists in nothing else than an exhibition of it (*Ibid.*).

Or again:

[Contradiction] is the root of all movement and vitality' (*WL* II. p. 75, M. p. 439).

This aspect of contradiction, however, will be considered later. The point, for the moment, is that motion is an actual phenomenon which, if Zeno were right, would be contradictory. Hegel's response to Zeno is, of course, inadequate. For one thing, he wishes to employ some notion of logical consequence in stating his position: Motion is contradictory, 'but it does not follow from that (*aber daraus folgt nicht*) that motion does not occur'. Our customary notion of logical consequence is subverted, however, once we concede the possibility of objective contradictions. To say that q follows from p means, or at least entails, that it is impossible that p but not q; to say that q does not follow from p means, or at least entails, that it is possible that p but not q. If the contradictory is not impossible, then what is? Hegel provides no satisfactory answer to this question.[105]

(ii) If Zeno were right, then motion would be contradictory. But most of the counterinstances which Hegel believes he has found to the 'laws of thought' do not even look much like contradictions or contraventions of the law of identity. If an animal is in pain or diseased, if a horse is born with five legs, there may be a sense in which it falls short of, or contradicts, its 'concept', but none of these states of affairs is an internally contradictory one. Neither does the following passage provide any case of genuine contradiction:

449

Although a circle with many angles and a rectilineal curve conflict with this proposition [viz. the law of contradiction] just as much [as a quadrangular circle], geometers do not hesitate to regard and treat the circle as a polygon with straight sides. But such a thing as a circle (its mere determinacy) is still not a *concept*; in the concept of a circle, the centre and the circumference are equally essential, both marks (*Merkmale*) belong to it; and yet circumference and centre are opposed and contradictory to each other (*Enz.* I. 119).

In his discussions of the laws of logic, the supposed counter-examples to them to which Hegel most commonly refers are such facts as that one man's debt is another man's credit, that there cannot be north poles without south poles, negative electricity without positive electricity, acids without alkalis, and so on.[106] Such cases as these do not, however, present any fundamental challenge to the law of contradiction or that of identity ('A = A'). They constitute a difficulty at most for a metaphysical offshoot of formal logic, the view, namely, that the world consists of sharply discrete entities, each of which has the properties it has independently of the others, and each of which is sheerly identical with itself and sheerly distinct from the others. Hegel believes that there are many groups of things, the members of which are neither flatly identical nor flatly non-identical with each other: the parts of an organism, a mind and its object, a person's mind and his body, the poles of a magnet, God and the world, the persons of the trinity, and so on. There is also a sense in which, on his view, nothing whatsoever is distinct from other things, since its having a definite character and the actual character it does have depends on its logical-cum-physical relations with other things. We have attempted to express Hegel's meaning by introducing the symbols '⇒' '⇔', instead of, or at least in addition to, the customary '=' and '≠'.[107] These examples are, however, different from each other and each of them deserves more consideration than can be given here. It is perhaps true that our traditional ways of viewing the world are as complex, or almost as complex, as Hegel conceives them to be, involving diverse types of polarity, interconnection, and so on. It is a further question whether the world is ultimately like this or whether it has a simpler underlying structure of a discrete or atomistic kind, which the imperfection of our knowledge prevents us from embodying in our language and thought. But whatever answers are given to these questions, the laws of logic do not seem to be at stake. In some areas, for example, it may be difficult or impossible to pick out distinct entities either on a single occasion or over a period of time. But this need only mean that it is difficult to find an application for 'A = A', not that we have encountered a counterinstance to it. Our inability to say whether x is or is not identical with y does not entail that x or y or both are not identical with themselves.

(iii) So far we have considered Hegel's attempts to find counter-examples to the laws of logic. Sometimes, however, he attacks the laws themselves in more direct ways. This is especially apparent in the case of the law of identity. He takes this law, 'A = A', as a recipe for the production of statements of the form 'x is x', where 'x' is to be replaced by the same word in each case, and as a prohibition on statements of the form 'x is y', where 'x' and 'y' are to be replaced by different terms:

> If e.g. to the question '*What is a plant?*' the answer is given '*A plant is — a plant*', then the whole company on which the truth of such a statement is tested will both concede its truth and equally unanimously declare that it says nothing (*WL* II. p. 43, M. p. 415).

Such a statement as, 'A plant is a plant' is, Hegel argues, in a way contradictory, for in purporting to say something and yet saying nothing, it defeats or contradicts the point of communication:

> the beginning, 'the plant is . . .', sets out to say *something*, to bring forth a further determination. But when it is just the same thing which returns, rather the opposite has happened, *nothing* has emerged. Such *identical* talk therefore *contradicts itself* (*WL* II. p. 44, M. p. 415).

This criticism rests, however, on a misunderstanding. The law of identity does not restrict us to statements of the type 'Socrates is Socrates' or 'A plant is a plant'. It does no more than forbid us to make such statements as 'Socrates is not Socrates', or at least it tells us that such statements cannot be true, as long as 'Socrates' refers to one and the same entity in each of its occurrences. It leaves us free to say such things as 'Socrates is the teacher of Plato' or 'Socrates is wise.' There are, indeed, two more substantial problems which Hegel may have had in mind here. First, how can a statement of identity be both true and informative, by referring, as does 'Thera is Santorini', to the same entity in two different ways? Secondly, how can a statement such as 'Thera is beautiful' fail to contravene the law of identity? As we have seen, he tends to regard subject-predicate statements as partially unsuccessful identity statements.[108] These are interesting problems, but it is doubtful whether Hegel contributed much to their solution.

It is true, as Hegel says, that the law of identity, 'A = A', is 'the expression of empty *tautology . . . without content* and leads no further' (*WL* II. p. 41, M. p. 413). One would expect statements which mark the boundaries of possibility to have an air of vacuity about them. But Hegel cannot maintain both that they are taut-ologous and that they are empirically false. If they are tautologous, it follows that there cannot be counterexamples to them. Such laws as that of identity are interpreted so as to accommodate the facts of change and interconnectedness to which he draws attention. They do not, as it were, mark a fixed and definite boundary which could be surmounted or demolished, but one that recedes before any assault on it.

(iv) Hegel often refers to the laws of identity and contradiction as *Denkgesetze* or 'laws of thought' (*Enz.* I. 115; *WL* II. p. 41, M. p. 413). This conception of them is probably associated with the view that the law of contradiction implies that contradictions are unthinkable or inconceivable: '[It is said that] the *contradictory* can be neither *conceived* nor *thought* ' (*WL* II. p. 75, M. p. 439). To say that a contradiction is unthinkable presumably means not simply that a contradictory proposition cannot be true, but that it cannot even be understood. Hegel counters this view, as we have seen, with examples of what he supposes to be actual contra-dictions: 'When they say that contradiction is not thinkable, it is rather, in the pain of the living creature, even an actual existence' (*WL* II. p. 481, M. p. 770).[109] If contradictions actually occur, then they must, on his view, be thinkable. Even if we discount such empirical counterexamples, however, Hegel still has at least two other arguments against the view that contradictions are unthinkable. In the first place, he believes that a philosopher should not make any assumptions.[110] From this it follows that the laws of logic, if they are to be accepted, must be justified. It is plausible to suppose, however, that if any significant justification of the law of contradiction is to be given, then we must be able to think contradictions. The law is commonly justified, for example, by arguing that a contradictory proposition entails any proposition whatsoever, that if any contradictory proposition were true, then any and every proposition would be true.[111] We could not under-stand this argument, if we were unable to entertain contradictory propositions or to understand the sentences which express them. And if we can do this, then contradictions must be in some sense thinkable. It is, of course, doubtful whether the law of contradiction can, in any case, be significantly justified, since any argument for it will in some way presuppose its truth. But if Hegel clings to his view that philosophy must be free of assumptions, this consideration

452

will presumably fortify rather than diminish his resistance to the law of contradiction.

The foregoing argument concludes that, if the law of contradiction implies that contradictions are unthinkable, then it cannot be coherently justified. The second argument available to Hegel concludes that, if the law is interpreted in this way, then it cannot be coherently accepted at all, with or without justification. For if the law is taken to set limits to thought or to what is thinkable, acceptance of it would presumably contravene Hegel's limits principle. Thought cannot assign limits to itself, discover what its limits are, or even discover that it has *some* limits *or other*, since to do so would involve its transcending those limits (*Enz.* I. 60).[112] The limits principle, however, and its application to this case might be taken in various ways. The argument might, for example, run like this: I cannot believe truly that I cannot think what is contradictory, for in order to believe it at all, I have to understand the expression 'what is contradictory' and, if I can do this, I must be able to think what is contradictory or to think contradictions. But this type of argument is, as we have seen, fallacious.[113] By the same token, we could show that no one can believe truly that he cannot think what is unthinkable, a proposition which is patently false. Alternatively, the argument might be that if we are to think of things or states of affairs as non-contradictory, then we must be able to think of things or states of affairs as contradictory. To this, however, the reply could be made that 'non-contradictory' and 'contradictory' are predicates not of things and states of affairs, but of sentences. Our ability to understand them as predicates of sentences need not involve our being able to think of or conceive contradictory states of affairs or even to understand contradictory sentences. There is, however, little point in pursuing any of these arguments to their conclusions, since none of them is presented explicitly by Hegel. One version is, however, found in Fichte:[114]

> Logically fluent thinkers rise to everything except this. They guard against *contradiction*. But how, then, is the principle of their very logic possible, that one can think no contradiction? For they must have conceived, thought, contradiction in some way, since they communicate about it.

(v) Even if we grant that contradictions are thinkable, it does not obviously follow that there are any. Hegel seems to have believed, however, that what is thinkable must exist. This need not be taken to extend to such entities as unicorns, of which we form an empirical conception. It can be restricted to pure thoughts, and the concept of contradiction is, on Hegel's view, a pure thought

(*Enz.* I. 119; *WL* II. pp. 64 ff., M. pp. 431 ff.). But why must every pure thought be exemplified? Presumably Hegel had in mind some such arguments as these. Firstly, on one account of his system, pure thought generates the world without any outside assistance.[115] Why should the thought of contradiction be exempt from this? If there is something thinkable which yet does not exist, it would be impossible to give an ultimate explanation of its failure to exist. Secondly, in theological or metaphysical terms, thought must realize itself in nature in order to become aware of itself. In more down to earth terms, there must be things which correspond to any given thought, if we are to derive conceptions from them and ultimately arrive at the thought itself.[116] If, that is, we have the thought of objective contradiction, there must be objectively contradictory things from which we have derived it. Finally, Hegel might have appealed to the principle that if there is (or is known to be) anything which is *F*, then there must be (or be known to be) something which is not *F*.[117] If, that is, there is (known to be) anything which is not contradictory, then there must be (known to be) something which is contradictory. It might be objected to this that, since Hegel believes that everything is contradictory, this principle is in any case contravened by the fact that consistency or non-contradictoriness remains unexemplified. But he could reply to this that the contradictory contains the non-contradictory — as '*p* and not-*p*' contains '*p*' — or that what is contradictory at one level is not so at another.[118]

These considerations perhaps show that the acceptance of objective contradictions is deeply-rooted in Hegel's system, but they do not show that it is correct. Firstly, any explanation involves some conception of impossibility. To explain something is to show that it is in some sense impossible for it to be otherwise. But the contradictory is the most fundamental notion of impossibility that we have. Hegel himself believes that there is no better explanation of the death or demise of something than to say that it contained a contradiction. Even if it is hard to explain why contradictions do not occur, therefore, once we admit that they do, we make it impossible to explain anything whatsoever. Secondly, the principles invoked in the second and third arguments are not acceptable. Either of them could be used to establish the existence of unicorns or of any other conceivable entity. Finally, contradictory states of affairs are not straightforwardly thinkable in the way that unicorns are. There is constant pressure to regard the contradictory as unimaginable or inconceivable. Such grasp as we have on the notion comes from our acquaintance with subjective contradictions. The objectively contradictory no more needs to exist for us to know what is meant by it, or for there to (be known to) be non-contradictory things, than there needs to be a perfect book for there to (be known to) be imperfect ones.

(vi) Hegel's *Logic*, as we have seen, falls into two parts, 'Objective Logic' and 'Subjective Logic'.[119] The first part, comprising 'The Doctrine of Being' and 'The Doctrine of Essence', considers the subject-matter, roughly speaking, of traditional metaphysics, such concepts, for example, as those of being, substance and causality. The second part, or at least the first of its three sections, covers the subject-matter of traditional logic, the concept, the proposition and the syllogism or argument. The natural supposition is that the items considered in objective logic and those considered in subjective logic differ in respect of their relationship to objective things. Things, for example, *are*, they are perhaps substances, and they are causally related to one another. But things are not concepts, propositions, or arguments. Concepts, propositions and arguments are employed in our thought or discourse about things, but they do not directly characterize them in the way that the thought-determinations of objective logic do. Hegel, however, is at odds with this view. He believes that the concept, the proposition and the syllogistic form are embedded in the nature of things in much the same way as, for example, causality is:

> *Logic* therefore coincides with *metaphysics,* the science of *things* grasped in *thoughts* which were felt to express the *essentialities* of *things.*
>
> The relation of such forms as concept, judgment, and inference to others like causality, etc. can only emerge within the *Logic* itself. But this much can be seen in advance, that when thought seeks to form a *concept* of things, this concept (and consequently its most immediate forms, judgment and inference too) cannot consist of determinations and relations which are alien and external to things. Meta-thinking . . . leads to the universal of things; but this itself is one of the elements of the concept' (*Enz.* I. 24).

In this passage Hegel restricts himself to claiming that our concepts, judgments, and inferences must be relevant to things and that things have universal features corresponding to the concepts which we apply to them. But his eventual conclusion is bolder than this implies. It is that the forms of subjective logic are embedded, or at least mirrored, in objective things. We have already seen the role that concepts play in Hegel's account of at least some types of entity.[120] Perhaps the most surprising feature of his doctrine, however, is the claim that the syllogistic forms are embedded in the structure of the universe, that 'everything is a syllogism' (*Enz.* I. 181).[121] For whereas things or states of affairs have sometimes been held to reflect the structure of our propositions, the form of an argument like

'All Greeks are mortal;
Socrates is a Greek;
Therefore Socrates is mortal'

is not generally supposed to mirror the structure of the things themselves. Hegel's point may be that everything is an individual, exemplifies some general or universal kind, e.g. mortal things, and belongs to some particular species of this kind, e.g. Greeks. But the examples which he considers at length are entities with a more complex 'syllogistic' structure than this. The solar system is one such case. Another is the political state:[122]

Like the solar system, so is e.g. in the practical sphere the state a system of three syllogisms. 1. The *individual* (the person) is coupled with the *universal* (society, justice, law, government) through his *particularity* (physical and spiritual needs, which when further developed on their own give civil society); 2. the will, activity of individuals is the mediating factor [or 'middle term'] which gives satisfaction to the needs in society, law, etc. and gives fulfilment and actualization to society, law, etc; 3. but the substantial mean (*Mitte*) is the universal (state, government, law), in which individuals and their satisfaction have and acquire their fulfilled reality, mediation and subsistence. Each of the determinations, when mediation couples it with the other extreme, therein coalesces with itself, produces itself, and this production is its self-preservation. – It is only through the nature of this coupling, through this triad of inferences of the same *termini,* that a whole is truly understood in its organization (*Enz.* I. 198).

It is not, however, only items within the universe that have a 'syllogistic' structure. The universe itself is, on Hegel's view, a triad consisting of a universal term – the logical idea, a specific or particular term – nature, and an individual term – mind. These are combined in three syllogisms, each term in turn playing the role of the middle term which links the other two:

Here nature is first the middle, combining term. Nature, this immediate totality, unfolds itself into both extremes, the logical idea and mind. But mind is only mind when it is mediated by nature. Then secondly the middle term is mind, which we know to be the individual activating element, and nature and the logical idea are the extremes. It is mind which cognizes the logical idea in nature and thus raises it to its essence. Thirdly the logical idea itself is likewise the mean; it is the absolute substance both of mind and of nature, the universal, the all-pervasive. These are the terms of the absolute inference (*Enz.* 1. 187Z. Cf. *Enz.* III. 575 ff.).

In this way Hegel provides some ontological support for his belief that arguments or proofs should reflect the structure of the subject-matter. The subject-matter itself has the structure of an inference proceeding from two premises to a conclusion.[123]

On the whole this is simply elaborate nonsense. Even if we grant that the appropriate relationships obtain between the institutions of a society, the needs of its members, and the individual members themselves, or between the logical idea, nature and mind, the identification of these terms as respectively universal, particular and individual seems more or less arbitrary. Their relationship to each other resembles only remotely that between mortality, Greekness and Socrates. Indeed Hegel's belief that there is a resemblance seems to rest to a large degree on the etymological connection between the words '*Schluss*' and '*schliessen*' ('inference', 'infer') and the word '*zusammenschliessen*' ('couple', 'combine'). In any case, it is hard to see why so much weight should be placed on the argument-forms of traditional logic. Paradoxically Hegel's hostility to orthodox logic goes together with an exaggerated respect for an ill-digested version of it.

These criticisms do not, however, affect our main point, which is that Hegel's tendency to see the forms of subjective logic embedded in the structure of things seems to be one source of his belief that objective contradictions occur. For subjective logic is the proper domain of contradiction and consistency. Concepts and propositions can be contradictory, that is subjectively contradictory. Arguments cannot, indeed, be straightforwardly contradictory, but the propositions of which they consist may contradict each other or themselves. If, then, we transpose the forms of subjective logic into the things themselves, it is not unnatural to suppose that things, like concepts, propositions and arguments, can also contradict each other and themselves.

(vii) Contradiction in Hegel's *Logic* is not confined, however, to the Subjective Logic. Indeed, contradiction is considered as a distinct thought-determination not in the Subjective Logic at all, but in the Doctrine of Essence, in the context of the examination of the concepts of identity and difference (*Enz.* I. 119; *WL* II.

pp. 64 ff., M. pp. 431 ff.). In any case, however, the Objective Logic itself deals with concepts or thoughts, thoughts which are in some way contradictory. Hegel believes, however, that things mirror thoughts. He takes seriously Spinoza's view that: 'The order and connection of ideas is the same as the order and connection of things.'[124] But if this is so, then it is natural to suppose that things are as contradictory as the corresponding concepts.

The parallelism between the logical idea and the world does not, however, automatically commit Hegel to the view that there are actual, objective contradictions. For although the contradictoriness of thoughts is essential to his *Logic* — it is the contradictions in thoughts which bind them together into a single system (*Enz.* I. 81) — there are two ways, as we have seen, in which this contradictoriness can be interpreted. Hegel might mean, firstly, only that a thought would be contradictory if it were detached from other thoughts. Its apparent contradictions are removed once it is properly incorporated into the logical idea. Alternatively, he might mean that a finite thought is actually contradictory whether or not it is taken in the appropriate relationships to other thoughts.[125] Corresponding to these two possible interpretations of the contradictoriness of thoughts, there are two possible accounts of the contradictions in things. On the first account, the contradictions are merely hypothetical and not actual. Hegel would then be saying not that things actually are contradictory, but that they would be contradictory if they were detached from their environment, if they did not interact with it at all or if they did not interact with it in the specific way in which they do. It would, for example, have been contradictory if Hegel had not died of cholera in 1831. On the second account, things actually are contradictory. Hegel, for example, contained one or more contradictions and this explains in general why he died.

The first of these views amounts to the claim that whatever is the case is so because it is logically necessary that it should be so and it clearly does not entail the occurrence of any actual contradictions. Sometimes Hegel speaks as if he held this view, suggesting for example that the disposition of things in space and time avoids contradictions which would arise if matters were arranged otherwise:

> But formal thinking makes identity its law, lets the contradictory content which it has before it fall into the sphere of conception, into space and time, in which the contradictory is held *asunder* in juxtaposition and succession, and appear before consciousness without reciprocal contact (*WL* II. pp. 562 f., M. p. 835).

Spatial and temporal 'asunderness' can be seen as ways of averting contradictions. It is, for example, contradictory for it to be both raining and not raining, but not if it is raining on Tuesday but not raining on Thursday, or raining in Paris but not in Berlin. Hegel, however, clearly holds the second view, that contradictions actually occur, and this accords with the parallelism between the logical idea and the world. For the logical idea or pure thoughts cannot, as we have seen, be distinguished from pure thinking.[126] But whatever Hegel may say about the atemporality of logic, pure thinking takes time. Since it develops by the emergence and over-coming of contradictions, there will be a time during which one's thoughts are contradictory and one has not seen that this is so, and there may be a further interval before one resolves the contra-diction in one's thought. In general, subjective contradictions, contradictions in one's thoughts or beliefs, may persist for a time, even though, once perceived, they may explain, in part, changes in one's thoughts or beliefs. If objective contradictions mirror subjective ones, then they too must persist for a time before they are resolved. The world can then be seen as developing in time in the way that our thoughts and beliefs develop over time, attempting to resolve contradictions which persist until they become intolerable.

This parallelism, however, is open to at least two objections. Firstly, in explaining why subjective contradictions persist for a time, we can exploit the fact that a contradiction might remain unnoticed or implicit; it is only when a contradiction is perceived or explicit that its resolution becomes urgent. In nature, however, there is no distinction between perceived and unperceived contra-dictions. Why, then, should contradictions persist for any length of time, or — alternatively — why does it ever become urgent to resolve them? It is hard to reconcile the actual occurrence of contradictions with their need for resolution.[127] The second difficulty is that there are, as we have seen, two distinct types of series in nature, the temporal series of change and dissolution, and the atemporal series, or hierarchy, of phases of nature.[128] Corresponding to these, there are two distinct ways in which contradictions might be resolved. The contradictions in one level of nature or type of entity might be resolved, firstly, by the existence of another, higher type of entity or level of nature. The contradictions in, for example, mechanical or chemical entities generate, and are in some sense resolved by, the existence of organic entities and processes. In the second place, however, the contradictions in a type of entity or a level of nature are resolved by what happens to those entities or at that level, by, for example, the occurrence of movement or change or by the death or destruction of the entities in question. Hegel, as we have seen, tends to run together these two types of contradiction-resolution, speaking as if the destruction of an entity of one level resulted in an entity of a higher level. His discussion of animals, for example, culminates both in the death of the individual animal and in a transition to spirit (*Enz.* II. 376).[129] But which of these series is analogous to human thought-processes? The temporal series, for example the deaths of successive generations of organisms, can perhaps be seen as parallel to the way in which we successively modify or discard our beliefs as we find them to be inconsistent. But it fails to capture the increasing adequacy and richness of our beliefs. The atemporal hierarchy, on the other hand, while it may do justice to the increasing complexity of our beliefs, cannot genuinely resolve contradictions. Since, on Hegel's view, stones and plants have always existed together, it cannot be the case that the contradictions in stones are relieved by the emergence of plants. *Either* stones are *actually* contradictory and the existence of plants does not remedy this *or* the contradictions are merely hypothetical: stones *would* be contradictory *if* plants did not exist, but they are not in fact contradictory. In the former case, the contradictions are not resolved; in the latter, the absolute has remained, as it were, one step ahead of the ever-threatening contradictions, never allowing them to emerge. If Hegel believes that there are actual contradictions, it is hard to see how they c?.. be resolved by the move to higher levels of nature.

(viii) As we have seen, one of Hegel's motives for the postulation of contradictions was his desire to explain change and dissolution. The general idea is that change and dissolution would not occur if there were not some flaw in things as they are, that to explain why the world does not remain in the state which, at any given time, it is in we must suppose that there is something wrong with this state. There are, however, two ways in which he might have stopped short of accepting actual contradictions. He might, firstly, have confined himself to such notions as those of conflict, tension, and stress. Or, secondly, he might have postulated only hypothetical contradictions: there would have been a contradiction in the world, if such and such a change had not occurred. Why does change require actual, persistent *contradictions*?

It is, of course, true that what Hegel calls contradictions are often no more than tensions, strains or conflicts, but it is fairly clear that he would have been reluctant to accept this diluted characterization of them. One reason for this is perhaps the fact that reference to a non-logical conflict or tension does not give a complete and final answer to the question why change occurs. A bridge or a partnership can endure a good deal of conflict or tension. Bridges, buildings and communities can be sustained, as well as destroyed, by tensions and opposition. Thus to explain the collapse of such entities by referring to their tensions leaves room for the question: Why could it not survive the tension? If the reply is that the tension became unendurable or intolerable, then either it is simply another way of saying that it had a certain effect or it points to a genuine kind or degree of tension whose fatality is assured. Contradiction seems made to measure for this role. One cannot sensibly ask why a thing or a state of affairs did not survive a contradiction. This advantage is lost, however, as soon as one concedes that things can sustain contradictions for a time, that a change results from a preceding contradiction of some duration. Hegel seems to believe that contradictions, like tensions, persist for a time before the occurrence of the change which relieves them. But then, if we are to explain why the change occurs when it does rather than earlier, contradictions, like tensions, must be qualified as 'unsupportable' or 'coming to a head'. Contradictions cannot be both occurrent and infallibly unsustainable.

If contradictions were postulated only in order to explain change, it would be natural to locate them in states of the world as a whole rather than in individual things in the world. The death of a man from a bullet, for example, could be explained by pointing to a contradiction, hypothetical or actual, in a world-state which includes a living man with a bullet in his brain or in a world-state which includes a living man with a bullet about to enter his brain. On Hegel's view, however, contradictions lie not simply in whole world-states, but in single items within the world, in the man (and in the bullet) taken individually. Indeed, if contradictions resided only in world-states and not in things taken separately, it would be hard to maintain that contradictions persist for a finite time. For it is possible that change is continuous and that the world does not remain in any given state for a period of time. By contrast, an individual thing can be regarded, despite the continual change which it undergoes, as relatively long-lasting, with contradictions which persist throughout at least a part of its life-span. But why did Hegel locate contradictions in individual things rather than world-states? There are at least two reasons for this. Firstly, he wants to connect contradictoriness with finitude, and things in the world are more obviously finite than are states of the world as a whole. Contradictions explain not only changes in things over time, but their entanglements with each other in space. Thus the death of a man, for example, is to be explained not only by a contradiction in the world to which he belongs, but by a contradiction in the man himself (*Enz.* I. 81Z.1).[130] We are inclined to distinguish between a person's dying under his own steam, of cancer perhaps or of old age, and his dying as a result of some external invasion by bullets or bacteria. The first sort of death may be the result of internal contradictions, or at any rate tensions or defects, but the second is not. Hegel seems to disagree with this, however, and he would perhaps argue somewhat as follows. Even if a man were closeted in a bullet- and bacteria-free environment, he would still die eventually. But, in any case, no man could be entirely insulated from his environment. We cannot distinguish between an inner core of persistent, tensionless vitality and external intrusions into it. External intrusions are essential to life and it must be receptive to them, the destructive or damaging ones as well as the sustaining ones. The distinction between dying of one's own accord and dying from external causes is not a sharp one. If a man's death is occasioned by some slight occurrence, the bursting of a paper bag, for example, or mild sexual exhilaration, there has to be some internal defect which accounts for its having had this effect on him. But this is true of any death from external causes. There must be something wrong, though not necessarily abnormally wrong, with a living creature to account for its vulnerability to external attack. Trivially, if x has a certain effect on y, then y must be capable of being affected by x in that way.[131] In general, then, Hegel's view seems to be that if anything dies, disappears or indeed changes in any way, there must be some intrinsic defect which explains its doing so.

A second reason for Hegel's locating contradictions in things rather than in world-states or complexes of things is the connection which he sees between the objective contradictions in things and the subjective contradictions in the concepts which are embedded in things. These concepts apply to individual things rather than to world-states or complexes of things. It is, for example, the man who is alive, not the complex of a man with a bullet approaching him. The concept of life, Hegel argues, is bound up with that of a genus, and this involves the death of the individual members of the genus (*Enz.* I. 221; *WL* II. pp. 484 ff., M. pp. 772 ff.). The argument is uncompelling, but the main point is clear. If the death of an organism is to be explained by the intertwining of the concepts of life and of death, then we cannot sharply separate a man's mortality from his vitality, attributing his death solely to adventitious intrusions. It can, of course, be objected that conceptual connections cannot explain what happens to things; that if the proposition that something is alive entails that it will die, then we simply cannot be sure that it is alive unless we have established, on empirical grounds, that it will die; that such conceptual links no more entitle us to explain a creature's death by its vitality than to account for a man's celibacy by his bachelorhood; that things and events do not mirror the entanglements of concepts with one another any more than they contradict themselves. The point, however, is that if (*per impossibile*) the interconnections of things were patterned on the interconnections of concepts, then what happens to an individual thing would be accounted for by features internal to it, and not simply by the state of the world as a whole.

These, then, are some of the sources of Hegel's belief that there are contradictions in things. In the following section we shall consider some criticisms of this belief.

14 *The overcoming of contradiction*

Hegel has attracted little support for his belief that objective contradictions occur, but the law of contradiction is too fundamental to our thought for it to be easy to say why they cannot occur. It is commonly held that, while we can construct coherent and fruitful formal systems which do not include the law of the excluded middle, a formal system which admitted contradictory propositions would be one in which any proposition whatsoever was a theorem, since a contradictory proposition entails any and every proposition.[132] Since Hegel believes that everything is contradictory, he might not object very strenuously to the view that anything follows from a contradiction. There is, after all, a sense in which he is prepared to assert even propositions with which he primarily disagrees.[133] But evidently the consequences of accepting this result would reduce his system to absurdity. It would commit him to granting, for example, that all his statements are false and that the sun is shaped like a banana. The view has indeed been challenged, and attempts have been made to construct a system in which a contradictory proposition does not entail *any* proposition, in which a contradiction can be kept, as it were, in quarantine so that it does not infect the rest of the system.[134] Hegel, however, was entirely unfamiliar with these issues and lacked the formal training to handle them effectively. There is little point, therefore, in attempting to defend him along these lines.

He can, however, be met on his own ground if we ask the question: Why, on his view, are subjective contradictions to be avoided? For he believes, as we have seen, that contradictions

463

in our thinking cannot be simply accepted. They are to be, if not avoided, at least resolved and overcome. But why? The obvious answer to this question is that contradictory concepts cannot be applicable and contradictory beliefs cannot be true. But since Hegel believes that states of affairs and things can contradict themselves, this answer is not available to him. Contradictory beliefs may be, in the ordinary sense, true beliefs. He does indeed hold that there is another sense of 'true', in which a belief, or anything else, which contradicts itself cannot be true. A contradictory belief is not a true belief and a contradictory concept is not a true concept in much the way in which a friend may fail to be a true friend. He presumably believes that just as things like societies, animals and projectiles must escape their (objective) contradictions, so we must escape our (subjectively) contradictory thoughts and beliefs. However, Hegel's belief that objective contradictions must be overcome depends to a large extent on his assumption that subjective contradictions are objectionable, an assumption which has yet to be justified. Unless something can be shown to be wrong with contradictoriness, it remains unclear why it should disqualify beliefs and concepts from being true ones or why, even if it did, they should therefore be avoided, abandoned or modified. If there are objective contradictions, then contradictory beliefs and concepts do their job as well or better than consistent ones.

One answer that might be given to our question is that contradictory thinking or contradictory speaking can be seen to be intrinsically pointless, without reference to the external world. We might, for example, invoke the view that a contradiction entails any proposition and suggest that thinking in which contradictions are permitted would be as pointless and anomic as a game in which every move is allowed. But, as we have seen, Hegel is unfamiliar with this view and, while he has reason to place *some* constraints on thinking, he has no special justification for assigning this role to the law of contradiction. In any case, since he believes that contradictions are empirically detectable, he could presumably subject it to empirical constraints, though to do so would impair its purity and autonomy. Another idea that might be of service is that contradicting oneself is a self-defeating activity like taking one step forward and one step back, knitting a garment and unravelling it as soon as one knits it, or pouring water into a sieve. It is easy, however, to think of contexts in which such activities as these have a point — in a dance, for example, or a game, or as a form of exercise. The thinking or assertion of contradictions might be assigned a similar point, if it were not for the fact that they already have one if Hegel is right, namely that of describing a contradictory world. The pointlessness of contradicting oneself would surely be removed if the world itself were contradictory.

In general, however, Hegel regards contradiction not so much as pointless and self-defeating as a source of psychological conflict and disharmony. It is, therefore, fruitful, an impetus to further advance. To think that p and not p involves the same sort of discomfort as wanting both to have one's cake and to eat it. However, while some of the things that Hegel calls contradictions, pains, for example, and unfulfilled desires, are intrinsically distressing and worthy of avoidance or resolution, in most cases the discomfort depends on an objective world, independent of the mental states of the subject, in which contradictory states of affairs cannot obtain. What is wrong with wanting to have one's cake and eat it, for example, can only be that one cannot actually have one's cake and eat it. Similarly, thinking contradictory thoughts and asserting contradictory propositions is not intrinsically stressful or unpleasant. What is wrong with it is that the thoughts cannot be applicable and the propositions cannot be true.

Hegel's belief that contradictions are intrinsically uncomfortable rests in part on his claim that, when thinking gets involved in them, it 'gets lost in the fixed non-identity of thoughts, [and] thus it does not attain to itself' (*Enz.* I. 11).[135] One idea here seems to be that contradictions arise when sharp boundaries are drawn between concepts.[136] Rigid distinctions of this sort may in themselves be a source of discomfort to the thinking self, in that whereas the self is or strives to be a unity, the thoughts which are its object are separate and disconnected, or at least sharply distinct, from each other. Disparity of this kind between the self and its object is, on Hegel's view, one of the primary motives for our efforts to understand and organize the world.[137] The tension must be all the greater if it is not simply the empirical world, but thoughts themselves that are out of accord with the ego. For thoughts are what the ego consists of. Hegel calls the contrast between the ego and its object a 'contradiction [which] must be resolved' (*Enz.* III. 425Z). Even if we grant, however, that this type of 'contradiction' must be resolved, that the disparity between the single, unified ego and its disconnected objects affords the sort of discomfort which must be relieved, it does not follow that all contradictions in thinking must be resolved. For, firstly, it is not obvious that contradictions arise only when thoughts are kept rigidly distinct from each other. The contradiction within the concept of a whole consisting of parts, for example, is not resolved when we connect this concept up with others.[138] Secondly, even if contradictions did arise only when concepts were separated from one another and consequently disappeared when the proper relationships were established between them, we would still need some independent reason for objecting to contradictions if we are to bring this about. For when the ego thinks purely, it is not presented with an array of disconnected thoughts which it has to bring into some relationship. Logic is, as we have seen, unilinear. Any given thought has some contradiction or other defect, the loose ends, as it were, which indicate that there is some other thought with which it is to be connected. But this second thought has not yet emerged before the ego. It is only if it is distressed by the contradiction, and therefore follows up the loose ends, that it will arrive at it. Any given segment of logic is already unified and, on one account at least, it is only if there is something wrong with contradicting oneself that we have any reason to go beyond it. Even if we agree, therefore, that disarray and discontinuity must be overcome, Hegel still needs to tell us what is wrong with contradiction, and this he has failed to do.

This is a serious omission. Contradiction is intended to be the force which drives both the universe and our thought about it. It is a familiar complaint against Hegel that he accepts and even welcomes contradictions. This, as we have seen, is not true. Contradictions are not to be tolerated, or at least they are not to be tolerated for very long. But this simply leaves Hegel with another problem, namely why there is anything wrong with them at all.

15 *Consistency and idealism*

Hegel's beliefs about contradictions are connected, as we have seen, with his idealism. In what sense, then, is he an idealist? If he believed that things are no more than the projections of thought, then clearly things might contain contradictions, just as the characters in a work of fiction might have contradictory characteristics conferred upon them by their author. There would, in this case, be no genuinely objective contradictions in things, but only those read into them by the creative thinker. Hegel clearly does not believe, however, that it is we men who produce the world in this way. If he did, he could not argue that it is a mistake, for example, to regard living organisms as merely wholes consisting of parts.[139] It would be up to us, or to me, what thoughts are deployed in what connection. Hegel is presupposing that there are things independent of us which have an implicit conceptual structure which we bring out but do not produce. Again, if

466

contradictions were simply imposed on things by us, they could not plausibly be supposed to do the work that Hegel requires of them, explaining movement, change and death. If such phenomena as these are to be seen as the results of a thinker's efforts to extricate himself from the contradictions in which he is entangled, it must be a single cosmic thinker rather than any one of us. Is Hegel, then, an idealist in this sense, ascribing the universe as a whole to a single divine thinker? The answer to this question is obscured by a variety of factors, by, for example, the sheer diversity of his arguments for the primacy of thought and by his conflation of thoughts with the features to which thoughts correspond. Hegel's central doctrine, however, seems to be this. Idealism and realism are commonly seen as *alternative* ways of regarding the world. If we start from the self and the features of it of which we are immediately aware, then we shall tend to be idealists, regarding the external world as in some sense a product or a construct of the self. If, on the other hand, we start from the external world, we shall tend to be realists, regarding the self and its features as a product of things. This is how, for example, Fichte viewed the matter:[140]

> *The thing,* which must be determined independently of our freedom and to which our knowledge must conform, and *the intelligence,* which must know, are in experience inseparably connected. The philosopher can leave one of the two out of consideration, and he has then abstracted from experience and raised himself above it. If he leaves out the former, he retains an intelligence in itself, that is, abstracted from its relation to experience, as a basis for explaining experience; if he leaves out the latter, he retains a thing-in-itself, that is, abstracted from the fact that it occurs in experience, as a similar basis of explanation. The first method of procedure is called *idealism,* the second *dogmatism.*

Fichte did not believe that either of these positions could strictly refute the other, though he did believe that there were rational grounds for preferring idealism to realism or, as he calls it, dogmatism. At all events, he seems to have held that one can be *either* an idealist *or* a realist but not consistently both. Hegel, by contrast, although he regularly calls himself an idealist, attempts, as we have seen, to combine both positions in his system, proceeding in a circular manner from the self to the world and from there back to the self.[141] In the light of this, it is hardly to be expected that we can assign to him a single, unequivocal doctrine about the status of the world.

This, then, concludes our account of Hegel's view of the universe. In the final chapter, something will be said about the ethical implications which he took this view to have.

XI

Freedom, Morality and the
End of History

Hegel was as concerned as any philosopher with practical and ethical questions, with questions about how one ought to live and with the ways in which such questions can be answered. In his mind, however, these questions are closely intertwined with logical, epistemological and theological questions. Moreover, whatever may have been the original motivation of his work, in his mature system logic is the central and dominant element. It is from this point of view, therefore, that his ethical doctrines will be considered.

1 *Freedom*

One important notion in Hegel's thought is that of freedom. It is not in fact, of course, a single notion, but rather a set of interconnected ones. He is, for example, less inclined than most of us are to draw a sharp distinction between freedom of the will and political or civil liberty.[1] The main point for the moment, however, is that freedom is a cognitive or theoretical concept as well as an ethical or practical one. A person's freedom can be impaired, for example, as much by getting him to believe certain things by hypnotic suggestion or indoctrination as it can by the use of such means in order to influence his conduct. Or, again, one way, for Hegel a very important way, in which a person may lack freedom is by his unquestioning acceptance of the norms of his society or the pronouncements of his church as guides for his action. But his theoretical autonomy is similarly impaired if he relies on authority, his society, his church or whatever, for unfailing guidance with respect to his beliefs. Autonomy of both kinds involves stepping back from or distancing oneself from accepted norms and dogmas and asking: 'Granted that the law or the ecclesiastical authorities tell me to do so-and-so, why, nevertheless, should I do it?' or 'Granted that the church or public opinion tell me that such-and-such is the case, why should I believe it?' The asking of such questions as these is, as we have seen, an essential feature of what Hegel conceives to be the fall from innocence.[2]

There are, however, at least two problems involved in such a transition to autonomy. The first is: Where is the line to be drawn between what does and what does not count as an impairment of my cognitive or practical autonomy? Once one type of authority has been questioned, it may begin to look as if nothing could be a reason for my doing or believing anything without thereby infringing my liberty, as if, in order to become autonomous, I must distance myself from everything which could conceivably lead to my doing or believing one thing rather than another. The second and related problem is: How are we ever to achieve the restoration which should, on Hegel's view, follow our descent from naiveté? How can we reconcile the claims of autonomy with the adoption of any settled way of deciding what to believe and how to act? The more we are led to reject in our pursuit of autonomy, the more difficult such a reconciliation will be. These problems will figure prominently in the following sections.

2 Autonomy and empiricism

The first problem becomes urgent when a pei   '˙ desires and his sensory intake are regarded as alien intrusions on his freedom in much the same way as laws and traditional dogmas are. Then to act on one's own desires or to believe one's own eyes is seen as an abandonment of one's autonomy, and the reassertion of it begins when one asks: 'Why should I do what I feel like doing?' or 'Why should I accept the testimony of my own senses?' This move is apparent, as we have seen, in Hegel's treatment of empiricism and the natural sciences. The pre-Kantian metaphysicians were on the right lines in so far as they believed that the truth was to be sought by thinking, but the inadequacy of their thinking led them to succumb to tradition and authority at crucial points (*Enz.* I. 31Z).[3] Empiricism, by contrast, was, in this respect at least, free or autonomous. The freedom which empirical scientists have and which their spokesmen insist upon is the freedom provided by reliance on sensory evidence at the expense of tradition and authority (*Enz.* I. 38).[4] As we have seen, however, there is a sense in which the empirical scientist is no more free than the person who relies on tradition and authority (*Enz.* I. 38Z).[5] My sensory data are, on Hegel's view, no more myself than are the dogmas of others, and to rely on them is as much a renunciation of my autonomy as it is to take on trust the assertions of priests and kings.

Hegel believes that empiricism carries certain ethical implications which make it, in this respect too, a 'doctrine of unfreedom'. Just as it rejects the idea of a supersensible world, ontologically or epistemically superior to our own phenomenal world, so it acknowledges no transcendent ethical standard in the light of which the actual world may be found wanting. He expresses both points in terms of a rejection of *das Sollen,* of the 'ought-to-be':[6]

> Empiricism contains the great principle that what is true must be in actuality and exist for perception. This principle is opposed to the *ought-to-be,* which reflection flaunts and uses to show contempt towards actuality and the present with a *beyond* (*Jenseits*) which has its seat and existence only in the subjective understanding (*Enz.* I. 38).

There is a sense in which Hegel approves of this, but he cannot accept what the empiricists take to be a consequence of it, namely that 'reason and unreason are only subjective, i.e. we have to content ourselves with the given, just as it is, and we have no right to ask whether and how far it is intrinsically rational' (*Enz.* I. 38Z). It was David Hume who, on Hegel's view, brought this standpoint to fulfilment, when he reduced universality and necessity to

> a subjective contingency, a mere habit, whose content can be constituted this way or that. An important consequence of this is that in this empirical manner legal and ethical determinations, like the content of religion, appear as something contingent and their objectivity and inner truth is abandoned (*Enz.* I. 39).

There cannot, on this account, be any genuinely objective standard for judging how things ought to be, whether embedded in the actual phenomenal world or supplied by some transcendent realm. Our decisions to act, therefore, can be based only on what we happen to desire: 'Everything in general then appears (*auftritt*) in the form of an irrational, unthought being; what is in itself true and right is not in thought, but in the form of an impulse, an inclination' (*VGP* III. p. 281, H. III. p. 375). Certain norms of conduct are, of course, widely accepted and acquire a sort of objective status, but this depends only on the fact that the corresponding desires or feelings happen to be widely shared:

> If it is presupposed that our knowledge is from experience and we must accept as true only what we have from that source,

then we find in our feeling e.g. the sentiment (*Empfindung*) that the murderer, the thief must be punished; others too feel this and thus it becomes universally valid (*VGP* III. p. 279, H. III. p. 373).

Hegel's primary objection to this doctrine seems to be that, if one acts only on one's own desires, then one cannot be properly free:

> The will which is at first only free in itself is the immediate or natural will. The determinations of the distinction which the self-determining concept puts into the will appear in the immediate will as a content which is immediately present — that is impulses, desires, inclinations by which the will finds itself determined by nature (*PR* 11).

Freedom of this sort is 'dependence on a content and material given from within or without' (*PR* 15. Cf. 10). My desires and impulses are no more me, or even determined by me, than are my sensory data. Empiricism is, then, a doctrine of practical and theoretical unfreedom. It makes our will dependent on our contingent desires, just as it makes our intellect dependent on our sensory experience.

Hegel's understanding of the empiricist tradition is, as we have seen, imperfect, and a number of questions could be raised about this account.[7] We shall here raise only one of them, however. Is Hegel claiming only that the empiricist account of human capacities implies that men are unfree in these ways, or is he also claiming that empiricists themselves actually are unfree in these ways? He believes that all persons at a certain stage of their life, and perhaps some people for the whole of their life, are unfree in the sense that they have only the 'immediate or natural will'. He also believes that the methods of the natural sciences, and empiricist philosophy, leave no place for proper freedom in their picture of the world (*Enz.* I. 8). It does not, however, follow that natural scientists and their philosophical spokesmen, the adherents of the 'doctrine of unfreedom', are unfree. It is true that there is, on Hegel's view, an essential connection between how people are and how they conceive themselves to be: 'That the mind attains to awareness of what it is constitutes its realization. The mind is essentially only what it knows (*weiss*) of itself' (*Enz.* III. 385Z).[8] But this does not imply, apparently, that people are invariably correct in the account they give of themselves. Jacobi, for example, believed incorrectly that he possessed exclusively immediate awareness.[9] Natural scientists believe incorrectly that they dispense with thought and rely solely on sense-experience.[10] In some cases, indeed, we can find discrepancies between an account of human capacities and the capacities presupposed by the ability to give that account.[11] It is a familiar criticism of Hume, for example, that whereas he ascribes to men only the capacities for experiential and for verbal reasoning, it is not obvious that his own thought involves only reasoning of these two types.[12] In view of the fact that Hegel regards such discrepancies in general terms as one of the mainsprings of intellectual development, it is perhaps surprising that he does not make more of them in particular cases than he does. The main point, however, is that, if there can be such discrepancies between what men think they are and do and what they actually are and do, it is possible that, on Hegel's view, natural scientists and empiricists are free in ways which their own theories exclude. It is, however, unlikely that he believed them to be fully and entirely autonomous. One strand in Hegel's thought is that freedom is conferred, and not merely described, by his own philosophy. At that stage, of course, there is no mismatch between how men conceive themselves and how they are. Before we turn to Hegel's own answers to these questions, however, we shall consider his account of Kant's view.

3 Kant and freedom

The parallel between intellectual autonomy and moral autonomy underlies Hegel's account of Kant. In one sense, Kant treated cognition and ethics in the same way. Reason in its theoretical capacity is intended to make claims which transcend our sensory intake, our experience, just as practical reason is intended to prescribe courses of action which transcend our desires, even our desire for happiness. Kant was at least prepared to ask the questions: 'Why should I/we follow my/our desires?' and 'Why should we accept (only) the beliefs which my/our sensory experience seems to impose on me/us?' At this point, however, the parallel, on Kant's view, ends. For transcendent cognitive claims cannot be legitimated by reason:[13]

> *Knowledge*, which as such is speculative, can have no other object than that supplied by experience; if we transcend the limits thus imposed, the synthesis which seeks, independently of experience, new species of knowledge, lacks that substratum of intuition upon which alone it can be exercised.

Practical reason, by contrast, can produce and legitimate transcendent imperatives:[14]

> Reason does not here follow the order of things as they present themselves in appearance, but frames for itself with perfect

spontaneity an order of its own according to ideas, to which it adapts the empirical conditions, and according to which it declares actions to be necessary.

Hegel is aware of this difference:

> What Kant denied to theoretical reason — free self-determination — he has expressly vindicated for practical reason . . . . Whereas . . . theoretical reason is, according to Kant, supposed to be merely the negative faculty of the infinite and, without any positive content of its own, is confined to seeing the finitude of experiential cognition, he has, by contrast, expressly acknowledged the positive infinity of practical reason, and indeed in such a way that he ascribes to the *will* the capacity to determine itself in a universal way, i.e. by thinking (*Enz.* I. 54Z).

Hegel, however, finds two difficulties in this view. The first is this. If Kant is right, then it is not enough for him to ascribe to the will the ability to distance itself from our desires. Practical reason will be in the same position as theoretical reason unless it has some way of finding out what we are supposed to do and what we are supposed not to do:

> This acknowledgement does not yet answer the question of the content of the will or of practical reason. When, then, it is said that man should make the *good* the content of his will, the question of the content of his will, i.e. the determinacy of this content, is immediately raised and the mere principle of the agreement of the will with itself, just like the requirement to do one's duty for duty's sake, gets one no further (*Enz.* I. 54Z).

How is such a content to be supplied? Kant believed that certain types of action, the breaking of promises, for example, and the telling of lies, could be ruled out *a priori,* without reference to what one's own desires or those of others happen to be. One of his formulations of the criterion for right action is this: 'I should always proceed in such a way that I can also will that my maxim should become a universal law.'[15] The application of this criterion, Kant believes, would exclude promise-breaking and lying for the reason that to will that such practices should become universal would involve an inconsistency or contradiction.

With some, but not excessive, oversimplification Hegel represents Kant's position as this:

> For what practical thinking is to make a law, for the criterion of its self-*determination,* nothing else is available but the *abstract*

identity of the understanding, that no contradiction occurs in the determining — *practical* reason thus does not get beyond the formalism which is supposed to be the ultimate (*das Letzte*) of theoretical reason (*Enz.* I. 54).

As this suggests, however, Hegel does not believe that consistency or absence of contradiction provides a criterion of right or permissible action. The example to which he most frequently refers is that of theft. Kant would attempt to establish the wrongness of theft by asking us if we could consistently will that theft, or perhaps theft in certain specified circumstances, should become a universal practice. To this procedure Hegel objects:

> That there should be no property contains, taken on its own (*für sich*), as little contradiction as that this or that people, family, etc. should not exist or that in general there should be no living men. Of course, if it is independently established and presupposed that there should be property and human life and they should be respected, then it is a contradiction to commit a theft or a murder; a contradiction must be a contradiction of something, that is, of a content which is presupposed in advance as a fixed principle. Only in relation to such a content is an action either in agreement or in contradiction (*PR* 135. Cf. *PG* pp. 306 ff., M. pp. 256 ff.).

At one level, Hegel believes, everything is contradictory. But this applies to abstention from stealing as much as to stealing, to property as much as to its absence. At the level with which Kant is concerned, however, nothing is contradictory, so that absence of contradiction would legitimate any action whatsoever. The traditional laws of thought, then, 'abstract identity', cannot provide us with guidance on how to act. But if we have no way of telling what the good is, the claim that we should not simply fulfil our desires and inclinations but rather will the good for its own sake has no more content than the claim that beyond our sense-experience there is an ultimate reality to which we have no access.

The second difficulty is that Kant is inconsistent, on Hegel's view, in treating, or at least attempting to treat, practical and theoretical reason differently. Hegel can see no ground for restricting theoretical reason to the organization of our sensory data, while liberating practical reason from dependence on our desires. There are, on the face of it, three possible views that might be taken on this question:

(i) The cases are not parallel. The most natural version of this view is Kant's own, namely that whereas a person's non-moral beliefs should (or must) depend on his/our sensory experience, his moral beliefs or attitudes can (or should) transcend his/our desires. Ethical imperatives are different in this respect from factual beliefs.

(ii) The cases are parallel in that thought can transcend neither my/our sensory experience nor my/our desires. There are various ways in which apparently transcendent cognitive or ethical claims may be treated. They may be regarded as meaningless, or as meaningful but unknowable or uncertifiable, or they may be seen as no more than disguised empirical claims, expressions of or statements about my/our desires or sensory data, based on, and answerable to, my/our sensory experience or desires just as any other claim is.

(iii) The cases are parallel in that transcendent claims of both sorts can and should be made.

If we are to be consistent, Hegel believes, only positions (ii) and (iii) are acceptable. Kant erred in attempting to occupy position (i). However, in view of the first difficulty, the difficulty of substantiating transcendent imperatives with only the equipment of traditional logic, Kant ends up, on Hegel's view, with a version of position (ii). He is unprepared to accept either our sensory experience or our desires as the final authority on what is true and what ought to be the case. In neither case, however, can reason legitimate transcendent claims, cognitive claims which go beyond our senses or imperatives which go beyond our desires. The freedom won by our readiness to distance ourselves from them is thus empty. If we wish to believe or to do anything definite at all, then we have no other option than to resort once more to our senses and our desires:

Kantian philosophy advances the principle of thinking and freedom in direct opposition to this [viz. materialistic, naturalistic] empiricism . . . . The one side of its dualism is still the world of perception and of the understanding which reflects upon it . . . . The other side, however, is the independence of self-apprehending thinking, the principle which it [viz. Kantian philosophy] has in common with the former, ordinary meta-physics, but empties of all content and cannot provide with any more. This thinking (here called *reason*), being stripped of all determination, is exempt from all *authority*. The main effect which Kantian philosophy has had is to have aroused the consciousness of this absolute inwardness, which, although on account of its abstraction it cannot develop into anything or produce any determinations, either cognitions or moral laws, yet absolutely refuses to admit and accept as valid anything which has the character of an externality (*Enz.* I. 60).

476

4 *Hegel's solutions*

To which of the three positions presented in the last section does Hegel adhere? Characteristically, and in keeping with his strictures on one-sided concepts, no single one of them can easily be ascribed to him. He can be excluded with some confidence from category (i). For he clearly believed that intellectual and moral autonomy were parallel, though, as we shall see, he did not succeed in establishing this. He does not, however, adhere to position (ii), that of the empiricist and of the 'eudaemonist':

> Now since happiness was understood as the satisfaction of man in his particular inclinations, wishes, needs, etc., the contingent and particular was thereby made the principle of the will and its activity. To this eudaemonism, which lacks all firm foundation and opens the door to any wilfulness and caprice, Kant opposed practical reason and therewith expressed the demand for a universal determination of the will, equally obligatory for all .... Now, of course, the will possesses this capacity and it is of great importance to be aware that man is only free in so far as he possesses it and uses it in his conduct (*Enz.* I. 54Z).

On the other hand, Hegel rejects any suggestion that there are, as it were, two worlds, an empirical world and a supersensible one accessible only to thought, a world of freedom and a world governed by causal necessity, or a world of values and a world of facts. The terms of such dualisms can no more be sharply distinct from, or flatly identical with, one another than God can be sharply distinct from, or flatly identical with, the world:

> Since reason [which 'has the infinite and unconditioned for its object'] is regarded in this way merely as the transcendence (*das Hinausschreiten*) of the finite and conditioned of the understanding, reason is thus reduced in fact to something finite and conditioned, for the truly infinite is not a mere beyond of the finite, but contains it sublimated within itself (*Enz.* I. 45Z).

Claims which genuinely transcend our sensory experiences or our desires are therefore excluded. There is no transcendent realm to which they could correspond or, for that matter, fail to correspond.

Hegel's position is, then, a complex one. In this section, we shall attempt to unravel his views about intellectual autonomy. One fundamental feature which he ascribes not only to the will, but to the ego in general is the 'absolute possibility of being able to abstract from every determination in which I find myself or which I have set up in myself, the flight from all content as a limit' (*PR*

5).[16] We have already seen, however, that pure thought is not simply a determination of the self, something from which, as a limitation, it can abstract or attempt to disentangle itself. We cannot abstract from our capacity for thought.[17] Such abstraction can be described, therefore, as 'the limitless infinity of absolute abstraction or universality, the pure thinking of oneself' (*PR* 5). Abstraction of this sort, moreover, is not merely an empty gesture, for, as we have seen, 'thinking of oneself' or thinking about thinking is a substantial cognitive enterprise. Hegel regularly associates it with freedom:[18]

> *Freedom* is immediately involved in thinking, because it is the activity of the universal, thus an abstract relating of oneself to oneself, a determinationless being at home with oneself (*Beisichsein*), with regard to subjectivity, while with regard to *content* it is only in the *subject-matter* and its determinations (*Enz.* I. 23).

An addition makes it clear that what Hegel has in mind is pure thinking. It contrasts pure thinking with acting on one's desires, though thinking differs in this respect not simply from practical activity, but from other cognitive procedures:

> In logic, thoughts are so conceived that they have no other content than one that belongs to thinking itself and is produced by it . . . . Thus the mind is purely at home with itself and therefore free, for freedom is just to be at home with oneself in one's other, to depend on oneself, to be what determines oneself. In all impulses I begin from an other, from something which is for me external. Here, then, we speak of dependence. Freedom is only there where there is no other for me which I myself am not. The natural man, who is determined only by his desires, is not at home with himself: however self-willed he is, the *content* of his willing and opining is yet not his own, and his freedom is only *formal* (*Enz.* I. 24Z.2).

Hegel does not distinguish these two types of freedom as well as he might. Too much weight is placed, for example, on the contrast between form and content. In §23 the thinker is said to be 'free with regard to form' owing to his abandonment of his 'subjective particularity', while in the addition the natural man is said to be *formally* free despite his retention of it. If we ignore, however, the vicissitudes of such terms as 'form' and 'formal', there seem to be at least four respects in which, on Hegel's view, desires, or for that matter sense-perceptions, differ from pure thoughts:

478

(i) My desires are not identical with myself, but are 'states' of myself. I might, for example, have had different desires from those I actually have. My pure thoughts, by contrast, are me, not simply things that I happen to have.[19]

(ii) A desire is a desire for something other than myself, for example for a piece of cake. Pure thoughts, however, are not thoughts of anything other than myself. This involves two distinct points. Firstly, pure thinking is thought about thoughts, and, secondly, the thoughts that it is about are themselves non-empirical concepts, concepts like that of being rather than conceptions like that of an elephant. One can, of course, have desires about desires, reflective, second-order desires, the desire, for example, that I should not have the (first-order) desire to smoke.[20] However, the first-order desires that second-order desires are about must be desires for something definite. They cannot be abstract in the way that thoughts or concepts can. In any case, the natural man's desires are intended to be of the first, not the second, order.

(iii) A desire for something is produced by something other than myself. My desire for cake, for example, may be produced by the sight of a cake or by some other circumstance which is, in the relevant sense, external to myself. It does not, of course, follow that, if I act on my desire, then my decision or my action is determined, causally or otherwise, by the circumstances which produced my desire. Hegel believes that men, unlike animals, can refrain from acting on, 'abstract from', any given desire.[21] The point is rather that, if one does choose to act on the desire, one's action is not fully autonomous, for one has submitted oneself to the authority of external circumstances (PR 11Z). My pure thoughts, by contrast, are not produced by anything external to myself, but are generated by thinking alone.[22]

(iv) People differ from each other in respect of their desires, but not in respect of their pure thoughts, just as they do not differ qua pure egos.[23] Paradoxically, Hegel associates freedom with conformity rather than with idiosyncrasy.

One can achieve intellectual liberty, then — and indeed practical liberty, in so far as to engage in a certain type of cognitive enterprise is itself a way of acting — by thinking about thinking. Intellectual autonomy is not restricted, however, to the pure thinker. The study of nature, for example, in so far as it involves the elevation of nature to thought, guarantees freedom of a kind, for it consists in the progressive disclosure that what we thought was alien to ourselves is in fact an embodiment of our own thoughts:

> The theoretical [as opposed to the practical] approach begins
> with the arrest of desire, is disinterested, lets things subsist and

go their own way; with this position we have at once established two things, a subject and an object, and the separation of the two, one of them on this side and the other beyond (*ein Diesseits und ein Jenseits*). But our intention is rather to grasp, to conceptualize nature, to make it our own so that it is not something alien and beyond (*Enz.* II. 246Z).

The natural scientist, as we have seen, begins this work of assimilation and the philosopher of nature completes it. They are autonomous, or at least achieve autonomy, in so far as they do their job properly.

There are, then, two distinct ways in which intellectual autonomy can be won, firstly by retreating from the apparently alien world into pure thinking, and secondly by advancing on the world and imposing one's thoughts upon it or, rather, discovering them in it. These two types of freedom correspond to the two types of self-consciousness mentioned earlier.[24] If one is free, then one is conscious of oneself, but this may mean *either* that one is aware of oneself as distinct from other things *or* that one is aware of an initially and apparently alien object as in some identical, or at least similar, to oneself. Hegel runs these two conceptions together in the following passage:

In the expression I = I is expressed the principle of absolute *reason* and *freedom*. Freedom and reason consist in my raising myself to the form of I = I, in my knowing everything as mine, as *I*, in my grasping each object as a term in the system of what I myself am, in short in my having my *ego* and the *world* in *one and the same* consciousness, finding myself again in the world and, conversely, having in my consciousness what *is,* what has *objectivity* (*Enz.* III. 424Z).

The two types of self-consciousness are more loosely connected than this implies, however. It is true that, if one is self-conscious in the first sense, then one is aware of something which is identical with oneself — namely oneself. But it does not follow that one must be aware of the world as an expression of thought. One might be self-conscious in this way and yet also be conscious of many other things which are not identical with oneself. Again, the consciousness of an object, or at least normal human consciousness of an object, involves self-consciousness of the first type. I am aware of the object as something of which *I* am aware. This generates a slide from the first to the second type of self-consciousness: 'I am aware of the object as mine (it is my conception); I am aware, therefore, of myself in it' (*Enz.* III. 424). But this transition needs to be supported by further argument. On the face of it, I can quite easily be aware of something 'as mine' without being aware of 'myself in it'. We have already seen a similar tendency on Hegel's part to confuse two senses in which something other than myself, even a state of myself, may involve thought: the thought, firstly, which lies in my awareness of it and, secondly, the thought which is embedded in it.[25] The argument, or type of argument, which is needed to sustain a connection between the two types of self-consciousness is one which shows that awareness of oneself goes hand in hand with one's conceptualization of the world or, as Hegel sees it, with one's recognition of oneself in the world. As we have seen, he does provide arguments to this effect.[26] There are, nevertheless, two distinct types of self-consciousness, on Hegel's implicit view, and, corresponding to them, two distinct types of intellectual autonomy.

If men can be free even when they are not thinking purely and if freedom consists in finding, or having found, thought in things, it might seem that Hegel should conclude that people are always intellectually autonomous, whatever their cognitive approach to things may be. For he never tires of repeating that 'man distinguishes himself from the beast by thinking' and that thought is involved in everything specifically human (*Enz.* I. 2,3; III. 400).[27] This might be taken to imply that the empiricist, or someone whose cognitive behaviour conformed to the empiricist model, is as free as anyone, except perhaps the pure thinker. But, as we have seen, Hegel seems to believe not simply that some conceptions of people represent them as more free than others do, but also that some people actually are more free than others are. The answer to this is that the embodiment of thought in our mental states and in our conception of the world is a matter of degree: '[Things] acquire the determination of universality for us or . . . we transform them into something universal. The more thinking enters into the conception, the more the naturalness, individuality and immediacy of things disappears' (*Enz.* II. 246Z). There is, for example, more thought involved in a conception of the world as the manifestation of a system of laws than in viewing it as a collection of things with properties, more thought in natural science or religion than in everyday sense-perception, more thought in watching a cricket match or signing a cheque than in scratching an itch. A person is free to the extent that his states, activities, and conception of the world are thought-ridden. He is presumably as free as he possibly can be with regard to the natural world when he is doing, or has studied, the philosophy of nature and is deriving, or has derived, the results of the sciences *a priori* from pure thought. He is, however, free in a higher way when he is actually engaged in doing logic.

5 *Pure thinking and pure willing*

This, then, is how Hegel conceived intellectual autonomy. Can a parallel account be given of practical autonomy or, as Hegel calls it, freedom of the will? There is an obvious objection to the view that this is possible. For, as we have seen, a person is primarily and incontestably free in his cognitive pursuits when he is engaged in pure thinking. But the realm of practice contains no analogue of pure thinking. While thinking or cognition can be pure or abstract, decision and action cannot. What I decide or plan to do may, of course, be characterized only in a general way, as, for example, 'enjoying myself' or 'doing something useful'. But the action which I perform in fulfilment of my decision must be some definite action like mowing the lawn or going for a swim. What I decide to do may, again, be to engage in some abstract cognitive activity like pure thinking. But when pure thinking is seen in this light, it is as definite and 'concrete' as any other activity in which I may decide to involve myself. Cognition, in short, can be abstract and unspecific, but action cannot.

Hegel believes that the will is simply a special way of thinking, not a distinct faculty alongside that of thought (*PR* 4 and Z).[28] This may be one of the reasons why he often speaks as if there were a practical counterpart to pure thinking. More is required for genuine freedom than the capacity for 'free reflection which abstracts from everything and dependence on content and material given from within or without' (*PR* 15). A will which has only these features is not strictly a free will, but only 'wilfulness' or *Willkür*. If the will is to be properly free, then it must in some sense will itself: 'Only when the will has itself as its object is it for itself what it is in itself' (*PR* 10). Or again:

> Reflection, the formal universality and unity of self-consciousness, is the will's abstract certainty of its freedom, but [reflection] is not yet the truth of freedom because it has not yet got itself as its content and aim, and thus the subjective side is still other than the objective side; the content of this self-determination, therefore, also remains an entirely finite one (*PR* 15).

And finally:

> Only in this freedom is the will entirely at home with itself, because it relates itself only to itself, and with that every relation

of dependence on something else falls away. The will is true or rather truth itself, because its determining consists in its being in its existence (*Dasein*), i.e. as standing over against itself, what its concept is, or the pure concept has the intuition of itself as its purpose and reality (*PR* 23).

The general idea behind these passages is clear enough. 'Reflection', the capacity for refraining from action on any given desire that one has, is not sufficient, if eventually one has to act on some desire or other. What is needed is that the will should determine its own goals and in that sense have itself as its object. That the will should have itself as its aim or object is a locution introduced on the analogy of 'thinking about thinking', but similar sense cannot be made of it. One might suppose that what Hegel has in mind here are second-order desires, desires about my desires. But there is, as we have seen, little temptation to suppose that my second-order desires could be the same as my first-order desires, in the way that, on Hegel's view, second-order thoughts are, ultimately at least, the same as the thoughts that they are about. The first-order desires would have to be ordinary ones like the desire to smoke, analogous to sensations or to empirical conceptions rather than to pure thoughts.[29] There is no such thing as pure willing or willing (about) willing.

Even if we dilute the doctrine so that it amounts only to the claim that the will should determine its own goals without outside help, the position seems no better. For Hegel has no confidence in any of the customary views about how this is to be done. He rejects, as we have seen, Kant's belief that the law of contradiction can legitimate any particular acts of commission or omission. Again, his criticisms of the doctrine of immediate awareness as an account of our knowledge of God can be as well applied to the view that we are immediately aware of what our duties are (*Enz.* I. 72; *PR* 140 (e)).[30] Finally, we have seen that, on Hegel's view, giving reasons for a decision or a course of action will not serve the purpose, since one can in this way justify theft — on the ground, for example, that one is hungry — as easily as respect for property.[31] In any case, the reasons for or against doing something are as likely as not to include desires that one happens to have and, if this is so, the decision in favour of a course of action, even if it is argued for, is not genuinely autonomous. If contingent desires and other factors which impair one's autonomy are to be excluded from the justification of actions, it must be shown that it is possible to reach a non-arbitrary decision without reference to them.

6 *Nature and society*

Hegel's own solution to this difficulty is analogous not to pure thinking, but to the subjection of our sensations and of the natural world to thought. Just as nature comes to be seen no longer as alien to us, but as permeated by thought, so the norms and institutions of the societies which we form are not alien to us, but pervaded by thought. Just as our sensations cease to be mere sensations and are ordered and organized by thought, so our desires cease to be raw urges and are organized and channelled in the thought-ridden forms of our social life.

Hegel's presentation of this solution in the *Philosophy of Right* is odd and complex. The *Introduction* to the work (1–33) is concerned primarily with those general features of the will which we have already considered. The remainder of the text deals consecutively with aspects of social life: property, contracts, morality, the family, industry and commerce, and, finally, the state. The move from an account of general features of the in-dividual will to a consideration of social and political life owes something to Hegel's belief that the individual is, in part at least, constituted by the social order to which he belongs:

> They [viz. 'the ethical substance, its laws and powers', 146] are not something alien to the subject, but his spirit bears witness to them as to its own essence, in which he has his feeling of self and lives therein as in his element, which is not distinguished from himself (*PR* 147).

Hegel recognizes that the relationship between an individual and his society is closer in some societies, in the Greek city-state for example, than in others:

> That relation, or rather relationless identity, in which the ethical (*das Sittliche*) is the actual vitality of self-consciousness, can, of course, pass into a [looser] relation of faith and of conviction, and a relation mediated by further reflection, into an insight based on reasons, reasons which can also proceed from some particular purposes, interests and considerations, from fear or hope, or from historical presuppositions (*Ibid.*).

But in any society the sort of decisions which a man can take, the actions which he can perform, depend to a large degree on the social framework to which he belongs.

This, then, is one reason for Hegel's transition from the individual to the social. There is, however, another reason for it and this lies in his constant preoccupation with the parallel between practice and cognition. For Hegel seems to conceive the relationship between the will, as it is presented in the *Introduction*, and the social forms considered in the rest of the work as similar to the relationship between the logical idea and the actual world of nature and men. The will is regarded as a sort of concept which finds increasingly adequate embodiments in the different forms or aspects of social life:

> The absolute determination or, if one will, the absolute impulse of the free mind is that its freedom should be an object for it — objective both in the sense that it should be the rational system of the mind itself and in the sense that this system should be immediate actuality — in order to be for itself, as idea, what the will is in itself — the abstract concept of the idea of the will is in general the free-will which wills the free-will (*PR* 27.).

Or again:

> But the purposive activity of this will is to realize its concept, freedom, in the externally objective side, so that the latter is a world determined by the concept, so that the will is at home with itself in it, joined up with itself, and thus the concept is perfected to the idea [viz. the unity of a concept and its actualization] (*Enz.* III. 484).

The expansion of the *Philosophy of Right* from an account of free-will in the abstract into an account of the social forms within which we exercise our freedom is presented as if the social forms were themselves the product of the willing of the abstract will, in much the way that the objective world as a whole is the product of abstract thought.

This, however, is a mistake. Firstly, what Hegel provides in the *Introduction* is not an account of abstract willing, on a par with abstract or pure thinking, but rather an abstract account of the will. Secondly, the features of the will thus described are not in general supposed to correspond to features of society in the way that phases of thought correspond, for example, to levels of nature. Only occasionally does Hegel suggest that this is so — when he argues, for example, that the ability of the will to abstract from our needs and desires is expressed in revolutionary Jacobinism, conceived not so much as the pursuit of some definite policy as the rejection of any policy whatsoever (*PR* 5). In general, however, the aspects of society which Hegel considers in the remainder of the work are intended to be more or less successful attempts to satisfy not individual features of the free-will, but the general requirement of freedom, namely that the will should in some sense will itself.

What Hegel seems to have in mind are two different ways in which pure thought, rather than pure willing, is related to social phenomena. In the first place, he believes, social arrangements can, in their broad outlines at least, be derived from pure thought and shown to be necessary:

> The method whereby in science the concept develops out of itself and is only an immanent advance and engendering of its determinations – the advance does not occur by means of the assertion that there are various states of affairs and then by the application of the universal to such material received from somewhere else, this method is here likewise presupposed from logic (*PR* 31).

The procedure is to this extent similar to that of the *Philosophy of Nature*. There is, however, the difference that whereas to engage in philosophy of nature is itself a display of intellectual freedom, freedom of a higher order than that which mere natural scientists possess, to engage in the philosophy of right is not itself a display of *practical* freedom. Cognition 'overreaches' practice in the sense that discourse about practice or about practical discourse is itself theoretical, and not practical, discourse. Practical freedom is secured and displayed by participation in the life of one's society. The *Philosophy of Right* can only make it clear that this is freedom, not confer extra freedom of this type upon us.

Hegel's solution to the problem of practical freedom is supplied by the second relationship of thought to social phenomena, namely that thoughts are embedded in them. When a man adheres to the laws and customs of his own society, he is in a sense 'willing his own will', following the autonomous dictates of his own will, since the institutions of his society embody the thought which he at bottom is. The justification of his doctrine takes up most of the *Philosophy of Right*. The central ideas, however, are relatively simple. One of them is that the laws of a society are rational in a way that a person's desires and impulses are not. They are, for example, universal in form and, if they are properly instituted, they are the same for everybody (*PR* 258; *Enz.* III. 485). One's desires and impulses, moreover, do not stand in stark contrast to laws and institutions, but are similarly purified and imbued with thought:

> [The content], freed of the impurity and contingency which it has in the practical feeling and the impulse and similarly moulded

into the subjective will, no longer in that form [viz. the form of practical feeling and impulse] but in its universality, as the habit, temper and character of the will, is now custom (*Sitte*) (*Enz.* III. 485).

Elsewhere Hegel speaks of duties as that into which our impulses are transformed: 'The same content which assumes the form of duties and then of virtues is also what has the form of impulses' (*PR* 150). These duties or customs are embodied in, and may be read off from, social institutions. Our sexual impulses, for example, are canalized into the institution of marriage, an institution which involves duties corresponding in their content to those impulses:[32]

[T]he natural impulse is reduced to the modality of a natural element, which is destined to vanish in its very satisfaction; the spiritual bond emerges in its right as what is substantial, thus as something elevated above the contingency of passions and of transient caprice, inherently indissoluble (*PR* 163).

To do one's duty, even under legel compulsion, is not an impairment of one's liberty:

Binding duty can appear as a restriction only on indeterminate subjectivity or abstract freedom, and on the impulses of the natural will or of the moral will which determines its indeterminate good out of its wilfulness. But in duty the individual has rather his liberation, liberation from the dependence in which he lies in mere natural impulse and from the depression which he suffers as subjective particularity in moral reflections on what ought to be and what may be (*in den moralischen Reflexionen des Sollens und Mögens*), liberation from the indeterminate subjectivity which does not attain to existence and the objective determinacy of action and remains within itself and unactualized (*PR* 149).

The intersubjective norms and laws of one's society, Hegel believes, are no more a restriction on one's freedom than the rules of football are a restriction on one's natural impulse to kick a ball, or the rules of language are a restraint on one's liberty to express oneself.[33]

Nature, as we have seen, involves an element of contingency, and sometimes Hegel speaks as if contingency were confined to nature and had no place in the higher realm of mind and society (*Enz.* II. 250).[34] In fact, however, he acknowledges contingency in social arrangements as well, and here it takes two different forms corresponding to the two ways in which thought is related to social phenomena. Contingencies of the first type are parallel to those of geography, biology and so on. Certain features of history and society just happen to be as they are and cannot be derived from pure thought. There are contingencies in history 'in so far as the idea is its essence, but its appearance lies in contingency and in the field of wilfulness' (*Enz.* I. 16). Again, such practical matters as taxation require firm and precise decisions on questions which '*lie* outside the *absolute determinedness (An-und-für-sich-Bestimmt-sein) of the concept*' (*Ibid.*). Philosophy or science can tell us that some taxation or other is required, but not, for example, the precise rate at which it is to be levied. It does not, of course, follow that, once the rate of taxation has been fixed, the individual is not obliged to pay it or that he is not free when he does so. For, firstly, even if the need for this particular arrangement lies beyond the scope of the 'concept', the need for some such contingent arrangement does not, and, secondly, the regulation, if it is a general one, involves pure thought, even though it is not derivable from it.

The second type of contingency in social affairs is quite different. It arises from the fact that the state should, on Hegel's view, accommodate an element of 'subjective' freedom. There should remain areas – for example, the choice of a profession or of a spouse – in which the individual is permitted to do, within certain limits, whatever he likes (*PR* 299). Hegel believes that the need for some degree of subjective freedom is certified by logic. But what any given individual chooses to do with his subjective freedom will be a matter of contingency. So too is it contingent what an individual ought to do. It is presumably in part because logic cannot tell us what any given person should do in given circumstances that he is to be permitted to do, within limits, whatever he likes in those circumstances. This type of contingency has no obvious counterpart in our cognitive affairs. Some matters of fact are indeed contingent, but if it is, or can be, known by empirical enquiry how they stand, one is not at liberty to believe whatever one likes about them. This does not, of course, mean that one should not be legally permitted to believe or say what one likes about them. Hegel holds that religious beliefs and worship other than those of Lutheran christianity should be tolerated by the state, but this is not because the beliefs are true or because the questions to which they are answers are not rationally soluble (*PR* 270). The point is rather that cognitive questions, unlike some practical ones, cannot be appropriately answered by a free choice or on the basis of one's desires and inclinations. There is no cognitive analogue of subjective freedom.

Despite his attachment to 'objective' freedom, Hegel clearly regards subjective freedom, at least in certain areas, as something of value. As we have seen, he criticizes Plato for excluding it from his ideal state (*PR* 299; *VGP* II. pp. 127 ff., H. II. pp. 112 ff.).[35] To acknowledge the need for a degree of subjective freedom is a concession to commonsense, but it is not clear that Hegel is entitled to make it. An individual presumably has no other way of making a choice in such cases than reliance on his desires, impulses and inclinations. Would his freedom not be secured more firmly, if general rules were to be laid down prescribing certain types of job and certain types of spouse for certain types of individual? Even if the rational support for such rules were flimsy, they would still be, in virtue of their universality, more thought-ridden than our personal whims. Hegel probably has no better answer to this than to say that subjective freedom corresponds to a phase of logic and must, therefore, be incorporated into a properly constituted state; just as lower types of entity have a place in nature or lower categories have a place in logic. He seems to have felt, as we have seen, that if a state or a society contains the leading features of some other state or society, as well as some of its own, then its superiority over the latter is guaranteed. No critic of Hegel's state, from the standpoint of Plato's ideal or, for that matter, from the standpoint of subjective freedom, can get a grip on it, because the Hegelian state embraces the standpoint from which the criticism is made, just as Hegelian philosophy embraces all other philosophical principles.[36,37]

This reply is unsatisfactory, however. The view that an area of society should be allocated to each political principle would commit us to assigning a special place to arbitrary tyranny, as well as to subjective freedom. For arbitrary tyranny has presumably been the leading feature of some societies. Hegel could reply that subjective freedom, doing what one feels like doing, can be seen to be valuable when compared with certain other arrangements, whereas arbitrary tyranny cannot. The fact remains, however, that he has argued that action in accordance with intersubjective rules confers a higher freedom than action on the basis of one's own desires. If this is so, then we should presumably eliminate subjective freedom in favour of law-governed behaviour wherever this is possible. Characteristically, Hegel has argued in favour of a novel position, from which he subsequently attempts to retreat under the pressure, not of consistency, but of common sense.

7 Freedom and dissent

Many questions can be, and have been, raised concerning Hegel's view of freedom. We shall consider, however, only one of these, namely: To what extent does it commit him to a conservative attitude towards social institutions?[38] Hegel is, as we have seen, opposed to *das Sollen,* the ought-to-be, the dichotomy between how things are and how they ought to be.[39] His objection rests in part on the difficulty or impossibility of substantiating claims about how things ought to be, whether on the basis of how they are or in some other way.[40] But it depends primarily on his rejection of a certain conception of action, the view that an action is an attempt to remedy some defect in the existing state of things, to bring about some state of affairs which ought to obtain, but does not (*Enz.* I. 233 f.; *WL* II. pp. 541 ff., M. pp. 818 ff.). It is easy to feel that, if this is what action is, then either we are engaged in a labour of Sisyphus, doomed to undertake endless attempts to complete a task which can never be completed, or, if we finally achieve our goal, a world in which what is and what ought to be perfectly coincide, then we shall cease to act altogether and live in endless repose. Most of our action, however, is not naturally viewed in this way, particularly after the rebellious idealism of adolescence (*Enz.* III. 396Z). It is, rather, an easy indulgence in social routines. If, for example, one is engaged in a natural, free-flowing conversation or a stroll in the country, one is not attempting to remedy some defect in the *status quo,* as one is if one is trying to break an awkward silence or running to catch a train. Much of our action is a matter of swimming with the tide. It does not follow, however, that the world is as it ought to be, that we cannot coherently criticize our society, or that its norms are the final arbiter of right and wrong.

Again, we can agree with Hegel that the picture of man as a rational ego confronting recalcitrant urges and desires is an exaggerated one. Brute, unconceptualized urges play as small a part in the life of the socialized adult as do brute, unconceptualized sensations. Just as, for example, our visual experience is not appropriately described in terms of shapes and colour-patches, but of trees, houses, causal processes and so on, so our primitive urges are socialized and thought-ridden, surrounded by ritual which would be lacking in a 'natural' state. Raw hunger becomes, for example, the desire to dine at 6 o'clock, the primitive desire for security becomes the desire to buy an annuity, to hoard wealth, and so on. This is as true of our deviant desires as it is of our conforming ones. Thought and the social life which surrounds us are major determinants of what we want to do, and should not be seen simply as obstacles in the way of our doing what we want to do. To regard them only as constraints would indeed be as absurd as seeing the rules of syntax as a constraint on our primitive urge to communicate or the rules of football as an impediment in the way of our desire to score goals. Again, however, it does not follow that one's own society is beyond criticism or that there is no room for the individualist question 'Why should I act in the ways prescribed in my society?' Some games, after all, ought not to be played and we can coherently advocate changes in the rules of games which it is permissible to play.

Did Hegel think otherwise? Did he believe that one cannot legitimately criticize one's own society? This question is not easy to answer, and the answer, when it comes, is not an unequivocal one. We shall begin by considering Hegel's criticisms of Kant's view of the matter.

8 *Morality and the final end*

Kant held that anyone who takes morality seriously is committed to the belief that his moral efforts will not be fruitless, that the world will be responsive to them and not simply wash them away, and that eventually the world will be, as a result of these efforts, just as it ought to be. This belief is not one that can be under-written by theoretical reason, but we must adhere to it if our moral endeavours are to make any sense:[41]

> But a final end (*Endzweck*) is merely a concept of our practical reason and cannot be derived from any data of experience for the theoretical judgment of nature nor related to knowledge of nature. No use of this concept is possible except only for practical reasons according to moral laws; and the final end of creation is that constitution of the world which harmonizes with what we can only determinately specify according to laws, namely with the final end of our pure practical reason and of this, indeed, in so far as it is supposed to be practical. Now we have by virtue of the moral law, which imposes this end upon us, a reason for assuming in practical intention, namely in order to apply our resources to its realization, the possibility (realizability) of this end, and thus a nature of things which harmonizes with it, because without the cooperation of nature in respect of a condition of its possibility which is not in our power its realization would not be possible. Thus we have a moral reason for conceiving of a final end of creation in the case of a world.

This final end of creation has not yet been reached. It is one that we must attempt to bring about:[42]

We are determined *a priori* by reason to advance the *summum bonum* to the limit of our resources. It consists in the combination of the highest welfare of the rational beings in the world with the supreme condition of the good in them, i.e. in universal happiness together with morality in the conformity with law.

This view does not, of course, entail that we are morally entitled or morally obliged to break the laws or disrupt the institutions of our society. But it does imply that the world is not currently as it ought to be, and this would presumably include social arrangements. Hegel seems to have at least three criticisms of it:

(i) Kant's conception of the good is taken, in so far as it can be given a determinate content at all, to be an anthropocentric one:

But the *good* in which the final end of the world is located is determined from the start only as *our* good, as the moral law of *our* practical reason; so that the unity goes no further than the harmonization of the state and events of the world with our morality (*Enz.* I. 60).

Hegel's train of thought seems to be this. The goodness in terms of which the final end of creation is conceived is only our view of what goodness is. There is no guarantee that it is objectively good. Other beings might with equal right form different conceptions of the good and, therefore, of the final end of creation. It does not, of course, follow from this that the world will not become good according to our conception of goodness, but it is arbitrary to suppose that it is destined to do so, if this conception is only one among several equally legitimate ones.

This line of objection is not cogent, however. In the first place, the phenomenal world with which we are acquainted is, on Kant's view, only the world as it appears to *us*.[43] It does not seem arbitrary to suppose that the world as it appears to *us* will become good according to *our* conception of goodness, as long as our conception means that of men in general and not that of, say, nineteenth century Germans. Other beings may believe that their world will become good in a different way, but then they inhabit a different phenomenal world from the one which we have constructed. Secondly, Kant seems to be claiming not that the world actually will become good, but only that morality commits one to believing that it will. It is not arbitrary to suppose that *our* morality commits us to believing that the world is destined to conform to *our* view of the good. This claim is compatible with holding that *anyone's* morality commits him to believing that the world will become good in *his* sense. Finally, Kant did not believe, as Hegel seems to imply, that our morality is anthropocentric in the way that our view of the phenomenal world is. Our theoretical conception of the world depends on the peculiar mental constitution of humans, but our moral laws and our conception of the good do not. They are, rather, such as would be arrived at by any rational being whatsoever, since they depend only on intellectual equipment — the laws of logic — which is indispensable to any rational creature.[44] Since no beings apart from rational ones could possibly have a view on the matter, our conception of the good is not, on Kant's view, subjective. What is subjective is the belief that the world can and will fully conform to it. Hegel is probably presupposing at this point his own argument to the effect that our conception of the good, or at least the one that Kant attributes to us, does not have the rational support which he claims for it.[45]

(ii) The belief that there is a final end of creation, that the world will become good, is regarded by Kant as in some sense subjective:

> [T]he harmony is determined as something only *subjective* — as something which only *ought* to be, i.e. which at the same time *lacks reality* — as an object of *faith*, which has only subjective certainty, not truth, i.e. *not* the objectivity which corresponds to the idea (*Enz.* I. 60).

Hegel's objection to this is similar to his argument against the view that the purposiveness of organic nature is merely subjective. He argued in that case that, if organisms are internally purposive, then we cannot distinguish within them between an objective core which is given to us and the purposiveness which we impose upon it.[46] Here he argues that to regard the final end of creation, the perfect world, as merely subjective or as something that merely ought to be, involves making distinctions which could not be drawn within the perfect world itself. In a perfect world there would be no distinction between the universal and the individual, between subjectivity and objectivity, or between what is and what ought to be:

> [T]he universality determined by reason, the absolute final end, *the good*, would be actualized in the world, and indeed by a third entity, the power which proposes and realizes this final end — *God*, in whom, as the absolute truth, those oppositions of universality and individuality, of subjectivity and objectivity are thus dissolved and declared to be non-self-subsistent and untrue (*Enz.* I. 59).

Kant is therefore inconsistent, Hegel implies, when he applies these contrasting concepts to the perfect world itself or to our beliefs about it: 'Against this harmony the opposition which is posited as *untrue* in the content of the harmony is revived and reasserted' (*Enz.* I. 60). It might be questioned whether in fact Kant believed that none of these oppositions would have a place in the perfect world. The main point, however, is that even if this were so, the argument which Hegel bases on it is clearly invalid. There is no inconsistency in applying to the perfect world, or to our beliefs about it, a distinction which could not be drawn within the perfect world itself. If there were then it would equally be inconsistent to doubt the possibility of a necessary being, to doubt whether there could be a world free of doubt, to ask whether there could be a language in which it was impossible to ask questions, or to say that what is the case ought to, but does not, coincide with what ought to be the case. Hegel's argument here has affinities with his belief that what can be said about the thoughts of objectivity and of subjectivity establishes the objectivity of thought. But neither argument is sound. Just as what is the case within the realm of thought cannot license claims about the objective status of thought itself, so the internal features of a perfect world cannot legitimate external claims about *its* objective status.[47]

(iii) Hegel implies that it was in order to escape this contradiction that Kant placed the realization of the final end in the future:

> If this contradiction seems to be concealed by locating the realization of the idea in *time*, in whatever future time the idea may be, such a sensuous condition as time is rather the opposite of a resolution of contradiction and the corresponding conception of the understanding, the *infinite progression*, is immediately no more than the contradiction continually posited (*Enz.* I. 60).

What is the contradiction that is supposed to be resolved, or at least concealed, by the adjournment of the final end to a future date? Hegel may mean that we could claim only at the cost of self-refutation both that the final end is already realized and that the belief in it is subjective, since the actual realization of the final end would preclude any discrepancy between the subjective and the objective. If, on the other hand, we claim only that the final end will be realized at some future time, this does not prevent us from conceding *now* that this belief is only subjective. Elsewhere, however, he locates contradiction within the final end itself, as it is conceived by Kant:

> [A]s theoretical reason remains opposed to the objective sensuous, so practical reason remains opposed to practical

sensuousness, impulses and inclinations. Perfected morality must remain a beyond; for morality presupposes the divergence of the particular and the universal will (*VGP* III. p. 369, H. III. p. 461).

Or again:

Nature would no longer remain nature if it were to become conformed to the concept of the good; we thus remain at the height of contradiction, they cannot be unified. The law of necessity and the law of freedom are different from one another. It is equally necessary to posit the unity of both; but the unity is not actual (*VGP* III. p. 371, H. III. p. 463).

The general idea is that the harmonization required by the final end cannot ever be fully realized and must, therefore, be continually postponed into an ever-receding future, as a goal which the world approaches asymptotically, but never actually reaches.

Hegel is also relying, however, on his general belief that contradictions often manifest themselves in the form of an infinite regress: 'The progress to infinity is in general the expression of contradiction . . . . The *infinite progression* is only the *expression* of this contradiction, *not* its *resolution*' (*WL* I. p. 262, M. p. 227). For example, things and qualities are what they are owing to their conceptual-*cum*-physical relations with other things and qualities, and are thus 'contradictory' in the sense that they involve or contain what is other than themselves. This contradiction generates the infinite regresses of things and qualities and of the physical changes of one thing into another: 'Something becomes an other, but the other is itself a something, and thus it similarly becomes an other, and so on to *infinity*' (*Enz.* I. 93; cf. *WL* I. pp. 125 ff., M. pp. 116 ff.). Characteristically, Hegel moves from such considerations as these to reflections on the 'ought' of Kant and Fichte:

The finite here *ought* to be only sublimated and the infinite ought to be not merely something negative, but also something positive. This 'ought' always involves the fact that something is recognized as justified and yet cannot establish its validity. Kantian and Fichtean philosophy have remained at this standpoint of the ought, as far as ethics is concerned. The continual approximation to the law of reason is as far as one gets along this route (*Enz.* I. 94Z. Cf. *WL* I. pp. 144 ff., M. pp. 133 ff.).

Hegel, as we have seen, has a general aversion to infinite regresses of any kind.[48] But what is particularly vicious about the regress in this case? Kant is claiming, at least as Hegel reads him, not that the final end will be realized at some definite future date — if that were so the regress would not be an infinite one — but that any moral agent must believe that it *will be* realized. The belief that it will be realized must, in that case, be subjective, since, if something is to happen in fact, its occurrence cannot always lie in the future. It does not follow, however, that to work for the realization of the final end is pointless in a Sisyphean way. Sisyphus made no progress at all. But, Kant would argue, if we work to bring about the final end, then we shall make the world not perfect, but better, and that the strictly false belief that the goal will actually be reached enables, or at least encourages, us to make the effort. There is, again, a cognitive counterpart to this ethical position, and Hegel's concentration on the notions of objectivity and subjectivity perhaps suggests that he had it in mind. One might argue that although we shall never acquire complete and unadulterated knowledge of the universe, we shall, if we apply ourselves in the appropriate way, continually reach ever closer approximations to it. The belief that there is an objective truth to be known, and perhaps that one day we shall find ourselves in possession of it, is, although strictly false, an essential or important incentive to unremitting inquiry. As we have seen, however, Hegel rejects both this doctrine and its ethical counterpart.[49]

9 *Is the world as it ought to be?*

Hegel's own views on this matter operate on several different levels. There are three apparently distinct questions which he in general treats together. They are:

1. Is the world as a whole, including human history, past, present and future, as it ought to be?
2. Is the world, at any given stage of its history, as it ought to be?
3. Is the world today, i.e. in Hegel's own day, as it ought to be?

The first of these questions will be considered in this section, the second and third in the two following sections.

It is a noticeable feature of Hegel's discussion of these questions, but particularly the first, that he takes the question 'Is goodness realized in the world, or is the world as it ought to be?' to be equivalent to asking: 'Is thought objectively realized, or embedded, in the world?' To commonsense, as well as to Kant, these questions seem distinct. The first is a question about goodness, about whether men are morally good and are happy in proportion to their deserts.[50] The second is a question about intelligibility, about the extent to which phenomena involve thoughts or categories, and about whether or not these thoughts are applicable to things-in-themselves. For Hegel, however, the problem about the goodness of the world and the problem about its intelligibility are one and the same problem with one and the same solution. The requirement that 'the good should have worldly existence, external objectivity' is just the requirement that 'thought should be not merely *subjective*, but objective in general' (*Enz.* I. 54). This equation is implicit in Hegel's dictum: 'What is rational is actual and what is actual is rational' (*PR* Preface; *Enz.* I. 6).[51] 'Rational', *vernünftig*, seems to mean both 'rationally intelligible', in the sense of exemplifying or embodying thought-determinations, and 'reasonable', in the sense of being more or less as it ought to be. This ambiguity becomes apparent in Hegel's explanation of the dictum:

> [Philosophy] sets out from this in its study of the spiritual universe and of the natural . . . . What matters is to come to know the substance which is immanent, and the eternal which is present, in the appearance (*Scheine*) of the temporal and transient.

But he infers from this that we should not attempt to 'construct a state as it ought to be', but rather to 'understand (*begreifen*) and exhibit the state as something intrinsically rational', to 'cognize reason as the rose in the cross of the present' (*PR* Preface). Similarly, in the *Encyclopaedia*, the doctrine that thought is actualized in the world is taken to imply that it is no part of our, or at least of the philosopher's, business to say that things ought to be other than they are or to say how they ought to be, if this is held to be different from how they are:

> This agreement [of philosophy with 'actuality and experience'] can be seen as at least an external criterion of the truth of a philosophy, just as to produce through knowledge of this agreement the reconciliation of self-conscious reason with *existing* reason, with actuality, is to be seen as the ultimate purpose of science (*Enz.* I. 6).

Understanding is taken to preclude criticism.

Hegel's account of the intelligibility of human history does not differ radically from his account of nature. Just as nature develops out of, and at its own level embodies, thought, so thought unfolds itself into human history. In this case, however, it does so in time as well as in space, and the subject-matter is conscious, in varying degrees, of what is happening to it. History develops in a mind-like way: different peoples and civilizations succeed one another like the stages of an argument, each presupposing and emerging from the 'contradictions' of its predecessor by a sort of reflection upon it. The structure of the process is intended to be that of pure thought and each phase of history corresponds to and embodies a phase of the logical idea (*VPG* pp. 86 ff., N. pp. 138 ff.). Hegel sometimes supports his thesis by invoking the fact that any historian needs some conceptual framework or other in order to make sense of the bewildering array of past events:

> Even the ordinary, mediocre historian who supposes and professes that he is only receptive in his attitude, devoting himself only to what is given, is not passive in his thinking and brings his categories with him and sees what is there through them; especially in everything that is supposed to be scientific, reason may not sleep and meta-thinking must be applied. Whoever looks rationally at the world will find that it looks rational to him, both are in a reciprocal relationship (*VPG* p. 23, N. p. 29).

But Hegel's thesis is stronger than this. It is that:

> [W]orld history has been rational, it has been the rational, necessary course of the world-spirit, of the spirit whose nature is always one and the same, but which reveals this nature in the existence of the world (*VPG* p. 22, N. p. 29).

If this were not so, if reason were simply our way of making sense of history, then the dichotomies of universality and individuality, and of objectivity and subjectivity, would re-emerge. On Hegel's view, however, they are dissolved in God (*Enz.* I. 59).[52] History, like nature, though in a higher degree, is ready-made for our cognition. Its inner structure is knowable, since it is no more than the structure of our own thought. In this sense the dichotomy between subjectivity and objectivity is overcome.

But why does it follow that the dichotomy between what is and what ought to be is similarly overcome? That the world is as it ought to be, or at least is not as it ought not to be? Hegel has several answers to this:

(i) Theology provides a link between his ontological and his ethical doctrines. If history is rationally intelligible, then it embodies the logical idea. But the logical idea is, on Hegel's view, God and to say that history is rational is therefore equivalent to the claim that it is governed by divine providence (*VPG* p. 27, N. p. 37; *Enz.* I. 6, 147Z).[53] If this is so, then it is not reasonable, at least from the point of view of theology, to maintain that history, or for that matter nature, ought to have been other than it is. It can be argued that this simply throws into question Hegel's theological assumptions. But at least we can see that the association of value and intelligibility is deeply embedded in his thought.

(ii) In its main outlines at least, history, like nature, is necessary (*Enz.* I. 7, 16). Our world is not, except for minor details, one among several possible worlds. The *Logic* is conceived of as the framework of any possible world; any world would have to be more or less like our own. But if something is necessarily so, it is hard to claim that it ought to be otherwise. Hegel presents this argument only in passing: '*You can, because you ought* – this expression . . . lies in the concept of ought' (*WL* I. p. 144, M. pp. 133f.). Or again:

> The equality which one might introduce perhaps in connection with the distribution of goods would in any case shortly be destroyed again, since wealth depends on diligence. But what cannot be executed ought not to be executed (*PR* 49Z).

But the belief that the evaluation of our world, or at least the unfavourable evaluation of it, depends on the logical possibility of significant alternatives underlies much of what he says on the matter.

(iii) Since our world is the only possible world, it is also the only thinkable or conceivable world.[54] Even if we were entitled to say, therefore, that our world ought to be other than it is, we could not say how it ought to be. For to say how it ought to be, we would have to think of a world significantly different from our own, and this cannot be done. This is not the result of some special limitation on our power of thought. As we have seen, Hegel believes that we cannot coherently suppose that our thought is limited in this way. It is, rather, because our world has run through and, as it were, contained all thinkable possibilities, in much the way that philosophy or the modern state has exhausted all the relevant possibilities.[55] But if this is so, there can be no sense to the claim that the world ought to be otherwise than it is. This would imply that there is some way the world ought to be, even though we cannot think of it. But this is open to all the objections which Hegel raises against the view that thought can assign limits to itself. We would be supposing that there is a realm which is inaccessible to thought, a supposition which is, on his view, a self-refuting one.[56]

(iv) Even if we were able to think of an alternative possible world, we could not justify the claim that that is how our world ought to be. One can only justify some proposed possible state of affairs by appealing to some feature of the actual state of affairs, to some ethical standard, for example, which is already accepted widely enough to stand as a premiss of the argument. But, if this is so, one's criticism of the world is not likely to be a very radical one. One is simply condemning certain features of it in terms of certain other features. In any case, Hegel seems to believe that the world, like our thought, is self-correcting. By the time one has adequate grounds for believing that some feature of it is other than it ought to be, a process of change which will remedy it is already in motion.[57] We can find no foothold within the world for criticizing the world as a whole. This argument, too, is parallel to one of Hegel's arguments for the limitlessness of thought. I cannot check the coherence and cogency of my thought as a whole against some external standard, since any such standard would have to be interpreted, accepted and applied by thought itself. Thought, if it is to be corrected at all, must be self-correcting.[58] Similarly, we cannot step outside the world as a whole and evaluate it against some standard which the world itself does not endorse. If it is to be corrected at all, the world must correct itself. These arguments do not, of course, license the conclusions that thought is unlimited and correct, or that the world is good and as it ought to be. To suppose that they did would be on a par with supposing that, because I can never say truly that I am dead, I shall never die. What, if anything, they establish is that thought as a whole and the world as a whole must be judged by standards which they themselves supply, and that no neutral, external evaluation of them, as good, bad or indifferent, is possible.

(v) It might be objected that the arguments presented in (iii) and (iv) do not exclude quite radical criticisms of the human condition. We can, for example, imagine, at least at a superficial level, a world in which people had never resorted to warfare in order to settle their differences. Such a world would be significantly different from our own. Yet there is sufficient material within our own world, in the form of human ideals, likes and dislikes, to present a plausible case that a world of this sort would be better than the actual one. In order to avert objections of this type, however, Hegel conducts his theodicy at the level of particular cases, like that of warfare, arguing both that it is a necessary feature of the world, an indispensable means by which the world spirit realizes its plan, and that there are various benefits which could not be secured without it.[59] It does not, of course, follow from this that particular acts of war may not be criticized. But this would not amount to a fundamental criticism of the world as a whole, especially if we remember that some such acts of injustice or barbarity are in any case inevitable.

10 *Critics, heroes and rebels*

These, then, are some of Hegel's reasons for giving an affirmative answer to the question: 'Is the world as a whole, including human history, past, present and future, as it ought to be?' This does not, however, entail that the same answer must be given to the second question, namely: 'Is the world, at any given stage of its history, as it ought to be?' If the general course of world history is necessary and inevitable, then it follows that any given stage of it is necessary and inevitable. This perhaps implies that one cannot legitimately say, of one's own phase of history, that it ought not to have been. But it does not follow that one may not properly judge, at a given stage, that the world or one's own society ought not to be as it now is. It must, after all, contain some radical defect in virtue of which it gives way to another stage or type of society and presumably unfavourable judgments passed on it by its occupants play a part in this transition. A person perhaps cannot legitimately criticize his own society in terms of some past society. A genuine restoration of a past society is not, on Hegel's view, possible, nor could one's own society, including as it does the fundamental features of any given past society, compare unfavourably with it.[60] But why could he not do so in the light of some possible future society? Or why should he not simply suggest ways of improving the current state of affairs without having in mind any detailed picture of the future state to which they might lead? Kant, for example, made a number of proposals for the elimination of warfare, for the attainment of 'perpetual peace'.[61] Hegel rejects these proposals (*PR* 324, 325, 333 ff., 351). But he cannot legitimately do so on the ground that they imply that the whole course of history could have, and ought to have, been other than it is. For Kant might disavow any intention to criticize history as a whole, arguing that his proposals are simply attempts, internal to history itself, to influence its future course. As we have seen, Hegel has definite objections to these particular proposals, but he also has reservations of a general kind about any prescription or proposal whatsoever for the improvement of society:

(i) He draws a distinction, as we have seen, between what exists and is also actual and what exists and yet is not actual, but only an appearance and contingent (*PR* Preface; *Enz.* I. 6).[62] The line between the actual and the apparent is drawn at different points for different purposes. Sometimes anything which is bad or defective is regarded as non-actual and therefore, by implication, as something which can be criticized. In that case, however, all the weight of Hegel's argument falls on the decision as to what is actual and what is not. More informatively, he implies that, while the central structure of any given society is actual and rational, there are inevitably certain contingent features which are not: 'external and transitory objects, regulations, conditions (*Zustände*), etc.' (*Enz*. I. 6). Features of this sort are legitimate objects of criticism, but such criticism is not the proper concern of the philosopher. The matters in question are too trivial to deserve his notice. Some philosophers, Plato and Fichte for example, have intruded into this area, but it is not to their credit that they have done so:

> Plato could have omitted his advice to nurses never to stand
> still with children, but always to rock them in their arms;
> similarly, Fichte could have omitted his so-called construction
> of the perfection of passport regulations, to the point where
> passports are required to carry not just the signature of suspects,
> but also painted portraits of them (*PR* Preface).

If this is so, then philosophers should not criticize any aspect of their own society or make proposals for altering it. What is actual could not have been otherwise and is not open to criticism; what is not actual may be criticized, but it is not the philosopher's job to do so.

This argument is inadequate, however. In the first place, Hegel provides no satisfactory criterion for distinguishing what is actual from what is not. Nor does he supply any guarantee that the various marks of the non-actual — contingency, transience, triviality, and so on — will inevitably coincide. A particular institution or practice may, for example, be contingent in the sense that its existence is not necessary and yet the question whether it should survive or not may be a far from trivial one, the answer to which has an important bearing on human welfare. If no deep philosophical issues are at stake in the explanation or assessment of it, then it may not be the philosopher's job to evaluate it or to recommend its elimination or alteration. But many non-philosophical tasks need to be performed, and the criticism of social institutions may be one of them. Secondly, Hegel has not yet established that it is a mistake to criticize those aspects of a society which are actual and rational. When he stresses the transitoriness of what is not actual, he implies that what is actual is permanent. If the actual were permanent, then it would, on his view, be necessarily permanent, and, if that were so, it would be inappropriate to criticize it. The fundamental institutions of a society, however, are not in general permanent. It may be true that, as Hegel believes, the essential features of the Greek city-state are contained in modern society, but the city-state as such has passed away. It is also perhaps true that the city-state was a necessary phase of world history. If that is so, then it would be pointless for the citizen of such a state or anyone else to say: 'It ought not to have been.' The radical critic is not, however, committed to denying that the fundamental features of his society ought to have been as they are, but only to making certain recommendations for the future, to saying, roughly: 'It ought not to be like this in the future.' Such recommendations would, on the present argument, be defective only if they proposed some social arrangement which could not possibly come about in the future or, perhaps, in the immediate future. The critic of the city-state would thus be at fault if he proposed, for example, the establishment of a community of primitive cave-dwellers, a populous, but technologically backward, direct democracy or, perhaps, an industrialized welfare state, but not if he were to recommend the formation of a Hellenistic empire. The emergence of such an empire was a possible and, on Hegel's view, a necessary, development of history. What, then, could be wrong with recommending it? To see this, we need to turn to Hegel's other arguments on this question.

(ii) 'As far as the individual is concerned', he maintains,

each one is a child of his time; so also is philosophy its own time grasped in thought. It is just as silly to imagine that any philosophy goes beyond its present world as that an individual leaps beyond his own time .... If his theory in fact goes beyond it, if he builds himself a world as it ought to be, then this world exists, but only in his opinions — a pliable element which can accommodate anything one likes (*PR* Preface).

The claim that an individual cannot leap beyond his own time is far from clear. It might be taken to be a mere tautology, for anything a man does is a feature of the period in which he does it. If, for example, we were to discover that Socrates had, in isolation, written the *Principia Mathematica*, constructed an electronic computer, and predicted the Russian Revolution, we might simply revise our conception of Greek society, so that it could accommodate such feats. Socrates, we might argue, did not leap beyond his own time, because, after all, he did what he did in the fifth century B.C. If we left the matter there, however, there would remain a sharp rift between Socrates' achievements and the rest of

Greek society. Hegel believes that a society must display the sort of coherence that a human mind has — that is a part of the point of his talk of *Geist* — and, if this is so, there are two responses available to him. Firstly, he might accept the evidence that Socrates had done all these things, but argue that, in that case, we must overhaul our conception of the rest of Greek society, so that no incoherence obtains between it and Socrates, so that he fits intelligibly into his social context. Secondly, he might deny that such things can happen. If evidence were discovered which appeared to suggest that it did happen, then we would have to interpret the manuscripts or artefacts in a way which did not commit us to attributing such novel achievements to Socrates. An example of this second type of response is seen in Hegel's treatment of Plato's *Republic*. In that work Plato presents and advocates an ideal society which differs in fundamental ways from all existing Greek societies. Hegel interprets it, unusually and implausibly, in a different way. On his view, Plato is simply giving an abstract description of the typical Greek city-state, a description which faithfully portrays its basic features and differs from it only in inessential respects (*PR* Preface; *VGP* II. pp. 105 ff., H. II. pp. 90 ff.).[63] The thesis, then, that no one can leap beyond his age hovers between a tautology, a resolve to interpret history in a certain way, and a plausible, but imprecise, empirical claim that certain things do not happen.

It might be objected, however, that Plato is not even an apparent counterexample to Hegel's thesis. The *Republic* is not, even on the customary interpretation, an achievement so strikingly out of accord with Greek society as those which we have hypothetically attributed to Socrates. In the second part of the passage quoted, however, Hegel gives a quite different sense to the notion of leaping beyond one's time. In the first part, to leap beyond one's time is, if not to indulge in time-travel, to do or think something which is not intelligibly connected with one's own social environment. It is plausible to suppose that, in this sense, nobody can leap beyond his own time. In the second part, to leap beyond one's time is to imagine, propose, or predict a state of the world or of society which is radically different from its present state. There is no obvious reason for thinking that someone who leaps beyond his time in this sense must also do so in the first sense. A person's imaginative utopias or even predictions may well intelligibly cohere with his social and intellectual environment. There is, therefore, no reason to suppose that one cannot, in this sense, leap beyond one's time. Nor does Hegel believe that one cannot. In the second part of the passage, he implies that a man, or at any rate his theory, can leap beyond his time. The point of denying that Plato did so is not that it would have been impossible for him to do so, but that, if he had done it, then the *Republic* would have been bad philosophy or perhaps not philosophy at all.

The thesis that one *cannot* leap beyond one's time (in one sense) has become, then, the thesis that one *ought not* to leap beyond one's time (in a different sense). But if a man, or his theory, can leap beyond his time, why should it not be done? It may be true that philosophy is a second-order discipline, confined more or less to reflection upon non-philosophical achievements.[64] It does not follow, however, that *nobody* could or should leap beyond his time. Hegel's point seems to be that a person cannot conceive a coherent and realistic alternative to his own society or civilization. If an ideal of this kind is not too similar to one's own society to count as a genuine alternative to it, then it will be too novel to be susceptible to any evaluative or predictive decision procedure. There will be no prospect of predicting that it will come about, of realizing it or of rationally recommending it to one's contemporaries. In the passages in which he discusses this question, however, Hegel does not supply any very compelling arguments for this conclusion. If one is to be provided for him, it will be something like this. A realistic prediction or proposal of some future social state of affairs would involve unravelling the logical idea beyond that segment of it which is embedded in history so far. For significantly novel historical stages embody different phases of logic. The predictions which we can make, primarily in the natural sciences, do not involve this. A predicted eclipse, for example, does not differ, in respect of the thought involved in it, from past eclipses. Nature, unlike history, is repetitive and cyclical. To predict or prescribe future social developments, therefore, is on a par, not with predicting an eclipse, but with deriving novel scientific results from pure thought before they have been established empirically. But this, as we have seen, cannot, on Hegel's view, be done. The appropriate conceptual materials are not available to us until they have been unearthed by empirical enquiry. In an analogous way, the pure thoughts required for the projection of future historical developments are not to hand until they have already been embodied in social institutions.[65]

(iii) Hegel does not mean, however, to exclude all social change or all social criticism. All past societies have had flaws in virtue of which they succumbed to historic dissolution. Even if the participants in a way of life were unable to leap beyond it to a conception of a later phase of history against which they could measure it, they were able to see, or perhaps only to feel, the flaws in it. If this is so, then there can be a legitimate critic of his own society, namely one who points to or expresses genuine defects or conflicts within it. In so far as he does this, however, he does not so much stand in opposition to the existing state of affairs as represent a process of change into a new type of social order. Even if the critic is right, he has failed to locate a discrepancy between what is the case and what ought to be the case, since what ought to be the case either has already become, or is in the course of becoming, the case. An example of such a respectable rebel is Socrates, who, on Hegel's view, represented the emergence of a new principle of individualism in the collectivist 'ethical life' (*Sittlichkeit*) of the Greek city-state.[66] Socrates did not outline a coherent alternative way of life against which the city-state was to be measured. He did, however, foreshadow a new way of life that was implicit in Greek civilization and which was already beginning to emerge.

Hegel believes that there is, in this respect, a parallel between action and cognition. The contrast between them, or between 'theoretical mind' and 'practical mind', is initially conceived as a distinction between two opposing, but complementary, ways of handling the discrepancy between oneself and one's object. In cognition the mind starts out from features of the object and attempts to make them its own; the mind is, roughly speaking, assimilated to the object. In our practical activity, by contrast, we set out from features of our minds, from purposes and interests, and alter the object in accordance with them; roughly, the object is assimilated to the mind (*Enz.* III. 443 and Z; *WL* II. pp. 487 ff., M. pp. 775 ff.). This sharp contrast is misleading, however. For, properly conceived, cognition and action converge on one another, so that they involve the same process: 'The absolute idea, as it has emerged, is the identity of the theoretical and the practical idea' (*WL* II. p. 548, M. p. 824. Cf. *Enz.* I. 236 and Z). The point seems to be that, whereas in cognition and action of the ordinary type and/or as they are ordinarily conceived there is a discrepancy between the subject and its object, there is no such discrepancy in the case of proper cognition and action. Paradigmatic cognition, pure thinking, is thought about thought itself, and this involves, on Hegel's view, the dissolution of the distinction between subject and object (*Enz.* I. 236Z; III. 577).[67] Similarly, the proper sort of action consists not in introducing a change into an object which is initially quite different from oneself, but in acting in accordance with the norms of one's society, that is, in contributing to the continued working of something that is at bottom the same as oneself.[68]

The analogy is not a clear one. What, for example, are we to say about the study of nature? Hegel may mean that the discrepancy between the subject and the object is dissolved once we have discerned the forms of thought in it. Or he may mean that it is dissolved in virtue of the fact that we can, so to speak, watch the emergence of minds, namely ourselves, as we pass higher up the *scala naturae* (*Enz*. III. 381 Z). Or he may mean that the discrepancy is only properly eliminated once we have extracted the logical idea from the objective world and devote ourselves to pure thought. Moreover, Hegel is mistaken if he believes that he has shown that cognition and action end up as one and the same thing. Even if cognition and action have been shown to be similar in the relevant respect, there is still a difference between the practical activity of the citizen and the theoretical or contemplative activity of the philosopher, and, apart from the fact that it is possible to perform, as Hegel did, both roles, no clear connection between them has been established. The main point for our present purposes, however, is that this account of action is not intended to exclude social or political change. Indeed, Hegel often cites political innovators as examples of people whose actions were of the approved type:

We have said that the mind negates the externality of nature, assimilates nature to itself and thereby idealizes it.[69] This idealization has a one-sided form in the case of finite mind which places nature outside itself; here an external material stands over against the activity of our will and of our thinking, a material which is indifferent to the alteration which we undertake with it, and which therefore experiences in an entirely passive way the idealization which thereby falls to its lot. A different relationship obtains, however, in the case of the mind which produces world history. There no longer stands, on the one side, an activity which is external to the object and, on the other, a merely passive object; the spiritual activity is directed against an object which is intrinsically active — against an object which has worked itself up to what is supposed to be brought about by that activity, so that one and the same content is present in the activity and in the object. Thus e.g. the people and the time, on which Alexander's and Caesar's activity operated as their object, had become ready by their own efforts for the achievements to be performed by those individuals; the time created those men, just as much as they created their time; they were the instruments of the spirit of their time and their people, just as much as, conversely, their people served those heroes as the instrument for the fulfilment of their deeds (*Enz*. III. 381 Z).

What Hegel means, then, is that, apart from people who simply behave in routine ways in their society, there are two types of social critic. They may be called, for convenience, 'external' critics and 'internal' critics. External critics include people like Fries in Hegel's own society and presumably also Kant.[70] They advance claims about how things ought to be which have no basis in the actual conflicts and developments in their society and therefore meet with little response among their contemporaries. They are viewed by Hegel not as the standard-bearers of a new order, but rather as flies to be swatted. Internal critics, on the other hand, are those referred to by Hegel as 'world-historical individuals' (*VPG* p. 45, N. p. 85). They include fairly isolated intellectual rebels like Socrates, but primarily the initiators of large-scale social changes like Alexander, Caesar and Napoleon. Such people are, in a sense, not critics at all, since what they believe ought to be the case already is, or is becoming, the case. They are no more at odds with their environment than is a person who performs his routine duties in a stable society. They are, as it were, swimming with the tide. Although he is normally thought of as a conservative, Hegel does not in this regard differ markedly from his wayward disciple, Karl Marx. Marx had little more respect than Hegel for external critics:[71]

> Historical action is to yield to their personal inventive action; historically created conditions of emancipation to phantastic ones; and the gradual, spontaneous class organisation of the proletariat to an organisation of society especially contrived by these inventors. Future history resolves itself, in their eyes, into the propaganda and the practical carrying out of their social plans.

The position is not, however, a satisfactory one. For the distinction between internal and external critics is difficult to draw. Any critic of his time is, to some degree, a product of his time. (One cannot, as Hegel attempts to do, both claim that no one can leap beyond his time and rebuke some people for doing so.) Any critic of his time is to some degree an internal critic, at least in the trivial sense that he is included in the general state of affairs which he is criticizing. This does not mean that such criticism is self-refuting, that in rejecting a state of affairs which includes oneself criticizing it one is thereby rejecting one's own criticisms of it. One can consistently criticize a state of affairs which includes and gives rise to one's own disapproval of it, just as one can legitimately propose changes in a club of which one is a member. But nor does it mean that the criticisms or the proposed alterations are necessarily realistic ones. The distinction turns on the extent to which the tide is running in the same direction as the critic, to which his contemporaries can, do or will accept and respond to the criticisms. This, however, is a question of degree and it is easier to answer in retrospect than at the time. Hegel's world-historical individuals have already proved successful. It is not obvious that he has any criterion for recognizing them that would ensure that, if he had been a contemporary of Socrates, he would have accorded him greater respect than he shows to Kant or Fries.

11 *What next?*

The considerations which apply to the question: 'Is the world, at any given stage of its history, as it ought to be?' apply, for the most part, to the less general question: 'Is the world today, i.e. in Hegel's own day, as it ought to be?' An early nineteenth-century European could no more leap beyond nineteenth-century Europe than a person of any preceding age could leap beyond that age. Hegel's Owl of Minerva doctrine forbids him to make predictions about the future or to recommend changes which have not already started to take place. The question to be asked, however, is not simply a special case of this general question. It is, rather, this: Does Hegel believe that his own society, like all past ones, contains flaws and contradictions which will lead to its dissolution and replacement by another type of society?

Hegel provides the materials both for an affirmative and for a negative answer to this question. On the one hand, he does not treat critics of his own society with the respect, or at any rate caution, that would be due to them if it were possible that a new Socrates or a new Napoleon might emerge from their ranks, though in general the reasons which he gives for his disapproval are such as would apply to an external critic of any society, and not just his own. He offers, on the other hand, a general suggestion as to what might happen next, which shows at least that he thought that something was going to happen next:

America is thus the land of the future, in which its world-historical importance should reveal itself in the times which lie before us, perhaps in the conflict between North and South America . . . . America has to depart from the ground on which world history has taken place up to now. What has happened there so far is only the echo of the Old World and the expression of alien vitality, and as a land of the future it does not in general concern us here; for in history our business is with what has been and with what is — while in philosophy our concern is neither with what only has been nor with what only will be, but with what *is* and eternally is — with reason (*VPG* p. 114, N. pp. 170 f.).

Such indications that Hegel was sensible, however, may be to the detriment of his consistency as a systematic philosopher. Does his philosophy in fact leave open the possibility of significant future developments in the structure of society, or indeed in anything else? Some commentators believe that it does. J. N. Findlay, for example, argues that Hegel believed that his own system was open to revision by future generations in the light of new discoveries and insights and, if this is so, there is no reason to suppose that our social institutions are not similarly revisable:[72]

[W]hile Hegel undoubtedly thought that the sequence of thought-phases described in the *Phenomenology* . . . was a necessary sequence, he still did not think it the only possible necessary sequence or pathway to Science, and certainly not the pathway to Science that would be taken by men in the future, or that might have been taken in other cultural and historical settings . . . . Hegel was obviously familiar with the branching variety of alternative proofs, all involving strictly necessary steps, that are possible in mathematics, and it is plain that he did not think that a similar branching of proof was impossible in his dialectical reasoning. Dialectic is, in fact, a richer and more supple form of thought-advance than mathematical inference, for while the latter proceeds on lines of strict identity, educing only what is explicit or almost explicit in some thought-position's content, dialectic always makes higher order comments upon its various thought-positions, stating relations that carry us far beyond their obvious content . . . . If mathematical identities can thus follow different routes to the same or to different goals, dialectical commentaries can even more obviously do the same, and Hegel in his varying treatment of the same material in the two Logics and in the *Phenomenology* shows plain recognition of this fact. A necessary connection, whether mathematical or dialectical, is not psychologically compulsive: it represents a track that the mind may or may not take, or that it may or may not prefer to other tracks, on its journey to a given conclusion. There is no reason then to think that Hegel thought that the path traced in the *Phenomenology,* though consisting throughout of necessary steps, was the only path that the conscious spirit could have taken in rising from sensuous immediacy to absolute knowledge. It was the path that *had* been taken by the World Spirit in past history, and that had been rehearsed in the consciousness of Hegel, in whom the notion of Science first became actual. But this involved no pronouncement as to what pathway to Science would be taken by men in the future, nor as to what pathway would have been taken in other thinkable situations. For Hegel admits an element of the sheerly contingent, and therefore also of the sheerly possible, in nature and history.

Findlay is arguing, then, that, on Hegel's view, both the pathway to 'Science' or logic and logic itself are optional, or at least variable in different historical circumstances. If this were so, then Hegel would be leaving some thing of intellectual significance for future generations to do. The arguments for this interpretation are not compelling, however:

(i) Hegel does indeed present different versions of the *Logic*. This does not establish, however, that he believed them to be equally legitimate alternatives between which one is free to choose. The *Encyclopaedia Logic* is an abbreviation of the *Science of Logic,* and this would explain some of the divergences between them. Where the two versions differ in the order in which material is presented, it may only be that Hegel was uncertain, or changed his mind about, which was the correct version. It does not follow that he ever doubted that there was a single correct version. Hegel claims that since the method which he pursues in the *Logic* is not distinct from its 'object and content', the *Logic* is more or less correct and more or less complete (*WL* I. p. 50, M. p. 54).[73] This surely suggests that what Hegel is presenting, more or less, but not entirely, correctly, is logic, rather than simply one of several alternative logics.

(ii) Hegel was aware, as we have seen, that mathematics allows for alternative proofs of a single theorem.[74] He also believed that his own method is superior to that of mathematics. It does not follow, however, that he is committed to accepting that his own dialectic, *a fortiori,* provides alternative routes to the same terminus. For the existence of alternative proofs is seen as a problematic feature of geometry rather than as an obvious merit. The fact that Pythagoras' theorem may either be proved from certain premises or serve, in turn, as a premiss for the derivation of them as theorems is regarded as a defect:

[T]he pythagorean theorem too, if taken as the definition of a right-angled triangle, would similarly yield by analysis the theorems proved earlier in geometry in order to prove it. The freedom to choose rests on the fact that both methods proceed from something *externally presupposed* (*Enz.* I. 231).

Such things, it is implied, cannot happen in logic, where nothing is 'externally presupposed'. It is indeed true that there are several distinct proofs of the existence of God. But in the first place, these are, as we have seen, not strictly alternatives. They depend on, and disclose to us, different aspects of God, and all of them are required for us to have an adequate conception of him. Secondly, these proofs are not taken by Hegel to be different routes to the same conclusion. They are, rather, integrated into the single, unilinear course of the *Logic* and correspond to different phases of it.[75] They provide no warrant for attributing to Hegel the view that there are alternative logics.

(iii) Hegel concedes that there is an element of contingency in nature and history, but this concession does not go far enough to support Findlay's case. Firstly, contingency does not extend to logic itself. Even if the invocation of contingency could show that future generations are able to arrive at a different logic, it could not establish that this logic was a *legitimate* alternative to Hegel's. If contingency alone is at issue and if what future generations believe is to be true, then their intellectual life can amount to no more than variations on the theme of Hegel's logic. How far they can legitimately innovate within this framework will depend on the proximity of the subject-matter to that of logic. Secondly, even in the realm of what men actually — not necessarily legitimately — think or believe, the scope of contingency is severely restricted. Hegel maintains that the history of philosophy at least 'exhibits no contingent succession, but the necessary succession in the development of this science' (*VGP* III. p. 461, H. III. p. 552). Findlay would reply that this does not mean that the history of philosophy had to be as it was, but only that each historical philosophy follows by intelligible and cogent steps from its predecessor; any given philosophy could have had a different, equally legitimate, successor. In that case, however, the appeal to contingency is irrelevant, for Hegel is here contrasting contingency with whatever kind of necessity he may have in mind.

Findlay's arguments are, then, inconclusive. There are, moreover, several objections to his interpretation:

(i) The view that there are alternative routes to the same conclusion is at odds with Hegel's belief that in philosophy the steps by which we reach a result are contained in the result itself. Mathematics is criticized just because its results are independent of the procedures by which we arrive at them.[76] It follows that, if past generations had taken a different route, they would have reached a different conclusion and that, if future generations do so, then they too will arrive at a different terminus.

(ii) If there were alternative routes to the same goal, or for that matter alternative routes to different goals, then each route would be 'a track that the mind may or may not take, or that it may or may not prefer to other tracks, on its journey to a given conclusion'. If this is the case with logic, however, the mind would have to be distinct from pure thoughts in the way that it is, on Hegel's view, distinct from the objects and procedures of mathematics. In deciding which of the alternative tracks to take, it would have to depend on whim or on some other consideration which thought itself fails to provide. But if this were so, Hegel would not be entitled to say that philosophy involves 'letting go *particular opinions and prejudices* and giving free rein to the *subject-matter in oneself*' (*Enz.* I. 23).[77] It would not, of course, follow from the fact that no single pure thinker has alternative options open to him that different generations of pure thinkers do not think differently. The subject-matter might change, and then immersion in it would give rise to different courses of thought. The logical idea, however, does not change or vary from individual to individual. It can only be supposed that it does, if we interpret the Owl of Minerva doctrine to mean that logic is not pure thought at all, but a sort of high-level empirical reflection on one's age.[78] But this, as we have seen, does not square with Hegel's central doctrines. What varies and changes is not the logical idea itself, but the extent to which we have access to it.

(iii) One of the purposes of Findlay's interpretation is to ensure that Hegel's system leaves something of intellectual significance for post-Hegelian thinkers to do. But it is not clear that it achieves this. Sometimes it is suggested that future generations will discover new routes to the goal which Hegel himself reached, to logic or to absolute knowledge or whatever. This would mean that their work will be of less consequence than that of Hegel and his predecessors, for it is surely of less interest to find new routes to a destination which has already been located than to discover it for the first time. In any case it is unclear why they should bother to find new routes, if they can achieve the same result by simply reading Hegel. Elsewhere Findlay suggests a different picture of post-Hegelian intellectual life:[79]

Hegel will, however, marvellously *include* in his final notion of the final state of knowledge the notion of an endless progress that can have no final term. For he conceives that, precisely in seeing the object as an endless problem, we forthwith see it as not being a problem at all. For what the object in itself is, is simply to be the other, the stimulant of knowledge and practice, which in being forever capable of being remoulded and reinterpreted, is also everlastingly pinned down and found out being just what it is.

As we have seen, it is not obvious that this is a correct account of what Hegel means.[80] Indeed, the view attributed to him corresponds better to Hegel's version of Fichte than to Hegel himself:

The Fichtean philosophy makes the ego the starting-point of philosophical development . . . . But now the ego appears here not as truly free, spontaneous activity, since it is regarded as first aroused by an impulse (*Anstoss*) from outside . . . . What in Kant is called 'the thing-in-itself' is, in Fichte, the impulse from outside, this abstraction of something other than the ego, which has no other determination than that of the negative or of the non-ego in general (*Enz.* I. 60Z. 2. Cf. *VGP* III. pp. 388 ff., H. III. pp. 481 ff.).

The main question, however, is: What, on this view, will future thinkers do? They may, on the one hand, continue to remould and reinterpret the object in the way that men in the past have done. Significant reinterpretations, however, will require the discovery of novel categories, and this would, in turn, involve either the construction of alternatives to Hegel's logic or the extension of it. Moreover, for them to continue indefinitely in this way would amount to a case of bad infinity, and this, as we have seen, is something to which Hegel has deep-rooted, if not very cogent, objections. They may, on the other hand, cease to mould and interpret the object in the light of their realization that it is no more than the indeterminate object of our own mouldings and interpretings. After all, why should the object retain its capacity to stimulate us, once Hegel has supplied us with this insight? There seems to be no way out of this dilemma. Either intellectual history is a case of fruitless bad infinity or it comes to an end. If it comes to an end, where else could it do so except with Hegel?[81]

12 *The close of Hegel's system*

The truth seems to be that Hegel's system leaves no room for significant developments after his own time. In order to do this, it would need to form, as it were, a straight line, a line which breaks off with Hegel and his time, but which can be extended beyond it. As we have seen, however, it forms not a straight line, but a circle, and a circle cannot be continued indefinitely, but is essentially complete. It might be objected that each age has, so to speak, its own philosophical circle, and this would leave open the possibility of future circles different from Hegel's. But this is not so. Past philosophies have not, on his view, formed circles in the way that his own does. They are generally regarded as one-sided and incomplete, a feature of them which provides Hegel with some of his criticisms of them.[82] Moreover, there is, on his view, only one philosophy (*Enz.* I. 13).[83] If each historical philosophy formed a circle, what, then, would be the relationship between them? If they did not together form a single higher circle, then this would be the same in effect as an indefinitely extendible straight line, open to all the objections that Hegel levels against bad infinity. If, on the other hand, they form a further circle of a higher order, then there is presumably no better place to look for this than Hegel's own system.

It seems to follow that Hegel cannot concede that his own philosophy will be developed or supplanted in the way that past philosophies have been. Philosophy, or the series of philosophies, is a gradual unravelling of the system of pure thoughts, and this system is a closed one, a circle and not a straight line. The closure of the circle corresponds to the luminous insight which Hegel claims to have achieved into the nature of philosophy and its history. This conclusion is implicit in Hegel's descriptions of philosophy: the work of an architect, however long it takes, comes to an end at some definite time, and the acquisition of self-consciousness is presumably a completable task (*Enz.* I. 13).[84] To suppose otherwise would, in any case, raise the prospect of bad, Sisyphean infinity. Roughly speaking, Hegel believes that philosophy has run through all logical possibilities and that the system which embraces them all and sees their interconnections is the complete and final philosophy. It also follows that Hegel cannot consistently countenance important future developments in the natural sciences. Within the terms of his thought, scientific developments fall into three categories. Firstly, there are those which could be accommodated by the *Encyclopaedia* as it stands, requiring the addition of some extra paragraphs or remarks, but no alteration of its basic structure or of the bulk of its content. The most obvious items in this category would be the detection of extra bits of information about matters which Hegel regards as contingent, but it might also include the discovery of some low-level generalizations, laws or theories. Secondly, there are those which would require a thorough-going change in the content of *Encyclopaedia,* though not in its structure nor, consequently, in the *Logic* itself. Thirdly, there might be developments which would require changes not only in the content of the *Encyclopaedia*, but in its structure, and, therefore, in the *Logic* itself. Such developments might include, for example, the abandonment of the category of inner purposiveness, or the addition of entirely novel categories.[85] If the *Logic* were not revised so as to accommodate such results, a gap would open up between pure thought and the empirical sciences. But this, on Hegel's view, cannot be. The sciences, if they are to be intelligible or more than piecemeal collections of information, must embody pure thoughts. He cannot, however, countenance the possibility of developments either of this or of the second type. The general results of the sciences, the main body of the content of the *Philosophy of Nature*, are, on his view, shown to be *a priori.* This is presumably intended to exclude the possibility that they will at some future date be shown to be false. Our general view of the logical idea, and therefore of the structure of science, is not open to revision. The completeness of Hegel's account of it is guaranteed by its closure in the absolute idea, the correctness of its main outlines by the fact that it was not, strictly speaking, Hegel who gave this account, but the logical idea itself.[86] Scientific innovations of the second and third types, that is significant innovations, are therefore excluded.

Finally, if Hegel's *Logic* is a closed and unrevisable circle, and if, as we have seen that they do, periods of history correspond to the phases of the *Logic,* it follows that there can be no significant historical developments after Hegel's own time. The closure of the circle in Hegel's own age means that in that age, but in no earlier one, the whole course of history, its purpose and rationality, has become entirely intelligible. Such self-knowledge is the terminus of history: '[I]t can be said of world history that it is the presentation of the way in which the mind acquires the awareness of what it is in itself' (*VPG* p. 31, N. p. 53). Hegel does not suggest that there could be any greater degree of self-awareness than that which he purports to provide. The mere fact that we could not say what greater self-awareness would consist in does not, of course, entail that there could not be any. But if there were such, we would expect our lack of it to make itself felt in present social and intellectual discomforts — of which Hegel provides hardly a glimpse — and the circle could not be closed with such emphasis. If there is none, if Hegel makes spirit entirely transparent to itself, then it follows that history, or at least interesting history, is at an end. The problem with the suggestion that America is the land of the future is not that we cannot predict what will happen there, but that there is nothing left to happen there.

13 *The end of history*

Hegel is not, of course, unique in supposing that history does, at some time or other, come to a close. At a general level, Marx and Engels describe communist society in terms similar to those which Hegel applies to his own society. History is, in each case, a development from necessity to freedom. Just as, for Hegel, *'the final end of the world* [is] the mind's consciousness of its freedom and thus the actuality of its freedom' (*VPG* p. 32, N. p.55. Cf. *Enz.* III. 381Z), so Engels speaks of the prospective proletarian revolution as 'humanity's leap from the realm of necessity into the realm of freedom'.[87] Once this transition has been made, history as we know it will come to an end. Thus Marx refers to capitalist society as 'the closing chapter of the prehistoric stage of human society'.[88] Marx locates the end of history − or rather that of 'prehistory' − not, as Hegel does, in the present, but in the future. He, therefore, needs to distinguish carefully between the question of the end of history and the question of the sort of criticism that can be appropriately made of any society by one of its members. Hegel, by contrast, fails to distinguish between what is true of any age and what is true of his own. Questions about what will come next are met by considerations about the scope of philosophy and the inaccessibility of the future, considerations which would apply with equal force to any phase of history. This is why he does not openly avow that history ends with him.

Nevertheless, Hegel's doctrines commit him, as we have seen, to this claim, and it might be felt that it is a peculiarly egotistical, or at least parochial, one. It is not immediately apparent, however, why this should be so. Hegel was not, after all, the first, or the last, thinker to believe that he, after centuries of endeavour, has at last discovered the truth about the universe. Aristotle and Spinoza did not acknowledge the prospect that their beliefs would be considerably modified, abandoned or forgotten in the future. If their beliefs had been true, then there would have been little of intellectual consequence for future generations to do. Hegel is not alone in holding that the world is a familiar, finite place about which the whole essential truth can be discovered in a finite time. Once this is known, nothing remains to be done apart from filling in the details and contemplating the knowledge which we have acquired. Nor is he alone in holding that the social order of his own day is in need of little improvement. Hegel has, moreover, some special defences against the charge of egotism. He acknowledges more explicitly than most a debt to his own age and to past history for whatever he has achieved. Again, the doctrine that the thinking ego is simply absorbed in its subject-matter implies that it is not, strictly speaking, Hegel who is thinking these thoughts rather than Kant or Jacobi. This, he believes, is a sort of humility or modesty (*Enz.* I. 23). Consequently, he often discusses philosophical doctrines without attributing them to named individuals, and he generally speaks, not of 'my system' or 'Hegel's philosophy', but of 'science' or the 'present standpoint' (*VGP* III. pp. 454 ff., H. III. pp. 545 ff.).

This last phenomenon, however, is more readily taken as a sign of conceit than of humility. It is not modest to claim to be a mere mouthpiece for one's subject-matter, particularly if one's subject-matter is God. There are, moreover, at least two additional reasons for the charge of egotism. The first is that Hegel's claim to be right is not a naïve and unconsidered one. He was more aware than most philosophers have been of the reasons there are for supposing that one's own beliefs, and even the beliefs and values generally accepted in one's time, are open to subsequent revision. This does not, however, lead him to attach an acknowledgement of his own fallibility to his pronouncements, but rather to devise ingenious reasons for believing them to be correct.[89] Secondly, Hegel believes not simply, as Aristotle or Spinoza believed, that he has discovered the truth about the universe, but, unlike them, that to the extent that he is a distinct individual, he himself, or at least his discovery of this truth, is a crucial feature, indeed the culminating feature, of the universe which he purports to describe:

> A new epoch has arisen in the world .... Finite self-consciousness has ceased to be finite; and, on the other side, absolute self-consciousness has acquired the actuality which it previously lacked .... Spirit produces itself as nature, as the state; that is its *unconscious* activity, in which it is for itself something different, not spirit; in the deeds and life of history as well as of art it brings itself forth in a *conscious* way, is aware of all kinds of modes of its actuality, but only as modes of it; only in science is it aware of itself as absolute spirit, and this awareness alone, spirit, is its true existence (*VGP* III. p. 460, H. III. pp. 551 ff.).

Hegel does, indeed, continue in a way which implies that this process has not ended: 'Now this is the standpoint of the present time and the series of spiritual formations is closed with it for now (*für jetzt*)'. But if there is more to come, it is wholly unclear what it could be. The tone of such passages as this and the role in which they implicitly cast Hegel are reminiscent of his obscure discussion of the difference between Christ and Socrates:

> According to that comparison Christ is a man like Socrates, a teacher who lived a virtuous life and brought to consciousness in man what the truth is in general, what must constitute the foundation of human consciousness. But the higher view is that the *divine nature* was revealed in Christ . . . . [God] is this life-process, the trinity, in which the universal opposes itself to itself and is identical with itself in it. In this element of eternity God is the coming together with himself (*das Sichzusammen-schliessen mit sich*), this closure (*Schluss*) of himself with himself. Faith simply grasps and is conscious that in Christ this truth which is in and for itself is intuited in its course and that this truth was first revealed through him (*VPR* II. p. 287, S.S. III. pp. 86 f.).

We have seen that there are a variety of reasons for rejecting Hegel's system. If it were true, however, Christ would be no more than his lisping precursor. Hegel, it might be said, took more seriously than others have done the historical significance of the claim to be right.

Conclusion

Anyone who writes about Hegel must eventually face the fact that Hegel has outlasted most of his critics. Why is this? How are we to account for his resilience? A preliminary answer might be that Hegel has already had an enormous influence and that influence is self-perpetuating. Under his more or less indirect inspiration, regimes have been established and overthrown. Hardly any of the human sciences remains unaffected by him: theologians, sociologists, political theorists, art-critics and historians have fallen under his spell, attempted to break it, or simply derived nourishment from his works. Philosophers of the stature of Marx, Kierkegaard, Peirce and Heidegger have developed their thought in opposition to him and, by the process of contagion through conflict, bear the marks of their encounter with him. A serious interest in Marx, for example, leads directly to Hegel — though conversely the current revival of Marxism owes much to its regeneration by the recovery of its Hegelian roots. But this cannot be a complete answer to our question. For influence does not entail merit. If Hegel's immense and diverse influence is not wholly undeserved — and it is no doubt improbable that it should be — then we should try to see what his intrinsic merits are. These merits are several and they lie at different levels. Hegel's survival-value consists in part in the fact that he is sufficiently rich, ambiguous and complex to provide something for different epochs and for different milieus.

This book has concentrated on the arguments to be found, explicitly or implicitly, in Hegel and most of them have been subjected to criticism. But this does not mean that he is only of interest as an antiquarian curiosity. Arguments may, in the first place, be novel and interesting and thus worthy of study, even if they are not valid. Most of Plato's arguments, for example, are not

520

valid, but few would doubt that they nevertheless deserve continued study. Hegel's *Logic* contains a wealth of arguments — many more than I have extracted from it — from which we have much to learn, if only in attempting to see why they are not valid. Secondly, the detection, reconstruction and evaluation of arguments is an open-ended business. The arguments (and doctrines) of any great philosopher are open to renewed interpretation and assessment in the light of subsequent interests and discoveries. Hegel's richness, complexity and self-awareness make him an especially good case of this. For whenever we criticize one of his arguments or doctrines, we can never be entirely sure not only that there is no reply which he *might* have made, but that there is no reply which he *did* make but which has escaped our notice. Kierkegaard was mistaken when he took this to be only a matter of ad hoc and retrospective adjustment:[1]

> In the case of committee reports, it may be quite in order to incorporate in the report a dissenting opinion; but an existential system which includes the dissenting opinion as a paragraph in its own logical structure, is a curious monstrosity .... [I]f a particular objection seems to attract a little attention, the systematic entrepreneurs engage a copyist to copy off the objection, which thereupon is incorporated in the System; and when the book is bound the System is complete.

But Hegel has an uncanny knack of anticipating apparent objections to his thought and incorporating them within it. An example of this is his account in the *Phenomenology* of the 'unhappy consciousness', which clearly foreshadows Kierkegaard's own existentialist alternative to Hegelianism.[2] It does not, of course, follow that Hegel is in the right as against Kierkegaard. Hegel's criticisms of the unhappy consciousness might, for example, be unacceptable. But it does suggest that the criticism of Hegel is an intricate matter. However glaring the flaw may appear, there is always the possibility that Hegel has been misunderstood or indeed that he is one or more steps ahead of his critics. There is no obvious end in sight to this interplay between criticism and interpretation. (Hegel's own account of the nature and role of arguments perhaps does something to illuminate it.) Finally, arguments — it might be argued — are not everything. Arguments are, of course, important within Hegel's system. Arguments, or something like arguments, are what bind the system together and they form the rungs for our ascent to the absolute idea. But if we are reluctant to swallow Hegel whole, we might nevertheless believe — as, for example, McTaggart did[3] — that better arguments can be found to support his enterprise, or we might feel that doctrines, systems, visions or ways of looking at things may well be better than the arguments advanced for them and provide benefits which withstand the arguments deployed against then. Who would maintain, for example, that Locke is better forgotten in the light of Berkeley's arguments against him? Or, for that matter, that Christianity is no stronger than its evidential support?

What, then, does Hegel provide apart from arguments? Above all he provides system: an attempt to assign everything its place in a single coherent whole. But his systematicity can be appreciated on more than one plane. At one level, he supplies an aesthetically satisfying, comforting picture in which man occupies a significant position within a meaningful universe. At another level, he attempts to fulfil the age-old promise of theology and metaphysics by giving an intellectually rigorous account of the universe as a whole together with a complete, presupposition-free explanation of it. This might appeal in at least two different ways. Some have believed that something like this must be possible and that Hegel has shown us what a fully worked out theology should look like. Others have felt that it cannot be possible and that Hegel has shown its absurdity. But the sceptics have at least tended to pay Hegel the compliment of choosing him as their adversary, for the reason that he has pursued the enterprise further than anyone and made an important contribution to showing what is wrong with it. There is merit, as Hegel himself saw, in taking a false position as far as it will go, for this enables us to detect and question the assumptions which made it seem plausible in the first place and to see what is required of an alternative. At a humbler level, however, system, unification, is perhaps not only desirable but possible. Hegel appeals to the craving for a unified science, to the desire for a single coherent account of the large categories and procedures that govern our thinking or, again, to the common experience that work in one area of philosophy raises problems which cannot be resolved without trespassing into other areas or even into other disciplines. His attempt to uncover connections — between ontology and action, between epistemology and ethics, or between almost anything and logic — is one source of his perpetual, or at least recurrent, attraction.

Associated with this is Hegel's tendency to ask what seem to be the right questions: questions about the relations between apparently disparate domains; large important questions about the relationship of reflective, autonomous individuals to the surrounding anonymous society or to nature as conceived by the sciences; and perennial philosophical questions about self-referentiality or the status of logic and its laws. The raising of questions is often as important as the answers given to them. It is better still if a whole range of questions can be answered in a systematic way, and even better if the answers are the right ones. Are Hegel's answers the right ones? Perhaps not. But nor are they negligible. He can be drawn, as a plausible participant and not simply as a historical reference point, into several current debates. For example, his legacy of Aristotelian teleology, together with his emphasis on intersubjective norms and institutions ('objective mind'), make him a rich source of insights in our understanding of human action.[4] But more than this, his answers, obscure and problematic as they are often seem to point in roughly the right direction. This is particularly noticeable in the case of those persistent dualisms on which so many philosophical (and other) problems depend: mind and body, individual and society, subject and object, internal and external, self and others, freedom and necessity, God and world, and so on. Hegel indicates an inviting path between blank dualism and reductionist monism. Correspondingly, his own system eludes most of the customary dyadic classifications. Is Hegel an idealist or a realist? Is he a theist or an atheist? Is he a metaphysician or an anti-metaphysician? Is he a descriptive metaphysician or a revisionary one? And descriptive or explanatory?[5] It is not easy to say. And that is all to the good, both because Hegel's position may ultimately prove to be the right one and because he makes us rethink our inherited ways of categorizing philosophical systems. Whether or not, and in what areas, Hegel may turn out to be (more or less) right is, of course, still an unsettled matter. For apart from the fact that the questions themselves are still in dispute, it is only recently that, avoiding the extremes of undiscriminating adoration and execration, analytical philosophers have begun to make use of what he has to offer.

Perhaps Hegel comes most forcefully into his own in those areas where there is an interplay, even a tension, between rationality and historicity. The attraction of Hegel's historicism is, at one level, a matter of mood or perhaps of perspective. His feeling for the grand sweep of the historical process elevates us above the petty conflicts and concerns of the present and opens our eyes to the transience of human affairs and institutions. Some, like Kierkegaard and the existentialists, have felt that this presents us with a false perspective on the human situation:[6]

[A Hegelian] probably finds compensation in the thought that in comparison with an understanding of China and Persia and six thousand years of the world's history, a single individual does not much matter, even if that individual be himself. But it seems otherwise to me, and I understand it better conversely: when a man cannot understand himself, his understanding of China and Persia and the rest must surely be of a very peculiar kind.

But whatever the strength of this objection may be, it is again significant that it is Hegel who is under attack: he is honoured by opposition as much as by agreement.

At another level, we surely have something to learn from Hegel in our understanding of, for example, the development of science, in particular of the replacement of one 'paradigm' by another. He at least provides one answer, or the materials for constructing an answer, to the question how this development can be both historical and rational, and it is not an answer to be dismissed without consideration.[7] In Hegel's own day, however, the development of the natural sciences was not in general felt to be a problem. Characteristically it was regarded as a paradigm of cognitive progress, with assured and significant results to its credit which far outshone anything which philosophers had to offer. Philosophy and its history was — and is — a problem. A conception of philosophy something like those which Hegel was attempting to combat is described by Stephen Spender in his autobiography. The passage will be quoted at length, both because it enhances by contrast Hegel's own more satisfying — not to say more flattering — conception of philosophy and its history, and because it tells us something about how not to handle Hegel himself:[8]

In the first lesson we were told that . . . for Mill, happiness was the criterion of moral value. In the next tutorial we were told that Mill was wrong because he had forced himself into the position where . . . a very happy pig might be considered morally better than a moderately happy human being. Obviously this was outrageous. Mill himself realized that it was unthinkable; accordingly, he introduced standards of higher and lower kinds of happiness . . . . Here he was caught out, because, if you talk of a higher happiness, your criterion . . . is not happiness but something else. Next please. The next philosopher is Locke. We were told what he thought and then why he was wrong. Next please. Hume. Hume was wrong also. Then Kant. Kant was wrong, but he was also so difficult to understand that one could not be so sure of catching him out.

This might be described as the Obstacle Race way of teaching philosophy. The whole field of human thought is set out with logical obstructions and the students watch the philosophers race around it. Some of them get further than others but they all fall sooner or later into the traps which language sets for them. It soon occurred to me that it was useless to enter a field where such distinguished contestants had failed.

The Obstacle Race conception of philosophy is introduced here to serve two purposes. It represents, firstly, one of the ways in which we should not treat Hegel — disqualifying him from the race altogether on account of his obscurity or allowing a simplified parody of him to stumble at an early stage. Hegel is in any case too self-reflective to accept the obstacles that *we* set for him: he brings with him his own conception of an obstacle and of what is to count as surmounting it, and in doing so he stimulates us to rethink *our* conception. Secondly, it brings into relief the virtues of Hegel's own conception of philosophy as a progressively unfolding unity with subtle interconnections with other areas of culture. Hegel's conception no doubt has problems of its own, but it has had a constant attraction for those who have attempted to do the history of their subject.[9] We might at least say that philosophy *ought* to be somewhat as Hegel saw it and that it is a problem if it is not.

One final question: Does Hegel's philosophy have anything to say about its own subsequent fate? Some philosophers have nothing special to say about the later reception of their ideas. Others do. It is often felt, for example, to be a problem for Marx that Marxism has found a readier audience in non-industrialized societies than in capitalist ones. For Marxism makes claims not only about its own truth, but also about its future acceptance. Does Hegel's system imply similar claims? Hegel's self-reflectiveness, his concern for history and for the role of philosophy within society might lead us to expect that it does. His reluctance to say what will happen after him pulls in the other direction, but his belief that he had reached the pinnacle of human self-consciousness surely carries certain general implications about the later history of his thought — that it will not, for example, be totally forgotten and neglected after his death. Can we say more than this? Not a great deal. No doubt it would have surprised Hegel — in the light of his views about the perspicuity of pure thought — that exegesis has played so great a role in the reception of his system by later generations, that its attractions (and repulsions) have been in part those of an undeciphered script. But what did he expect to happen to it? Was it to be 'sublimated' or overcome, as the philosophies of his predecessors had been? Was it to form the basis of a unified and institutionalized science? Or to become a new, rational state religion? Occasionally he contemplates a more modest prospect:

> philosophy . . . is a sequestered sanctuary and its servants form an isolated priesthood, which must not mix with the world and has to preserve the possession of truth. How the temporal empirical present is to find its way out of its diremption, what form it is to take, are matters to be left to itself to settle and are not the *immediately* practical business and concern of philosophy (*VPR* II. pp. 343 f., S.S. III. p. 151).

This, however, looks more like a refusal to forecast the *long-term* prospects for his thought, or, if it is not, it does not present an accurate picture of its subsequent history, a history whose predominant feature has been the influence of Hegel outside academic philosophy. What might Hegel have said about this complex history? About the periods of neglect and dismissal, about the dispersal of his insights throughout various disciplines, about the transformation of his system into the potent political force of Marxism — on which its intermittent revivals partly depend? It is hard to tell. But the long view characteristic of Hegel's own historical vision suggests greater caution in assigning him his place in history: it is too early to say. For one prediction is sure: if the civilization to which he has already contributed so much endures, we have not seen the last of Hegel.

Notes

INTRODUCTION

1 'My own dialectical method is not only fundamentally different from the Hegelian, but is its direct opposite. For Hegel the thought process, which he even transforms into an independent subject under the name of "idea", is the demiurge of the actual; the actual forms only its outer appearance. For me, on the contrary, the ideal is only the material when it is transposed and translated inside the human head . . . . In Hegel, the dialectic is standing on its head. One must turn it the right way up (*umstülpen*) in order to disclose the rational kernel in the mystical covering' (*Das Kapital*, Preface to 2nd edition of 1872 (Paul and Paul, 1930, vol. II, p. 873)).

2 Harris, 1972, provides such an account for the years 1770–1801.

3 First published in Nohl, 1907. On these, see Kroner, 1948; Kaufmann, 1954; Walsh, 1963, pp. 133 ff.; Harris, 1972; Lukács, 1975.

4 Cf. Inwood, 1979.

I PERCEPTION, CONCEPTION AND THOUGHT

1 Cf. esp. Ch. VIII.

2 But cf. Ch. II, 1.

3 E.g. *Enz*. I. 38Z.

4 Cf. Ch. III, 1.

5 Cf Ch. X, 1.

6 Cf. Ch. IX, 4.

7 Cf. Ch. III, 8.

8 *Enz*. I. 87; *WL* I. pp. 82 ff., M. pp. 82 ff.

9 *WL* II. p. 228, M. p. 562. Cf. Ch. X, 10.

10 *Enz*. I. 135Z. Cf. Ch. X, 10.

11 Cf. Findlay, 1958, pp. 89 ff.

12 For discussions of this passage, see Soll, 1969, pp. 92 ff.; Taylor, 1972; Solomon, 1974; Taylor, 1975, pp. 140 ff.; Soll, 1976.

13 But cf. Ch. VII, 8.

14 Cf. Ch. I, 5, Ch. VIII, 6, 7.
15 Cf. *Enz*. I. 8, where Hegel assents to the dictum '*Nibil est in intellectu quod non fuerit in sensu.*'
16 E.g. *Enz*. I. 33 on pre-Kantian metaphysics; 42 on Kant's categories; *WL* I. pp. 50 f., M. p. 55 on formal logic.
17 E.g. *Enz*. I. 12.
18 Cf. Waismann, 1959, pp. 1 ff., 235 ff.
19 E.g. *PG* pp. 35 ff., M. pp. 24 ff.; *WL* I. pp. 239 ff., M. pp. 209 ff.
20 Cf. Ellis, 1968, pp. 4 ff.
21 Cf. Ch. VIII, 8.
22 E.g. *Enz*. I. 99Z. Cf. Ch. VIII, 24.
23 E.g. *WL* I. pp. 32 f., M. pp. 41 f.
24 Cf. Chs VIII–X.
25 Cf. Ch. VI, 6.
26 Christian Wolff (1679–1754), a follower and systematizer of Leibniz, is Hegel's stock example of an arid metaphysician of the pre-Kantian sort. Cf. esp. *VGP* III. pp. 256 ff., H. III. 348 ff.
27 Cf. Chs VI, VII.
28 Cf. Ch. IX.
29 Cf. Ch. VIII, 17, 18.

II THINKING AND THE SELF

1 Cf. Ch. V.
2 Cf. Ch. XI.
3 Cf. Ch. VII, 24.
4 E.g. *Enz*. I. 2; *WL* I. pp. 19 ff., M. pp. 31 ff.
5 E.g. *Enz*. I. 20; *PG* pp. 88 f., M. p. 66.
6 The egocentricity, not of all desires, but of our most primitive ones is Hegel's primary reason for associating desires, rather than cognitive states and activities, with self-consciousness: *PG* pp. 133 ff., M. pp. 104 ff.; *Enz*. III. 426. See further O'Brien, 1975, pp. 90 ff. But for a different account, see Norman, 1976, p. 46.
7 Cf. Ch. III, 1, 4.
8 On F. H. Jacobi (1743–1819) and Hegel's criticisms of him, see Ch. VII, esp. 1.
9 Cf. Ch. I, 7, Ch. VII, 24.
10 But cf. Ch. IX.
11 Cf. Ch. VIII, 15.
12 E.g. *Enz*. I. 42 and Z.1.
13 E.g. *Enz*. I. 57 f. Cf. Ch. VIII, 23.
14 E.g. *Enz*. I. 3.
15 Cf. Solomon, 1970.
16 Cf. Ch. II, 3.
17 Cf. *Enz*. III. 408Z, where it is said that I can imagine that I am a dog or that I am able to fly.
18 *Enz*. III. 424 ff.; *PG* pp. 133 ff., 175 ff., M. pp. 104 ff., 139 ff. Cf. Ch. XI, 4. Hegel's account of self-consciousness is affected by the fact that

'*selbstbewusst*' commonly means 'proud, self-confident, self-assertive' – almost the opposite of the ordinary sense of 'self-conscious'. Cf. Soll, 1969, pp. 7ff.

19 *Enz.* III. 389, 410Z; *PG* pp. 141 ff., 221 ff., M. pp. 111 ff., 180 ff.

20 For this objection, see Cousin, 1957-8.

21 Cf. Ch. II, 2.

22 *KdrV.* B 131. When Hegel cites this passage, he often speaks simply of 'the I' rather than of 'the "I think"' (e.g. *Enz.* I. 20).

23 *KdrV.* B 157.

24 Cf. Ch. VIII, 20.

25 Cf. *Enz.* III. 398, 402 and Z, 406Z, 408 and Z. Many of these passages occur in the course of discussions of various types of mental derangement.

26 Cf. Ch. II, 1.

27 '*Übergreifen*' is felicitously translated as 'outflank' by Wallace, 1892, p. 38. The word is discussed by Fackenheim, 1967, pp. 98 ff.

28 *Enz.* I. 20; *PG* p. 88, M. p. 66; *WL* I. pp. 20 f.; M. pp. 31 f.

29 Cf. Ch. V, 2 on the possibility of alternative conceptual systems.

30 Cf. Chs I, VIII.

31 E.g. *Enz.* I. 125; *WL* II. pp. 129 ff., M. pp. 484 ff.; *PG* pp. 89 ff., M. pp. 67 ff. Cf. Ch. V, 2, Ch. VI, 6, Ch. VII, 12.

32 Hegel does not himself accept this account of God, for he does not believe that an infinite deity can be related to anything other than itself. Cf. Ch. VII, 12.

33 *PG* pp. 239 f., M. pp. 196 f. Cf. Ch. VIII, 17. For a discussion of Hegel's views on the brain, see MacIntyre, 1972b.

34 Cf. Chs VIII, XI.

35 *Ibid.*

36 Cf. Ch. I, 2.

37 *PG* pp. 133 ff., M. pp. 104 ff.; *Enz.* III. 424.

38 *PG* pp. 102 ff., M. pp. 79 ff.: 'Force and Understanding'.

39 For a discussion of Thales (6th century BC), see Barnes, 1979, vol. I. pp. 5 ff.

40 E.g. *Enz.* I. 24Z.3; *VGP* III. p. 512, H. I. p. 44.

41 Cf. Chs I, VIII, IX.

42 Cf. Ch. XI, 4.

43 Cf. Ch. II, 2.

44 *Enz.* III. 459 on language; 465 ff. on thinking. But for a different view, see Derrida, 1970, who believes that Hegel lived up to the standard which he implicitly set himself when he said: 'Usually the *sign* and *language* are inserted somewhere in psychology or also in logic as an *appendix,* with no thought being given to their necessity and connection in the system of the activity of intelligence' (*Enz.* III. 458).

45 For a different account of degrees or levels of self-consciousness, see Norman, 1976, pp. 46 ff.

46 Cf. Ch. VIII, 14.

III EXPERIENCE, META-THINKING AND OBJECTIVITY

1 Cf. Ch. II, 1.
2 E.g. *Enz.* I. 12; II. 246.
3 Cf. Ch. II.
4 Cf. Ch. II, 1.
5 Cf. *Enz.* I. 36, 49 ff.
6 It is also connected, however, with deeper confusions about the nature of the empirical. Cf. Ch. III, 3.
7 E.g. *Enz.* I. 38Z, II. 246Z; *PG* pp. 29 ff., M. pp. 18 f.
8 Cf. Ch. II, 1.
9 Newton, *Philosophiae Naturalis Principia Mathematica*, Bk I, Law I.
10 Cf. Ch. I, 4.
11 Cf. Ch. III, 8.
12 E.g. *Enz.* III. 385Z. Cf. Ch. II, 4.
13 Cf. Ch. III, 3, Ch. V, 8, Ch. XI, 2.
14 Cf. Ch. VI.
15 E.g. *Enz.* I. 38Z. Cf. 7, where the rise of empirical science is associated with the Lutheran Reformation.
16 Cf. Ch. XI, 1.
17 But cf. Ch. III, 3.
18 Cf. Smart, 1964, pp. 40 f.
19 *Enz.* I. 61 ff.; II. 246Z. Cf. Ch. VII, esp. 1.
20 Cf. Ch. X, 1.
21 Cf. *Enz.* II. 286 and 334, where Hegel claims to be more empiricist than the scientists in his criticisms of their classification of the elements.
22 It was not, however, strictly irrefutable, since it was refuted, as Hegel is aware, by the experiments of Count Rumford (*Enz.* II. 304). See Petry, 1970, vol. II, pp. 300 f., 302 f.
23 Cf. Ch. I.
24 Cf. Ch. VII, 15.
25 Hume, *Enquiry concerning the Human Understanding*, VII; Kant, *KdrV.* B4 f.; A111 ff.; A195 f., B240 f.
26 *KdrV* A189 ff., B232 ff.
27 *KdrV* A565 ff., B593 ff.
28 Cf. *Enz.* I. 43, where Kant's objections to the application of categories to the soul are misinterpreted in a similar way.
29 *KdrV* B143.
30 *KdrV* A295 f., B352 f.
31 Cf. Chs VI, VII.
32 Cf. Ch. VII, 2, 5.
33 Cf. Ch. III, 5.
34 Hegel, or his editor, confuses matters by giving as an example of the thesis the introduction of Solon's laws, a product of thinking, into Athenian society (*Enz.* I. 22Z). Solon's laws changed Athens, and not simply our conception of it, but this is because their introduction and enforcement involved more than mere thinking.
35 Cf. Ch. VII, 18.

36 Cf. Ch. II, 1.
37 Hegel distinguishes between gravity and attraction, e.g. at *Enz*. II. 262, but the distinction does not matter here.
38 Cf. Ch. VII, 25.
39 But cf. Ch. VII.
40 Cf. Ch. XI, 12.
41 Cf. Ch. V, 7.
42 Cf. Ch. V, 9.
43 Cf. Ch. III, 1.
44 Cf. Ch. IX.
45 Hegel is apparently trying to remedy this situation at *Enz*. II. 267.
46 Cf. Ch. III, 8.
47 Cf. Ch. III, 2.
48 Cf. Ch. II.
49 Cf. Ch. XI.
50 Cf. Ch. III, 4.
51 Hegel may have other points in mind in his criticism of analysis. He may mean, for example, that to analyse something into its elements leaves out the relations between these elements. If what is at issue, however, is mental analysis rather than physical dissection, there seems to be no reason why these relations should not figure among the elements into which the entity is analysed. He may, again, mean that, in the case of some entities, their 'parts' or 'constituents' are, as it were, constituted by the relationships between them, so that physical dissection destroys the parts, as well as the whole which they compose: cf. Ch. VIII, 22. Hostility to analysis was a commonplace of Hegel's time: see *Logic* (Wallace, 1892), p. 398, and Buchdahl, 1961, esp. pp. 28 ff.
52 Cf. Ch. VI.
53 E.g. *PG* pp. 102 ff., M. pp. 79 ff. Cf. Ch. XI, 4.
54 Cf. Ch. III, 1.
55 Cf. Ch. III, 3.
56 Cf. Ch. VI.
57 E.g. *Enz*. I. 38. Cf. Ch. VII, 1.
58 Hegel has Goethe primarily in mind: cf. Ch. VIII, 3. One might question the rigour of the empirical constraints on this type of experience, since 'religious feeling, naive trust, love, fidelity, and natural faith' are also placed under this heading (*Enz*. I. 24Z. 3).
59 Cf. Ch. VI.
60 Cf. Chs VI, VIII.
61 Cf. Ch. IX, 2.
62 Cf. Ch. VII, 24.
63 Cf. Ch. I, 2.
64 Cf. Ch. III, 1.
65 Cf. *PG* pp. 133 ff., 175 ff., M. pp. 104 ff., 139 ff.
66 Cf. Ch. II, 2.
67 Hume, *Enquiry Concerning the Principles of Morals*, IX, 1, 222. This idea naturally suggests that of an 'impartial spectator' who has no 'private and particular situation' — a postulate adopted by some philosophers, though

not by Hume himself : cf. Raphael, 1972. It is tempting to regard Hegel's *Geist* — in one of its several senses — as the ideal spectator, cognitive as well as ethical, who sees the world as it is in itself and not simply as it appears to be from some particular perspective. This idea was not, however, developed by Hegel, perhaps because it would imply that God straightforwardly transcends the world and individual people. But it was proposed by some philosophers under his influence : see, e.g., Royce, 1897, pp. 22 ff.

68 Cf. Ch. II, 3.

69 Cf. Ch. III, 2.

70 Cf. Ch. III, 9.

71 Cf. Ch. V, 2.

72 Cf. Chs V, VIII.

73 Cf. Ch. III, 3.

74 E.g. *Enz.* II. 286, 305.

75 E.g. *Enz.* I. 38Z, 60, 99Z. Hegel even has doubts abou the hypothesis that lightning is electricity, mainly for the reason that moisture dispels the electricity produced in the laboratory, while lightning occurs in moist air (*Enz.* II. 286Z). He does not doubt, however, that it is the expression of a *force*.

76 Hegel attributes this expression to Schelling. For references to *similar* expressions in Schelling's writings, see *Logic* (Wallace, 1892), pp. 392 f.

77 Cf. Chs IX, X.

78 Hegel would probably disagree with this account of laws. Cf. *PG* pp. 114 ff., M. pp. 90 ff.

79 Cf. Ch. III, 1.

80 Cf. Ch. X, 1.

81 Cf. Ch. X.

82 Cf. Ch. 1, 2.

83 Cf. *Enz.* I. 24Z. 1, quoted on p. 81.

84 Cf. Ch. IX, 4.

85 Poíncaré, 1914, pp. 27 f.

86 Cf. Ch. X, 4.

IV   PHILOSOPHY AND THE FALL OF MAN

1 Cf. Ch. VI.

2 But cf. Ch. VI.

3 Cf. Ch. V.

4 Cf. Ch. V, 5.

5 Cf. Ch. VIII, 7.

6 E.g. *Enz.* I. 10. Cf. Ch. V, 10.

7 Cf. *VPR* II. pp. 257 ff., S.S. III. pp. 53 ff.

8 Cf. *Enz.* III. 425; *PG* pp. 133 ff., 175 ff., M. pp. 104 ff., 139 ff.

9 Cf. Elster, 1978, pp. 60 ff.

10 E.g. *VGP* I. pp. 39 ff., L. pp. 75 ff., H. I. pp. 20 ff.

11 Cf. Ch. X, 11.

12 *VGP loc. cit.* Cf. *PR* 57.

13 Cf. Ch. V, 4, Ch. VIII, 8.
14 The word 'perception' (*Wahrnehmung*) is used by Hegel in at least two ways. In the *Phenomenology* and elsewhere (e.g. *Enz.* III. 420 f.), it refers to that 'form of consciousness' in which the world is regarded as a collection of things with properties. At e.g. *Enz.* I. 39, by contrast, it seems to refer to the mere reception of sensory material, independently of any conceptualization of it. Perception in this sense has more in common with sense-certainty than with perception in the *Phenomenology*. This ambiguity is similar to the ambiguity in Hegel's use of the word 'experience' (cf. Ch. III, 1). It may be connected with deeper confusions in his notion of what it is to think (about) phenomena (cf. Ch. III, 1, Ch. VII, 15, 20).
15 *Enz.* I. 26 ff. Cf. *Enz.* I. 24Z. 3 on '*Reflexion*'.
16 Cf. Ch. VI.
17 *Enz.* I. 28, 48. Cf. Ch. III, 2, Ch. VI.
18 Cf. Inwood, forthcoming.
19 Cf. Ch. X, 14.
20 Cf. *Enz.* II. 249Z, 252Z, 339Z.
21 E.g. *VA* II. pp. 33 ff., K. I. pp. 443 ff.
22 Chs VII, XI.
23 Cf. Ch. III, 7.
24 Cf. Ch. VIII.
25 The body is not, however, a perfectly adequate expression of the mind. This position is reserved for language (*Enz.* III. 411).
26 E.g. *PG* pp. 168 f., M. pp. 135 f.
27 Cf. Ch. X, 11.
28 E.g. *Enz.* III. 389, 410Z; *PG* pp. 227 ff., M. pp. 185 ff. Cf. Ch. VIII, 17.
29 Cf. Ch. IX.
30 Cf. Ch. XI, 6.
31 E.g. *Enz.* I. 23, 24Z. 2. Cf. Ch. XI, 4.
32 Cf. Ch. XI, 4, 6.
33 Cf. Ch. XI, 10.
34 Cf. Ch. III, 6.
35 Cf. Ch. XI, 10.
36 Cf. Ch. IX, 1.
37 Walsh, 1947, pp. 66 ff. suggests three roles that the philosophy of nature might perform : (a) 'the analysis and clarification of the concepts used by natural scientists'; (b) 'setting out the *a priori* presuppositions of natural science' with perhaps 'some criticism or justification of these'; (c) 'producing from its own resources necessary truths about the natural world.' His conclusion is that Hegel 'would like, if he could', to engage in (c), but 'his good sense holds him back at the last moment and he falls into a hybrid theory whose basis and justification are far from obvious.'
38 Cf. Ch. II, 1, VII, 24.
39 Cf. Ch. III.
40 Cf. Ch. XI, 11.
41 From a piece entitled 'On the essence of philosophical criticism in general and its relation to the present state of philosophy in particular.' This was

written as an introduction to, and published in the first issue of, a journal under the joint editorship of Hegel and Schelling: *Kritisches Journal der Philosophie,* Bd. I, Stück I, 1802.

42 But cf. Ch. V, 4, Ch. VIII, 8.

43 Cf. Chs V, VIII.

V   KNOWLEDGE AND ASSUMPTIONS

1 Cf. Chisholm, 1973; Chisholm, 1977, pp. 119 ff.

2 Cf. Chisholm, 1977, pp. 62 ff.

3 Cf. Ch. III, 6.

4 Cf. *KdrV* A28 f., B44 f.

5 On these and other problems, see Hegel's discussion of the ancient sceptics: *VGP* II. pp. 358 ff., H. II. pp. 328 ff.

6 Cf. *KdrV* Axiff.

7 In this context Hegel often says that to attempt 'to know before one knows' is as absurd as trying to 'learn to swim before one ventures into the water' (*Enz.* I. 10). But it is not logically impossible to learn to swim before entering water.

8 *KdrV* A426 f., B 454 f. Cf. Ch. VI, 10.

9 *KdrV* A49, B66.

10 Cf. Ch. VI, 1.

11 Cf. Ch. X, 12.

12 *KdrV* A46 ff., B64 ff. on space and time.

13 Cf. Ch. IX.

14 Cf. Ch. X, 2.

15 Cf. Ch. V, 9. This may be the point of the words '*doch etwas Reelles*', though this may rather be a challenge to Kant's view that our knowledge, if the assumption held good, would still be knowledge and not mere illusion (cf. *WL* I. p. 39, M. p. 46).

16 Cf. Walsh, 1947, pp. 10 f.

17 Cf. Ch. VI, 9.

18 E.g. *Enz.* I. 124; *WL* II. pp. 129 ff., 135 f., M. pp. 484 ff., 489 f. Cf. *PG* pp. 89 ff., M. pp. 67 ff.

19 E.g. *PG* pp. 89 ff., M. pp. 67 ff.; *WL* II. pp. 129 ff., M. pp. 484 ff.; *Enz.* I. 36, 124 ff. Cf. Ch. II, 3.

20 Cf. Ch. III, 6.

21 Cf. Ch. V, 5.

22 Cf. Ch. XI, 11.

23 But cf. Ch. IX.

24 Cf. Ch. VIII.

25 Cf. *Enz.* I. 116 ff.; *WL* II. pp. 46 ff., M. pp. 417 ff. on the notion of difference.

26 Cf. Ch. IX, 8.

27 But cf. Ch. IX, 3.

28 For similar arguments against things-in-themselves, see Rorty, 1972, and, for an alternative view, Williams, 1978, pp. 64 ff. Hegel's position is

ultimately equivocal, but Rorty is unjustifiably confident that his is an opponent rather than an ally.

29 Cf. Chs VI, VIII.
30 Cf. Carnap, 1950, and Solomon, 1974.
31 Cf. Ch. VIII, 23.
32 Cf. Ch. IV, 5.
33 Much of what Hegel says suggests that he had in mind the fact that a form of consciousness characteristically involves a *substantial* account of what things are in fact like, as well as an account of how they appear to us. One might hold, for example, that while objects *appear* to us as coloured, smelly, etc., they consist, in *reality,* of colourless, odourless, etc. atoms. Various problems, epistemological and otherwise, might arise from the attempt to combine both accounts: see e.g. Ryle, 1954, pp. 68 ff.; Russell, 1962, p. 13 (quoted Ch. VII, 21); Collingwood, 1965, p. 103 (quoted Ch. V, n. 83). The substantial conception of (our beliefs about) the object as it is in reality is, of course, distinct from the empty conception of the object as it is in itself (apart from *all* our beliefs about it); Hegel may, however, have conflated the two: cf. Ch. X, 6. But for a different account of Hegel's arguments, see Taylor, 1975, pp. 127 ff.
34 E.g. *WL* I. p. 35, M. p. 43. Cf. Ch. III, 7.
35 Cf. Ch. VIII.
36 E.g. *Enz.* I. 33 on pre-Kantian metaphysics; 42 on Kant. Cf. Ch. I, 5.
37 E.g. *Enz.* I. 28. Cf. Ch. VI.
38 Cf. Ch. VIII.
39 Cf. Ch. VIII, 10.
40 E.g. *PG* pp. 35 ff., M. pp. 24 ff.; *WL* II. pp. 526 ff., M. pp. 806 ff. Cf. Ch. VII.
41 Cf. Ch. XI, 11.
42 Cf. Ch. I, 5.
43 Cf. *Enz.* I. 78, 81, 82.
44 There are familiar complications in cases where the subject-term refers to a non-existent entity, as in 'Pegasus is white', or where the subject could not have any of the range of properties, one of which is ascribed to it, as in 'The note B is red.' But these are not relevant here. Cf. Ch. VI, n. 85.
45. Cf. Ch. IV, 2.
46 *Enz.* I. 11. Cf. Ch. VIII, 9.
47 Cf. Ch. IV, 3, Ch. VIII, 8.
48 According to Copi, 1971, p. 107, the idea was originated by Russell:

> These difficulties suggest to my mind some such possibility as this: that every language has, as Mr. Wittgenstein says, a structure concerning which, *in the language,* nothing can be said, but that there may be another language dealing with the structure of the first language, and having itself a new structure, and that to this hierarchy of languages there may be no limit (Russell, 1922, p. 23, quoted by Copi, *loc. cit.*).

The idea has often been attributed to Hegel, of course in an implicit form: see e.g. Findlay, 1963; Solomon, 1975; Inwood, 1977.

49   Cf. Ch. V, 10.

50   Cf. Ch. V, 5.

51   Cf. e.g. Martin, 1958, pp. 62 ff.

52   Such scepticism was expressed by G. E. Schulze, in his *Kritik der theoretischen Philosophie* (Hamburg, Bohn, 1801). This book was reviewed at length by Hegel in the *Kritisches Journal der Philosophie*, Bd. I, Stück 2, 1802, in a piece entitled 'Relation of scepticism to philosophy. Account of its different modifications and comparison of the most recent with ancient scepticism' (*JS*, 1801-7, pp. 213 ff.).

53   Cf. Ch. V, 1.

54   *KdrV* A542 ff., B 570 ff.

55   *KdrV* A470 f., B498 f.

56   *Enz.* I. 60. Cf. Ch. IX, 3, Ch. XI, 4.

57   E.g. *Enz.* I. 71. Cf. Ch. VII, 5.

58   Cf. Ch. IX, 4, esp. pp. 374 f.

59   Cf. Solomon, 1974, p. 280, n. 7:

> The best definition I know of '*aufheben*' has been preferred by the hardly Hegelian philosopher Frank Ramsey in his *Foundations of Mathematics* (pp. 115-16): 'the truth lies not in one of the two disputed views but in some third possibility which has not yet been thought of, which we can discover by rejecting something assumed as obvious by both the discussants.

This represents a part, but not the whole, of what Hegel has in mind. If a position is to be shown to be intrinsically superior to one or more others, we cannot rely on the contingent historical fact that what is *implicitly* assumed by the latter is *explicitly* denied by the former. On '*aufheben*', cf. Ch. VIII, n. 42.

60   Cf. Ch. VI, 1.

61   Cf *VGP* I. pp. 284 ff., 319 ff., S.S. I. pp. 249 ff., 278 ff.; *WL* I. pp. 84 f., M. pp. 83 f. On Parmenides and Heraclitus, see also Barnes, 1979, vol. I. pp. 155 ff. and 57 ff. On Hegel and Heraclitus, see Saintillan, 1974, and, on Hegel and the Greek beginnings of philosophy, Ramnoux, 1974. On Hegel's history of philosophy in general, see Walsh, 1965.

62   Cf. Ch. VI, 7, on propositions and concepts.

63   Cf. Ch. VIII, 10. In any case, Hegel seems not to have identified a philosophy of nothing.

64   Even in the case considered, there is the difficulty that the modern consensus seems to be that Heraclitus preceded Parmenides: Barnes, 1979, vol. I. pp. 155, 311.

65   Cf. Ch. V, 4.

66   Cf. Ch. XI, 6.

67   The views ascribed to Hegel in this section are similar to, and perhaps influenced by, some doctrines of Aristotle: (i) Aristotle believed that the views held on any given topic by all, most, or especially distinguished people were unlikely to be wholly incorrect. The true account, therefore,

will probably contain something of each of them. His discussion of incontinence, for example, begins as follows:

> Our proper course with this subject as with others will be to present the various views about it (τιθέντας τὰ φαινόμενα), and then, after first reviewing the difficulties they involve, finally to establish if possible all or, if not all, the greater part and the most important of the opinions (τὰ ἔνδοξα) generally held with respect of these states of mind; since if the discrepancies can be solved, and a residuum of current opinion left standing, the true view will have been sufficiently established (δεδειγμένον ἂν εἴη ἱκανῶς) (*Nicomachean Ethics*, VII. 1, 1145b 2 ff.).

This procedure is not confined to ethical subjects. His *Metaphysics* begins, for example, with an account and criticism of the views of his predecessors concerning the causes of things, and this is motivated by a similar desire to confirm Aristotle's own, more comprehensive, account (*Met.* A). For discussion of this with special reference to Aristotle's *Physics*, see Owen, 1961. (ii) Aristotle also holds that some types of entity are such that their species are not co-ordinate with one another but form an ascending series or hierarchy. This is true, for example, of the soul or ψυχή, the principle of life. The three species of soul – the plant-soul, the animal-soul and the human soul – form such a series because the plant soul involves, or consists in, only the capacity for nutrition and growth; the animal-soul involves *both* this capacity *and* the capacity of perception; the human soul involves *both* these preceding capacities *and* the capacity for thought. There are additional refinements within this hierarchy, but the general idea is that any member of the series presupposes its predecessors, but can exist independently of its successors (*De Anima*, II. 3, 414b 20 ff.). Aristotle believes this to be true not only of souls, but also of rectilinear figures (*loc. cit*), numbers (*Metaphysics*, 999a 6 ff.), political constitutions (*Politics*, 1275a 35 ff.) and categories of being (*Nicomachean Ethics*, 1096a 17 ff.). In such cases, he argues, the search for a definition which gives the common features of all the members of the series is problematic:

> For this reason it is foolish to seek both in these cases and in others for a common definition (τὸν κοινὸν λόγον), which will be a definition peculiar to no actually existing thing and will not correspond to the proper indivisible species, to the neglect of one which will (*De Anima*, II. 3, 414 b 25 ff.).

The idea behind this difficult passage may be that what is common to *all* the members of the series is the first member of it, but to give an account of this alone will tell us nothing about its successors. For further discussion of this doctrine, see Wilson, 1904; Lloyd, 1962. The doctrine is commended by Hegel in his account of Aristotle's psychology (*VGP* II. pp. 203 f., H. II. pp. 185 f.), and he attempts to draw from it a general lesson about the nature of the universal. There is, however, some confusion over what the universal is. The candidates are:

(a) What is common to all the terms of the series, expressed in a general definition which fits no single one of the terms (Hegel approves of Aristotle's rejection of the search for such a universal.)

(b) the first term of the series, e.g. the vegetable or nutritive soul

(c) the final term of the series which presupposes or embraces all the rest.

It looks as if Hegel is conflating (a) and (b), believing, perhaps, that the first term of the series cannot exist on its own but must develop into higher ones. He clearly wants to say that the proper universal is (c), just as the universal philosophy is the final, all-embracing one, not the simplest one. But there is no sign that Aristotle had either of these points in mind. It should be added that Aristotle did not combine these two doctrines in the way that Hegel does. He does not seem to regard his own philosophy as the culmination of a series of philosophies, related to earlier members of the series as the human soul is related to plant- and animal-souls. For further discussion of Hegel's relationship to Aristotle, see Stace, 1924, pp. 18 ff.; Mure, 1940; Hartmann, 1957; Aubenque, 1974.

68 Cf. Ch. V, 2.
69 Cf. Ch. I, 5.
70 Cf. Martin, 1958, pp. 70 ff.
71 Cf. Martin, 1958, pp. 99 ff.; Tarski, 1944.
72 Cf. Ch. V, 4.
73 Cf. Ch. III, 5.
74 Blanché, 1962, p. 27.
75 Blanché, 1962, pp. 61 ff.
76 Cf. Ch. V, 4.
77 E.g. Plato, *Republic*, V. 476A ff. Cf. *VGP* II. pp. 37 ff., H. II. pp. 27 ff. On Hegel's relationship to Plato in general, see Stace, 1924, pp. 7 ff.; Delhomme, 1974.
78 Cf. Ch. V, 2.
79 Cf. Ch. V, 1.
80 Cf. Ch. VIII, 2.
81 *Ethics*, I. Prop. XXXI.
82 Cf. Ch. VII, 12. On Hegel's relationship to Spinoza, see McMinn, 1959-60; Janicaud, 1970; Macherey, 1979. On the position of Spinoza in German philosophy, see Jacobi, *Über die Lehre des Spinoza*; Herder, *Gott*; Burkhardt, 1940, pp. 28 ff.; Copleston, 1946.
83 Cf. Collingwood, 1965, p. 103: 'man [is] regarded by Galileo as transcending nature; and rightly, because if nature consists of mere quantity its apparent qualitative aspects must be conferred on it from outside, namely by the human mind as transcending it.'
84 Cf. Williams, 1978, pp. 64 f.
85 L. Tieck, *Der gestiefelte Kater* (Puss-in-Boots), 1797, and *Die verkehrte Welt*, 1797; Diderot, *Jacques le fataliste et son maître*, 1773, published 1796.
86 Spinoza draws a similar distinction between two types, or two conceptions, of infinity, the infinity of the intellect and that of the imagination:

Ethics, I, Note to Prop. XV, and Letter XXIX (Elwes, 1955, vol. II, pp. 317 ff.). The infinity of the intellect is, like Hegel's true infinity, the favoured variety. Hegel refers to this distinction with approval (e.g. *VGP* III. pp. 170 ff., H. III. pp. 261 ff.). But Spinoza's distinction is not obviously the same as his own. On Hegel's conception of infinity, see further Ch. IX, 3.

87 Cf. Popper, 1963a, p. 178:

> [Kant] was concerned with the knotty problem . . . of the finitude or infinity of the universe, with respect to both space and time. As far as space is concerned a fascinating solution has been suggested since, by Einstein, in the form of a world which is both finite and without limits.

Hegel did not of course apply his idea to space, his reflections on which are for the most part disappointing: cf. Ch. VI, 1, Ch. IX, 3.

88 Cf. Ch. VIII, 16.
89 Cf. Ch. V, 3.
90 Cf. Ch. IV, 5.
91 Cf. Ch. VI, 7; Ch. VIII.
92 Cf. Ch. VII, 14.
93 Cf. Ch. VIII, 4.
94 Cf. Ch. VIII, 7.
95 But cf. Ch. VIII, 17.
96 Cf. Passmore, 1961, pp. 19 ff. On Hegel's arguments against bad infinity, the comment of Royce, 1959, First Series, p. 508 n. 1 — 'There is a certain question-begging involved in condemning a process because of one's subjective sense of fatigue' — is not altogether unfair.
97 Cf. Ch. VIII, 18.
98 For a statement, and rejection, of the view that there is no such thing as 'epistemological order', see e.g. Russell in Schilpp, 1963, vol. II. pp. 710 ff.
99 Cf. Ch. V, 2, Ch. IX, 3.

VI INFINITE OBJECTS AND FINITE COGNITION

1 Cf. Ch. III, 5.
2 *VBDG* V in *VPR* II. pp. 378 ff., S.S. III. pp. 188 ff.; *Enz.* I. 19Z. 1. Cf. Ch. IV.
3 Cf. Ch. IV, 5.
4 Cf. Ch. V, 10.
5 But cf. Ch. VIII.
6 The use of this term as a substantive is at least as old as Nicholas of Cusa (1401-64): e.g. *De Docta Ignorantia* II, 9. It is a close relative of Kant's 'Unconditioned' (*das Unbedingte*): e.g. *KdrV* BXX. For further references, see *Logic* (Wallace, 1892), p. 410 and Hoffmeister, 1955, pp. 6 f.
7 Cf. Ch. VII.
8 Cf. Ch. V, 1.
9 *VBDG* V in *VPR* II. pp. 381 ff., S.S. III. pp. 192 ff. Cf. Ch. VII, 4.

10 *Enz.* I. 36, 163 ff.; *WL* II. pp. 273 ff., M. pp. 600 ff.
11 Cf. Ch. III, 5.
12 Cf. Ch. VI, 3.
13 Cf. Ch. VII.
14 Hegel prefers the term *'Geist'* ('mind' or 'spirit') to *'Seele'* ('soul'), in part because the latter term is associated with the conception of the soul as a thing (e.g. *Enz.* I. 47, *'Seelending'*). In his *Philosophy of Mind*, however, the *Seele* is distinguished from the *Geist* as a sort of middle-term between the body and the mind; it is what makes the body alive, and thus has more in common with the Aristotelian than with the Cartesian soul (e.g. *Enz.* I. 34Z, III. 388 ff.).
15 Cf. Ch. II, 2. Hegel claims that this expression, *'absolute Aktuosität'*, was applied by the scholastics to God. For references, see *Logic* (Wallace, 1892), pp. 396 f.
16 Cf. Ch. VII, 8, Ch. X, 13.
17 Cf. Ch. II.
18 Cf. Ch. IX, 2.
19 Cf. Ch. VII, 6.
20 Cf. Ch. IX.
21 Aristotle held that because the intellect is capable of thinking of or about anything, it cannot have any determinate character of its own: *De Anima,* III. 4. Hegel discusses this doctrine at *VGP* II. pp. 212 f., H. II. pp. 194 f.
22 Cf. Ch. II.
23 *Enz.* I. 145 ff.; *WL* II. pp. 202 ff., M. pp. 542 ff.
24 Cf. Ch. VIII.
25 Cf. *Enz.* I. 94Z; *WL* I. pp. 166 ff., 264 ff., M. pp. 150 ff., 228 ff.
26 Cf. Ch. VIII, 8, Ch. IX, 4.
27 A similar mistake seems to be involved in Hegel's remark, in the course of a discussion of the distinction between clear and confused (*dunkle*) concepts, that we cannot say clearly what a confused concept is, for it would in that case be a clear and not a confused concept. We cannot, that is, form a clear concept of a confused concept or a clear idea of confusion (*WL* II. p. 290, M. p. 613).
28 Cf. Ch. VI, 5.
29 Cf. *WL* I. pp. 271 ff., M. pp. 234 ff.; *Enz.* I. 94Z. The infinity in question is bad infinity: cf. Ch. V, n. 87.
30 *VBDG* XIV in *VPR* II. pp. 470 ff., S.S. III. pp. 293 ff.
31 Cf. Ch. VII.
32 Cf. Ch. V, 5.
33 Cf. Ch. VII, 6.
34 Cf. Chs X, XI.
35 Cf. Ch. VIII, 13.
36 Proudhon, *Qu'est-ce que la propriété?* (1840). His short answer to this question was that property is theft.
37 Cf. Ch. XI, 6.
38 Cf. Chs IX, X.
39 Hegel's views seem to contrast, in this respect, with those of the later Wittgenstein as expounded by e.g. Hudson, 1968, pp. 42 ff. '

40 Cf. Chs VII, VIII.
41 Cf. Ch. V, 10.
42 But cf. Chs VII, IX.
43 E.g. *WL* I. p. 50, M. p. 54.
44 See Herder, *Gott.*
45 Cf. Solomon, 1975; Inwood, 1977.
46 But cf. Ch. X, 10.
47 Cf. Ch. VII, 22.
48 *Enz.* I. 153 ff.; *WL* II. pp. 222 ff., M. pp. 558 ff.
49 Cf. Ch. VIII, 7.
50 Cf. Ch. VIII.
51 Cf. Ch. VIII, 9.
52 Cf. Ch. VIII, 22, Ch. X, 10.
53 Cf. Ch. VI, 1.
54 Cf. Ch. VI, 3.
55 Cf. Ch. IX, 3.
56 Cf. Ch. VI, 1.
57 Spinoza, *Ethics* II. Prop. VII. Cf. Ch. X, 13.
58 Hegel attributes this discovery to J. F. Blumenbach (1752–1840): *WL* II. p. 516, M. p. 798. On Blumenbach, see further Petry, 1970, vol. III. pp. 348 ff.
59 Cf. *PG* p. 187, M. p. 149; *Enz.* III. 246Z; *VBDG* II. in *VPR* II. pp. 360 f., S.S. III. pp. 168 f.
60 Cf. *Enz.* I. 89 ff.; *WL* I. pp. 115 ff., M. pp. 109 ff.
61 E.g. Leibniz, *Discourse on Metaphysics,* VIII (Wiener, 1951, pp. 299 f.).
62 Cf. Ch. VIII, 15.
63 Cf. Ch. VIII, 13.
64 Cf. Ch. VI, 3. On Hegel's criticisms of the judgment (*Urteil*) and the proposition (*Satz*), see also Aquila, 1973.
65 Cf. Ch. VI, 2.
66 Cf. Ch. X, 8.
67 Cf. Ch. VI, 1, 2.
68 Cf. Ch. II, 3.
69 Cf. Ch. VI, 1, 8.
70 Cf. Ch. II, 3, Ch. VII, 12.
71 Cf. Ch. II, 2, VI, 1.
72 E.g. *Enz.* I. 33, where Hegel says that if concepts are introduced unsystematically, then 'their more precise *content* can only be based on *conception*.' Cf. Ch. I, 6.
73 This addition contains a characteristic panegyric to the free thinking of ancient Greece in contrast to the orthodoxy-ridden thinking of modernity: see further Gray, 1969.
74 Cf. Ch. V, 7.
75 Cf. *Enz.* I. 87, 99, 115, 160Z, 181, 213.
76 Ch. VI, 6.
77 Cf. Ch. X, 13.
78 E.g. *Enz.* I. 33. Cf. Ch. VI, 1.
79 Cf. Ch. VIII, 20.

80 Cf. Ch. VIII, 8.
81 Cf. Chs I, VIII.
82 Cf. Ch. IV, 3.
83 Cf. *KdrV* A341 ff., B399 ff.
84 Cf. Ch. III, 3, Ch. VII, 15.
85 Cf. Ch. VI, 1. Hegel's discussion of 'infinite' judgments is relevant here. Examples of infinite judgments are 'The mind is not red' and 'The mind is not an elephant.' They differ from ordinary negative judgments like 'This rose is not red' or 'Fido is not an elephant' in that the rose, unlike the mind, is of some other colour and Fido, unlike the mind, is an animal of some other type (*Enz.* I. 173; *WL* II. pp. 324 ff., M. pp. 641 ff.). Hegel does not however introduce this idea in the present context. ('Infinite' judgments have little to do, of course, with infinity in Hegel's usual sense. He may believe that there is a connection, however, and this would explain why he gives examples which have 'the mind' as their subject-term rather than, say, 'This rose is not ambitious.'
86 Cf. Chs VIII, X.
87 From this point of view, a more appropriate criticism of Kant's views about the soul than that which Hegel in fact advances would be that the ascription of categorical activity to the self is inconsistent with the limits which Kant places on our knowledge of it, that it is at least paradoxical to claim both that the ego imposes certain categories on our sensory data and that it is entirely unknowable: cf. Ch. V, 8.
88 Cf. Ch. VI, 1.
89 Cf. Ch. VII.
90 Cf. Ch. VI, 1.

VII   FAITH, PROOFS AND INFINITY

1 *VBDG.*
2 J. J. Lalande (1732-1807), a French astronomer. See *Logic* (Wallace, 1892), p. 407.
3 The accuracy of Hegel's account in detail is not relevant to our purposes. Hegel refers especially to Jacobi's *Über die Lehre des Spinoza*, 2nd ed., 1789, Appendix VII (*Jacobi Werke*, IV, 2, pp. 125 ff.). For further references to Jacobi's works, see *Logic* (Wallace, 1892), pp. 406 ff. For Hegel's attitude to Jacobi, see also *Glauben and Wissen* (*JS*, 1801-7, pp. 287 ff., esp. 333 ff.); Hegel's review of the third volume of Jacobi's works (*NHS*, 1808-17, pp. 429 ff.); and *VGP* III. pp. 315 ff., H. III. pp. 410 ff. Cf. Colletti, 1979, pp. 139 ff. and also Anstett, 1946.
4 Cf. Ch. III, 5.
5 But cf. Ch. III, 4.
6 Cf. Ch. VII, 18.
7 Cf. Ch. I, 6.
8 Cf. *VBDG* IV, V.
9 *Enz.* I. 7. Cf. Ch. III, 2.
10 Cf. Ch. VII, 22.
11 *Über die Lehre des Spinoza* (*Jacobi Werke*, IV, 1, p. 211).

12 The *Cogito* is presented in Descartes, *Discourse on Method,* IV, and *Meditations on First Philosophy,* II. The same works also provide a version of the ontological argument for the existence of God (*Discourse,* IV; *Meditations,* III). But Descartes does not connect the two arguments in the way that Hegel does; he does not suggest, that is, that they are one and the same argument.

13 Ch. VI, 3. But cf. Ch. X, 10.

14 Cf. *VGP* III. pp. 130 ff., H. III. pp. 227 ff., where both arguments are said to establish the 'unity of thinking and being'.

15 Cf. Ch. VIII, 14.

16 But cf. Ch. VIII, 8, on the *Cogito.*

17 Cf. Ch. X, 1.

18 Cf. Ch. VII, 6.

19 Cf. Ch. V, 2.

20 Cf. Cicero, *De Natura Deorum,* i. 16, ii. 4, '*De quo autem omnium natura consentit, id verum esse necesse est.*' These and other passages are cited by Wallace, 1892, p. 408 (*Logic*).

21 But cf. Ch. VII, 15.

22 Voltaire, *Philosophical Dictionary,* p. 239.

23 Cf. Geach, 1969.

24 Cf. Ch. II, 3.

25 Cf. Ch. VI, 2.

26 Cf. *PR* 139 on subjectivism in ethics; 217 f. on property.

27 Cf. Ch. VI, 1.

28 Cf. Ch. VII, 23.

29 Cf. Ch. VII, 19.

30 Cf. Ch. VII, 3.

31 Cf. Ch. VII, 18.

32 Cf. Ch. VI, 1.

33 Cf. Ch. VII, 18.

34 Cf. Ch. VII, 6.

35 Cf. Ch. I, 3.

36 Cf. Ch. III, 2.

37 Cf. Bennett, 1974, pp. 66 ff.

38 Cf. Ch. V, 7.

39 Cf. Ch. VII, 18.

40 Cf. Ch. V, 5.

41 *Enz.* III. 572 ff.

42 Cf. Ch. V, 5.

43 Cf. Ch. III, 7.

44 Cf. Ch. VII, 6.

45 Cf. Ch. II, 1.

46 Cf. *PR* 147, where naïve faith is distinguished from reflective faith, the latter being a response to sceptical doubts which have not arisen for the former.

47 Kant has a similar conception of the proofs: e.g. *KdU, Allgemeine Anmerkung zur Teleologie* (Vorländer, ed., 1924, pp. 349 ff.; Meredith, 1952, Part II, pp. 150 ff.).

48 Cf. Ch. VI, 7.

49 Cf. Ch. VII, 22.

50 Cf. Ch. II, 3.

51 Cf. Ch. VI, 3.

52 Cf. Ch. VII, 4.

53 Cf. Ch. V, 8.

54 *Ethics* I, Defn. IV, The Latin original reads as follows: '*Per attributum intelligo id, quod intellectus de substantia percipit tanquam eiusdem essentiam constituens.*'

55 *Ethics*, I. Prop. XXXI.

56 *Ethics*, I. Prop. XI; Letter LXVI (Elwes, 1955, vol. II. pp. 398 ff.).

57 Cf. Ch. VII, 4.

58 *Monadology*, 41 (Wiener, 1951, p. 541).

59 *Monadology*, 45 (Wiener, 1951, pp. 541 f.).

60 E.g. *Enz.* I. 91Z; *WL* II. p. 195, M. p. 536. The dictum is invariably quoted in this form by Hegel and also by Marx, who speaks of 'Spinoza's proposition: Determination in negation (*Bestimmung ist Verneinung*)' (*Das Kapital*, p. 549, n. 25 (Paul and Paul, 1930, vol. II. p. 656, n.1)). The closest approximation to it occurs in Letter L (Elwes, 1955, vol. II. p. 370): 'As the figure is nothing else than determination, and determination is negation (*figura non aliud quam determinatio et determinatio negatio est*), figure, as has been said, can be nothing but negation.' Cf. further Ch. IX, 9.

61 'Pure light is pure darkness.'

62 *Theodicy*, Preface, quoted by Wallace, 1892, pp. 397 f. (*Logic*).

63 Cf. Hepburn, 1963, p. 42:

> If 'singling out', 'identifying' God is a logically necessary task, it is also one that can easily be represented as blasphemous. It may be taken to imply that God belongs among finite, limited entities. For if he can be singled out, God can hardly be infinite in every possible way. There must exist that from which he is being singled out − over against him, as it were.

64 Cf. Ch. VII, 17.

65 Cf. Ch. VI, 7.

66 Cf. Ch. V, 4.

67 Cf. *VPR* II. pp. 421 ff., S.S. III. pp. 237 ff.

68 Cf. *VPR* II. pp. 501 ff., S.S. III. pp. 328 ff.

69 Much of what Hegel says about *philosophical* proofs is reminiscent of what Wittgenstein says about *mathematical* proofs. Wittgenstein says, for example: 'A psychological disadvantage of proofs that construct *propositions* is that they easily make us forget that the *sense* of the result is not to be read off from this by itself, but from the *proof*' (*Remarks on the Foundations of Mathematics*, II. 25). Or again: 'the proof shews me a new connexion, and hence it also gives me a new concept' (*Ibid.* IV. 45). And: 'I once said: "If you want to know what a mathematical proposition says, look at what its proof proves"' (*Ibid.* V. 7). Wittgenstein saw that this involves difficulties: 'ought I to say that the same sense can only

have *one* proof? Or that when a proof is found the sense alters?' (*Ibid.* V. 7) – difficulties to which Hegel believed he had an answer. For an assessment of Wittgenstein's views on this, see Ambrose, 1959, and, more generally, Dummett, 1959; Wright, 1980.

The similarities should not be exaggerated, however. Hegel takes this view only of philosophical proofs; his account of mathematical proofs is one that Wittgenstein would have opposed. More generally, both philosophers stressed that what something means depends on its place, or role, in a system, and this implies that we should interpret Hegel's doctrines in the light of their connections with the rest of his thought and not by comparing them piecemeal with the doctrines of other philosophers.

70 Quoted Ch. III, 3.
71 Cf. Ch. III, 3.
72 Cf. Ch. IV, 1, Ch. VIII, 17.
73 Cf. Ch. V, 3.
74 Cf. Ch. VII, 24.
75 Cf. Ch. VII, 5.
76 Cf. Ch. VII, 24.
77 Cf. Ch. VI.
78 Cf. Ch. X, 13.
79 Cf. Ch. VII, 19.
80 Cf. Ch. X, 3.
81 Cf. Ch. VII, 8.
82 For a good account of the different types of ground or reason, see Schopenhauer, *The Fourfold Root of the Principle of Sufficient Reason.*
83 Cf. Ch. XI, 11.
84 Cf. Ch. III, 7.
85 Cf. Ch. VI, 5.
86 Cf. Ch. VII, 6.
87 Cf. Ch. VII, 12.
88 Cf. Ch. VIII, 17.
89 On the significance and history of these terms, see *Logic* (Wallace, 1892), pp. 400 ff.; Hoffmeister, 1955, pp. 645 f.
90 Cf. Ch. VII, 15.
91 Cf. Ch. X, 2.
92 Cf. Ch. II, 3.
93 Russell, 1962, p. 13.
94 Cf. Chs VIII, IX, X.
95 Cf. Ch. V, 9.
96 Cf. Ch. VII, 24, Ch. VIII, 18, Ch. XI, 13.
97 Cf. Chs VIII, IX.
98 Versions of this argument are to be found in St Anselm (*Proslogion,* II), in Descartes (cf. Ch. VII, n. 2), and in most of Descartes's pre-Kantian successors. On the history of the argument, see Henrich, 1967, esp. pp. 189 ff. on Hegel. For non-Hegelian, and largely critical, discussions of it, see Schelling's Munich lectures of 1827, esp. the first, on Descartes (*Schellings Werke,* V, pp. 84 ff.); and, more recently, Hick and McGill,

1967. Recent attempts to resuscitate the argument by e.g. Plantinga (1974, pp. 197 ff.) have little to do with Hegel's attempt.

99 Cf. *KdrV* A592 ff., B620 ff.

100 Cf. Ch. VII, 2.

101 See, e.g., the first set of objections to Descartes's *Meditations* (Caterus) and his reply (Haldane and Ross, 1931, vol. II. pp. 7 f., 20 f.).

102 *WL* I. pp. 88 ff., M. pp. 86 ff., on 'being'; II. pp. 125 ff., M. pp. 481 ff., on 'existence'; II. pp. 402 ff., M. pp. 705 ff., on 'objectivity'. Cf. Ch. VI, 1.

103 Cf. *WL* II. pp. 245 ff., M. pp. 577 ff.

104 Cf. Ch. VIII, 19.

105 Cf. Ch. VII, 11.

106 Cf. Ch. III, 5.

107 Cf. Ch. IX.

108 *KdrV* A606 ff., B634 ff.

109 Cf. Ch. VIII, 20.

110 Cf. Ch. VIII, 6.

111 Eg. *Enz.* I. 128Z, 163Z.2. Cf. Ch. VIII, 20, Ch. IX, 4, 7.

112 Cf. Ch. VII, 26, Ch. IX, 10, Ch. X.

113 Cf. Ch. VIII, 17.

114 The reference is to no. 286, '*Der Teleolog*', of Goethe's and Schiller's '*Xenien*' (1796-7), a series of 926 epigrams. See further Petry, 1970, vol. I. pp. 293 f.

115 Cf. Ch. VIII, 22.

116 *VPR* II pp. 243 ff., S.S. III. pp. 36 ff. Cf. Ch. VIII, 19.

117 *Enz.* III. 564 ff.

118 Cf. *VPR* II. pp. 533 f., S.S. III. pp. 365 f.

119 Cf. Ch. II, esp. 1.

120 Cf. Ch. II, 4.

121 Cf. Ch. III, 1.

122 Cf. Ch. XI.

123 Cf. Ch. VII, 15.

124 Cf. Ch. VII, 19.

125 *Enz.* III. 413 ff.

126 Cf. Ch. I. 2.

127 Cf. Ch. V, 5.

128 Cf. Ch. III, 4.

129 Cf. *WL* II; *Enz.* I. 112 ff.

130 Cf. Ch. V.

131 Cf. Ch. III, 9.

132 Cf. Ch. X.

133 Cf. Ch. III, 4.

134 Cf. Ch. VII, 12.

135 *Ethics,* I. Prop. XXIX. Cf. Ch. IX, 1.

136 Cf. Ch. VI, 1.

137 Cf. Ch. IV, 4.

138 Cf. Ch. V, 6.

139 Cf. Ch. VII, 24.

140 *KdrV* A348.
141 *Grundlage der gesamten Wissenschaftslehre* (*Fichtes Werke* I. p. 96 n., Heath and Lachs, 1970, p. 97, n. 3.).
142 Cf. *VPR* II. pp. 533 f., S.S. III. pp. 365 f.; *WL* II. pp. 304, 466, M. pp. 625, 758.
143 Cf. Ch. X, 13.
144 For a similar objection to Spinozism, see Kant, *Lectures on Philosophical Theology*: Wood and Clark, 1978, pp. 74 f.
145 Cf. Ch. V, 9, Ch. VIII, 18.
146 Cf. Ch. XI, 13. For a brief summary of Hegel's theological views, and doubts about their orthodoxy, see Meynell, 1964, pp. 122 ff.

VIII LOGIC: THINKING ABOUT THINKING

1 But cf. Ch. XI, 11.
2 Cf. Ch. VIII, 17.
3 Cf. Ch. X, 13.
4 *KdrV* A50 ff., B74 ff.
5 Cf. Ch. VIII, 19.
6 *WL* I. pp. 56 ff., M. pp. 59 ff.; II. pp. 550 ff., M. pp. 825 ff.; *Enz.* I. 6, 14, 15 on the 'idea'; *Enz.* I. 9 on the 'concept'.
7 Cf. Ch. III, 5.
8 Cf. Ch. VI, 3.
9 Cf. Ch. V, 9.
10 Cf. Ch. VI, 1.
11 Cf. *KdrV* B146 f.
12 Cf. Ch. VI, 10.
13 Cf. Ch. V, 2.
14 Cf. Ch. V, 8,; Ch. IX, 3.
15 *KdrV* B135.
16 *KdrV* B145.
17 E.g. *Enz.* I. 55 ff.; *VGP* III. pp. 379 ff., H. III. pp. 472 ff.; *WL* II. pp. 260 ff., 440 ff., M. pp. 588 ff., 737 ff.
18 Cf. Ch. VI, 2, 3.
19 But cf. Ch. VI, 1.
20 Cf. Ch. V, 8.
21 Kant's most extended discussion of the intuitive understanding is at *KdU* 76 ff. For more recent discussion, see Walsh, 1946; Walsh, 1947, pp. 64 ff.
22 Another idea with which Hegel explicitly associates his enterprise is that of the sort of thinking which Aristotle attributes to God or the Prime Mover. God is supposed to 'think himself' or to 'think of thinking' (*Metaphysics,* xii, 7 and 9). Thus, speaking of the absolute idea, Hegel says:

> So far *we* have had the idea in its development through its different stages for our object; but from now on the idea is objective to itself. This is the νόησις νοήσεως which even Aristotle termed the highest form of the idea' (*Enz.* I. 236Z).

The *Encyclopaedia* concludes with a quotation from Aristotle's Metaphysics on this theme (*Enz*. III. 577, quoting *Met*. xii, 7, 1072b 18-30). For discussions of Aristotle's views on this, see *VGP* II. pp. 157 ff., H. II. pp. 143 ff., and, more recently, Norman, 1969; Lloyd, 1970; Lloyd, 1981, pp. 10 ff. On Hegel's Aristotelianism, cf. Ch. V, n. 67. On his ascription of divine activities to human beings, cf. Ch. IV, Ch. VIII, 17, Ch. XI, 13.

23 Cf. Ch. VI, 1.
24 Cf. Ch. IV, 3.
25 Cf. Ch. VII, 24.
26 Cf. Ch. I, 6.
27 Cf. Ch. III, 5.
28 Cf. Ch. X, 14.
29 Cf. *Enz*. I. 14; *WL* I. pp. 19 ff., 35 ff., M. pp. 31 ff., 43 ff.
30 Cf. Ch. V, 9.
31 For some remarks on reflexivity in psychology, see Bannister, 1970, pp. 416 ff.
32 Cf. Ch. VIII, 2.
33 Quoted Ch. V, 7.
34 Quoted Ch. V, 10.
35 Cf. Ch. II, 4.
36 Cf. Ch. V, 2.
37 Cf. Ch. II, 3.
38 Cf. Ch. V, 7.
39 Cf. Ch. VIII, 13.
40 Cf. Ch. V, 3, Ch. VIII, 14.
41 Cf. Ch. V, 10.
42 Cf. Ch. V, 10.
43 '*Aufheben*' is a crucial Hegelian word. Hegel prizes it for its ambiguity: 'By "*aufheben*" we mean firstly "get rid of", "negate", and we say accordingly that a law, a regulation, etc. is "*aufgehoben*". But further "*aufheben*" means also "preserve"' (*Enz*. I. 96Z. Cf. *WL* I. pp. 113 ff., M. pp. 106 ff.). '*Aufheben*' has, however, more than the two meanings which Hegel ascribes to it. It also means, for example, 'raise up' (cf. Hoffmeister, 1955, p. 92). I have generally translated it as 'sublimate', following a suggestion of Kaufmann, 1966, pp. 159, 191 f., but I have sometimes used other expressions, e.g. 'eliminate', where they seemed more appropriate. On the idea of *Aufhebung*, see Ch. V, 5, and esp. n. 59.
44 Cf. Ch. IV, 5.
45 Cf. Ch. VII, 23.
46 Cf. Ch. I, 4, Ch. IX, 10.
47 Cf. Ch. VI, 6.
48 Cf. Ch. I.
49 Cf. Ch. V, Ch. VI, Ch. VIII, 8.
50 Cf. Ch. V, 7.
51 But cf. Ch. VI, 9.
52 Cf. *EGP* pp. 95 f., *VGP* III. pp. 493 ff., H. I. pp. 70 ff.
53 But cf. Gardner, 1958, p. 28, who speaks of a curious tendency among

certain logicians to peer down their noses at logic diagrams as though they were barbaric attempts to picture a structure more appropriately represented by words or notational symbols. One might as well look down upon the graph of a parabola as somehow of a lower status than the algebraic equation that produces it. Clearly, the parabola and its formula are simply two different ways of asserting the same thing . . . . It would be foolish to ask which of the two, considered in itself, is superior to the other.

54 Cf. Ch. I, 7.
55 Cf. Ch. VI, 9.
56 Cf. Ch. II, 3, Ch. IV, 4.
57 E.g. *Ur-sache*, 'cause' or 'original thing' (*WL* II. pp. 223 ff., M. pp. 558 ff.; *Enz.* I. 153); *Ur-teil*, 'judgment' or 'original division' (*Enz.* I. 166. Cf. Ch. VII, 26); and *aufheben* (Cf. Ch. VIII, n. 42).
58 Cf. Ch. VIII, 15.
59 Cf. Ch. II, 4.
60 E.g. *Enz.* I. 104Z. 3; *WL* I. pp. 243 ff., M. pp. 212 ff.
61 J. G. Herder, *Abhandlung über den Ursprung der Sprache*. On Herder's views on language, see Guttenplan, 1975; Taylor, 1975, pp. 13 ff. On Hegel's views about language, see Cook, 1973.
62 E.g. *Enz.* I. 1, 12. Cf. Ch. I, 5.
63 Cf. *Enz.* II. 312 on the magnet; *Enz.* I. 198 on the state and the solar system as each a 'system of three syllogisms'. For further discussion, see Ch. X, 13.
64 *Enz.* I. 181 ff.; *WL* II. pp. 351 ff., M. pp. 664 ff.
65 Cf. Ch. VII.
66 Cf. Ch. VIII, 4.
67 Cf. Ch. V, 10.
68 Cf. Ch. VI, 4.
69 Cf. Ch. IX, 8.
70 Cf. *Enz.* II. 343 ff., esp. 345 and Z on Goethe's *Die Metamorphose der Pflanzen*.
71 Cf. Ch. V, 4.
72 Cf. Ch. V, 10.
73 Cf. Ch. V, 2, 6.
74 Cf. Ch. I, 2.
75 Cf. Ch. V, 2, Ch. VII, 9.
76 Cf. Ch. VI, 1.
77 Cf. Ch. V, 4, Ch. VII, 25.
78 Cf. Ch. VII, 24, Ch. VIII, 3.
79 Cf. Ch. X, 10.
80 Cf. Ch. V, 6.
81 *Enz.* I. 86 ff.; *WL* I. pp. 82 f., M. pp. 82 f. Cf. Ch. VIII, 14.
82 Cf. Ch. VI, 1, 9.
83 Cf. Ch. VIII, 1.
84 Cf. Ch. VI, 4.
85 Cf. Ch. V, 4.

86 Cf. Ch. VIII, 5.
87 Cf. Ch. V, 4.
88 Cf. Ch. VI, 4.
89 A similar, but more interesting, case is given — for a different purpose — by Henle, 1949.
90 Cf. Henle, 1949, p. 278: 'Of course, to show that a statement is ineffable, one must have a broader symbolism in which it can be expressed, but this does not prevent a statement being ineffable with regard to some particular symbolism.'
91 Cf. Ch. X, 13.
92 Cf. Ch. X, 14.
93 Cf. Ch. IV.
94 Hegel attempts to connect this sense of 'speculative' with such expressions as 'matrimonial speculation' and 'commercial speculation' (*Enz*. I. 82Z *Heirats- oder Handelsspekulationen*). In fact it has little to do with such usages, but is derived from the Latin '*speculari*' — to spy out, observe or explore (Cerf, 1977, pp. xi ff.; Hoffmeister, 1955, pp. 570 f.). There is, in Hegel's use of the word, no suggestion of risk or uncertainty. It is perhaps also to be associated with the Latin '*speculum*', a mirror (Reardon, 1977, p. 128, n. 28; Hoffmeister, *loc. cit.*). The notion of a mirror seems to underlie some of Hegel's uses of such words as '*Reflexion*', '*Schein*', and '*scheinen*': Cf. Ch VIII, 17 and n. 150, Ch. X, 2. On light and mirrors, see *Enz.* II. 275 ff., esp. 278 and Z. But most of Hegel's uses of the word 'speculative' seem to involve no special reference to mirrors.
95 Cf. Ch. VII, n. 89.
96 Cf. *Enz*. I. 78; *PG* pp. 68 f., M. p. 51.
97 Cf. Ch. V, 4.
98 Cf. *WL* II. pp. 60 ff., 70 ff., M. pp. 427 ff., 435 ff.
99 Cf. Ch. VIII, 8, 14.
100 Hegel did not use the words 'thesis', 'antithesis' and 'synthesis' to denote the three terms of a triad. Kaufmann, 1960, p. 166 writes: 'The triad of thesis, antithesis, and synthesis is encountered in Kant, Fichte, and Schelling, but mentioned only once in the twenty volumes of Hegel's works (ed. Glockner) — not approvingly but at the end of his critique of Kant.' See also Mueller, 1958.
    It is, however, misleading to say that the triad is not mentioned 'approvingly'. The passage occurs at *VGP* III. p. 385 f., H. III. 477 f.:

> [Kant] has delineated the rhythm of cognition, of the scientific movement, as a universal schema and has everywhere proposed thesis, antithesis, and synthesis, the modes of the mind, through which it is mind, being conscious that it thus distinguishes itself . . . . He has given the aspects of the whole historically; it is a good introduction to philosophy.

    It seems clear that Hegel is endorsing the triplicity of Kant's thought, and objects only to the fact that the terms are introduced 'historically', that is, without establishing the logical connections between them.

Thus, although most of Hegel's triads do not in fact conform to the pattern of thesis–antithesis–synthesis (cf. Kaufmann, 1960, p. 167), it is not obvious that the use of these words misrepresents his intentions.

101 Cf. Ch. VIII, 8.

102 *Enz.* I. 99 ff.; *WL* I. pp. 209 ff., M. pp. 185 ff.

103 On quantity and measure, see Taylor, 1975, pp. 244 ff. Cf. also Haldane, 1927; Doz, 1970.

104 Cf. Ch. VI, 1.

105 Cf. Ch. VI, 4, Ch. X, 10.

106 Cf. Ch. V, n. 67.

107 Cf. Aristotle, *De Generatione Animalium*, 1, 726b 23 ff.: 'for the hand also, or any other part, if without the capability of soul or some other capability, is no hand or part except homonymously.'

108 For a similar account, see Vlastos, 1963.

109 Cf. Ch. X, 10.

110 Cf. Ch. VI, 5.

111 Cf. Ch. X, 13.

112 Cf. Ch. X, 7.

113 Cf. Ch. V, 1.

114 Cf. Ch. X, 13.

115 Cf. Ch. V, 4.

116 *PG* p. 16, M. p. 7; *VGP* I. pp. 39 ff., H. I. pp. 20 ff. Cf. Ch. IV, 3.

117 Cf. Ch. V, 2, 6.

118 Cf. *Enz.* I. 121Z; *WL* II. pp. 105 ff., M. pp. 463 ff.

119 Cf. Ch. VI, 2.

120 Cf. Ch. III, 7, Ch. V, 3.

121 Cf. Ch. X, 13.

122 Cf. Ch. II.

123 Cf. Ch. VII, 24.

124 Cf. Ch. VI, 10 and n. 87.

125 For similar doubts about the propriety of Hegel's introduction of becoming, see McTaggart, 1910, pp. 17 ff.; Taylor, 1975, pp. 232 f.

126 E.g. *WL* II. pp. 222 ff., M. pp. 558 ff.

127 *Ethics*, V. Prop. XXXVI. A similar view is to be found in, or has been read into, Aristotle: See Allan, 1952, pp. 81 ff.

128 For discussion of these passages, see Soll, 1969, pp. 91 ff.; Taylor, 1972; Taylor, 1975, pp. 140 ff.; Soll, 1976.

129 Cf. Chisholm, 1976. But Chisholm believes, in apparent contrast to Hegel, that 'I am able to individuate myself *per se* . . . because I know that I have the property of *being me*' (p. 130).

130 At *Enz.* III. 418, Hegel suggests a revision of the account given in the *Phenomenology*:

> Spatial and temporal individuality, *here* and *now*, as I have determined the object of sensuous consciousness in the *Phenomenology of Mind* . . . belongs strictly to intuition (*Anschauen*). The object is here at first to be taken only in the relationship in which it stands to *consciousness*, namely as something *external* to it, and is not yet to

be determined as external in itself or as asunderness (*Aussersichsein*).

This qualification does not, however, importantly affect the present argument.

131 McTaggart, 1908, argued for the unreality of time on the basis of the egocentricity of the words 'past', 'present' and 'future'. He did not, however, apply the argument to other token-reflexive terms. He believes, for example, in the existence of a plurality of 'spirits': e.g. McTaggart, 1918, pp. 4 ff. For an account of McTaggart's argument and a defence of the restriction of it to time, see Dummett, 1960, and Geach, 1979, pp. 89 ff. Although Hegel's argument is similar, he did not believe time to be unreal in the sense in which McTaggart did: cf. *Enz.* II. 247Z: 257 ff.

132 Cf. Ch. VIII, 17.

133 Cf. Ch. I, 2.

134 Cf. Chs IX, X.

135 At *PG* pp. 85 f., M. pp. 63 f., Hegel considers the device of pointing, but not its use in conjunction with a definite description.

136 Quoted Ch. II, 3.

137 Cf. Ch. X.

138 Cf. Ch. V, 2.

139 Cf. V, 2, Ch. IX, 5.

140 *Enz.* I. 116 ff.; *WL* II. pp. 46 ff., M. pp. 417 ff. Cf. *Enz.* I. 98.

141 Cf. Ch. V, 10, Ch. VIII, 4.

142 Cf. Ch. V, 5, Ch. VII, 24.

143 Cf. Ch. IV, 4.

144 Cf. Ch. II, 4.

145 Cf. Ch. V, 9.

146 Cf. Ch. V, 10, Ch. VIII, 11.

147 Cf. Ch. II, 3.

148 Cf. Ch. V, 9.

149 Cf. Ch. VII, 26.

150 For the acquisition of a third-person perspective on my own visual field, and more generally on myself, I am heavily dependent on other people. This accounts in part for the role assigned to other people in Hegel's discussion of self-consciousness (*PG* pp. 141 ff., M. pp. 104 ff.). Mirrors are also important, and this may be connected with some of his uses of the word '*Reflexion*'. He sometimes compares the ego with light (*Enz.* II. 275Z). Cf. Ch. VIII, n. 94.

151 See further Bennett, 1974, pp. 69 ff.; Williams, 1978, pp. 68 ff., 93 ff., 295 ff.

152 Quoted Ch. II, 3.

153 Cf. Ch. II, n. 33.

154 Cf. Ch. II, 3.

155 Cf. Ch. VI, n. 14.

156 Cf. Williams, 1978, p. 100.

157 Cf. Ch. VIII, 15.

158 Ayer, 1947, pp. 194 f.

159 Cf. Ch. II, 4.
160 Ayer, 1947, p. 195.
161 On Hegel's teleology, see Findlay, 1964.
162 Cf. Ch. VII, 21.
163 Cf. Ch. X.
164 Cf. Ch. VII, 24.
165 Cf. Ch. V, 10.
166 Cf. Ch. VIII, 16.
167 Cf. *VPR* II. pp. 243 ff., S.S. III. pp. 37 ff.; *VBDG* VII in *VPR* II. pp. 395 ff., S.S. III. pp. 207 ff.
168 Cf. Ch. VII, 24.
169 Royce, 1959, First series, p. 504.
170 Cf. Ch. VIII, 16.
171 Cf. Ch. VII, 24.
172 Cf. Ch. VI, 1, Ch. VII, 26.
173 Cf. *PG* pp. 178 f., M. pp. 142 f. on *the* 'category'.
174 Cf. Ch. VIII, 4.
175 Cf. Ch. VIII, 11.
176 Cf. Ch. V, 10, Ch. VIII, 4.
177 Cf. Ch. II.
178 Cf. Ch. IX, 4.
179 Cf. Ch. VIII, 16, Ch. XI, 6.
180 Cf. Ch. VIII, 4.
181 Cf. Ch. IX, 1.
182 Cf. Ch. VI, 3.
183 Cf. Ch. VI, 4, Ch. VIII, 7, 12.
184 Cf. Ch. VII, 24.
185 E.g. *WL* II. p. 83, M. p. 446. Cf. *WL* II. pp. 436 ff., M. pp. 735 ff. Cf. Ch. X, 5.
186 Cf. Ch. VI, 1.
187 Cf. Ch. XI.
188 Cf. Ch. III, 8.
189 *KdrV* A77 ff., B102 ff.
190 Cf. Ch. VIII, 12.
191 Cf. Ch. VI, 5. For a similar view, see Ayers, 1974.
192 Cf. Ch. VI, 3, Ch. VII, 12.
193 Cf. Ch. II, 3.
194 Cf. Ch. VIII, 7, Ch. X, 10.
195 E.g. *WL* I. pp. 243 ff., M. pp. 212 ff. Cf. Ch. VIII, 6.
196 Cf. Ch. VIII, 7, 12.
197 Cf. Ch. VI, 3.
198 Cf. Ch. V, 2.

IX   THOUGHT AND THINGS: THE TRANSITION TO NATURE

1 This seems to be the view of Petry, 1970: 'The subject matter of "Logic" is, therefore, as revisable as the subject matters of "Nature" and "Spirit"'

(p. 43) and: 'The transition from "Logic" to "Nature" is therefore no different from any other transition in the "Encyclopaedia"' (p. 45).
2 Cf. Ch. VIII, 14.
3 Cf. Ch. V, 2.
4 Cf. Ch. VI, 9.
5 Cf. Ch. III, 8.
6 Cf. Ch. III, 4.
7 Cf. Ch. XI, 11.
8 E.g. *Enz.* I. 6, 147Z, 213Z; *PR* 343.
9 *Ethics* I. Prop. XXXIII.
10 Cf. Ch. VII, 25.
11 Cf. Ch. V, 8, Ch. VI, 6, Ch. VII, 12, Ch. IX, 3.
12 Cf. Ch. III, 5.
13 Cf. Ch. VI, 3.
14 Cf. Ch. VIII, 22.
15 Cf. Ch. VI.
16 Stace, 1924, argues that Hegel's admission of an element of contingency in nature 'lends some colour to the suggestion that he was still, in spite of all his assertions to the contrary, infected with the Kantian idea of the unknowable. And this in turn would explain his fumbling over the transition from logic to nature' (p. 308).
17 Cf. Ch. VII, 24.
18 Cf. Ch. V, 9.
19 Cf. Ch. III.
20 Cf. Ch. III, 5.
21 Cf. Ch. III, 3.
22 Cf. Ch. I, 1, Ch. II, 3.
23 Cf. Ch. VII, 24.
24 Cf. Ch. II, 2.
25 Cf. Ch. II, 1.
26 Cf. Ch. III, 8.
27 Cf. Ch. VII, 26.
28 Cf. Hegel's review of some of Krug's works in *Kritisches Journal der Philosophie*, Bd. 1, Stück 1, 1802: '*Wie der gemeine Menschenverstand die Philosophie nehme — dargestellt an den Werken des Herrn Krug*' (*JS*, 1801-7, pp. 188 ff.).
29 Cf. Ch. VIII, 15.
30 Cf. Ch. IX, 7.
31 Cf. Ch. VI, 1.
32 Cf. Ch. V, 10.
33 See Quinton, 1962.
34 Cf. Ch. V, n. 87.
35 *Ethics* I. Defn. IV, Props. X, XXI; II. Prop. I.
36 *Ethics* I. Defn. II.
37 Cf. Ch. V, 2.
38 Spinoza cannot allow that there might be, or might be known to be, two distinct spaces. The uniqueness of substance presumably implies the uniqueness of space, and the close attachment of the mind to a 'mode of

extension' would preclude its successive occupation of distinct spaces: 'The object of the idea constituting the human mind is the body, in other words a certain mode of extension which actually exists, and nothing else' (*Ethics*, II. Prop. XIII).

39 Cf. Ch. IX, 1, 5.
40 Cf. Ch. VI, 5.
41 Cf. Ch. VIII, 15.
42 Cf. Ch. V, 2.
43 Cf. Ch. I.
44 Cf. Ch. VIII, 4.
45 Cf. Ch. VIII, 4.
46 Cf. Ch. VIII, 5.
47 Cf. Ch. II, 3.
48 Cf. Ch. III, 8.
49 Cf. Ch. VIII, 2.
50 Cf. Ch. VI, 5, Ch. VIII, 5.
51 Cf. Ch. XI, 5.
52 Cf. Ch. II.
53 Cf. Ch. VI, 3, Ch. VIII, 23.
54 On the state, see further Ch. XI, 6. Cf. also McTaggart, 1918, pp. 177 ff.
55 Cf. Ch. III, 8.
56 *Ibid.* See also *Enz.* I. 227.
57 *Ibid.*
58 Cf. Ch. IX, 7, Ch. X, 4.
59 Cf. Chs V, VIII.
60 Cf. Strawson, 1954.
61 Cf. Ch. VIII, 10.
62 Cf. Ch. VI, 1, Ch. VIII, 8.
63 Cf. Ch. III, 1.
64 Cf. Ch. II, 1.
65 Cf. Kant, *KdrV* A832, B860: 'By a system I understand the unity of the manifold modes of knowledge under one idea. This idea is the concept provided by reason − of the form of a whole − in so far as the concept determines *a priori* not only the scope of its manifold content but also the positions which the parts occupy relatively to one another.'
66 Cf. Ch. VIII, 19.
67 Cf. Ch. II, 3.
68 Cf. Ch. IX, 3.
69 *First Dialogue between Hylas and Philonous* in Berkeley (1962). See also Williams, 1966.
70 Cf. Ch. III, 3.
71 E.g. Mackie, 1976, p. 53.
72 Cf. Ch. VIII, 14.
73 Cf. Ch. V, 9, Ch. VIII, 18.
74 Cf. Borges, 1964.
75 Cf. Ch. VIII, 19.
76 Cf. Ch. VI, 1, Ch. VIII, 8.
77 Cf. Chs VI, VIII.

78 Cf. Ch. IX, 4.
79 Cf. Ch. IX, 4.
80 Cf. Ch. IX, 1.
81 Wolff, 1963, p. 152 n.
82 Cf. Ch. III, 8, Ch. IX, 1.
83 Cf. Ch. X, 4.
84 Cf. Ch. VIII, 17.
85 Cf. Ch. I, 1.
86 Cf. Ch. II, 3.
87 Cf. Ch. I, 2, Ch. VIII, 15.
88 Cf. Ch. VIII, 15.
89 Cf. Ch. VIII, 15, Ch. IX, 2.
90 Cf. Ch. III, 8, Ch. IX, 4.
91 For a discussion of these concepts, in relation to Aristotle, see Ackrill, 1973.
92 Cf. Ch. X, 6.
93 Cf. Ch. IX, 3, 4.
94 Cf. Ch. I, 7.
95 Cf. Ch. VII, 24.
96 Cf. Ch. VIII, 15.
97 Cf. Ch. VI, 5.
98 For discussion of the inverted world, see Gadamer, 1975; Solomon, 1974; Solomon, 1975; Inwood, 1977.
99 This accounts for Hegel's tendency to speak of the 'like-named' rather than of the 'like'. What are at issue here are not genuine differences and similarities, but differences and similarities in what we *call* things.
100 Cf. Ch. VII, 13, and n. 60. Hegel's ideas on this perhaps have something Gardner, 1970, pp. 182 ff. On opposition in general, see Ogden, 1967.
101 Cf. Ch. VII, 13, and n. 60. Hegel's ideas on this perhaps have something in common with the structuralism of Saussure, Lévi-Strauss and others: see e.g. Culler, 1976, pp. 23 ff.
102 Cf. Ch. VIII, 7.
103 Cf. Ch. VI, 5.
104 Cf. Ch. VI, 5.
105 Cf. Black, 1949.
106 Cf. Ch. VIII, 7. The idea that pure thoughts are 'determined' by relations between them which are themselves thoughts — though not necessarily the same thoughts — might help to explain why Hegel postpones the account of his method to the end of the *Logic*, when, that is, all the relevant thoughts have been considered (*WL* II. pp. 550 ff., M. pp. 825 ff.). Something of this sort underlies the introduction of the concept: cf. Ch. VIII, 24.
107 Cf. Ch. VII, 21, Ch. VIII, 18.
108 *Enz.* I. 87, 88; *WL* I. pp. 82 f., M. p. 82. Cf. Ch. VIII, 14.
109 Cf. Ch. V, 1.

X IDEALISM, APPEARANCE AND CONTRADICTION

1 Cf. Ch. VIII, 17.
2 McTaggart, 1910, p. 9, n. 2, writes: 'Such a perception would, of course, be held by Hegel to be more or less erroneous. Nothing really exists, according to his system, but Spirits. Bodies only appear to exist.' Cf. Ch. VIII, n. 131.
3 E.g. *Enz.* I. 38Z, 62, 127 ff. Cf. Ch. III.
4 Cf. Ch. IX, 6.
5 E.g. *Enz.* I. 42Z, 45Z, 46.
6 Cf. Ch. III, 8.
7 Cf. Ch. VII, 2.
8 Cf. Ch. III, 8, Ch. IX, 1.
9 Cf. Ch. VIII, 2.
10 Cf. Ch. VII, 6.
11 *KdrV* A20, B34. See further Quinton, 1975.
12 *KdrV* B69.
13 E.g. *Enz.* I. 131Z; *WL* II. pp. 19 ff., M. pp. 395 ff.
14 E.g. *Enz.* I. 76 quoted Ch. X, 1.
15 Cf. *Enz.* I. 131 f; *WL* I. pp. 172 ff., M. pp. 154 ff.
16 Cf. Ch. XI, 9.
17 Cf. Ch. IX, 2.
18 Cf. Ch. X, 10.
19 Cf. Ch. VIII, 17.
20 Cf. Ch. X, 8.
21 Cf. Ch. VI, 3.
22 Cf. Ch. VIII, 23.
23 Cf. Ch. IX, 2.
24 Cf. Ch. IX, 8.
25 Cf. Ch. III, 5.
26 Cf. Ch. VII, 11.
27 Cf. Ch. VII, 19.
28 Cf. Copleston, 1979.
29 Cf. Ch. VIII, 22.
30 Cf. Ch. I.
31 Cf. Ch. III, 8, Ch. IX, 4.
32 Cf. *Enz.* I. 42Z on Kant.
33 Cf. Ch. III, 9.
34 Cf. Ch. VI, 5, Ch. VIII, 23.
35 Cf. Ch. I, 2.
36 Cf. Ch. VIII, 12. See also Ackrill, 1973.
37 Cf. Ch. IX, 7.
38 Cf. Ch. VIII, 22. For a discussion of Kant's views, see McFarland, 1970.
39 *KdU* 61 (Meredith, 1952, Part II, p. 4).
40 Cf. Ch. VIII, 22.
41 Cf. Ch. X, 4.
42 But cf. Ch. VIII, 23.
43 Cf. *KdrV* B131 ff.

44 E.g. *Enz.* III. 388 ff.; *PG* pp. 133 ff., M. pp. 104 ff. Cf. Ch. II, 4.
45 Cf. Ch. V, 2.
46 Cf. Ch. III, 9.
47 Cf. Ch. IX.
48 Cf. Ch. V, 1, 2.
49 Cf. Ch. III, 8.
50 Cf. Ch. V, 2.
51 *KdrV* Bxx.
52 Cf. Ch. VIII, 18.
53 Cf. Ch. VI, 1.
54 Cf. Ch. VIII, 19.
55 Cf. Ch. VI, 5, Ch. VIII, 13.
56 Cf. Ch. VI, 4.
57 Cf. Ch. VIII, 12.
58 Cf. Ch. VIII.
59 Cf. Ch. VIII, 10.
60 Cf. Ch. VIII, 17.
61 Cf. Ch. VIII, 13.
62 Cf. Ch. VIII, 13.
63 Cf. *Enz.* II. 286 and Z.
64 Cf. Ch. IX, 4.
65 Cf. Ch. X, 2.
66 Cf. Ch. VIII, 16.
67 Cf. Ch. V, 5.
68 Cf. Ch. VIII, 10.
69 Cf. Ch. X, 13.
70 Cf. Ch. VI, 3.
71 Cf. Ch. VI, 4.
72 Cf. Ch. VI, 3.
73 Cf. Ch. III, 8, Ch. VI, 3.
74 Cf. Ch. VI, 4.
75 Cf. Ch. II, 1.
76 Cf. Ch. X, 11.
77 Cf. Ch. VIII, 8.
78 Cf. Ch. VI, 3.
79 E.g. *PR* 5. Cf. Ch. II, 3, Ch. XI, 1.
80 For a discussion of this aspect of causality, see Bunge, 1963, pp. 173 ff.
81 Cf. Ch. VI, 6.
82 Cf. Ch. VI, 4.
83 Cf. Ch. X, 12, 13.
84 Cf. McTaggart, 1918, pp. 4 ff.
85 Cf. Ch. II, Ch. VIII, 17.
86 *KdrV* A811, B839.
87 Cf. Ch. XI, 8.
88 E.g. *VPR* II. pp. 261 ff., S.S. III. pp. 57 ff.; *VPR* II. pp. 302 ff., S.S. III. pp. 104 ff.
89 Cf. Ch. XI, 9.
90 Hegel does indeed attribute an ethical significance to a person's death.

The deliberate risking of one's life, for example, is important for the growth of self-consciousness, for it signifies one's detachment from all external, sensuous things and concentration on one's own bare individuality or ego (*PG* pp. 144 ff., M. pp. 113 ff.). Again, in an account of the 'ages of man', death appears as the natural culmination of the pattern of a person's life, when one has become fully integrated into the social order and fully accustomed to its routines — when, that is, one has nothing left to do (*Enz.* III. 396Z). These passages do not imply any *post mortem* survival, but, if anything, the contrary. Cf. Ch. XI, n. 59. See also Ariès, 1974, pp. 27 ff.

91   Cf. Ch. X, 10.
92   Cf. Ch. V, 4, Ch. VIII, 9.
93   Cf. Ch. VI, 10.
94   Cf. Ch. V, 1.
95   Cf. Ch. VI, 1.
96   Cf. Ch. VI, 10.
97   Cf. Ch. VI, 1, Ch. VII, 6.
98   Cf. Ch. V, 2.
99   Cf. Ch. X, 11.
100   Cf. Ch. VI.
101   See further Barnes, 1979, pp. 261 ff.
102   Aristotle, *Physics*, Z.9. 239b 14 ff.
103   Aristotle, *Physics*, Z.9. 239b 30 ff.
104   Cf. *Enz.* I. 89; II. 298; *VGP* I. pp. 295 ff., H. I. pp. 261 ff.
105   Cf. Ch. X, 14.
106   E.g. *Enz.* I. 119 and Z; *WL* II. pp. 74 ff., M. pp. 439 ff.
107   Cf. Ch. VII, 19.
108   Cf. Ch. VI, 6.
109   Cf. Ch. X, 11.
110   Cf. Ch. V, 7, Ch. VIII, 4.
111   See e.g. Popper, 1963b.
112   Cf. Ch. V, 2.
113   Cf. Ch. V, 2.
114   *Darstellung der Wissenschaftslehre*, 1801, § 24 (*Fichtes Werke*, vol. II. p. 53).
115   Cf. Ch. IX.
116   Cf. Ch. I, 4, Ch. VIII, 5.
117   Cf. Ch. VI, 5.
118   E.g. *PG* pp. 307 f., M. pp. 257 ff. Cf. Ch. XI, 3.
119   Cf. Ch. VIII, 1.
120   Cf. Ch. VIII, 23.
121   Cf. Ch. VIII, 7.
122   *WL* II. pp. 360 f., 424 ff., M. pp. 671, 723 f.
123   Cf. Ch. VII, 18.
124   *Ethics*, II. Prop. VII. Cf. Ch. VI, 5.
125   Cf. Ch. VIII, 12.
126   Cf. Ch. VIII, 14.
127   Cf. Ch. X, 14.

128 Cf. Ch. X, 9.
129 Cf. Ch. X, 11.
130 Cf. Ch. VIII, 13.
131 Cf. Ch. X, 10.
132 Cf. Ch. X, n. 111.
133 Cf. Ch. V, 5.
134 Popper, 1963b, argues that 'a system of logic in which contradictory statements do not entail every statement . . . turns out . . . to be an extremely weak system. Very few of the ordinary rules of inference are left, not even the *modus ponens* which says that from a statement of the form "If *p* then *q*" together with *p*, we can infer *q*' (p. 321). He adds:

> I have a simple interpretation of this calculus. All the statements may be taken to be modal statements asserting possibility. From '*p* is possible' and '"if *p* then *q*" is possible', we cannot indeed derive '*q* is possible' (for if *p* is false, *q* may be an impossible statement). Similarly, from '*p* is possible' and '*non-p* is possible' we clearly cannot deduce the possibility of all statements (p. 321, n. 8).

More recently, however, attempts have been made to construct 'Relevance Logics', deductive systems which, while preserving our customary intuitions about implication (such as the validity of the *modus ponens*), avoid the so-called paradoxes of implication (such as the deducibility of any statement from a contradiction). See e.g. Anderson and Belnap, 1962, and, for brief accounts of the matter, Haack, 1978, pp. 198 ff., and Bradley and Swartz, 1979, pp. 228 ff.
135 Cf. Ch. VIII, 9.
136 Cf. Ch. VI.
137 E.g. *Enz.* III. 425Z; *PG* pp. 133 ff., M. pp. 104 ff. Cf. Ch. III, 6.
138 Cf. Ch. VI, 4.
139 Cf. Ch. VI, 4, Ch. X, 10.
140 *Erste Einleitung in die Wissenschaftslehre,* § 3 (*Fichtes Werke,* vol. I. pp. 425 f., Heath and Lachs, 1970, pp. 8 f.).
     In the *Phenomenology,* Hegel seems to be attempting to consider the whole experience associated with each form of consciousness, leaving neither the thing (or object) nor the intelligence (or subject) out of account: perhaps cf. Ch. X, 6. See further Norman, 1976, pp. 29 ff.
141 Morowitz, 1980, interprets modern science in a way that is reminiscent of Hegel's view:

> First, the human mind, including consciousness and reflective thought, can be explained by activities of the central nervous system, which, in turn, can be reduced to the biological structure and function of that physiological system. Second, biological phenomena at all levels can be totally understood in terms of atomic physics, that is, through the action and interaction of the component atoms of carbon, nitrogen, oxygen, and so forth. Third and last, atomic physics, which is now understood most fully by means of quantum mechanics,

must be formulated with the mind as a primitive component of the system.

We have thus, in separate steps, gone around an epistemological circle — from the mind, back to the mind (p. 16. I owe this reference to Mr R. B. Ware).

Husserl considers, and rejects, a circle that is closer to Hegel's: 'We are playing a pretty game: man evolves from the world and the world from man: God creates man and man God' (*Logical Investigations,* vol. I. p. 143).

XI FREEDOM, MORALITY AND THE END OF HISTORY

1   Cf. Ch. XI, 6.
2   Cf. Ch. IV.
3   Cf. Ch. VI, 7.
4   Cf. Ch. III, 2.
5   Cf. Ch. III, 5.
6   Cf. Ch. III, 5.
7   Cf. Ch. III.
8   Cf. Ch. IV, 3.
9   Cf. Ch. VII, 8.
10 Cf. Ch. III, 3.
11 Cf. Ch. V, 8.
12 See e.g. Passmore, 1961, pp. 1 ff.
13 *KdrV* A471, B499.
14 *KdrV* A548, B576.
15 *GzMdS* p. 20 (Paton, 1948, p. 70).
16 Cf. Ch. II, 3, Ch. X, 10.
17 Cf. Ch. II, 3.
18 Cf. Ch. III, 7, Ch. IV, 5, Ch. VIII, 4.
19 Cf. Ch. II, 3.
20 On this see Frankfurt, 1971.
21 Schacht, 1972, seems to be mistaken on this:

> [Hegel] would agree with Kant, however, that if what prompts one to act in a certain way is some mere impulse or inclination, one's action is not really free at all. For then the decision or choice upon which the action is based does not have its 'originative source' or 'determining ground' in the mind of the agent at all; rather, *it is just as completely determined by the operation of laws of sensuous nature as is any other natural event* (pp. 297 f.; italics added).

Nor is it clear that *Kant* holds the view here attributed to him:

> freedom of the will (*Willkür*) is of a wholly unique nature in that an incentive can determine the will to an action *only so far as the individual has incorporated it into his maxim* . . . only thus can an incentive, whatever it may be, co-exist with the absolute spontaneity of the will (*i.e.* freedom).

... If, now, this [viz. the moral] law does not determine a person's will ... an incentive contrary to it must influence his choice; and since, by hypothesis, this can only happen when a man adopts this incentive ... into his maxim ... it follows that his disposition in respect to the moral law is never indifferent, never neither good nor evil (Kant, *Religion within the Limits of Reason alone*, Book One, I (Greene and Hudson, 1960, pp. 19 f.)).

If this were not so, it is hard to see how, on Kant's view, a person who acted wrongly on the basis of some non-moral incentive could be held responsible for his action.

22 Cf. Ch. II, 3.
23 Cf. Ch. II, 3.
24 Cf. Ch. II, 2.
25 Cf. Ch. II, 2.
26 Cf. Ch. II, 3, 4.
27 Cf. Ch. II, 1.
28 Cf. Ch. IX, 4.
29 Cf. Ch. XI, 4.
30 Cf. Ch. VII, 6.
31 Cf. Ch. VIII, 13.
32 Hegel is not, as this passage might suggest, opposed to the legality of divorce (e.g. *PR* 176, 270). His point is simply that marriage is intended to outlast the ebb and flow of sexual desire.
33 Cf. Walsh, 1969, pp. 62 ff.
34 Cf. Ch. IX, 4.
35 Cf. Ch. V, 5.
36 *Ibid.*
37 On Hegel's attitude to Plato's ideal state, see Foster, 1935; Carritt, 1936; Inwood, 1984.
38 On Hegel's account of freedom, see e.g. Parkinson, 1972; Schacht, 1972. On his political beliefs, see Marx, *Critique of Hegel's 'Philosophy of Right'*; Kaufmann, 1970; Riedel, 1975.
39 Cf. Ch. XI, 2.
40 Cf. Ch. XI, 5.
41 *KdU* § 88 (Meredith, 1952, Pt II, p. 124). Cf. *Enz.* I 60, where Hegel quotes a part of this passage in a footnote.
42 *Ibid.* (Meredith, 1952, Pt II, p. 122).
43 Cf. Ch. V, 1.
44 *GzMdS* pp. 28 f. (Paton, 1948, p. 76). But see also Rescher, 1974.
45 Cf. Ch. XI, 3.
46 Cf. Ch. X, 5.
47 Cf. Ch. IX, 5.
48 Cf. Ch. V, 10.
49 Cf. Ch. V, 10, Ch. X, 6, Ch. XI, 11.
50 Cf. Ch. XI, 8.
51 Cf. Ch. X, 2.
52 Cf. Ch. XI, 8.

53 Cf. Ch. IX, 1.
54 Cf. Ch. X, 13.
55 Cf. Ch. V, 2, 5.
56 Cf. Ch. V, 2.
57 Cf. Ch. VII, 15.
58 Cf. Ch. VIII, 4, 13.
59 Hegel's belief that the state is to a high degree self-determining and self-articulating (cf. Ch. IX, 4) does not prevent him from regarding warfare as the primary way in which a state defines itself in relation to other states: 'Individuality, as exclusive being-for-self, appears *as a relation to other states,* each of which is independent *vis-à-vis* the others' (*PR* 323). This is similar to the way in which different (species of) animals define themselves by means of their teeth and claws (cf. Ch. VI, 5). Warfare, however, emphasizes and reinforces the 'infinity' of the state, since everything in the state is subordinated to it and put at risk. War is

> its actual infinity as the ideality of everything finite in it — the aspect in which the substance as the absolute power over against everything individual and particular, against life, property and its rights, also against wider spheres, brings their nullity into existence and consciousness (*PR* 323).

Warfare does for states what individual combat does for persons (*PG* pp. 144 f., M. pp. 113 ff.). It is perhaps not clear what Hegel's attitude is towards individual combat in war. In so far as the individual is risking his own life, this should enhance his importance as an individual (cf. Ch. X, n. 90), while in so far as he does so at the behest of the state, it should reduce him, or at least his life, to nullity. See further *PR* 324, 325, 333 ff., 351, and also Avineri, 1961.
60 Cf. Ch. V, 5, Ch. XI, 6.
61 Kant, *Zum ewigen Frieden.*
62 Cf. Ch. X, 2.
63 See Inwood, 1984.
64 Cf. Ch. IV, 5.
65 Cf. Ch. IX, 10.
66 Plato's *Republic* is interpreted by Hegel as a restatement of the traditional values of ethical life in the face of this disruptive innovation.
67 Cf. Ch. VIII.
68 See Inwood, 1982.
69 Hegel seems to imply, in the interests of his analogy between cognition and practice, that our cognitive activities idealize nature, produce a change in it which makes it ideal, rather than discover that it is ideal. This is not his usual view: cf. Ch. III, 4, and n. 34; Ch. X, 4. But his thought on this matter is ambiguous.
70 J. F. Fries (1773-1843). Cf. *PR* Preface and 15; *VGP* III. pp. 418 ff., H. III. pp. 510 ff. See further Nelson, 1971, vol. II, pp. 157 ff.
71 *Manifesto of the Communist Party,* III. 3 (Adoratsky, 1943, vol. I. pp. 237 f.).

72 Findlay, 1977, pp. v ff.
73 Quoted Ch. VIII, 13.
74 Cf. Ch. V, 4.
75 Cf. Ch. VII.
76 Cf. Ch. VIII, 14.
77 Cf. Ch. VIII, 5, 14.
78 Forbes, 1975, criticizes Stace, 1924, for being 'worried by what he regards as logical lapses or breaks in the chain of reasoning'. He adds:

> But the dialectic is not like that at all. It was the result of Hegel's desire 'to think life'; it is a way of thinking concretely and seeing things whole, whose conclusions cannot be proved or disproved, but which can be seen to be more or less true to life; its purpose is to provide insight (p. xiii).

If that is what logic is, then we can presumably have as many logics as we like. For a similar view, see Ch. IX, n. 1.
79 Findlay, 1977, p. xiv.
80 Cf. Ch. X, 8.
81 For these criticisms of Findlay, cf. Inwood, 1979.
82 Cf. Ch. V, 8.
83 Cf. Ch. V, 5.
84 Cf. Ch. V, 4.
85 Cf. Petry, 1970, vol. I. p. 43:

> Many of the categories recognized by Hegel are still in use, some are obsolete however, and not a few of the complexity relationships he formulates need revision in the light of the developments that have taken place since the work [sc. the *Logic*] was published.

This is true. What is false is the implication that the structure of Hegel's system can allow for it. Cf. Ch. IX, n. 1.
86 Cf. Ch. VIII, 13, Ch. XI, 11.
87 *Socialism: Utopian and Scientific*, III (Adoratsky, 1943, vol. I. p. 186).
88 *A Contribution to the Critique of Political Economy*, Preface (Adoratsky, 1943, vol. I. p. 357).
89 Cf. Ch. V.

CONCLUSION

1 Kierkegaard, 1968, pp. 111 f.
2 See Bernstein, 1972, pp. 84 ff.
3 See McTaggart, 1910.
4 See Riedel, 1976; Bernstein, 1977; Bubner, 1981, pp. 203 ff.
5 On these dichotomies, see Copleston, 1979.
6 Kierkegaard, 1968, p. 272.
7 See Bernstein, 1977; Bubner, 1981, pp. 134 ff.
8 Spender, 1964, pp. 39 f.
9 See Bubner, 1981, pp. 1 ff., 219 f.

Bibliography

Works by Hegel

Werke, 18 vols, ed. P. Marheineke *et al.,* Duncker & Humblot, Berlin, 1832–45.

Sämtliche Werke, Jubildumsausgabe, 20 vols, ed. H. Glockner, Frommann, Stuttgart, 1927–30.

Sämtliche Werke, Kritische Ausgabe, ed. G. Lasson, J. Hoffmeister, F. Nicolin and O. Pöggeler, Felix Meiner, Hamburg, 1911–.

Werke, 20 vols, ed. E. Moldenhauer and K. M. Michel, Suhrkamp, Frankfurt, 1970–1.

A new critical edition of Hegel's works has been undertaken by the Rheinisch-Westfälischen Akademie der Wissenschaften, to be published by Felix Meiner, Hamburg, 1968–. Some volumes have already appeared.

Theologische Jugendschriften, ed. H. Nohl, Mohr, Tübingen, 1907.

Briefe von und an Hegel, 3 vols, ed. J. Hoffmeister, Felix Meiner, Hamburg, 3rd ed., 1969.

Translations

Early Theological Writings, tr. T. M. Knox, intro. by R. Kroner, University of Chicago Press, 1948.

Difference between the Systems of Fichte and Schelling, tr. H. S. Harris and W. Cerf, State University of New York Press, 1977.

Faith and Knowledge, tr. W. Cerf and H. S. Harris, State University of New York Press, 1977.

Natural Law, tr. T. M. Knox, intro. by H. B. Acton, University of Pennsylvania Press, 1975.

System of Ethical Life and First Philosophy of Spirit, tr. H. S. Harris and T. M. Knox, State University of New York Press, 1979.

Political Writings, tr. T. M. Knox, intro. by Z. A. Pelczynski, Clarendon Press, 1964.

Phenomenology of Spirit, tr. A. V. Miller, intro. by J. N. Findlay, Clarendon Press, 1977.

Science of Logic, tr. A. V. Miller, Allen & Unwin, London, 1969.

Philosophy of Right, tr. T. M. Knox, Clarendon Press, 1942. Also translated by H. Nisbet as *Elements of the Philosophy of Right,* ed. A. Wood, Cambridge University Press, Cambridge, 1991.

Logic, tr. W. Wallace, Clarendon Press, Oxford, 2nd edn, 1892 *(Enz.* I). Also translated by T. Geraets, H. Harris and W. Suchting as *The Encyclopedia Logic, Hackett,* Indianapolis, 1991.

Philosophy of Nature, tr. A. V. Miller, Clarendon Press, 1970 *(Enz.* II).

Philosophy of Nature, 3 vols, tr. M. J. Petry, Allen & Unwin, London, 1970 *(Enz.* II).

Philosophy of Mind, tr. W. Wallace and A. V. Miller, Clarendon Press, 1971 *(Enz.* III).

Philosophy of Subjective Spirit, 3 vols, tr. M. J. Petry, Reidel, Dordrecht and Boston, 1978 *(Enz.* III).

The Philosophy of History, tr. J. Sibree, Dover, New York, 1956.

Lectures on the Philosophy of World History: Introduction, tr. H. B. Nisbet, intro. by D. Forbes, Cambridge University Press, 1975.

Hegel's Aesthetics, 2 vols, tr. T. M. Knox, Clarendon Press, 1975.

Introductory Lectures on Aesthetics, trans. B. Bosanquet, ed. M. Inwood, Penquin, Harmondsworth, 1993.

Lectures on the Philosophy of Religion, 3 vols, tr. E. B. Speirs and J. B. Sanderson, Kegan Paul, London, 1895. Also *Lectures on the Philosophy of Religion,* trans. P. Hodgson and R. Brown, University of California Press, Berkeley, 1984–6.

Lectures on the History of Philosophy, 3 vols, tr. E. S. Haldane and F. H. Simson, Kegan Paul, London, 1892.

Introduction to the History of Philosophy, tr. Q. Lauer, in *Hegel's Idea of Philosophy,* Fordham University Press, 1971.

Correspondance, 3 vols, tr. J. Carrère, Gallimard, Paris, 1962 (French tr. of *Briefe von und an Hegel,* ed. J. Hoffmeister).

Other works cited

Ackrill, J. L. (1973), 'Aristotle's Definitions *of Psyche',* *Proceedings of the Aristotelian Society* 73 (1972–3), pp. 119–33.

Adoratsky, V., ed. (1943), Marx, K. and Engels, F., *Karl Marx: Selected Works,* 2 vols, Lawrence & Wishart, London, 1943.

Allan, D. J. (1952), *The Philosophy of Aristotle,* Oxford University Press, 1952.

Ambrose, A. (1959), 'Proof and the Theorem Proved', *Mind,* 68, pp. 435–45.

Anderson, A. R. and Belnap, N. D. (1962), 'The Pure Calculus of Entailment', *Journal of Symbolic Logic,* 27, pp. 19–52.

Anselm, St, *Proslogion,* in *The Devotions of St Anselm,* ed. C. C. J. Webb, Methuen, London, 1903.

Anstett, J. J., tr. (1946), *Oeuvres philosophiques de F. H. Jacobi,* Aubier, Paris.

Aquila, R. E. (1973), 'Predication and Hegel's Metaphysics', *Kant-Studien,* 64, pp. 231–45.

Ariès, P. (1974), *Western Attitudes toward Death: From the Middle Ages to the Present,* Johns Hopkins University Press.

Aristotle, *De Anima, Bks II and III (with passages from Bk I)*, tr. D. W. Hamlyn, Clarendon Press, 1968.

Aristotle, *De Partibus Animalium I and De Generatione Animalium I*, tr. D. M. Balme, Clarendon Press, 1972.

Aristotle, *Nicomachean Ethics*, tr. H. Rackham, Heinemann, London, 1934.

Aristotle, *Metaphysics*, tr. J. Warrington, J. M. Dent, London, 2nd ed., 1961.

Aristotle, *Physics*, 2 vols, tr. P. Wicksteed and F. M. Cornford, Heinemann, London, 1934.

Aristotle, *Politics*, tr. H. Rackham, Heinemann, London, 2nd ed., 1944.

Aubenque, P. (1974), 'Hegel et Aristote', in D'Hondt, 1974, pp. 97–120.

Avineri, S. (1961), 'The Problem of War in Hegel's Thought', *Journal of the History of Ideas*, 22, pp. 463–74.

Ayer, A. J. (1947), 'Phenomenalism', *Proceedings of the Aristotelian Society*, 47 (1946-7), pp. 163–97.

Ayers, M. R. (1974), 'Individuals Without Sortals', *Canadian Journal of Philosophy*, 4, pp. 113–48.

Bannister, D. (1970), 'Comment' on H. J. Eysenck, 'Explanation and the Concept of Personality', in *Explanation in the Behavioural Sciences*, ed. R. Borger and F. Cioffi, Cambridge University Press, pp. 411–18.

Barnes, J. (1979), *The Presocratic Philosophers*, 2 vols, Routledge & Kegan Paul, London.

Bennett, J. F. (1974), *Kant's Dialectic*, Cambridge University Press.

Berkeley, G. (1962), *Three Dialogues between Hylas and Philonous*, in *The Principles of Human Knowledge with other Writings*, ed. G. J. Warnock, Fontana, London.

Bernstein, R. J. (1972), *Praxis and Action*, Duckworth, London.

Bernstein, R. J. (1977), 'Why Hegel Now?' *Review of Metaphysics*, 31, pp. 29–60.

Black, M. (1949), 'Linguistic Method in Philosophy', in M. Black, *Language and Philosophy*, Cornell University Press, pp. 1–22.

Blanché, R. (1962), *Axiomatics*, Routledge & Kegan Paul, London.

Borges, J. L. (1964), 'Partial Magic in the *Quixote*', in J. L. Borges, *Labyrinths*, ed. D. A. Yates and J. E. Irby, Penguin, 1970, pp. 228–31.

Bradley, R. and Swartz, N. (1979), *Possible Worlds*, Blackwell, Oxford.

Bubner, R. (1981), *Modern German Philosophy*, Cambridge University Press.

Buchdahl, G. (1961), *The Image of Newton and Locke in the Age of Reason*, Sheed & Ward, London.

Bunge, M. (1963), *Causality: the Place of the Causal Principle in Modern Science*, Meridian, Cleveland and New York.

Burkhardt, F. H., tr. (1940), Herder, J. G., *God, Some Conversations*, Bobbs-Merrill, Indianapolis.

Carnap, R. (1950), 'Empiricism, Semantics and Ontology', *Revue internationale de Philosophie*, 4, pp. 20–40.

Carritt, E. F. (1936), 'Hegel's Sittlichkeit', *Proceedings of the Aristotelian Society*, 36 (1935-6), pp. 223–36.

Cerf, W. (1977), 'Speculative Philosophy and Intellectual Intuition: an Introduction to Hegel's Essays', in G. W. F. Hegel, *Faith and Knowledge*, tr. W. Cerf and H. S. Harris, pp. xi–xxxvi.

Chisholm, R. M. (1973), *The Problem of the Criterion*, Marquette University Press.

Chisholm, R. M. (1976), 'Individuation *per se*', in *Contemporary Aspects of Philosophy*, ed. G. Ryle, Oriel Press, Stocksfield, pp. 122–131.

Chisholm, R. M. (1977), *Theory of Knowledge*, Prentice-Hall, Englewood Cliffs, N.J., 2nd ed.

Colletti, L. (1979), *Marxism and Hegel*, Verso Editions, London.

Collingwood, R. G. (1965), *The Idea of Nature*, Clarendon Press.

Cook, D. J. (1973), *Language in the Philosophy of Hegel*, Mouton, The Hague.

Copi, I. M. (1971), *The Theory of Logical Types*, Routledge & Kegan Paul, London.

Copleston, F. (1946), 'Pantheism in Spinoza and the German Idealists', *Philosophy*, 21, pp. 42–56.

Copleston, F. (1979), 'The Nature of Metaphysics', in *On the History of Philosophy*, F. Copleston, Search Press, London, pp. 116–30.

Cousin, D. R. (1957-8), 'Kant on the Self, *Kant-Studien*, 49, pp. 23–35.

Cutler, J. (1976), *Saussure*, Fontana/Collins, Glasgow.

Delhomme, J. (1974), 'Hegel et Platon', in D'Hondt, 1974, pp. 85–96.

Derrida, J. (1970), 'Les puits et la pyramide: Introduction a la semiologie de Hegel', in Hyppolite, 1970, pp. 27–84.

D'Hondt, J., ed. (1974), *Hegel et la pensée grecque*, Presses Universitaires de France, Paris.

Doz, A., tr. (1970), G. W. F. Hegel, *La Théorie de la Mésure*, Presses Universitaires de France, Paris.

Dummett, M. (1959), 'Wittgenstein's Philosophy of Mathematics', *Philosophical Review*, 68, pp. 324–48.

Dummett, M. (1960), 'A Defense of McTaggart's Proof of the Unreality of Time', *Philosophical Review*, 69, pp. 497–504.

Ellis, B. (1968), *Basic Concepts of Measurement*, Cambridge University Press.

Elster, J. (1978), *Logic and Society: Contradictions and Possible Worlds*, John Wiley, Chichester.

Elwes, R. H. M., tr. (1955), Spinoza, B., *Chief Works of Spinoza*, 2 vols, Dover, New York.

Fackenheim, E. L. (1967), *The Religious Dimension in Hegel's Thought*, Indiana University Press.

Fichte, J. G. (1971), *Fichtes Werke*, 11 vols, ed. I. H. Fichte, de Gruyter, Berlin.

Findlay, J. N. (1958), *Hegel: a Re-examination*, Allen & Unwin, London.

Findlay, J. N. (1963), 'The Contemporary Relevance of Hegel', in MacIntyre, 1972a, pp.1–20.

Findlay, J. N. (1964), 'Hegel's Use of Teleology', in J. N. Findlay, *Ascent to the Absolute*, Allen & Unwin, London, 1970, pp. 131–47.

Findlay, J. N. (1977), 'Foreword' to *Phenomenology of Spirit*, tr. A. V. Miller, Clarendon Press, pp. v-xxx.

Forbes, D. (1975), 'Introduction' to *Lectures on the Philsophy of World History: Introduction*, tr. H. B. Nisbet, Cambridge University Press, pp. vii-xxxv.

Foster, M. B. (1935), *The Political Philosophies of Plato and Hegel*, Clarendon Press.

Frankfurt, H. G. (1971), 'Freedom of the Will and the Concept of a Person', *Journal of Philosophy*, 68, pp. 5–20.

Gadamer, H. G. (1975), 'The Inverted World', *Review of Metaphysics*, 28, pp. 401–22.

Gardner, M. (1958), *Logic Machines and Diagrams*, McGraw-Hill, New York.

Gardner, M. (1970), *The Ambidextrous Universe*, Penguin.

Geach, P. T. (1969), 'On Worshipping the Right God', in P. T. Geach, *God and the Soul*, Routledge & Kegan Paul, London, pp. 100–16.

Geach, P. T. (1979), *Truth, Love and Immortality*, Hutchinson, London.

Gray, J. G. (1969), *Hegel and Greek Thought*, Harper & Row, New York, 2nd ed.

Greene, T. M. and Hudson, H. H., tr. (1960), Kant, I., *Religion within the Limits of Reason Alone*, intro. by J. R. Silber, Harper & Row, New York.

Guttenplan, S. (1975), 'Introduction' to *Mind and Language*, ed. S. Guttenplan, Clarendon Press, pp. 1–6.

Haack, S. (1978), *Philosophy of Logics*, Cambridge University Press.

Haldane, J. B. S. (1927), 'On Being the Right Size', in J. B. S. Haldane, *Possible Worlds and Other Essays*, Chatto & Windus, London, pp. 18–26.

Haldane, E. S. and Ross, G. R. T., tr. (1931), Descartes R., *Philosophical Works*, 2 vols, Cambridge University Press, 2nd ed.

Harris, H. S. (1972), *Hegel's Development: Toward the Sunlight*, Clarendon Press.

Hartmann, N. (1957), 'Aristoteles and Hegel', in N. Hartmann, *Kleinere Schriften*, Bd II, de Gruyter, Berlin, pp. 214–52.

Heath, P. and Lachs, J., tr. (1970), Fichte, J. G., *Science of Knowledge*, Appleton-Century-Crofts, New York.

Henie, P. (1949), 'Mysticism and Semantics', in *Philosophy of Religion*, ed. S. M. Cahn, Harper & Row, New York, 1970, pp. 274–82.

Henrich, D. (1967), *Der Ontologische Gottesbeweis*, Mohr Tübingen, 2nd ed.

Hepburn, R. W. (1963), 'From World to God', *Mind*, 72, pp. 40–50.

Herder, J. G. (1969), *Essay on the Origin of Language*, abridged trans. in *J. G. Herder on Social and Political Culture*, tr. F. M. Barnard, Cambridge University Press.

Herder, J. G. (1978), *Werke*, 5 vols, ed. R. Otto, Aufbau, Berlin and Weimar, 5th ed.

Herder, J. G., see also Burkhardt, 1940.

Hick, J. H., and McGill, A. C., eds (1967), *The Many-Faced Argument*, Macmillan, New York.

Hoffmeister, J. (1955), *Worterbuch der philophischen Begriffe*, Felix Meiner, Hamburg, 2nd ed.

Hudson, W. D. (1968), *Ludwig Wittgenstein: the Bearing of his Philosophy on Religious Belief*, Butterworth Press, London.

Hume, D. (1902), *Enquiries Concerning the Human Understanding and Concerning the Principles of Morals*, ed. L. A. Selby-Bigge, Clarendon Press, 2nd ed.

Husserl, E. (1970), *Logical Investigations,* 2 vols, tr. J. N. Findlay, Routledge & Kegan Paul, London.

Hyppolite, J., ed. (1970), *Hegel et la pensée moderne,* Presses Universitaires de France, Paris.

Inwood, M. J. (1977), 'Solomon, Hegel and Truth', *Review of Metaphysics,* 31, pp. 272–82.

Inwood, M. J. (1979), 'Hegel's *Phenomenology of Spirit*', *New Lugano Review,* 1, pp. 74-5.

Inwood, M. J. (1982), 'Hegel on Action', in *Idealism Past and Present,* ed. G. Vesey, Cambridge University Press, pp. 141–54.

Inwood, M. J. (1984), 'Hegel, Plato and Greek *Sittlichkeit*', in *The State and Civil Society,* ed. Z. A. Pelczynski, Cambridge University Press.

Jacobi, F. H. (1980), *Werke,* 6 vols, ed. F. Roth and F. Koppen, Wissenschaftliche Buchgesellschaft, Darmstadt. (See also Anstett, 1946.)

Janicaud, D. (1970), 'Dialectiqueet substantiality: Sur la refutation hégélienne du spinozisme', in Hyppolite, 1970, pp. 161–92.

Kant, I. (1930), *Kritik der reinen Vernunft,* ed. R. Schmidt, Felix Meiner, Hamburg, 2nd ed.

Kant, I. (1929), *Immanuel Kant's Critique of Pure Reason,* tr. N. Kemp Smith, Macmillan, London.

Kant, I. (1925), *Grundlegung zur Metaphysik der Sitten,* ed. K. Vorländer, Felix Meiner, Hamburg, 6th ed. (See also Paton, 1948.)

Kant, I. (1924), *Kritik der Urteilskraft,* ed. K. Vorländer, Felix Meiner, Hamburg, 6th ed. (See also Meredith, 1952.)

Kaufmann, W. (1954), 'Hegel's Early Anti-theological Phase', *Philosophical Review,* 63, pp. 3–18.

Kaufmann, W. (1960), *From Shakespeare to Existentialism,* Doubleday, New York, 2nd ed.

Kaufmann, W. (1966), *Hegel,* Weidenfeld & Nicolson, London.

Kaufmann, W., ed. (1970), *Hegel's Political Philosophy,* Atherton Press, New York.

Kierkegaard, S. (1968), *Concluding Unscientific Postscript,* tr. D. F. Swenson and W. Lowrie, Princeton University Press.

Kroner, R. (1948), 'Introduction' to G. W. F. Hegel, *Early Theological Writings,* tr. T. M. Knox, University of Chicago Press.

Lloyd, A. C. (1962), 'Genus, Species and Ordered Series in Aristotle', *Phronesis,* 7, pp. 67–90.

Lloyd, A. C. (1970), 'Non-discursive Thought: an Enigma of Greek Philosophy', *Proceedings of the Aristotelian Society,* 70 (1969-70), pp. 261–74.

Lloyd, A. C. (1981), *Form and Universal in Aristotle,* Francis Cairns, Liverpool.

Lukács, G. (1975), *The Young Hegel: Studies in the Relations between Dialectics and Economics,* Merlin, London.

McFarland, D. J. (1970), *Kant's Conception of Teleology,* University of Edinburgh Press.

Macherey, P. (1979), *Hegel ou Spinoza,* Maspero, Paris.

MacIntyre, A. C., ed. (1972a), *Hegel: A Collection of Critical Essays,* Doubleday, New York.

MacIntyre, A. C. (1972b), 'Hegel on Faces and Skulls', in MacIntyre, 1972a, pp. 219–36.

Mackie, J. L. (1976), *Problems from Locke*, Clarendon Press.

McMinn, J. B. (1959-60), 'A Critique of Hegel's Criticism of Spinoza's God', *Kant-Studien*, 51, pp. 294–314.

McTaggart, J. M. E. (1980), 'The Unreality of Time', *Mind*, 17, pp. 457–74.

McTaggart, J. M. E. (1910), *A Commentary on Hegel's Logic*, Cambridge University Press.

McTaggart, J. M. E. (1918), *Studies in Hegelian Cosmology*, Cambridge University Press, 2nd ed.

Martin, R. M. (1958), *Truth and Denotation*, Routledge & Kegan Paul, London.

Marx, K. (1970), *Critique of Hegel's 'Philosophy of Right'* tr. A. Jolin and J. O'Malley, Cambridge University Press.

Marx, K. (1932), *Das Kapital*, ed. G. Salter, intro. by K. Korsch, Kiepenheuer, Berlin.

Marx, K., see also Adoratsky, 1943; Paul and Paul, 1930.

Meredith, J. C., tr. (1952), Kant, I. *The Critique of Judgement*, Clarendon Press.

Meynell, H. (1964), *Sense, Nonsense and Christianity*, Sheed & Ward, London.

Morowitz, H. J. (1980), 'Rediscovering the Mind', *Psychology Today*, 14(8), pp. 12–18.

Mueller, G. E. (1958), 'The Hegel Legend of "Thesis-Antithesis-Synthesis"', *Journal of the History of Ideas*, 19, pp. 411–14.

Mure, G. R. G. (1940), *An Introduction to Hegel*, Clarendon Press.

Nelson, L. (1971), *Progress and Regress in Philosophy*, 2 vols, Blackwell, Oxford.

Norman, R. (1969), 'Aristotle's philosopher-God', *Phronesis*, 14, pp. 63–74.

Norman, R. (1976), *Hegel's Phenomenology: a Philosophical Introduction*, Sussex University Press.

O'Brien, G. D. (1975), *Hegel on Reason and History*, University of Chicago Press.

Ogden, C. K. (1967), *Opposition: A Linguistic and Psychological Analysis*, Indiana University Press.

Owen, G. E. L. (1961), 'ΤΙΘΕΝΑΙ ΤΑ ΦΑΙΝΟΜΕΝΑ' in *Aristote et les problèmes de la méthode*, Editions Nauwelaerts, SPRL, Louvain, pp. 83–103.

Parkinson, G. H. R. (1972), 'Hegel's Concept of Freedom', *Royal Institute of Philosophy Lectures*, 5 (1970-1), ed. G. N. A. Vesey, Macmillan, London, pp.174–95.

Passmore, J. A. (1961), *Philosophical Reasoning*, Duckworth, London.

Paton, H. J., tr. (1948), Kant, I., *The Moral Law*, Hutchinson, London.

Paul, E. and Paul, C., tr. (1930), *Capital*, 2 vols, J. M. Dent, London.

Petry, M. J., tr. (1970), Hegel, G. W. F., *Philosophy of Nature*, 3 vols, Allen & Unwin, London.

Plantinga, A. (1974) *The Nature of Necessity*, Clarendon Press.

Poincaré, J. H. [1914], *Science and method*, tr. F. Maitland, Dover, New York, n.d.

Popper, K. R. (1963a), 'Kant's Critique and Cosmology', in K. R. Popper, *Conjectures and Refutations*, Routledge & Kegan Paul, London, pp. 175–83.

Popper, K. R. (1963b), 'What is Dialectic?' in *Conjectures and Refutations,* op. cit., pp. 312–35.

Quinton, A. (1962), 'Spaces and Times', *Philosophy,* 37, pp. 130–47.

Quinton, A. (1975), 'The Concept of a Phenomenon', in *Phenomenology and Philosophical Understanding,* ed. E. Pivcević, Cambridge University Press, pp. 1–16.

Ramnoux, C. (1974), 'Hegel et le commencement de la philosophie', in D'Hondt, 1974, pp.9–26.

Raphael, D. D. (1972), 'The Impartial Spectator', *Proceedings of the British Academy,* 58, pp. 335–54.

Reardon, B. M. G. (1977), *Hegel's Philosophy of Religion,* Macmillan, London.

Rescher, N. (1974), 'Kant and the "Special Constitution" of Man's Mind', in N. Rescher, *Studies in Modality,* Blackwell, Oxford, pp. 71–84.

Riedel, M., ed. (1975), *Materialien zu Hegels Rechtsphilosophie,* 2 vols, Suhrkamp, Frankfurt.

Riedel, M. (1976), 'Causal and Historical Explanation', in *Essays on Explanation and Understanding,* ed. J. Manninen and R. Tuomela, Reidel, Dordrecht, pp. 3–25.

Rorty, R. M. (1972), 'The World Well Lost', *Journal of Philosophy,* 69, pp. 649–65.

Royce, J. (1897), *The Conception of God,* Philosophical Union, Berkeley/Macmillan, London.

Royce, J. (1959), *The World and the Individual,* 2 vols, Dover, New York.

Russell, B. A. W. (1922), 'Introduction' to L. Wittgenstein, *Tractatus Logico-Philosophicus,* Kegan Paul, London, pp. 7–23.

Russell, B. A. W. (1962), *An Inquiry into Meaning and Truth,* Penguin.

Ryle, G. (1954), *Dilemmas,* Cambridge University Press.

Saintillan, D. (1974), 'Hegel et Héraclite ou le "Logos" qui n'a pas de contraire', in D'Hondt, pp. 27–84.

Schacht, R. L. (1972), 'Hegel on Freedom', in MacIntyre, 1972a, pp. 289–328.

Schelling, F. W. J. (1927), *Schellings Werke,* 12 vols, ed. M. Schröter, Beck, Munich.

Schilpp, P. A., ed. (1963), *The Philosophy of Bertrand Russell,* 2 vols, Harper & Row, New York.

Schopenhauer, A. (1974), *The Fourfold Root of the Principle of Sufficient Reason,* tr. E. F. J. Payne, Open Court, La Salle, Illinois.

Smart, N. (1964), *Philosophers and Religious Truth,* SCM Press, London.

Soll, I. (1969), *An Introduction to Hegel's Metaphysics,* University of Chicago Press.

Soll, I. (1976), 'Charles Taylor's *Hegel'*, *Journal of Philosophy,* 73, pp. 697–710.

Solomon, R. C. (1970), 'Hegel's Concept of "Geist"'; *Review of Metaphysics,* 23, pp. 642–61.

Solomon, R. C. (1974), 'Hegel's Epistemology', *American Philosophical Quarterly,* 11, pp. 277–89.

Solomon, R. C. (1975), 'Truth and Self-Satisfaction', *Review of Metaphysics,* 28, pp. 698–724.

Spender, S. (1964), *World within World,* Hamish Hamilton, London.

Stace, W. T. (1924), *The Philosophy of Hegel: a Systematic Exposition*, Macmillan, London.

Strawson, P. F. (1954), 'Particular and General', *Proceedings of the Aristotelian Society*, 54 (1953–4), pp. 233–60.

Tarski, A. (1944), 'The Semantic Conception of Truth and the Foundations of Semantics', *Philosophy and Phenomenological Research*, 4, pp. 341–76.

Taylor, C. (1972), 'The Opening Arguments of the *Phenomenology*', in MacIntyre, 1972a, pp. 151–87.

Taylor, C. (1975), *Hegel*, Cambridge University Press.

Vlastos, G. (1963), 'Organic Categories in Whitehead', in *Alfred North Whitehead: Essays on his Philosophy*, ed. G. L. Kline, Prentice-Hall, Englewood Cliffs, N.J., pp. 158–67.

Voltaire, F.-M. A. de (1971), *Philosophical Dictionary*, tr. T. Besterman, Penguin.

Waismann, F. (1959), *Introduction to Mathematical Thinking*, Harper & Row, New York.

Walsh, W. H. (1946), 'Hegel and Intellectual Intuition', *Mind*, 54, pp. 49–63.

Walsh, W. H. (1947), *Reason and Experience*, Clarendon Press.

Walsh, W. H. (1963), *Metaphysics*, Hutchinson, London.

Walsh, W. H. (1965), 'Hegel on the History of Philosophy', *History and Theory*, 4 Beiheft 5, pp. 67–82.

Walsh, W. H. (1969), *Hegelian Ethics*, Macmillan, London.

Wiener, P. P., ed. (1951), Leibniz, G. W., *Selections*, Scribner, New York.

Williams, B. (1966), 'Imagination and the Self, in *Studies in the Philosophy of Thought and Action*, ed. P. F. Strawson, Clarendon Press, 1968, pp. 192–213.

Williams, B. (1978), *Descartes: The Project of Pure Enquiry*, Penguin.

Wilson, J. Cook (1904), 'On the Platonist Doctrine of the ἀσύμβλητοι ἀριθμόι', *Classical Review*, 18, pp. 247–60.

Wittgenstein, L. (1964), *Remarks on the Foundations of Mathematics*, tr. G. E. M. Anscombe, Blackwell, Oxford.

Wolff, R. P. (1963), *Kant's Theory of Mental Activity*, Harvard University Press.

Wood, A. W. and Clark, G. M., tr. (1978), Kant, I., *Lectures on Philosophical Theology*, Cornell University Press.

Wright, C. (1980), *Wittgenstein on the Foundations of Mathematics*, Duckworth, London.

Index

INDEX

body, 96 f., 195, 197 ff., 322 ff.
books, 497 f., 412, 455
Boyle, R., 255
brain, 40 f., 232, 239, 322 ff., 401 f.

Caesar, Julius, 507 f.
categories, 36, 57 ff., 65, 70 ff., 79, 143,
146 f., 170 ff., 190 ff., 194 f., 266 ff.,
283 ff., 335, 405 f., 416 ff., 436 ff.,
497, 514, 516, 542
catholicism, 270
causality, 11 ff., 17, 21, 37, 43, 58, 170,
194 f., 336, 338 ff., 419 ff., 438 ff.
change, 302 f., 429 ff., 446 f., 460 ff.,
467, 495, 500, 505 ff.
chemism, 289 f., 335 f., 436 f.
chemistry, 64 f., 255
children, 43, 95 ff., 156
Chinese, 43, 100 f., 282
Chisholm, R. M., 551
Christ, 54, 258, 519
christianity, 196, 202 ff., 251 ff., 522
Cicero, M. Tullius, 203, 543
circles, 2 f., 112, 143, 150 ff., 162, 169,
213, 258, 270, 274 f., 287, 317 ff.,
364, 378f., 403 f., 425, 467, 515 ff.,
560 f.
classification, 49, 178 ff.
climate, 255, 438
cogito, 197 ff., 211, 543; cf. Descartes
cognition, 469 ff., 488, 496, 498, 506 f.;
cf. knowledge
Collingwood, R. G., 538
colours, 69, 179 f., 285, 392 ff.
completeness, 128 ff., 144 ff., 424 f.,
515 f.
conceiving (Vorstellen), 18
concept, 10 ff., 18, 27 ff., 40, 84, 87, 151,
157 ff., 170 ff., 195 f., 197 ff., 207,
209 f., 216 ff., 239 ff., 262 f., 304 ff.,
334 ff., 355, 366 ff., 413 f., 434 ff.,
455 ff., 485; cf. thoughts
concept, clear and confused, 540
concept, the, 21, 36, 199, 241 ff., 262 ff.,
271 ff., 333 ff., 353 ff., 375, 383 f.,
390 f., 413 f.
conceptions, 10 f., 36 f., 77 f., 84 f.,
185 f., 221, 247, 273, 279 ff., 313 ff.,
385 ff., 392 ff., 479
conceptions, non-empirical, 22 ff., 186
conceptualization (Begreifen), 18, 37
concrete, 68 f., 289 f., 295 f., 366 ff.;
cf. abstract, abstraction
concrete universal, 136, 184, 366 ff.
conflict, 460 ff.
consciousness, 1, 208, 246 f., 257, 370 f.
content and structure, 393 ff.
contingency, 72, 203, 217, 235 ff., 355 ff.,

410, 487 ff., 501 f., 511 f., 554
contradictions, 20, 101 ff., 116 f., 131,
137 f., 158, 174 f., 191 f., 255, 269 f.,
292 ff., 299 ff., 433, 442 f., 445 ff.,
474 f., 494 ff., 498, 509, 560
contradictions, objective and subjective,
117, 302 ff., 433, 445 f., 454 f.,
457 ff., 462 ff.
cosmological proof, 224, 235 f., 242 f.,
244, 249
creation, 24, 242 ff., 247, 252, 390
crime, 407 f., 410
criticism, 496 ff.
criticism, external and internal, 305 ff.,
508 f.
crystals, 343, 350 f.

Dalai Lama, 201, 207 f.
Dalton, J., 59, 255
death, 303 ff., 429, 441 ff., 454, 461 f.,
467, 558 f.
deduction, 228 f., 447
definition, 537
Democritus, 255
Derrida, J., 529
Descartes, R., 197 ff., 211, 406, 540, 543,
545 f.
desire, 28, 32 f., 41 f., 76 f., 97 f., 106,
440, 465, 470 ff., 478 ff., 486 ff., 528
determinacy, 124, 206 ff.
determinate being (Dasein), 13 ff., 241,
264, 283, 288, 349
determination (Bestimmung), 70 ff., 221,
286, 311, 349, 385, 544
determinism, 136
dialectic, 294 ff., 348, 427 ff., 510 ff.,
527
dialectic, external and internal, 304 ff.
Diderot, D., 149
difference, 124, 317, 386, 425
division of labour, 54, 106
Don Quixote, 149, 382
dualism, 102, 106, 135, 227, 231 ff.,
256 f., 359 f., 403, 477, 523
duty, 22 ff., 483, 487

ear-lobes, 178, 373
eclipses, 505
ego, 333 f., 337, 364, 371, 421 ff., 443,
465 f., 477 ff., 514, 518, 542, 559;
cf. I, self
egotism, 517 ff.
Einstein, A., 138, 140, 255
electricity, 49 ff., 57, 59 ff., 66 f., 77 f.,
80 ff., 395 f., 450, 532
empirical testability, 52 f.
empiricism, 51 ff., 65 ff., 69 f., 414 ff.,
470 ff.

576